P9-CLE-171

THE LIST

THE LIST

A Week-by-Week Reckoning of Trump's First Year

AMY SISKIND

BLOOMSBURY PUBLISHING
NEW YORK • LONDON • OXFORD • NEW DELHI • SYDNEY

BLOOMSBURY PUBLISHING
Bloomsbury Publishing Inc.
1385 Broadway, New York, NY 10018, USA

BLOOMSBURY, BLOOMSBURY PUBLISHING, and the Diana logo are trademarks of Bloomsbury Publishing Plc

First published in the United States 2018

ISBN: HB: 978-1-63557-271-1; eBook: 978-1-63557-272-8

Library of Congress Cataloging-in-Publication Data is available

2 4 6 8 10 9 7 5 3 1

Typeset by Westchester Publishing Services
Printed and bound in the U.S.A. by Berryville Graphics Inc., Berryville, Virginia

To find out more about our authors and books visit www.bloomsbury.com and sign up for our newsletters.

Bloomsbury books may be purchased for business or promotional use. For information on bulk purchases please contact Macmillan Corporate and Premium Sales Department at specialmarkets@macmillan.com.

To the Resistance

In the darkest days, comes the brightest light

CONTENTS

Foreword ix

Introduction 1

The List 5

Acknowledgments 401

Notes 403

Index 493

FOREWORD

By Sarah Kendzior

On January 22, 2017, two days after the inauguration of Donald Trump, U.S. counselor to the president Kellyanne Conway went on television to make a case for a new concept: "alternative facts." Conway was defending lies that Press Secretary Sean Spicer had made the day before about the size of Trump's inauguration crowd—lies that could be disproven simply by looking at photographs of the event.

The audacity of Conway's claim left most Americans reeling. After all, what is the purpose of lying when one could be so easily caught? And if likely to be caught, shouldn't one be more subtle, rather than contriving a catchphrase that sounds straight out of a George Orwell novel? What many Americans missed is that the audacity of the lie *was* the point. Lies are not merely false statements but signals of power. Conway's goal was not to convince Americans of an alternate narrative but to tell them, "We know that you know that we're lying, and we don't care, because there's absolutely nothing you can do about it."

If there is a Trump Doctrine, it is written in Alternative Facts. Throughout 2017, the Trump administration unleashed a firehose of falsehoods designed to prompt Americans to frantically search for the truth, in the hope that they would ultimately stop valuing it. The difficulty in merely gathering accurate information under these conditions—much less organizing in response to it—was intended to exhaust both the critical thinking and political drive of the administration's opponents. *What is the point of speaking truth to power,* citizens would ultimately wonder, *if power is the only truth?*

Though the nomenclature may be new, the tactic is not: Alternative facts have long been a hallmark of authoritarianism, and a propaganda onslaught has never been easier to achieve than it is today. In 1941, Nazi propagandist Joseph Goebbels put forth his theory of "the big lie": "If you tell a lie big enough and keep repeating it, people will eventually come to believe it." Today the big lie finds new reinforcement in digital media: in twisted narratives invented by state officials, validated through retweets and trending topics, and repeated through aggregated content that often seeps into the mainstream press. The big lie is big not only in its audacity but in its pervasiveness, as armies of trolls work to drown out opposing views and a news media unprepared for autocracy scrambles to catch up.

Thankfully, in 2016, Amy Siskind sought to keep people caught up—by writing everything down. Inspired by articles I and other scholars of authoritarian regimes wrote advising citizens to keep track of changes shortly after Trump won the election, Siskind began writing a weekly list of things that were, in her words, "not normal." Given that this is the Trump administration, the list started long and ended longer, with Siskind logging one hundred items per week by midyear and surpassing that number by the time 2017 drew to a close.

Trump's election and first year in office were a brutal awakening for many Americans who did not realize how greatly our democracy rested on norms instead of laws. Having been falsely assured that America's institutions could withstand an authoritarian onslaught, they learned the hard way that checks and balances are only as good as the people willing to enforce them, and that the constitution is but a piece of paper without officials who will honor its principles in practice.

In contrast to all previous presidents, Trump does not appear to recognize the branches of government as separate administrative organs designed to serve the people, but instead sees them as mechanisms of personal power. He treats the attorney general as his private attorney, asked the head of the FBI for a loyalty oath, and demands blind fealty from Republicans in Congress while flatly labeling the Democrats his enemies, often baselessly calling for them to be prosecuted. The United States has always had corruption in government as well as presidents who abused power for personal gain, but we have never had a president who viewed the entire apparatus of government as designed to serve only himself. Previous controversies, like Nixon's Watergate, now seem refreshingly manageable.

Throughout his campaign, Trump swore he would make America great again, but never specified a particular era as embodying his vision. In many respects, he combines the worst elements of U.S. history, exposing and exacerbating authoritarian tendencies that have been there from the nation's birth, but which—until now—faced staunch and successful opposition in Congress, in law, and in society.

The United States is a country founded on democratic ideas that were radical when first introduced in the eighteenth century and now are taken for granted across much of the world. A respect for empirical truth was critical to the revolution that challenged the myths that had governed aristocratic Europe for centuries. The most radical truth entailed the equality of man, that inherited position or wealth should not confer privilege, that people had a right to self-government. America's progress toward these ideals has certainly been halting. The country was established on stolen land and built by black slaves, and it went on to enforce anti-democratic, inhumane policies such as World War II internment camps, Jim Crow, and the "Red Scare" purges of the McCarthy era. But throughout the centuries, the United States has generally moved in the direction of freedom and progress. Trump's words and actions—his disdain for truth, his tolerance of Nazis, his targeting of black citizens, his ban on Muslims, his abandonment of Puerto Ricans—are not entirely without precedent, but his wholesale and public rejection of basic constitutional principles have pulled America into a new era of chaos and overt white supremacy in the executive branch.

Trump rose to power by exploiting not only America's most vicious elements, but its most vulnerable. By the time Trump launched his campaign, the United States was in its seventh year of recovering from the Great Recession. The recovery was not distributed equally—expensive coastal cities thrived while much of the Midwest and South was drained of jobs and resources. Nationwide, wages continued their forty-year stagnation, costs of living soared, and income inequality rivaled that of the Gilded Age. Historically, demagogues thrive in times of economic desperation, and Trump was no exception, nor was the United States immune to his con.

Trump had spent his career as a businessman preying on the vulnerable and cheering events such as the 2007 housing bubble collapse as an opportunity to swoop in and make a profit. He viewed the presidency the same way, and operates like a typical kleptocrat, using his position as president to enrich his family's businesses while passing bills designed to exacerbate poverty and obliterate the safety net. Again, some of these policies are not new—America has always stood out from other modern democracies in its refusal to provide health care and other basic social services—but they have never been put into practice in such a blatantly authoritarian matter, with citizens unable to read the laws their representatives pass and representatives seemingly utterly divorced from the public's very negative reaction.

The end result of this mismanagement and malice was mass upheaval, and *The List* tracks each devastating development in detail. The scope of each weekly list is enormous: encapsulating corruption, propaganda, the erosion of civil rights, and other assaults on truth, justice, and the American way. As the year wore on, every day seemed to contain a month's worth of news, and scandals that would in earlier eras have been covered for weeks were now forgotten in hours. What I warned of in November 2016 came to pass: Standards of both decency and democracy shifted, and events that were once shocking now seemed predictable, albeit still appalling. Our expectations were recalibrated. This psychological change is typical when a country begins a shift from a democracy to an autocracy, and it happens even to citizens who resolutely oppose the transformation.

But there is a difference between expecting autocracy—which is a realistic approach to take under the Trump administration—and accepting it. In order to not accept it, you need to keep your expectations high, even if you assume they will not be met. That means maintaining the standard you had of what is "not normal" from before Trump took office even as a rapid and often terrifying rupture of political and social norms is occurring around you. It means remembering what we had, and realizing what we have lost.

Siskind's lists are essential to that endeavor. By recording events chronologically and in real time, she left a trail of truth in the fog of alternative facts, allowing both continuities and hypocrisies to be more easily exposed. Armed with *The List*, you can see exactly which promises were broken and when, who lied about what and how cover-ups were constructed, which political figures transformed from principled opponents to seemingly terrified lackeys, and how Trump and his colleagues attempted to achieve one of their professed goals: what former adviser Steve Bannon called "the deconstruction of the administrative state."

While some of Trump's challenges to democracy were quick and blatant—executive orders ultimately deemed unconstitutional, for example—others, like Trump and his team's ties to Russia, came to light gradually over the time period Siskind documented, with greater clarity as to their significance emerging only as a large number of abnormal occurrences were viewed in tandem. *The List* is an excellent guide to understanding that crisis, among others.

The lists don't editorialize; they simply document. That is one of this book's advantages in an era of hyperpartisanship and information silos—it is up to the reader to make sense of the material and to decide what to do in response. I hope Americans do not take this opportunity for granted. I have worked with activists and journalists in authoritarian and semiauthoritarian states, and in many of those countries, a collection like this—a simple weekly tally of events—would be banned (as would, of course, any news outlet that does not flatter the regime or that reveals things it would rather be kept secret).

Though the Trump administration has threatened the media in ways typical of authoritarian states—deeming journalists "members of the opposition party" and "enemies of the people," threatening both individual reporters and entire outlets—it has not succeeded in stifling the free press. That may change in the next year or two, especially given the crackdown on independent outlets and the repeal of net neutrality. It is therefore more important than ever that events be recorded thoroughly and accurately, as Siskind did, and that a record of what transpired is preserved. As scholars of authoritarianism have long noted, rewriting the past is an excellent way to control the future.

While many of us might like to forget 2017, it is very important that we do not. In addition to the problems that have long plagued American society—systemic racism and misogyny, economic inequality, rancid partisanship—2017 brought a host of new problems that would have seemed unthinkable just a few years ago. New concerns include the likelihood of nuclear war, the question of whether a federal investigation of the Trump campaign's Kremlin ties will be obstructed, a surge in neo-Nazi rallies, and the emergence of a dynastic kleptocracy as the Trump family abuses executive privileges to enhance its personal wealth.

It is normal to feel depressed or exhausted in the face of such horror and upheaval. It is normal to want to look the other way. But it is essential that we do not. Reading *The List* may horrify you, but it should also reassure you. No, you were not imagining things—that really did happen, he really did say that, and the only reason this particular atrocity is no longer discussed is because it was dwarfed by something even more outrageous.

The List is an antidote to the firehose effect of nonstop scandal as well as the gaslighting carried out by purveyors of alternative facts—and as such, it stands as a unique challenge to aspiring autocrats. In authoritarian states, the Internet has proven a double-edged sword. While social media is arguably the greatest tool of surveillance and propaganda ever conceived, it is also a mechanism through which researchers like Siskind can quickly gather information and recirculate it. This methodical task is essential to democracy. Without documentation—without a reliable and shared sense of what happened—demanding accountability is tremendously difficult. Reading *The List* may jar your memory in unpleasant ways, but hopefully it will also bring forth a push to right administrative wrongs.

The more cynical of pundits greeted Conway's declaration of "alternative facts" by proclaiming we live in a "post-truth world," one where accuracy is irrelevant and injustice a foregone conclusion. This argument is rendered moot by the fact that if the truth did not matter, the Trump administration would not work so hard to suppress it. There would not be countless cover-ups, threats to the free press, blatant lies, or displays of distracting spectacle. While pundits accurately depicted the administration's desire to block a critical assessment of its actions, the administration did not take into account the refusal of many citizens to play along.

I am grateful that Amy Siskind did not play along, and insisted on chronicling the Trump administration's first year despite the difficulty that entails. Writing *The List* was likely not an easy task, or a pleasant task, but it was certainly a necessary one. So let the record speak for itself—while we still have the freedom to read it.

INTRODUCTION

On the morning of Saturday, November 19, 2016, I found myself driving up to Val-Kill, the home of Eleanor Roosevelt. The week before, Trump had stunned the country by winning the election, and I was still reeling. The country's reaction to his victory was swift and hideous: The bigots in America took it as a legitimization of their hatred of others, and acts of hate were ubiquitous. Trump had ratcheted up his criticism of free speech, tweeting insults that morning at *Saturday Night Live*, the *New York Times*—even the cast of *Hamilton*. *This isn't normal*, I found myself thinking. *We are in great danger.*

I needed to take a break from the steady stream of e-mails flooding my inbox. *This is the worst day since 9/11 . . . What do we do now?* How could I assure others that we were going to be okay when I wasn't sure myself? I needed the steadying influence of my personal heroine. I found myself wondering, *What would Eleanor do today?*

That Saturday was a crisp, sunny day, and Val-Kill a familiar vision of peace in what already felt like a country in chaos. I first started by reading Eleanor's quotes on government and democracy and courage, walked by the old typewriter she used to write her weekly newspaper column, My Day, then took my dogs along the trails she had walked each morning with her Scottish terriers. My heart felt heavy, but somehow, in Eleanor's presence, I felt less scared playing her words in my mind again and again, "Courage is easier than fear."

As I walked, I found myself thinking about some of the articles I'd read in the aftermath of the election. Experts in authoritarianism—Masha Gessen, Sarah Kendzior, and Ruth Ben-Ghiat—wrote about the tools of autocrats: using hatred as fuel, silencing dissent, disregarding norms, and breaking down trusted institutions. All described how things would be changing, slowly and subtly, warning us not to be fooled by small signs of normalcy on our march into darkness. Sarah

Kendzior suggested that citizens write things down, starting that day, making a list of the specific things they never would have believed, things that they never would have done, before the regime came into power.

On the ride home, I knew what I had to do, and I started that night.

The List didn't start with any grand ambitions or even a vision. I just had an instinct to write down all of the things that were happening—things that were not normal. Each Saturday, I shared The List on Facebook and Twitter. Week 1 had nine items, but by Week 2, The List had doubled to eighteen items and concluded with, "I'm sure there are more. This list is overwhelming already." Little did I know. A few weeks in, as the readership started to take off, people asked that I add source links so they could read the articles: Already the chaos was building, there was so much to keep track of, and people were missing news items. A professor from my alma mater who read The List e-mailed to say, "We are the frog in the water who doesn't notice it is getting to boil degree by degree."

The weekend before Trump took office, January 14, 2017, The List went viral for the first time: Week 9, with thirty-six not-normal items, was picked up by several prominent progressive bloggers and had close to two million views. I wrote a short note that week observing that in normal times, "any one of these items would be a shock" and the "lack of consequences has changed me, and I suspect us all." I told readers I hoped The List would help us "trace our way back to normal when this nightmare is over."

The Women's March was the next weekend, and I chose to walk in my home city of New York, thinking that in a smaller crowd I would run into my friends. More than four hundred thousand showed up—a sign that Americans, especially women and members of marginalized communities, would not go quietly. In the coming weeks, as Trump took office and power, the weekly lists grew to sixty items, and my Saturdays were spent catching up on documenting our falling norms.

Even as The List grew longer week by week, the themes remained consistent: Trump was interested in making money and staying in power, and he would take whatever steps necessary to make these things happen. Every week he fanned the flames of hate: from signing the Muslim Bans to the Transgender Military Ban, to ending DACA, to increasing ICE roundups, to repealing the Global Gag Rule, to taking swipes at NFL players. He took steps to consolidate power such as installing regime members to undermine the very agencies they were meant to lead, silencing dissent and our free press, intimidating the legislative branch, and stuffing the judicial branch full of extremists. At the same time, Trump transformed our standing in the world, alienating our closest allies while cozying up to authoritarians, including, of course, Putin.

In May, as Trump continued staffing up the regime, the lists of not-normal items were approaching one hundred per week. Now there were many hands involved in the work of destabilizing our fragile democracy, but key roles at federal agencies were left vacant and many seasoned veterans had departed. Especially noteworthy was the loss of diplomatic channels in our state department. Meanwhile, the Trump-appointed agency heads had open-door policies for lobbyists and executives from the industries the agencies are designed to regulate. Week by week, rules and regulations put in place to protect the environment, consumers, marginalized communities, women, the poor, and people with disabilities were being rolled back.

In late June, I received a message from Margaret Sullivan at the *Washington Post*, asking if she could interview me about The List. I was thrilled! I had been waiting for the right columnist and publication for The List's coming-out story. Margaret's article went viral, reaching the top of the most-read pieces at *Washington Post* online with more than two million views. Shortly thereafter, someone who read the article nominated The List to be archived at the Library of Congress. I was incredibly grateful that The List would now be preserved for posterity, and would also have a home safe from hackers. At the suggestion of journalism professor Jay Rosen, I wrote a blog post memorializing this development. The very next day, I became the target of Russian-state media outlets and blogs: Sputnik and RT manufactured a storyline accusing me of "intense Russiaphobia," and a pro-Russia blog published a foreboding piece, calling me a "radicalized lesbian."

By mid-July, I realized the items I was listing weren't the only things subtly changing—I was changing as well. I felt like the character Carrie on *Homeland*, with thousands of items and trails of connections to Trump's end mapping out in my head. Naïvely, that day at Val-Kill months earlier, I imagined justice would catch up and Trump would be gone by the summer. The injustices were piling up, but there was no accountability or consequences! I headed to Vermont for some solitude and space to marinate on my new reality. At this point, I was devoting more than twenty hours a week to The List, and my old life and plans for what came next were sidelined. I decided I should record how this was affecting me and visited my favorite bookstore to pick out a diary. The first entry reads, "I am on the toughest climb of my life, and the hill feels steep and unrelenting."

A personal challenge throughout was staying engaged and dispassionate without losing my empathy and humanity. The country I love was under siege, and I was heartbroken and devastated. There were events, like Charlottesville and Myeshia Johnson standing over her husband's casket, where I found myself staring at the computer screen with tears streaming down my face. There were weeks when, with my growing public voice, I spoke out against hate and became a target myself. After Week 39, in August, I tweeted at web-hosting company GoDaddy, complaining about the neo-Nazi website the Daily Stormer's inflammatory attack on Charlottesville heroine and martyr Heather Heyer. Within twenty-four hours, the Daily Stormer was taken down, but my home address and phone numbers were posted online. That week I hired an armed security guard to be stationed outside my home.

As summer came to an end, I was spending some thirty hours a week on the lists, which were now approaching 120 items each. When I cracked a tooth and made an appointment with my endodontist, she gave a diagnosis without missing a beat: "This is what happens in dictatorships. You're screaming in your sleep!" She advised getting a mouth guard, which, she offered up, many of her patients were doing. Ironically, as I sat in her office waiting to be seen, I was reading an op-ed by Dana Milbank, "President Trump Is Killing Me. Really," describing the impact on his physical health. Psychotherapists remarked on their patients' focus on politics—a feeling of outrage, fear, and loss of control. Our country was truly suffering, physically, emotionally, and mentally, under the Trump regime.

As year one of The List drew to a close, I reread the articles by the experts on authoritarianism, and their predictions were coming true: Trump was still holding his campaign-style rallies with chants of "Lock her up!" as he encouraged the FBI and DOJ to do the same. He was still complaining about the "rigged system," which he assured his raucous crowds he would fix by silencing the fake media and dismantling what was left of the Deep State corrupt institutions that hampered him from assuming full control. It turns out authoritarians do follow a fairly predictable game plan—even if new to us and our fragile democracy. Our country has spent a year in chaos, and so often people worry out loud about forgetting all the events that happened in a single week. And so I am grateful I took the experts' advice and constructed a trail map for us to follow back to normalcy and democracy—a journey, sadly, I suspect will take years if not decades to travel.

Week 1: Experts in authoritarianism advise to keep a list of things subtly changing around you, so you'll remember.

NOVEMBER 13–20, 2016

1. Acts of hate—Of the first four hundred acts of hate cited by the Southern Poverty Law Center (SPLC), I had seen many covered by the media. Then I noticed the updated count exceeded seven hundred, and I realized I knew very little about those additional three hundred.

2. Reporters critiqued their own paper's coverage of Trump, then deleted their tweets.

3. A president-elect was openly (on Twitter!) trying to take away our freedom of expression and First Amendment rights: targets this week included *Saturday Night Live* (*SNL*), the *New York Times* (*NYT*), and *Hamilton*.

4. The media, including traditional media, covered an alt-right conference (annual gathering for the National Policy Institute, headlined by alt-right leader Richard Spencer) and published the conference's demands, which included a fifty-year ban on immigration of anyone not white and an all-white nation.

5. Reporters from major media outlets were following Trump's reality show story lines on Twitter, instead of reporting as traditional journalists.

6. Democrats were advocating for a Mitt Romney appointment as secretary of state (SoS)—a man with whom we agree on almost nothing on policy, but accept because he is competent and not a racist or a bigot.

7. The untraditional, unorthodox acts and conflicts of interest by Trump were coming so fast and furiously, they were barely getting coverage.

8. Utter outrage by the left at the general complacency and silence of our elected leaders. Watch for a Tea Party–type uprising.

9. A request for tolerance for, and understanding of, white supremacists. Following a white nationalist conference held in D.C. during which participants gave Nazi salutes and chanted "Hail Trump, hail our people, hail victory!," Trump issued a statement that avoided condemning the actions directly and instead claimed that he "will be a leader for every American."

Week 2

NOVEMBER 21–26, 2016

1. Melania and Barron Trump will not be living in the White House.

2. Melania's Wikipedia bio was changed overnight to reflect that she did not go to college.

3. Donald Jr. met with Russian representatives in Paris during the campaign to discuss Syria.

4. Aleppo has devolved into the worst humanitarian crisis in our lifetimes, and Russian president Vladimir Putin is emboldened to tell the U.S. to get out of the way.

5. Putin moved missiles into Kaliningrad—within striking distance of Germany—"in response to NATO aggression."

6. Russian propaganda was the source of much of the "fake news" during the campaign.

7. Trump selectively met with the media and groomed them by yelling at them at Trump Tower. They all showed up for this.

8. The next day he met with *NYT* editors at their offices, and the paper's coverage of the meeting totally normalized his porous positions and outrageous actions so far.

9. Trump has been furthering his business affairs and using his presidency to get licensing opportunities and other favors.

10. Trump's daughter Ivanka and son-in-law Jared Kushner have joined him in meetings and calls with heads of state and other senior officials from other countries.

11. Trump openly stated that he does not care about conflicts of interest and that he does not feel compelled in any way to separate his business dealings from his role as president.

12. Trump admitted to breaking the law! He signed off on the Trump Foundation's tax statement and now has admitted the foundation was in violation of tax laws.

13. In Wisconsin, five thousand votes out of Trump's twenty-seven-thousand-vote lead were proven to be fake votes.

14. In true dictatorial form, Trump demanded that Mitt Romney publicly apologize for criticizing Trump publicly during the presidential campaign if he wants the position of SoS.

15. Trump is selling Trump merchandise in Trump Tower and online, including Christmas tree ornaments.

16. CNN aired a segment with the subline on the chyron, "Are Jews People?"

17. Hate crimes continued nationwide against Muslim, Jewish, female, black, LGBTQ, and Hispanic Americans. On a Delta flight, one Trump supporter screamed "Hillary bitches" and didn't get kicked off.

18. Trump adviser Steve Bannon received $376,000 from a small foundation in Tallahassee to pay him for his work at *Breitbart*.

I'm sure there are more. This list is overwhelming already.

Week 3

NOVEMBER 27-DECEMBER 3, 2016

Observation: Each week the list is getting longer and more troubling/frightening.

1. SPLC issued a startling report on the profoundly negative impact of the election results on our schools and children. This is in addition to 867 cases of hate attacks in the ten days postelection, and 892 active hate groups.

2. There were reports nationwide, including on college campuses, of women being grabbed by the genitals and being told a variation of "it's no big deal."

3. Trump continued to be disinterested in availing himself of daily intelligence briefings.

4. Our news cycles are now being led by Trump's Twitter account. Our media seems unable to do anything but follow along.

5. Trump sent a total of thirteen tweets about Green Party candidate Jill Stein's recounts, the most consecutive tweets he has made on any subject. Still not a single tweet condemning nationwide hate crimes carried out in his name.

6. Trump tweeted that there were "millions of people who voted illegally." Trump adviser Kellyanne Conway and other loyalists parroted and embellished this false claim during the week.

7. Despite his claims of millions of illegal votes, Trump and the GOP apparatus aggressively filed lawsuits to prevent vote recounts in Michigan, Wisconsin, and Pennsylvania.

8. Trump retweeted a sixteen-year-old's tweet attacking a CNN reporter. The sixteen-year-old complained that Trump edited his tweet.

9. Kellyanne Conway scolded a seventeen-year-old, in response to the girl's question about working for a man with a history of sexual assault.

10. Unprovoked by events or any reason, Trump suggested—again via a tweet—consequences for burning the American flag: "perhaps loss of citizenship or year in jail!"

11. Senate Majority Leader Mitch McConnell awoke from a seeming slumber to condemn the flag-burning tweet, while House Speaker Paul Ryan assured America he was tutoring Trump on the Constitution.

12. Trump's online store held a Cyber Monday sale on Trump merchandise.

13. Russia claimed to be in talks with several people on the Trump team regarding Syria, before Trump takes office.

14. After spending the entire general election criticizing Hillary Clinton's e-mail practices, Trump considered General David Petraeus for SoS—despite a

requirement that the general notify his probation officer in order to leave North Carolina (fortunately, there's no travel entailed in the SoS position). In 2015 Petraeus pleaded guilty to leaking classified information to his mistress and biographer, Paula Broadwell, and lying to FBI agents about the breach.

15. Trump continued to conduct his SoS selection like episodes of *The Bachelor*. Romney was shamed into public apology–lite remarks after feasting on frog legs, only to find days later that the current and former CEOs of Exxon had been added to the contestant list.

16. Under continued pressure, Trump tweeted that he would leave his businesses, but offered little detail or comfort that this would be anything but having his children run things. Hardly arm's length.

17. Eight members of the Senate Intelligence Committee wrote a letter to President Obama, urging him to declassify information related to Russia's interference with our election. Although seventeen intelligence agencies have said Russia was involved in hacking, the public is aware of no response or actions that have been taken.

18. Bahrain—the country that Trump falsely claimed donated money to the Clinton Foundation in exchange for favorable treatment by Hillary Clinton when she was SoS—booked space at the Trump International Hotel in D.C. for a reception.

19. Even Trump loyalists rebelled at Trump's appointment of Goldman Sachs execs to his cabinet and inclusion of them in his inner circle. Since Election Day, GS stock has rallied by 23 percent, or a 347 percent annualized return.

20. Seemingly disinterested in the fact that the campaign is over, Trump embarked on a "Victory Tour"—later rebranded as a "Thank You Tour"—visiting only the states he won. His first rally, in Cincinnati, was half empty.

21. At the Cincinnati rally, after being egged on by Trump, supporters chanted, "Lock her up! Lock her up!" and Trump did nothing to stop them. The same night, Trump loyalist Corey Lewandowski told a panel that *NYT* editor Dean Baquet should be imprisoned.

22. In kicking off the tour, Trump and Vice President Mike Pence engineered a saving of one thousand American jobs at the Carrier Corporation, at a cost of seven million dollars to Indiana taxpayers. A *Wall Street Journal* (*WSJ*) editorial referred to the ploy as "Trump's Carrier Shakedown."

23. In a forty-eight-hour period, Trump did incredible damage to our country's global standing, conducting conversations with foreign leaders without being briefed by or consulting with the State Department.

24. According to the Pakistani government, Trump told Pakistan's prime minister, Nawaz Sharif, in a phone call that Sharif was "a terrific guy" who made him feel as though "I'm talking to a person I have known for long."

25. Trump invited Philippine president Rodrigo Duterte to the White House and congratulated him on handling the drug war the "right way."

26. Trump became the first U.S. leader to have a phone conversation with a Taiwanese leader since diplomatic ties were cut in 1979. Trump explained it away in two tweets. China promptly responded in protest.

Week 4

DECEMBER 4–11, 2016

1. This was the week of Trump silencing dissent:

- the arts (comedy)—on Twitter, Trump attacked Alec Baldwin and called *SNL* "unwatchable."
- corporate America—Trump sent a false tweet about the cost of Air Force One after Boeing's CEO spoke out against starting a trade war with China. Boeing stock cratered.
- private citizens—Trump's tweet at union leader Chuck Jones, after Jones spoke out on the Carrier deal, led to death threats against Jones.
- protest marchers—Trump tried to squash the Million Women March by changing permitting. A new location was found.

2. *Variety* reported that Trump will continue in his role as executive producer of *Celebrity Apprentice*. Two days later, Trump called it "fake news" and blamed CNN.

3. NBC, which broadcasts *Celebrity Apprentice*, refused to release tapes of Trump rumored to be damaging during the election.

4. The *Washington Post* (*WaPo*) reported on a Central Intelligence Agency (CIA) report that claimed Putin interfered in our election to help Trump win. Trump's response amounted to defending Russia and questioning the CIA's capabilities.

5. According to *WaPo*, Mitch McConnell had refused to allow the CIA report to be put out before the election. McConnell's wife, Elaine Chao, was appointed by Trump to a cabinet position.

6. The day after Chao's appointment, Trump appointed Exxon CEO Rex Tillerson as SoS. Tillerson has no experience with government or diplomacy, but has a close relationship with Putin.

7. In responding to why he has availed himself of only four of thirty-one intelligence briefings, Trump responded, "I'm, like, a smart person."

8. Attacks against Muslim Americans, including a congresswoman in D.C. and a teenager in New York, were reported nationwide.

9. An *Atlantic* article titled "Are Jews White?" drew a response by former Ku Klux Klan (KKK) leader David Duke.

10. Trump is seeking ways to include both his daughter and son-in-law in his administration, despite laws prohibiting their involvement.

11. Trump appointed three generals into leadership positions in his cabinet—a disturbing trend, indicative of authoritarian leadership.

12. Trump appointed another Goldman Sachs executive to a major leadership role. GS stock is up 33 percent since Election Day and comprises one-third of the Dow Jones Industrial Average's rise.

13. Trump invited celebrity campaigners on the environment—Al Gore, Leonardo DiCaprio—for well-promoted, reality-TV-like meetings at Trump Tower, while appointing an Environmental Protection Agency (EPA) head who doesn't believe in climate change.

14. The Republican National Committee (RNC) will hold its holiday party at a Trump hotel (and pay him for it). Several GOP appendages are doing the same.

15. Trump continues to keep full ownership of his businesses, brushing off the need to explain conflicts of interest.

16. Trump's economic team is all men and all white. Five of the thirteen are named Steven or Stephen.

17. Reality TV producer Mark Burnett will help Trump plan the inauguration, with a reality-TV-type build-up.

18. Rudy Giuliani "withdrew" his candidacy for a cabinet position. A lawyer filed a Freedom of Information Act (FOIA) request for documents about Giuliani's connection to the FBI search warrant seeking additional material in the Clinton e-mail case.

19. Trump changed the legend on his iconic hat from MAKE AMERICA GREAT AGAIN to simply USA. Said hat is sold exclusively by Trump for forty dollars.

20. Trump put out his first policy-related post on Facebook.

21. Trump continued his Thank You Tour in states he won.

22. Trump, with the help of the GOP apparatus, shut down the recount efforts in Michigan, where he won by ten thousand votes out of 4.8 million cast, with many anomalies. Efforts to do the same in Wisconsin failed. Efforts in Pennsylvania also have led to recount efforts being stifled.

Week 5

DECEMBER 12-17, 2016

1. CIA employees feared reprisals from Trump over their findings on Russian interference in the election, while his team threatened to bring in new leadership.

2. A Trump press conference, scheduled for December 15 to discuss dealing with his conflicts of interest, was "postponed" indefinitely.

3. A *WSJ* reporter later revealed that Trump will not divest from his businesses—the excuse given is that the sale would bring in too little money.

4. *Vanity Fair* (*VF*) issues a scathing review of Trump Grill. Trump responds with a Twitter attack, saying of *VF*, "Way down, big trouble, dead!" The same day, *VF* picked up a record number of subscriptions.

5. The Trump team announced that Trump plans to change the traditional daily White House briefings.

6. Ivanka will be taking a White House office typically reserved for the first lady.

7. Conway says Trump is looking at ways to get around nepotism rules so he can include Ivanka and Jared in his regime.

8. Trump continues to deny Russian hacking of the election, saying it could have been China or a four-hundred-pound man.

9. The RNC, meanwhile, says it was not hacked by Russia.

10. A battle opened between Obama's press secretary and the Trump team, threatening a smooth transition of power. Conway said Obama would end this feud if he loved "the country enough."

11. The Federal Bureau of Investigation (FBI), the CIA, and other intelligence agencies reached agreement that Russia interfered with our election, with a goal of getting Trump elected.

12. The General Services Administration (GSA) told Trump he would violate his D.C. hotel lease "the moment he takes office." Word spreads that Trump will replace the leadership of the GSA.

13. General Michael Flynn, Trump's pick for national security adviser, was found guilty by the army of sharing classified information. Flynn also deleted his tweet promoting Pizzagate.

14. Ivanka auctioned off a coffee date, with a fifty-thousand-dollar floor. As rumblings of conflict started to stir, the online posting mysteriously disappeared.

15. The Trump team asked the Department of Energy for a list of scientists who have worked on climate science. The request was denied. Scientists are said to be backing up their data, for fear it, too, will disappear.

16. Trump continued his Thank You Tour to only states he won. He stood before Christmas trees only—no reference to other religions.

17. Trump issued a negative tweet about Lockheed just before the stock market opened. Like Boeing's, Lockheed's stock cratered. It was discovered that

traders are starting to anticipate Trump's tweets by taking long or short positions.

18. Trump continued to pick white men for his cabinet—many of whom have no experience with the area they are about to lead. His cabinet is the least diverse since 1989.

19. Trump held meetings with tech leaders at Trump Tower and included his three children, but excluded the CEO of Twitter for his unwillingness to produce a "Crooked Hillary" emoji.

20. Hillary Clinton adviser Huma Abedin joined lawyer E. Randol Schoenberg's calls to release the FBI search warrant that led to FBI director James Comey's October 28 letter to Congress on the FBI's investigation of Clinton's e-mails.

Week 6

DECEMBER 18–24, 2016

1. Trump will keep his private security force while in office. This is unprecedented and potentially dangerous.

2. Upon winning the Electoral College vote, Trump's first official statement was a lie (about his electoral landslide).

3. The FBI search warrant used to gain access to Huma Abedin's computer before the election was made public. Most legal experts agreed that there was no probable cause to issue the warrant. Blogger Nate Silver released additional data showing major moves to Trump in swing states in the final days before the election, around the time of the Comey letter. There was almost no media follow-up on this story. No politicians have followed it up, either.

4. A *Politico* article claimed that Trump was browbeating fellow Republicans into silence by targeting, via *Breitbart* and his tweets, those who speak out against him.

5. On air, Fox News's Bill O'Reilly said, "The left wants power taken away from the white establishment."

6. A Jewish family in Lancaster, Pennsylvania, was targeted by *Breitbart* and Fox News with a false claim that they were behind the cancellation of an elementary school Christmas play.

7. *Teen Vogue* reported that Michael Flynn, Trump's national security adviser, met with the head of Austria's neo-Nazi party.

8. Not a single A-list celebrity is willing to perform at Trump's inauguration (at which he tweeted his anger). Several Rockettes spoke out in protest against having to perform.

9. Former congressman Newt Gingrich suggested that Trump should pardon his advisers who break the law.

10. Gingrich, after saying Trump wouldn't actually drain the swamp, was forced by Trump to publicly apologize and say Trump would.

11. The embassy of Kuwait, citing political pressure, canceled its long-standing reservation to host its National Day celebration at the Four Seasons and changed it to Trump Hotel D.C.

12. Trump met the CEOs of Lockheed and Boeing, after tweeting false or negative information that caused their stocks to crater more.

13. A senior executive at Oracle resigned over that company's CEO's participation on Trump's transition team.

14. Eric Trump and Donald Trump Jr. offered a million-dollar hunting trip, which included access to their dad, via a foundation. Upon calls of conflict of interest and investigation into the foundation, the offer was canceled.

15. Trump's team instructed the State Department to turn over a list of "gender-related staffing, programming, and funding."

16. Trump tweeted a planned buildup of our nuclear arms, reversing three decades of disarmament.

17. Days later, he and Putin shared an admiring exchange of letters. Putin publicly castigated Hillary as a "sore loser," and Trump agreed via a tweet. No U.S. elected officials responded to either.

Week 7

DECEMBER 25-31, 2016

Please note this was a holiday week, but nonetheless busy.

1. Trump continued to take credit for jobs he didn't create—this week with Sprint's five thousand jobs. Companies needing things from government agencies—like Sprint with an upcoming merger—have started to play into this to gain favor.

2. Obama announced sanctions of Russia. Trump tweeted in support of Putin and pinned that tweet. Trump also used "V. Putin," which is the Russian convention for writing names.

3. The same day Putin said Russia will not expel U.S. diplomats, a U.S. utility in Vermont was hacked and Russia was suspected to be behind it.

4. Trump continued to deny Russian hacking, saying we should "get on with our lives," and dismissing it with "I think the computers have complicated lives very greatly."

5. It has been 157 days since Trump held a press conference (the one where he encouraged Russia to hack more American e-mails).

6. Trump sent a congratulatory tweet to himself for higher consumer confidence numbers that he had nothing to do with.

7. Paul Ryan introduced rules banning lawmakers from taking pictures or videos of procedures on the House floor.

8. Trump announced on Christmas Eve that he will be shutting down the Trump Foundation. The New York attorney general said the foundation is still under investigation.

9. Mar-a-Lago sold hundreds of tickets at more than five hundred dollars for a New Year's celebration attended by Trump and his family.

10. My friend Kevin Sessums, a prominent author and writer, had his Facebook account suspended and a post calling Trump supporters "fascists" deleted.

11. Simon & Schuster paid a $250,000 advance for a book by alt-right author and troll Milo Yiannopoulos. In reaction, the *Chicago Review of Books* said it would not review any S&S books during 2017.

12. The RNC sent out a Christmas message comparing Trump to Jesus.

13. Senator John McCain announced he would hold hearings during the first week of January, before Trump takes office, on Russian hacking—which Trump denies happened.

14. A second round of FOIA requests was filed to gain access to FBI e-mails relating to the Comey letter, to see if there were ties to Giuliani or Flynn as both indicated they had been given leaked information about the Clinton investigation.

15. Neo-Nazis in Whitefish, Montana—hometown of Richard Spencer—planned an armed march to harass Jews.

16. Trump sent out a bizarre New Year's tweet chastising his enemies.

17. After a morning tweet about Obama not cooperating with the transition, Trump appeared with Don King that evening and said the opposite.

Week 8

JANUARY 1-7, 2017

Although the bar is high, this week was the most devastating for our country so far.

1. Trump announced that he will make major policy announcements via Twitter.

2. Trump's executive producer credit appeared in the *Celebrity Apprentice* premiere.

3. Trump's divisive, incendiary New Year's tweet was contrasted with departing President Obama's warm and generous one.

4. On New Year's Day, Trump promised a revelation on hacking, either Tuesday or Wednesday. This was a lie—it never came.

5. In a puzzling exchange, MSNBC's Joe Scarborough tweeted that he spent New Year's Eve watching TV with his children, but a photo showed him and cohost Mika Brzezinski chatting up Trump at Mar-a-Lago.

6. Trump appointed yet another Goldman Sachs executive to an economic leadership position, this one overseeing markets (chair of the Securities and Exchange Commission [SEC]). GS stock is up 35 percent since Election Day.

7. *WSJ* editor Gerard Baker said his paper would not refer to Trump's lies as "lies."

8. Trump repeatedly tweeted support for Julian Assange and WikiLeaks—despite at one point saying the media was lying about their alliance. Trump ally Sean Hannity interviewed Assange for his Fox News show.

9. Trump repeatedly dismissed U.S. intelligence agencies' findings on Russian hacking and referred to the agencies in quotes: "Intelligence."

10. Trump announced he would appoint Pam Bondi, the former Florida attorney general who received an illegal payment of twenty-five thousand dollars from the Trump Foundation in exchange for not investigating Trump University, to a top White House spot.

11. Senator McCain held a publicly televised Senate Armed Services Committee hearing on Russian hacking of our election. For the first time, Americans got to hear from intelligence leadership.

12. Senators McCain and Lindsey Graham said they had given up on efforts to push Majority Leader McConnell for a special panel on Russia interference.

13. Trump lashed out in tweets at General Motors and Toyota, causing both stocks to plummet. In the case of Toyota, Trump's allegations were false.

14. Trump falsely took credit for added jobs at a Ford plant. Ford's CEO publicly stated that the rationale for choosing the U.S. over Mexico was not related to Trump.

15. *WaPo* announced the launch of a weekly column on what Trump got wrong on Twitter each week.

16. The House GOP took a secret vote to take power over the independent Office of Congressional Ethics. After public outcry and calls to representatives by voters, the plan was scuttled. Trump had tweeted that he was for the change but against the timing.

17. Trump started referring to Senate Minority Leader Chuck Schumer as a "clown."

18. The House GOP revived an obscure 1876 rule that allows them to cut the annual salary of individual federal workers to one dollar.

19. Trump said he would ask the American taxpayers to pay for his infamous wall on the Mexican border.

20. Trump promised to downsize intelligence agencies, including the CIA and the Office of the Director of National Intelligence (DNI), saying both were politicized.

21. Ex-CIA director James Woolsey resigned from Trump's transition team, saying he did not want to "fly under false colors" any longer.

22. Breaking decades of precedent, Trump said he would recall all Obama overseas envoys immediately on January 20, before their replacements have been appointed.

23. Trump tweeted his apparent displeasure with the ratings of *Celebrity Apprentice* under Arnold Schwarzenegger, saying he got "swamped" compared with when Trump hosted the show.

24. A briefing filed by a bipartisan group of lawyers claimed that fifty Trump electors were allegedly illegally seated. During Congress's electoral vote count Representative Maxine Waters and other Democratic representatives stood to protest, but couldn't find a single senator to join them.

25. After meeting with the DNI and the heads of the CIA and FBI, Trump continued to deny the Russian hacking and instead pressed for a congressional investigation of leaks to NBC (something Congress doesn't investigate). Trump said there was no impact on the election.

26. Later that day, an intelligence report was made public detailing Putin's desire to hurt Clinton and help Trump, and the many ways Russia interfered. The report did not assess whether Russia's interference had an impact on the election, despite Trump's claim that the activity had no effect.

27. Trump blamed the Democratic National Committee (DNC) and Democrats for being hacked. The intelligence report also indicates Republicans were hacked, although that info was not leaked.

28. Trump continued to side with WikiLeaks and Russia, and against U.S. intelligence. Even after learning Russia had hacked our election, he called the actions of the intelligence agencies a "political witch hunt," and the next day tweeted that only "stupid" people or fools would think having a good relationship with Russia was a bad thing.

Week 9

JANUARY 8-14, 2017

This was not a good week for our country: this is the longest and most troubling list so far. I want to note that the purpose of the authoritarian list is to highlight subtle changes, and so business as usual, as upsetting as it may be—like the GOP's attempt to repeal the Affordable Care Act (ACA)—is not covered. Again, this is a list that is not meant to be partisan, but rather to capture changes in the fabric of our country, so we can refer back and recall what used to be normal and acceptable.

1. The Office of Government Ethics (OGE) director publicly lamented, "We seem to have lost contact with the Trump-Pence transition since the election."

2. Three vendors have placed liens on the Trump International Hotel in D.C., for unpaid bills of over five million dollars.

3. The OGE said they had not completed ethics reviews of Trump's cabinet nominees. Senator McConnell said the Democrats need to "grow up" and not delay confirmations.

4. Sean Hannity endorsed a tweet that said, "Make Russia Great Again" with the word "Amen." Hannity later deleted his tweet.

5. Meryl Streep used her Golden Globes speech to eloquently attack Trump, without mentioning his name.

6. Trump responded via a tweet that Streep is an "over-rated" actress and denied he had mocked a disabled reporter.

7. Trump took credit for a Fiat Chrysler plant and jobs in Michigan and Ohio. Fiat Chrysler responded that Trump had nothing to do with it.

8. Trump appointed Jared Kushner, his son-in-law, to a top White House post, possibly violating the 1967 federal anti-nepotism statute.

9. Trump told the *NYT* that all the dress shops in D.C. are sold out for his inauguration. This was a lie.

10. Trump dismissed the head of the National Nuclear Security Administration (NNSA) and his deputy, responsible for maintaining our nuclear arsenal, as of January 20. Trump also dismissed the commanding general of the D.C. National Guard.

11. Cory Booker became the first U.S. senator to speak out against a fellow sitting senator at a confirmation hearing (Jeff Sessions for attorney general).

12. CNN reported a bombshell: intelligence chiefs had briefed Trump that Russia had gathered a dossier of information to blackmail him.

13. The same day, *BuzzFeed* published contents of the dossier, which apparently had been in the hands of the FBI and some in the media since the summer. Contents include references to the infamous golden shower video.

14. Trump denied having been briefed and said the contents of the dossier were confirmed by intelligence to be fake. DNI James Clapper issued a public statement indicating the dossier's contents are still being verified (not fake), and the media reported that Comey met with Trump one-on-one to review the dossier the prior Friday.

15. Trump held his first press conference since July. Trump packed the room with paid employees, who applauded him, and jeered at reporters.

16. At the press conference, Trump said he had no plans to release his tax returns or resolve conflicts of interest, saying, "I have no conflict situation because I'm president."

17. Trump bullied reporters at two news outlets, calling them "fake news," and used other news outlets as evidence.

18. The director of the OGE publicly blasted Trump's non-plan for dealing with conflicts of interest. The next day, Representative Jason Chaffetz threatened to investigate the OGE.

19. The next day, while meeting with the CEO of AT&T at Trump Tower (AT&T needs approval for its merger with Time Warner, parent company of CNN), Trump tweeted that CNN is "FAKE NEWS" and tanking.

20. Representative Barbara Lee said she would not attend Trump's inauguration. During the week, the list grew to twelve members of Congress who will not attend.

21. Trump encouraged his followers in a tweet to "buy L.L. Bean," in violation of a White House policy prohibiting the endorsement of products.

22. The Justice Department inspector general opened an investigation into allegations of misconduct by the FBI and Comey leading up to the election.

23. C-SPAN's online broadcast was interrupted by Kremlin-backed broadcaster RT while Representative Maxine Waters was speaking (C-SPAN called it a "technical error"). Waters has said she will not meet with Trump. The broadcast was also interrupted that morning when a senator discussed Russian hacking.

24. *WaPo* reported that Michael Flynn, Trump's national security adviser, spoke to Russia's envoy on December 29, the day Obama announced sanctions on Russia. Trump's team initially denied this, then later said they spoke only once that day. Reuters reported they spoke five times that day.

25. Trump continued to deny Russian hacking and to use quotes around "intelligence" in his tweets.

26. Trump appointed Rudy Giuliani to a cybersecurity role through a private company, despite Giuliani's lack of experience.

27. Trump appointed a sixth Goldman Sachs (past or present) employee to a major role in his administration.

28. After Congress was briefed by intelligence chiefs, Representative John Lewis said, "I don't see Trump as a legitimate president."

29. The next morning, Trump tweeted a disparaging attack on Lewis, on Martin Luther King Day weekend, saying he was "All talk."

30. Democrats in Congress were furious with FBI director Comey's unwillingness to answer their questions and fully brief them.

31. The *Independent* reported that Christopher Steele, the former British agent who gathered the info in the dossier, had shared his findings with the FBI, starting in the summer, and had become concerned that a cabal within the FBI was compromised and attempting to cover up information.

32. The Senate announced hearings on possible Russia-Trump ties and said subpoenas would be issued if necessary.

33. The Federal Elections Commission (FEC) sent Trump a letter listing 247 pages of illegal contributions to his campaign.

34. In the wake of the Trump dossier becoming public, Russia's cybersecurity head is out of a job.

35. Human Rights Watch issued its annual report of threats to human rights around the world. For the first time in twenty-seven years, the U.S. was listed as a top threat because of the rise of Trump.

36. A Quinnipiac poll showed Trump's favorability ratings continuing to slide to historic lows for modern-day presidents before their inauguration: only 37 percent of Americans view Trump favorably.

Week 10

JANUARY 15-21, 2017

An observation: this week's list includes two articles, one by McClatchy and one by the NYT, *with breaking news on Russian interference in our election, including possible Trump team complicity. Both articles are shocking and disturbing, yet garnered little attention. It's as if the American people are losing faith and trust in our institutions, and giving up that there will be accountability and consequences.*

1. The Sunday *Times* of London reported that Trump's first meeting as president will be with Putin.

2. In interviews with the *Times* of London and Germany's *Bild*, Trump referred to NATO as "obsolete."

3. The next day, the front page of *Le Monde* showed Trump standing with his back turned, accompanied by the headline TRUMP CONTRE L'EUROPE (Trump Against Europe).

4. The Trump transition team is considering a plan to evict the press corps from the White House. Trump later clarified, saying he won't evict all press, but he will pick who is allowed to come.

5. Trump's war of words with Representative Lewis continued for four days.

6. Trump canceled his plan to visit the National Museum of African American History and Culture on Martin Luther King Day. Trump spokesperson Sean Spicer said Monday that Trump never planned to be in D.C. that day, after Conway said the prior Friday that Trump was going.

7. A dossier provided to U.S. intelligence alleged that Trump agreed to sideline the issue of Russian intervention in Ukraine after Russia promised to feed the e-mails it stole from prominent Democrats' inboxes to WikiLeaks.

8. Trump ally Representative Todd Rokita is considering legislation that would allow Trump to fire federal employees for no cause.

9. Trump publicly traded barbs with outgoing CIA director John Brennan. Brennan said Trump "does not yet" fully appreciate what embracing Russia might mean, and called Trump's response "repugnant."

10. After Trump said at his press conference that the American people don't care about his tax returns, an ABC poll found that 74 percent of Americans want Trump to release his returns.

11. In a 2014 interview, Trump identified Russia as the U.S.'s "biggest problem" and greatest geopolitical foe.

12. On Sunday talk shows, Trump's pick for White House chief of staff, Reince Priebus, and Representative Jason Chaffetz warned and attacked the director of the OGE, who has publicly challenged Trump's conflicts of interest.

13. In a speech, Putin defended Trump and said the Obama administration was trying to undermine Trump's legitimacy.

14. Trump's cabinet-level appointees are the least diverse in decades: eighteen of twenty-three are white men, and none are Latino. Trump defended his choices, saying his cabinet has the highest IQ of any cabinet ever.

15. Michael Flynn's son tweeted an article from a Kremlin-funded website that said Flynn should take control of the sixteen U.S. intelligence agencies.

16. A disturbing *WaPo* article detailed Trump's isolation at Trump Tower, including his leaving the building only once over several days and interacting with very few people.

17. NBC and the *WSJ* reported that jobs at General Motors and Bayer that Trump took credit for were in the works for years, and that corporate leaders are crediting him to avoid his Twitter wrath.

18. In Greenwich, Connecticut, a Republican official grabbed a woman by her genitals, bragging, "I love this new world, I no longer have to be politically correct." He was caught on tape and later arrested.

19. Trump was sued for defamation by one of the woman who accused him of unwanted sexual advances. Attorney Gloria Allred said she will subpoena unseen footage from *The Apprentice*.

20. SoS nominee Tillerson's disclosure says he intends to stay away for only one year from State decisions that might benefit Exxon.

21. Media was banned from Trump Hotel D.C. in the days leading up to his inauguration. Trump did, however, stop by the hotel, and Spicer told the press, "I encourage you to go there, if you haven't been." Trump still benefits financially from the hotel.

22. Passwords used by Rudy Giuliani, Trump's incoming cybersecurity adviser, and thirteen other Trump team staff were leaked in a mass hack.

23. A CBS News poll found that Trump's approval rating had fallen to 32 percent. Similarly, a Fox News poll had him at 37 percent favorability. Trump is the first incoming president to have a net-negative approval rating.

24. Trump bragged about "displaying our military," including possible military parades in major U.S. cities.

25. Trump also wanted to include tanks and missile launchers in his inaugural parade.

26. McClatchy reported that the FBI and five other law enforcement and intelligence agencies have been investigating how money may have covertly moved from the Kremlin to help Trump win.

27. Nearly seventy members of Congress and SoS John Kerry boycotted Trump's inauguration.

28. Representative Elijah Cummings, who did attend, explained that "members of Congress have a lot of information that the public does not have," and eventually the American people would understand the boycotts.

29. As Trump took office, he had the fewest cabinet members confirmed of any modern-day president. Trump had nominated only 28 of 690 Senate-confirmable jobs in the executive branch.

30. The day before his inauguration, Trump asked fifty Obama administration officials to stay on in their roles.

31. As Trump took office, the State Department said they have not been instructed on whether to attend upcoming Syria peace talks.

32. The Trump team tried an additional form of suppressing the media, serving CNN with a retraction request, which the network is forced to respond to, for a routine story about potential Trump appointee Tom Price.

33. In a parting interview, Vice President Joe Biden told *Vanity Fair* that he is worried Trump might destroy Western civilization.

34. The *NYT* reported that law enforcement and intelligence agencies are examining communications and financial transactions between Russian officials and Trump advisers Paul Manafort, Carter Page, and Roger Stone.

35. Despite Trump's efforts to promote ticket sales through a heavily advertised online video, the Trump inauguration and the events surrounding it were poorly attended, and no well-known celebrities agreed to perform.

36. The *Guardian*'s editorial board described Trump's inaugural speech as "bitter, blowhard and banal," and said that, in contrast to FDR's message of overcoming fear, Trump "told the world to be very afraid."

37. The streets along the inaugural parade had thin crowds, and many parade stands were empty.

38. Trump's team banned the Department of the Interior from Twitter after the department retweeted photos of small crowds on Inauguration Day. A National Park Service spokesperson apologized.

39. Within hours of Trump's being sworn in, all mention of climate change, civil rights, and LGBT issues was removed from the White House web page.

40. Upon taking office, Trump was likely in violation of the federal lease of his D.C. hotel.

41. An estimated 2.5 million Americans participated in the Women's March, in cities all over the country, ten times more than showed for Trump's inauguration. The Associated Press (AP) reported that five hundred thousand marched in D.C. alone, doubling the expected attendance.

Protesters flood Independence Avenue during the Women's March on Washington January 21, 2017, in Washington, D.C. Large crowds attended the anti-Trump rally a day after he was sworn in. The Women's March was the largest single-day protest in U.S. history. (Getty Images)

Week 11

JANUARY 22-28, 2017

This week was chaos. Journalist Dan Rather described it as "the Twilight Zone," and author Stephen King as "the ugliest first week of a presidency in the history of the American republic." This week, there were numerous articles about Trump transforming America into an authoritarian state.

1. The revised tally for the Women's March came at over four million, making it the largest protest march in U.S. history.

2. Hundreds of protesters coming to the Women's March from Canada were turned away at the U.S. border.

3. Trump defensively responded with outright lies about his inauguration crowd. Press Secretary Sean Spicer said, "This was the largest audience to ever witness an inauguration—period." When pressed about this lie on NBC, Conway said Spicer's false claims were "alternative facts."

4. Numerous reporters were arrested while covering the inauguration protests. NBC reporters were released, while others were charged.

5. In true authoritarian form, Trump declared his inauguration day to be the National Day of Patriotic Devotion.

6. On the Monday after he was sworn in, a group of constitutional scholars, Supreme Court litigators, and White House ethics lawyers filed a suit claiming Trump violated the Constitution by receiving foreign payments.

7. The *Boston Globe* ran an op-ed titled "The President's House Is Empty." In Week 2 Melania and Barron were living in New York City and now apparently Trump is too. We have normalized this item.

8. The *WSJ* reported that Flynn—in addition to Page, Manafort, and Stone—is under investigation for links to Russia.

9. National Park Service spokesman Tom Crosson confirmed that days after the inauguration, Trump called the National Park Service. Trump was reportedly upset about the retweet of a side-by-side photo of his inauguration next to one of Obama's.

10. As of the Sunday evening after being sworn in, Trump still hadn't severed his ties to his businesses as promised. After the media reported this, documents were filed the next day.

11. The White House comment line switchboard no longer has a person answering the phone.

12. Conway said Trump, breaking decades of precedent, would never release his tax returns, saying the American public is not focused on this, despite last week's ABC poll showing that 74 percent of Americans want his returns released.

13. Despite Trump's proclamation of having a "great meeting" and "long standing ovations" at a meeting with the CIA, it turned out that Trump's

paid employees were the ones cheering, and his relations with intelligence agencies may be getting worse.

14. Without explanation, the Centers for Disease Control and Prevention (CDC) canceled a Climate and Health Summit scheduled to take place in Atlanta.

15. Trump's staff continued to tell multiple outright lies daily, including statements about the size of the federal workforce, the inauguration crowd size, and voting fraud.

16. Massive leaks coming from the White House staff portrayed Trump as impulsive and childish, in stories published by the *NYT* and *WaPo*.

17. The State Department's statement of apology for past LGBT discrimination was scrubbed from the official website.

18. Trump signed an executive order reinstating and expanding to an unprecedented degree the Global Gag rule, which bars federal funding to any NGO that offers or educates on abortion services. He signed the order in the company of all white men.

19. Days after being sworn in, Trump told lawmakers that three to five million illegal ballots cost him the popular vote. The next day, Spicer repeated the same lie.

20. Trump froze EPA grants.

21. Trump banned EPA employees from providing information to reporters or on social media about new contracts or grants.

22. Later, Trump banned multiple federal agencies from communications with members of Congress and the media.

23. Trump threatened to send federal troops to Chicago, citing false claims about crime rates.

24. Republican legislators around the country proposed a series of bills that would criminalize peaceful protests.

25. Russian media reported on multiple arrests, disappearances, and deaths of Russian intelligence agency officers for leaks related to Trump's dossier and interference with the U.S. election. There was also news of a possible public trial.

26. Trump's attorney general nominee, Sessions, said he would not commit to recusing himself from Trump-related investigations. This is counter to requirements of Department of Justice (DoJ) rules.

27. Advisers to Germany's chancellor, Angela Merkel, said they were still struggling to open communications channels with the Trump administration days after the inauguration, and that they have "given up" on him acting "presidential."

28. On Wednesday, the White House sent an e-mail to the press titled "Praise for President Trump's Bold Action."

29. Trump ordered billions of dollars in funding cuts to UN agencies and took action toward pulling the U.S. out of treaties, including the Paris climate agreement.

30. *Mother Jones* reported that some of Trump's foreign business partners attended his inauguration and were given VIP treatment.

31. Trump mandated that EPA scientific studies undergo a review by his political staff before being released publicly.

32. Trump called for an investigation into voter fraud, then delayed signing the executive order. Media uncovered that several Trump insiders are registered to vote in two states.

33. Trump said torture "absolutely works," putting him at odds with his staff on a draft torture order. For now, Trump said Secretary of Defense James Mattis could override him.

34. In his CIA speech, Trump said of Iraq, "We should've kept the oil. But, okay, maybe we'll have another chance." He kept that mantra alive during the week, endangering our troops serving in Iraq.

35. Protests continued around the country, including major marches in Philadelphia and New York City.

36. In a bizarre interview with ABC, Trump continued to maintain his false claim about voter fraud and his fixation on the crowd size at his inauguration, showing David Muir a photo and also saying, "We had the biggest audience in the history of inaugural speeches."

37. The *Economist* downgraded the U.S. on its democracy scale to a "flawed democracy."

38. The entire senior staff of the State Department left ahead of the arrival of SoS Tillerson, who has no diplomatic or government experience. It was unclear if they resigned or were fired.

39. Trump signed an executive order to build the wall. The Mexican president said Mexico would not be paying for the wall and canceled a previously scheduled trip to meet with Trump in D.C.

40. The *WSJ* editorial board slammed Trump for his treatment of Mexico and for floating a 20 percent tariff, calling him a "foreign-affairs neophyte."

41. Steve Bannon said the media should "keep its mouth shut" and referred to news organizations as "the opposition party."

42. National Public Radio (NPR) reported that Trump signed a record number of executive actions in his first week; in a shift from his predecessors' first orders, none of Trump's addressed ethics.

43. Trump replaced the leader of a federal agency that oversees the use of federal land, including the controversial Trump Hotel D.C.

44. *Business Insider* reported on a memo between Igor Sechin, the CEO of Rosneft, Russia's state oil company, and Trump ally Carter Page, offering Page and his colleagues a stake in Rosneft in exchange for lifting U.S. sanctions.

45. Trump issued a statement on Holocaust Memorial Day that did not mention Jews, breaking a precedent of past Democratic and Republican presidents.

46. The same day, Trump signed an executive order banning citizens from seven Muslim-majority countries from entering the U.S. for the next ninety days. Trump also announced plans to increase the number of countries on this list.

47. Trump said Christian refugees would be given preference, a clear violation of the Constitution.

48. The Trump immigration ban did not include any countries in which Trump has business interests.

49. Trump hinted at dropping U.S. sanctions against Russia in the lead-up to his first official call with Putin. In response, McCain said that if Trump lifts sanctions, Congress will restore them.

50. Much of Trump's foreign policy is decided and carried out by two men, Bannon and Kushner.

Week 12

JANUARY 29–FEBRUARY 4, 2017

An observation on Week 12: several of the most important items in this very long list are the ones not getting coverage, including the surge in violence in Ukraine and the many abuses of power to silence dissent and stomp on ethics. Conflicts of interest abound, unfettered.

1. Protests over Trump's Muslim ban took place all over the country and around the world. Thousands protested in major airports and cities, including in many red states.

2. Trump's executive order was criticized by many and supported by few. Christian leaders spoke out against prioritizing Christian refugees.

3. Innumerable horrid stories about the impact of the Muslim ban surfaced during the week. Spicer minimized its impact. Presidents of 598 colleges and universities wrote a letter of concern about the ban.

4. Trump promoted Bannon, in a reorganization of the National Security Council (NSC), to a regular seat on the principals committee. This move prompted widespread criticism and outrage. Democrats proposed a bill to remove Bannon from the NSC.

5. A federal judge in New York issued a temporary order blocking the Muslim ban. The next morning, the DHS issued a statement that it would not abide by the court order and would continue to enforce Trump's order. Four other federal judges issued similar temporary orders.

6. The judicial branch was removed from the White House website. It was later restored.

7. An op-ed published on Medium, "Trial Balloon for a Coup?," which included a diagram showing an almost completely gutted State Department, trended for an entire day.

8. In just twelve hours, more than 900,000 people in the UK signed a petition demanding Trump's state visit to Britain be canceled.

9. Germany's Chancellor Merkel, according to her spokesperson, had to explain to Trump the Geneva Convention and the requirement for the international community to take in war refugees on humanitarian grounds.

10. Books topping the Amazon list included *1984*, *It Can't Happen Here*, and *Brave New World.*

11. Trump continued to say his executive order should not be termed a "Muslim ban." Trump insider Rudy Giuliani told Fox News that Trump had called him seeking advice for a "Muslim ban" and how to do it legally.

12. According to Senator Marco Rubio, the State Department was instructed not to speak to Congress about Trump's Muslim ban.

13. On the day when the *NYT* described Bannon's elevation and Michael Flynn's stumbling, Flynn's Twitter account was taken down.

14. The AP reported that the voter fraud expert chosen by Trump to conduct his voter fraud investigation is registered to vote in three states.

15. *Politico* reported that several House Judiciary Committee aides secretly worked on the Muslim ban. Their bosses were not aware of the ban or their staffs' involvement.

16. Acting Attorney General Sally Yates directed the Justice Department not to defend the Muslim ban, saying the ban is not legal.

17. Hours later, Trump fired her, saying she "betrayed" the DoJ. Her memo was rescinded that same night. Trump's action, named for a similar firing by Nixon, became known as the "Monday Night Massacre."

18. The *WSJ* reported that Trump's tax plan, unlike a plan proposed by congressional Republicans, would preserve millions in tax benefits for Trump's companies.

19. Days after Trump's phone conversation with Putin, Russia escalated hostilities in Ukraine. Among the chaos of the Muslim ban, etc., few in the U.S. noticed.

20. Six were killed in a mosque shooting in Quebec. The perpetrator was a white man who had "liked" Trump's Facebook page. The next day, the Eiffel Tower went dark overnight in support of the victims. Trump, however, said nothing publicly about the attack.

21. The White House publicly stated that any State Department employees who disagree with Trump's Muslim ban should resign.

22. As Trump prepares to name his first Supreme Court pick, for the first time in decades, no one is bothering to advocate for diversity anymore.

23. In retaliation for its coverage, Trump said he would no longer send his spokespeople to appear on CNN. One reporter noted, "They're trying to cull CNN from the herd."

24. Trump announced his Supreme Court nominee in the style of a reality TV show, claiming he had invited both finalists to the prime-time announcement.

25. Trump's sons, who are running his business supposedly without input from their father or participation in his administration, sat in the front row for the Supreme Court announcement and mingled with politicians, including the chair of the Senate Finance Committee.

26. *WaPo* reported that Eric Trump's business trip to Uruguay in January for the Trump Organization cost taxpayers nearly one hundred thousand dollars in hotel rooms for Secret Service and embassy staff.

27. For a second day in a row, Trump personally attacked Schumer on Twitter: "Fake Tears Chuck Schumer."

28. Trump canceled a trip to Milwaukee, where he was scheduled to deliver an economic address, given the threat of protests.

29. The House Oversight Committee stopped accepting calls relating to investigating Trump.

30. As part of Black History Month, Trump cited Frederick Douglass, whom he described as still alive, and Pence tweeted about a white man.

31. Trump's first overseas raid, in Yemen, ended in failure. Among the dead were a Navy SEAL and fifteen women and children, including an eight-year-old American. Trump has relaxed Obama's stance on protecting civilians.

32. The Yemen raid garnered little media attention for days, until Reuters reported via U.S. military officials that Trump "approved his first covert counterterrorism operation without sufficient intelligence, ground support or adequate backup preparations."

33. Spicer admitted that Trump was not in the White House Situation Room during the Yemen raid. He issued the green light while at dinner, and during the raid itself, he was busy sending unrelated, incendiary tweets.

34. In the third wave of mass disruption in January, seventeen Jewish community centers (JCCs) received bomb threats.

35. First Lady Melania Trump said she and Barron may never move to the White House.

36. Reuters's editor in chief announced that its reporters would cover the Trump administration as an authoritarian regime.

37. On the day Tillerson was confirmed, the House killed a transparency rule that required oil companies to report payments to foreign governments. As Exxon CEO, Tillerson had lobbied against this provision.

38. The House's move on transparency also impacts the ability to trace the owner of a 19 percent stake of Rosneft, mentioned in Week 11's list.

39. In a phone call, Trump threatened his Mexican counterpart with sending the U.S. military to stop "bad hombres down there." The next day, Trump said this was just meant to be "lighthearted."

40. Trump's first call with the prime minister of Australia, Malcolm Turnbull, one of our closest allies, went terribly and ended prematurely after, according to Australian media, Trump berated Turnbull.

41. Later that night, at 7:55 P.M., Trump tweeted that Obama had agreed "to take thousands of illegal immigrants from Australia." This was a lie: Obama accepted 1,250 refugees. The next day, John McCain called Turnbull to express U.S. support. Representative Steny Hoyer also issued a statement of support.

42. Trump opened his remarks at the National Prayer Breakfast by attacking Arnold Schwarzenegger for *Celebrity Apprentice*'s low ratings. Trump continued to hold the role of executive producer of the show.

43. Later at the National Prayer Breakfast, Trump promised to "totally destroy" the Johnson Amendment, which forbids churches from political activity in order to maintain their tax-exempt status.

44. Trump lifted sanctions, introduced by Obama in December, on Russia's intelligence and security agency, the Federal Security Service (FSB). A former head of the FSB claimed in the Duma that this was the start of a formal "antiterror alliance."

45. Virginia filed a contempt motion against Trump over his Muslim ban, asking the U.S. District Court to make sure that the federal government complied with the temporary restraining order.

46. At the hearing, the Justice Department said over one hundred thousand visas had been revoked as part of Trump's Muslim ban. The State Department later said the number was closer to sixty thousand.

47. NBC reported, via a FOIA request, that e-mails reveal ethics officials warned Trump against an "unprecedented" effort to staff his cabinet without ethics vetting. Trump aides rebuffed OGE efforts.

48. As noted in Week 11, Trump issued a Holocaust statement without mentioning Jews. This week, *Politico* reported that the State Department's draft statement did reference Jewish victims, but the Trump team took the reference out.

49. Due to lower sales caused by boycotts, both Nordstrom and Neiman Marcus announced that they will no longer carry Ivanka Trump's brand.

50. A poll by Public Policy Polling (PPP) revealed that 40 percent of registered voters support impeaching Trump. Polls asking during the Nixon years didn't reach this level until sixteen months after the Watergate break-in.

51. A former prime minister of Norway was detained for hours at Dulles Airport because his passport showed a visit to Iran in 2014.

52. Trump ordered female staffers to "dress like women." Twitter mocked his words, with a campaign using the hashtag #DressLikeAWoman.

53. Kellyanne Conway continued telling outright lies, citing a fabricated "Bowling Green massacre" as a rationale for Trump's Muslim ban.

54. Trump said he would be "cutting a lot out of Dodd Frank" since his friends with "nice businesses" are having a hard time borrowing money because of rules and regulations.

55. NPR reported that Trump faces fifty-five lawsuits in his first two weeks—as compared with five for Obama, four for George W. Bush, and five for Clinton.

56. The *New Yorker* and *Vanity Fair* canceled their involvement with White House Correspondents' Dinner parties.

57. As the week came to a close, a federal judge appointed by President George W. Bush ruled that Trump's Muslim ban be halted nationwide, immediately.

Protesters rally during a demonstration against the new immigration ban issued by Trump at John F. Kennedy International Airport on January 28, 2017, in New York City. President Trump signed the controversial executive order that halted refugees and residents from predominantly Muslim countries from entering the United States. (Getty Images)

Week 13

FEBRUARY 5-11, 2017

Given that we're thirteen weeks into this tracking exercise, starting this week I'll be adding a section at the bottom of the list, "Some Things We've Already Normalized." The goal is to remind us of items in the early lists that at the time were unprecedented and shocking, but have long since been accepted and forgotten. We must remember what normal used to be if we are to resist and find our way back—and so we begin!

1. In a Fox News interview, when Bill O'Reilly referred to Putin as a "killer," Trump responded, "Well, you think our country is so innocent?"

2. Trump's comments were condemned by leaders and commentators on both sides. Putin demanded an apology from Fox News.

3. The *NYT* ran a disturbing story describing Trump's first two weeks. Trump is reportedly still isolated—going upstairs alone at 6:30 P.M. and maintaining a small inner circle.

4. The *NYT* also reported that Trump wasn't fully briefed on the executive order he signed giving Bannon a National Security Council seat. Trump tweeted that he calls his own shots, and referred to the story as fake news.

5. The *WSJ* reported that arrests of Russian intelligence officers are likely linked to Russia's U.S. hacking.

6. House Minority Leader Nancy Pelosi called on the FBI to probe Trump's personal and financial ties to Russia, to explore whether Russia may be blackmailing him.

7. By the end of the week, six New England Patriots said they would not attend the Super Bowl celebration ceremony at the White House.

8. McClatchy reported on efforts to silence public opinion: the White House comment line is shut down, signatures aren't being counted on petitions, and federal agencies are no longer allowed to respond to requests.

9. On *SNL*, Melissa McCarthy delivered a devastating portrayal of Sean Spicer. Days later, Trump was reportedly rattled, and rumored to be seeking a replacement for Spicer.

10. Spurred by a petition signed by 1.5 million citizens, UK officials announced that Trump would not be allowed to address the UK Parliament during his upcoming visit.

11. As of this week, numerous key roles in the executive branch remain unfilled. Of the 658 positions that are open and require Senate confirmation, Trump has appointed only thirty-five (eight are confirmed, and twenty-seven await confirmation).

12. Trump continued to assert that the "very dishonest press" doesn't report terrorist attacks. At first, the source of his claim appeared to be *InfoWars*. The White House later released a list of attacks, with several misspellings; all attacks on the list had in fact been covered.

13. The White House is still not open to the public. Tours typically resume shortly after the new president takes office.

14. As part of her lawsuit against the *Daily Mail Online*, Melania Trump mentioned the "once-in-a-lifetime" merchandising possibilities she envisioned as first lady.

15. Republicans on the House Administration Committee voted to eliminate the agency charged with protecting voting machines from being hacked.

16. Without explanation or warning, the USDA purged a page on animal welfare from its website.

17. Trump attacked the federal judges ruling on his Muslim ban, and questioned the independence of the judicial branch, saying, "The courts seem to be so political," and threatening that any terrorist attacks would be the fault of these judges if they don't rule his way.

18. Trump also referred to federal judge James Robart, a George W. Bush appointee who ruled against Trump's Muslim ban, as a "so-called judge."

19. Trump's nominee for the Supreme Court, Neil Gorsuch, called Trump's remarks "demoralizing" and "disheartening." Trump said Gorsuch's comments were misrepresented. In response, a spokesperson for Gorsuch said his comments had been reported accurately.

20. During a debate on the confirmation of Jeff Sessions, Senator Elizabeth Warren was formally silenced by Mitch McConnell after she tried to read a letter by Coretta Scott King on the Senate floor. McConnell's refrain will go down in history books: "She was warned. She was given an explanation. Nevertheless, she persisted." The rule cited by McConnell, Rule XIX, was not used on GOP men like Ted Cruz.

21. A *Huffington Post* story seemed to call Trump's mental health into question, citing via leaks that Trump called Flynn at 3 A.M. to ask him about a weak dollar and the economy. A member of George W. Bush's NSC added, "I genuinely do not think this is a mentally healthy president."

22. In response to Trump's failed raid in Yemen, according to the *NYT*, Yemenis withdrew permission for the U.S. to use Yemen for antiterror ground missions. More stories came out questioning Trump's decision-making process and truthfulness on the Yemen raid.

23. The *WSJ* reported that Trump's appointee as acting SEC chair is seeking to get rid of the requirement under Dodd Frank that companies disclose the pay gap between CEOs and their employees.

24. Trump tweeted, from both his personal account and the POTUS account, that Nordstrom has treated his daughter unfairly. He included a veiled threat: "She's a great person—always pushing me to do the right thing." Nordstrom cited lagging sales, and their stock rose 4.1 percent that day.

25. Trump's attack against Nordstrom was widely condemned by ethics experts as a clear violation of federal ethics rules.

26. The next day, Kellyanne Conway said on Fox News, "Go buy Ivanka's stuff is what I would say." Spicer, later that day, said Conway was "counseled." Trump sided with Conway.

27. Jason Chaffetz, head of the House Oversight Committee, called Conway's statement "wrong, wrong, wrong." The next day, Conway made a snide remark about Chaffetz's stormy town hall.

28. France's spy agency, the DGSE, said Russia is actively working to get Marine Le Pen elected. Le Pen announced that if she wins, Jews would have to leave France if they did not give up their Israeli citizenship.

29. A bipartisan group of senators introduced a bill that would require congressional approval for Trump to lift sanctions on Russia.

30. A Hitler Valentine's Day card was handed out by College Republicans at Central Michigan University. Nationwide, anti-Semitic incidents continue to escalate since Election Day.

31. Reuters reported that Trump did not get briefed prior to his phone call with Putin and had to ask aides about the New START treaty.

32. Breaking seven decades of presidential precedent, Trump said he will not rely on the White House Council of Economic Advisers.

33. Democrats in the House moved to force a debate on Trump's Russia business conflicts and ties.

34. Rachel Maddow reported that in order to shield himself from having to pay for the cleanup of a polluted business site in South Carolina formerly owned by his son, Trump claimed to have no relationship to the former owner.

35. Town halls hosted by Republicans in Utah, Tennessee, and other states had huge crowds show up and vociferously show their displeasure.

36. A national poll conducted by PPP found that 51 percent of Trump supporters think the "Bowling Green massacre"—a lie put forward by Conway in Week 12—is justification for Trump's Muslim ban.

37. Courts again turned back Trump, this time in his efforts to scale back an Obama-era consumer protection designed to avoid conflicts of interests when brokers give retirement advice.

38. First Lady Melania Trump again broke with tradition by not hosting the first lady of Japan during her tour of Washington, D.C.

39. *WaPo* reported that despite his earlier denials, Flynn did indeed have conversations with Russia's ambassador about sanctions while Obama was still in office. Flynn changed his story to say that he had "no recollection" of the conversations.

40. Aides for Pence, who had vouched for Flynn on Sunday TV, said Flynn had lied to Pence, and that Flynn was his only source. When asked about this story, Trump feigned ignorance, despite *WaPo* having it on page 1.

41. In a meeting with senators, Trump again asserted voter fraud, citing alleged buses of Massachusetts residents who voted in New Hampshire.

42. Trump has still not come to an agreement with federal officials over the Trump International Hotel's violation of its lease.

43. After a conversation with the leader of Taiwan in Week 3, an action not taken by an American president in decades, Trump asserted that his bumble was intended to show strength to China. Unceremoniously this week, Trump changed course and said he would honor the "One China" policy.

44. Without notice, days after Sessions was confirmed as attorney general, federal agents started conducting mass immigration raids in at least six states. Citizens reported seeing checkpoints in several major cities.

45. CNN reported that U.S. intelligence has corroborated some parts of the infamous Russian dossier. Spicer responded by attacking CNN for fake news reporting.

46. Gallup found that only 29 percent of Americans think Trump is respected in the world, while 67 percent believe he is not.

47. Trump continued to actively lie this week. Protests and marches continued nationwide.

SOME THINGS WE'VE ALREADY NORMALIZED:

- The first family is not living in the White House.
- Trump is not receiving daily intelligence briefings.
- Trump remains an executive producer of *Celebrity Apprentice.*
- Media coverage of Trump includes images of his tweets.
- Our secretary of state is a former CEO of Exxon who has close ties to Putin and no government or diplomatic experience.

Week 14

FEBRUARY 12-18, 2017

After a slight reprieve last week, this week was again chaos, resulting in the longest weekly list so far. An overarching theme to watch is the consolidation of power: positions in the executive branch are going unfilled and layoffs continue. Meanwhile, Trump, his children, and his small circle of insiders are making all major decisions domestically and abroad.

1. Trump was tested in his first national security incident, as North Korea launched intermediate-range ballistic missiles. Trump, at Mar-a-Lago hosting Japanese prime minister Shinzo Abe, conferred with a small circle of aides *and* Abe, using a flashlight app that could have been compromised. Trump then proceeded to stop by a wedding at his club for a photo op.

2. The public exchange with Abe was captured in photos by a member of the Mar-a-Lago club, who posted them publicly on his Facebook page.

3. After staying mum about Flynn over the weekend, Trump spokespeople went from saying Flynn "does enjoy the full confidence of the president" to Trump is "evaluating the situation" on Monday. That evening, Flynn "resigned."

4. Flynn became the third Trump adviser to resign over inappropriate ties to Russia (others are Manafort and Page).

5. After firing Flynn, Trump pivoted to blaming the media and intelligence for leaks. He referred to "intelligence" in quotes, again. Trump also denied any wrongdoing by Flynn.

6. The *NYT* reported that several Trump campaign aides had repeated contact with Russia in the year before the election. CNN reported that, in fact, Trump aides had been in constant contact with Russian officials.

7. Chaffetz, chair of the House Oversight Committee, chose to investigate leaks, but not Trump and his regime's connections to Russia.

8. Attorney General Sessions refused to recuse himself from investigations into Trump and his regime's ties to Russia, despite his ties to Trump during the campaign.

9. As Trump's battle with intelligence agencies intensified, he brought in loyalist billionaire hedge fund manager Stephen Feinberg to lead a broad review of the intelligence agencies.

10. The FBI released four hundred pages of records from their race discrimination probe of Trump's real estate company in the 1970s.

11. The *WSJ* reported that the Pentagon has no records of approving Flynn's Russian-TV payment.

12. *WaPo* reported that Trump staffers are so scared of being accused of leaking to the media that they are now using a secret chat app called Confide to communicate.

13. After Betsy DeVos's Senate confirmation as secretary of education, the Department of Education removed a website for disabled students. After outrage by Democratic senators and the public, it was restored.

14. A Gallup poll found that Americans see the U.S. world standing as the worst in decades. Only 29 percent think world leaders respect Trump.

15. The Windsor, Ontario, school board canceled all student trips to the U.S., citing "safety and equity" concerns.

16. Trump picked longtime friend Patrick Park for the post of ambassador to Austria, saying Park is a big fan of *The Sound of Music.*

17. Democrats in public, and Republicans in private (mostly), voiced concern about Trump's mental health. Mental health professionals also warned about Trump.

18. White House senior policy adviser Stephen Miller was awarded "bushels of Pinocchios" (by *WaPo*) for a series of lies told on Sunday talk shows. Pundits compared his tone, his demeanor, and the content of his statements to those of a propaganda minister.

19. In one of his first actions as AG, Sessions signaled he would not pursue states that refused to enforce Obama's transgender policy.

20. The list of stores dropping Trump product lines continued to grow.

21. In joint press conferences with heads of state from Japan, Canada, and Israel, Trump took two questions each time from only friendly news sources, and refused to take any from the major media present.

22. Bloomberg reported that while Trump was making calls about the cost of Lockheed's F-35 fighter plane, the CEO of rival Boeing was in the room.

23. SoS Tillerson irked his Russian counterpart in their first meeting, when he made journalists leave the room before his opening remarks. "Why did you shush them out?" Ambassador Sergey Lavrov said.

24. A federal judge in Virginia granted an injunction against Trump's Muslim ban. By the end of the week, Trump said he would not appeal.

25. Trump's efforts to deport immigrants broadened to include a Dreamer; Immigration and Customs Enforcement (ICE) detained a woman who was seeking a protective order against an abusive boyfriend. ICE refused to respond to inquiries by Democrats as deportations escalated.

26. CNN reported that the Pentagon may propose sending troops to Syria in response to Trump's order to come up with proposals to fight ISIS.

27. After meeting with Trump, Canadian prime minister Justin Trudeau urged deeper EU-Canadian ties in response to Trump's isolationist policies.

28. The director of the Office of Government Ethics said there was "strong reason" to think Kellyanne Conway violated rules and that disciplinary action is warranted for her on-air endorsement of Ivanka's brand.

29. In a room of all white men, Trump signed the repeal of transparency rules for oil companies to disclose foreign payments.

30. The twenty-three Republicans on the House Ways and Means Committee voted not to require Trump to release his tax returns.

31. Russia dealt Trump several provocations, including placing a ship outfitted with spying equipment thirty miles off Connecticut's coast; deploying a cruise missile, in violation of an arms control treaty; and buzzing a U.S. warship in the Black Sea.

32. Meanwhile, Russian-backed forces continued to escalate violence in Ukraine.

33. Russian TV's coverage of Trump started to become less flattering.

34. The *WSJ* reported that Trump's nominee for secretary of commerce, Wilbur Ross, wants to keep his stake in eleven entities whose fortunes he would affect in his new job.

35. The week after Trump announced he would support the "One China" policy, China awarded Trump a ten-year trademark for construction services.

36. When asked about the alarming rise of anti-Semitism in the U.S. during his press conference with Israeli Prime Minister Benjamin Netanyahu, Trump shifted to bragging about his Electoral College victory.

37. The *WSJ* reported that U.S. intelligence agencies are withholding information from Trump, citing concerns that information would be leaked or compromised. The DNI and CIA denied this is happening.

38. SoS Tillerson was conspicuously absent from Trump's meetings with heads of state. Tillerson also did not invite the customary press corps to accompany him on a truncated trip to a Group of Twenty meeting.

39. *Politico* reported on the frustration of Tillerson, Secretary of Defense Mattis, Secretary of Homeland Security John Kelly, and CIA director Mike Pompeo for being left out of decision-making. Kushner was described as a "shadow Secretary of State," running his own foreign policy.

40. The already gutted State Department conducted additional layoffs, a sign that key foreign policies will be made at the White House.

41. *Mother Jones* reported on a classified memo for intelligence on how to prepare Trump's daily briefing: "less material, less nuance, less dissent."

42. Rachel Maddow reported on the Kushner family's desire to buy the Miami Marlins, as the owner, Jeffrey Loria, who is selling the baseball team, is being considered by Trump for the plum job of ambassador to France.

43. Trump hit his lowest approval level in a Pew Research poll: 39 percent approve of his performance, 56 percent disapprove; in the Gallup Daily tracking poll, 38 percent approve, 56 percent disapprove.

44. Six of Trump's staffers were escorted out of the White House after failing their FBI background checks.

45. *Newsweek*'s Kurt Eichenwald reported that U.S. allies in Europe are conducting their own intelligence operations to assess Trump ties to Russia.

46. Ten members of Trump's Advisory Commission on Asian Americans and Pacific Islanders resigned, citing "portrayal of immigrants, refugees, people of color, and people of various faiths as untrustworthy, threatening, and a drain on our nation."

47. Trump hosted an unhinged, lie-ridden, impromptu eighty-minute press conference. A GOP senator texted CNN's John King, "He should do this with a therapist, not on live television."

48. Also at the press conference, Trump insulted reporter April Ryan when she asked if he planned to arrange a meeting with the Congressional Black Caucus. Trump replied, "Do you want to set up the meeting? Are they friends of yours?"

49. Also, when asked by a Jewish reporter about anti-Semitism, Trump called him a liar, told him to sit down, and said anti-Semitism was coming from "the other side."

50. *WaPo* reported that Michael Flynn lied in a January 24 FBI interview, denying sanction discussions with Russian ambassador Sergey Kislyak. Lying to the FBI is a felony offense.

51. Retired vice admiral Robert Harward turned down the offer to replace Flynn, citing a chaotic White House. According to a friend, Harward described Trump's offer as a "shit sandwich."

52. David Petraeus also bowed out of consideration for national security adviser, citing the inability to pick his own staff.

53. Kushner met with Time Warner executives to complain about CNN's coverage of Trump. Time Warner has a pending merger with AT&T, which requires governmental approval.

54. Trump held his first 2020 campaign event today in Florida. A Craigslist ad that offered money to enthusiastic attendees was taken down.

55. The AP reported on a leaked draft memo that shows Trump is considering using one hundred thousand National Guard troops to round up unauthorized immigrants.

56. Germany's minister of defense warned the U.S. against hurting European cohesion, abandoning core Western values, and cozying up to Russia.

57. Trump tweeted, then deleted, then expanded his list of enemy media outlets and tweeted that the media is the "enemy of the American people"—a slogan also used by Lenin and Stalin.

58. After a closed-door meeting between FBI director James Comey and the Senate Intelligence Committee before leaving for recess, Marco Rubio tweeted, "I am now very confident Senate Intel Comm I serve on will conduct thorough bipartisan investigation of #Putin interference and influence."

59. The cost of protecting Trump and his family is staggering. Obama averaged $12 million a year, while Trump's three weekend visits to Mar-a-Lago alone cost $10 million, and the guards at Trump Tower in New York cost $183 million per year.

60. Representative Barbara Lee introduced legislation signed by more than seventy House Democrats urging the removal of Steve Bannon from the NSC.

61. PBS, AmeriCorps, the Legal Services Corporation, and the National Endowment for the Arts are all set to be eliminated in Trump's preliminary budget.

SOME THINGS WE'VE ALREADY NORMALIZED:

- Trump continues to financially benefit from his businesses and to gain additional revenues from his position of power.
- Very few open positions in the executive branch are getting filled.
- Trump has still not come to agreement on the lease of his D.C. hotel on federal land.
- Without an official government role, Ivanka Trump continues to attend meetings with heads of state and leaders of corporate America.

Week 15

FEBRUARY 19–25, 2017

This week had two themes. The first was Trump's lack of empathy—the cruelty and heartlessness toward Americans who are not white, straight, Christian, and male. Trump and his regime continued to target the defenseless, including transgender individuals, Native Americans, and people of color. The second theme was Russia: evidence of ties between the Trump regime and Russia is continuing to pour out; meanwhile, the regime is actively seeking to suppress information.

1. Despite Trump saying his company would not enter any new overseas deals once he took office, Donald Jr. and Eric announced the opening of a Trump-branded golf course in Dubai. U.S. taxpayers continue to pay the cost for the security detail that covers Trump's sons on such trips.

2. At Trump's campaign rally in Florida, he referenced a Swedish terrorist attack that never happened as a rationale for his anti-immigrant policies.

3. When questioned about his source, Trump tweeted he learned about the Sweden attack that never happened by watching Fox News.

4. The DHS ordered the creation of a new office in ICE named VOICE (Victims of Immigration Crime Engagement), and ordered all resources set aside to advocate for "illegal aliens" moved over to VOICE.

5. The *NYT* reported on a back-channel plan, originally handed in a sealed envelope by Trump's attorney Michael Cohen to Flynn, for a Ukraine and Russia "peace plan" calling for new leadership in Ukraine, in exchange for the U.S. lifting sanctions on Russia. Other Trump connections to Ukraine involved with the plan include Ukrainian politician Andrii Artemenko, Paul Manafort, and businessman Felix Sater.

6. The Ukraine lawmaker, Artemenko, who allegedly worked with two Trump associates on the back-channel plan, faces a treason inquiry.

7. *Talking Points Memo* (*TPM*) reported on the significance of Sater's involvement, and his ties to Russia and Trump, dating back to construction of the Trump SoHo hotel.

8. The *Daily News* reported that as Trump's Muslim ban faced court challenges in New York after the rollout, Stephen Miller called the Brooklyn U.S. attorney at home and told him how to defend it.

9. The *WSJ* reported that the Trump regime is using unrealistically rosy growth forecasts to hide that his tax plan would lead to a soaring deficit.

10. The *WSJ* also reported that the Trump regime is considering changing the way the U.S. trade deficit is calculated—again to hide reality.

11. The *NYT* reported on struggles within the *WSJ* between journalists and owner Rupert Murdoch over the direction of the paper and coverage of Trump.

12. NBC News reported that the Kremlin is preparing a psychological dossier on Trump for Putin. Preliminary findings are that Trump is a "risk taker" who can be "naïve."

13. The *WSJ* reported that the Senate Intelligence Committee is looking at possible collusion between Russia and Trump staff, including Manafort, Trump's former campaign chair.

14. The Senate Intelligence Committee sent letters to a dozen intelligence agencies, organizations, and individuals demanding they preserve communications related to Trump's possible ties to Russia.

15. In the past two months, there have been sixty-nine threats at fifty-four JCCs in twenty-seven states. Also, this week more than 170 gravestones at a Jewish cemetery in Missouri were vandalized.

16. Bowing to pressure, and perhaps a tweet by Hillary, Trump finally blandly responded to the alarming rise of anti-Semitism, calling it "horrible," but offering no actions or solutions.

17. The Anne Frank Center issued a harsh statement, including, "The President's sudden acknowledgment is a Band-Aid on the cancer of anti-Semitism that has infected his own administration." Spicer scolded the Anne Frank Center for its statement.

18. Edward Price, the NSC spokesperson, resigned over Trump's disturbing and repeated attempts to undermine U.S. intelligence.

19. Republicans home for break and attending town halls all over the country were greeted by overflowing rooms of angry constituents, questioning them on repealing ACA and holding Trump accountable. Chants of "Do your job!" were heard at many meetings.

20. By the end of the week, numerous elected Republicans disappeared or refused to meet with constituents. Representative Louie Gohmert blamed his refusal on the Gabby Giffords shooting, to which she replied, "Have some courage. Face your constituents."

21. After Trump's announced Muslim ban, interest in trips to the U.S. has declined, which is likely to cost jobs in the tourism sector.

22. An NBC News/Survey Monkey poll found that two-thirds of Americans fear the U.S. will become involved in another war.

23. The Trump regime issued new immigration enforcement policies, which included, among other things, hiring ten thousand additional ICE officers and expanding the definition of "criminals" to include people who have been charged but not convicted.

24. The *NYT* editorial board called Trump's "deportation force" an assault on American values.

25. Horrific and heartless stories of deportations continued, including a twenty-six-year-old woman with a brain tumor who was taken from a hospital.

26. *WaPo* reported that Deputy National Security Adviser K. T. McFarland was once accused of violating voter registration laws by being registered to vote at two different addresses. In New York, this is a felony offense.

27. More than one million people signed a White House petition—a White House petition record—requesting that Trump release his tax returns.

28. Prime Minister Trudeau said Canada will continue to accept asylum seekers from the U.S.

29. The air force said it cannot account for the one billion dollars in savings that Trump alleges he negotiated for the development of two new Boeing airplanes.

30. Mexico rejected Trump's plan to deport migrants illegally crossing the U.S. border, including non-Mexicans, to Mexico.

31. Trump touted his immigration raids, referring to them as a "military operation." While visiting Mexico to assure our seemingly former ally, Kelly attempted to clarify that it wasn't really a military operation.

32. As Kelly and Tillerson visited Mexico, relations between the U.S. and Mexico are now at their lowest point in decades. Of note, Kelly and Tillerson's stance differs from Trump's.

33. *WaPo* reported that Tillerson has largely been offstage, without power, and has not been included in meetings with Trump.

34. The State Department continues to be dysfunctional, conducting no daily briefings.

35. The State Department issued a warning to its employees on leaking—which was promptly leaked.

36. Trump rescinded rules that had provided protection for transgender individuals to use bathrooms corresponding to their gender identity.

37. The U.S. Interagency Council on Homelessness's page on LGBT youth homelessness was taken down.

38. The *Huffington Post* reported additional detail on Trump's activities during the failed Yemen raid. As the raid went awry, putting Navy SEALS and civilians at risk, Trump was at dinner with Bannon and Kushner, and later tweeting and deleting and tweeting about an upcoming show on CBN.

39. In another case of nepotism, Eric Trump's brother-in-law was appointed to a key position at the Department of Energy.

40. *Politico* reported that while serving as Trump's campaign manager, Paul Manafort faced a blackmail attempt by a Ukrainian parliamentarian to expose him and Trump as Russia-friendly.

41. The *NYT* reported that National Security Adviser H. R. McMaster may reorganize the NSC and that Trump didn't understand the significance of the executive order that elevated Bannon and took the intelligence director and Joint Chiefs of Staff chairman off the council.

42. At the Conservative Political Action Conference (CPAC), Bannon was openly hostile to the media, which he referred to as "corporatist, globalist media" and "the opposition party."

43. Bannon also vowed a daily fight for "deconstruction of the administrative state." This comes as only thirty-four out of nearly seven hundred open positions in the executive branch that require Senate confirmation have nominees.

44. The White House assigned DHS to work with intelligence to write a report to back Trump's Muslim ban and the danger caused by the seven countries named in the ban. Sources said intelligence is concerned, including about the veracity of the claim.

45. The DHS report was later leaked out—it found there is not a threat from the seven countries targeted by the Muslim ban.

46. *WaPo* calculated that Trump has lied an average of four times per day since taking office. He has not yet had a day in office without a lie.

47. A shocking op-ed in the *Atlantic*, "I Was a Muslim in the Trump White House," described a woman working for the NSC who lasted for eight days under Trump—and described how diversity was viewed as a weakness.

48. The remnants of a Dakota Access Pipeline protest camp was set ablaze by opponents as the government deadline for getting off the land approached.

49. CNN reported that Reince Priebus tried to get the FBI to publicly refute recent reporting on Trump's ties to Russia. The FBI refused. Such communication is problematic because of decades-old restrictions.

50. The White House confirmed conversations between Priebus and the director and deputy director of the FBI, but denied there was anything wrong with these conversations occurring.

51. Trump continued his gaslighting strategy of castigating leakers while not acknowledging the growing evidence of his ties to Russia.

52. The Russian ambassador to the UN died suddenly in New York City. Vitaly Churkin was the fifth Russian ambassador to die in the past three months.

53. A group of law professors filed a misconduct complaint against Kellyanne Conway. The letter said Conway should be "sanctioned for violating government ethics rules" and "conduct involving dishonesty, fraud, deceit or misrepresentation."

54. Border patrol agents stopped travelers on a domestic flight from San Francisco to New York and asked passengers departing the plane to show identification.

55. Reporters from the *NYT*, *BuzzFeed*, CNN, the *Los Angeles Times*, and *Politico* were excluded by Sean Spicer from a closed-door White House briefing on Friday. The BBC, the *Guardian*, and the *Daily Mail* were also excluded.

56. In protest, ABC and *Time* chose not to attend the briefing, and the *WSJ* issued a statement objecting and saying they will not participate in closed briefings in the future.

57. At CPAC, a section of the audience waved Russian flags until staff came and took the flags away.

58. At CPAC, Trump delivered yet another dystopian speech, but failed to acknowledge actual hate crimes happening in our country, including a Kansas bar shooting where a white man yelled "get out of my country" at two Indian American men before shooting into a crowd and killing one.

59. The father of the slain man appealed to parents in India not to send their children to the U.S., saying, "There is a kind of hysteria spreading that is not good because so many of our beloved children live there."

60. *WaPo* reported that in addition to the Trump regime's efforts to discredit news on its ties to Russia, they also sought the help of senior intel officials and GOP leaders Senator Richard Burr and Representative Devin Nunes, who head the Senate and House Intelligence Committees.

61. A NBC/*WSJ* poll found that 53 percent of Americans want Congress to look into Trump's ties to Russia; only 25 percent do not.

62. Breaking with Trump, McMaster advised his staff that use of the label "radical Islamic terrorism" is not helpful. Nonetheless, Trump continued to use the term in his CPAC speech.

SOME THINGS WE'VE ALREADY NORMALIZED:

- Our economy and economic policy is being run predominantly by former employees of Goldman Sachs.
- U.S. taxpayers are footing the bill for three Trump residences: the White House, Trump Tower in New York, and Mar-a-Lago.
- Meanwhile, Melania does not appear to be conducting much if any of the typical FLOTUS duties.
- Power continues to consolidate in the hands of a few.

Week 16

FEBRUARY 26–MARCH 4, 2017

This week's theme was undoubtedly the continued taint of the Trump regime's ties to Russia. For the first time since Election Day, Trump seems unable to drive the media story lines.

1. Trump announced he would not attend the White House Correspondents' Association dinner, amid growing tension with the media.

2. Further to the stories on Priebus reaching out to the FBI in Week 15, *Axios* reported that Spicer made calls to the CIA, and Republican leaders Nunes and Burr, asking they discredit the *NYT* story about Russian ties.

3. Before the investigation even begins, Nunes, the House Intelligence Committee chair, said he hasn't found evidence of the Trump team's ties to Russia.

4. Citizens for Responsibility and Ethics in Washington (CREW) filed under the FOIA to see communications between Priebus and the FBI.

5. Trump accused Obama of being behind the town hall protests: "I think [Obama] is behind it. I also think it's politics."

6. Early in the week, Trump pronounced, "I haven't called Russia in ten years," a statement then thoroughly discredited by video clips of his numerous statements otherwise.

7. In an NBC interview, former president George W. Bush said that "we need answers" on Trump ties to Russia.

8. Another Trump cabinet pick, Wilbur Ross, has deep ties to Russia, including investing more than a billion dollars in the Bank of Cyprus and becoming a vice chairman of the bank. Putin appointed the other vice chairman.

9. Rachel Maddow reported the Bank of Cyprus also has ties to a Russian oligarch who helped Trump make a sixty-million-dollar profit flipping a home in Florida he owned for just two years.

10. As Trump continued his attacks on Sweden, O'Reilly booked a supposed Swedish "national security adviser" for his Fox News show. After Swedish officials indicated this expert was not known, O'Reilly was forced to issue a watered-down apology. Since then, Trump has stopped attacking Sweden.

11. A massive wave of anti-Semitism continued, including two more cemeteries desecrated, and thirty-one threats against JCCs in one day alone. The Anti-Defamation League (ADL) has said anti-Semitism in the U.S. is the worst since the 1930s.

12. Seeming to follow David Duke's lead, Trump said it could be Jews behind the rash of anti-Semitic attacks.

13. Another mosque was burned down—the fourth in seven weeks.

14. *WaPo* reported the FBI had once planned to pay the British spy behind the Trump-Russia dossier, lending credibility to the contents.

15. The Senate Intelligence Committee may call Christopher Steele, the British spy who gathered the information for the infamous dossier, to testify. If they can find him (he's in hiding).

16. The father of the SEAL killed in the failed Yemen raid told the *Miami Herald* he wants answers.

17. Trump sought to blame the generals for the SEAL's death.

18. Trump also tried to blame Obama, saying he finished what Obama had started. This was refuted by a former aide, who said Obama had never approved the raid.

19. NBC reported that despite Trump's claims to the contrary, senior U.S. officials said there was no significant intel yielded from the Yemen raid.

20. Dianne Feinstein and other Democratic senators demanded more information from the State Department on China's sudden decision to grant a trademark to the Trump organization. As noted in Week 14's list, this occurred shortly after Trump declared his support of the "One China" policy.

21. The Trump White House let Conway off the hook on an ethics investigation, saying she acted "inadvertently" in promoting Ivanka's brand—despite recommendations by the OCE for discipline.

22. Amid protests and ethics concerns, Donald Jr. and Eric Trump cut the ribbon on a new hotel in Vancouver, built and financed by one of Malaysia's richest families.

23. A businesswoman who touts access to China purchased a sixteen-million-dollar penthouse at Trump Park Avenue. Trump retains an economic interest in the property.

24. Although an order to stay Trump's Muslim ban is in place, problems continued, including Muhammad Ali Jr. being detained in a Florida airport and French historian and expert on the Holocaust Henry Russo being threatened with deportation while traveling to a discussion at Texas A&M University.

25. Stories continue to describe the State Department's diminishing role. Department staff are being excluded from meetings with foreign leaders, leadership posts are going unfilled, and many employees are quitting. Trump also has threatened to slash the department's budget by one-third.

26. The State Department has not held a single daily briefing under Tillerson. Daily briefings had been the norm since the 1950s. Limited daily briefings are set to begin next week.

27. The State Department tweeted, then deleted, a congratulatory message to an Iranian director for winning an Oscar.

28. Trump escalated his war on the media, telling *Breitbart* that the *NYT*'s "intent is so evil and bad" and that "they write lies."

29. Trump delivered a de facto State of the Union (SOTU) speech, read from a teleprompter. Although his manner was mild, the content continued to be nationalistic and dystopian. The Center for American Progress said that of sixty-one claims made in the speech, fifty-one were false.

30. Refuting Trump's claims about crime rates in his SOTU, the Brennan Center for Justice noted, "Nationally, crime remains at the bottom of a 25-year downtrend, half of what it was at its peak in 1991. Last year, rates of overall crime fell for the 14th year in a row."

31. Justice Ruth Bader Ginsburg did not attend Trump's SOTU, nor did Maxine Waters.

32. The Democratic women of the House wore the white of the suffragists at Trump's SOTU to show support of women's rights.

33. Ahead of the SOTU, Trump officials fed news outlets misinformation on a shift in Trump's immigration plans—hinting that the time might be right for an immigration bill. CNN reported that Trump misled reporters to get positive coverage.

34. The *NYT* reported that the Obama administration had rushed to preserve information on the Trump team's ties to Russia, spreading it to government agencies.

35. Also reported by the *NYT*: American allies, including the British and the Dutch, provided the Obama administration with information on meetings between Russian officials and the Trump regime in European cities.

36. A bombshell story by *WaPo* reported that Sessions met with Kislyak twice, but did not disclose those meetings when asked during his Senate confirmation hearing.

37. Sessions first spoke with Kislyak in Cleveland on July 18—the same day the Trump campaign gutted the GOP's platform of its anti-Russia stance on Ukraine. On July 23, WikiLeaks released stolen e-mails from the DNC.

38. The *WSJ* reported that Sessions used campaign funds to pay for his trip to the Republican National Convention (RNC), where he met the Russian ambassador.

39. At a press conference the next day, Sessions recused himself from the investigation of Russia's meddling in the 2016 election.

40. As the controversy continued, Sessions said he would submit an amended testimony to address Democratic senators' questions.

41. *Politico* reported that Trump adviser Carter Page also met with Kislyak at the RNC. While in office, former senator Harry Reid had asked Comey to investigate Carter, saying Carter was also meeting with "high ranking sanctioned individuals" in Moscow.

42. Carter told MSNBC he had met with Kislyak, then seemed to backtrack on CNN to say he never spoke with him for more than ten seconds.

43. Kushner and Flynn also met with Kislyak, at Trump Tower in December. Of note, given the venue and people involved, this points to Trump having direct knowledge of the meeting.

44. CNN reported that U.S. intelligence considers Kislyak to be one of Russia's top spies and spy recruiters in Washington.

45. Kislyak did not attend the Democratic National Convention.

46. The Trump team forced Nikki Haley, ambassador to the United Nations, to fire career staffers who she had asked for advice on how to talk tough with Russia.

47. A front-page story in *USA Today* reported that e-mails released to the *Indianapolis Star* under a FOIA request show Pence used personal e-mail for state business while governor, including for sensitive matters and homeland security issues, and that his personal AOL account was hacked.

48. The next day, Pence turned over thirteen boxes of government-related e-mails to the Indiana statehouse, so that they could be archived in accordance with the law.

49. *Politico* reported that Trump's transition team canceled planned training on ethics for his staff, appointees, and cabinet members.

50. Maddow reported on a leaked DHS assessment document indicating that most U.S.-based extremists radicalized years after entry into the U.S. These findings negate the main argument made by the Trump regime for its Muslim ban, and may explain why it has yet to release the new version frequently promised to be coming soon.

51. Inhumane roundups by ICE continued, including the detention of a father of four U.S.-born children who has lived in the U.S. for twenty years. He was seized while dropping his kids off at school.

52. A twenty-two-year-old immigrant was detained by ICE moments after a press conference. She was seven when her family moved to the U.S. from Argentina, placing her under Deferred Action for Childhood Arrivals (DACA) immigration policy.

53. Spicer was reported to be checking his staff's phones for leaks.

54. Reuters reported on stepped-up efforts by the Trump regime to plug leaks, including Secretary of the Treasury Steven Mnuchin using his first senior staff meeting to inform his aides that he would not tolerate leaks.

55. Top talent continues to leave the already thinly staffed executive branch over poor morale and fear of Trump.

56. *Foreign Policy* reported that the Trump White House is considering using high-end security software for its networks in an effort to stop leaks.

57. Schwarzenegger quit *Celebrity Apprentice*, citing too much "baggage"—a clear shot at Trump. Trump continues his role as executive producer of the show (which we've normalized!).

58. Trump fired back via Twitter the next day, claiming Schwarzenegger was fired because of low ratings. Schwarzenegger told him to hire a fact-checker.

59. As stories continued all week about Trump and his team's ties to Russia, Trump, offering no proof, accused Obama of wiretapping phones in Trump Tower, tweeting, "This is Nixon/Watergate. Bad (or sick) guy!"

60. As the week closed out, Trump yet again headed to Mar-a-Lago for the weekend, after leaving the White House at 3 P.M. on Friday. Trump has yet to visit Camp David.

SOME THINGS WE'VE ALREADY NORMALIZED:

- Trump's sons are continuing to conduct business from which Trump receives a direct economic benefit.
- Our executive branch is vastly understaffed, and Trump and his regime seem to make little effort at hiring (consolidation of power).
- Some in our media continue to push the notion of a Trump "reset," and seek to normalize Trump and his regime.
- Comey continues to not cooperate with Congress in hearings. We also do not know the status of the DoJ inquiry into Comey and the FBI, and whether this has been allowed to continue under Sessions.

Week 17

MARCH 5-11, 2017

This week, some threads from past weeks' lists continue to unwind: Trump and his regime's ties to Russia, conflicts of interest, and the dysfunctional and largely unstaffed executive branch. But the broader story of Week 17 is an underlying shift away from democracy, and it's not subtle at all!

Under the auspices of Trump's top adviser Steve Bannon, our democracy as we know it is transitioning under a term used widely this week: the Deep State. Know this term! As referenced this week, the Deep State is a paranoid, authoritarian vision of a regime under siege and being infiltrated—in this case by Obama and his loyalists. This authoritarian vision has been used by the Trump regime as justification for its ever-increasing need to consolidate power into the hands of a trusted few—transforming our democracy into an authoritarian state and making it harder to get to the truth on many troubling matters.

1. Trump refused to back off his claims tweeted Saturday morning in Mar-a-Lago that Obama wiretapped Trump Tower. Trump demanded that Congress investigate his claim.

2. Trump provided no evidence for his wiretap claim. Sunday morning on *Meet the Press*, former DNI Clapper said, "I can deny" that Trump Tower was wiretapped.

3. Sunday, the FBI's Comey also denied Trump's wiretapping claim and asked the DoJ to publicly reject it. The DoJ has not rejected Trump's assertion.

4. A White House spokesperson rejected Comey's assertion that Trump's wiretapping claim is false. Trump regime members continued to dance around the lack of evidence all week, refusing to deny Trump's false claim.

5. *WaPo* reporters, in a disturbing piece, described Trump's fury and instability over the weekend. Further to the story, reporter Robert Costa tweeted: "Trump woke up in good spirits, per his confidants. Read the papers and watched early cable shows, liked that they covered his allegations."

6. Upon Trump's return to the White House, Monday was the first weekday that his schedule was entirely closed to the press.

7. Other members of the Trump regime acted erratically, including adviser Roger Stone, who was suspended from Twitter for his misogynistic rants. Later in the week, Stone admitted to being in contact with Guccifer 2.0, the DNC hacker, during the campaign.

8. After his flip-flopping on Russian contact in Week 16, this week Page, without offering evidence, said his phone may have been tapped.

9. As the week closed out, Trump had still not been in contact with Comey or the FBI about his wiretapping claims. Trump's sources for his claim were *Breitbart* and right-wing radio host Mark Levin.

10. Trump signed a second Muslim ban order, ignoring the findings of the DHS report he ordered, this time targeting six countries.

11. Four states sued to stop the ban, including the state of Hawaii, which used Stephen Miller's own words on TV, that the revised travel ban is really just like the original, as evidence.

12. Alex Orono, the Ukrainian businessman who arranged the "peace plan" meeting between Cohen, Sater, and Artemenko mentioned in Week 15, died suddenly.

13. The first imports of Russian steel arrived at a port in New Jersey.

14. The Trump White House announced, contrary to an executive order that Trump signed requiring the use of domestic steel in U.S. pipelines, that the Keystone XL builders can use non-U.S. steel.

15. The AP reported on how Trump Hotel D.C. has become the central hub of political capital in D.C. Several of Trump's cabinet members are living at his hotel as well. Trump still financially benefits from the property.

16. The top official in charge of public buildings at the GSA, who was in charge of overseeing Trump's D.C. hotel, resigned. Trump will get to appoint his replacement.

17. Cork Wine Bar in D.C. sued Trump for unfair competition over Trump's D.C. hotel, saying, "President Donald Trump's ownership constitutes unfair competition and we are asking the courts to stop it."

18. Young people in a Sweden suburb said a Russian TV crew tried to bribe them to riot. Trump has largely gone quiet on his assertions of a terrorist attack in Sweden.

19. McClatchy reported on the curious overlap on the tarmac between the luxury plane of the same Russian billionaire who bought Trump's Florida home (delivering Trump a sixty-million-dollar profit) with Trump's plane in Charlotte, North Carolina. A spokesperson for the oligarch, Dmitry Rybolovlev, said, "Mr. Rybolovlev has never met Donald Trump."

20. CNN reported on a speech given by Kislyak in October 2016 in which he denied meeting Trump or his campaign team during the 2016 election. We now know that is a lie on many counts.

21. On Sunday, after North Korea launched a ballistic missile into the Sea of Japan, Trump and the State Department had no response for over five hours. The State Department eventually issued a statement after 10 P.M.

22. Shortly after Trump had lunch with Tillerson, the White House issued a statement congratulating Exxon on a new program.

23. The White House press release contained full paragraphs copied verbatim from Exxon's press release.

24. Bureau chiefs wrote a letter saying they were "deeply concerned" that Tillerson did not bring the press on a trip to Asia to visit important allies: "It gives the American people no window whatsoever into the views and actions of the nation's leaders." Spicer claimed this was due to cost savings by Tillerson.

25. MSNBC's Andrea Mitchell was kicked out of two State Department press briefings for trying to ask Tillerson questions. The briefings turned out to be solely photo ops.

26. Mexico's top diplomat came to D.C. and skipped the normal channels, going straight to the White House to meet with Kushner, McMaster, and Trump's economic adviser Gary Cohn. The State Department did not know about the meeting.

27. In a statement, the State Department asked the New York City medical examiner not to disclose the cause of death of Russian UN ambassador Churkin.

28. Tillerson still doesn't have a deputy, and most of the diplomats with expertise in senior roles have been fired or left the State Department. Former ambassador to Iraq Christopher Hill said the vacuum of leadership is "unprecedented."

29. *ProPublica* reported that Trump has quietly installed four hundred insiders to be his ears and eyes in the federal government. Hires include former lobbyists and campaign workers.

30. As of March 10, 96 percent of key positions in the executive branch remain unfilled. Trump has nominees in the confirmation process for only 8 percent of positions requiring Senate confirmation.

31. More reporting emerged of Trump's failed Yemen raid which revealed carelessness with civilian casualties, and that despite the White House's taking credit for a successful mission in which they recovered intelligence, that was not in fact the target of the mission; rather, the goal was to kill a key member of al Qaeda.

32. A top general took responsibility for the failed Yemen raid. Trump had blamed the generals in Week 15—atypical of a commander in chief.

33. Widespread instances of anti-Semitism continued across the country, including a bomb threat to the Jewish Children's Museum in Brooklyn, vandalism at the largest synagogue in the Pacific Northwest on Shabbat, and incidents at two Maryland schools.

34. WikiLeaks announced another data dump they claim came from the CIA. This time, the media largely did not bite, questioning instead whether Russia was the source of the data and whether the purpose was to distract from Trump's wiretap claims and Russian ties.

35. A large portion of the WikiLeaks dump is from the CIA's Center for Cyber Intelligence, the unit assigned by Obama to respond to Russia's interference in our election.

36. Two days after the WikiLeaks dump, British politician Nigel Farage visited Assange at the Ecuadorian embassy in London (March 9). On February 25, Farage had had dinner with Trump, Ivanka, and Kushner.

37. Costco started stocking the popular Orwell book *1984*.

38. Gold Star father Khizr Khan canceled a speaking engagement in Toronto, saying he was notified that his travel privileges were under review. At the end of the week, there were still open questions about this curious case.

39. The American Civil Liberties Union (ACLU) filed an ethics complaint against Sessions in Alabama over his Senate confirmation testimony about contact with Russia to "determine whether he violated the Alabama Rules of Professional Conduct."

40. The Office of Government Ethics director wrote a letter to Trump's deputy White House counsel on the decision not to discipline Conway, saying he remains "concerned" about the Trump aide's "misuse of position" and that her evading punishment risked "undermining the ethics program."

41. Bannon and *Breitbart* increasingly used the term "Deep State" to describe an imagined "covert resistance" to Trump, largely composed of Obama loyalists. "Deep State" is a term generally used by authoritarian regimes.

42. Fox News's Hannity tweeted Thursday it was time for Trump "to purge the deep state saboteurs from the government."

43. On Friday, Representative Steve King also suggested that a purge of federal staff needs to happen.

44. The same day, when asked in the White House daily briefing, Spicer did not reject the concept of the Deep State.

45. That afternoon, without any notice, Sessions asked all forty-six remaining Obama-appointed U.S. attorneys to resign.

46. Three watchdog groups, Democracy 21, CREW, and the Campaign Legal Center, asked the U.S. attorney for the Southern District of New York (home to the Trump Organization) to investigate whether Trump effectively receives benefits from foreign entities, in violation of the Constitution.

47. The U.S. attorney for the Southern District of New York, Preet Bharara, was invited to Trump Tower in November and asked by Trump to stay on, only to be asked to resign in the Sessions sweep on Friday. As of today, Bharara refused to resign.

48. *Politico* reported that Europeans are concerned about Bannon and Trump's efforts to undo the European Union. Commerce Secretary Ross, who has ties to Russia per Week 16, is also anti-EU.

49. Trump golf properties enjoyed an unprecedented boom in sales, as people seek access to Trump. Eric Trump bragged, "I think our brand is the hottest it has ever been."

50. The *New Yorker* reported on one of Trump's questionable and likely illegal deals in Baku, Azerbaijan (a former Soviet republic). Ivanka oversaw the deal, which was linked to corrupt oligarchs and terror financiers.

51. Russia broke a thirty-year-old nuclear treaty with the U.S., deploying a missile with nuclear capability that threatens Europe. U.S. generals briefed Congress, but the Trump regime did nothing about it.

52. Muhammad Ali Jr. was again detained at an airport, this time, ironically, in D.C., after meeting with lawmakers to discuss his being detained last month.

53. In a filing this week, Flynn admitted that he had worked as a foreign agent during the campaign, lobbying Trump on behalf of the Turkish government, and earning $530,000 for his work.

54. Examples emerged of how Flynn's lobbying role may have interfered with U.S. policy, such as during the transition, when Flynn delayed approval of a Kurdish plan to seize Raqqa. The Obama White House had worked for months on this plan.

55. Flynn also had written an op-ed, published on Election Day, calling Turkey "our strongest ally" against ISIS and recommending we extradite "radical cleric" Fethullah Gulen from his home in Pennsylvania back to Turkey.

56. Information in Flynn's filing also revealed a possible bribe attempt to get an e-mail sent by Hillary regarding Benghazi re-marked as classified.

57. Spicer said Friday that Trump did not know that Flynn was working as a secret foreign agent, as evidence mounted to suggest otherwise.

58. In a morning interview with MSNBC, a former Trump transition team member said Trump and the transition team knew about Flynn.

59. Pence said he didn't know about Flynn. It was uncovered that Representative Elijah Cummings had sent Pence a letter on this topic in November. In an awkward interview with Fox News's Bret Baier Friday, Pence offered up twice that this was the first he had heard of it—not responding to a question asked.

60. A story that had been dismissed four months ago about Russia's Alfa Bank pinging the Trump Organization's servers re-emerged. Sources reported the FBI is investigating.

61. Trump's former campaign manager Manafort may face charges in Ukraine for his involvement with mass police shootings of protesters in Kiev in 2014 allegedly backed by Russian interests.

62. At a White House press briefing Friday, some members of the media literally laughed at Spicer for his explanation of why Trump accepted and took unwarranted credit for this month's jobs report, while in the past saying the jobs report was phony.

63. As Week 17 drew to an end and Trump marked his first fifty days in office, the media was widely critical of the frequent lies and assertions without evidence made by Trump. A concern emerged about Trump's credibility should a crisis emerge.

64. On Friday morning, Spicer broke a 1985 federal rule that forbids government officials from publicly commenting about the jobs report within one hour of the release, when he commented via a tweet.

Week 18

MARCH 12-18, 2017

Events and actions this week lend credence to an evolving theme: Trump isn't all that interested in typical legislative stuff like passing health care or his budget—his passion and focus are on enriching himself and making America white.

This week was also unfamiliar territory for Trump: he couldn't control the narrative the entire week. We're learning Trump is great on offense, but inept on defense.

1. As Trump's wiretap claim entered its second week, Trump still offered no evidence to support it. Conway backed Trump, saying, "Microwaves that turn into cameras" can spy on us. Spicer said Trump didn't mean wiretapping literally when he tweeted about wiretapping.
2. Office of Management and Budget (OMB) director Mick Mulvaney claimed Obama had been "manipulating" jobs data.
3. The Trump regime had its second e-mail scandal in two weeks. The *WSJ* reported that Tillerson used an e-mail alias, "Wayne Tracker," while at Exxon, to discuss climate change.
4. Kushner is set to net four hundred million dollars on the sale of a New York City office building to a Chinese firm with murky links to the Chinese power structure.
5. Ivanka imported fifty-three metric tons of Chinese goods while her father was making "Buy American" speeches.
6. A businesswoman with ties to Chinese intelligence and the Chinese ruling elite purchased a penthouse in a Trump property for $15.8 million.
7. Items 5 and 6, along with the thirty-eight trademarks granted to Trump in Week 14, are examples of increasing financial ties between the Trump regime and China as Trump readies to host China's premier at Mar-a-Lago. Trump has shifted on both his "One China" policy and trade war threats in recent weeks.

8. Trump insider Roger Stone told the AP that he may have been the subject of surveillance by U.S. intelligence for his possible role as a foreign agent for Russia.

9. Former White House staffer Monica Crowley, who was fired for plagiarism, took a job as a foreign agent for a Ukrainian oligarch with ties to Russia.

10. Reuters uncovered that Russian elites have invested close to one hundred million dollars in Trump luxury towers in South Florida.

11. The yacht of Trump financial backer Robert Mercer was spotted in the British Virgin Islands next to the yacht of Dmitry Rybolovlev, the Russian oligarch mentioned in Week 17 for his multiple connections to Trump.

12. Mercer also has close ties to Bannon, and collaborated with him on at least five ventures, including *Breitbart News*.

13. A document released Thursday showed that Flynn received three formerly undisclosed payments from Russian interests, totaling seventy thousand dollars.

14. The *WSJ* also reported that Flynn had an interaction with a Russian-British national while serving as head of the Defense Intelligence Agency, which he failed to report as required.

15. Russia continued provocations: a Russian spy ship reappeared off the U.S. eastern seaboard, just twenty miles south of a U.S. Navy submarine base.

16. News of the DoJ's findings that Russian agents were behind the 2014 Yahoo hacking brought Russia interference back front and center. The hacking exposed personal data of 500 million Yahoo accounts.

17. As things heated up on Russia in the Senate, McCain accused Senator Rand Paul, on the Senate floor, of "working for Vladimir Putin."

18. Further to Week 17's Deep State theme, Trump opened the week by signing an executive order on a "reorganizing" of the executive branch, which opened the door for the Trump regime to dismantle federal agencies.

19. *Politico* reported on the growing paranoia and dysfunction in Trump's executive branch. One staff member said, "People are scared."

20. Tillerson mirrored Trump, saying the proposed slashing of the State Department's budget would make it "much more efficient," while offering no vision or strategy for foreign policy.

21. As mentioned in Week 17, much to the consternation and objections of our media, Tillerson did not bring press along on his first trip to Asia. He did, however, bring one reporter from the conservative website *Independent Journal Review* (*IJR*)—who coincidentally had written a glowing piece about him two weeks prior.

22. Friday, Tillerson said the U.S. was prepared to take military action against North Korea if necessary. Tillerson cut his trip to South Korea short, citing fatigue.

23. Saturday, Tillerson stood by his decision not to allow the media along on his trip to Asia, saying, "I'm not a big media press access person."

24. A federal judge in Hawaii halted Trump's second Muslim ban the day before it was set to go into effect, saying the ban is unconstitutional and discriminates based on religion.

25. The federal judge also cited remarks made by Miller and Giuliani on TV in his ruling.

26. The *IJR* speculated that Obama's visit to Hawaii was behind the ruling. The next day, the *IJR* added an editor's note to the article, and soon thereafter, the reporter resigned.

27. *BuzzFeed* reported that Nick Ayers, a top adviser to Pence, is an investor in the *IJR*.

28. Trump held a campaign rally in Nashville on Wednesday at which he chastised the federal judge who ruled against his Muslim ban, claiming incompetence, before transitioning the crowd to cheers of "Lock her up!"

29. Trump's ranting at the Nashville rally about the halt of his second Muslim ban—"This is a watered-down version of the first one"—could be a death blow to his chances at an appeal, which he does plan to file.

30. *WaPo* reported on two internal reports prepared for the Trump regime, with data undercutting the premise of his Muslim ban.

31. Trump's Nashville campaign rally was half full, while thousands of protesters outside chanted things like "Bless your heart" (a Southern insult) to drown out Trump supporters.

32. Sebastian Gorka, Trump's top counterterrorism adviser, was reported to be a sworn member of a Hungarian group listed by our State Department as "under the direction of the Nazi Government of Germany" during World War II.

33. In Netherland's race for prime minister, the candidate associated with Trump lost with unexpectedly poor results. Some in Europe noted that Austrian and Dutch elections point to a Trump backlash.

34. At a photo op before his Michigan speech, Trump said publicly to the governor, "Come on, governor—even though you didn't endorse me . . . I never forget."

35. *WaPo*'s David Fahrenthold followed up on three promises made by Trump on November 8: donating his salary, giving away leftover funds from the Inaugural Committee, and donating profits derived from foreign governments that use Trump hotels to the U.S. Treasury. Trump has given nothing so far.

36. On Friday, the Trump Organization announced that it will wait until 2018 to start donating profits from foreign government use of his hotels.

37. Anti-Semitic threats continued. CNN created a map to show how widespread Jewish bomb threats have become: so far in 2017, 159 bomb threats in thirty-eight states.

38. Trump's Muslim ban took another blow from a federal judge in Maryland, who suspended the part of the ban that prevented visas from being issued. Trump and his surrogates continued talking about the need to contain "judicial overreach."

39. Trump's budget director's first week got off to a disastrous start when Mulvaney said of cutting funds to Meals on Wheels that it's a program "not showing results." The words "Meals" and "Wheels" trended on Twitter for the rest of the day.

40. The *WSJ* reported that tax cuts for the wealthy in the GOP's tax plan would save Trump millions.

41. Part of Trump's 2005 tax return was leaked to reporter David Cay Johnston, who shared them on *The Rachel Maddow Show*. Trump called it "fake news"; Maddow called the scoop "a drop of water in the desert."

42. The New Jersey legislature passed a bill requiring presidential candidates to disclose their tax returns.

43. Trump nominated his fifth Goldman Sachs employee, to a role as deputy treasury secretary.

44. Ethics documents showed that Chris Liddell, Trump's director of strategic initiatives, has three to four million dollars' worth of stock in eighteen of the companies whose CEOs attended a meeting with him and Trump.

45. By midweek, Republicans including Nunes, chair of the House Intelligence Committee, were turning on Trump for his wiretapping claim. Ryan joined him, too.

46. The Senate Intelligence Committee issued a formal statement that there is no evidence of any surveillance (going beyond wiretapping) on Trump Tower during or after the campaign. The statement was issued fifteen minutes before the White House daily briefing.

47. At the daily briefing, which started an hour late, Spicer said Trump stands by his allegation that Obama wiretapped Trump Tower.

48. Spicer also parroted allegations first made on Fox News that Obama used British intelligence agency GCHQ to spy on Trump. GCHQ issued a strongly worded refutation of this ridiculous claim.

49. Friday morning, UK media reported the U.S. made a formal apology to Britain for the White House accusation that the GCHQ wiretapped Trump Tower.

50. That afternoon, Spicer denied that an apology was made, saying, "I don't think we regret anything," while Trump commented on the matter, "We said nothing. All we did was quote a very talented legal mind."

51. With cameras rolling, Trump refused when Merkel asked him to shake her hand.

52. Multiple pictures surfaced of Ivanka inexplicably seated next to Chancellor Merkel at the meeting.

53. Trump misspoke during the press conference with Merkel, referring to the U.S. as a "company" instead of a country.

54. Also at the press conference, Trump turned to Merkel in answering about his wiretap claims by Obama and said, "At least we have something in common perhaps," a reference to Obama's 2010 approval to monitor Merkel's phone. He claimed he got the information from Fox News.

55. After the press conference, Fox News's Shep Smith said on his show, "Fox News knows of no evidence of any kind that now-President of the United States was surveilled at any time, in any way. Full stop."

56. Oklahoma representative Tom Cole became the first congressional Republican to call on Trump to apologize to Obama for his false wiretapping claim.

57. Friday it was announced that Trump's DoJ is working to speed deportations, shifting immigration judges to twelve U.S. cities where the DoJ claims there are more immigrants who have committed crimes.

58. Cases continued to surface of noncriminals being targeted for deportation, including a mother of six in Chicago during a routine check-in with ICE. Her congressman was handcuffed while trying defending her.

59. Canada's version of the Girl Scouts—the Girl Guides—canceled all trips to the U.S., citing concerns over Trump's Muslim ban and its message.

60. Representative Steve King said blacks and Hispanics "will be fighting each other" before overtaking whites in population. Few in the GOP condemned him as King continued to the TV circuit reiterating his white nationalist beliefs.

61. The Trump regime went to court to try to bring the consumer protection agency created by Senator Warren after the 2008 recession under direct control of Trump, opening the door to dismantling it.

62. The White House "1600 Daily" e-mail blast mistakenly included a very obviously satirical article from *WaPo*, "Trump's budget makes perfect sense and will fix America, and I will tell you why."

63. Continuing his pattern of hiring insiders, Trump plans to nominate Kellyanne Conway's husband to a powerful post overseeing the federal government's lawsuits, including the Muslim ban.

64. Republicans continue to face energized, raucous crowds when returning home. Senator Joni Ernst faced a packed crowd, which frequently booed her.

65. The House Intelligence Committee sent a letter to the FBI, the CIA, and the National Security Agency (NSA) demanding info on whether Flynn was being surveilled. The committee oversees the FBI, CIA, and NSA, yet the agencies did not comply. Rachel Maddow called the noncompliance "nuts" and "not normal."

66. Open hearings in Congress on Russian interference start next week: March 20 in the House and March 30 in the Senate. McCain said of upcoming Trump-Russia probes, "I think there's a lot of shoes to drop from this centipede."

Week 19

MARCH 19-25, 2017

Of all the weeks so far, this was the most exhausting. In normal times, any one item below would be a top story for days or weeks—the flow of not normal is so heavy right now, it's a challenge to keep track. Newsman Dan Rather best summarized the feel of Week 19: "I have seen a lot in my lifetime. But I have never seen anything like this. No one has. The cauldron of chaos and confusion which engulfs President Trump in his early days in office is simply unprecedented."

1. Three weeks have passed since Trump's tweet that Obama wiretapped Trump Tower. He has yet to offer any evidence, or apologize.

2. As Week 19 opened, Trump's Gallup daily approval rating hit a new low: 37 percent approve, 58 percent disapprove.

3. After Trump's embarrassing meeting with Merkel last week, Germany's defense minister refuted a claim by Trump that Germany owes NATO "vast sums of money" by saying that "there is no debt account in NATO."

4. New York attorney general Eric Schneiderman hired a prosecutor who worked under fired U.S. Attorney Preet Bharara to focus on issues specifically related to the Trump regime.

5. An op-ed penned by two former chief White House ethics lawyers, titled "Trump's Unprecedented War on Ethics," detailed a long laundry list of ethics breaches already committed by Trump and his regime.

6. Continuing the Deep State theme, the Trump regime installed insiders in executive branch agencies to spy on fellow employees. At the same time, leadership roles remain largely unfilled (61 of 553 have a nominee).

7. *Politico* reported that federal career staffers are living in fear of being targeted and singled out by *Breitbart* and other conservative media outlets for not being loyal to Trump.

8. At the first day of the House Intelligence Committee's hearing into Russia, Comey said the FBI is conducting a counterintelligence investigation of both Russian interference in our election and whether there was any coordination between the Trump campaign and Russia.

9. Comey also said there is "no information" to back Trump's wiretapping claim.

10. During the hearing, Trump live-tweeted from the @POTUS Twitter account. His tweets contained false and misleading information.

11. When asked by Representative Jim Himes during the hearing, Comey refuted and corrected information in Trump's tweets. The AP fact-checked Trump's tweets vs. what was actually said in testimony.

12. McClatchy reported that the FBI is also investigating the role of conservative media outlets like *Breitbart* and *InfoWars* in the Russian hacking of our election.

13. Ivanka got a West Wing office and was granted security clearance, but did not get a formal government role or title.

14. Government watchdogs called on Trump to give Ivanka an official title to avoid conflicts of interest between her government roles and financial interests.

15. Eric Trump filed to bring in foreign workers to work at his Trump Winery. A lawyer working for him said, "It's difficult to find people."

16. Modern Appealing Clothing filed a class action suit against Ivanka's brand over "unfair competition," citing Trump and Conway's publicity.

17. As Trump's bad week continued, the *WSJ* reported Kushner's sale of 666 Fifth Avenue to a Chinese buyer, for a four-hundred-million-dollar profit, was teetering.

18. Trump International Hotel will host an event on American-Turkey relations, sponsored by an organization whose chair is a Turkish businessman with ties

to the Turkish government. The Four Seasons had hosted previous events for the organization.

19. James Woolsey said while on the Trump transition team, he attended a September meeting in which Flynn discussed how to get Fethullah Gulen to Turkey without going through the legal extradition process.

20. The Trump Organization is pursuing a hotel deal in Dallas with a man known as the "Turkish Trump," whose real estate company has business ties in Russia, Kazakhstan, and at least two dozen other countries.

21. Trump threatened Republicans in the House who were considering voting against Trumpcare: "I'm gonna come after you."

22. NBC reported that the Trump Organization is in violation of New York City law for not being registered with the New York City Department of Housing Preservation and Development.

23. Deutsche Bank—a major lender to Trump—was fined $630 million for laundering more than $10 billion for Russia from the bank's Moscow office in a scheme dubbed "Global Laundromat."

24. Maddow reported that Senator Chris Van Hollen asked Sessions to recuse himself from the U.S. investigation of Deutsche Bank, formerly conducted by U.S. Attorney Bharara, and asked if this investigation is why Bharara was fired.

25. The Trump Organization launched a new hotel chain, triggering all sorts of ethics concerns, including that investors may invest in order to gain favor from and access to the new administration.

26. According to a *New York* magazine reporter, Trump is "obsessive" in recording and watching cable news: "a source close to the White House told me that he does DVR basically all of the cable news."

27. In the Trump regime's second major e-mail scandal—Tillerson's use of an alias account (Wayne Tracker)—Exxon claimed to have lost all e-mails from the alias account.

28. Trump's newly appointed GSA head said the Trump International Hotel lease is valid. An expert on government procurement law at George

Washington University called the GSA decision harmful to the "integrity—and thus credibility—of the GSA."

29. Hawaii's Representative Beth Fukumoto resigned from the GOP and said she would become a Democrat. Her open letter cited Trump's "marginalizing and condemning minorities" and demeaning women.

30. The AP reported a bombshell: former Trump campaign manager Manafort was under a ten-million-dollar-per-year contract with a Russia-related entity, starting in 2006, to covertly promote the interests of the Russian government.

31. The White House responded that Trump was not aware of Manafort's work for a Russian billionaire while Manafort worked as Trump's campaign manager.

32. Manafort is also being investigated for transactions with banks in Cyprus, known as a haven for laundering money for Russian billionaires. Wilbur Ross was previously vice chair of the Bank of Cyprus.

33. Maddow reported that the attorney general of Cyprus is cooperating with U.S. officials in turning over information related to Manafort.

34. Five Democratic senators sent a letter to Wilbur Ross asking for clarification about his ties to the Bank of Cyprus. The response was due March 24, but as of now, Ross has not responded.

35. A Ukrainian lawmaker released documents showing that Manafort laundered payments from former Ukrainian president Viktor Yanukovych, who has been hiding in Russia since his overthrow in 2014.

36. CNN reported that the FBI has information that members of the Trump regime possibly coordinated with Russia on the release of information damaging to Hillary Clinton.

37. Tillerson gave a surprisingly frank interview to *IJR*, saying, "I didn't want this job. I didn't seek this job. My wife told me I'm supposed to do this." Tillerson said he had planned to retire in March 2018 to spend time with his grandkids.

38. On Thursday, House Intelligence Committee ranking Democrat Adam Schiff said he has been presented with new evidence on collusion between the Trump regime and Russia that merited a grand jury investigation.

39. Russian lawyer Nikolai Gorokhov, who represents the family of Sergei Magnitsky, a Russian who died in prison in 2009 after uncovering massive fraud, mysteriously "fell" from his fourth-floor apartment the night before he was set to appear in court in Moscow. He survived.

40. Gorokhov was also scheduled to be a witness in a U.S. case connected to the largest money-laundering scheme in Russian history, *USA v. Prevezon*, which was on the brink of going to trial in Manhattan. Fired U.S. attorney Bharara had been spearheading the case, which alleged that the real estate company Prevezon, owned by a Russian national, had engaged in fraud.

41. Two days later, former Russian parliamentarian Denis Voronenkov, who fled Russia after criticizing Putin, was assassinated on the streets of Ukraine's capital. Voronenkov was said to be a key witness in Ukraine's investigation of Yanukovych and Russian military support of anti-government forces in Ukraine.

42. On Wednesday, offering no evidence, Nunes held an impromptu press conference during which he claimed that some in the Trump transition team, including Trump, had been inadvertently surveilled by U.S. intelligence.

43. Nunes bypassed protocol of reporting his findings to the House Intelligence Committee, instead briefing Ryan and then the White House before his press conference, even while the White House is under investigation by the FBI.

44. On Thursday, Nunes apologized to the members of the Intelligence Committee for not going to them first. Nunes also said he was unsure if Trump or any of his transition team members were party to the phone calls or other communications intercepted.

45. Thursday night on Hannity's show, in explaining his actions, Nunes said he felt a "duty and obligation" to Trump.

46. On Friday, Nunes backed down from his assertion that Trump was surveilled. He also refused to reveal his sources.

47. On Friday, Nunes abruptly canceled an open hearing scheduled for Tuesday, in which former DNI Clapper, former CIA director John Brennan, and former acting attorney general Yates were scheduled to testify.

48. The *Daily Beast* reported that Tuesday, the night before his Trump surveillance claim, Nunes left the Uber car he was riding in with a senior staffer to take a phone call, then mysteriously disappeared for hours, leaving his staff member behind without explanation.

49. The *WaPo* editorial board called for Nunes to be removed as chair of the House Intelligence Committee and investigated for leaking.

50. As the week closed, a Quinnipiac poll found that 66 percent of Americans want an independent commission to investigate Trump-Russia ties.

51. The House Oversight Committee requested documents from the White House and FBI on any communications between Flynn and Russia.

52. The Senate Intelligence Committee asked Trump adviser Stone to preserve any Russian-related documents.

53. Richard Painter, George W. Bush's chief White House ethics lawyer, tweeted that he testified to the House Oversight Committee that "treason is an oversight issue."

54. It was revealed that the RNC, while chaired by Priebus, hired a firm with intelligence connections to Russia to dig up dirt on Hillary Clinton.

55. Andrea Mitchell reported on her MSNBC show that a single source had told her Trump transition team members are purging their phones.

56. All week, Spicer and the Trump regime tried to distance Trump from Manafort, Flynn, and others under FBI investigation. The Trump-supporting *National Enquirer* ran a cover story on Flynn, "Trump Catches Russia's White House Spy."

57. A Russian-organized money-laundering network with offices in Trump Tower, three floors below Trump's penthouse, was under a court-approved wiretap by the FBI. The investigation led to the indictment of thirty people, including a Russian mafia boss.

58. The *WSJ* editorial board issued a blistering attack on Trump: "A President's Credibility," in which they described how Trump's constant lies and falsehoods were eroding public trust, abroad and at home.

59. Canada's largest school district canceled travel to the U.S., citing worries about Trump's Muslim ban.

60. A waiter in California refused to serve four Latina customers until they showed proof of residency, saying "I need to make sure you're from here."

61. Organizers of a Cinco de Mayo festival in Philadelphia canceled it, fearing an ICE raid. The festival, celebrating Mexican culture, had been a tradition since 2006.

62. Trump continued to take credit for jobs he didn't create, this time twenty thousand jobs at Charter Communications announced last October.

63. The federal judge in Hawaii who ruled against Trump's second Muslim ban has received multiple death threats and is under twenty-four-hour protection.

64. Despite a forty-four-seat advantage in the House, Trump's first major legislative attempt, to repeal and replace Obamacare, failed—a sign of incompetence, but also of his weakened political capital amid Russian allegations and record low favorability.

65. The *NYT* reported that Ryan had told Trump he didn't have the votes, but Trump, Bannon, and Trump's director of legislative affairs, Marc Short, wanted to force a public vote to create a GOP enemies list. Ryan said no.

66. Trump blamed the loss on Democrats, calling Pelosi and Schumer "losers." The conservative *WSJ* editorial board blamed Republicans.

67. The *NYT* reported that a U.S.-led coalition is investigating a strike in Mosul that killed up to two hundred civilians—the highest toll for an American attack in Iraq since 2003. Unlike Obama, who acted in a way to protect civilians, this and Yemen showcase Trump's complete disregard for human life.

Week 20

MARCH 26–APRIL 1, 2017

For the third week running, Trump has lost control of the narrative. His legislative agenda has ground to a halt, a sign of his waning political capital; however, he continues to fundamentally change the values and fabric of our country in myriad alarming ways. Russia's interference in our election is now an accepted notion, and words like "collusion" and "cover-up" entered the fray this week as all eyes turned to examining the Trump regime's role.

1. Four weeks have passed since Trump's tweet accusing Obama of wiretapping Trump Tower. He has yet to offer any evidence or apologize.

2. The Sunday *Times* of London reported that during Merkel's visit to the White House, Trump handed her a £300 billion invoice for money he falsely claimed Germany owed to NATO.

3. On Sunday, Trump announced that Kushner would lead a newly formed White House Office of American Innovation, giving him broad authority over federal bureaucracy. Kushner already has a significant portfolio.

4. On Monday, the *NYT* reported that the Senate Intelligence Committee will question Kushner about two meetings he arranged with Kislyak during the transition.

5. Kushner will also be questioned on a previously unreported meeting with Sergey Gorkov, the head of Russia's state-owned development bank, Vnesheconombank (VEB). Gorkov is former KGB and was appointed by Putin to run VEB, a bank that has been under U.S. sanctions for three years.

6. Kushner and VEB gave different public accounts of why they met.

7. As a secret "third party," VEB paid the bill for its employee Evgeny Buryakov's legal defense at his trial for spying on the U.S. for Russia.

8. Kushner arrived for a ski vacation in Aspen on the same day as Russian billionaire Roman Abramovich, one of Putin's closest confidants. Abramovich's wife is also friends with Ivanka.

9. China's Anbang Insurance Group walked away from the planned purchase of 666 Fifth Avenue, which would have netted Kushner $400 million—a possible sign that the Chinese government is uncertain about the Trump regime's longevity.

10. Changing course, Ivanka will become a federal employee. In her new role of assistant to the president, the highest staff title, Ivanka will have the same rank as National Security Adviser McMaster.

11. In January, Trump attorneys had said Ivanka would resign from her business positions. She is still listed as CEO of a New York–based business.

12. Ethics filings released on Friday showed that Ivanka and Kushner, despite their new roles, will remain as beneficiaries of real estate and investment businesses worth about $741 million.

13. Ivanka will also maintain her stake in the controversial Trump International Hotel in D.C., which netted her between one and five million dollars from January 2016 to March 2017; her stake is worth as much as twenty-five million dollars.

14. Ethics filings also revealed that Bannon earned $917,000 in the past twelve months, more than half of which comes from Mercer-related entities.

15. Trump again took credit for jobs created before he took office: this time a $1.2 billion investment by Ford that was planned in 2015.

16. Per *WaPo* tracking, so far Trump has taken credit for jobs created before he took office eleven times.

17. Trump's anti-immigrant policies are scaring eligible families away from safety net programs like SNAP, Medicaid, the Children's Health Insurance Program, and free school lunches.

18. ICE arrested five green card applicants in Lawrence, Massachusetts, when they showed up for their scheduled appointments at a U.S. Citizenship and Immigration Services office. All are scheduled to be deported.

19. A federal judge in Hawaii extended the order blocking Trump's second Muslim ban.

20. Trump has been named in more than fifty lawsuits filed by individuals in response to his Muslim bans.

21. Trump signed an executive order that legalizes discrimination against LGBTQ federal employees.

22. Trump excluded LGBTQ people from documentation by the U.S. Census, removing categories for "sexual orientation" and "gender identity."

23. At a White House women's event, Trump said, "If I weren't president, [women's empowerment] would be a very scary statement. We can't compete!" He also asked the crowd if they knew about Susan B. Anthony.

24. Trump's lawyer said the Summer Zervos sexual harassment–related lawsuit, in which Zervos is suing Trump for defamation, should be put on hold because it will "distract the president from his duties." Zervos was a contestant on *The Apprentice* in 2007 and alleges that Trump repeatedly sexually attacked her during the filming of the show.

25. Following the failed Yemen raid and the Mosul bombing that left two hundred civilians dead, Trump declared Somalia a war zone and lifted Obama's civilian protection rules for air strikes.

26. *WaPo* reported a growing sense of panic and mistrust among civilians in Iraq and Syria amid a record number of casualties from U.S.-led air strikes.

27. NBC reported that 40 percent of U.S. colleges reported a drop in international student applications because of Trump's policies like the Muslim ban. Foreign students generate thirty-two billion dollars in revenue and 400,000 jobs.

28. Trump's approval hit a new low at Gallup: 35 percent approve, 59 percent disapprove. Ratings this week are the lowest ever for a new president.

29. Trump will not throw the ceremonial first pitch on the Nationals opening day, making him only the second president since Taft in 1910 not to do so.

30. *USA Today* reported that Trump and his companies have been linked to at least ten former Soviet businessmen with alleged ties to organized crime or money laundering.

31. WNYC reported three all-cash real estate purchases by Manafort in New York. One purchase was for ten million dollars at Trump Tower in 2006—the same time Manafort entered a ten-million-dollar contract with a pro-Putin Russian oligarch, Oleg Deripaska, to help strategize on influencing U.S. elections as reported in an AP exclusive.

32. Deripaska took out a quarter-page advertisement in *WaPo* and the *WSJ* denouncing the AP story and offering to testify to Congress.

33. On Monday, Nunes unilaterally canceled all scheduled hearings and meetings for the week. He refused to share his source for the leaks.

34. On Tuesday, *WaPo* reported that the Trump regime tried to block Sally Yates from testifying at the House hearing on Russia's involvement with the Trump campaign.

35. *WaPo* also reported that both Yates and John Brennan had made clear that parts of their testimony contradict statements made by the White House.

36. On Thursday, the *NYT* identified two White House officials, Ezra Cohen-Watnick and Michael Ellis, who gave Nunes intelligence reports. Ellis formerly worked for Nunes, and Cohen-Watnick was brought in by Flynn and kept on by Trump, Bannon, and Kushner despite McMaster's desire to fire him.

37. *WaPo* identified a third White House source involved in leaking information to Nunes: John Eisenberg, top lawyer for the National Security Council, on which Bannon sits.

38. E. Randol Schoenberg uncovered that Ezra Cohen-Watnick's wife, Rebecca Miller, did public relations work for Putin.

39. Barton Gellman raised the specter of uncharted territory—that the leaks to Nunes could indicate that the Trump White House is spying on the FBI.

40. On Friday, Representative Adam Schiff met with Trump and was given the materials that were leaked to Nunes. In a statement, Schiff said nothing he had seen warranted a departure from normal review procedures. He also questioned why senior White House staff leaked to Nunes, who then shared the info back with Trump's White House.

41. CREW and Democracy 21 requested an OCE inquiry into whether Nunes violated House ethics rules.

42. Robert Wasinger, a former Trump campaign official, transition team staffer, and Trump appointee who served as White House liaison to the State Department, became the second staffer to leave without signing an ethics pledge. Wasinger is now working as a lobbyist.

43. *ProPublica* reported that the Trump regime is refusing to respond to inquiry letters from congressional Democrats, including the letters sent by Senate Democrats to Wilbur Ross in Week 19.

44. Louis Marinelli, the man behind the #Calexit Campaign—an effort to break California from the rest of the country—splits his time between living in San Diego and Russia, and has ties to a group reportedly backed by the Kremlin.

45. The BBC verified a key claim in Steele's dossier—a Russian diplomat named Kalugin (misspelled in the dossier as "Kulagin"), who was head of the Russian embassy's economic section in Washington, was a spy.

46. The BBC also confirmed contact between the Trump campaign and Russia, including sharing of voter rolls in key states like Michigan and Pennsylvania.

47. The identity of "Source D" in the Steele dossier, source of the most salacious details, was confirmed to be Belarusian American businessman Sergei Millian, who also had ties to Trump campaign officials.

48. The FBI raided an obscure casino in Saipan run by a Trump protégé, which has attracted attention over its huge revenue and cash flows. Board members include Trump transition team member Woolsey.

49. On Thursday, Flynn's lawyer said he had offered his testimony to the FBI and the House and Senate intelligence committees in exchange for immunity. According to his lawyer, Robert Kelner, the committees have not taken him up on the offer.

50. The next morning, Trump tweeted that Flynn should ask for immunity in this "witch hunt."

51. Robert Kelner tweeted on November 12, 2016, "A prediction: Donald Trump will make novel and unusual use of the President's pardon power. An under-utilized tool of political power."

52. Jeremy Bash, an ex-intel official, said Flynn could only get immunity if he could deliver evidence against someone higher up the chain: Trump.

53. A federal judge approved the twenty-five-million-dollar judgment against Trump University for defrauding more than six thousand students, and with all the news, no one really noticed.

54. NBC reported that the Obama administration was so concerned that Trump would destroy documents related to the Russia probe, they created a list of

the documents, with each identified by a serial number, and hand-delivered it to all members of the Senate Intelligence Committee.

55. At a press conference before Senate Intelligence Committee hearings, Senator Richard Burr said Russia hired more than one thousand hackers to create fake, anti-Hillary news. Senator Mark Warner added that Russia targeted key swing states, including Michigan, Pennsylvania, and Wisconsin.

56. The Senate Intelligence Committee held its first day of hearings on Thursday. All experts who testified concurred on Russia's involvement with the U.S. election.

57. Former FBI special agent Clint Watts testified that one reason Russia's attacks were so successful is that Trump and his team amplified and seemingly coordinated with propaganda coming out of Russia.

58. As proof that Russia was aiming not only to hurt Hillary but to buoy Trump, Watts testified that Russia interfered in the Republican primary to undermine other candidates, including Rubio.

59. Rubio shared at the hearing that during his presidential campaign, his staff detected hack attempts from Russian IP addresses. Also, this week a second attempt was made to hack former members of his campaign staff.

60. CBS reported that the FBI is probing whether the Trump campaign coordinated with Russian intelligence to carry out cyberattacks on the DNC and other targets in 2016

61. Marc Kasowitz, Trump's personal lawyer of more than fifteen years, was named lead attorney for Sberbank, a Russian bank which is majority owned by the Russian government. Sberbank faces charges in U.S. federal court for racketeering.

62. *WaPo* reported that nearly one out of every three days while in office, Trump has visited a Trump-branded property.

63. The Center for Public Integrity noted that Wilbur Ross, while charged with Trump's trade policy, maintains a stake in a shipping company that flies the Chinese flag, and visits Iran and Russia.

64. Trump insider Rudy Giuliani is defending an alleged Iranian money launderer. Giuliani did not notify the court of his role, as is generally required. He also visited Turkey to discuss the case with President Recep Tayyip Erdogan. The case is being heard in the Southern District of New York (formerly Bharara's district).

65. In a letter to the federal judge on Friday, the federal prosecutor on the case disclosed that Giuliani tried to go around him and cut a deal between the Turkish and U.S. governments.

66. Senate Democrats called for an ethics probe of Mnuchin for promoting a movie he produced during a public interview on March 24. Mnuchin said Friday it was not his intention to promote the movie.

67. *ProPublica* reported that while in Congress in 2016, Secretary of Health and Human Services (HHS) Tom Price bought stocks in six pharmaceutical companies, then used his connections to help scuttle a rule that would have hurt the companies' profit.

68. The Oklahoma bar launched an investigation into whether Scott Pruitt, administrator of the Environmental Protection Agency (EPA), lied under oath during his Senate confirmation hearing by saying while attorney general of Oklahoma he only used his professional e-mail for AG business.

69. The State Department has gone dark. Since the *IJR* interview of Tillerson in which he signaled regret over taking the SoS job, both John Bolton and Condoleezza Rice have been invited to the White House by Trump.

70. *WaPo* reported that many career diplomats in the State Department have been instructed not to speak to Tillerson directly or to make eye contact.

71. Senators in the House Armed Services oversight subcommittee urged Trump to fill Pentagon positions in the Office of the Inspector General and the Office of Special Counsel to "ensure that the American people know about and have a means to address instances of waste, fraud and abuse in their government." Only one position of fifty-two has been filled (Mattis). Bannon and Kushner have blocked other picks.

72. Trump friend and insider Carl Icahn stands to significantly benefit from several of Trump's policies, including a regulation that if put in place will save CVR Energy, of which Icahn owns 82 percent, $206 million per year.

73. *Newsweek* reported that Comey wanted to go public in July with information on Russia's campaign to influence the election, but in a meeting with

Secretary of State John Kerry, Attorney General Loretta Lynch, Secretary of Homeland Security Jeh Johnson, and National Security Adviser Susan Rice, was told not to proceed.

74. When asked by a reporter about Flynn during an executive order signing ceremony, Trump walked out of the room without signing the orders.

75. NPR reported that Trump has started to employ "whataboutism"—a Russian propaganda tactic commonly used by Putin. When criticized, Trump will say someone else is worse.

Week 21

APRIL 2-8, 2017

Over the past three weeks, Trump's approval has plummeted as he struggled to take back the narrative amid legislative failures and ubiquitous questions about Russia. He floated several attempts to deflect and replace Russia as the lead story: the Obama wiretap, the Nunes brouhaha, the Susan Rice unmasking—but none seemed to work. This week he figured out a way to take back the narrative, one commonly used by autocrats: he edged toward starting a war.

1. Five weeks have passed since Trump's tweet accusing Obama of wiretapping Trump Tower. He has yet to offer any evidence or apologize.

2. Seeking to deflect from his growing unpopularity and Russia stories, Trump segued his Obama story to "a crooked scheme" involving Susan Rice spying on the Trump regime.

3. Citing no evidence, Trump said Susan Rice had committed a crime. Experts debunked his claim, saying unmasking is routine for an NSA.

4. The *Los Angeles Times* editorial board launched a scathing six-part series on the Trump presidency: "Our Dishonest President."

5. Since taking office, Trump has made 367 false or misleading claims, according to *WaPo*.

6. Rejecting Trump's defense, a Kentucky federal judge said a lawsuit against Trump for inciting violence at a campaign event could proceed.

7. Trump's popularity plunged this month to 34 percent in an April IBD/TIPP poll, including a significant loss of support among rural voters (56 percent to 41 percent) and white men (58 percent to 49 percent).

8. A Quinnipiac poll found a similar drop in approval this month by the key Trump demographic of white men: 58 percent to 47 percent.

9. The U.S. jobs report for March was dismal, the weakest in almost a year. Unlike in February, when Trump took credit for a strong report despite his short time in office, this time there was no comment.

10. *ProPublica* reported that despite his pledge to remove himself from his business interests, Trump can pull money from any of his businesses, at any time, without disclosing it.

11. At a White House press briefing, Spicer defamed *ProPublica*, calling it a "left-wing blog." *ProPublica* issued a strong response and statement of facts, including Trump trust documents that were revised on February 10.

12. While under consideration for a major national security role, Stephen Feinberg said he wants to keep his stake in Cerberus, which was the seventeenth-biggest U.S. Army contractor in 2015.

13. *Politico* reported that Trump ex-staffers are cashing in through foreign lobbying work, breaking from Trump's pledge to "drain the swamp."

14. Trump has left the White House Office of Science and Technology vacant, filling just one position with the former chief of staff for billionaire investor Peter Thiel. As discussed in past lists, Trump is installing "spies" into agencies while leaving key roles unfilled.

15. Researchers said the Trump regime has been deleting scientific data collected by government agencies. One scientist said, "It's a bloodbath."

16. In violation of the Hatch Act, Dan Scavino Jr., White House social media director and adviser, tweeted at a member of the Freedom Caucus that he was a "big liability" and should be primaried. He later changed his Twitter bio to "Personal @Twitter Handle."

17. Without public announcement, Trump issued an executive order changing the order of succession within the DoJ.

18. Twitter filed a lawsuit after the Department of Homeland Security requested the company reveal the identity of an anonymous account that has been critical of the U.S. Citizenship and Immigration Services office.

19. On Friday, DHS dropped its request, and Twitter withdrew its lawsuit.

20. The Twitter account for the agency that controls the U.S. nuclear force, U.S. Strategic Command, tweeted an article by *Breitbart*.

21. Expanding his already huge portfolio of responsibilities, Kushner traveled to Iraq with General Joseph Dunford. The trip became the stuff of parody in a piece in *Task & Purpose* titled "Jared Goes to Iraq! A Picture Story."

22. *WaPo* reported that Kushner's Iraq trip violated protocol in that it was publicized before they landed.

23. Kushner's increasing foreign relations portfolio led to questions of whether he has become the "de facto secretary of state."

24. The city council in Cambridge, Massachusetts, passed a resolution calling for Congress to begin an impeachment investigation into Trump.

25. Trump invited Egyptian president Abdel Fattah el-Sisi to the White House and did not mention human rights abuses. Families of Americans being held prisoner in Egypt also said Trump had ignored their pleas for help, after Trump, on the campaign trail, excoriated Obama for not prioritizing prisoners in Iran.

26. On #EqualPayDay it was noted that Trump had quietly signed an executive order taking away Obama-era protection for women workers.

27. Trump cut all U.S. funding to the United Nations Population Fund, an agency that works on maternal and reproductive health.

28. Trump defended serial sexual harasser Bill O'Reilly during Sexual Assault Awareness Month, calling him "a good person" and saying, "I don't think Bill did anything wrong."

29. In the first three months of 2017, hate crimes in New York City doubled over the total in the same period last year. Most crimes were anti-Semitic, with an uptick in anti-black incidents as well.

30. The New York State Supreme Court ruled that New York City can destroy immigrants' municipal ID information, as part of the city's effort to protect undocumented immigrants from being deported by the Trump regime.

31. An Indiana restaurant owner was deported overnight by ICE to Mexico, despite pending legal actions. According to NPR, none of his lawyers were notified.

32. The *Financial Times* reported that the FBI plans to create a special unit to coordinate its investigation of Russian interference with the election.

33. It was reported that before resigning as national security adviser, Flynn did not reveal income he received from Russian-related entities during 2015 for speaking fees.

34. Yahoo reported that Trump abruptly pulled out of a meeting scheduled for February with Alexander Torshin, the deputy governor of the Bank of Russia and a close ally of Putin, over disclosed ties to organized crime.

35. ICE whisked away Evgeny Buryakov, the Russian spy mentioned in Week 20. At trial, Buryakov's attorney fees were paid by his employer VEB, the Russian bank whose head secretly met with Kushner in December.

36. *BuzzFeed* reported that former Trump adviser Page met with an undercover Russian spy in 2013 and passed along documents about the energy industry.

37. *WaPo* reported that Erik Prince, Trump insider and brother of Betsy DeVos, attended a secret meeting arranged by the United Arab Emirates with a Russian close to Putin in Seychelles on January 11, to open a communication back channel between Trump and Russia.

38. A UAE crown prince also had a meeting with Flynn, Kushner, and Bannon in December in New York City. In an unusual breach of protocol, the UAE did not notify the Obama administration in advance.

39. CNN reported that the FBI is investigating links between Alfa Bank and Trump Organization servers, indicating an intention to communicate. During the campaign, 80 percent of Trump Organization server lookups were done by Alfa Bank and 19 percent by Spectrum Health, which is led by Betsy DeVos's husband.

40. The *NYT* reported that Kushner omitted his multiple meetings with Russians in filling out his questionnaire for national security positions.

41. In a video obtained by the *Forward*, Trump's chief counterterrorism adviser, Gorka, was seen publicly supporting a violent anti-Semitic militia group.

42. On Thursday, Nunes temporarily stepped away from chairing the House Intelligence Committee's investigation of Russia, citing an ethics complaint by the Office of Congressional Ethics.

43. In a letter that afternoon, the Republican chair of the House Ethics Committee announced that they, too, are investigating Nunes for the "unauthorized disclosure of classified information."

44. Confusion reigned in the Trump regime after Syrian president Bashar al-Assad used chemical weapons on Syrians. Without citing specifics, Trump said he changed his Syria policy, but no one else in the regime seemed to know details.

45. Without a formal announcement, Trump removed Steve Bannon from the National Security Council. Jennifer Jacobs, a Bloomberg reporter, broke the story after reading it in a notice published in the *Federal Register*.

46. *Politico* reported that megadonor Rebekah Mercer convinced her close ally Bannon not to resign. Reporter Jane Mayer has uncovered that the Mercers stand to avoid $6.8 billion in taxes under Trump.

47. The National Security Council page on whitehouse.gov is blank, save for these words: "Check back soon for more information."

48. The *NYT* reported that as early as July 2016, the CIA had evidence of Russia's efforts to get Trump elected, and that Trump advisers were likely working with the Russians.

49. In August, CIA director John Brennan met with Congress's Gang of Eight to share his findings. Harry Reid pushed repeatedly to inform the American public, but Mitch McConnell questioned the findings and pushed for a softer version of a public letter, striking any reference to Russia.

50. As noted in Week 4, McConnell had also been the roadblock to Obama's going public in October with more explicit information on Russia's attempted interference with our election.

51. Also as noted in Week 4, shortly after the election, Trump chose McConnell's wife as his nominee for transportation secretary.

52. On Friday, McConnell passed the filibuster-ending "nuclear option" for Supreme Court picks. One columnist referred to him as "the man who broke America."

53. Trump had also pushed McConnell toward the nuclear option. One expert in authoritarianism said of autocrats, "They will continue to rewrite major rules and disregard norms."

54. Wars within the Trump regime continued this week, with open animus between Kushner and Bannon, and rumors that Bannon and Priebus could be on their way out.

55. All the while, power continues to consolidate into the hands of Trump, Ivanka, and Kushner. In the executive branch, only 4 percent of key roles are filled and 92 percent still have no nominee.

56. In a PR stunt that fell flat, Trump donated his $78,333 paycheck to the National Park Service. Ironically, Trump's budget calls for cuts to the Interior Department, which includes the Park Service, of 12 percent, or $1.5 billion.

57. On Thursday, amid a continued fall in approval and a growing drumbeat of Russia news, Trump used provocations by North Korea and Syria as an opportunity to threaten war against both.

58. On Thursday night, while in Mar-a-Lago meeting with China's president, Xi Jinping, Trump launched an attack on Syria.

59. Trump did not seek approval or notify Congress ahead of time. He did, however, give advance notice to Russia.

60. Trump cited Assad's use of chemical weapons against Syrian civilians, including children, as justification. Ironically, one of Trump's first actions in office was his Muslim ban, which banned Syrian refugees. Also, per PolitiFact, on the campaign trail, Trump promised to remove existing Syrian refugees from the U.S.

61. Also of note, the Trump regime has been responsible for killing hundreds of innocent civilians, including children, in the failed Yemen raid and then in Mosul, where pamphlets told citizens not to leave their homes.

62. The Pentagon released a video of the U.S. strike Thursday night, claiming, "Initial indications are that this strike has severely damaged or destroyed Syrian aircraft and support infrastructure and equipment."

63. Nine civilians, including four children, were killed by Trump's air strike.

64. By the next day, the Assad regime was again launching air strikes from the airfield Trump's attack had supposedly destroyed.

65. The media loved Trump's show of force, and on Friday Syria become story one, displacing Russian interference and ties to Trump.

66. The *Onion* ran the perfect parody of the situation on Friday, "Trump Confident U.S. Military Strike on Syria Wiped Out Russian Scandal." Other pundits used the euphemism "wag the dog."

67. To complete the stagecraft, the Trump regime released its version of the famous photo of the White House Situation Room during the raid that killed Osama bin Laden. This version was taken at Mar-a-Lago and included Spicer, two Goldman Sachs executives, Commerce Secretary Ross, and Kushner glaring over at Bannon.

Week 22

APRIL 9-15, 2017

Week 22 has, by far, the most items related to Trump-Russia ties. This week, the word "probe" progressed to "scandal," signaling an acceptance that some sort of collusion occurred. Trump continued his attempts to divert attention from this story by bombing and provocation without a strategy or plan. Two days of bombings have earned him his first two days of positive press. Meanwhile, as we approach the one-hundred-day mark, Trump has accomplished little and his regime is in disarray.

1. Six weeks have passed since Trump's tweet accusing Obama of wiretapping Trump Tower. He has yet to offer any evidence or apologize.

2. Trump continues to claim, without evidence, that Susan Rice committed a crime by spying on the Trump campaign.

3. The Trump regime has articulated five different policies for Syria in the last two weeks. As the week closed, he still hadn't settled on one.

4. Reuters reported that the Assad regime was warned by Russia (after Russia was warned by Trump) of the impending U.S. strike, and was able to mostly evacuate the target.

5. Secretary of State Tillerson attended a G7 meeting, where he was a dissenting voice on imposing more sanctions on Russia. Tillerson said of Russia's involvement in Ukraine, "Why should U.S. taxpayers be interested in Ukraine?"

6. Tillerson ditched his press pool while meeting with Putin. Tillerson claimed he and Putin found very little to agree on.

7. As news about the Trump-Russia collusion in our election seeped out this week, Trump and Putin sought to display a deteriorating U.S.-Russia relationship, with Trump saying relations were "at an all-time low."

8. The next day, Trump tweeted an odd, unprompted reassurance, "Things will work out fine between the U.S.A. and Russia. At the right time everyone will come to their senses & there will be lasting peace!"

9. *BuzzFeed* reported that Pyotr Levashov (Severa), a Russian hacker, was detained in Spain for ties to a computer virus linked to the U.S. election. His wife said he was arrested for being "linked to Trump's win."

10. *WaPo* reported that the FBI had obtained a FISA warrant to monitor Carter Page as part of an investigation of the Trump campaign's connection to Russia's effort to swing the election in Trump's favor.

11. *WaPo* also reported that the first ninety-day FISA warrant was issued in July 2016 and has since been renewed by the FISA court more than once.

12. In an ABC interview, Page said he couldn't guarantee he did not discuss easing of sanctions with Russian contacts at a meeting in July in the Russian capital: "We'll see what comes out in this FISA transcript."

13. According to the Steele dossier, also discussed at that July meeting was the sale of a 19.5 percent stake in Rosneft, Russia's state oil company—allegedly in exchange for lifting sanctions.

14. CNN reported that classified documents reviewed by Democrats and Republicans on the House Intelligence Committee contradict Nunes's and Trump's claims that Susan Rice did anything unusual or illegal.

15. Financial records obtained by the AP confirmed at least two payments totaling $1.2 million were paid to Manafort by a pro-Russian political party in Ukraine. The payments were discovered on a handwritten ledger known as the Black Ledger that surfaced in Ukraine.

16. After consulting with federal authorities, Manafort said he would register as a foreign agent for his past work on behalf of pro-Russia interests in the Ukraine.

17. Manafort became the second in Trump's inner circle to retrospectively register as a foreign agent, Flynn being the first for his work with Turkey.

18. A D.C. lobbying firm that was directed by Manafort and his deputy Rick Gates also retroactively registered as a foreign agent for work to promote a pro-Russian Ukrainian political party's interests in Washington.

19. The day after Manafort stepped down from the Trump campaign, he set up a shell company that secured $20 million in loans, including $3.5 million from Spruce Capital, which has connections to a post-Soviet fertilizer oligarch, Alexander Rovt, who also has ties to Trump.

20. *BuzzFeed* reported on a bizarre story involving Trump attorney Michael Cohen taking a $350,000 check from a Russian NHL player, which was meant to be passed along to Cohen's client, a Russian woman in Florida, for payment on a condo, but instead Cohen kept the check and cashed it.

21. Former MI6 chief Sir Richard Dearlove said Trump borrowed from Russia as a lender of last resort after the 2008 financial crisis.

22. The *Guardian* reported that British spies were the first to spot the Trump team's links to Russia, in late 2015. GCHQ shared the suspicious activity with their counterparts in U.S. intelligence.

23. Germany, Estonia, Poland, the Netherlands, France, and Australia also relayed material on the Trump campaign's links to Russia to U.S. intelligence during 2016.

24. The head of GCHQ met with CIA chief Brennan in July 2016—per the *Guardian*, the matter was deemed so sensitive it was handled at "director level." This meeting allegedly precipitated Brennan's one-on-one meetings with the Gang of Eight, described in Week 21.

25. CNN confirmed the *Guardian* report, citing sources in the U.S. Congress and law enforcement and U.S. and European intelligence.

26. CIA director Pompeo had harsh words for WikiLeaks, calling it a "hostile intelligence service," and said Russian military intelligence used WikiLeaks to release hacked DNC e-mails.

27. Pompeo also described RT as Russia's "primary propaganda outlet" and said it actively collaborated with WikiLeaks.

28. Ironically, while part of Trump's campaign, Pompeo had cheered on WikiLeaks, tweeting a *RedState* article, "BUSTED: 19,252 Emails from DNC Leaked by WikiLeaks."

29. Offering no evidence, Roger Stone told *Politico* the Obama administration got a FISA warrant on him. Stone has admitted communication with both Guccifer 2.0 and Julian Assange, the founder of WikiLeaks.

30. Rachel Maddow observed the serious press and agencies rushing in this week to take credit for having uncovered the Trump regime's collusion with Russia—meaning it's now generally agreed that there is some substance behind the allegations.

31. The House Intelligence Committee sent Representative Mike Quigley to Cyprus as part of its Trump-Russia probe. Week 19's list noted some of the extensive ties between Cyprus and the Trump regime.

32. The Department of Justice released ninety pages under the FOIA about voting machine malfunctions in Pennsylvania, Michigan, Wisconsin, Florida, and North Carolina.

33. As Trump neared the one-hundred-day judgment mark, *Politico* described the White House as a "pressure cooker" to show results, when little has been accomplished.

34. As power continued to consolidate in the hands of the Trump family, Trump's White House drew comparisons to a "family business."

35. Unabated personnel drama plagued the White House the entire week, as snipes continued between Bannon, Kushner, and Trump.

36. After Trumpcare failed (twice), Trump had promised to take on tax reform next, saying a plan was forthcoming. This week Trump's White House scrapped this effort, saying they would not produce a tax plan.

37. The *WSJ* reported that Trump's federal hiring freeze, put in place on day 1 of his administration, put correctional officers at risk, could delay payments to veterans, and could prevent the disabled and retirees from getting Social Security payments.

38. The day after the report, Trump lifted his federal hiring freeze.

39. During the hiring freeze, thousands of positions remained vacant, including more than 350 at the EPA alone. CNBC blamed the pace on "Trump's close involvement" and "turf wars" in his inner circle and cabinet.

40. Trump threatened to undermine Obamacare to get Democrats to the negotiating table. Specifically, he would hold back subsidy payments to health care companies providing insurance to low-income Americans.

41. The Government Accountability Office said it's investigating whether the Trump transition team followed federal guidelines and ethics rules during the transition.

42. Education Secretary Betsy DeVos said she would scrap Obama's plan for tougher federal oversight and new rules for student-loan servicers. Coincidentally, DeVos has significant holdings in one such servicer, Performant Financial Corp.

43. Trump appointed crony Don Benton, a salesman, as director of the Selective Service System, overseeing the military draft. This is the first time since 1941 that a person with no military experience has been chosen.

44. Allan Lichtman, the American University professor who predicted the winner of the last eight presidential elections, predicted Trump will be impeached.

45. CREW and others sued DHS under the FOIA for failing to disclose visitor logs of the White House, Mar-a-Lago, and Trump Tower.

46. On Friday, the Trump regime said it will not release the White House visitor logs, breaking with a practice started under President Obama.

47. The rationale for not releasing visitor logs was "security risks" and to save taxpayers $700,000 over the next three years. Each weekend Trump spends at Mar-a-Lago costs taxpayers an estimated $3 million.

48. Trump is on track to spend more on travel in his first year than Obama spent in all eight years in office.

49. The Trump International Hotel in D.C. is facing new legal challenges under the emoluments clause from a watchdog group represented by constitutional lawyer Laurence Tribe, who noted a "major infusion of value" from the General Services Administration decision to let the Trump Organization keep the lease.

50. A deal for a Trump-branded hotel in Dallas with developer Mukemmel Sarimsakci, known as the "Turkish Trump," collapsed. Sarimsakci said the Trump Organization had been vetting potential investors in the deal.

51. Bloomberg found that of Trump's ten most engaged followers on Twitter, five are confirmed robots and three appear to be bots.

52. A Florida court of appeals ruled against Trump, saying he owed a paint company $300,000 for stiffing them on work done and supplies provided at the Trump National Doral Miami golf resort.

53. Trump completely reversed himself on several key campaign positions this week. China is no longer a currency manipulator, NATO and the Export-Import Bank are no longer obsolete, and he likes the job Federal Reserve chair Janet Yellen is doing.

54. Trump credited President Xi Jinping and the Boeing CEO with his newfound knowledge on North Korean history. Boeing donated one million dollars to Trump's inauguration, and as mentioned in prior weeks, China has granted many goodies to Trump, including thirty-eight new trademarks.

55. Trump's Treasury Department oddly placed Germany on its new special currency "monitoring list." Germany's currency is the euro.

56. In a Fox Business News interview, Trump described eating "the most beautiful piece of chocolate cake" with China's leader—giving a free advertisement to Mar-a-Lago catering—then got the country he bombed wrong (he said Iraq, not Syria).

57. Spicer made shocking statements regarding Hitler and the Holocaust at Tuesday's press briefing. He used the term "Holocaust center" rather than concentration camp, and in comparing Hitler to Assad, said the former had never used chemical weapons on his own people.

58. The Anne Frank Center called on Trump to fire Spicer. The Trump regime has amassed a steady stream of anti-Semitic behavior, including omitting Jews from the White House International Holocaust Remembrance Day statement.

59. No one from the Trump family attended the White House Passover seder, unlike President Obama and Michelle, who attended every year.

60. NBC reported on Gorka's ties to Vitezi Rend, a Nazi-linked group, including wearing his honorary medal from the group at Trump's inaugural ball.

61. In a speech on Tuesday, AG Sessions ordered prosecutors to crack down on illegal immigrants more aggressively, claiming gangs and cartels are turning U.S. cities into "war zones."

62. ICE detained 367 immigrants this week in raids across the country. ICE claims the raids are focused on "criminal aliens, illegal re-entrants and immigration fugitives." Advocates say this is not true.

63. A mother of four in Cincinnati was deported after appeals. Maribel Trujillo had no criminal record in her fifteen years here and has children aged three to fourteen years old, the youngest of whom has special needs.

64. On Thursday, the "mother of all bombs" (MOAB)—the largest non-nuclear bomb ever used in combat—was dropped in Afghanistan. Trump refused to say if he had ordered the strike or even if he knew about it.

65. Trump said he gave total authorization to "my military"—a reference appropriate for a dictatorship, not a democracy.

66. While his popularity continues to flounder, Trump got his second day of positive press for dropping the MOAB (the first was after the Syrian bombing).

67. Trump has yet to declare a strategy in Afghanistan or appoint an ambassador. The sixteen-million-dollar MOAB killed thirty-six ISIS fighters—a cost of roughly half a million per fighter.

68. Late Thursday, Trump issued confrontational statements about North Korea, threatening a preemptive strike. North Korea's vice foreign minister says Trump is "making trouble" with "aggressive" tweets.

69. Trump spent Friday at Mar-a-Lago, golfing and avoiding the press. Friday marked Trump's eighteenth time golfing, compared with other presidents at this point: Obama, zero; George W. Bush, zero; Clinton, three.

70. As tax day, April 18, approaches, thousands are expected to march today in cities around the country to protest Trump being the only modern-day president to not release his tax returns.

Week 23

APRIL 16–22, 2017

This week the Trump-Russia scandal continued to unfold, but that wasn't the big story. What stands out in Week 23 is the kleptocracy—a pattern of conflicts of interest and pay-to-play arrangements—and the Trump regime's utter irreverence toward ethics and past standards.

As the hundred-day mark approaches, Trump has no legislative accomplishments, and his foreign policy can best be described as an embarrassing mess. Instead, Trump seems focused on enriching himself, members of his regime, and his business contacts. The pace and boldness of corruption have the whiff of a man who is aware his days in this gig are numbered.

1. Seven weeks have passed since Trump's tweet accusing Obama of wiretapping Trump Tower. He has yet to offer any evidence or apologize.

2. American Oversight, a group of liberal lawyers, is suing the DoJ and FBI seeking proof for Trump's wiretapping claim.

3. Trump has yet to offer any evidence or apologize for his accusations that Susan Rice committed a crime by spying on his campaign.

4. The *New Yorker* reported that not only did members of the House from both parties find nothing in the Rice intercepts, but also the rationale became clear: per an intelligence source, the White House said, "We are going to mobilize to find something to justify the President's tweet that he was being surveilled."

5. Trump hosted a disastrous Easter Egg Roll, which included him telling the children, "We will be stronger and bigger and better as a nation than ever before," and forgetting to lift his hand to his heart during the National Anthem.

6. The *NYT* reported on violations and a raft of potential conflicts of interest as Trump appoints former lobbyists, lawyers, and consultants to craft policies in industries where they formerly worked.

7. OGE director Walter Shaub noted that Trump rolled back an Obama requirement that appointees not accept jobs in agencies they recently lobbied for, and that Trump has granted waivers allowing appointees to take up matters that benefit their former clients.

8. *WaPo* reported that 168 corporate interests have made requests to Trump for relief from regulations, all likely to be granted, "especially those designed to advance environmental protection and safeguard worker rights."

9. On tax day, breaking precedent with every modern-day president, Trump did not release his tax returns, nor explain why.

10. The *WSJ* reported that in the first quarter, Trump's campaign funds paid $500,000 to Trump's companies, including hotels, golf clubs, and restaurants.

11. Trump raised $107 million for his inaugural, double the amount Obama raised for his 2009 inauguration, although Trump's crowds and festivities were markedly smaller. It's unclear where unspent money has gone, meanwhile numerous "pay-to-play" stories are emerging.

12. For example, Rachel Maddow reported on a $666,000 gift from a businessman named R. W. Habboush, which led to meetings between his son and both an NSC official and Bannon to discuss how to open up business with Venezuela, which is heavily sanctioned by the U.S.

13. After meeting with pharma lobbyists, Trump dropped his campaign promise to let Medicare negotiate bulk discounts on prescription drugs.

14. Ivanka was granted China trademarks during dinner with Chinese president Xi Jinping at Mar-a-Lago. As reported in Week 22, Trump also changed his position, saying China does not manipulate its currency.

15. The *Financial Times* reported that Paul Manafort stepped into the China action, advising Chinese billionaire Yan Jiehe on how to broker deals as part of Trump's trillion-dollar infrastructure plan.

16. CREW filed an amended complaint to its emoluments challenge against Trump in federal court, adding new plaintiffs who claim they've been "directly harmed by a loss of business and wages."

17. Dow Chemical donated one million dollars to Trump's inauguration, then asked the regime to ignore a study on one of its pesticides, which was "originally derived from a nerve gas developed by Nazi Germany."

18. Billionaire Trump adviser Stephen Schwarzman, CEO of Blackstone, which has significant holdings in China, stands to gain from U.S.-China policies he helped to shape.

19. *USA Today* reporters pieced together that Trump companies own more than four hundred luxury condos and homes worth $250 million that are up for sale or rent, presenting individuals, corporations, or foreign interests an opportunity to gain influence through purchases.

20. Further, since Trump launched his presidential bid, Trump companies have sold at least fifty-eight units for ninety million dollars—almost half to LLCs. Since Election Day, fourteen units have been sold for twenty-three million dollars—half to LLCs.

21. The House Oversight Committee sent a letter asking Trump for details on how and when he will donate profits made from foreign government officials' use of his company's properties. Representatives Cummings and Chaffetz signed the letter.

22. Two days earlier, without explanation, Chaffetz said he would not run for reelection in 2018 and that he may leave office early to return to the private sector.

23. Despite denials by Trump, Erik Prince has close ties to the Trump regime, including riding the Acela with Conway, providing advice to Trump's inner circle (including Flynn), and entering Trump Tower through the back entrance.

24. As mentioned in Week 21, Prince had a one-on-one meeting with a Putin insider in Seychelles on January 11. He is also Betsy DeVos's brother.

25. Without explanation, the national security official leading the DoJ investigation into whether the Trump regime colluded with Russia abruptly resigned.

26. CNN reported that the FBI used information in the Steele dossier, which they independently confirmed, for their FISA warrant against Page.

27. CNN reported that Russia tried to use Trump advisers, including Page, to infiltrate the campaign. Page is one of several advisers U.S. and European intelligence found to be in contact with Russian officials during the campaign.

28. The DoJ said it is preparing charges against WikiLeaks founder Assange, with Sessions saying Assange's arrest is a priority. Strangely, the Trump regime has turned on Assange, after lauding him during the campaign.

29. Sessions left open the possibility of prosecuting U.S. news organizations for publishing leaked information as stories on the Trump-Russia scandal continue to pour out.

30. As part of a custody battle, *InfoWars*' Alex Jones said he is a "performance artist." As noted in Week 19, *InfoWars* and *Breitbart* are under FBI investigation for their roles in the Russian hacking of our election.

31. NBC compiled a seating chart of attendees at Putin's December 2015 RT celebration dinner. Flynn was seated next to Putin, Jill Stein was also at Putin's table, and Assange appeared via satellite. NBC also reported on efforts by RT to promote Stein (and hurt Hillary) in the primary.

32. The House Intelligence Committee announced that it will reopen its Trump-Russia probe. Yates, Comey, Mike Rogers, Brennan, and Clapper have all been invited to testify.

33. Nikolai Andrushchenko, a Russian journalist and Putin critic, was beaten to death by strangers. He is the twelfth "mysterious" Russian death in recent months.

34. Similar to the way they interfered in the U.S. election, Russian sources are flooding French social media with fake news ahead of France's election.

35. Reuters reported on a Putin-linked think tank that purposefully and carefully orchestrated an attack on the U.S. election. Fake news, pro-Kremlin bloggers, and cyberattacks were all part of the plan.

36. Exxon sought a U.S. waiver to resume drilling in their Russian joint venture with Rosneft—a deal forged by Tillerson, who is ring-fenced from Exxon for only one year. Amid outcry, permission was denied by the Treasury Department.

37. The UK Election Commission has launched an investigation of the funding of Nigel Farage's Leave.EU campaign. The involvement of Cambridge Analytica—which also allegedly has ties to Bannon and the Mercers, and to the Russian hacking of the U.S. election—was not declared to the Commission.

38. Sessions said he was "amazed" that a U.S. judge "on an island in the Pacific" (aka Hawaii) could block Trump's Muslim ban.

39. Sessions took a fact-free swipe at another ethnically diverse city, saying New York City was soft on crime and plagued by gang murders.

40. ICE immigrant arrests were up 33 percent in the first two months of the Trump regime, including a doubling of arrests of noncriminals.

41. Trump deported his first Dreamer, Juan Manuel Montes, who is twenty-three and has lived here since age nine.

42. Trump ally Representative Steve King celebrated the deportation by tweeting a photo of a frosty beer mug with the words, "First non-valedictorian DREAMer deported. Border Patrol, this one's for you."

43. Ironically, a federal lawsuit brought on behalf of Montes has been assigned to Judge Gonzalo Curiel, the jurist infamously attacked by Trump for his Mexican heritage during the Trump University case.

44. Trump signed an executive order to review high-skilled H-1B immigration visas.

45. Trump's order does not, however, impact low-skilled H2A or H2B visas. According to CNN, Trump businesses have received 1,024 H-2B visas since 2000, and Trump Vineyards has received 64 H-2A permits since 2006.

46. In a troubling provocation, Russian aircraft were spotted flying off the coast of Alaska four times in four days this week.

47. Amid silence from Trump and our State Department, pogroms of gay men in Russia's Chechnya region escalated. Russia also banned Jehovah's Witnesses, claiming "extremist activities."

48. Trump shocked U.S. and international officials when he called Turkey's Erdogan to congratulate him on passage of a referendum that allows Erdogan to further consolidate power as an autocrat. International monitors have said the vote was not "genuinely democratic."

49. Trump held a secret meeting at Mar-a-Lago with former presidents of Colombia, threatening to undermine the country's peace agreement with rebel leaders. The meeting was arranged by Rubio, a member of the Senate Intelligence Committee, and was not on Trump's schedule.

50. Meanwhile, at a speech in Wisconsin, Trump called some of Canada's trade practices a "disgrace" and claimed NAFTA is "a disaster for our country."

51. In another example of Trump's embarrassing statements on U.S. foreign policy, Trump promised that "we are sending an armada"—the USS *Carl Vinson* carrier group—to waters off the Korean peninsula. This was not true.

52. Mattis and McMaster also made similar misstatements about the USS *Carl Vinson*'s location. While traveling in the region, Pence assured our allies the misstatements were "not made intentionally."

53. On Wednesday, Tillerson said that Iran is in compliance with the nuclear deal. On Thursday, Trump said Iran was not in compliance.

54. Trump offended our South Korean allies with a claim that the country "actually used to be part of China." Trump apparently gleaned this "knowledge" from his conversation with Xi Jinping.

55. For his upcoming visit to London, Trump demanded a carriage ride with Queen Elizabeth II down a strip that leads to Buckingham Palace.

56. Three months in, Trump has filled only 4 percent of key roles in the executive branch. And with all the international hot spots and conflicts, the State Department remains largely vacant, lacking even a deputy secretary.

57. A State Department official who helped shape the Iran nuclear deal was summarily reassigned for criticizing *Conservative Review* and *Breitbart*.

58. The surgeon general was also quietly dismissed on Friday evening, without explanation or a full-time replacement.

59. DeVos's pick to head the Department of Education's Office for Civil Rights said she faced discrimination for being white.

60. In his first three months of office, Trump has made 417 false or misleading claims.

61. Trump first-quarter job approval stood at 41 percent, the lowest of any modern-day president by fourteen points, in Gallup polling.

62. The Resistance claimed a major victory, bringing down Fox News icon Bill O'Reilly. Some speculated that the rise of Trump, and his backing of O'Reilly after recent allegations, laid the groundwork for O'Reilly's fall.

63. Hundreds of thousands are expected to march on Earth Day in the global March for Science in D.C. and at 609 satellite locations.

Week 24

APRIL 23-29, 2017

Today marks day 100 of the Trump regime. Despite the Republicans having control of the House and Senate, Trump has yet to tally a single legislative accomplishment. He was obsessive this week in pushing for Trumpcare 3 ahead of the 100-day mark, but the Resistance, which continues to grow in number and fervor, headed him off.

And all the while, the drumbeat of Russia grows louder. This week, Speaker Ryan acknowledged Russian interference. Trump's involvement has evolved from a "Trump-Russia probe" to a "Trump-Russia scandal," and this week, to a "Trump-Russia cover-up." As this unfolds, concern grows that Trump will seek to distract attention by starting a war. The one constant throughout the weeks is Trump's attempts to enrich himself and his regime through a growing list of conflicts of interest and corruption.

1. Speaker Ryan acknowledged that Russia interfered with our election and said U.S. probes could help our allies prevent similar interference.

2. As Le Pen advanced to the French presidential election runoff, Putin is using many of the tools successfully employed in the U.S. to target France.

3. WikiLeaks released more top-secret CIA documents. Our media has by and large stopped covering the WikiLeaks document dumps.

4. A group of psychiatrists at a conference held at Yale Medical School cited a "Duty to Warn" about Trump being dangerously ill.

5. Of the ten items listed on Trump's contract with the American people for the first hundred days of his administration, he accomplished none of them.

6. The State Department and two U.S. embassies promoted Mar-a-Lago on their websites with a four-hundred-word blog post. After public outrage, the post was removed.

7. The *NYT* reported that the State Department is likely to remain largely unstaffed into 2018. Trump has yet to fill two hundred leadership jobs that require Senate confirmation. Tillerson is taking no action, either.

8. Similarly, as the Trump regime launched its tax plan, the Treasury Department does not have a single confirmed appointee in positions tasked with reforming the tax code.

9. Trump's tax reform plan was launched with Mnuchin handing out a one-pager with broad details and no numbers.

10. Democrats, including former Obama ethics chief Norm Eisen, noted that Trump's tax reform could save him hundreds of millions of dollars. Without tax returns, it's impossible to know his total benefit.

11. Beyond State, the slow pace of nominations in the first hundred days has left cabinet agencies in limbo. Only 26 of the 556 senior positions that require Senate confirmation have been filled.

12. Nikki Haley was the only member of the Trump regime to condemn the abuse and killings of gay men in the Russian republic of Chechnya. Days later, the State Department said it wants to clear her remarks in advance.

13. UN diplomats were invited to the White House, but Tillerson was not included. Haley was there, and Trump publicly threatened to fire her: "Does everybody like Nikki? Good, otherwise she could easily be replaced."

14. In his first hundred days, Trump has an unprecedented number (fifteen) of appointees who got fired, withdrew, or quit.

15. Carl Bernstein said there is a "serious belief" in the FBI and Congress that there is an active cover-up under way by the Trump regime of their involvement with Russia.

16. On Monday, Yahoo reported that the Senate Intelligence Committee's Russia probe had stalled because of a lack of staffing and Senator Richard Burr's unwillingness to sign off on witness requests.

17. Democrats on the Senate Intelligence Committee hired April Doss, the former head of intelligence law at the NSA. Burr refused to bring on additional staffing, saying staffing levels were already sufficient.

18. Trump picked ally Dana Boente to take over the Justice Department unit's probe of Trump-Russia. Boente was previously named by Trump as an interim acting attorney general on the occasion of the Monday Night Massacre (the firing of Sally Yates).

19. On Tuesday, *Politico* reported that Michael Flynn's lobbying work for Turkey came to him via Dmitri Zairian, a Russian with ties to the Putin regime.

20. The White House denied a request by House Oversight Committee leaders Jason Chaffetz and Elijah Cummings to release documents related to Flynn.

21. Shortly thereafter, Chaffetz and Cummings addressed the press, saying Flynn may have broken the law by not disclosing payments from Russia.

22. The next day, Chaffetz posted an explanation on Facebook of why he was leaving office, citing a foot injury. His explanation was met with much skepticism.

23. Friday, Cummings said the White House is "covering up" for Flynn. Senator Richard Blumenthal said there is "powerful, mounting, incontrovertible evidence" of a violation of criminal law.

24. The Pentagon's internal watchdog group opened an investigation into whether Flynn took payments from foreign governments after leaving the military.

25. Democrats on the House Oversight Committee released documents showing that the Pentagon warned Flynn not to take foreign payments without advance approval from the military. Flynn did not seek approval.

26. Spicer blamed Obama for Flynn having security clearance, neglecting the fact that Obama fired Flynn, and Trump appointed him as national security adviser.

27. NBC reported the Trump team did do a background check on Flynn as part of his becoming national security adviser. Despite their public denials, senior transition team members like Pence and Sessions would have seen the information.

28. Michael Cohen said he may sue *BuzzFeed* for publishing the Steele dossier, which includes allegations that Cohen traveled to Prague in August to meet with Russians.

29. The *Guardian* reported that Steele had also alerted the UK government with two memos about collusion between Trump and Russia. His contact in the U.S. appears to have been with Senator John McCain, not James Comey.

30. Steele's memo also reported that four members of the Trump team traveled to Prague for secret discussions with the Kremlin in August/September 2016 on how to pay hackers for penetrating the Democratic Party computer systems.

31. Pyotr Levashov, the Russian hacker whose wife said he was "linked to Trump's win" in Week 22, was indicted in Bridgeport, Connecticut, on eight counts related to the Kelihos botnet, which he used to steal log-in information, install malware, and distribute spam.

32. Representative David Cicilline, the ranking minority member of the House Judiciary Committee, requested that the inspector general open an investigation into the firings of Yates and Bharara. Yates will testify on May 8 in a Senate hearing.

33. Trump made sixteen false claims in a bizarre interview with the AP. He also made at least fifteen comments that the AP classified as "unintelligible."

34. Also in the AP interview, Trump bragged that his appearance on "Face the Nation" earned the show's highest ratings since its 9/11 coverage.

35. Trump said he planned to keep on his controversial press secretary, Sean Spicer, because "the guy gets great ratings."

36. After a second executive order was blocked, Trump said he would "absolutely" consider proposals to break up the Ninth Circuit Court of Appeals. This threat was compared in a *Slate* article with the type of action a dictator might take.

37. The Trump regime's VOICE (Victims of Immigration Crime Engagement) hotline for callers to report on immigrants has reportedly been flooded with calls with reports of space aliens.

38. A federal judge in San Francisco temporarily blocked the Trump regime's efforts to withhold money from sanctuary cities.

39. *WaPo* reported on ICE data showing that half of the immigrants arrested had no criminal convictions or had committed traffic offenses.

40. Supreme Court Justice John Roberts spoke out against Trump's immigration plan, describing the regime's interpretation as inviting "prosecutorial abuse" by making it easy to strip citizenship for lying about even minor infractions.

41. Trump's Muslim ban suffered another setback as the Ninth Circuit Court of Appeals denied his request for an eleven-member court review.

42. A report by the ADL revealed that anti-Semitic incidents in the U.S. rose by 86 percent in the first three months of 2017, over the same period last year.

43. Trump's proposed budget would strip all funding from a State Department bureau that promotes the rights of women around the world.

44. A Trump supporter stormed a cafeteria at a Kentucky university and asked people about their political affiliation before stabbing two women.

45. Trump's USDA rolled back Michelle Obama's school nutrition standards.

46. Mnuchin said Trump will not release his tax returns, adding that Trump "has given more financial disclosure than anybody else."

47. The *NYT* reported that Kushner recently financed real-estate transactions in New York City through the Steinmetz family, who are under investigation for bribing a government official in Guinea to secure mining rights.

48. The investigator who found that Florida attorney general Pam Bondi did nothing wrong by accepting $25,000 of campaign cash and then dropping the investigation of Trump University ignored key evidence already unearthed.

49. *Politico* reported that Lewandowki's D.C. firm is offering foreign clients in-person meetings with Trump, Pence, and other senior regime members.

50. The *Huffington Post*'s Christina Wilkie compiled a public spreadsheet to identify $107 million of donations to Trump's inauguration. Discrepancies have been found, and the regime has yet to explain where unspent monies went.

51. Ivanka was booed for defending her father at a conference for female business leaders in Berlin.

52. *WaPo* reported that workers endured long hours and low pay working at factories used by Ivanka's company in China.

53. Facebook revealed that fake accounts were used on its platform to sway the U.S. election. Facebook also indicated that its findings do "not contradict" the January 6 report issued by the U.S. Director of National Intelligence.

54. Commerce Secretary Ross said the Trump regime would impose a 20 percent tariff on Canadian softwood lumber.

55. On Wednesday morning, Trump said he was considering withdrawing from NAFTA. By the evening, amid confusion and without a reasonable explanation, he changed course and said the U.S. would remain.

56. Trump ceremoniously summoned the entire U.S. Senate onto a bus to the White House for a closed-door meeting on North Korea. To the senators' frustration, nothing was offered beyond public information. Stagecraft.

57. Trump gave another disturbing one-hundred-days interview to Reuters, for which the first headline to break was "there is a chance of a 'major, major conflict with North Korea.'"

58. Trump also told Reuters he missed his past life and added, "This is more work than in my previous life. I thought it would be easier."

59. Trump brought a printed map handout to his Reuters interview to showcase his electoral win.

60. In another one-hundred-days interview, Trump asked *WaPo* to put his Electoral College handout on their front page.

61. The U.S. economy grew at just 0.7 percent in the first quarter, the weakest showing in three years. Expectedly, Trump did not comment or tweet.

62. The Resistance claimed another victory as Trumpcare 3 failed to muster support in the House, despite the GOP's forty-seven-seat advantage.

63. Fallout from the O'Reilly ouster continued, as CNN reported Fox News is now under federal investigation by the U.S. Postal Inspection Service and the Justice Department regarding settlement payments potentially involving mail or wire fraud. The probe is also examining misconduct allegations and inquiring about the atmosphere at the company.

64. A new CNN/OCR poll found that two thirds of Americans do not believe Trump is honest and trustworthy.

65. Koi, the restaurant in Trump SoHo, became the latest Trump business to suffer a decline in revenue and close. Unlike Trump Hotel D.C., Koi didn't have the benefit of foreign diplomats patronizing it to win favor.

66. The Trump regime announced Friday that the EPA website would be undergoing changes, then removed information about climate science from public view.

67. The White House Correspondents' Dinner will go on without Trump tonight. He will instead hold a campaign rally in Pennsylvania.

Week 25

APRIL 30–MAY 6, 2017

The fabric and values of our country are transforming before our eyes. The Trump regime of billionaires and sycophants—with most Republicans cowering along in lockstep—continue to act and take actions that are greedy and cruel. As we hit Week 25, every subgroup of Americans not white, straight, and male has been a target.

The beat of Trump-Russia continues, as does Trump's mentally imbalanced leadership—about which there is increasing concern. This week the authoritarian themes of silencing dissent and consolidating power and wealth were also front and center.

1. Trump delivered a campaign speech in Harrisburg, Pennsylvania, to mark his first hundred days. One pundit called it "the most hate-filled in modern history."

2. Frustrated by his failures in the first hundred days, Trump took to Twitter and Fox News to demand changes to "archaic" rules of the House and Senate, so he could consolidate his power.

3. Trump called for a government shutdown in September to fix what he called a "mess." Republican leaders rejected this idea.

4. Trump also blamed constitutional checks and balances for the chaos of his first hundred days, saying, "It's an archaic system . . . It's really a bad thing for the country."

5. Trump said he is open to meeting North Korean leader Kim Jong-un, saying, "I would absolutely be honored to do it."

6. Trump ally Erdogan fired thirty-nine hundred people from the Turkish civil service and military as "threats to national security" in his second post-referendum purge. Trump has filled 5 percent of key roles in the executive branch.

7. Tillerson sent a survey to employees ahead of a major State Department overhaul involving significant job and budget cuts. Tillerson has yet to name a deputy or fill the key roles vacated by early resignations.

8. In a CBS interview, Trump denied that Russia hacked our election, saying, it "could've been China, could've been a lot of different groups."

9. A massive coordinated hack and online leak of Emmanuel Macron's e-mails occurred just one and a half days before the French presidential election. Macron's campaign blamed Russia for the attack.

10. The leaks came within an hour of the midnight campaign blackout, during which politicians, media, and citizens are legally required to pull back from any public election discussion.

11. The head of Germany's domestic intelligence agency accused Russia of gathering large amounts of political data in cyberattacks ahead of Germany's September election.

12. Sparking shock and outrage, Trump invited Philippine president Duterte, an authoritarian known for brutality, to the White House. Trump did not clear the invitation with the State Department.

13. According to Duterte's spokesman, Trump praised Duterte, saying, "You're doing a great job."

14. Amid concern with Trump's embrace of authoritarian rulers, Tillerson said American values, such as human rights, should not be a condition for U.S. foreign policy.

15. Trump Tower in the Philippines continues to use videos of Trump and Ivanka as a key selling point.

16. The *Moscow Times* reported that someone is throwing chemicals at Russian opposition activists, causing them to go partially blind.

17. *USA Today* compiled a list of thirty-eight Russians opposed to Putin who were victims of unsolved murders or suspicious deaths in the past three years. Two such deaths were related to the Steele dossier/Trump-Russia ties.

18. John McCain said he was "looking at other options" after Trump ally Senator Bob Corker backed off from imposing more sanctions on Russia.

19. In violation of the Hatch Act, Secretary Ross accompanied Trump to Pennsylvania for a campaign event to raise money for Trump's 2020 campaign, and White House staffer Sarah Huckabee Sanders tweeted about it.

20. Sean Spicer walked out of a press conference without taking questions after Trump negotiated with Senate Democrats to avoid a government shutdown.

21. The OGE sent a letter to the White House and executive branch agency heads asking for copies of any waivers for Trump regime members from ethics rules. According to the *NYT*, at least two such waivers have been granted.

22. The OGE says it wasn't consulted about Ivanka's job, saying she should be considered a federal employee and subject to those rules.

23. Voice of America, a government-funded news agency, posted a story and tweeted about Ivanka's new book, raising questions about the Trump regime's use of government sources to promote private business interests.

24. A State Department account (@GenderAtState) also likely violated federal rules by retweeting a post promoting Ivanka's book.

25. After pushback from his cabinet, Trump started to dismantle his "shadow cabinet"—young, inexperienced spies placed at federal agencies.

26. The IRS is demanding seven billion dollars in back taxes from the Mercer family's hedge fund. The Mercers' donations and ties to the Trump regime make it unlikely they will pay.

27. Congress allocated a whopping $120 million for the Trump family's security costs. Costs include business trips to Vancouver and Dubai by Trump's sons, and ski weekends in Aspen and Whistler for Ivanka.

28. The *WSJ* uncovered that Kushner had failed to report one billion dollars' worth of loans in his financial disclosure. He also omitted his stake in Cadre, a tech startup with ties to Goldman Sachs, George Soros, and Peter Thiel.

29. *Politico* reported that at least nine members of Trump's transition team have registered as lobbyists, despite a five-year lobbying ban.

30. Wilbur Ross said the Syria strike—which he viewed with Trump and Chinese president Xi at Mar-a-Lago—was "after-dinner entertainment."

31. Priebus told ABC that the Trump regime "looked at" changing libel laws to go after the media for articles "that have no basis or fact," and for "writing stories about constant contacts with Russia."

32. Desiree Fairooz, a Code Pink activist who briefly laughed during Sessions's confirmation hearing, was convicted in Virginia. Two others will also face charges. Fairooz was found guilty of disorderly and disruptive conduct and a charge of parading or demonstrating on Capitol grounds.

33. Trump's new Federal Communications Commission (FCC) chairman, Ajit Pai, said the FCC would investigate talk show host Stephen Colbert for a joke made about Trump and Putin and "take appropriate action."

34. The AP reported that Republican House Financial Services Committee chair Jeb Hensarling told dozens of government agencies to exclude communications with his committee from FOIA requests. He was widely criticized.

35. Citing e-mails obtained under the FOIA, CBS reported that Trump had direct involvement in tracking down the National Park Service official who tweeted photos of Trump and Obama's inauguration crowds. Trump contacted the acting director of the department about the tweeted photo.

36. Seemingly to counter his unpopularity, Trump has mentioned the election results on 39 percent of the days since November 8.

37. In an article in the *New Yorker*, writer Evan Osnos reported that Trump's fitness to serve is "officially part of the discussion in Congress."

38. Breaking a tradition of eighteen years, a school district in Seattle canceled its international field trip over concerns about Trump's border enforcement.

39. Trump did away with a sixteen-year-old tradition of celebrating Cinco de Mayo at the White House.

40. Senator Bob Casey blasted Trump and his regime for deporting a mother and her five-year-old son back to Honduras, where they would face grave danger. Despite Casey's efforts to intervene, the deportation is moving forward.

41. According to the ACLU, Texas is about to become the first "show me your papers" state, forcing law enforcement officers to demand proof of citizenship from anyone they detain.

42. The Trump regime fired chief usher Angella Reid, the first woman and second African American to hold the job. The job typically involves a long tenure, so this Friday afternoon firing was viewed with curiosity by presidential historians and those who have worked in the White House.

43. Trump said he may not continue to fund the twenty-five-year-old Historically Black College and University Capital Financing Program, saying it may be unconstitutional to allocate funds on the basis of race, ethnicity, and gender.

44. In a memo, Trump ordered his regime to end Michelle Obama's girls' education program, "Let Girls Learn."

45. After campaigning on cracking down on drugs, a line of attack that seemed racially based, Trump proposed cutting funding for the Office of National Drug Control by 95 percent.

46. Rape charges were dropped against an immigrant teen in Maryland. Fox News had devoted days of coverage to the case, using it to validate Trump's immigration agenda.

47. Several outlets reported that Gorka would accept a role outside the White House after being denied security clearance and because of his associations with a Hungarian hate group. Gorka said these reports were "very fake news."

48. The *Daily Beast* reported that Trump and Bannon intervened to save Gorka, and for now, he will remain.

49. On Wednesday, *Politico* reported that Lewandowski's firm, Avenue Strategies, quietly signed a deal to represent Citgo, a U.S.-based oil company owned by Venezuela, in its proposed sale to Russia's Rosneft.

50. Citgo donated $500,000 to Trump's inauguration. According to the *Daily Beast*, that money may have come from the Kremlin, at least indirectly.

51. The owner of the 19.5 percent stake in Rosneft sold shortly after Carter Page's July meeting with Putin allies in Russia is still not known.

52. A bipartisan group of senators called on Trump to block Citgo's sale to Rosneft, citing concern that with control of Citgo, Russia could use its influence to counter U.S. trade sanctions imposed in 2014.

53. Amid reports on Citgo and other questionable dealings, Lewandowski resigned from Avenue Strategies, the firm he cofounded.

54. Friday afternoon, Mark Green, Trump's second pick for Army Secretary, withdrew as a nominee. Senators had expressed alarm at Green's public homophobic statements, something Trump's vetting missed or ignored.

55. Rachel Maddow cited that Trump has yet to fill fifty-seven of fifty-eight senior-level Pentagon positions that require Senate confirmation.

56. Trump reportedly speaks to Rupert Murdoch almost every day. Some had speculated that Murdoch might be the biggest winner of Trump firing Bharara, as Fox News is under investigation in the Southern District of New York.

57. The Senate Intelligence Committee sent letters to several Trump insiders, including Flynn, Manafort, Page, and Stone, requesting records of their communication with Russia.

58. Page said he planned to cooperate, but his records as a private citizen would be "minuscule in comparison" to what the FBI had collected under a FISA warrant. Page was asked to list any Russian official or business executive he met with between June 16, 2015, and January 20, 2017.

59. *WaPo* reported that Trump transition staffers warned Flynn about contact with Kislyak. Flynn was warned on both Kislyak's background and that contact with him would likely be monitored.

60. *WaPo* reported that Marshall Billingslea was among a small group of national security hands in the Trump transition team who were concerned about Flynn and Trump's pro-Russia stance.

61. The AP reported that the Obama administration was concerned about the Trump transition team's request for info on Kislyak and about Flynn's contact with Russia. The Obama administration also delayed telling the Trump team about planned sanctions against Russia for their interference in the 2016 election.

62. One punishment was to close two Russian compounds. The AP reported the Obama administration feared if they told Trump's team too far in advance, they might give Moscow lead time to clear information out.

63. NBC further reported that the Obama administration gave the Trump team only a few hours' notice about closing Russian compounds.

64. The AP reported that the Obama administration was also concerned about sharing info with the Trump transition team after classified documents were copied and removed from a secure room in their Washington headquarters.

65. Sally Yates will testify Monday before the Senate that she gave a formal warning to Trump's White House that Flynn was lying three weeks before he was fired. This contradicts the Trump regime's version of what happened.

66. Nine weeks have passed since Trump's tweet accusing Obama of wiretapping Trump Tower. This week Trump said it has "been proven very strongly."

67. Rand Paul, a supporter of Trump's false claim, also said he thinks Obama spied on him. Paul tweeted that he has requested info on whether he "was surveilled by Obama admin" or the intelligence community.

68. At an open Senate hearing, Comey reiterated that there was no spying on Trump Tower.

69. On Thursday, Trump and the GOP passed a series of measures, including passage of Trumpcare/the American Health Care Act (AHCA) in the House, a watering down of Dodd Frank, and a "religious liberty" executive order that allows religious institutions to participate in politics and to decide whether to cover birth control for their employees.

70. Beer was rolled in as the votes on Trumpcare were cast in the House, followed by a celebration at the White House—this, as more than twenty-four million Americans stood to lose health insurance.

71. After the vote and celebration, it became apparent that many House members never read Trumpcare or considered how it would impact their district. As House members returned home for an eleven-day vacation, many avoided the public or turned off their phones.

72. Jason Chaffetz, who in Week 24 was noted to have left D.C. and halted his investigation of Flynn in order to get foot surgery, slithered back to D.C. to vote for Trumpcare.

73. After Trumpcare passed the House, the nonpartisan *Cook Political Report* said the vote hurt the reelection prospects of twenty Republicans.

Week 26

MAY 7-13, 2017

What stands out in Week 26 is our normalization of a leader who tells bald-faced lies to us and the ease with which Trump continues to indulge in this behavior. We've entered uncharted territory: Trump fired the FBI director in charge of investigating him and his regime's ties to Russia, and admitted he did so because of the investigation.

The other takeaway of Week 26 is what you missed. We're in such a state of constant chaos, it's easy to overlook the ways the Trump regime continues to tear the fabric of our values, to loot every cent it can, and to move the U.S. further away from democracy.

1. Despite Russian involvement, Macron defeated Le Pen handily in France's presidential election, marking the third European country since the U.S. election (after Austria and the Netherlands) to reject a Trump-like candidate.

2. A shocking *Guardian* article detailed the use of data to influence the outcome of the Brexit vote and the U.S. election, as Cambridge Analytica was able to harvest vast data sets from Facebook and other places and weaponize them to influence outcomes. Cambridge Analytica has ties to Trump, Nigel Farage, Peter Thiel, Steve Bannon, and Robert Mercer.

3. The article also warned that the Trump regime is already weaponizing U.S. data for future elections, reporting that allegedly Cambridge Analytica has "been awarded contracts in the Pentagon and the U.S. state department."

4. While in Beijing for a meeting with potential investors for the family's New Jersey project, Kushner's sister mentioned Jared's role in the Trump administration and the project's use of the EB-5 visa program. EB-5 visas allow immigrants a path to a green card for investing $500,000 in a project that creates U.S. jobs.

5. The Kushner family later apologized after being accused of kleptocracy by critics including former George W. Bush attorney Richard Painter.

6. A *WaPo* researcher who attended the meeting tweeted, "I was threatened, harassed and forced to delete recordings and photos of The Kushner family recruiting Chinese investors in US Green cards."

7. Carter Page said he would no longer cooperate with the Senate Intelligence Committee's request, saying he wants information he requested from the Committee on the "unjustified civil rights violations by the Clinton/Obama regime."

8. Eric Trump reportedly told a reporter back in 2014, when asked about funding golf courses, "Well, we don't rely on American banks. We have all the funding we need out of Russia."

9. Eric Trump later denied having said this, but Donald Jr. had similarly said at a real estate conference in 2008: "We see a lot of money pouring in from Russia."

10. Trump-connected lobbyists are making millions from major companies and foreign governments by touting their access to the Trump regime.

11. Goldman Sachs hired a top Trump campaign staffer, David Urban, as a lobbyist.

12. Eight Senate Democrats asked regulators to investigate whether Trump friend Carl Icahn violated insider trading laws in the biofuel market.

13. Wilbur Ross doubled down on the Trump regime rhetoric about tariffs on Canadian softwood lumber, and warned Canada that "threats of retaliatory action" are "inappropriate."

14. Nikki Haley issued a strong statement on Venezuela, citing President Nicolás Maduro's "disregard for the fundamental rights of his own people." As Venezuela's state-owned oil company donated $500,000 to Trump's inauguration, the rest of the regime has been silent.

15. The State Department has yet to resume daily press briefings.

16. Chicago mayor Rahm Emanuel revived the deleted EPA climate change webpage, which in Week 24 was mysteriously taken down on a Friday night, and put the information up on Chicago's website.

17. Minutes after an ABC reporter asked Spicer why Trump's campaign website still calls for a Muslim ban, that reference was deleted.

18. Despite Trump's promises to keep jobs in the U.S., Rexnord—in Pence's home state of Indiana, near Carrier, which Trump visited earlier to much ballyhoo—is moving jobs to Mexico. Trump tweeted to blame Obama.

19. On CBS's *60 Minutes*, residents of Granger, Indiana, lamented their neighbor, who had no criminal record and had been in the U.S. for twenty years, being deported and separated from his wife and children, who are all citizens.

20. The AP reported that the Trump regime targeted Haitian immigrants, seeking evidence of crimes as an excuse to deport them.

21. A bill that passed the Texas House would allow adoption agencies to reject families on the basis of religion or sexual orientation.

22. Dan Heyman, a Public News Service reporter, was arrested Tuesday night in West Virginia for persistently questioning HHS Secretary Tom Price.

23. Price commended the police who arrested the journalist.

24. The EPA dismissed five scientists from a major scientific review board and replaced them with representatives from industries the EPA regulates.

25. Later in the week, two EPA science board members resigned in protest.

26. Trump signed an executive order creating a commission on "election integrity" to reexamine Hillary's three-million-vote win and "fraud," to be led by Pence and noted xenophobe Kris Kobach, Kansas secretary of state.

27. Representative John Lewis issued a statement on the commission, saying, "It's only been 54 years since we were jailed, beaten, and killed for trying to cast a vote," and stated that the commission was "nothing more than a cover for them to threaten our progress."

28. Reversing progress, Sessions instituted a tougher new criminal charging and sentencing policy—a noted failure in the 1980 and 1990s. Sessions's policy will disproportionately impact people of color.

29. ICE arrested 1,378 suspected "gang members" in what Fox News characterized as the largest gang sweep ever.

30. Trump tweeted that China "just agreed that the U.S. will be allowed to sell beef, and other major products" in China again. This deal was brokered by Obama last September.

31. *Foreign Policy* reported on Bannon's attempts to get National Security Adviser McMaster fired, calling it the White House "Game of Thrones for morons." McMaster remains one of the few Trump senior officials who was not part of the campaign.

32. When asked about NSC's functions at a daily press briefing, McMaster said that "a lot of what we do at the NSC is trying to keep up with the president."

33. During the day of the Sally Yates/James Clapper hearing, Trump addressed a total of seven tweets to Yates, including one from the @POTUS account.

34. CNN anchors Dana Bash and John King likened Trump's tweets ahead of the hearing to "witness intimidation."

35. Yates testified that she met with White House counsel Don McGahn twice to warn him that Michael Flynn had lied to Pence about his conversations with the Russian envoy, therefore Pence's public statements were false.

36. Yates warned McGahn that Flynn was compromised and could be blackmailed by the Russians. Yates met with McGahn on January 26 and 27, and was fired on Monday, January 30, allegedly for saying she would not defend the Muslim ban.

37. Despite her warning, Flynn remained as national security adviser for eighteen more days, sitting in on important foreign policy meetings and receiving classified information.

38. The day after the Yates/Clapper hearing, Senator Lindsey Graham said that based on what he heard, he wants to investigate Trump's business dealings.

39. After Trump blamed Obama for Flynn having security clearance, NBC reported that Flynn never received the broader security clearance required for a national security adviser.

40. Trump briefly changed his Twitter cover Monday night to a statement that Clapper said "there is 'no evidence' of collusion w/Russia and Trump." Trump repeated this lie all week, including in a Friday morning tweet.

41. On Friday, Clapper told Andrea Mitchell that he didn't say what Trump claimed.

42. *ProPublica* reported that part of Comey's testimony to the Senate Judiciary Committee about Huma Abedin was inaccurate. The FBI issued corrections just hours before Trump fired Comey.

43. Following Clapper's testimony on Monday, the Senate Intelligence Committee asked Treasury Department's Financial Crimes Enforcement Network (FinCEN) for more information on Trump's business dealings.

44. The *WSJ* reported that FinCEN will provide info on businesses owned by Trump and family members to the Senate Intelligence Committee and the FBI. Ranking member Senator Ron Wyden is interested in shell companies and money laundering through property transfers.

45. *Vanity Fair* reported that FBI sources said there are multiple inquiries about Russia in progress, including the cyber investigation of the hacking, and questions about money laundering from Russian plutocrats through Trump's businesses. Bharara would have been investigating the business side as U.S. attorney for the Southern District of New York.

46. Late Friday night, Joon Kim, the acting U.S. attorney for the Southern District of New York, tweeted, "We will not allow the U.S. financial system to be used to launder proceeds of crimes committed anywhere—here or in Russia."

47. On Friday, a bipartisan group of 178 former U.S. attorneys and assistant U.S. attorneys for the Southern District of New York wrote a letter to Deputy Attorney General Rod Rosenstein calling for a special prosecutor.

48. Law firm Morgan, Lewis & Bockius provided a letter from their firm to Trump showing that Trump has limited business dealings with Russia. ABC reported that the firm has deep ties to Russia and received a "Russia Law Firm of the Year" award in 2016.

49. Trump's initial stated basis for firing Comey was a letter from Attorney General Sessions and Deputy Attorney General Rosenstein relating to Hillary's e-mails and accusing Comey of handling the investigation poorly. Of note, Sessions had agreed to recuse himself from the Trump-Russia investigation.

50. Comey became the third person, after Yates and Bharara, to be fired by Trump while investigating him. Mary McCord, who was the assistant attorney general overseeing the Trump-Russia probe, also resigned without explanation.

51. Shortly after the firing, CNN reported grand jury subpoenas for business records have been issued to Flynn as part of the FBI's Russia investigation.

52. The Senate Intelligence Committee also subpoenaed Flynn after he declined to comply with their April 28 letter unless he was offered immunity.

53. Trump's popularity hit a new low in a Quinnipiac poll: 36 percent approve, 58 percent disapprove. The poll was conducted before the Comey firing.

54. The morning after firing Comey, Tillerson and then Trump met with Russian foreign minister Lavrov.

55. Lavrov scolded Andrea Mitchell for asking Tillerson a question: "Who was giving you your manners, you know?" Tillerson did not intervene.

56. Trump's meeting took place at the White House, and included Lavrov and Kislyak. Photos credited to Russian news agency TASS emerged, showing a joyous meeting. U.S. media was excluded from both meetings.

57. The White House readout of the meeting with Lavrov did not mention Kislyak. If not for Russian news agency photos, no one would have known he was there.

58. *Politico* reported that the idea to exclude U.S. press came from Putin, as did the insistence that the meeting be held at the White House.

59. The Senate Intelligence Committee invited Comey to testify next Tuesday. He declined for now, saying he needed some time off first.

60. The *NYT* reported that days before the firing, Comey had asked Deputy Attorney General Rosenstein for a significant increase in resources for the FBI's investigation into Russian interference in the U.S. election.

61. General Michael Hayden, former director of the CIA and NSA, said of Trump's successive firing of Yates, Bharara, and Comey, "it's beginning to feel a little bit like Nicaragua around here."

62. The *Financial Times* said of Comey's firing, "Putin chalked up another victory," as Trump's action resembles that of a nondemocracy.

63. Trump claimed that he followed the recommendation of Rosenstein that Comey be fired over his handling of Hillary's e-mails. By the next day, leaks led to multiple stories that contradicted that claim.

64. This story would change again and again in the coming days—leaving surrogates having lied to the media. Pence said Trump fired Comey at the "recommendation of the deputy attorney general" seven times during a presser.

65. *WaPo* reported that in fact Trump made a decision to fire Comey, then met with Sessions and Rosenstein to craft a plan for how. Trump was totally unprepared for the media explosion and political backlash.

66. Trump himself said in an NBC interview Thursday that he was thinking about the Russia investigation when he fired Comey, saying, "Russia is a made-up story."

67. *WaPo* also reported that Trump was angry that Comey would not back his false Obama wiretapping claim and that Comey focused on the Trump-Russia probe rather than leaks.

68. Reuters reported that Trump was infuriated that Comey would not preview his Senate testimony for Trump, Sessions, and Rosenstein ahead of the May 3 hearing.

69. The *NYT* reported that Trump and Comey dislike each other. Comey told associates that Trump was "outside the realm of normal," even "crazy."

70. The *WSJ* reported that Comey had started getting daily instead of weekly briefings in the past three weeks because of the quantity of potential evidence of collusion.

71. The *WSJ* also reported that on Monday, Comey had briefed lawmakers on his request to boost the investigation and requested additional personnel from Rosenstein.

72. In an open letter to Rosenstein, twenty state attorneys general called for an independent investigation, saying Trump's firing of Comey was a violation of the public trust.

73. Trump abandoned plans to visit the FBI after the Comey firing. According to NBC, Trump was told agents might not provide a warm reception.

74. McClatchy reported that Comey sought to expand his Trump-Russia probe to include Manafort, who earned eighty to one hundred million dollars for political and business consulting work done for clients, including a Russian billionaire.

75. Rachel Maddow reported that despite earlier indications he would do so, Manafort has yet to register as a foreign agent. Also, Sessions would not confirm if he has recused himself from matters involving Manafort.

76. The *WSJ* reported that the Justice Department requested Manafort's bank records as part of a probe into the Trump campaign's possible collusion with Russia in the 2016 election.

77. The *WSJ* also reported that New York State attorney general Eric Schneiderman and Manhattan district attorney Cyrus Vance have been examining real estate transactions by Manafort.

78. On Thursday, acting FBI director Andrew McCabe testified at a televised Senate Intelligence Committee hearing. McCabe said he will not update the White House on the Russian investigation.

79. McCabe contradicted the Trump regime's assertion that Comey was not well liked at the FBI, saying that "the vast majority of employees enjoyed a deep, positive connection to Director Comey."

80. Also contradicting White House claims, McCabe called the Trump-Russia investigation "highly significant."

81. Trump still claimed on Thursday that he had spoken to Comey three times about whether he was under investigation. When Senator Susan Collins asked if that was standard practice, McCabe answered, "It is not."

82. *Politico* reported that Rosenstein arrived at the Senate Intelligence Committee's office while the televised hearing was taking place. Senators Burr and Warner left the hearing, for what Burr said was a meeting "we can't push off."

83. Sarah Flores, a DoJ spokesperson, lied that the meeting with Burr was previously planned and is "nothing unusual."

84. The *NYT* reported that at a White House dinner shortly after Trump took office, at Trump's request, Comey declined to pledge his loyalty or discuss the Trump-Russia investigation.

85. The dinner took place on January 27, the day after Yates initially informed the White House counsel that Flynn was compromised and subject to blackmail.

86. Rudy Giuliani, who was photographed at the Trump International Hotel in D.C. the night of the Comey firing, was given a May 19 deadline by a judge in Detroit to produce his memo for Trump on the Muslim ban.

87. In a series of erratic early morning tweets Friday, Trump threatened to cease daily press briefings and tweeted, "Comey better hope that there are no 'tapes' of our conversations before he starts leaking to the press!"

88. A source close to Comey said he is "not worried about any tapes."

89. Presidential historian Michael Beschloss noted in a tweet, "Presidents are supposed to have stopped routinely taping visitors without their knowledge when Nixon's taping system was revealed in 1973."

90. Top House and Senate Democrats demanded that Trump release any tapes of communication between him and Comey.

91. Jason Chaffetz asked the DoJ inspector general to look into Comey's firing. Democrats also asked him to look into whether Sessions has recused himself and whether the FBI investigation into Russia is properly staffed.

92. Senators Dick Durbin and Dianne Feinstein called on Rosenstein to resign if he refuses to appoint a special counsel. Senator Amy Klobuchar said senators plan next week to further push this demand in closed-door meetings.

93. On the backs of visits by Duterte and the Russian envoy, Trump will host brutal authoritarian Erdogan for a White House visit on May 16.

Russia's foreign minister Sergey Lavrov, Trump, and Russian ambassador to the United States Sergey Kislyak (L-R) talking during a meeting in the Oval Office at the White House. (Getty Images)

SOME PERSPECTIVE (AFTER 26 WEEKS—HALF A YEAR)

MAY 20, 2017

When I started the Weekly Authoritarianism List in November, early weeks had ten to twenty items: things that were not normal, subtle changes to our democracy and the fabric of our country.

The week of the Women's March, as Trump took office, the list grew to thirty-something items, and from there, in his first hundred days in office, steadily grew and found a new resting point of sixty- to seventy-something items per week.

Last week the list had ninety-three items. This week we likely will top that.

I point this out to acknowledge what we are all feeling—as if we're living in chaos. We are! But I also urge you to be aware of what we are normalizing and accepting each week amid the chaos, and to notice the items you missed in the news because of the overwhelming number of stories. Please also be aware of the items from the early weeks that we have now normalized, despite being shocked back then.

This man is not going to give up power without a fight. His compass and mental health lead him to believe he is in the right, always, and those who fight to take back our democracy are part of the Deep State or out to get him. We must stay woke and resist each and every day because, truly, our democracy and way of life are at risk.
#StandTogether #resist

Week 27

MAY 14–20, 2017

This week's list has over one hundred items and increasingly our country feels like complete chaos: bombshell after bombshell about Trump's ties to and efforts to undermine the investigation into Russia.

Although the biggest headline of the week was the appointment of a special counsel to investigate Trump-Russia, of equal importance were the diurnal signs of our fading democracy. Trump's White House invitation to yet another brutal authoritarian, Erdogan of Turkey, and the ensuing melee outside the Turkish embassy in D.C., is a wake-up call for us all.

1. The *WSJ* reported that three former employees of the Trump Organization saw him tape phone calls from Trump Tower. Trump still has not revealed if his alleged taped conversations with Comey really exist.

2. The *Economist* interviewed Trump about his economic policy and described his strategy to be "unimaginative and incoherent." The interview revealed alarming lack of knowledge of basic concepts.

3. General Michael Hayden said on CNN that he's usually not in favor of special prosecutors, but after Trump fired Comey, "I've changed my mind."

4. Richard Spencer and his torch-carrying white supremacist followers marched in Charlottesville, Virginia, to protest the removal of a Confederate monument, chanting, "You will not replace us."

5. Merkel's party seized a key state from rivals in an election, putting her in a strong position for Germany's general election in September. This would mark the fourth setback for Putin, who often clashes with Merkel, since Trump's election.

6. An NBC poll found that just 29 percent approve of Trump's firing of Comey, and 78 percent want an outside special prosecutor.

7. Trump spent Mother's Day on the golf course and did not see Melania or Barron.

8. The Trump regime issued a statement on North Korea's latest missile test, which, oddly, started out with a Russian perspective.

9. *New York* magazine reported that candidates for FBI director were being screened for their loyalty to Trump.

10. *WaPo* reported on the ways Trump has leveraged his presence at Mar-a-Lago to enhance his club's event business and enrich himself.

11. *Axios* reported Sunday that Trump is considering a sweeping shake-up in his regime. One confidant said, "He's frustrated, and angry at everyone."

12. The Trump regime has hidden massive amounts of data on issues such as workplace violations monitored by OSHA, energy efficiency, and animal welfare abuses—lessening the "naming and shaming" effect on corporate behavior.

13. Clapper said U.S. institutions are under assault—both externally, with Russian interference in our election system, and internally from Trump.

14. WNYC reported that New Jersey Republican representative Rodney Frelinghuysen wrote a letter to a constituent's employer complaining about her progressive activism: "P.S. One of the ringleaders works in your bank!"

15. Page wrote a bizarre letter to Rosenstein, complaining about Obama and Clinton, and citing Maroon 5 lyrics in the footnotes.

16. A *WaPo* reporter noted, "This Is Not Normal," when the paper accidentally published Mattis's personal cell phone number, which was on a yellow sticky note in a photo of Trump bodyguard Keith Schiller.

17. Russian aluminum oligarch Oleg Deripaska is suing the AP for libel in connection with its reporting on his ties to Manafort.

18. *Mother Jones* reported that fifty farmworkers outside of Bakersfield, California, were poisoned by a pesticide just green-lighted by Trump's EPA.

19. Trump met with UAE crown prince Sheikh Mohammed at the White House Monday. In Week 21 it was noted that this crown prince brokered a meeting between Erik Prince and a Putin ally in Seychelles.

20. On Monday, *WaPo* reported that Trump revealed highly classified information on ISIS to Lavrov and Kislyak at the White House meeting. As mentioned in Week 26, U.S. media was excluded.

21. *WaPo* also noted that they withheld the most significant details from the story at the urging of White House officials who warned "revealing them would jeopardize important intelligence capabilities."

22. *BuzzFeed* confirmed *WaPo*'s story, adding that an official who was briefed on Trump's leak said, "It's far worse than what has already been reported."

23. Reuters and the *NYT* also confirmed the story, with the *NYT* adding that the leaked information came from an ally. The White House continued to deny the *WaPo* story Monday night.

24. Trump took to Twitter Tuesday morning, saying he leaked to Russia for "humanitarian reasons," which he has "the absolute right to do." Trump also ironically tweeted a complaint about "the LEAKERS."

25. Former U.S. ambassador to Russia Michael McFaul said Trump does not "have the right to leak classified information obtained from other countries, without their permission."

26. A European official told the AP that their country "might stop sharing intel with U.S. if Trump gave classified info to Russian diplomats."

27. At a press conference Tuesday, McMaster claimed that Trump decided to leak highly classified info to the Russians on the spur of moment, and wasn't aware where the information came from.

28. The *NYT* reported that Israel was the source of the intelligence given to Russia. The leak raises concerns that the information could be passed to Iran, "Russia's close ally and Israel's main threat in the region."

29. *BuzzFeed* reported that an Israeli intelligence official said that knowing Trump leaked to Russia without Israel's prior knowledge was Israel's "worst fears confirmed."

30. ABC reported that Trump's leak endangered an Israeli spy placed inside ISIS.

31. The *WSJ* reported that the Israeli information Trump leaked was considered so sensitive, it wasn't shared with our closest allies.

32. For the first time, more Americans support Trump's impeachment (48 percent) than oppose it (41 percent), according to Public Policy Polling. Its poll was conducted before the Russia leak.

33. Trump hosted Turkey's Erdogan at the White House, another in a string of brutal authoritarians invited to the White House despite human rights abuses at home.

34. After the meeting, a video captured Erdogan's bodyguards viciously attacking protesters outside the Turkish embassy in D.C. Later, a video surfaced of Erdogan watching as his guards beat protesters.

35. D.C. police chief Peter Newsham said diplomatic immunity could limit what the city can do to hold Erdogan's bodyguards accountable.

36. Republicans and Democrats spoke out against the attack, with McCain calling for Turkey's ambassador to be expelled.

37. Ceren Borazan tweeted a photo and wrote: "Dear @POTUS I'm being attackd in this photo. I was assaulted by this man, strangled for protesting. Please help me find & prosecute this man." The tweet was retweeted over 55,000 times. Trump has not responded to the assaults.

38. Following an outcry, the State Department summoned the Turkish ambassador; but two bodyguards who were detained were released and allowed to leave without redress.

39. The @VP account tweeted, then deleted, a photo of Trump's and Erdogan's sons-in-law—both in government positions of power—seated across from each other at lunch.

40. The *NYT* reported that Comey had been writing memos on his interactions with Trump, including a February 14 meeting at which Trump asked Comey to end the FBI investigation of Flynn.

41. The *NYT* also reported that the meeting took place in the Oval Office, and before it started, Trump asked Sessions and Pence to leave the room.

42. According to a Comey associate, Trump also told Comey he should consider putting reporters in prison for publishing classified information.

43. *WaPo* reported that Comey had shared his notes with a small circle in the FBI and DoJ—raising questions of whether Sessions and Rosenstein were aware of them before they wrote the memo to back Trump's firing of Comey.

44. That evening, and the following morning, TV networks—including Fox News—complained that elected Republicans were refusing to go on-air.

45. Russian foreign minister Lavrov advised Americans not to believe the *WaPo* story on Trump leaking to Russia. A spokesperson wrote on Facebook about American newspapers: "You shouldn't read them."

46. Wednesday morning, Putin offered to hand over records of Trump and Lavrov's conversation to the U.S. House and Senate.

47. NBC reported that the FBI subpoenaed Manafort for a $3.5 million mortgage taken out on his Hamptons home just after leaving the Trump campaign. Mortgage documents were never filed, and taxes never paid, on the loan.

48. Eleven Democratic senators called for an investigation of Sessions's involvement with the Comey firing after his stated recusal from the Trump-Russia investigation.

49. In another sign of U.S. decline under Trump, France's prime minister, economic minister, and national security adviser are all experts on Germany, indicating the rise of Germany's importance on the global stage.

50. Twenty-seven-year-old Jean Jimenez-Joseph became the seventh person this year to die while in ICE custody. Jimenez-Joseph committed suicide, but ICE said he "passed away" while at a detention center.

51. ICE data revealed forty-one thousand arrests in Trump's first hundred days, a 38 percent increase over the same period in 2016.

52. As crises loom this week, a new NBC/*WSJ* poll found that only a quarter of Americans find Trump to be honest.

53. The *WSJ* reported that Russian state-run bank VEB indirectly provided hundreds of millions of dollars in financing to a Ukrainian steel mill owned by Alexander Shnaider, who then funded construction of a Trump project in Toronto.

54. Delivering a commencement speech at the Coast Guard Academy, Trump said, "No politician in history . . . has been treated worse or more unfairly."

55. On Wednesday, Rosenstein appointed a special counsel, Robert Mueller, to oversee the federal investigation into Russian interference in the 2016 election and possible collusion between Russia and the Trump regime.

56. Rosenstein was set to appear before the full Senate on Thursday and House on Friday.

57. The White House was blindsided by the special counsel news and given only thirty minutes' advance notice.

58. White House PR strategy was in chaos, with Conway canceling a scheduled appearance on Tucker Carlson's show an hour before airtime. No members of Trump's inner circle appeared on TV Wednesday.

59. *WaPo* reported that a month before Trump clinched the GOP nomination, in a private conversation with fellow GOP leaders, House Majority Leader Kevin McCarthy said Trump could be getting money from Putin: "There's two people I think Putin pays: [Representative Dana] Rohrabacher and Trump."

60. Some GOP leaders laughed, and McCarthy continued, "Swear to God." Speaker Ryan swore the attendees to secrecy.

61. When called for comment, spokespeople for Ryan and McCarthy denied the *WaPo* story—until the *Post* told them they had audio.

62. Pence registered a PAC on Wednesday, typically a signal of seeking higher office. Neither Joe Biden nor Dick Cheney had active PACs while in office.

63. The *NYT* reported that Flynn officially disclosed to the Trump transition team on January 4 that he was under federal investigation for secretly working as a paid lobbyist for Turkey.

64. Pence headed Trump's transition team, but he continued to deny he knew about Flynn's lobbying. Pence was also notified about Flynn by Representative Cummings in a letter dated November 18.

65. The *NYT* reported that the Trump team was aware of Flynn's business dealings in early November, even before his infamous pro-Turkey op-ed on November 8.

66. The *NYT* also reported that acting FBI director McCabe confirmed to Congress a "highly significant" investigation into possible collusion between the Trump regime and Russia to sway the 2016 election.

67. FBI prosecutor Brandon Van Grack is leading a grand jury inquiry in Virginia looking into Flynn's foreign lobbying and has started issuing subpoenas.

68. NBC reported that both Manafort and Flynn are considered "subjects" of a criminal investigation.

69. Also per NBC: the FBI, with help from the Treasury Department, the CIA, and other agencies, is examining contacts, money transfers, and business relationships between the Trump regime and Russia.

70. McClatchy reported that one of the Trump regime's first foreign policy decisions, involving the fight against ISIS, was made by Flynn in coordination with outgoing national security adviser Susan Rice. Flynn went against Obama administration advice, delaying a military operation that would retake ISIS's capital city, Raqqa. The delay was in accordance with Turkey's wishes. It was revealed that Flynn was paid $530,000 by the Turkish government to represent their interests.

71. Reuters reported that the Trump campaign had at least eighteen undisclosed contacts with Russian officials in the seven months leading up to the election.

72. Six of the undisclosed contacts involved Kislyak with Flynn and three other Trump operatives. The other twelve involved Russian officials or people close to Putin and Trump campaign advisers.

73. Reuters also reported that after the election, Flynn and Kislyak had conversations about setting up a back-channel communication between Trump and Putin that could bypass the U.S. national security bureaucracy.

74. Yahoo reported that Trump was in touch with Flynn as recently as April 25, telling him to "stay strong."

75. On Thursday, Flynn's lawyer said his client will not honor the Senate Intelligence Committee's subpoena.

76. White House advisers and personal associates are urging Trump to hire an experienced outside attorney to deal with the Trump-Russia probe.

77. *Time* reported that Russia tried to hack the Department of Defense (DoD)'s Twitter accounts by sending more than ten thousand tailored messages in an effort to get someone at DoD to click on a link, which would have enabled hackers to control the account.

78. Chaffetz, the chair of the House Oversight Committee, resigned from Congress without explanation.

79. *Newsweek* reported that Trump staffers are starting to look for new jobs and are worried about the taint of having worked for the Trump regime.

80. Rosenstein briefed the Senate. Claire McCaskill and other senators said that Rosenstein knew Comey was going to be fired before he wrote his memo.

81. Trump tweeted that the special counsel's investigation is the "single greatest witch hunt of a politician," and continued to cite Rosenstein's memo as justification for his firing of Comey.

82. Trump denied collusion between his campaign and Russia in the 2016 election, but said, "I can only speak for myself."

83. Rosenstein released his opening remarks to the House and Senate. On the subject of the Comey firing, the remarks stated, "My memorandum is not a statement of reasons to justify a for-cause termination."

84. After Rosenstein briefed the House, Cummings told the media, "This is about the fight for the soul of our democracy. We cannot afford to lose this one."

85. The *NYT* reported that Trump called Comey weeks after taking office and asked when he was planning to publicly state that Trump was not under investigation. Comey tried to explain proper chains of communication.

86. According to a friend, Comey was troubled by many of his encounters with Trump, including a January 22 ceremony in the White House Blue Room, where Comey tried to blend into the blue curtains to avoid Trump's attention.

87. *WaPo* also reported on Comey's apprehension about meetings with Trump, his extensive preparations with staff, and his writing out notes in his car directly after meetings.

88. The *NYT* also reported that Priebus asked Comey to push back on media reports in mid-February that the Trump regime had been in contact with Russia during the election.

89. Kushner, while in a White House room with a high-level delegation of Saudis, called the chief executive of Lockheed Martin and asked if she would cut the price on a hundred-billion-dollar weapons deal with Saudi Arabia.

90. CNN reported that despite his recusal, Representative Devin Nunes continues to review intelligence relating to Russia, including as part of the Gang of Eight. Nunes had recused himself over his close ties to the Trump regime.

91. Pence's team continued to spin stories and distance him from Trump, indicating that Pence was kept in the dark on Flynn and Russia, and that he's a "loyal soldier" but that the news cycle is wearing on him.

92. In Trump's first 119 days, he has made 586 false or misleading claims.

93. As Trump floated former senator Joe Lieberman as his potential pick for FBI director, Lieberman's Wikipedia page was mysteriously edited to remove Donald Trump as a notable client of his firm.

94. As Trump leaves for his first overseas trip, foreign leaders have been instructed to praise him for winning the Electoral College. The *NYT* reported that foreign officials and their consultants have created rules for meetings with Trump: "Compliment him on his election win. Contrast him favorably with former President Obama."

95. Representative Carlos Curbelo became the first Republican to call for Trump's impeachment.

96. Spicer issued a statement in response to *NYT* stories, accusing Comey of "grandstanding" and "politicizing" the Russia probe, and hurting our ability "to engage and negotiate with Russia."

97. The *NYT* reported on a document detailing conversations between Trump and Lavrov and Kislyak in the Oval Office. According to the document, Trump said, "I just fired the head of the FBI. He was crazy, a real nut job."

98. Stepping closer to obstruction of justice charges, Trump also allegedly told Russian officials that firing Comey had relieved "great pressure" on him and that he is not under investigation.

99. *WaPo* reported that law enforcement has identified a current White House official as "a significant person of interest."

100. Reuters reported that the Trump regime is exploring ways to use obscure ethics rules to undermine the special counsel's investigation of Trump-Russia. Since Kushner and Manafort were clients of Mueller's former firm, Trump's advisers think Mueller should be barred from investigating them.

101. *New York* magazine reported that the person of interest in the *WaPo* story is Kushner.

102. CNN reported that intercepts of Russian communications reveal that Russian officials bragged during the presidential campaign that they could use Flynn to influence Trump.

103. Trump's pick for deputy treasury secretary, James Donovan, withdrew from consideration on Friday.

104. A former Trump campaign official who has hired counsel for the Russia probe told a CNN reporter that Trump should help pay for his legal costs.

105. As Trump left for his first foreign trip, one reporter tweeted, "Almost palpable relief the circus has left town for a few days." It truly was a different feel from the not-normal chaos of recent months.

Week 28

MAY 21–27, 2017

This week the Trump-Russia scandal reached the inner circle of Trump's White House, as a bombshell revealed that Kushner is a central focus of the FBI investigation. The Trump regime established a war room as the walls of the Trump-Russia probe are increasingly caving in on them, with breaking news daily.

Also of note this week are myriad examples of Trump distancing our country from our traditional allies and instead cozying up to brutal authoritarians. Human rights abroad are no longer a priority—the focus seems to have shifted to countries where the Trump Organization has properties.

1. Trump's attorney said he wouldn't sign his 2016 financial disclosure, a major departure from the norm. After OGE pushback, Trump said he would sign, but has yet to do so.

2. The White House also blocked disclosure of names of former lobbyists who have been granted waivers to work in the White House or for federal agencies. Late Friday, the White House said it would comply, but has yet to do so.

3. GOP senators are considering changing rules to make it harder for Democrats to block Trump's picks for circuit court judges. This follows implementation of the "nuclear option," which eased the path for Trump's Supreme Court pick.

4. Tillerson held a press conference in Riyadh on a new U.S.-Saudi partnership. U.S. media was excluded.

5. NPR reported there's been an unprecedented spike of white supremacist activity on college campuses since Trump was elected.

6. Shortly after announcing his resignation from Congress, Jason Chaffetz said individuals leaking info to the press should go to jail.

7. Trump considered vetoing the temporary spending bill. Priebus asked former House Speaker John Boehner to talk Trump into signing and keeping the government open.

8. As Tillerson visited Saudi Arabia, the kingdom announced it would invest twenty billion dollars in Blackstone's new forty-billion-dollar infrastructure fund.

9. Saudi Arabia will also invest one hundred million dollars in Ivanka's Women Entrepreneurs Fund. In addition to other human rights abuses, the kingdom has one of the worst records globally for treatment of women.

10. During a photo op with Netanyahu on his visit to Israel, Trump confirmed the source of his leak to Lavrov and Kislyak at the White House by telling the press he "never mentioned the word or the name Israel."

11. *Foreign Policy* reported that Israel changed its rules for intelligence sharing with the U.S. after Trump's leak to Russia.

12. Turkey summoned the U.S. envoy to complain about the treatment of Erdogan's bodyguards after they beat up U.S. protesters.

13. Amid rising tensions, Turkey signed a $1.5 million contract with longtime Trump lobbyist Brian Ballard. Ballard's firm has also recently signed contracts with the Dominican Republic and the Socialist Party of Albania.

14. A leaked transcript prepared by the Philippine government of a phone call between Trump and Duterte described Trump praising the brutal authoritarian: "What a great job you are doing" with the drug problem.

15. Also on the call with Duterte, Trump revealed the location of two U.S. nuclear submarines.

16. U.S. officials were chastised for leaking the identity of the bomber who attacked a concert in Manchester to the press before British police officially named him.

17. UK officials were also outraged when photos of the aftermath of the Manchester attack were published in the *NYT*, and said they would stop sharing information about the attack with their U.S. counterparts. Later that day, sharing reportedly resumed.

18. Flynn's lawyer said his client would invoke his Fifth Amendment rights rather than comply with a Senate Intelligence Committee subpoena. Senators Burr and Warner said they are considering holding Flynn in contempt.

19. New Jersey governor Chris Christie told reporters that as head of Trump's transition team, he told Trump not to hire Flynn in any capacity. Pence took over as head next.

20. Sessions canceled his Monday testimony before Congress on DoJ funding, for fear the hearing would be overtaken by questions about the Trump-Russia scandal.

21. Representative Elijah Cummings said the House Oversight Committee has documents that show Flynn lied to security clearance investigators in 2016. Flynn claimed he was paid by "US companies," not Russia's RT, for his 2015 Moscow trip.

22. CNN reported that Mueller visited FBI headquarters and was briefed on the contents of Comey's Trump memos.

23. *WaPo* reported that Trump asked Director of National Intelligence (DNI) Dan Coats and NSA director Michael Rogers to publicly say there was no

collusion between Russia and Trump in the 2016 election. The goal was to "muddy the waters" about the FBI probe.

24. Like Comey, Rogers was concerned about his conversations with Trump and kept contemporaneous notes.

25. *WaPo* also reported that White House staffers tried to get senior intel officers and members of Congress to push back on the stories that the Trump regime members were in frequent contact with Russian officials.

26. Senator Tammy Duckworth sent a letter to the NSA requesting info on security sweeps of the Oval Office after Trump's meeting with Lavrov and Kislyak.

27. A member of the Federal Elections Commission (FEC) called for an investigation into Russia's purchase of Facebook ads to possibly boost Trump in the election.

28. At a House hearing, former CIA director Brennan testified that he was convinced last summer that "the Russians were trying to interfere in the election. And they were very aggressive."

29. Brennan also testified on significant contact between the Trump campaign and Russia, citing Russian efforts to get U.S. persons "to act on their behalf either wittingly or unwittingly."

30. Brennan also said he alerted the FBI about the troubling pattern in July, seeming to form the basis for the start of the FBI investigation.

31. Despite the Trump regime's efforts to limit the scope of Mueller's investigation by noting that Kushner, Ivanka, and Manafort are clients of his former law firm, the DoJ cleared Mueller to lead the Russia probe.

32. The Senate Intelligence Committee subpoenaed two Flynn companies. Corporations cannot avoid testifying by invoking the Fifth Amendment.

33. On Thursday, the Senate Intelligence Committee voted to give Senators Burr and Warner blanket authority to issue subpoenas in the Trump-Russia probe.

34. Burr and Warner asked Trump's political organization to produce all Russia-related documents, e-mails, and phone records going back to his campaign's launch in June 2015.

35. STAT reported that experts think the deterioration in Trump's linguistic capabilities could reflect changes in the health of his brain.

36. *InfoWars* was given White House press credentials.

37. William Adams, the chairman of the National Endowment for the Humanities (NEH), resigned amid Trump's budget rollout, which calls for huge cuts to domestic programs.

38. A top Education Department official resigned after refusing DeVos's orders to testify before a congressional oversight hearing.

39. Trump released his budget with a two-trillion-dollar double-counting error. Larry Summers described it as "the most egregious accounting error in a presidential budget in the nearly 40 years I have been tracking them."

40. Trump's Caribbean estate was quietly put on the market at a significantly higher price than he paid in 2013, again raising ethical concerns of potential buyers paying above market to gain access to the president.

41. The *NYT* reported on ethical concerns over the Trump family golf business, as the Professional Golf Association tournament comes to Trump National. Access to Trump, who frequents his courses, is being touted as a marketing point for membership.

42. Demonstrating how Trump's friends continue to influence policy, Carl Icahn is set to save sixty million dollars for his oil refinery company CVR Energy in the first quarter given planned easing of regulations.

43. Giuliani attempted to distance himself from Trump's Muslim ban, despite his bragging on Fox News months ago that he was consulted by Trump.

44. DeVos said states should have the flexibility to discriminate against LGBTQ students, and schools will not be at risk of losing federal funds.

45. Although before taking office Trump promised to donate all profits earned from foreign governments back to the U.S. Treasury, according to NBC, the Trump Organization is not tracking these payments. The Constitution bans presidents from receiving foreign government gifts.

46. Ninety-three percent of key roles in the executive branch remain unfilled.

47. *BuzzFeed* reported that the guest reception manager at Mar-a-Lago, wife of a twice-convicted felon who likes to brag about his wife's access, was assigned a White House e-mail address and phone number and helped with Trump's overseas plans.

48. A new study found that tourism to the U.S. has been on the decline since Trump took office, dropping by as much as 16 percent.

49. The Carrier plant in Indiana, where, to much ballyhoo, Trump showcased saving eight hundred jobs, announced mass layoffs before Christmas. The jobs are being moved to Mexico.

50. *Foreign Policy* reported that NATO countries were frantically preparing for their summit with Trump. One official said, "It's like they're preparing to deal with a child—someone with a short attention span and mood who has no knowledge of NATO, no interest in in-depth policy issues, nothing."

51. At the NATO summit in Brussels, Trump pushed the prime minister of Montenegro aside, before chastising participants for not paying their share of NATO costs. His behavior was met with uniform disgust by our allies.

52. Trump also refused to clearly back Article 5, the one-for-all, all-for-one principle of NATO, and remained at odds with our allies over Russia.

53. Trump also said of Germany, our close ally, "The Germans are bad, very bad."

54. Aya Hijazi, whose release from an Egyptian prison Trump had bragged about negotiating, told PBS's Judy Woodruff that Trump did not understand that it was el-Sisi's regime that had held her.

55. On Wednesday, Greg Gianforte, running for Montana's open congressional seat, body-slammed *Guardian* reporter Ben Jacobs when asked about the Congressional Budget Office (CBO)'s scoring of Trump's American Health Care Act (AHCA). Like Trump, Gianforte has had harsh things to say about the media. Gianforte was charged with assault the night before the election, which he won.

56. Weeks before, Jacobs had reported on Gianforte's ownership of Russian index funds, whose holdings include companies like Rosneft that are under U.S. sanctions.

57. Paul Farhi in *WaPo* cited four violent clashes between the press and public officials in the past month, saying Trump's rhetoric has led to a "climate of anger, disrespect and hostility" toward the press.

58. *Politico* reported that Trump reached out to former campaign staffers Corey Lewandowski and David Bossie about becoming crisis managers as the Trump-Russia scandal unfolds.

59. In a surprising move, Trump hired his longtime personal lawyer Marc Kasowitz to represent him in the special counsel's Trump-Russia probe.

60. CNN reported that the Trump regime is establishing a war-room-type operation aimed at developing a rapid response to Trump-Russia news.

61. As the CBO came out with alarming scoring on Trumpcare/AHCA, Trump ally Gingrich called for the abolishment of the CBO.

62. Trump's budget targets undocumented immigrants by denying them tax credits and jobs, while significantly beefing up his deportation force.

63. The Trump regime kept U.S. reporters largely in the dark during his overseas trip this week: delaying readouts, keeping reporters at a distance, and refusing to hold press conferences.

64. Trump ally Sheriff David Clarke directed his staff waiting at a Dallas/Fort Worth International Airport terminal to hassle a plane passenger after a brief exchange. The passenger is suing Clarke and the deputies involved.

65. The Fourth Circuit Court of Appeals upheld a nationwide injunction against Trump's second Muslim ban by a 10–3 vote. The chief judge said the ban "drips with religious intolerance, animus, and discrimination."

66. In their efforts to highlight crimes committed by undocumented immigrants through the VOICE program, Trump's DHS published a database with the personal information of abuse victims.

67. For the first time in almost two decades, the State Department declined to host a Ramadan event.

68. In Portland, Oregon, a suspect hurled insults at Muslim women on a MAX train before stabbing men who tried to stop him. Two were killed.

69. According to the DoJ, Sessions did not disclose his meetings with Kislyak in his security clearance application.

70. Sessions remains attorney general despite having lied both to the Senate under oath and on his security clearance application about Russia, as well as playing a role in Comey's firing despite being recused from Trump-Russia matters.

71. Members of the House Financial Services Committee asked Deutsche Bank to produce documents on Trump family loans. As mentioned in Week 18's list, Deutsche Bank has been fined for laundering money for Russia.

72. The *NYT* reported that U.S. spies collected info last summer that top Russian officials were discussing how to exert influence on Trump through Manafort and Flynn.

73. *Politico* reported that despite the Trump spin that Manafort was a minor player and not in touch with his regime, Manafort called Priebus the week before the inauguration to discuss the growing Russia scandal.

74. *WaPo* reported that a fake Russian document, which claimed that Attorney General Loretta Lynch had given assurances to the Clinton campaign not to worry about the e-mail investigation, influenced Comey's handling of the investigation, including his unusual news conference in July, which he gave without conferring with the DoJ.

75. Although Comey had the Russian document for months before the July news conference, the FBI did not take the simple steps needed to prove it to be bad intelligence until after July.

76. *Wired* magazine reported that Russian hackers are weaponizing "tainted" leaks—planting altered materials with disinformation alongside legitimate leaks.

77. The *WSJ* reported that a GOP political operative, Aaron Nevins, worked with the Russians to hurt Clinton and Democrats during the election—the first direct evidence of collusion.

78. *WaPo* reported that the FBI "person of interest" in the White House referenced in its reporting last week is Kushner. The FBI is investigating Kushner for the extent and nature of his contacts with Russian officials.

79. Further, *WaPo* reported that the FBI is investigating possible coordination between the Trump campaign and Russia to influence the 2016 election, as well as possible financial crimes.

80. The FBI informed House Oversight Committee chair Chaffetz that it will not turn over Comey's memos, leaving open the prospect that Mueller is investigating Trump for obstruction of justice.

81. Joe Lieberman became the fourth candidate under consideration by Trump for FBI director to withdraw from consideration.

82. After demurring on whether Trump would lift sanctions on Russia Thursday, a top Trump adviser, under media scrutiny, said Friday that the sanctions would remain in place.

83. A Quinnipiac poll found that most Americans believe Trump is abusing his power (54–43 percent), and most believe he is not honest (59–36).

84. *WaPo* reported that at a meeting at Trump Tower in early December, Kushner proposed to Kislyak setting up a secret communication channel between the Kremlin and the Trump regime using Russian diplomatic facilities.

85. Kislyak was reportedly taken aback by the suggestion and concerned that Kushner's request would expose Russian communication capabilities.

86. Kushner's goal was to avoid U.S. intelligence monitoring. Flynn attended the meeting with Kislyak, too.

87. Of note, both Kislyak and Flynn secretly met with a UAE crown prince around the time that prince was setting up a meeting between Erik Prince and a Russian official in Seychelles (see Week 21's list). Trump met that same UAE crown prince at the White House last week.

88. Reuters reported that Kushner had at least three previously undisclosed contacts with Kislyak during and after the 2016 presidential campaign.

89. Reuters reported that FBI investigators are examining whether Russians suggested to Kushner or other Trump aides relaxing U.S. sanctions in exchange for making bank financing available to the Trump regime.

90. In response to the Reuters piece, Kushner's lawyer issued a statement that Kushner "has no recollection of the calls as described."

91. Russian oligarch Oleg Deripaska has offered to cooperate with Congress in their investigation of Manafort, in exchange for immunity. As noted in Week 27, Deripaska is suing the AP for libel for reporting his ties to Manafort.

92. The owners of Russian Alfa Bank, Mikhail Fridman, Petr Aven, and German Khan, sued *BuzzFeed* Friday in state court in Manhattan for publishing the Steele dossier.

93. Amid the Trump-Russia turmoil, Trump canceled his Iowa campaign rally scheduled for next week.

Week 29

MAY 28–JUNE 3, 2017

This was an abbreviated week, with Memorial Day and Congress out of session. Republicans were largely in hiding. Without the background noise in D.C., two major themes played out: the spreading Russia crisis and the shaping of a new world order.

Even before Megyn Kelly's prime-time interview of Putin, Russia has become a national obsession. Several bombshells on Trump-Russia broke this week, as the collusion puzzle continues to piece together. And seemingly at Putin's behest, a new world order is being shaped, with Trump distancing himself from our democratic allies and cozying up to brutal authoritarian states.

1. As the Trump-Russia scandal spread, Donald Jr,. Eric, and Eric's wife, Lara, met with GOP leaders to discuss strategy. Donald Jr. and Eric were supposed to steer clear of politics while running the family business.

2. Secretary of State Tillerson, Exxon's former CEO, was present in Saudi Arabia at the same time Exxon's current CEO was signing a major deal with state-owned Saudi Basic Industries Corporation (SABIC).

3. The Trump regime planned to quietly sell $1.2 million worth of semiautomatic handguns to Erdogan's security guards. After these guards beat American protesters at the Turkish embassy in D.C., members of Congress objected.

4. Belgian newspaper *Le Soir* reported that during his Brussels visit, Trump complained to the Belgian prime minister about his difficulties in setting up golf courses in the EU.

5. In the final leg of his trip, Trump continued to ignore the U.S. press. Trump was the only G7 leader to not hold a press conference after the summit.

6. The White House omitted the name of the husband of Luxembourg's gay prime minister from the caption of a photo taken at the NATO summit. The caption was later corrected.

7. Merkel warned Europeans that the U.S. and Britain are no longer reliable partners and that Europe "must take its fate into its own hands."

8. Macron said his prolonged, white-knuckled handshake with Trump was "not innocent," telling French media, "We must show that we will not make small concessions, even symbolic ones."

9. In an interview with Megyn Kelly, Putin said it would be a good thing for Moscow if NATO were completely "falling apart."

10. In sharp contrast to Trump, on Monday France's Macron stood onstage next to Putin and called Russian media outlets "organs of influence and propaganda." France also accepted LGBTQ refugees from Chechnya.

11. While visiting Australia, McCain sought to reassure our important ally, saying in a speech that Trump's actions have "unsettled many Americans as well."

12. CNN reported that Trump's return from his first foreign trip finds him lonely and angry. One source said, "I see him emotionally withdrawing. He's gained weight. He doesn't have anybody whom he trusts."

13. A furious Trump threatened a White House shake-up again this week amid the broadening Russia crisis; however, it also became clear that few are interested in working for Trump.

14. Trump's communications director Mike Dubke quit Tuesday. Other than that, no changes were made this week despite all the drama.

15. Kellyanne Conway's husband, George Conway, withdrew his name from consideration to lead the Civil Division of the DoJ.

16. Reuters reported that Trump's FBI director search has become "chaotic," and said Trump interviewed candidates for ten to twenty minutes. In one interview, he mostly talked about himself.

17. The AP reported that Trump gave his cell number to world leaders and urged them to call him directly, raising concerns about security and secrecy.

18. Trump's Twitter account experienced a strange surge of followers in the month of May. Nearly half his new followers are likely fake accounts.

19. Rolling back forty years of progress, the Trump regime plans to disband the Labor Department division responsible for policing discrimination among federal contractors.

20. Also as part of this move, Trump will roll back protections for the LGBTQ community and for victims of campus sexual assault.

21. Amid racial tensions in Portland, Oregon, after two men were killed by a white supremacist while coming to the aid of Muslim women, a Republican said the party should use militia groups at public events.

22. Three days after the Portland attack, Trump tweeted that the attack was "unacceptable," although he did so through the @POTUS Twitter account, not the personal account he typically uses.

23. One hundred eighth graders on a field trip to D.C. refused to pose with Paul Ryan. One student said, "I don't want to be associated with him."

24. WNYC reported that Trump SoHo plans layoffs; in the past five months room and event bookings are down sharply.

25. As Trump lost the appeal in federal court on his second Muslim ban, the regime gave U.S. embassies broad discretion to limit travelers through intensified screening measures for visa applicants.

26. In another act of violence against U.S. media, several windows at Kentucky's *Lexington Herald-Leader* were shattered by bullets.

27. Texas's House passed SB 4, which attempts to abolish "sanctuary cities" by making local officials who refuse to enforce the Trump regime's extremist measures subject to removal from office.

28. A Texas state representative, Matt Rinaldi, called ICE on SB 4 protesters. He also threatened to "put a bullet in one of his colleague's heads" during a scuffle on the House floor.

29. A man arrested for failing to pay the fare on Minneapolis light rail faces deportation after undergoing inappropriate questioning by a transit officer about his immigration status. The exchange was captured on video.

30. In Michigan, ICE agents ate breakfast at an Ann Arbor restaurant, complimented the chef on the waffles, bacon, eggs, and toast, and then went to the kitchen area and arrested three restaurant workers.

31. A *Guardian* article described ICE agents as "out of control" and "getting worse" as arrests of nonviolent undocumented immigrants multiply across the country. Agents have also been accused of targeting protesters.

32. The Trump regime filed a petition with the Supreme Court to appeal the second Muslim ban rulings. Ironically the ban, marketed as imperative to protecting America, had a ninety-day limit. It is now over 120 days later.

33. A noose was found at the segregation exhibition of the National Museum of African American History and Culture.

34. New York City sculptor Alex Gardena, upset about the "Fearless Girl" statue looking at the Wall Street bull, placed a statue of a urinating dog next to the girl.

35. Signaling his lack of knowledge about governing and his authoritarian bent, Trump tweeted the Senate "should switch to 51 votes, immediately, and get Healthcare and TAX CUTS approved."

36. China arrested one activist, and two others disappeared, after they investigated alleged labor abuse at a factory that makes Ivanka's shoes.

37. Senate Judiciary Committee chair Chuck Grassley called for an investigation into a Chinese company marketing investments in a property partly managed by Kushner using EB-5 visas (visas granted in exchange for $500,000 investments).

38. McCain said Russia is a bigger threat to the U.S. than ISIS, and added, "We have done nothing since the election last November to respond to Vladimir Putin's attempt to change the outcome of our elections."

39. *Politico* reported that as Mueller ramps up his Russia investigation, Trump aides are responsible for preserving materials, despite many using auto-delete apps. Destroying materials could expose aides to criminal charges.

40. On *Meet the Press*, former DNI Clapper said of the Kushner-Russia reports that his "warning light was clearly on," and "all of us in the intelligence community [are] very concerned about the nature of these approaches to the Russians."

41. The *NYT* reported that the FBI is investigating Kushner's motives for meeting with Gorkov, head of VEB, the Russian state bank, and whether it had anything to do with Russia's interference in the 2016 election.

42. CNN reported on intercepted conversations during the 2016 election that reveal Russians believed they had "derogatory" information on Trump and some of his tops aides that could be used to influence them.

43. At the Code Conference, Hillary said the Russians "could not have known how best to weaponize that information" without help from Americans, referring to the "fake news" that Russia spread during the election.

44. Trump's close confidant and personal attorney Michael Cohen was asked by House and Senate investigators "to provide information and testimony" on contacts he had with Russia. So far Cohen has declined.

45. The House Intelligence Committee sent a preliminary request for information to former Trump aide Boris Epshteyn.

46. The *New Yorker* reported that Trump reached out to ally Roger Stone, who is at the center of congressional and FBI investigations, on May 11 and told him, "Good job."

47. CNN reported that Congress is investigating a possible third undisclosed meeting between Sessions and Kislyak.

48. The House Intelligence Committee issued seven subpoenas Wednesday on the Trump-Russia probe—four subpoenas were related to the Russia investigation, and three were issued to the NSA, FBI, and CIA on "unmasking," in which names are un-redacted. Several Trump campaign and transition team names were unmasked in leaked intelligence reports.

49. Representative Adam Schiff said no Democrats were consulted on the "unmasking" subpoenas. Democrats on the House Intelligence Committee said that Nunes violated his Russian recusal by issuing these subpoenas.

50. The White House finally disclosed waivers granted. *Vox* reported that Trump has granted more lobbyist waivers in four months than Obama did in eight years!

51. The waiver granted to Bannon for communicating with *Breitbart* may have violated ethics rules, as it was granted retroactively.

52. White House OMB director Mulvaney said the day of the CBO "has probably come and gone."

53. It has been thirty-six days since the State Department held a daily press briefing. Daily press briefings were a decades-old tradition in the department before Tillerson took office.

54. *Politico* reported that the White House ordered agencies not to comply with Democrats' oversight requests, as Republicans fear the information could be used against Trump. None of these requests have been honored so far.

55. Trump tweeted at 12:06 A.M.: "Despite the constant negative press covfefe." While Twitter stayed awake lambasting Trump, the tweet remained up until morning, when Trump replaced it with a joke.

56. When Spicer was asked about the Trump tweet the next day, he refused to admit a mistake, instead saying, "The president and a small group of people know exactly what he meant."

57. Amid outrage by corporate CEOs, U.S. and international politicians and experts, and a clear majority of U.S. citizens, Trump formally withdrew from the Paris Accord with another of his hallmark dystopian speeches.

58. While delivering his speech, Trump referred to a casino robbery in a Manila casino as an "act of terrorism." This was a false statement.

59. Trump also bragged in his speech about adding one million jobs. The actual number is closer to 600,000. Trump's top economic adviser, Gary Cohn, said Trump was using the ADP number, ignoring his own government's report. ADP, a company that prints and direct deposits paychecks, publishes a job report based on their check printing.

60. May's nonfarm payroll number came in Friday well below expectations (138,000 actual vs. 185,000 expected).

61. After Trump pulled out from the Paris Accord, Ivanka sought to re-create her image, tweeting support for the LGBTQ community and being featured by CNN as the "most powerful Jewish woman." Both statements were met with outrage on Twitter.

62. A poll by *Politico*/Morning Consult found support for Trump's impeachment is rising: 43 percent this week, up from 38 percent last week.

63. *WaPo* reported that the Trump regime is moving to return the two U.S. compounds the Obama administration had taken away from Russia as punishment for interfering in the 2016 election.

64. Yahoo reported that days after taking office, the Trump regime tasked the State Department with finding ways to lift economic sanctions, to return the two U.S. compounds, and to relieve tensions with Russia.

65. As these were the same State Department employees who helped develop punitive measures, they were alarmed and rallied congressional allies.

66. *WaPo* reported that while Kushner and VEB's Gorkov have given different accounts of why they met, shortly after their meeting, Gorkov met with Putin in Japan.

67. Congressional investigators are looking into whether Kushner was vulnerable to Russian influence because his real estate holdings are overleveraged, and whether this led to his meeting with Gorkov.

68. *WaPo* reported that Kushner financed a luxury skyscraper in Jersey City using federal loans meant to help poor, job-starved areas.

69. NBC reported that five current and former officials say Trump participated in a private meeting in April 2016 with Kushner, Sessions, and Kislyak at the Mayflower Hotel.

70. Nigel Farage is a "person of interest" in the FBI's Trump-Russia scandal, in part for meeting with Assange at the Ecuadorian embassy in London in March.

71. James Comey is scheduled to testify in front of the Senate Intelligence Committee next Thursday and is expected to say that Trump asked him to back off the investigation of Flynn.

72. ABC reported that Comey is angry, saying Rosenstein and Sessions never relayed any concerns about his job performance before firing him.

73. The *NYT* reported that Trump could try to block Comey from testifying by citing executive privilege. As of today, Trump has not decided if he will try to block Comey's testimony.

74. Going a step further than Trump, Putin said maybe "patriotically minded" private Russian hackers meddled in the U.S. election.

75. DoJ's Andrew Weissmann, who oversaw foreign bribery and bank cases, is joining Mueller's Russia investigation team.

76. The AP reported that Mueller has taken over a separate DoJ criminal probe into Manafort, which predates the 2016 election.

77. Mueller may also expand his inquiry to investigate Sessions's and Rosenstein's roles in firing Comey.

78. Reuters reported that the special counsel will also probe Flynn's ties to Turkey.

79. *Politico* reported that the Trump regime is pushing Congress for legislative victories as Trump grows impatient, but as the Trump-Russia scandal heats up, it's unlikely any legislation will be passed in coming months.

80. Today, Americans in more than 150 cities will participate in the "March for Truth" to demand urgency and transparency on Trump-Russia.

A closing note: the number of items we have normalized and/or forgotten about from the early lists is astounding. Each week brings new bombshells and scandals—stories that in normal times would be front-page news for weeks or months—for example, Pence's (Week 16) and Tillerson's (Week 19) e-mail scandals. In the chaos, we have forgotten.

Week 30

JUNE 4–10, 2017

This week all eyes were on the Comey testimony, which opened the door for a possible obstruction of justice charge against Trump, an impeachable offense. Despite Republicans controlling the House, Senate, and White House, legislative progress has largely come to a halt amid weekly and sometimes daily bombshells, as all eyes turn to the

Trump-Russia scandal. Also of note are the complete disarray of the Trump regime and the difficulty Trump is having hiring staff and finding legal representation.

1. In the aftermath of terrorist attacks in London Saturday night, Trump attacked Mayor Sadiq Khan, tweeting, "At least 7 dead and 48 wounded in terror attack and Mayor of London says there is 'no reason to be alarmed!'"
2. The U.S. ambassador to the UK contradicted Trump, tweeting from the embassy account that we "commend the strong leadership" of the mayor.
3. Trump used the attack as an opportunity to promote his Muslim ban: "I am calling it what we need and what it is, a TRAVEL BAN!" Ironically, the Trump regime spent months denying it was a "ban."
4. Trump also criticized Sessions, tweeting that the DoJ should have stayed with the first Muslim ban, "not the watered down, politically correct version."
5. Experts said Trump's tweets would likely hurt the chances of a successful appeal at the Supreme Court.
6. The *NYT* reported that Trump is fuming at Sessions, especially over his decision to recuse himself from the Russia investigation.
7. Mattis tried to reassure allies at a conference in Singapore, asking them to "bear with us" after Trump's disastrous foreign trip.
8. *Politico* reported that Trump's national security team was blindsided when he left out the planned language reaffirming U.S. commitment to Article 5 from his NATO summit speech in Brussels.
9. A noose was found at a construction site in D.C., marking the third noose found in the D.C. area this week.
10. The Ku Klux Klan applied to hold a rally in Charlottesville on July 8.
11. Reuters reported that the Trump regime is seeking to reopen hundreds of cases of illegal immigrants who were granted a reprieve under Obama.
12. *BuzzFeed* reviewed more than fifty reports of school bullying and found that kids nationwide are using Trump's words to taunt their classmates.
13. Democrat Kim Weaver dropped her run for Congress against Trump ally Steve King after receiving multiple death threats.

14. *Politico* reported that Tillerson has made himself largely inaccessible to staff and outsiders, funneling all inquiries through two staffers.

15. The mayor of Los Angeles said ICE's aggressive raids could cause high tensions in his city to boil over: "I fear a tinderbox out there."

16. Canadian searches for flights to U.S. cities have dropped by 43 percent since Trump's first proposed Muslim ban.

17. Ivanka continued her efforts to reset her image, appearing on the cover of *Us Weekly* with the headline "Why I Disagree with My Dad."

18. Questions arose of whether it is constitutional for Trump to block users, given that he uses Twitter to communicate about domestic and foreign policy.

19. Trump filed a six-month extension for filing his 2016 taxes. His rationale for the extension is unknown.

20. The *WSJ* reported Saudi Arabia's lobbyists and consultants spent $270,000 at the Trump International Hotel in D.C. as part of an effort to lobby Trump against a bipartisan act that lets Americans sue foreign countries over terrorist attacks.

21. The DoJ argued that Trump can accept payments from foreign governments, saying the emoluments clause doesn't apply to "fair-market commercial transactions" like payments for hotel rooms and golf club fees.

22. As questions remain on why Kushner met with VEB's Gorkov, Bloomberg reported that Kushner is seeking a $250 million loan to pay back Chinese investors for a New Jersey luxury tower. U.S. banks are wary to lend.

23. WNYC reported that the Kushner family is set to lose $6.5 million in annual tax credits for a property in Jersey City.

24. The acting U.S. ambassador to China resigned over Trump's decision to withdraw from the Paris Accord.

25. The head of the U.S. Patent Office resigned.

26. Eighty-five percent of the top science jobs in Trump's executive branch remain unfilled and do not have a nominee.

27. The chief executive of Newseum warned that Trump's denigration of the media would lead to the "delegitimization of journalists" and encourage authoritarians to target reporters and newspapers around the world.

28. Representative Gianforte agreed to pay fifty thousand dollars to the Committee to Project Journalists in a civil settlement for assaulting journalist Ben Jacobs.

29. Mueller brought in several well-known attorneys with relevant experience to join his Russia probe, including Michael Dreeben, the DoJ's top criminal law expert.

30. Yahoo reported that four top law firms turned down requests to represent Trump, citing his unwillingness to listen to advice, potential harm to recruiting and client relationships, and his history of not paying bills.

31. *Forbes* reported that at a charity golf tournament run by Eric Trump for St. Jude Children's Research Hospital, $1.2 million of expenses paid to the Trump Organization had no documented receipts.

32. Additionally, five hundred thousand dollars was redonated to other charities (four of which subsequently held tournaments at Trump golf courses), and one hundred thousand dollars was funneled through the Eric Trump Foundation to the Trump Organization.

33. The New York attorney general's office said it will look into these payouts by Eric Trump's foundation.

34. Flynn turned over more than six hundred pages of documents to the Senate Intelligence Committee. Most are business records, but some are personal documents.

35. The *Intercept* published a leaked top-secret NSA document that detailed the efforts of Russian hackers to target a voting-software supplier and more than one hundred local election officials just prior to Election Day.

36. The FBI arrested the leaker: twenty-five-year-old Reality Winner, a federal contractor in Augusta, Georgia. The FBI was able to track the leak to Winner after the *Intercept* provided a copy to the NSA for comment.

37. Warner, the ranking Democrat on the Senate Intelligence Committee, said Russian attacks on our election were broader and targeted more states than reported in the *Intercept*.

38. Senator Klobuchar asked that the Senate Rules Committee get a classified briefing on the Russian vote-hacking attempts.

39. Deutsche Bank ignored the House Democrats' request for information on Trump's accounts and possible ties to Russia.

40. Deutsche Bank blamed privacy laws for preventing the bank from disclosing the information requested.

41. At a Senate Intelligence Committee hearing, Coats, Rogers, and Rosenstein largely refused to answer senators' questions. One conservative journalist called it contempt of Congress.

42. A pro-Trump PAC ran ads attacking Comey as a "showboat" and a failure on the day of his testimony.

43. *WaPo* reported that Coats told associates that Trump asked him to intervene to get Comey to back off the FBI's investigation of Flynn in its Russia probe.

44. Sources said the request was made at the end of a briefing at the White House, when Trump asked everyone to leave the room except Coats and Pompeo.

45. The *NYT* reported that the day after Trump asked Comey to end the investigation of Flynn, Comey told Sessions not to leave him alone with Trump.

46. ABC reported that Trump lashed out repeatedly at Sessions in private meetings about recusing himself from the Russia issue, and that Sessions in turn suggested he could resign.

47. After allegations that Nunes was behind the House Intelligence subpoenas on "unmasking," Nunes refused to confirm if he had stepped aside from the Russia probe.

48. *Vox* reported that Comey had spoken to three senior FBI officials (Jim Rybicki, James Baker, and Andrew McCabe) who could vouch for his story that Trump asked him to shut down the Flynn investigation.

49. Trump's approval hit a new low in a Quinnipiac poll: 34 percent approve of him, 57 percent disapprove. Of note, Trump is almost underwater with white men!

50. A senior State Department official, Under Secretary of State for Political Affairs Tom Shannon, will travel to Russia to help solve the "irritants" in our relationship.

51. Putin threatened Sweden with a military response to "eliminate the threat" if the country joins NATO.

52. Former DNI Clapper said that "Watergate pales" compared with what the U.S. is confronting now.

53. Ahead of his testimony Thursday, on Wednesday the Senate Intelligence Committee released seven pages of a prepared statement by Comey to open his testimony.

54. In the testimony, Comey noted that he had unusually frequent contact with Trump, and that Trump requested that Comey sign a loyalty pledge. Comey also stated that he documented all contact with Trump, that the president was focused on the Steele dossier, and that Trump asked Comey to "let this go" in reference to Flynn.

55. Trump's pick for FBI director, Christopher Wray, works for a law firm that counts among its clients Russian state-controlled oil companies Rosneft and Gazprom.

56. Comey testified in an open session Thursday. Major networks covered the testimony and over nineteen million watched. Many in D.C. caught "Comey fever" and played hooky to watch at restaurants and pubs.

57. Comey said Trump lied about him and the FBI, that Sessions had no choice but to recuse himself, and that he was fired because of the Russia investigation.

58. Comey said he took notes starting directly after his first meeting with Trump, on January 6, because he was concerned Trump "might lie." Comey did not feel the need to take notes with Obama or George W. Bush.

59. On Trump's threat of having taped his conversations, Comey said, "Lordy, I hope there are tapes." This spurred another round of demands by Democrats for Trump to either produce the tapes or admit he lied.

60. Comey said Sessions seemed uncomfortable when Trump asked him to leave the room: "My sense was the attorney general knew he shouldn't be leaving." Comey said the same of Kushner.

61. Comey said he leaked a memo about one of his meetings with Trump to the *NYT* through a friend at Columbia University, in hopes of getting a special counsel appointed.

62. Comey testified that he has given his memos to Mueller and suggested the special counsel is investigating Trump for obstruction of justice.

63. Comey said there was no doubt that Russia interfered in our election, saying, "They're coming after America" and "they will be back." He also noted this is an attack on our democracy, not a particular political party.

64. Trump's lawyer Kasowitz responded with a written statement in which he misspelled "President." He also got the timeline of the Comey memo wrong and falsely accused Comey of leaking classified information.

65. After the Comey testimony, Republicans mostly shied away from the camera this week, while Speaker Ryan offered a tepid defense for Trump's actions: "He's just new to this."

66. Numerous Trump surrogates spent the days surrounding Comey's testimony by trying to smear him as a liar and an attention seeker.

67. NBC reported that during the Senate Intelligence Committee's closed hearing, senators learned about a third, undisclosed meeting between Sessions and a representative of Russia. This confirms an item in Week 29 that the DoJ denied.

68. British prime minister Theresa May suffered a major setback in the UK elections, as her Conservative Party lost the majority. Her party's loss also could spell trouble for Brexit.

69. Senate Intelligence Committee staff will interview Kushner next week. NBC reported that Congress wants to ask Kushner if he was seeking Russian funding for his New York City tower.

70. Representative Nancy Pelosi told MSNBC that she is looking into why Trump picked Saudi Arabia as his first country to visit. Past presidents, going back to Reagan, had visited close allies Canada or Mexico first.

71. Pelosi also said she is looking into why, during the visit in Saudi Arabia, Trump had "cleared the room."

72. Trump and Tillerson had an embarrassing difference on Qatar, as Tillerson said there should "be no further escalation by parties in the region," and Trump sided with Saudi Arabia and others, slamming Qatar as a sponsor of terrorism.

73. Trump's attorney said he would file a complaint against Comey for leaking his memo to his friend at Columbia.

74. According to a letter from the U.S. Office of Special Counsel, Trump's social media director Daniel Scavino violated the Hatch Act in April when he tweeted a call to oust a member of the House. He was issued a warning.

75. In a joint press conference with the president of Romania in the White House Rose Garden, Trump switched course again and said he would support Article 5 of the NATO pact.

76. Trump also called Comey a liar and a "leaker," and claimed that Comey's testimony showed there was "no collusion, no obstruction."

77. Trump also said he would be willing to tell his side of story under oath, "100 percent," but still would not confirm if the "tapes" really exist.

78. Top Democratic donor Tom Steyer called for impeachment hearings over obstruction of justice.

Week 31

JUNE 11-17, 2017

Another week for the history books: Trump is under investigation for obstruction of justice—a fact he confirmed through a tweet. With his increasingly erratic behavior, Trump has become his own worst enemy. While investigations by the House, Senate, FBI, and the special counsel into Trump-Russia steam ahead, Trump's continued efforts to interfere with investigations may prove to be his ultimate undoing.

This week the tentacles of the Trump-Russia probe reached new members of the Trump regime, and several chose to lawyer up. Congress is singularly focused on Trump-Russia, save for McConnell's odd, clandestine AHCA efforts.

1. Trump canceled his UK visit, saying he didn't want to come until the British public supports him. Large-scale protests were expected.

2. Trump National Golf Club in Bedminster, New Jersey, has been coined "the summer White House," and similar to Mar-a-Lago, offers access—such as Trump's crashing parties—as part of the marketing plan.

3. Since taking office, Trump has been at one of his properties every 3.5 days and at one of his golf courses every 6.2 days.

4. On Sunday, Trump attorney Jay Sekulow said Trump is considering firing Robert Mueller.

5. Trump allies, including Newt Gingrich and Kellyanne Conway, attacked Mueller, claiming he was biased in favor of Comey and that members of his staff have donated to Democrats and liberal causes.

6. Gingrich also accused Mueller of being part of the "Deep State" plot to undermine Trump.

7. Preet Bharara said on ABC's "This Week" Sunday that Trump called him three times. Bharara was fired the day after he did not return the third call. Bharara noted that Obama did not call him once.

8. Bharara also described his contact as "a little bit uncomfortable," and said reading about Trump's contact with Comey "felt a little bit like déjà vu."

9. Marc Kasowitz bragged that he was behind the firing of Bharara. According to a *ProPublica* source, Kasowitz told Trump, "This guy is going to get you."

10. In response to a FOIA request, the Secret Service said it has no audio or transcripts of any tapes made in the White House. Trump has still not verified if he lied about the existence of tapes, despite promises to do so soon.

11. Hundreds of Kremlin critics were arrested amid anticorruption protests, including opposition leader Alexei Navalny, who was detained near his home.

12. A Moscow court sentenced Navalny to thirty days in prison for staging an unsanctioned rally. The White House and State Department were silent on all of this.

13. Representative Greg Gianforte was sentenced to a 180-day deferred sentence and ordered to complete forty hours of community service and twenty hours of anger management counseling for assaulting reporter Ben Jacobs.

14. The Ninth Circuit upheld an injunction blocking part of Trump's second Muslim ban. In their ruling, the judges cited Trump's own tweets.

15. Trump changed the expiration date of the Muslim ban in an effort to prevent the Supreme Court from declaring it moot.

16. Monday, in a bizarre display in front of cameras, Trump's cabinet members took turns praising him.

17. A journalist noted: "Putin televises the beginnings of his cabinet meetings."

18. Representative Mike Quigley introduced the "COVFEFE Act," to require the preservation of Trump's tweets. The original covfefe tweet was deleted.

19. Also of note, Trump has been actively blocking users on Twitter, despite using his Twitter account for policy and other announcements.

20. Trump's approval sunk again in a new AP-NORC poll, with his net favorability falling to –29 (35 percent approve, 64 percent disapprove).

21. The AP-NORC poll also found that seven in ten Americans are at least moderately concerned that Trump or his campaign associates had inappropriate ties to Russia.

22. A survey of CEOs, business executives, government officials, and academics at the Yale CEO summit found that 50 percent gave Trump an F and 21 percent a D for his first 130 days in office.

23. Bloomberg reported that the Russian cyber hack of the U.S. electoral system was far wider than reported—including thirty-nine states in all. The attacks included incursions into voter databases and software systems.

24. Further, in Illinois, which became known as "Patient Zero" in the government probe, Russian hackers gained access to personal information of fifteen million people, half of whom were active voters.

25. Cindy McCain agreed to join the State Department, after being aggressively courted by Trump.

26. Dana Shell Smith, the U.S. ambassador to Qatar, resigned.

27. Trump's EPA head, Scott Pruitt, skipped much of the G7 environmental summit.

28. The Department of Energy said it will close an office that works with other countries to develop clean energy technology.

29. At a Senate Appropriations Committee hearing, Tillerson said he would not be staffing the State Department until next year.

30. Trump's Commerce Department removed sexual orientation and gender identification from the list of categories covered by its anti-discrimination policies.

31. Trump appointed loyalist Lynne Patton, who planned Eric's wedding and golf tournaments at Trump courses, to run the office that oversees federal housing programs in New York. She has no housing experience.

32. Office of Government Ethics director Shaub responded to a request from four Senate Democrats, saying that Steve Bannon had in fact violated White House ethics rules, and noting that Bannon's ethics waiver was retroactive and neither dated nor signed.

33. *USA Today* reported that in the last twelve months, 70 percent of Trump property buyers have been LLCs, compared with 4 percent two years ago.

34. China approved nine Trump trademark requests that had previously been rejected. Intellectual property lawyers suggested "special treatment."

35. The AP reported that a company that partners with both Trump and Kushner is a finalist for a $1.7 billion contract to build the new FBI headquarters.

36. While Ivanka has made attempts to reset her public image, the *Guardian* reported that at her clothing factory in China, workers complain of verbal abuse, impossible targets, and poverty pay.

37. During Senate Judiciary Committee testimony, Rosenstein said he now agrees that Russia interfered in our election. Rosenstein had not taken a position during his confirmation hearings.

38. Reporters at the Capitol were told they were no longer allowed to interview senators in the hallways, contrary to years of precedent.

39. Karen Tumulty, a reporter for *WaPo*, was expelled from the Capitol for doing just that.

40. Following a backlash, later that day Senate Republicans backed off from their restrictions on the media.

41. D.C. police said they will charge twelve of Erdogan's security guards for assaulting protesters outside the Turkish embassy.

42. In response to FOIA requests, a D.C. judge ordered the DoJ to produce Sessions's clearance form, on which he was required to disclose contacts with Russians, within one month.

43. The D.C. judge also ordered the DoJ and FBI to release any records of Priebus reaching out to the FBI to request they refute reports of communications between the Trump campaign and Russia.

44. Sessions testified in front of the Senate Intelligence Committee, but largely refused to answer important questions. He did not mention any further contact with Russian officials, nor confirm the third meeting.

45. McCain asked Sessions at the hearing if he had had "any contacts with any representative, including any American lobbyist or agent, of any Russian company." Sessions said, "I don't believe so."

46. The *Guardian* reported that Richard Burt, a lobbyist for Russia who helped craft a foreign policy speech for Trump, said he attended two dinners hosted by Sessions during the 2016 campaign.

47. Burt also served on the advisory board of Alfa Capital Partners, a private equity fund in which Alfa Bank was an investor. Per Week 21, the FBI is looking at links between Alfa Bank and Trump during the campaign.

48. Senator Kamala Harris was interrupted by Senators McCain and then Burr during her questioning of Sessions. Harris was also scolded by Burr for not being "courteous" in the hearing last week of Coats, Rogers, and Rosenstein.

49. By a 98–2 vote, the Senate passed a new Russian sanctions bill that would impose additional sanctions and limit Trump's ability to lift them.

50. *Wired* reported on Mueller assembling a "dream team" of lawyers, including attorneys who specialize in money laundering and organized crime, and a former prosecutor for the Watergate investigation.

51. On Wednesday, a lone gunman, who had volunteered for Bernie Sanders, shot at congressional Republicans who were practicing for a baseball game at a park in Alexandria, Virginia. Extreme rhetoric was blamed.

52. The next night, as the bipartisan game was being played, the Trump regime rescinded Obama's protections for parents of Dreamers and reduced protections for Dreamers themselves.

53. In Ossining, New York, ICE detained a nineteen-year-old on the day of his prom and weeks before his high school graduation.

54. On Wednesday, *WaPo* reported that Mueller is investigating Trump for obstruction of justice.

55. *WaPo* also reported that Mueller will interview Coats, Rogers, and former NSA official Rick Ledgett as part of the investigation.

56. In a poignant moment, Lester Holt said on *NBC Nightly News*, "NBC News has learned the president of the United States is now under criminal investigation."

57. Rosenstein issued an odd statement scolding the media for "anonymous allegations" on Russia, and saying "Americans should exercise caution before accepting as true" anonymous sources.

58. Representative Nancy Pelosi predicted that Trump will "self-impeach."

59. In a tweet, Trump acknowledged he was under investigation and described the investigation as a "Witch Hunt."

60. Trump's tweet also took a swipe at Rosenstein, raising questions of whether Trump would fire him. Doing so could make it possible for Trump to put in place a process to fire Mueller.

61. Senator Dianne Feinstein said she is increasingly concerned that Trump will fire Mueller. In a strong statement she noted, "We're a nation of laws that apply equally to everyone, a lesson the president would be wise to learn."

62. The AP reported that Trump's advisers and confidants describe him as increasingly angry over the investigation and yelling at televisions carrying coverage.

63. The *NYT* reported that Trump's private attorney, Kasowitz, has advised White House staffers not to hire private lawyers yet.

64. Kasowitz was hit with ethics complaints in New York and D.C. over this advice.

65. *WaPo* reported that Mueller is investigating Kushner for his finances and business dealings. This is in addition to previously reported investigations of Kushner's meetings in December with Kislyak and Gorkov.

66. *WaPo* also reported that the FBI and federal prosecutors are investigating the financial dealings of Flynn, Manafort, and Page.

67. CNN reported that the House Intelligence Committee is planning to call Brad Parscale, the digital director for Trump's campaign, in their investigation of possible collusion between the Trump campaign and Russia.

68. CNN also reported that Kushner is under federal investigation for his role in overseeing Trump's data operations, and is expected to talk to Senate investigators about the campaign's data operation.

69. Pence hired Richard Cullen, a top-dollar lawyer with Watergate experience, to represent him in the Russian probe.

70. Pence's PAC held a fund-raiser in Indianapolis. When Rachel Maddow's staff asked whether funds raised would go toward legal costs, the response was: "His legal fees will be paid by non-tax dollars."

71. Trump personal lawyer Michael Cohen hired counsel for the Russian probe. Cohen is under investigation by the special counsel and will testify in front of the House Intel Committee on September 5.

72. Michael Caputo, a Manafort ally who served as a senior communications adviser on Trump's campaign, hired a lawyer. Caputo lived in Moscow, and in 2000 worked to improve Putin's image in the U.S.

73. Manafort and Page also hired counsel for the Russia probe.

74. CNBC reported that the Trump regime is touting the creation of coal jobs that might not actually exist.

75. Putin offered Comey political asylum in Russia, continuing to publicly insert himself into U.S. politics.

76. *BuzzFeed* reported that fourteen recent deaths in the UK appear tied to Russia.

77. Frustrating House Republicans, Trump called their version of AHCA/ Trumpcare—which he had celebrated in the Rose Garden—"mean," and said he hoped the Senate would pass a better version.

78. McConnell has been leading an oddly closed-door effort to pass AHCA in the Senate with no hearings or input. Open frustration was expressed by Democrats, some Republicans, and major patient advocacy groups.

79. The OGE released Trump's most recent financial disclosure Friday. Trump reported $315 million of loans, including $130 million from Deutsche Bank, the bank with Russian ties that refused Democrats' request for information.

80. The ninety-eight pages of financial disclosure showed a sharp rise in revenue at places Trump frequented, including Mar-a-Lago and nearby golf courses.

81. Trump also made twenty million dollars at the newly opened Trump International Hotel in D.C. Despite his early promise to turn over payments from foreign governments to the U.S. Treasury, Trump is not tracking all payments.

82. The attorneys general for D.C. and Maryland sued Trump for breaching his constitutional oath by accepting millions in payments and benefits from foreign governments.

83. Nearly two hundred Congressional Democrats filed an emoluments lawsuit against Trump, saying he has violated constitutional restrictions on taking gifts and benefits from foreign leaders.

84. A Russian oil tycoon parked his giant yacht in front of the Statue of Liberty. The yacht was a gift from Roman Abramovich, who, as noted in Week 20, was skiing in Aspen at the same time as Kushner and Ivanka.

85. In an early sign of cracks from unfilled key roles in the executive branch, after the USS *Fitzgerald* collision, Trump was criticized by Brandon

Friedman, a former Obama administration official, for leaving the positions of U.S. Navy secretary and ambassador to Japan unfilled.

Week 32

JUNE 18–24, 2017

There were signs this week that our democracy is fading: the unusual process undertaken by McConnell in attempting to pass AHCA without Senate input or public support; alarming evidence that Russia may have tampered with 2016 Election Day results, possibly with help from the Trump campaign; and the Trump regime taking steps to shut down access for the media, while our country burns in bigotry and hate.

Trump-Russia is still the dominant theme, as investigations open on new fronts and Trump regime members go quiet and lawyer up. Trump continues to deny Russian interference, which will undoubtedly lead to it continuing in upcoming elections—to his benefit, of course.

1. For the first time since taking office, Trump visited Camp David.
2. Russia renewed six unused Trump trademarks in 2016. Four of the six approvals were officially registered on November 8, Election Day.
3. The Department of Education said it will scale back civil rights investigations at public schools and universities, including rolling back Obama's efforts to end campus sexual assault and protect transgender students.
4. Six members of the Presidential Council on HIV/AIDS angrily resigned in a public letter, saying Trump doesn't care or have a strategy.
5. Rick Perry, the Secretary of Energy, denied that man-made carbon dioxide emissions are the primary cause of global warming.
6. Sessions's DoJ is exploring new legal theories to take on sanctuary cities in court and force them to aid in Trump's deportation efforts.
7. A Muslim teen was brutally beaten and killed while walking to a mosque with her friends in Sterling, Virginia. A funeral vigil drew many, while the murder has yet to be charged as a hate crime.
8. Trump International Hotel in D.C. will host a conference for an anti-Islamic group, ACT for America, including a private tour. Neither the Trump

Organization nor ACT would answer *WaPo*'s questions about the event and its cost.

9. An attorney said his client was acting within his First Amendment rights when he disrupted a Black Lives Matter rally in Tennessee by wearing a gorilla mask and carrying a rope and bananas.

10. NPR reported that the Trump regime will not collect LGBTQ census data despite a HUD document obtained under the FOIA which cites this data as "essential." Trump's DoJ questions the "appropriateness" of sexual orientation and gender identity topics.

11. Trump and his White House have made no mention or acknowledgment of June being LGBT Pride month.

12. McConnell continued to secretly push AHCA in unusual ways. Not only is the closed-door bargaining not bipartisan, most Republicans haven't seen the bill.

13. The *NYT* reported that Kushner's team quietly reached out to high-powered criminal lawyers to represent him in the Russia probe.

14. Sessions hired a lawyer to represent him in the Russia probe.

15. Pence's use of a private AOL e-mail account to conduct government business is costing Indiana one hundred thousand dollars in legal fees to process a large backlog of records requests.

16. A lawsuit alleges private prison company GEO Correction donated to a Trump super PAC, in violation of federal law. Trump has adopted a pro-private-prison policy.

17. Andrew Weissmann, a lawyer who joined Mueller's team in Week 29, has expertise in witness-flipping.

18. Speculation grew that Flynn is cooperating with the FBI, including by Senator Sheldon Whitehouse, a ranking member of the Senate Judiciary Committee.

19. Flynn failed to report a 2015 Middle East trip on his security clearance forms. The trip was to discuss a U.S.-Russia partnership, financed by Saudi Arabia, to build nuclear reactors throughout the Middle East.

20. The *NYT* reported that despite concerns about Flynn being a security risk, CIA director Pompeo continued to give him classified briefings for three weeks.

21. The *NYT* also reported that even though he gave Trump briefings almost daily, Pompeo did not raise the issue of Flynn's ties to Russia.

22. ABC reported that Senate investigators are looking into financial ties between the Trump campaign and Russian and Eastern European businessmen to see if any of their interactions involved organized crime or organizations subject to U.S. sanctions.

23. Several names associated with financing for the Trump SoHo have alleged ties to money laundering or Russian organized crime.

24. One of those names is Felix Sater, a Russian-born former partner with New York property developer Bayrock who was twice convicted and served jail time, and, as noted in Week 15, worked with Michael Cohen on a back-channel plan for a Ukraine "peace plan" (with new leadership in Ukraine).

25. Felix Sater worked with Trump and his children on projects around the world.

26. Bloomberg reported that an employee of Bayrock, Jody Kriss, said he quit because the firm was a front for money laundering. A federal judge said a lawsuit by Kriss against Bayrock could proceed as a racketeering case.

27. In a CBS poll, Trump's approval hit a new low (36 percent). He is also losing Republican support: 83 percent approval on day 100 vs. 72 percent now.

28. Mueller brought in a second lawyer from the solicitor general's office. Elizabeth Prelogar is fluent in Russian; while at Harvard Law, she won an Overseas Press Club scholarship to study Russian media and censorship.

29. Spicer did an off-camera, no-audio-broadcast press briefing. The Trump regime's access to the media has become increasingly erratic.

30. When Spicer was asked if Trump believes that Russia interfered with our election on Tuesday, he said, "I have not sat down and asked him."

31. While Spicer acknowledged that he is helping Trump find his replacement, Trump is considering new measures including limiting press briefings to once a week and asking reporters to submit written questions in advance.

32. Former Secretary of Homeland Security Jeh Johnson testified to the House Intelligence Committee that "Putin himself orchestrated cyber-attacks on our nation for the purpose of influencing our election—plain and simple."

33. Also at the hearing, Jeanette Manfra, acting deputy undersecretary at DHS, said that so far evidence exists that Russia targeted election-related systems in twenty-one states.

34. The *Daily Beast* reported that the DHS never ran a formal federal audit to see if votes were hacked.

35. *WaPo* calculated that in Trump's first 151 days, he has made 669 false and misleading claims.

36. A *NYT* op-ed, "Trump's Lies," cataloged every lie told by Trump since he took office, noting that "as regular as they have become, the country should not allow itself to become numb to them."

37. Trump held a campaign rally in Iowa and gave a speech full of factually incorrect statements. The *NYT* described the rally as a "venting session."

38. At the Iowa rally, Trump defended his wealthy cabinet picks, saying, "In those particular positions, I just don't want a poor person."

39. Boeing announced layoffs at the South Carolina plant Trump visited earlier this year, where he promoted his "Buy American" pledge.

40. Trump will hold his reelection campaign kickoff event on June 28 at the Trump Hotel D.C. The cost is thirty-five thousand dollars per head, or one hundred thousand dollars for a spot on the host committee.

41. While ignoring atrocities committed by numerous authoritarian leaders, Trump tweeted a falsehood, "Mexico was just ranked the second deadliest country in the world," about our former close ally.

42. Trump called newly appointed Saudi crown prince Mohammed bin Salman to congratulate him on his new role.

43. Further to a *BuzzFeed* article in Week 31 citing multiple deaths in the UK at the hands of Russian operatives, the *New Yorker* reported on similarly mysterious deaths of Putin critics in the U.S.

44. Tillerson proposed a three-point plan aimed at improving relations with Russia, including working together on cybersecurity.

45. The *NYT* reported that Trump's White House is trying to get the House GOP to weaken the Senate bill that imposes sanctions on Russia.

46. Representative Kevin Brady tried to block the Senate's Russia sanction bill, saying it was a "blue slip" violation—revenue bills must originate in the House.

47. Democrats on the House Oversight Committee questioned why Kushner still has security clearance, and why Flynn kept his clearance, after public reports that both had had undisclosed meetings with Kislyak.

48. Rachel Maddow reported on a second bipartisan letter to the Trump White House and acting FBI director McCabe questioning Kushner's security clearance.

49. *BuzzFeed* reported that Bharara wrote a memo on March 9 to several senior DoJ officials outlining his concern about a third call from the White House. Bharara was fired on March 11.

50. *Politico* reported that Trump has frequently lashed out at White House counsel McGahn for not doing more to quash the Trump-Russia probe early on.

51. CNN reported that Coats and Rogers both told Mueller and the Senate Intelligence Committee in a private session that Trump suggested they say publicly there was no collusion between his regime and Russia.

52. Coats told House investigators that Trump seemed obsessed with the Russia probe and repeatedly asked him to publicly state there was no evidence of collusion.

53. In a cryptic tweet, Trump admitted he did not tape Comey, raising questions of whether his initial tweet was witness intimidation.

54. Trump also continued to deny that Russia hacked our election and tweeted blame at Obama: "if Russia was working so hard on the 2016 Election, it all took place during the Obama Admin. Why didn't they stop them?"

55. Rachel Maddow reported on the many ways Russia, possibly with the help from the Trump regime, may have tampered with actual voting results on Election Day.

56. The *WSJ* reported that Deep Root Analytics, a GOP data firm, left a proprietary data set with personal information on nearly two hundred million voters unprotected online—where anyone could see it.

57. *Gizmodo* reported that the data leak contains detailed personal information on about 61 percent of the U.S. population—including address, birthday, party registration, and views on issues for almost all registered voters.

58. The RNC paid Deep Root $983,000 in 2016, but much of the data leaked came from the Data Trust, the GOP's primary voter file provider. The RNC paid the Data Trust $6.7 million during the 2016 election cycle.

59. The president of the Data Trust was Johnny DeStefano, who is now in charge of personnel for Trump.

60. Dallas County, Texas, a heavily Democratic area, said its web servers were targeted multiple times by Russian hackers.

61. Of the six hundred IP addresses provided by DHS as possible Russian hackers, seventeen associated with Russian computers tried to gain access to Dallas servers.

62. Rachel Maddow reported that adjoining counties that were heavily Republican did not have any matches from the six hundred IP addresses.

63. The *WSJ* reported on VR Systems, a software company whose products were used to check in voters in twenty-one of North Carolina's one hundred counties. VR Systems software failed in heavily Democratic Durham County.

64. Durham County was forced to issue ballots by hand, meaning longer lines and likely depressed voter turnout. Trump won North Carolina, but the race was very close.

65. *Time* reported that the Russian hacking of our election was more widespread than previously reported and included at least one successful attempt to alter voter information and the theft of personal information on thousands of voters.

66. CBS reported that the House Intelligence Committee investigation on Russia has expanded to probe whether Trump associates received information from hacked voter databases.

67. Brad Parscale, digital director for the Trump campaign, emerged as a central figure in the Trump-Russia probe. Parscale, known as "Jared's boy" according to an unnamed insider, reported to Kushner. His firm was paid ninety-one million dollars by the Trump campaign.

68. The House Intelligence Committee will interview Parscale to ascertain if information stolen by Russian hackers made its way to the Trump campaign.

69. As he takes over as House Oversight Committee chair, unlike his predecessor, Chaffetz, Representative Trey Gowdy said the committee will no longer probe Trump-Russia ties or violations of the emoluments clause.

70. An NBC/*WSJ* poll found that by a two-to-one margin, Americans believe Comey over Trump. Just 27 percent approve of Trump's firing of Comey.

71. Trump told *Fox & Friends* he tweeted his lie about the existence of tapes in order to influence Comey's account of their conversation—further raising the specter of witness intimidation.

72. Also in the *Fox & Friends* interview, Trump left open the option of firing Mueller because of his "bothersome" friendship with Comey.

73. A *WaPo* bombshell discussed a CIA report delivered only to Obama and three top officials in August, revealing Putin's specific instructions to defeat or at least damage Hillary and help elect Trump.

74. *WaPo* also reported that in the months ahead of the election, the FBI became alarmed by an unusual spike in temporary visa requests by Russia for officials with technical skills to enter the U.S. Permission was denied.

75. The Obama administration's response was mild and fairly muted, due in part to worry that their action would be perceived as political interference in an already volatile election, and concern it would lead Russia to escalate attacks, according to *WaPo* reporting.

76. *WaPo* also reported on GOP efforts to block intelligence agencies from informing the public and from acting on concerns of interference. In response to Homeland Security Secretary Jeh Johnson's proposal to shore up voting infrastructure, Georgia SoS Brian Kemp called the efforts an assault on state rights.

77. After the *WaPo* story, Trump again tweeted about Obama and Russian interference: "Obama Administration knew far in advance of November 8th about election meddling by Russia. Did nothing about it. WHY?"

78. Trump continued to deny intelligence that Russia influenced our election, but said it "probably was Russia" who had done the hacking and indicated other countries could have been behind the attacks as well.

79. NBC reported that Trump has taken little meaningful action and shown no interest in stopping Russia from hacking our next election, despite a slew of intelligence warnings that Russia will be back.

80. McConnell rolled out the Senate version of AHCA, which only a small group of white male senators and lobbyists were involved in crafting. The public is overwhelmingly against the bill. One journalist referred to the process in a column titled "Our Fake Democracy."

81. Trump has yet to pass a single piece of major legislation despite control of the House and Senate. He seems largely uninterested and disengaged in this sphere.

U.S. Capitol police arrest a protester against the Senate Republican's draft health care bill outside the office of Senate Majority Leader Mitch McConnell, Republican of Kentucky, on Capitol Hill in Washington, D.C., June 22, 2017. (Getty Images)

Week 33

JUNE 25–JULY 1, 2017

This week the first evidence of possible collusion between the Trump campaign and Russia surfaced. Several key members of the Trump regime could be ensnared—big news, with major ramifications! Yet most of our country was distracted by Trump's Twitter war with Joe and Mika.

This week, Trump continued to keep his base engaged by attacking those not white, straight, Christian, and male. Through deportation and immigration bans, and continually peeling away rights and protections from women, people of color, LGBTQ people, and Muslim and Jewish Americans, Trump is changing the character of our country, and the world is noticing.

1. California added four more states to its ban on state-funded and state-sponsored travel, citing these states (eight in total) for laws allowing discrimination against LGBTQ people.

2. Overruling experts and diplomats, and without explanation, the State Department removed Iraq and Myanmar from the list of the world's worst offenders in the use of child soldiers.

3. Trump's DHS pulled a grant given by Obama given to Life After Hate, a group dedicated to countering neo-Nazis and white supremacists.

4. The State Department's anti-Semitism monitoring office will be unstaffed as of July 1. The ADL reports that anti-Semitic incidents have almost doubled in 2017.

5. A court in Mississippi lifted an injunction on an anti-gay law, freeing individuals and government workers to discriminate against gay and transgender people on religious grounds.

6. North Carolina's Supreme Court ruled that a woman cannot revoke consent after sexual intercourse begins.

7. Trump ended an almost two-decade-long tradition of celebrating Ramadan at the White House.

8. Six Afghan girls were denied one-week visas to show their robot at FIRST Global Challenge in D.C. Roa Mahboob, the first female tech CEO in Afghanistan, who sponsored the team, said, "They were crying all the day."

9. The historical marker for civil rights icon Emmett Till on the Mississippi Freedom Trail was vandalized.

10. Trucker Rene Flores, who was featured in a *USA Today* article on how poor immigrants who speak little English have become modern-day indentured servants, was fired the day after the article ran.

11. Five months after Trump's ninety-day Muslim ban was introduced, the Supreme Court allowed part of the second version to take effect, banning travel from six Muslim countries where Trump doesn't have properties.

12. Attorneys general from ten states and Idaho's governor threatened to sue the government to stop granting and renewing Deferred Action for Childhood Arrivals ("DACA") permits by September 5.

13. Trump's White House said Chicago (Trump regime code for black American) gun violence is "driven by morality more than anything else."

14. Trump invited families of victims killed by undocumented immigrants to the White House for an on-camera, anti-immigrant display.

15. *Politico* reported that the White House Council for Women and Girls, set up by Obama, has gone dark under Trump and will likely be shuttered.

16. Secretary Mattis will delay the Pentagon's decision on allowing transgender recruits into the military for six months. Ash Carter, his predecessor under Obama, had ended the ban on transgender people serving.

17. *WaPo* reported that one month before Election Day, Kushner's firm finalized a $285 million refinancing loan from Deutsche Bank. Kushner and his brother are guarantors of the loan.

18. Kushner did not report the loan or his personal guarantee on his financial disclosure form filed with the Office of Government Ethics.

19. The loan came at a time when Deutsche Bank was negotiating with New York State regulators to settle a federal mortgage fraud case and charges of money laundering for Russia.

20. In Week 19's list (March 25), it was revealed Deutsche Bank was fined $630 million for laundering more than $10 billion of Russian money, and settled the case in May.

21. The *Financial Times* reported that VEB, the state-owned Russian bank whose chairman, Gorkov, met clandestinely with Kushner, has no banking license or capital, and is essentially a special-purpose vehicle to support the Kremlin's priorities.

22. Kushner retained Abbe Lowell, one of the country's leading criminal defense attorneys, to represent him in the special counsel probe.

23. *WaPo* reported that Manafort retroactively filed as a foreign agent on Tuesday for $17.1 million in payments received by his firm between 2012 and 2014 from a pro-Russia political party that controlled Ukraine's government.

24. Also in the filing, Manafort revealed that in 2013 he met with California congressman Dana Rohrabacher, an outspoken pro-Russia advocate.

25. *Roll Call* reported that Manafort donated to Rohrabacher three days after their meeting.

26. ABC reported that congressional investigators will question Trump's longtime bodyguard, Keith Schiller, who now serves as a White House aide, as part of their Russia probe. Schiller delivered Comey's termination letter in person.

27. The *Miami Herald* reported on Igor Zorin, a Russian government official who, on his seventy-five-thousand-dollar bureaucrat's salary, purchased three units at the ritzy Trump Palace in South Florida worth $5.4 million.

28. CNN reported that Trump's own advisers are struggling to convince him that Russia still poses a threat.

29. CNN also reported that NSA director Mike Rogers expressed frustration to lawmakers about his inability to convince Trump that Russia interfered in our election, and Trump's lack of focus on the continued threat.

30. Further, even as the intelligence community continues to brief him on Russian interference, Trump has not convened any meetings on Russian meddling.

31. Intelligence officers and lawmakers expressed concern about the State Department's unwillingness to crack down on Russian diplomats traveling within the U.S., despite evidence that Moscow is trying to conduct intelligence operations.

32. Trump continued to distract from Russian interference and possible collusion, tweeting "Hillary Clinton colluded with the Democratic Party in order to beat Crazy Bernie Sanders. Is she allowed to so collude?"

33. A former CIA analyst and targeting officer explained how Trump's tweets are being used by foreign spies to determine his vulnerabilities.

34. The Kremlin recalled Kislyak amid the election controversy. Flynn, Kushner, and Sessions all had undisclosed meetings with Kislyak.

35. *WaPo* reported that the FBI met with Carter Page five times in March about his contacts with Russia and claims in the Steele dossier. At the time, Page did not have a lawyer.

36. Ivanka was ordered to testify in a dispute with an Italian shoemaker that accused her of copying one of its shoe designs.

37. Chinese authorities released on bail, pending trial, the three activists who were investigating low pay, excessive overtime, crude verbal abuse, and possible misuse of student labor at Ivanka's China factories.

38. The *Guardian* reported that a nonprofit run by Trump attorney Jay Sekulow will be investigated by authorities in two states for steering tens of millions of dollars to his family and their businesses.

39. The CBO report indicated that the Senate version of AHCA/Trumpcare would result in twenty-two million more uninsured. The White House issued a statement trashing the credibility of the office.

40. Polls showed the Senate version is wildly unpopular: the *USA Today*/Suffolk poll found that 12 percent approve; the NPR/*PBS NewsHour*/Marist poll found that 17 percent approve.

41. A pro-Trump PAC ran negative ads targeting Senator Dean Heller in his home state for not supporting AHCA. Amid backlash, the ads were pulled.

42. News reports on the Senate's failure to pass AHCA cited Trump's lack of interest and loss of political capital. Some senators also didn't trust him after he called the House version he had backed "mean."

43. On Monday late evening, the White House issued a cryptic statement warning of potential preparations for a chemical attack in Syria, and saying Syria would "pay a heavy price."

44. NBC reported that Trump's own senior national security officials were caught off guard by the White House statement. NBC noted the disconnect demonstrates how Trump "is making foreign policy on the fly."

45. The U.S. image has plunged under Trump. Pew Research found that three-quarters of respondents in the countries surveyed have little to no confidence in Trump to handle foreign affairs. Our democratic allies were the most negative.

46. In the same poll Pew found that only 22 percent are confident in Trump's handling of foreign affairs, compared with 64 percent during the Obama administration.

47. Also of note in the Pew Research survey, for the first time in thirty-five years, a majority of Canadians have an unfavorable view of the U.S.

48. The *Toronto Star* has also been keeping track of the false claims by Trump, and has so many that it chose to sort them by topic.

49. The EPA chief of staff pressured a scientist on the agency's scientific review board to change her testimony before the House Science Committee.

50. *Politico* reported that Trump Hotel D.C. has become a go-to meeting place. Conway said, "They look at it as a piece of the president." Trump continues to profit from the hotel and has not tracked foreign government receipts as promised.

51. The White House abruptly changed course and disinvited the media from covering Trump's first reelection fund-raiser. As mentioned in Week 32, the high-priced event will be held at Trump Hotel D.C.

52. *WaPo* reported that a fake *Time* magazine cover is hanging at several of Trump's golf clubs. After the report, a spokesperson for *Time* said the magazine had asked the Trump Organization to remove them.

53. Trump remarked to an Irish reporter in the Oval Office with him that she had a "nice smile" during a telephone call in the Oval Office with the newly elected Irish prime minister, Leo Varadkar. Trump told Varadkar, "I bet she treats you well."

54. Trump told the Irish prime minister, "We have so many people from Ireland in this country. I know so many of them, too. I feel I know all of them."

55. Rachel Maddow reported that Republicans and conservative media have started a campaign to smear FBI interim director McCabe, who can corroborate Comey's statements on conversations with Trump.

56. Maddow also reported that Deutsche Bank added a lawyer with a background in tax crimes and money laundering.

57. Deutsche Bank again denied Democratic lawmakers' request for information on Trump's accounts, saying individual members of Congress don't have the same standing as a committee (in addition to their previous refusal on the grounds it would violate privacy).

58. Senators Lindsey Graham and Chuck Grassley requested the FBI and DoJ provide copies of surveillance requests made in their investigation of Russian interference in the election. If shared with Trump, this could bolster his defense.

59. Pence and Kris Kobach, heads of Trump's commission on election integrity, asked all fifty states to release voter roll data, including names, birthdays, the last four digits of Social Security numbers, and voting history back to 2006.

60. Amid cries of voter suppression and privacy concerns, within twenty-four hours almost half of all states had rejected the request in part or whole.

61. Kobach said Kansas would not hand over some of the information, nor will Pence's home state of Indiana. Mississippi's secretary of state said, "They can go jump in the Gulf of Mexico."

62. The next morning, Trump tweeted his dismay at states' unwillingness to turn over voter information, "What are they trying to hide?" leading to a conversation on Twitter on why Trump has yet to share his tax returns. We have normalized this and stopped asking.

63. The AP reported that the EPA's Pruitt met with the CEO of Dow Chemical before deciding to reverse an agency ban on a widely used pesticide that studies have found can harm children's brains.

64. Dow spent $13.6 million on lobbying in 2016 and wrote a one-million-dollar check to Trump's inauguration festivities. Dow's CEO stood by Trump in February as he signed an executive order rolling back government regulations.

65. At the Aspen Ideas conference, Sally Yates said that while acting attorney general, she found out about the Muslim ban by reading about it in the *NYT.*

66. Yates slammed the Trump regime for ignoring legal and political norms, and said the regime's behavior "should be alarming to us as a country."

67. ABC reported that federal authorities are investigating a breach of at least one nuclear plant's computer system.

68. *Politico* reported that Tillerson blew up at Trump's head of personnel, Johnny DeStefano, for torpedoing his picks for senior State Department roles. The State Department remains largely unstaffed.

69. In Week 32, DeStefano's data company was involved in the leak of private information of two hundred million U.S. voters, which was left unprotected online ahead of the 2016 election.

70. Kasowitz failed to follow through on his threatened legal complaint against Comey, part of a pattern for Trump's attorneys.

71. As stories on Russia and other controversies continued to break, Trump continued his efforts to weaken the media's credibility, tweeting, "They are all Fake News!"—about CNN, ABC, NBC, CBS, *WaPo,* and the *NYT.*

72. Trump shared videos of CNN commentator and producer Van Jones being secretly recorded by Project Veritas's James O'Keefe to his seven million followers on Instagram. Jones made statements casting doubt on Russia's influence on the election. O'Keefe is known for conducting politically motivated sting operations against ACORN and Planned Parenthood and was arrested and convicted for entering Senator Mary Landrieu's office under false pretenses in 2010.

73. CNN's Brian Stelter gave three examples of press access being rolled back: Trump and the South Korean president didn't hold a joint news conference; Pentagon's non-answer on why Mattis traveled to Germany and Belgium without the customary TV journalists; and journalists were told to leave a DoJ event marking Pride month.

74. The Senate Intelligence Committee will get Comey's memos on his conversations with Trump. It is unclear when or if the public will see them.

75. Trump directed a set of highly offensive tweets at Joe Scarborough and Mika Brzezinski, including the epithets "low I.Q. Crazy Mika" and "Psycho Joe." The tweet to Mika was widely condemned as sexist and beneath the office.

76. Conservative pundit Charles Krauthammer told Fox News of Trump's tweets, "This is what it's like in a banana republic."

77. Amid the uproar, Trump quietly announced that he will meet with Putin in person at the G20 gathering next week. Numerous experts and lawmakers expressed grave concern.

78. *Vox* reported that Trump aides said he doesn't have an agenda or plan much preparation for the meeting, raising concerns that Putin, a master tactician who arrives meticulously well prepared, will outplay Trump.

79. Trump also succeeded at distracting from the bombshell of possible collusion, Kobach and Pence's voter roll request, and other highly controversial stories.

80. The *WSJ* reported the first solid evidence of collusion between the Trump campaign and Russia. A Republican operative, Peter W. Smith, tried to get Hillary's thirty-three thousand deleted e-mails from Russian hackers in concert with Flynn.

81. Smith passed away in May. The Trump campaign said that if Flynn coordinated with Smith, "it would have been in his capacity as a private individual."

82. The *WSJ* also reported that Smith's story is consistent with intelligence agencies' intercepts of Russian hackers discussing how to obtain e-mails from Hillary's server and transmit them to Flynn via an intermediary.

83. Late Friday, the *WSJ* broadened its story, saying that Smith named other key Trump associates—Bannon, Conway, and Sam Clovis—in his September 7, 2016, recruitment document for his effort to get Hillary's thirty-three thousand deleted e-mails.

84. On Friday, *New York* magazine reported on Trump's efforts to possibly blackmail Scarborough and Brzezinski by using a story to be published at

Trump ally David Pecker's *National Enquirer* making their affair public. Kushner was the go-between for communication. He told Scarborough he would need to personally apologize to Trump for negative coverage for the story not to run. Scarborough would not, and the story ran.

85. *Law & Crime* explained that Trump's alleged attempted blackmail of Joe and Mika, including persistent phone calls by reporters to Mika's teenage children, could be an impeachable offense.

86. Bloomberg reported that Kushner almost bought the *National Enquirer* three years ago, and the *New Yorker* reported that David Pecker is considering a bid for Time Inc., owner of *Time* magazine.

87. On Friday, as the Senate left for break, Trump tweeted that they should just repeal Obamacare and replace it later. The CBO estimated in that scenario eighteen million would lose coverage in the first year and thirty-two million more would by 2026.

88. Twenty-five House Democrats, including the ranking member of the Judiciary Committee, backed a bill that would create an "oversight" commission that could declare the president incapacitated under the Twenty-fifth Amendment.

Week 34

JULY 2–8, 2017

This is arguably the most alarming weekly list so far. A plot that has played out week by week: Trump is alienating our allies while cozying up to authoritarians, as witnessed by his embarrassing behavior at the NATO and G7 meetings, culminated this week at the G20 summit with U.S. isolationism. Putin is the winner in this new world alignment.

This week Trump amped up his assault on the media, including encouraging violence against reporters. With this, Trump has distracted the country and media, and taken back the narrative. In the atmosphere of chaos, this week also stands out for the number of important stories that received little or no media coverage.

1. More and more states refused to comply with what Trump described as his "very distinguished VOTER FRAUD PANEL."

2. By midweek, forty-four states and D.C. refused to provide some or all of the voter roll data requested by Trump's Election Integrity Commission.

3. States are denying the request based on concerns over privacy and federal overreach, and also concern that the effort of identifying voter affiliation will be used to purge Democrats from voter rolls.

4. The Lawyers' Committee for Civil Rights Under Law filed a Hatch Act complaint against Kobach, saying he used Trump's commission to solicit political campaign money.

5. A Maryland official, Deputy Secretary of State Luis Borunda, resigned from Trump's commission.

6. Several experts on the regulatory process told *The Hill* that Trump's commission may have violated the law by failing to submit the requests to states through the Office of Information and Regulatory Affairs (OIRA), as required by the Paperwork Reduction Act.

7. A DoJ letter sent to forty-four states' election officials on the same day Kobach and Pence made their requests asks states to detail their compliance with the National Voter Registration Act of 1993 (NVRA). This request also raised concerns about voter purging.

8. At a rally in D.C., Trump continued his attacks on the "fake" media, saying, "I'm president and they're not."

9. Trump tweeted a video created by a Reddit user from both his personal account and the official @POTUS account, showing him violently wrestling down a person whose face is the CNN logo.

10. The Reddit user was named "HanAssholeSolo" and his posts were full of anti-Muslim, anti-Semitic, and other white supremacist materials.

11. The Reddit user later apologized, but Trump did not. The parents and wife of the CNN reporter who covered the story, Andrew Kaczynski, received around fifty harassing phone calls given a line he included in the piece that CNN reserved the right to publish the Reddit user's real identity should he repeat his behavior. According to Ben Smith, a journalist and mentor of Kaczynski, CNN did not defend the reporter.

12. As Trump continued his anti-CNN rhetoric, the cable network's anchors and executives received death threats and other harassing messages.

13. Following Trump's tweet, three media watchdog groups have started to do something they never imagined: documenting violent threats and actions against the media in the U.S.

14. Maine's governor, Paul LePage, said he makes up stories to mislead the press. LePage also called the media "vile" and "inaccurate."

15. The *NYT* reported that the Trump regime discussed using the pending merger between Time Warner and AT&T as leverage over CNN.

16. Trump media ally the *Daily Caller* reported that the White House doesn't support the merger if Jeff Zucker still heads CNN.

17. Trump ally and Bannon patron Robert Mercer bought 2.5 million shares of Time Inc., owner of *Time* magazine, in the first quarter of 2017. As noted in Week 33, David Pecker, owner of the *National Enquirer*, is also interested in Time Inc.

18. Rachel Maddow reported that *The Rachel Maddow Show* was sent a forged NSA document. Maddow speculated that this was an attempt to trick her show into reporting a false story, hence weakening her credibility and dulling that storyline.

19. Maddow said that other media outlets may be receiving forged documents as well, citing recently retracted stories at CNN and *Vice*.

20. *Politico* reported on the Trump regime's obsessive crackdown on leaks from the intelligence community, which has led to an "increasingly tense and paranoid working environment" in the national security community.

21. Protesters gathered at rallies in dozens of cities around the country to call for Trump's impeachment.

22. NBC reported that in Trump's first 168 days in office, he spent fifty days at Trump properties and thirty-six days at Trump golf resorts.

23. The *NYT* reported that while consulting with industry representatives, not EPA staff, Pruitt has moved to undo, delay, or block thirty environmental rules, a rollback larger in scope than any other in the agency's forty-seven-year history.

24. Several states sued over the EPA's decision to keep a Dow pesticide, which studies show can harm children's brains, on the market. As noted in Week 33, Dow spent millions lobbying and donated to Trump's inauguration.

25. The Wisconsin assembly passed a bill that would block students from protesting conservative speakers on college campuses.

26. The *NYT* reported that the Trump regime's latest anti-immigrant tactic is to target undocumented parents suspected of having paid to have their children smuggled into the U.S.

27. *Politico* reported that Trump insider Stephen Miller has been holding meetings with agencies on how to further curb the entry of refugees. Miller clashed with Tillerson, who demanded autonomy.

28. A new law in Florida allows parents and other residents of school districts to file complaints with school boards to challenge what's taught in science classes.

29. Attorneys general for eighteen states and D.C. sued DeVos and the Department of Education over a decision to roll back rules put in place to help students who have been defrauded by their colleges.

30. DeVos's Department of Education may stop publishing the list of colleges and universities in violation of Title IX for mishandling campus sexual assault. The Obama administration started the list to hold schools accountable for an issue that impacts one in five college women and one in twenty college men.

31. *WaPo* reported that the White House gender pay gap has more than tripled under Trump, with female staffers earning on average 63 percent of what their male counterparts make. This is the biggest White House gender pay gap in decades.

32. Female journalists were banned from the Speaker's Lobby, a room where reporters speak to members of Congress, because their sleeveless dresses were not viewed as "appropriate attire."

33. In a fifty-three-page memo to the court, Trump attorney Kasowitz argued for the dismissal of a sexual harassment lawsuit against Trump, claiming Trump cannot be sued in state court while in office.

34. The Auschwitz Memorial condemned a political video posted by Louisiana Republican Clay Higgins, which the congressman filmed inside an Auschwitz gas chamber.

35. At a protest outside Senator Rob Portman's office in Columbus, Ohio, a woman in a wheelchair was pushed out of her chair to the ground by a police officer.

36. The KKK plans a rally in downtown Charlottesville today and warned that many of its eighty to one hundred members and supporters will be armed.

37. Pro-Trump Twitter operatives are marketing their services to candidates and others, promising to mobilize their followers and networks for pay.

38. The *Guardian* reported that investigators are looking into whether the Trump campaign and far-right websites coordinated with Russia in spreading fake news. Senator Mark Warner noted that voters in swing states were targeted.

39. *Motherboard* reported on an analysis of the Twitter bots that helped Trump, and found the same bots and alt-right narrative emerged in the French election against Macron.

40. On July 4, NPR tweeted the Declaration of Independence and was attacked by Trump supporters who called it "propaganda" and "spam."

41. A new NPR/*PBS NewsHour*/Marist poll found that Trump's net approval with independents has fallen by seventeen points since he took office.

42. The poll also found that the majority (54 percent) of Americans believe Trump personally did something illegal or unethical with Russia.

43. While his predecessors Clinton, George W. Bush, and Obama celebrated July 4 by visiting troops, Trump spent the day on a Trump-branded golf course. Senators John McCain, Elizabeth Warren, and Lindsey Graham visited troops in Afghanistan.

44. Despite his recusal, Sessions spoke to *Fox & Friends* about the Trump-Russia probe, offering advice to Mueller on hiring practices and tempo.

45. The *WSJ* reported that the Office of Government Ethics will release an additional two dozen ethics waivers just filed for Trump regime members working on issues they handled in their private-sector jobs. Trump has already granted as many waivers to White House officials as Obama did in his eight years in office.

46. The State Department's Office of the Inspector General said the State Department and the U.S. Agency for International Development (USAID) have failed to adequately track more than $30 billion of foreign aid annually.

47. In a survey of thirty-five thousand employees in the State Department and USAID, workers said they were concerned about the future of their agencies and the lack of support from the Trump regime and Tillerson.

48. An Indiana nonprofit is suing Pence's successor as governor for keeping residents in the dark on the deal between the Trump regime and Carrier. The group's request for information in December went unanswered.

49. In another sign the Trump regime won't take civil rights seriously, Trump nominated Eric Dreiband to the DoJ's Civil Rights Division. Dreiband has spent his career defending companies against charges of discrimination.

50. One of the DoJ's top corporate crime watchdogs, Hui Chen, resigned, saying the Trump regime has been engaging in conduct that she would never tolerate in corporations, "creating a cognitive dissonance that I could not overcome."

51. Walter Shaub, director of the OGE, resigned in frustration, six months before his term ended, saying, "It's clear that there isn't more I could accomplish." Shaub and OGE have twenty-four items in the *Weekly List* up to this point.

52. Shaub said in a postresignation interview that Trump's ethics program is "a very serious disappointment" and that his efforts to get basic information from the regime was "like pulling teeth."

53. CREW filed an ethics complaint against Kushner, saying he failed to make the required disclosure of his ownership interest in Cadre. The online real estate investment company has a value of eight hundred million dollars.

54. The Russian sanctions bill, which passed in the Senate 98–2, stalled in the House as Republican Pete Sessions, chair of the House Rules Committee, said it would make American energy companies less competitive.

55. The *WSJ* reported that energy companies including Exxon and Chevron, and companies in other industries, are lobbying against the Russian sanctions bill, saying it would hurt their business with Russian partners.

56. The Trump Organization renewed more than one thousand web domains, including many which refer to Trump and Russia, like TrumpTowerMoscow.com, indicating possible interest in future development.

57. *Axios* reported that Russian-government-owned Sputnik news is coming to the D.C. airwaves after taking over an FM radio station. The FCC has not yet been notified, according to a spokesperson.

58. Matt Tait, a cybersecurity expert who is cited in a *WSJ* story on possible Trump campaign collusion with Russia over Hillary's deleted e-mails, wrote an op-ed, "The Time I Got Recruited to Collude with the Russians," to tell his story.

59. Tait said it was clear to him that Peter W. Smith knew Michael Flynn and his son well and that they knew the contact from the "dark web" who offered up Clinton's e-mails was likely Russia, but didn't care. Tait warned it could be "part of a wider Russian campaign against the U.S."

60. Tait also received a document from Smith titled "A Demonstrative Pedagogical Summary to Be Developed and Released Prior to November 8, 2016," which list four groups involved—one group includes Bannon, Conway, Clovis, Flynn, and Lisa Nelson.

61. McClatchy reported on a Kremlin document that shows that Kaspersky Lab, a leading global seller of antivirus programs, has ties to Russia's spying apparatus. Kaspersky's certification has an FSB military intelligence unit number.

62. Kaspersky security software is available globally, including at Target and Walmart. The company also serves as a subcontractor for U.S. federal software contracts, and was used by the DNC last summer.

63. CNN reported that Russia is stepping up spying efforts in the U.S. since the U.S. elections. Officials cited said Russia feels emboldened by the lack of a significant retaliatory response by Trump and Obama.

64. U.S. intelligence estimates that Russia has 150 espionage operatives in the U.S. Since the election, many have tried to sneak in under the guise of business.

65. Strangely, the State Department reportedly continues to grant temporary duty visas to suspected Russian intelligence officers, despite this knowledge.

66. The AP reported on a lawsuit filed by Coalition for Good Governance, saying Georgia's Sixth Congressional District election results should be voided because of previously identified problems with the touch-screen voting system.

67. The suit cites the work of a private cybersecurity researcher who found that a misconfigured server had left Georgia's 6.7 million voter records exposed to hackers last August.

68. Georgia's Republican secretary of state, Brian Kemp, blamed the media for developing a false narrative about Russian hacking. He said states are doing enough to keep elections secure and "anything to the contrary is fake news."

69. The *WSJ* reported that Mueller has hired an "absolute cream of the crop" team of fifteen top attorneys with experience in national security, public corruption, and financial crimes for the Russia probe.

70. The *Financial Times* reported that Russian-born Felix Sater has agreed to cooperate with an international investigation into a money-laundering network. As noted in Week 32, Sater has extensive ties to both organized crime and the Trump family.

71. In its campaign for the upcoming election, Merkel's party has dropped the reference to the U.S. as a "friend." Four years ago, her party referred to the U.S. as Germany's "most important friend" outside Europe.

72. Bloomberg reported that China and Germany have stepped up to lead this year's G20 summit, a role formerly held by the U.S.

73. Pew Research found that seventeen of the nineteen G20 countries in its survey look to Merkel, not Trump, to lead in world affairs.

74. The *Guardian* reported that Trump considered a sneak visit to Downing Street in order to avoid massive UK protests en route to or from the G20 summit. After the story broke, the White House said Trump would not visit.

75. Instead, on his way to the G20 summit, Trump chose to stop off in Poland, despite the new far-right government's authoritarian leanings, including cracking down on judges and the media.

76. The AP reported that the Polish government promised the White House cheering crowds as part of the invitation. Members of the ruling party and pro-government activists bused in groups of people for Trump's speech.

77. Trump gave another of his dystopian speeches in Poland, saying Western civilization was at risk of decline because of "radical Islamic terrorism" and government bureaucracy.

78. At a news conference in Poland, Trump said he thinks meddling in the U.S. election was done by Russia, but that "it could have been other people in other countries" and that "nobody really knows for sure."

79. Also on his trip to Poland, Trump continued to dismiss and belittle U.S. intelligence, saying, "Do we even have seventeen intelligence agencies?"

80. The day before Trump was set to meet with Putin, seemingly as a bargaining chip, the *Moscow Times* reported that the Russian embassy to the U.S. is accusing the U.S. of "kidnapping" a man accused of cyberfraud.

81. Ahead of his meeting with Putin, top Senate Democrats sent a letter to Trump saying that not raising Russia's interference in our election would be "a severe dereliction of the duty of the office to which you were elected."

82. The *Los Angeles Times* reported that in preparing Trump for his meeting with Putin, aides had written a list of "tweet-length sentences" that summarize the main points.

83. Trump met with Mexican president Enrique Peña Nieto at the G20 summit. After the meeting, Trump was asked if Mexico will pay for the wall, to which he responded, "Absolutely." Mexico's foreign minister said the wall was not discussed.

84. On Friday, without provocation or reason, Trump tweeted a random lie about Democratic strategist John Podesta: "Everyone here is talking about why John Podesta refused to give the DNC server to the FBI and the CIA. Disgraceful!"

85. At the G20 summit, Trump and Putin met for two hours and sixteen minutes off camera, behind closed doors. The meeting was originally scheduled to last thirty minutes.

86. Only Tillerson and Trump were present from the U.S. side, despite media speculation that McMaster and Trump adviser Fiona Hill would be included.

87. Lavrov and Tillerson gave different accounts of what happened behind closed doors. Lavrov said Trump told Putin that some circles in America were "exaggerating" allegations of Russian interference in the U.S. election.

88. Sally Yates tweeted that Trump's refusal to confirm Russian interference "insults career intel pros & hinders our ability to prevent in future."

89. Tillerson's version differed from Lavrov's, but both said they agreed to put whatever happened behind them: "There was not a lot of re-litigating of the past." Tillerson added, "This is a very important relationship."

90. Russia faces no consequences from Trump for interfering in our election. It was unclear if Trump returned the two Russian compounds seized by Obama as punishment for Russia interfering in our election.

91. In an op-ed, "Trump Caves to Putin," conservative journalist Stephen Hayes laid out an indictment of how Trump bowed to Putin on Russian interference and foreign policy. Elected Republicans, however, were silent.

92. The AP reported on Saturday that Putin said "he thinks Trump believes his denial of Russian meddling in U.S. vote, but better to ask Trump himself."

93. Ivanka took her father's seat at a G20 meeting on Saturday. Normally, government ministers or senior officials would take such a role.

94. Trump isolated the U.S. from other G20 countries on a series of policies ranging from climate to free trade.

95. The U.S. abstained from signing onto the G20 communiqué on climate-related issues, the sole country at the summit to do so.

96. As the summit came to a close, leaders feared that G20 summits may be ineffective while Trump is in office. President Macron said, "Our world has never been so divided."

Week 35

JULY 9–15, 2017

I'm pleased to share that the Weekly List *has found a safe home at the Library of Congress. May future generations learn from our slow slide to authoritarianism, and never let it happen again!*

This week the bombshell story about Donald Jr.'s e-mails, the first direct evidence of possible collusion and intent between the Trump campaign and Russia, dominated media coverage and conversation. But as with each week, amid the bedlam, there were myriad less-covered, important stories on how the fabric of our country is changing and kleptocracy is omnipresent.

1. After the G20 summit, Pope Francis warned about "dangerous" international alliances, including the one between the U.S. and Russia.
2. On Sunday, after returning from the G20 summit, Trump sent a bizarre set of tweets, including his apparent acceptance that Putin did not meddle in our election and his plan to set up a "Cyber Security unit" with Putin.
3. After widespread condemnation of his "Cyber Security unit" idea, Trump tweeted the same night that he didn't really mean it.
4. U.S. officials say Russia government hackers were behind recent cyber-intrusions into the administrative and business networks of a U.S. nuclear power plant and other energy companies.
5. Reuters reported that European infrastructure networks have also recently been hacked, and the Russian government is thought to be the culprit.
6. An Arkansas bill scheduled to go into effect July 30 would make it illegal for a woman to have an abortion without notifying the man who impregnated her, even in cases of rape.
7. On Monday, Capitol police arrested citizens protesting the GOP health care bill outside Republican senate offices.
8. A federal judge halted the deportation of fourteen hundred Iraqi nationals, including many Christians fearing persecution. The Trump regime's efforts to deport took on new urgency because Iraq has agreed to accept deportees.

9. An Iranian cancer researcher traveling on a valid visa to the U.S. to work as a visiting scholar at Boston's Children's Hospital was detained at Logan Airport, along with his wife and three children.

10. Pew Research found that the percentage of refugees arriving in the U.S. who are Muslim has steadily declined under Trump from 50 percent in February to 31 percent in June, while the percentage of Christian refugees has increased from 41 percent to 57 percent.

11. A federal judge's ruling in Hawaii narrowed the scope of Trump's Muslim ban by vastly expanding the list of family relationships with U.S. citizens that visa applicants can use to get into the U.S.

12. Trump ally Steve King called for using federal funds set aside for Planned Parenthood and welfare programs like food stamps to be reallocated for funding Trump's Mexican wall.

13. *Politico* reported that Trump and his regime are quietly working with conservative senators Tom Cotton and David Perdue to cut the number of legal immigrants allowed into the U.S. by half over the next decade.

14. According to a memo obtained by *WaPo*, the Trump regime is considering expanding the DHS's power to expedite the deportation of illegal immigrants, a major expansion of the agency's power.

15. DeVos met with "men's rights" groups who believe campus sexual assault is a hoax, including the National Coalition for Men, an organization with a history of harassing and intimidating alleged sexual-assault survivors.

16. DeVos also met with Stop Abusive and Violent Environments (SAVE), an organization the SPLC described as promoting misogyny. SAVE has lobbied against efforts to address military sexual assault, calling it a "witch hunt."

17. Ahead of these pivotal meeting, Candice Jackson, the acting assistant secretary for civil rights at the Education Department, said 90 percent of campus sexual accusations come after drunk sex or breakups. She later apologized.

18. Sessions delivered a speech to Alliance Defending Freedom, a group designated as an "anti-LGBT hate group" by the SPLC in 2016, off camera on Tuesday. The DoJ refused to release his remarks.

19. Representative Martha McSally stood on the House floor Wednesday in a sleeveless dress and open-toed shoes to say she would not comply with the dress code in the chamber and Speaker's Lobby.

20. On Friday, female members of the House wore sleeveless clothing to work, tweeting in support of "Sleeveless Friday."

21. Price's HHS quietly defunded teen pregnancy programs designed by the Obama administration to fund scientifically valid ways to help teenagers make healthy decisions that avoid unwanted pregnancy.

22. The ACLU filed a suit against Trump's Election Integrity Commission, saying it isn't following federal law requiring it to be open to the public.

23. Trump's Election Integrity Commission published a 112-page document of public feedback (mostly negative), which exposed personal information including e-mail addresses, phone numbers, and home addresses of some commenters.

24. More than three thousand Colorado voters have canceled their registrations since Trump's Election Integrity Commission requested voter roll information.

25. A nonpartisan campaign finance watchdog group filed a complaint with the Federal Election Commission (FEC) alleging that Price improperly used his congressional campaign fund to promote his confirmation to HHS secretary.

26. The Center for Public Integrity reported that Bannon failed to properly disclose more than two million dollars in mortgage debt on his financial disclosure form.

27. Trump's expected pick for chief of the Wage and Hour Division of the Department of Labor, Cheryl Stanton, was named in a lawsuit last year for allegedly not paying her house cleaners.

28. *WaPo* reported that while Trump has chastised companies for outsourcing jobs and Ivanka branded herself a feminist, Ivanka's clothing lines are exclusively produced at low-wage foreign factories, and women employees are treated terribly.

29. After Trump's much ballyhooed deal with Carrier to keep American jobs, Indiana has lost five thousand manufacturing jobs since February.

30. The *WSJ* reported that the CEO of OpenGov, a small technology start-up that Kushner's brother has a stake in, got a seat at a White House roundtable for prominent technology-industry leaders last month. Kushner owned the stake before selling it to his brother early in the year.

31. *Politico* reported that conservative Sinclair Broadcasting increased "must run" segments featuring former Trump adviser Epshteyn to nine times per week, across its affiliates.

32. Sputnik, a Russian-government-funded news outlet, started broadcasting on 105.5 FM last week from K Street offices a few blocks from the White House.

33. Within twenty-four hours of the announcement that the *Weekly List* will be archived in the Library of Congress, I was the target of two hit pieces in Sputnik, one in RT, and others in various Russia-friendly blogs.

34. The *NYT* reported that Pence has quietly hosted at least four private dinners, and has more in the works, to court big donors and corporate executives.

35. The Trump regime's deregulation teams are full of appointees with deep industry ties. The *NYT* and *ProPublica* reported on seventy-one appointees with industry links, including twenty-eight with potential conflicts.

36. The *Intercept* reported Kushner tried to get a half-billion-dollar loan bailout for his 666 Fifth Avenue property from a Qatar sovereign wealth fund, and the deal's not coming to fruition may have influenced U.S. policy toward Qatar.

37. *USA Today* reported that a U.S. Golf Association executive told USGA executive committee members that Trump threatened to sue the organization if it moved the 2017 U.S. Women's Open from Trump's golf club in Bedminster.

38. Trump tweeted: "I will be at the @USGA #USWomensOpen in Bedminster," advertising one of his properties again.

39. Documents released to *WaPo* under the FOIA show that the State Department spent more than fifteen thousand dollars in February for rooms at the new Trump hotel in Vancouver.

40. At the behest of Bannon, Trump aides Prince and Feinberg, who both benefited from military contracting, developed an alternative plan to the one proposed by the Pentagon for Afghanistan. Their plan was to rely on contractors (mostly non-American) instead of American military troops.

41. Twitter users who were blocked by Trump's personal account are suing him in federal court, saying he violated their First Amendment rights.

42. Trump tweeted that Comey had "leaked CLASSIFIED INFORMATION" and "That is so illegal!" The Columbia law professor who received some of Comey's memos said the memos he received were not classified.

43. On Saturday evening, the *NYT* reported that Donald Jr., Kushner, and Manafort met with Natalia Veselnitskaya, a lawyer with close Kremlin ties, at Trump Tower on June 9, 2016.

44. Donald Jr. initially claimed the meeting was related to an adoption program. Kushner had failed to disclose the meeting in his security clearance. Manafort, who was Trump's campaign manager at the time, had no comment on the meeting.

45. On Sunday, the *NYT* reported that Donald Jr. met with Veselnitskaya after being promised damaging information on Hillary Clinton. The meeting took place two weeks after Trump became the GOP nominee.

46. On the question of whether the Trump campaign colluded with Russia, the *NYT* noted that Donald Jr.'s meeting is "the first public indication that at least some in the campaign were willing to accept Russian help."

47. A spokesperson for Trump's lawyer told the *NYT*, "The president was not aware of and did not attend the meeting."

48. Donald Jr. hired attorney Alan Futerfas to represent him in the Russia probe, adding to a long list of attorneys defending Team Trump.

49. *WaPo* reported that the acquaintance who set up the Trump Tower meeting was Rob Goldstone, who was active in the Miss Universe pageant and works as a manager for Russian pop singer Emin Agalarov.

50. As news was breaking on Donald Jr., Russia's Lavrov threatened that Russia is "considering specific measures" as retribution for Trump not returning two compounds seized by the Obama administration.

51. On Tuesday, Donald Jr. preemptively tweeted his e-mail exchange in setting up the Trump Tower meeting. Donald Jr. had been contacted by the *NYT* for comment, asked for more time, then tweeted.

52. Shortly after his tweet, the *NYT* reported on Donald Jr.'s e-mails and detailed the changing accounts of the Trump Tower meeting by all involved parties.

53. According to the e-mails, Donald Jr. was offered information that "would incriminate Hillary and her dealings with Russia and would be very useful to your father," and was told, "This is obviously very high level and sensitive information but is part of Russia and its government's support for Mr. Trump."

54. Donald Jr.'s response: "If it's what you say I love it especially later in the summer."

55. Donald Jr. forwarded the e-mail chain—with the subject line "Re: Russia—Clinton—private and confidential"—to Kushner and Manafort ahead of the meeting.

56. The e-mail was sent by Rob Goldstone on behalf of a mutual friend, Emin Agalarov. Emin is the son of Aras Agalarov, a real estate tycoon referred to as the Donald Trump of Russia, who has close ties to—and was awarded the Order of Honor of the Russian Federation by—Putin.

57. The meeting took place in Trump Tower, one floor below Trump's offices. Trump continued to deny knowledge or involvement all week.

58. According to e-mails, the meeting took place at 4 P.M. Donald Jr. said it lasted twenty to thirty minutes. At 4:40 P.M. the same day, Trump tweeted in response to a tweet by Hillary, "where are your 33,000 emails that you deleted?"

59. Julian Assange tweeted, "Contacted Trump Jr this morning on why he should publish his emails (i.e with us)."

60. *WaPo* reported that Donald Jr. changed his story about the meeting with Veselnitskaya four times in the first four days after the story came to light.

61. The *NYT* reported that Trump personally signed off on Donald Jr.'s first statement Saturday night saying his meeting with a Russian lawyer was to discuss adoption policy—a known lie.

62. After releasing his e-mails, Donald Jr. gave an interview to Fox News telling his side of the story. Trump called his son "a high-quality person" and added, "I applaud his transparency."

63. Yahoo reported that Trump had a Moscow real estate deal with Aras Agalarov, to construct a Trump Tower in Moscow.

64. A letter of intent was signed by Trump; then, as the presidential campaign got under way, Donald Jr. was assigned to take the lead. Ivanka also looked at spots for Trump Tower Moscow with Emin Agalarov.

65. The deal did not happen because the Russian economy floundered, in part because of U.S. and EU sanctions imposed after Russia annexed Crimea away from Ukraine. Doing away with U.S. sanctions could help put the deal back on track.

66. In April 2016, Emin and Aras Agalarov told *WaPo* they wanted Trump to be elected. Emin said Trump's election would be "an amazing breakthrough" that would forge peace between Russia and the U.S.

67. CNN reported that Mueller's investigators plan to examine the meeting and e-mail exchanges disclosed by Donald Jr. as part of their broader Russian-meddling investigation.

68. On *The Late Show* Tuesday night, Joe Scarborough announced that he is leaving the Republican Party. "It's a shame there are so few Republicans speaking truth to power," Scarborough tweeted.

69. The *NYT* reported Tuesday that Trump's longtime personal attorney and lead counsel for the Russia probe, Kasowitz, has been the target of Trump's frustration and ire, and may resign.

70. *ProPublica* reported that as Trump's lead attorney on the Russia probe, Kasowitz is unable to see classified information because he isn't seeking security clearance and may have trouble getting one.

71. On Wednesday night, Kasowitz threatened an unidentified man who wrote Kasowitz urging him to resign. In an e-mail, Kasowitz wrote, "I'm on you now," "Watch your back, bitch," etc. Later, he apologized through a spokesperson, saying he had been working late that night.

72. McClatchy reported that Congressional and DoJ investigators are focusing on whether Trump's campaign pointed Russian cyberoperatives to certain voting jurisdictions in key states.

73. Kushner, who is already a "person of interest" for the DoJ investigations, will be investigated for his role overseeing the digital operations and for possible cooperation with Russian efforts.

74. Of note, the Russians knew to target women and African Americans in two of the three decisive states, Wisconsin and Michigan. Clinton lost Wisconsin, Michigan, and Pennsylvania by a combined 77,744 votes out of 13.9 million ballots cast.

75. The *WSJ* reported that in light of Donald Jr.'s e-mails, U.S. intelligence investigators are reexamining recordings captured in the spring of 2015 of Russian government officials discussing associates of Trump.

76. Representative Brad Sherman of California introduced articles of impeachment against Trump. Representative Al Green of Texas was the only other Democrat to join.

77. The AP reported that Trump's mysterious friend "Jim," whom Trump referenced frequently on the campaign trail and more recently ahead of his trip to Paris, may not actually exist.

78. Trump faced heavy criticism after telling France's first lady during his first state visit to the country, "You're in such good shape."

79. Democratic members of the House Judiciary Committee sent a letter to Sessions asking why the DoJ settled a $230 million Russian money-laundering case against Prevezon for six million dollars two days before trial in May.

80. Veselnitskaya represented the family of Pyotr Katsyv, whose son owns Prevezon. Democrats want to know if she was involved at any point in settlement negotiations.

81. Prevezon was part of Russia's largest tax fraud scheme. Sergei Magnitsky, the lawyer who exposed the alleged fraud, was jailed, tortured, and killed in Russia. Veselnitskaya has been trying to undo the U.S. law named after him, the Magnitsky Act, which imposes sanctions on foreign officials responsible for human rights abuses.

82. The case against Prevezon was initially brought by U.S. Attorney Preet Bharara, who was fired by Trump.

83. *Axios* reported that Trump's outside legal team wants him to wall off Kushner from discussing the Russia investigation with Trump.

84. On Thursday morning, NPR reported that Sessions had defied a judge's order by not supplying an SF86 form listing his foreign contacts. The court's thirty-day deadline expired Wednesday.

85. Later that afternoon, a day late, the DoJ did release one heavily redacted page of Sessions's SF86, showing only that he had checked "no" in response to the question of whether he had met with any foreign governments in the past seven years.

86. The *New Republic* reported that Trump's relationship with Russia dates back to the 1980s and that over decades Russia has laundered money through Trump's buildings and casinos.

87. Gorka told CNN that Trump is considering returning the Russian compounds because "we want to give collaboration" a chance. U.S. intelligence found evidence that the compounds were used for spying on the U.S.

88. Trump said he would invite Putin to the White House at the right time. Trump also continued to not acknowledge that Russia hacked our election, saying it could have been China or North Korea.

89. The *NYT* reported that Kushner has supplemented his federal disclosure form three times, adding more than one hundred names of foreign contacts.

90. The *Chicago Tribune* reported that Peter W. Smith, the GOP operative who detailed his efforts along with members of the Trump campaign to get Hillary's deleted e-mails from Russian hackers, committed suicide.

91. Smith's interview with the *WSJ*'s Shane Harris was the first report of possible collusion between the Trump campaign and Russia. Smith's suicide, on May 14, happened nine days after the interview occurred.

92. Smith left a curious suicide note, citing a bad turn in his health and writing, "NO FOUL PLAY WHATSOEVER." Harris said when he spoke to Smith, he had no indication "he was ill or planning to take his own life."

93. NBC reported that at the June 9 meeting, Veselnitskaya was accompanied by Rinat Akhmetshin, a Russian-American lobbyist and former Soviet counter-intelligence officer with ongoing ties to Russian intelligence.

94. The AP confirmed that Akhmetshin attended the meeting. Donald Jr. had not disclosed Akhmetshin's attendance, nor had Kushner in his forms.

95. The *Daily Beast* reported that Akhmetshin was previously accused in federal and state courts of orchestrating an international hacking conspiracy.

96. Chuck Grassley, chair of the Senate Judiciary Committee, called on Donald Jr. to testify as early as next week. Grassley said he would subpoena him if necessary.

97. Grassley filed a complaint against Akhmetshin in March, saying he was effectively engaged in lobbying work as an unregistered agent for Russian interests. Akhmetshin lobbied for Congress to repeal the Magnitsky Act.

98. *Foreign Policy* reported that the private e-mail account of a top U.S. intelligence officer working in the secretive arm of the State Department focusing on Russia was hacked. Russia is suspected of being behind the hack.

99. Yahoo reported that Trump lawyers knew about the e-mails between Donald Trump Jr. and Veselnitskaya three weeks ago, although Trump claimed he learned about them "a couple of days ago."

100. On Friday, CNN said there were at least eight people at the Donald Jr.–Veselnitskaya meeting.

101. On the Friday Fox News hand-off from Shepard Smith to Chris Wallace, Smith said "Why is it lie after lie after lie? . . . The deception, Chris, is mind-boggling . . . Where are we, and why are we getting told all these lies?" Wallace answered, "I don't know what to say."

102. Veselnitskaya told the *WSJ* that she had been meeting regularly and sharing information with Russian authorities and Russia's top prosecutor, Yuri Chaika—the "Crown prosecutor" referenced in Goldstone's e-mails to Donald Jr.

103. Amid a legal team shake-up, Trump hired Ty Cobb to become point person inside the White House for matters related to Russia, and Kushner lawyer Jamie Gorelick stepped away from representing him on Russia.

104. Maddow reported on a lawsuit filed by United to Protect Democracy on behalf of three citizens against Trump and Stone for their role in the public sharing of information hacked by the Russians. If it goes to trial, discovery could reveal information on how stolen info was disseminated.

105. Friday, a judge ordered a retrial of Desiree Fairooz, the Code Pink activist who was arrested after she laughed during Sessions's confirmation hearing.

106. Lawyers for the only known Dreamer to be deported filed supporting statements showing that ICE agents wrongly forced him across the border.

Week 36

JULY 16–22, 2017

This week Trump's ties to Russia came increasingly front and center, as news of a second clandestine meeting between Trump and Putin at the G20 summit surfaced and Trump moved forward with actions that seemed oddly pro-Moscow. Trump also caused alarm on both sides by raising the specter of firing Mueller and the possibility of pardoning himself and members of his regime.

For the first time, this week there was bipartisan reaction: there were resignations, and pushback from national security officials who called out Russia for election meddling. Also of major importance, Congress agreed on an outline for a bipartisan bill to impose sweeping sanctions on Russia—a direct repudiation of Trump.

1. According to an FEC filing, Trump's reelection campaign paid fifty thousand dollars to Donald Jr.'s attorney on June 27, six days after Kushner updated his security clearance form to include the meeting with Veselnitskaya.

2. *Wired* reported that according to FEC filings, the Trump reelection campaign has already paid out six hundred thousand dollars to Trump-owned properties.

3. Trump lawyer Jay Sekulow was the sole representative of the Trump regime on all five of the Sunday shows.

4. Sekulow suggested that the U.S. Secret Service would have vetted Donald Jr.'s meetings. The Secret Service issued a statement denying that they screened anyone: "Donald Trump, Jr. was not a protectee of the USSS in June, 2016."

5. The U.S. Women's Open, hosted at a Trump golf course, posted its lowest final-round rating in at least thirty years. Trump had tweeted about attending the event.

6. The *WSJ* reported that there were nearly 150,000 attempts to penetrate South Carolina's voter-registration system on Election Day, even though South Carolina was not a competitive state. So far, there is evidence that twenty-one states were targeted.

7. *Time* reported on a previously undisclosed fifteen-page plan produced by Obama's cybersecurity officials that shows how concerned the administration was about Russian hacking.

8. The concern was so grave that on November 1, the Obama administration did a war-game practice attack. Obama's NSC ran a fictional attack and rehearsed how federal agencies would communicate and respond.

9. *Time* reported concern over a California primary election in which some voters were prevented from voting because their registrations had been altered. Russia was suspected of the hacking.

10. A *WaPo*/ABC poll showed that Trump's approval rating has fallen to 36 percent, from 42 percent in April. His net approval fell from –11 to –22. Trump's support from independents has fallen to 32 percent.

11. A Monmouth poll found that 41 percent of Americans support impeaching Trump, significantly higher than Nixon at the start of Watergate (24 percent).

12. A PPP poll found that 45 percent of Americans support impeaching Trump and 43 percent are opposed.

13. CNN tracked highlights of Trump's first six months: he passed no major legislation, held just one press conference, sent 991 tweets, golfed 40 times, and spent 21 of 26 weekends at Trump properties.

14. Criticism of Kobach and the Election Integrity Commission continued from all sides as their first public meeting took place, with many calling it a veiled attempt at voter suppression and purging.

15. Kobach responded to MSNBC when asked if Hillary won the popular vote, "We will probably never know the answer to that question."

16. The *Daily Beast* reported that civilian casualties have skyrocketed under Trump from the U.S.-led war against ISIS. Trump's air war has already killed more than two thousand civilians.

17. CREW won a legal battle to compel Trump to turn over the Mar-a-Lago visitor logs by September 8. CREW said they will make the information available to the public, when and if they receive it.

18. Outgoing Office of Government Ethics chair Shaub told the *NYT* that actions by Trump and his regime have created a historic ethics crisis. On the world stage, this has rendered the U.S. "close to the laughingstock," and it "affects our credibility."

19. DHS announced a one-time increase of fifteen thousand H-2B visas, an increase of 45 percent from the amount normally issued in the second half of the fiscal year. The change came after lobbying by industries that rely on temporary foreign workers.

20. The AP reported that the Trump Organization has asked the federal government to grant dozens of special visas to allow foreign nationals to work at two of Trump's private clubs in Florida.

21. Of note, this occurred during Trump's Made in America week. Also of note, none of Ivanka's products are produced in the U.S.

22. In a vote along party lines, the Senate confirmed political blogger John Bush, Trump's most controversial nominee yet, to the federal court of appeals in Kentucky. Bush's blog posts disparage gays, women, and people of color, and contain conspiracy theories and false information.

23. Poland, the country chosen by Trump for a major speech en route to the G20 summit, may be stripped of EU voting rights in response to the right-wing government's plan to abolish the independence of the country's judiciary.

24. Former diplomats and national security officials urged Tillerson not to eliminate the State Department's Bureau of Population, Refugees and Migration (PRM), citing the "profound and negative implications" of doing so.

25. *Foreign Policy* reported that Tillerson is set to also shutter the State Department's War Crimes Office, the office that for two decades held war criminals accountable.

26. Christopher Painter, the top diplomat responsible for cybersecurity issues, will leave his State Department job at the end of the month. Painter has led the American delegations to international cybersecurity meetings since 2011.

27. The U.S. Treasury fined Exxon-Mobil two million dollars, saying the company showed "reckless disregard" for Russian sanctions while Tillerson was CEO.

28. House Republicans will seek to defund the Election Assistance Commission (EAC), the only federal agency that exclusively works to ensure the voting process is secure.

29. The defunding comes as the EAC is working with the FBI to examine an attack late last year on the agency's computer systems by a Russian hacker.

30. Manafort filed reports with the DoJ showing his firm received nearly seventeen million dollars for two years of work for a Ukrainian political party with links to the Kremlin—more than the party's operations reported spending.

31. The Manhattan district attorney's office subpoenaed Federal Savings Bank, a Chicago bank run by Steve Calk, for records on sixteen million dollars in loans made to Manafort in November and January. At the time, Manafort was underwater on loans for a Brooklyn townhouse and a family investment in California properties.

32. The loans to Manafort represent 24 percent of the bank's reported sixty million dollars of equity capital. Calk was a member of Trump's economic advisory panel and had expressed interest in becoming army secretary.

33. On Tuesday, Russian Deputy Foreign Minister Rybakov said the Russian government is "almost" at a deal to get their seized compounds returned.

34. On Tuesday, Trump again tweeted his demand that the Senate must change its rules to make repealing Obamacare easier.

35. In a memo sent to station news directors, Sinclair's vice president of news defended the company from charges of being biased. In Week 35, Sinclair mandated broadcast appearances by Trump ally Epshteyn.

36. Sessions said he would be issuing a new directive aimed at increasing police seizures of cash and property.

37. Senator Rand Paul called on Sessions to abandon the directive, tweeting, “Asset forfeiture is an unconstitutional taking of property without trial.”

38. After Republicans failed in their efforts to repeal and replace the ACA, and then failed again at repeal, Trump said Republicans should “let Obamacare fail,” adding, “I’m not going to own it.”

39. CNN reported that Trump aides could face scrutiny by Mueller over their role in strategizing with Trump to craft the initial statement issued by Donald Jr. as the *NYT* story broke about the June 9 meeting.

40. The AP reported that according to Akhmetshin, Veselnitskaya brought a plastic folder with printed-out documents thought to be damaging to Clinton to the meeting with Donald Jr., Kushner, and Manafort.

41. *WaPo* reported that the eighth person in the Donald Jr.-Veselnitskaya meeting was Irakly “Ike” Kaveladze, who attended as a representative of Aras and Emin Agalarov.

42. Kaveladze’s attorney said he had received a phone call over the weekend from a representative of Mueller, asking to set up an interview.

43. Kaveladze was once the focus of a Congressional money-laundering probe involving Russian oligarchs.

44. In an interview with Charlie Rose, political scientist Ian Bremmer said Trump and Putin had a second, hour-long private meeting on the sidelines of the G20 summit.

45. Trump’s White House was forced to confirm the meeting Tuesday, as reports surfaced that some guests had been surprised that it occurred.

46. Trump’s White House sought to minimize the disclosure, claiming in a statement that the private meeting was “just a brief conversation at the end of dinner.” Spicer said of the meeting, “It was pleasantries and small talk.”

47. The *Daily Beast* reported that after being sent a secret document by officials in Moscow in April 2016, GOP Representative Dana Rohrabacher, a long-time Russia advocate, aimed to alter the Magnitsky Act by holding up the act in committee.

48. Without stated rationale, Trump ended a covert CIA program to train and arm moderate Syrian rebels battling Assad, a victory for Russia.

49. The day after a shocking announcement that he had been diagnosed with brain cancer, John McCain issued a statement condemning Trump's action in Syria, saying it is "playing right into the hands of Vladimir Putin."

50. Reuters reported that Russia says it is in talks with the U.S. to create a cybersecurity working group.

51. Trump gave a bizarre, wide-ranging interview to the *NYT*, which made it apparent he believes he is accountable to no one and has full control over who occupies positions of power.

52. Trump said he would never have hired Sessions if he knew he would recuse himself from the Trump-Russia probe. Expectations for Sessions's resignation followed, but Sessions said he would stay on.

53. Trump started to diminish Deputy Attorney General Rosenstein for appointing a special prosecutor, saying, "There are very few Republicans in Baltimore, if any. So, he's from Baltimore."

54. On the topic of his private conversation with Putin at the G20 summit, Trump repeated Donald Jr.'s initial false claim: "We talked about Russian adoption. Yeah. I always found that interesting."

55. Trump also claimed he spoke to Putin because he was seated next to the first lady of Japan and didn't have a Japanese language interpreter. Videos surfaced of Akie Abe speaking fluent English.

56. Trump also opened the door to firing Mueller, saying the special prosecutor would cross a red line if investigations delve into Trump family finances unrelated to Russia.

57. Bloomberg reported that Mueller has expanded the probe into Trump's business ties to Russia, including Russian purchases of apartments in Trump buildings, Trump SoHo, the 2013 Miss Universe pageant in Moscow, and Trump's sale of a Florida mansion to a Russian oligarch.

58. Mueller's team is also absorbing the money-laundering probe of Manafort, started by federal prosecutors in New York.

59. The *WSJ* reported that the Senate and House Intelligence Committees are also investigating Manafort for possible money laundering. The Senate committee received reports by the Treasury Department's FinCEN unit, which tracks Russian ties.

60. Manafort has borrowed and spent tens of millions of dollars over the past decade to finance real estate purchases in New York and California.

61. The *NYT* reported that Deutsche Bank is under investigation by regulators for its lending relationship with Trump. The bank is also likely to have to provide information to Mueller as part of the Trump-Russia probe.

62. As noted in Week 19, Deutsche Bank recently paid a $630 million settlement over charges of laundering ten billion dollars for Russia from the bank's Moscow office.

63. In the past six years, Deutsche Bank's private wealth management unit financed three Trump deals, lending three hundred million dollars.

64. The bank's commercial real estate lending division, which would typically lend for such transactions, would not finance the deals. It is also highly unusual for a private wealth division to lend so much money, especially after the real-estate division says no.

65. The *NYT* also reported that Deutsche Bank was the referenced European financial institution that had partnered with Russia's Prevezon, the massive money-laundering tax fraud mentioned in Week 35.

66. Prevezon's case was settled by Sessions's DoJ two days before trial.

67. The AP reported that Trump's repeated overtures toward Russia are increasingly putting him at odds with his national security and foreign policy advisers. The second meeting with Putin at the G20 summit exacerbated the rift.

68. The AP reported that it was highly unusual for only Tillerson, but not McMaster, to have attended the meeting with Putin at the G20 summit. McMaster has been warning Trump that Putin is not to be trusted.

69. The legal team defending Trump in the Russia probe had a shake-up on Thursday, with longtime personal attorney Kasowitz leaving. Mark Corrallo, a spokesperson for Trump's legal team, also resigned.

70. Sean Spicer resigned Friday after Trump appointed New York financier Anthony Scaramucci to be White House communications director. Sarah Huckabee Sanders was named Spicer's replacement as press secretary.

71. Senators Ben Cardin and Elizabeth Warren have pushed for an investigation into whether Scaramucci's company, SkyBridge Capital, violated sanctions against Russia.

72. On Friday, following Spicer's resignation, Sanders held an on-camera press briefing, the first one since June 29 (a twenty-two-day span).

73. CIA director Pompeo, Homeland Security secretary Kelly, and White House Homeland and Counterterrorism adviser Bossert, breaking from Trump, said they believe Russia meddled in our election.

74. Reuters reported Veselnitskaya, the Russian lawyer who met with Donald Jr., had Russian spy agency FSB as a client.

75. After interviewing Susan Rice as part of the Senate Intelligence Committee, Republican chairman Burr commented, "The unmasking thing was all created by Devin Nunes."

76. Michael Flynn opened a new consulting firm, Resilient Patriot, LLC. Flynn's new firm will advise private equity firms.

77. Trump named a temporary director, David Apol, to replace Walter Shaub as head of the OGE as he seeks a permanent director. Watchdogs groups expressed concern that Trump bypassed Shaub's designated successor, Shelley Finlayson.

78. *WaPo* reported that some of Trump's lawyers are exploring ways to limit or undercut Mueller's Trump-Russia probe, building a case around alleged conflicts of interest of Mueller and his staff.

79. Sekulow said Mueller's investigation of Trump's business dealings, including transactions like a Russian oligarch's purchase of Trump's Palm Beach mansion, "is far outside the scope of a legitimate investigation."

80. *WaPo* also reported that Trump has asked his advisers about his power to pardon aides, family members, and himself.

81. Mark Warner, the top Democrat on the Senate Intelligence Committee, warned Trump that pardoning targets of the Russia probe would be "crossing a fundamental line."

82. Trump loyalist Newt Gingrich told Fox News Friday, "The Mueller investigation has so many conflicts of interest, it's almost an absurdity."

83. A *New Republic* op-ed titled "We're on the Brink of an Authoritarian Crisis" cited Trump's *NYT* interview, efforts to attack Mueller, and questions about issuing pardons as causes for concern.

84. *WaPo* reported that Kislyak told his superiors he discussed campaign-related matters, including policy issues important to Moscow, with Sessions. The conversations were intercepted by U.S. spy agencies.

85. In March, Sessions said he had never had meetings with Russian operatives or intermediaries about the Trump campaign. He also lied under oath during the Senate confirmation hearings about the meetings.

86. *WaPo* reported that Sessions had three meetings with Kislyak, including at his Senate office in September, at the Republican National Convention in July, and at the Mayflower Hotel in April.

87. Kushner agreed to testify in front of the Senate Intelligence Committee next Monday and the House Intelligence Committee on Tuesday.

88. Bypassing Tillerson and the State Department after a contentious meeting, Trump assigned a White House team of loyalists to review the Iran nuclear deal and give him the option to say Tehran was not in compliance.

89. *WaPo* reported late Friday that Kushner filed a revised financial disclosure form, showing he had failed to disclose dozens of financial holdings that he was required to declare when he joined the White House.

90. Of note, Kushner had failed to disclose a $285 million loan that his company received from Deutsche Bank one month before the election.

91. A separate form filed Friday showed that Ivanka has personally profited from her outside businesses by as much as five million dollars since Trump took office, despite a promise to distance herself from her private holdings.

92. Also late Friday, a deal between Donald Jr., Manafort, and the Senate Judiciary Committee was announced, in which the two will provide records and be interviewed in a closed-door session to avoid being subpoenaed.

93. On Saturday morning, starting at 6:30 A.M. EST, Trump sent a bizarre litany of tweets on topics ranging from his usual trashing of the media, Hillary, and Comey to the topic of pardons and Mueller.

94. Trump continued to tweet, despite a new ABC/*WaPo* poll that showed 67 percent of Americans disapprove of his using Twitter; 68 percent of those who disapprove say his tweets are inappropriate and half say his tweets are dangerous.

95. On Saturday, in a repudiation of Trump, Congress reached a deal on sweeping sanctions to punish Russia for election meddling. The legislation will limit Trump's ability to suspend or terminate sanctions.

Week 37

JULY 23–29, 2017

This was a week of complete disarray within the Trump regime: firings, resignations, withdrawals. Trump distracted and played to his remaining base all week by targeting marginalized groups and ramping up hateful rhetoric.

Also of note, and a continuation from Week 36: Republicans are turning on Trump—not just in words this week, but also in actions. And in response, by firing Priebus and replacing him with a general, Trump seems to be preparing for an aggressive approach toward the legislative branch.

1. On Sunday, Trump's communications director Anthony Scaramucci told *State of the Union* that Trump is still not sure if Russia interfered in our election. This, just after CIA director Pompeo, DNI Daniel Coats, and Joint Chiefs of Staff chair Joseph Dunford confirmed that Russia meddled (Week 36).

2. As Trump floated the idea of firing Robert Mueller, former CIA director Brennan said elected officials need to "stand up" if this happens.

3. After Trump said, "We'll let Obamacare fail," he has taken several steps to sabotage ACA.

4. Since taking office, Trump has spent nearly one in three days at a Trump property and one in five days at a Trump golf property.

5. CNBC reported that investors have dumped the majority of "Trump trades." Investors are no longer confident tax reform, deregulation, and fiscal stimulus will happen.

6. The *New Yorker* interviewed a veteran ICE agent who is disillusioned by Trump. He said agents are explicitly encouraged to pursue undocumented aliens as aggressively as possible, adding, "We're going to get sued."

7. The ICE agent also noted that agents no longer look at the "totality of the circumstances," and that it's not just the person being removed, but "their entire family."

8. Several people were arrested by ICE at the Houston INS office when they went for their marriage interviews for green cards.

9. Pew Research Center found that 75 percent of Muslim Americans believe there is a lot of discrimination against Muslims in the U.S., and 74 percent believe Trump is unfriendly toward them.

10. Thousands marched in Warsaw to protest their right-wing government's attempted control of the Supreme Court and judiciary. Trump chose Poland en route to the G20 summit to deliver a nationalistic speech (Week 34).

11. On Monday, Trump continued to signal the possibility of firing Jeff Sessions, referring to him in a tweet as "our beleaguered A.G."

12. Trump floated the idea of Rudy Giuliani as a replacement for Sessions. *WaPo* reported that replacing Sessions is viewed by some Trump associates as part of a possible strategy to fire Mueller.

13. Trump continued to target Sessions on Tuesday, tweeting that he "has taken a VERY weak position on Hillary Clinton crimes," and asking on a phone call with an associate, "What would happen if I fired Sessions?"

14. Trump continued attacking Sessions on Twitter Wednesday, questioning why he hadn't fired acting FBI director McCabe.

15. *WaPo* reported that Trump spoke privately with confidants and advisers about the possibility of replacing Sessions with a recess appointment.

16. Senator Chuck Grassley responded by tweeting that the agenda for the Senate Judiciary Committee is set for the rest of 2017, and the committee would not have time for an AG nomination. Democrats threatened to block recess appointments.

17. Breaking their typical silence, several Senate Republicans spoke out against Trump's treatment of their former colleague Sessions. Senator Pat Roberts of Kansas said, "It's very difficult, it's disconcerting, it's inexplicable."

18. Sessions told Fox News that Trump's attacks are "kind of hurtful," but that he intended to stay on and serve as long as Trump will let him.

19. In an op-ed, Sally Yates warned that Trump is trying to "dismantle the rule of law, destroy the time-honored independence" of the DoJ, and if we're not careful, "our justice system may be broken beyond recognition."

20. Yates cited as examples Trump's efforts to bully Sessions into resigning, his goading Sessions to reopen an investigation of a former political rival, and his efforts to get Comey to back off from Flynn before firing him.

21. The *NYT* reported that David Apol, Trump's choice to replace Shaub, has clashed with Office of Government Ethics employees over his efforts to roll back or loosen ethics requirements on federal employees, including those in the White House.

22. The Center for Public Integrity reported that Steve Bannon is potentially violating the Antideficiency Act by using an outside shadow press office not employed by the Trump regime and providing services for free.

23. In another blow to the credibility of Trump's Election Integrity Commission, a federal judge upheld a fine against Kobach, citing a "pattern" of "misleading the Court" in voter-ID cases.

24. A lawyer in West Palm Beach filed a lawsuit with a federal judge in Florida, saying Trump is violating the Constitution by making money from renting rooms in his hotels or other buildings to federal agencies.

25. According to Gallup, Trump's approval is underwater in eleven of the states he won in November, including North Carolina (–11), Michigan (–10), Wisconsin (–9), and Pennsylvania (–9).

26. Trump's Boy Scout Jamboree speech turned into a political rally, as Trump led the crowd to boo Hillary and Obama, chided the "fake news" and the Washington "cesspool," and promised to bring back Christmas.

27. The Boy Scouts of America faced a backlash after Trump's speech, which some compared to Hitler's. Former Scouts called for a public denouncement and called the speech "a disgrace."

28. Randall Stephenson, the national president of the Boy Scouts of America, is also CEO of AT&T, whose pending merger with Time Warner requires government approval. In Week 34, the Trump regime discussed using this pending merger as leverage over CNN's reporting and president.

29. The day after reporting on Stephenson's role as CEO of AT&T, the chief scout executive of the Boy Scouts of America issued an apology for anyone who may have been offended by Trump's speech.

30. After the State Department's cyber coordinator resigned (Week 36), Tillerson plans to shutter the State's Office for the Coordination of Cyber Issues.

31. The State Department's head of diplomatic security, Bill Miller, resigned. Miller is one of a long list of senior State Department officials who have resigned since Trump took office.

32. CNN reported that Tillerson is considering resigning, citing his frustration and doubt that "the tug-of-war" with the White House would subside. Tillerson is also upset about Trump's unprofessional treatment of Sessions.

33. Many of the State Department's typical responsibilities have been reassigned to the White House in a consolidation of power, including Kushner taking responsibility for Middle East diplomacy and, as noted in Week 36, the White House taking over Iran compliance certification.

34. On Tuesday, Tillerson said he would taking time off. The State Department refused to comment on whether he is happy.

35. Longtime NBC chief foreign affairs correspondent Andrea Mitchell criticized the lack of transparency from and access to Trump's State Department.

36. Speculation grew that McMaster may resign. *Politico* reported on a meeting on Afghan policy, described as a "s*** show." *Axios* reported that McMaster is frustrated by the "disorganization and indiscipline."

37. Scaramucci threatened mass firings, saying he will purge aides who are not loyal to Trump or who leak. The first victim of the purge was Assistant Press Secretary Michael Short, who is close to Priebus and Spicer.

38. Trump's nominee to lead the DoJ's criminal division, the attorney Brian Benczkowski, disclosed to Congress that he previously represented Alfa Bank, one of Russia's largest banks, whose owners have close ties to Putin.

39. The FBI is investigating data transmission between Alfa Bank and the Trump Organization's servers during the election, which may indicate back-channel communications.

40. Benczkowski took on representing Alfa Bank after serving as part of Trump's transition team. He continued despite reports of the FBI investigation (Week 21) until his nomination in June.

41. A complaint filed by the Treasury's Office of Foreign Asset Control alleges that Trump ally Rohrabacher violated the Magnitsky Act by trying to get Russia's deputy general prosecutor removed from the U.S. sanctions list.

42. Ahead of his closed-door testimony to the Senate Intelligence Committee, Kushner publicly released the full text of his statement given to the committee in which he denied participating in, or knowledge about, collusion with Russia.

43. After his Senate testimony, the White House set up a podium with the White House seal for Kushner to make a follow-up statement to the media.

44. Kushner stood at the podium and said, "I did not collude," adding that he did not know anyone in the campaign who did. He said his actions were "proper and occurred in the normal course of events of a very unique campaign."

45. About the June 9 Trump Tower meeting with Russians, Kushner claimed he was unaware of the promise of damaging information, despite the e-mail subject line: "Re: Russia—Clinton—private and confidential."

46. Kushner claimed he met with four Russians but did not discuss specific policies, including U.S. sanctions against Russia.

47. Kushner also said, "I have not relied on Russian funds for my businesses." "Relied" seemed a carefully chosen term for its possibility to obfuscate.

48. The *Guardian* reported that Kushner bought several floors of the old *New York Times* building from Lev Leviev, known as the "king of diamonds," for $295 million in 2015.

49. Kushner's recently disclosed $285 million loan from Deutsche Bank was used to refinance this deal. The purchase is part of Mueller's investigation of Trump-Russia ties.

50. Leviev also sold properties to Prevezon, the Russian company represented by Veselnitskaya: apartments at 20 Pine Street in New York City. The property was part of a money-laundering case.

51. The Prevezon money-laundering case, originally brought by Bharara for $230 million before he was fired, was settled by Sessions two days before trial for six million dollars. The 20 Pine Street apartments were also released.

52. *Mother Jones* reported that former senator Carl Levin sent a letter to Mueller about his 2000 investigation of Ike Kaveladze, whom he described as a "poster child" for Russian money laundering.

53. Levin said Kaveladze circulated more than $1.4 billion through U.S. bank accounts. Kaveladze was Aras Agalarov's representative at Donald Jr.'s June 9 Trump Tower meeting.

54. Ivanka hired a defense lawyer to represent her in the Russia investigation. Donald Jr. hired an additional lawyer with congressional experience to his legal team.

55. On Tuesday, Manafort testified in front of the Senate Intelligence Committee about the June 9 meeting at Trump Tower. He was also subpoenaed by the Senate Judiciary Committee.

56. On Tuesday, Kushner testified behind closed doors for the House Intelligence Committee. Democratic leader Adam Schiff said Kushner had agreed to come back.

57. On Thursday, Bill Browder, founder and CEO of Hermitage Capital Management, which was looted by Russian kleptocrats in a case that gave rise to the Magnitsky Act, testified in front of the Senate Judiciary Committee.

58. Browder testified that he believed there was more than one meeting between Veselnitskaya and Donald Jr., Kushner, and Manafort, and that Veselnitskaya's goal would be to repeal the Magnitsky Act.

59. Browder also testified that Russian intelligence knew about the June 9 meeting in advance, and that he believes Fusion GPS—the firm behind the Russian dossier to get dirt on Trump—was hired by the Russians.

60. On Tuesday, by a vote of 419–3, the House passed a Russian sanctions bill, punishing Russia for election interference and curbing Trump's power to roll back sanctions.

61. Russia warned of a "painful" response if Trump backed the sanction bill, calling it "anti-Russian hysteria."

62. The *Weekly Standard* reported that its interview with Vladimir Kara-Murza, a Russian journalist, politician, and filmmaker, started late because he was in the hospital being treated for poisoning, again.

63. *BuzzFeed* filed a lawsuit to compel the release of information about the death of Putin's former media czar, Mikhail Lesin, who was brutally murdered in D.C. the night before a planned meeting with the DoJ in November 2015.

64. The Senate passed a motion to proceed on a health care vote, with no input, no debate, no CBO score, and with no knowledge of what they would be voting on once the motion passed. Thirteen percent of Americans support Obamacare repeal.

65. The vote was 50–50, with Pence casting the tie-breaking vote. After the passage, uncharacteristic chants erupted on the Senate floor of "Kill the bill" and "Shame, shame, shame."

66. Ahead of the vote, reporters were blocked from the Senate halls, where protesters were being arrested. Reporters were told, "No photos. Delete your photos."

67. A hot mic in the Senate captured a conversation between Senators Jack Reed and Susan Collins, with Reed saying of Trump, "I think—I think he's crazy," and Collins responding, "I'm worried."

68. Trump's actions have galvanized many who care about health care, climate change, and research funding to run for office. A PAC called 314 ACT (named for the number pi) was set up to recruit and assist scientists to run.

69. At a rally in Ohio, Trump said he could act more presidential than any other president except "the late, great Abraham Lincoln." He also joked that he should be on Mount Rushmore.

70. Trump also told a graphic tale about illegal immigrants slicing up beautiful teenage girls with knives: "They don't want to use guns because it's too fast and it's not painful enough." The story is a lie.

71. *WaPo* reported that between the Ohio rally and the Boy Scout Jamboree speech, Trump made twenty-nine false or misleading statements.

72. Trump tweeted that the U.S. government would "will not accept or allow . . . Transgender individuals to serve in any capacity in the U.S. Military."

73. The Pentagon was not informed of Trump's announcement ahead of time and was left scrambling with no plan in place for implementation, including how to deal with transgender individuals now serving.

74. The House and Senate Armed Services Committees were also not notified. The committees were awaiting results from a six-month review of potential impact ordered by Mattis in Week 33.

75. The day after Trump's tweet, the chair of the Joint Chiefs of Staff announced that the military policy on who is allowed to serve would not change until the White House sends DoD new rules and the secretary of defense issues new guidelines.

76. Secretary Mattis was on vacation when Trump tweeted. According to the *NYT*, he was given only one day's notice of the decision, and according to people close to him, was appalled that Trump used Twitter for the announcement.

77. Even Republicans spoke out against Trump's plan to ban transgender individuals. Conservative senator Orrin Hatch said, "Transgender people are people, and deserve the best we can do for them."

78. Trump's candidate for a senior position at the DHS, John Fluharty, withdrew from consideration because of Trump's transgender ban.

79. In a second attack on the LGBTQ community, Sessions's DoJ filed a brief saying that Title VII of the Civil Rights Act of 1964 does not cover employment discrimination "based on sexual orientation."

80. Representative Blake Farenthold said of "some female senators from the Northeast" who were against an Obamacare repeal, if they were a guy from south Texas, "I might ask him to step outside and settle this Aaron Burr style."

81. Wednesday, Trump chastised Senator Lisa Murkowski, tweeting she had let the Republicans and country down by not voting to repeal Obamacare.

82. Later that afternoon, Interior Secretary Ryan Zinke called both of Alaska's senators, saying Murkowski's vote would impact the Trump administration's view on issues that are a priority for Alaska.

83. Of note, all during the week, Republican men insulted and threatened their female colleagues for not supporting their health care bills. Male senators not in support did not face the same harassment.

84. On Thursday, Senator Lindsey Graham said that "there will be holy hell to pay" if Trump fires Sessions, and said if Trump fires Mueller without good reason, it would be "the beginning of the end" of Trump's presidency.

85. Later that day, Graham and Booker said they will introduce a bipartisan bill next week that will limit Trump's ability to fire Mueller.

86. On Wednesday night, Scaramucci accused Priebus of leaking his financial disclosure information and said he would be contacting the FBI. Shortly after *Politico* indicated that the information is public, he deleted the tweet.

87. Scaramucci gave an interview to the *New Yorker* Thursday, saying of his colleagues, "Reince is a fucking paranoid schizophrenic, a paranoiac," and "I'm not Steve Bannon, I'm not trying to suck my own cock."

88. Scaramucci also threatened leakers, saying, "What I want to do is I want to fucking kill all the leakers."

89. Later that evening, Scaramucci tried to shift the blame to the reporter, tweeting, "I made a mistake in trusting in a reporter," but Ryan Lizza shot back saying he had a recording of the call, which was "100% on the record."

90. On Thursday, the Senate passed a new sanction bill by a 98–2 vote, which would sharply limit Trump's ability to suspend or lift sanctions on Russia. With House and Senate passage, the bill now goes to Trump.

91. On Friday, Russia retaliated, expelling a large number of U.S. diplomats and seizing U.S. diplomatic properties.

92. Late Friday, the White House announced that Trump plans to sign the bill.

93. In a speech to police Friday on Long Island addressing the gang MS-13, Trump encouraged officers to be rough with suspects: "When you guys put somebody in the car and you're protecting their head . . . you can take the hand away, okay?"

94. Trump also used the speech to encourage Congress to find money to pay for ten thousand more ICE officers "so that we can eliminate MS-13."

95. After the speech, the Suffolk County Police Department tweeted, "As a department, we do not and will not tolerate roughing up of prisoners."

96. Later that evening, a second police department, in Gainesville, Florida, also rejected Trump's remarks, stating, "The @POTUS made remarks today that endorsed and condoned police brutality. GOP rejects these remarks."

97. The International Association of Chiefs of Police issued a statement Friday night countering Trump, saying officers are trained to treat all individuals "with dignity and respect."

98. After all other versions of Senate health care bills failed, late Friday, the Senate voted on the "Skinny Repeal." An eight-page copy of the bill was provided to Democrats at 10 P.M., ahead of a midnight vote.

99. The night prior, GOP senators Ron Johnson, Lindsey Graham, and Bill Cassidy announced they would vote for the "Skinny Repeal" only if House Republicans assured them it would never become law. Still the vote proceeded.

100. Ahead of the vote, Senator Mike Enzi filibustered the Senate floor for an hour. Democrats tried to interrupt and ask questions. Enzi told Senator Patty Murray, "Perhaps your time might be better spent taking a look at the bill."

101. At 1:30 A.M. Saturday, after over an hour spent by Pence and other Republicans to change Senator McCain's mind, the Skinny Repeal bill was voted down 49–51: Collins, Murkowski, and McCain voted with Democrats.

102. After the failed vote, at 2:25 A.M., Trump tweeted, "let ObamaCare implode, then deal. Watch!"

103. Trump also again pushed for the Republicans to end the legislative filibuster, a longtime norm in the Senate, so all bills can pass with fifty-one votes.

104. Trump unceremoniously fired Priebus as chief of staff, informing press and staff shortly after Air Force One landed in D.C. The *WSJ* reported that part of Trump's rationale was that Priebus did not retaliate at Scaramucci.

105. Priebus served the shortest time of any chief of staff in a president's first term since World War II.

106. The *WSJ* editorial board excoriated Trump over the Priebus firing, writing that "this shuffling of the staff furniture won't matter unless Mr. Trump accepts that the White House problem isn't Mr. Priebus. It's him."

107. *WaPo* tracked the Trump regime's unusually long list of firings, resignations, and withdrawals from consideration. Trump also has far fewer appointed and confirmed candidates for key executive roles than previous presidents at this time.

108. Trump appointed General John Kelly, current secretary of DHS, to the role of chief of staff. Kelly has little political or legislative experience. One Priebus ally said the next phase of the Trump presidency will be warfare against the GOP Congress.

109. On Saturday morning, Trump tweeted attacks at Republicans, saying they "look like fools" and that Democrats "are laughing at R's."

110. Trump also commanded Republicans to change norms: "Republican Senate must get rid of 60 vote NOW!" and he threatened if health care did not pass, he would end "BAILOUTS for Insurance Companies and BAILOUTS for Members of Congress."

Week 38

JULY 30–AUGUST 5, 2017

This week, as his popularity hit new lows, Trump and his regime's white nationalist push became more conspicuous and aggressive. Trump continues to irreverently lie—one such false statement, on Donald Jr.'s June 9 meeting, could directly implicate him in covering up the Russia scandal, which entered a new phase as Mueller impaneled a grand jury in Washington, D.C.

As a continuation of a theme over the past two weeks, the Republicans are finally pushing back on Trump, as Congress took steps to keep him in check. Trump seems prepared to fight Congress, along with battles he is already waging against the judicial branch and the media.

1. In a Fox News interview, Kellyanne Conway advised White House staffers not to address Trump by his first name and to treat him with "deference and humility."

2. On his Sunday show, Fareed Zakaria cautioned that with Trump in power, the U.S. faces something worse than being feared or derided—the U.S. is "becoming irrelevant."

3. On Sunday, Putin ordered the U.S. diplomatic missions in Russia to reduce their staff by 755 personnel, the single largest forced reduction, comparable only to the reduction in months after the Communist revolution in 1917.

4. The Trump regime had no response to Putin's order on Sunday, or for the entire week.

5. *ProPublica* reported that Customs and Border Protection is set to jump-start Trump's wall in a Texas national wildlife refuge. The agency will use money allotted by Congress for other purposes.

6. A spokesperson for Pruitt's EPA told *WaPo* the agency will make changes to the EPA Museum. For example, the exhibit on Obama's Clean Power Plan will be removed, and an exhibit on coal may be added.

7. CBN News reported that nearly all of Trump's cabinet officials attend Bible lessons with a pastor who compares Trump to biblical heroes.

8. In a statement released Tuesday, fifty-six retired generals and admirals came out against Trump's transgender military ban, arguing that it would be disruptive and degrade military readiness.

9. CBC News reported that Montreal's Olympic Stadium is being used to house a surge in asylum seekers crossing from the U.S. More than one thousand crossed from the U.S. into Quebec in July alone.

10. The National Association for the Advancement of Colored People (NAACP) issued its first-ever travel advisory for a U.S. state. NAACP cited Missouri legislation making discrimination cases harder to win, recent racist incidents, and racial disparities in traffic enforcement.

11. Kobach appealed an order requiring him to answer questions under oath about two documents containing plans for changes to U.S. election law.

12. A top EPA official, Elizabeth Sutherland, resigned after thirty years at the agency. In a scathing letter, she wrote, "The environmental field is suffering from the temporary triumph of myth over truth."

13. The Trump regime will redirect resources of the DoJ toward investigating and suing universities over affirmative action admissions policies, which the regime claims discriminate against white applicants.

14. *ProPublica* reported that Candice Jackson, DeVos's pick to head the Education Department's Civil Rights Office, said she faced discrimination for being white while at Stanford because of a calculus class help section reserved for minority students.

15. *WaPo* reported that Lizandro Claros Saravia, a standout soccer player who had a scholarship to play college soccer, was deported to El Salvador along with his brother after going to ICE to report that he got into college.

16. Documents released to the *Daily Beast* under the FOIA show high-level DHS officials ordered staff to stiff-arm members of Congress and treat lawyers with deep suspicion in the first hours of Trump's Muslim ban.

17. In an ICE press release, the agency admitted that in Kelly's final sweep as DHS head, designed to catch Central Americans who had come to the U.S. as family unit, 70 percent of those captured were not people being targeted.

18. Tillerson's State Department is considering eliminating the promotion of democracy from its mission statement.

19. Amateur hackers at the Def Con conference in Las Vegas were able to exploit vulnerabilities in five voting machine types within twenty-four hours.

20. *Politico* reported that by firing Priebus, Trump severed one of his few remaining ties to the Republican Party.

21. In a bombshell story, *WaPo* reported that Trump dictated Donald Jr.'s misleading statement claiming that Russian adoption was the rationale for the June 9 meeting, while flying back from the G20 summit.

22. While Trump was at the G20 summit, the *NYT* asked for comment on its pending story. Ivanka, Trump, and Kushner met on the sidelines with advisers, who recommended telling the truth. Trump disregarded all advice.

23. *WaPo* further reported that Kushner's lawyers first learned about the June 9 e-mail trail while researching their response to congressional investigators weeks earlier. Advisers and lawyers for Trump, Donald Jr., and Kushner had mapped out a strategy for disclosing the information.

24. *WaPo* further reported that with this misleading statement, Trump is now directly implicated in trying to cover up the Russia scandal.

25. The day after reports that Trump crafted Donald Jr.'s statement, CBS reported that congressional investigators requested Donald Jr.'s phone records around the time of the June 9 meeting.

26. Trump ally and former sheriff Joe Arpaio was found guilty of criminal contempt of court for defying a court order to stop detaining suspected undocumented immigrants.

27. *Phoenix New Times* reported that Arpaio was a no-show for his presentencing hearing on Thursday.

28. Ahead of his first cabinet meeting with Kelly as chief of staff, Trump referred to the Cabinet Room as a "boardroom."

29. Secretary of the Interior Zinke told *GQ* in an interview that Rick Perry didn't understand what his position is about: "I think he thought his department was more about energy than . . . science. Mostly, it's science."

30. *WaPo* reported that lobbyists are taking credit in the Trump era for writing bills to protect their industry that are passed in Congress with minimal input from the public and little or no discussion in Congress.

31. The *NYT* reported that Lewandowski has a new "advisory" business, and is taking on clients who may have interests that could be served by the Trump administration. Lewandowski is a frequent visitor to the White House.

32. *WaPo* reported that the Secret Service vacated its command post inside Trump Tower following a dispute over terms of the lease for the space. The post has been relocated to a trailer on the sidewalk.

33. Six months after leaving the Indiana governor's office, Pence handed over state-related e-mails transmitted from his personal AOL account. Some requests for Pence's e-mails are more than a year old.

34. Pence's attorney, also a top fund-raiser for Trump and Pence, determined which e-mails to release, raising concerns from watchdog groups.

35. A U.S. Court of Appeals ruled that seventeen states and D.C. could intervene against the Trump regime for its efforts to sabotage Obamacare.

36. Ivanka said, "We are committed to supporting the American worker," even as 100 percent of her companies' goods are manufactured overseas and the Trump Organization and Eric's winery seek to bring in foreign workers.

37. The *WSJ* reported that the U.S. attorney for the Southern District of New York issued subpoenas to Kushner Companies. Employees and Kushner family members have allegedly been offering green cards in exchange for five-hundred-thousand-dollar investments in their properties.

38. Kelly asserted his authority as chief of staff on Monday, firing Scaramucci immediately.

39. Kelly's first priority will be to gain control of the information that reaches Trump, with a goal of cutting out back channels and bad information.

40. Kelly reportedly called Sessions to tell him his job is safe.

41. CNN reported that Kelly was so upset about the handling of Comey's firing, Kelly called Comey afterward and said he was considering resigning.

42. On Tuesday, bowing to criticism on transparency, Tillerson held his first press briefing, saying he is not "very happy" with Congress's vote to sanction Russia.

43. Tillerson acknowledged the understaffed State Department: twenty-two of twenty-four assistant secretary slots are either unfilled or staffed by Obama holdovers.

44. On Tuesday, Greg Andres, a former DoJ official, became the sixteenth member of Mueller's team. Andres has vast experience with white-collar crime, including fraud and illegal foreign bribery.

45. On Tuesday, a story on Golf.com recounted a scene at Trump's Bedminster golf club, in which he tells members the reason he stays away from Washington is because the White House is a "real dump."

46. On Wednesday, Trump tweeted, "I love the White House, one of the most beautiful buildings (homes) I have ever seen," and referred to Golf.com as "Fake News."

47. On Thursday, Golf.com responded with a podcast about the story, saying at least eight people heard Trump call the White House a dump.

48. At a tense July 19 meeting with generals, Trump complained about the options in Afghanistan, saying, "We are losing." Trump also compared U.S. efforts to the renovation of the 21 Club, infuriating the generals.

49. Trump complained the U.S. wasn't getting a piece of Afghanistan's mineral wealth and said he was considering firing General John Nicholson.

50. As Kelly established an organizational structure, McMaster fired two Bannon loyalists from the NSC: Rich Higgins and Ezra Cohen-Watnick.

51. As the turf battle heated up between McMaster and Bannon, rumors circulated that Trump may send McMaster off to Afghanistan to replace Nicholson.

52. On Thursday, McMaster cleared Susan Rice after it was reported that she was responsible for unmasking members of Trump's team in intelligence reports, and said she will keep her top-secret security clearance. *Circa* reported that Trump was not aware of McMaster's decision.

53. Conservative media turned on McMaster, calling him a "sycophant" and "deeply hostile to Israel and Trump." A new app that tracks Russian troll activity also found "firemcmaster" as the most tweeted item.

54. NPR reported on a lawsuit that alleges that Fox News and Ed Butowsky, a wealthy Trump supporter, with the knowledge of the White House, created a fake story about murdered DNC staffer Seth Rich leaking DNC e-mails to WikiLeaks to help Trump deflect from Russian involvement.

55. The story started May 10, the day after the Comey firing. A few days later, Butowsky texted Rod Wheeler, the expert suing for being inaccurately cited in the story, that Trump "wants the article out immediately."

56. ABC reported that Spicer met with two Fox News contributors at the White House about the Seth Rich story and asked to be "kept abreast of developments."

57. Yahoo reported that the lawyer who is suing Fox News on behalf of Wheeler will seek to depose Trump and Spicer.

58. Reporter Andrew Feinberg, who worked at Sputnik, said he was pushed to cover the Seth Rich story: "It's really telling that the White House is pushing the same narrative as a state-run Russian propaganda outlet."

59. *Newsweek* reported that Russia is using LinkedIn to target critics by damaging their reputations and chances for employment, and possibly exposing them to physical harm beyond social media.

60. On Wednesday, flanked by Senators Cotton and Perdue, Trump introduced a bill to slash immigration levels in half over the next decade.

61. Trump said the bill, named the RAISE Act, will favor green card applicants who speak English, financially support themselves, and contribute to the economy.

62. AP fact-checked Trump's speech and found it was full of false statements.

63. The bill was sharply rebuked by Democrats and Republicans. Catholic bishops issued a strong statement against RAISE, saying it will weaken family bonds and impact the country's ability to respond to those in crisis.

64. At a contentious press briefing after the RAISE Act announcement, Stephen Miller said the 1883 "huddled masses" poem inscribed at the base of the Statue of Liberty doesn't matter since it was "added later."

65. Miller also acted aggressively toward *NYT* and CNN reporters. Miller said CNN's Jim Acosta, son of Cuban immigrants who did not speak English, had a "cosmopolitan bias."

66. "Cosmopolitan" is an anti-Semitic term used by twentieth-century authoritarian regimes.

67. The Anne Frank Center tweeted that Nazis found Anne Frank on August 4, 1944, after her family was denied entrance to the U.S. in 1941, for "reasons refugees hear now."

68. Trump told the *WSJ* that the head of the Boy Scouts called him to say his jamboree speech was "the greatest speech that was ever made to them." The Boy Scouts denied that any call from national leadership was made.

69. Trump also told the *WSJ* that Mexican president Peña Nieto called him and told him fewer people were crossing the border. This is also a lie.

70. White House press secretary Sanders revised Trump's statements to say an individual Boy Scout leader called Trump, and the statement from Peña Nieto took place in a conversation at the G20 summit.

71. On Wednesday Trump signed the Russia sanctions bill, behind closed doors and with no press coverage. Trump criticized Congress but said nothing of Russian election interference or the 755 U.S. embassy employees expelled from Russia.

72. In a statement, Trump called the measure "significantly flawed." Trump also said it "encroaches on the executive branch's authority to negotiate," adding, "I built a truly great company worth many billions of dollars."

73. On Thursday, Trump again attacked Congress, tweeting, "Our relationship with Russia is at an all-time & very dangerous low," and you can thank "the same people that can't even give us HCare!"

74. McCain responded, "You can thank Putin for attacking our democracy, invading neighbors & threatening our allies" for the dangerous low.

75. Russia's prime minister, Dmitry Medvedev, said the Trump regime "has demonstrated full impotence." He also tweeted that the Trump regime has shown its "total weakness" in handing power to Congress "in the most humiliating way."

76. On Wednesday, Trump's approval dropped to new lows: Rasmussen (38 percent approve), Gallup (36 percent approve, 60 percent disapprove), and Quinnipiac (33 percent approve, 61 percent disapprove). Trump used to cite Rasmussen as his favorite poll when his approval there reached the high fifties.

77. Quinnipiac also found that 54 percent of American voters say that they are embarrassed to have Trump as a leader.

78. On Thursday, two bipartisan pairs of senators (Lindsey Graham/Cory Booker, Thom Tillis/Christopher Coons) introduced legislation to block Trump from firing Mueller without good reason.

79. *BuzzFeed* reported that the RNC has instructed staff not to delete or modify any documents related to last year's campaign, given "the potentially expansive scope of the inquiries and investigations."

80. The *WSJ* reported that Mueller impaneled a grand jury in Washington to investigate Russia's interference in the 2016 election, a sign his inquiry is growing in intensity. Trump's special counsel, Ty Cobb, was not aware.

81. A grand jury is already impaneled in Alexandria, Virginia, to investigate Flynn. The second grand jury and recent hires show that the investigation has entered a new phase. The location gives Mueller's team easy proximity.

82. Reuters reported that grand jury subpoenas have been issued in connection to the June 9 meeting between Donald Jr., Veselnitskaya, and others.

83. On Thursday, Trump held a campaign rally in West Virginia in which he called the Russia investigation a "hoax," and presided over cheers of "Lock her up!" as he called for an investigation into Hillary's deleted e-mails.

84. Also of note at the rally, the supporters standing behind Trump as he spoke, a group typically carefully selected by staffers, were 100 percent white.

85. As the Senate adjourned for the summer, *WaPo* reported that this is a historically unproductive period of governance, as Republicans had no major legislative achievements despite controlling Congress and the White House.

86. The Senate unanimously agreed to a "pro forma" session before leaving for break, meaning Trump cannot make recess appointments. Senator Lisa Murkowski, attacked by Trump in Week 37, did the Senate wrap-up.

87. The Interior Department's Office of the Inspector General launched a preliminary investigation of Zinke's threats to the Alaska senators in an apparent effort to sway Murkowski to vote for the Obamacare repeal.

88. NBC reported that SCL Group, a private British behavioral research company related to Cambridge Analytica, was awarded several contracts by the State Department.

89. On its website, SCL Group advertised "our methodology has been approved by" followed by the State Department and NATO logos. After NBC's report, NATO and the State Department asked that their logos be removed.

90. The AP reported that Flynn will file an amended public financial filing to show he entered into a consulting agreement with SCL Group, a subsidiary of Cambridge Analytica.

91. Cambridge Analytica is funded by Trump allies the Mercer family, who, as noted in Week 26, are under investigation for possible interference in both Brexit and the 2016 U.S. election.

92. Flynn's amended filing will also include twenty-eight thousand dollars from the Trump transition team and five thousand dollars for working as a consultant for an aborted Middle East nuclear power deal. As noted in Week 32, that Middle East deal was a venture with Russia.

93. CNN reported that one year into the FBI's Russia investigation, now headed by Mueller, the probe has expanded to focus on possible financial crimes, some of which are not connected to the 2016 elections.

94. Investigators are looking into whether financial laws were broken by Trump and his associates, and whether Trump's business dealings could put members of the regime in a compromising position with Russia.

95. Further, the FBI noticed a spate of curious communications between the Trump campaign and Russian intelligence in the summer of 2016, including contact with Manafort about information damaging to Hillary.

96. CNN also reported that Page has been under a FISA warrant since 2014.

97. *Vox* reported that at least ten senior intelligence officials, including Comey and McCabe, are likely to be interviewed as part of Mueller's obstruction of justice investigation.

98. *WaPo* released the transcripts of Trump's phone calls with Mexican president Peña Nieto and Australian prime minister Turnbull during Trump's first week in office.

99. When Peña Nieto said Mexico would not pay for the wall, Trump responded, "You cannot say that to the press," acknowledging that talk about the wall was more about image management than economic policy.

100. Trump told Peña Nieto he won New Hampshire (a lie) because the state "is a drug-infested den."

101. Despite Trump claiming early on that reports of him berating Turnbull on the call were "fake news," the transcript does confirm this. Trump told Turnbull he had had a more pleasant call earlier with Putin.

102. Trump balked at taking refugees from Australia, as required in a deal struck by Obama, saying he hates taking these people and they could "become the Boston bomber in five years."

103. As Trump departed for a three-week vacation at his golf course in Bedminster, *GQ* labeled him "the laziest president in American history."

104. Likewise, the cover of *Newsweek* referred to Trump as "Lazy Boy" and pictured him in a chair watching television and eating junk food. The accompanying article refers to him as "America's boy king."

105. Staffers of Republicans on the House Intelligence Committee traveled to London to track down Steele, author of the dossier. *Politico* reported growing tensions as Democrats on the House and Senate Intelligence Committees, and Mueller, were not notified.

106. In a press conference Friday, Sessions threatened that the DoJ may prosecute journalists over suspected leaks. Sessions also said he is reviewing the DoJ's policies affecting media subpoenas.

107. The *NYT* reported that Mueller made his first formal request to the White House to hand over documents. Mueller seeks information on the financial dealing of Flynn related his company's work for Turkey.

108. Flynn was paid $530,000 by Inovo BV, owned by Ekim Alptekin. Investigators want to know if the Turkish government was behind the payments, and if Flynn Intel Group made kickbacks to Alptekin for concealing the source of the money.

109. Flynn's now third version of financial disclosure forms list $1.8 million in income, four hundred thousand dollars more than in his prior forms.

110. Failing to register as a foreign agent is a felony, and trying to hide a source of money by routing it through a private company, and using kickbacks to a middleman, could lead to criminal charges.

Week 39

AUGUST 6-12, 2017

Despite Congress being out of session and Trump on vacation, this was one of the most alarming weeks so far. Without provocation, Trump made aggressive statements toward three countries and escalated the possibility of nuclear war with North Korea. The country continued to burn in hate as violence surrounding a white supremacist rally in Charlottesville led to a state of emergency in Virginia.

Other troubling trends continued this week, including an increase of media controlled by Trump and his allies, an unstaffed and unprepared executive branch, and steps taken to suppress the vote in future elections. Even with his new chief of staff, it is apparent Trump is consolidating power and answering to no one. He is also stepping up his attacks on the legislative branch.

1. On Sunday, reminiscent of authoritarian propaganda, Trump launched the first broadcast of "real" Trump TV on his Facebook page featuring Kayleigh McEnany, formerly a commentator on CNN.

2. On Monday, the RNC named McEnany to be its national spokesperson, meaning she will get paid by the RNC for her Trump TV work.

3. Lara Trump will run Trump TV as part of her job with consulting group Giles-Parscale. As noted in Week 31, Brad Parscale has been called by congressional investigators to testify on his role in the Trump campaign and Russia.

4. Trump's FCC chair, Ajit Pai, revived a regulatory loophole allowing Sinclair Broadcasting to vastly exceed federal limits on media ownership. When a pending deal closes, Sinclair will reach 72 percent of U.S. households.

5. *Vox* analyzed seventeen months of *Fox & Friends* transcripts and found a symbiotic relationship between Trump and the show. Since the election, data reveals the show's primary goal is to talk to Trump, not its audience.

6. On *Fox News Sunday*, Rosenstein said he has not been directed by Trump to investigate Hillary's e-mail, as suggested by Trump. Rosenstein added, "That wouldn't be right. That's not the way we operate."

7. Rosenstein also dismissed the idea that the Russia probe is a "total fabrication"—the reference by Trump. He also said Mueller can investigate any crimes he discovers within the scope of his probe.

8. Conway suggested White House staffers may be required to take lie detector tests as part of the regime's efforts to find leakers.

9. *WaPo*'s editorial board wrote that Trump's DoJ is joining the GOP's crusade to suppress voting, citing an Ohio case of culling voters that will be argued before the Supreme Court. The Obama administration found this behavior unlawful; Trump's does not.

10. The Indiana chapter of the NAACP and Priorities USA are suing the state over a law that results in closing voting precincts in black and Latino areas.

11. A *WaPo* survey found that 52 percent of Republicans believe Trump won the popular vote and would support postponing the 2020 election to make sure that only eligible American citizens could vote if Trump proposed it.

12. The AP reported that Ivy League schools are bracing for scrutiny from the Trump regime for their efforts to make their campuses diverse.

13. A bomb was tossed through the window of a mosque in Bloomington, Minnesota. Minnesota's governor declared the bombing "an act of terrorism."

14. Trump did not acknowledge the bombing. Tuesday, Gorka said the White House would "wait and see" in case the blast turned out to be a hoax. By week's end, Trump still had no comment.

15. On Wednesday, Trump tweeted out a Fox News story about a vehicle ramming into soldiers in France, which the news agency insinuated, without having evidence yet, was carried out by Islamic terrorists.

16. The NAACP Legal Defense Fund will appeal a federal judge's ruling allowing a white Alabama town to secede from a racially mixed county school district and start its own system.

17. CNN fired conservative pundit Jeffrey Lord after he tweeted the Nazi salute, "Sieg Heil!" at a prominent liberal activist.

18. A study by the Kaiser Family Foundation found Trump's moves to undermine Obamacare have already triggered double-digit premium increases on individual health insurance policies in many states.

19. The *NYT* reported that government scientists are concerned that a report by scientists from thirteen federal agencies, which finds a drastic impact of climate change in the U.S., will be suppressed by Trump.

20. In a series of e-mails obtained by the *Guardian*, the Trump regime advised staff at the Department of Agriculture (USDA) not to use certain terms like "climate change" and "climate change adaptation."

21. Karina Brown, an Asian American woman who attended a Bon Jovi concert in Columbus, Ohio, was told by a fellow concertgoer, "You don't belong in this country."

22. Five transgender troops sued Trump over his tweet to instate a transgender military ban.

23. The Canadian military is building a refugee camp in Saint-Bernard-de-Lacolle, near Plattsburgh, New York, to house up to five hundred U.S. asylum seekers. This is in addition to the shelter at Montreal Olympic Stadium noted in Week 38.

24. CNN reported that Sam Clovis, Trump's nominee to be chief scientist at the USDA, had on his conservative radio show stoked the birther conspiracy, called former attorney general Eric Holder a "a racist black," and called former secretary of labor Tom Perez "a racist Latino."

25. More than seventy-five consumer, health, and other advocacy groups came together to stop the Trump regime from stripping nursing home residents and their families of rights to take facilities to court over alleged abuse or neglect.

26. As the Trump Organization tweeted about the launch of the Trump Estates and Golf Club in Dubai, concerns continued to surface about ways U.S. foreign policy has been impacted by the Trump family's investments.

27. *WaPo* reported on how the Trump International Hotel in D.C. has become a center of influence, where members of industry and others seeking access meet with Trump regime members. And Trump financially benefits.

28. The D.C. hotel turned a two-million-dollar profit for the first four months of 2017, far exceeding the Trump Organization's projected loss of $2.1 million. Driving profits were sky-high room prices and spending on food and beverages.

29. The *WSJ* reported that Trump International Hotel's average daily room rate was $660, compared with $496 for comparable hotels. The room rates are 60 percent higher than predicted in the hotel's original budget.

30. The eighteen Democrats on the House Oversight Committee sent letters to fifteen cabinet departments and nine executive branch agencies requesting information on their spending at Trump Organization businesses.

31. *Politico* reported that Trump's slow pace in filling vacancies at the Federal Energy Regulatory Commission (FERC) has caused thirteen billion dollars' worth of infrastructure projects, expected to create twenty-three thousand new jobs, to be indefinitely delayed.

32. The *NYT* and *ProPublica* continued to track Trump appointees put in charge of dismantling government regulations. Eighty-five appointees have been identified, many with industry or legal ties, or other conflicts of interest.

33. A U.S. District Court judge in New York will hear arguments in the Trump foreign emoluments lawsuit starting on October 18.

34. According to a letter to the Senate, the OGE has rejected retroactive waivers for the Trump regime.

35. Trump ally Robert Mercer donated three hundred thousand dollars to Senator Jeff Flake's Republican primary challenger after Flake spoke out against Trump. Among other benefits, the Mercers' hedge fund has avoided $6.8 billion of back taxes under Trump.

36. The AP reported that Trump companies applied for a casino trademark in Macau, the world's largest gambling market. Past applications by Trump had been rejected. Trump had pledged that his companies would pursue no new foreign deals while in office.

37. Two top aides for UN ambassador Nikki Haley—her chief of staff and communications director—resigned. Haley said on Twitter it was because of "family concerns."

38. Four top cybersecurity officials resigned from their posts, including the chief information security officer for the EPA and the chief information officer for the DHS, both of whom had been in their jobs for just a few months.

39. *Fortune* reported that vegetable prices may be going up soon: Trump's immigration policies have led to a farmworker shortage, and crops are rotting in the fields.

40. The *Toronto Star* reported that Trump has made five hundred false claims in his first two hundred days in office.

41. A CNN poll taken at two hundred days found that just 24 percent of Americans trust most of what they hear from the White House.

42. In another sign of Trump's waning popularity, Democrat Phil Miller won a special election by ten points in an Iowa district Trump had won by twenty-two points in 2016.

43. The AP reported that Pence has been quietly carving out his own political footprint, noting that Republicans privately admit Trump could be the first president since Nixon to leave office or not to seek reelection.

44. After Senator Richard Blumenthal appeared on CNN to discuss the Russia probe, Trump attacked him on Twitter for two days, calling him a "phony Vietnam con artist," and saying he "should take a nice long vacation in Vietnam."

45. Trump tweeted, "Thank you Nicole!" to the account @ProTrump45. The account, under the name Nicole Mincey, was deleted and appears to have been a bot, part of the Russia-backed disinformation campaign.

46. *Vice* reported that since taking office, Trump receives a folder full of positive news about himself twice a day. Some in the White House refer to the folder as "the propaganda document."

47. Bloomberg reported that Manafort and Donald Jr. turned over thousands of documents in August to the Senate Judiciary Committee in the Russia probe.

48. Bloomberg also reported that Fusion GPS, a company linked to the dossier, and its CEO have yet to turn over requested documents. Senate Judiciary Committee chair Grassley wants to know if Russians paid for the dossier.

49. *Page Six* reported that Trump's story about a renovation at the 21 Club, which Trump told the generals while berating them about losing in Afghanistan (Week 38), was "completely wrong in every detail."

50. On Wednesday, *WaPo* reported that the FBI conducted a predawn raid on Manafort's home in Alexandria, Virginia, seizing documents and other materials related to Mueller's Russia probe.

51. The raid occurred on July 26, the day Manafort was scheduled to testify before the Senate Judiciary Committee and a day after he met with the Senate Intelligence Committee.

52. The FBI search warrant was for documents relating to tax, banking, and other matters. Sources said the FBI agents left with a "trove of material."

53. ABC reported that Manafort was awoken in the predawn hours by a group of armed FBI agents knocking on his bedroom door.

54. On July 26 Trump had called for Sessions to replace acting FBI director McCabe. Also, that morning he inexplicably tweeted his transgender military ban without notifying the DoD or having a strategy in place.

55. Bloomberg reported that Manafort alerted congressional investigators about the June 9 Trump Tower meeting three months ago.

56. Trump ally the *National Enquirer* posted a story, "Trump Advisor Sex Scandal—Paul Manafort's Sick Affair," shortly after the *WaPo* article hit.

57. *Politico* reported that federal investigators sought cooperation from Jeffrey Yohai, Manafort's son-in-law, early in the summer, in an effort to increase pressure on Manafort.

58. On Thursday, Manafort fired WilmerHale and switched to Miller and Chevalier, a boutique firm in Washington that specializes in complicated financial crimes.

59. A story in the *New Yorker* noted that with Manafort's sophistication and links to Russia oligarchs, he was in a good position to "understand what Vladimir Putin wanted from the Trump campaign."

60. ABC reported that congressional investigators want to question Rhona Graff, Trump's assistant for thirty years, on the e-mail exchange and meeting at Trump Tower on June 9 with Russians.

61. The Senate Judiciary Committee asked the White House to respond to questions about changes to Kushner's security clearance forms related to undisclosed meetings with Russians. The deadline to reply was July 6.

62. On Tuesday afternoon, *WaPo* reported that analysis by the Defense Intelligence Agency (DIA) concluded that North Korea has passed the key threshold of producing missile-ready nuclear weapons.

63. Later Tuesday, from his golf course in Bedminster, Trump warned North Korea against threatening U.S. cities, saying threats "will be met with fire and fury like the world has never seen."

64. Late Tuesday, in reaction to Trump's "red line" of N. Korea threatening U.S. cities, Kim Jong-un's regime said it may strike Guam.

65. Trump's "fire and fury" comments broke the Dow's ten-day winning streak.

66. Trump's comments were condemned by Democrats, Republicans, and nuclear weapons experts, who said his incendiary rhetoric would make things worse.

67. The *Toronto Star* reported on the numerous times Trump has used varieties of the hyperbolic phrase "like the world has never seen" to make a point, including while a businessman and running for office.

68. Wednesday, the *NYT* reported that Trump's "fire and fury" threat to North Korea was improvised. The sheet of paper in front of him was about the opioid crisis, and he ad-libbed without input from his team on wording.

69. As the North Korea crisis unfolds, Trump has yet to appoint an ambassador to South Korea. As noted in Week 38, twenty-two of twenty-four assistant secretary positions in the State Department are either unfilled or staffed by Obama holdovers.

70. Senator Blumenthal told MSNBC that the Senate Armed Services Committee has been informed as North Koreans moved from milestone to milestone, indicating Trump also should have known of their progress and not been alarmist.

71. A thirty-foot inflatable chicken with Trump-like hair floated next to the White House on Wednesday. The balloon was set up by documentary filmmaker Taran Singh Brar to protest Trump's "being a weak and ineffective leader."

72. *Foreign Policy* reported that a seven-page memo written by NSC staffer Rich Higgins about the "Deep State" targeting Trump is thought to be behind the recent NSC shake-up, including McMaster's firing Higgins.

73. On Thursday, Trump escalated the rhetoric on North Korea further, saying his "fire and fury" comment may not have been "tough enough." Asked how he could have been tougher, Trump replied, "You'll see. You'll see."

74. Shortly after, flanked by Pence and McMaster in Bedminster, Trump conducted a twenty-minute lie-ridden press conference. A historian said Trump's bizarre outpouring was as if "he was a dam that had suddenly burst free."

75. Trump called it a "disgrace" that the Senate didn't pass a bill to repeal and replace Obamacare, placing blame on McConnell and saying he wants him to get back to work and get it done.

76. Trump also twice tweeted about McConnell's failure to repeal and replace Obamacare, and retweeted a *Fox & Friends* story Friday saying Trump was leaving the door open on whether McConnell should step down.

77. On the other hand, Trump said he was "very thankful" to Putin for expelling hundreds of U.S. diplomats "because now we have a smaller payroll." This is a false statement: those diplomats remain on the payroll.

78. Reuters reported that the State Department was "horrified and rattled" by Trump's remarks on expelling diplomats. The third-ranking State member under George W. Bush called the remarks "grotesque."

79. Also at the press conference, Trump, seemingly impromptu, declared opioids a federal emergency: "I'm saying officially, right now, it is an emergency."

80. Also, on the transgender military ban, Trump said, "I think I'm doing the military a great favor"; and on the transgender community, "I think I have great support . . . I got a lot of votes."

81. On Kim Jong-un, Trump said, "He got away with it for a long time . . . He's not getting away with it. This is a whole new ball game." He added, "And nobody, including North Korea, is going to be threatening us with anything."

82. Also at the press conference, Trump said, "I don't think Iran is in compliance" on the 2015 deal to curtail nuclear weapons.

83. Trump also said there was "no collusion between us and Russia. In fact, the opposite. Russia spent a lot of money on fighting me."

84. Gordon Humphrey, a former GOP senator, suggested Congress should use the Twenty-fifth Amendment to remove Trump from office, saying of Trump, "He is sick of mind, impetuous, arrogant, belligerent and dangerous."

85. Tillerson sought calm on North Korea, saying Wednesday that "Americans should sleep well at night." Gorka told BBC radio, "The idea that Secretary Tillerson is going to discuss military matters is simply nonsensical."

86. On Friday, Trump escalated tensions further, tweeting that the U.S. military is "locked and loaded" should North Korea "act unwisely."

87. As tensions rose, U.S. allies and adversaries urged caution. German prime minister Merkel said, "Verbal escalation will not contribute to a resolution," and Russian foreign minister Lavrov said Trump's rhetoric was "over the top."

88. In a phone call Friday night, China's President Xi Jinping also urged Trump to exercise restraint, according to Chinese state media.

89. As tensions heightened with North Korea, former defense secretary Leon Panetta told CNN that "we're dealing with probably the most serious crisis involving a potential nuclear war since the Cuban missile crisis."

90. In Hawaii, emergency management officials are working on reinstating alarm sirens, last used during the Cold War, to warn of a nuclear attack.

91. On Friday evening, Trump spoke to reporters with Tillerson, McMaster, and Haley by his side. Speculation was that this was to assure Americans that diplomacy was also being used with North Korea.

92. Instead, Trump escalated the rhetoric yet again, saying Kim "will not get away with" what he's doing, and if he attacks Guam, or any other American territory or ally, "he will truly regret it and he will regret it fast."

93. When asked about Venezuela, Trump said we have many options, "including a possible military option if necessary."

94. His threat played into Venezuelan president Nicolás Maduro's hands. Venezuelan officials have long said the U.S. is planning an invasion. Maduro requested a phone call with Trump on Friday, which was rejected.

95. A DoD spokesperson said Friday evening that the U.S. is not planning to invade Venezuela, and "any insinuations by the Maduro regime that we are planning an invasion are baseless."

96. Trump called the governor of Guam Friday night to reassure him of U.S. protection. He also joked that Governor Eddie Calvo has become "extremely famous," and offered, "Your tourism [is] going to go up like tenfold."

97. On Friday night, hundreds of white supremacists marched on the University of Virginia's campus in Charlottesville in a "Unite the Right" rally, carrying torches and chanting, "White lives matter," "You will not replace us," and "Jew will not replace us."

98. On Saturday morning, the Charlottesville marchers carried Confederate flags and flags with Nazi swastikas. Militia groups carrying guns also attended.

99. Violent clashes between white supremacists and protesters broke out. Local police declared a state of emergency.

100. Later Saturday, the Virginia governor declared a state of emergency in response to the white nationalist rally. White supremacists were ordered to vacate the park before the rally.

101. Trump addressed Charlottesville hours later, but failed to condemn white supremacists, many of whom were wearing Trump gear, instead tweeting, "We ALL must be united & condemn all that hate stands for."

Peter Cvjetanovic (center) along with neo-Nazis, alt-righters, and white supremacists encircle and chant at counterprotesters at the base of a Thomas Jefferson statue after marching through the University of Virginia campus with torches in Charlottesville, Virginia, on August 11, 2017. (Getty Images)

Week 40

AUGUST 13–19, 2017

This week's list is not the longest, but it is certainly the most heartbreaking. Trump's comments on Charlottesville legitimized the ugliest side of America and spawned a watershed moment for our country. His remarks were met with widespread condemnation and precipitated a mass exodus of corporate CEOs from Trump's American Manufacturing Council, wiping away any lingering doubts that Trump's goals were ever truly linked to job creation. For the first time, real questions about fitness for office were raised out loud by both sides.

This week in Trump's shrinking, chaotic regime it became even clearer that Trump answers to no one but himself. He attacked and attempted to intimidate Republicans as part of his continuing effort to consolidate power.

1. In an impromptu news conference on Charlottesville late Saturday afternoon, Trump said, "We condemn in the strongest possible terms this egregious display of hatred, bigotry, and violence on many sides."

2. White supremacists and neo-Nazi leaders cheered Trump's "on many sides" comment, taking his words as a defense, or even as a tacit approval, of their action.

3. On Sunday, the White House issued a statement to "clarify" Trump's Saturday comments, saying Trump condemns all forms of "violence, bigotry, and hatred" while naming white supremacists, the KKK, and neo-Nazis.

4. Thirty-two-year-old Heather Heyer was killed Saturday after a car driven by James Fields rammed into a crowd of counterprotesters in Charlottesville. Nineteen others were injured.

5. The *Daily Caller* and Fox News deleted a post titled "Here's a Reel of Cars Plowing Through Protesters Trying to Block the Road," which included a video encouraging people to drive through protests.

6. Two state troopers, Lieutenant Jay Cullen and Trooper Berke Bates, who were keeping watch on the demonstrations in Charlottesville, were killed when their helicopter went down.

7. On Sunday, a candlelight vigil planned for Heather Heyer in Charlottesville was canceled because of a "credible threat from white supremacists."

8. Neo-Nazis disparaged Heyer, and the KKK celebrated her death. Neo-Nazi website the *Daily Stormer* was taken down after activists, inspired by my Sunday tweet, contacted domain hosts including GoDaddy and Google.

9. After U.S. hosting companies refused to host the *Daily Stormer*, the website briefly relocated to Russia, for which they thanked Trump, before being kicked off there, too. China also rebuffed them.

10. In the wake of Charlottesville, numerous tech companies, including Facebook, Google, Spotify, Uber, and Squarespace, took action to curb use of their services and platforms by alt-right groups.

11. A Unite the Right organizer was disavowed by his family. Several marchers who were identified on social media lost their jobs. Others were asked to denounce their activities or were expelled by colleges.

12. On Sunday, Trump's popularity hit a new low at Gallup, with 34 percent approving and 61 percent disapproving (–27).

13. On Monday, Jeff Sessions said the car ramming into Heather Heyer and nineteen others "does meet the definition of domestic terrorism" under U.S. law.

14. On Monday morning, Merck's CEO resigned from Trump's American Manufacturing Council, saying that as a "matter of personal conscience, I feel a responsibility to take a stand against intolerance and extremism."

15. Later Monday, Trump tweeted that @Merck is a leader in "higher & higher drug prices" and "taking jobs out of the U.S."

16. Later Monday and Tuesday, four more CEOs resigned from Trump's American Manufacturing Council over his handling of Charlottesville.

17. Trump countered, "I have many to take their place. Grandstanders should not have gone on." Trump offered no new names publicly.

18. On Wednesday, the *NYT* reported that the CEOs in Trump's Strategic and Policy Forum held a morning conference call to discuss whether to disband the policy group. The Manufacturing Council planned a call that afternoon.

19. Before the policy forum and the manufacturing council could formally disband, at midday Wednesday Trump tweeted that "rather than putting pressure on the businesspeople," he was ending both.

20. On Thursday, the White House announced that the Presidential Advisory Council on Infrastructure, which was still being formed, would not move forward.

21. On Monday, Trump said he is "seriously considering" a pardon for ex-sheriff Joe Arpaio, saying, "He's a great American patriot."

22. In the aftermath of Charlottesville, the Phoenix mayor called on Trump to delay his planned rally next week, saying Trump's plan to pardon Arpaio could "enflame emotions and further divide our nation."

23. Minutes after the Phoenix mayor's statement, Trump tweeted a link for tickets to his Phoenix event.

24. Advocates said there has been a spike in reports of anti-LGBTQ violence since Trump took office. As of August, there are already more hate-related homicides than in all of 2016, excluding the Pulse nightclub shooting.

25. A Virginia high school sent a letter to parents saying that selection for AP and Honors classes would be at least partly based on race.

26. On Monday, the New England Holocaust Memorial in Boston was vandalized for the second time this summer.

27. On Monday, reading from a teleprompter, Trump gave his third version of comments on Charlottesville, calling the KKK, neo-Nazis, and white supremacists "repugnant" and saying, "racism is evil."

28. On Tuesday morning, Trump tweeted, then deleted, an image of a train running over a CNN reporter.

29. On Tuesday at Trump Tower, with Mnuchin, Chao, and Cohn by his side, Trump turned what were supposed to be remarks about his infrastructure plan into an "off-the-rails" news conference on Charlottesville.

30. Reversing himself for the fourth time in four days, Trump said, "I think there's blame on both sides"—insinuating that the "alt-left" was just as much to blame as white supremacists and neo-Nazis.

31. Trump claimed not all the white supremacists and neo-Nazis were bad people, "you also had people that were very fine people, on both sides."

32. When asked about Bannon, Trump said, "He's a good man. He's not a racist," and that the press treats him, "frankly, very unfairly."

33. Trump claimed alt-right protesters had a permit, but counterprotesters "came charging in without a permit" and "were very, very violent." *WaPo* gave the claim that counterprotesters had no permit four Pinocchios.

34. Trump equated taking down the statue of Robert E. Lee in Charlottesville to taking down statues of Washington ("George Washington was a slave owner") and Jefferson ("because he was a major slave owner").

35. Trump's staff, expecting brief remarks on infrastructure, were stunned by his action. One senior White House official told NBC that Trump "went rogue."

36. *Politico* reported that Trump was "in good spirits" Tuesday night and felt the "news conference went much better" than his Monday speech.

37. Alt-right leaders praised Trump's Tuesday comments. Richard Spencer said he was "really proud of him," and David Duke tweeted, "Thank you President Trump for your honesty & courage to tell the truth."

38. *Axios* reported that within the Trump White House, Bannon unapologetically supported Trump's instinct to blame "both sides," and that he and Trump "instinctively searched for 'their' people in that group of protesters."

39. Mnuchin's Yale classmates wrote an open letter calling on him to resign immediately, saying Trump "declared himself a sympathizer with groups" whose values are antithetical to Yale and decent human beings.

40. In a Republican primary in Alabama Tuesday, Trump's chosen candidate, Luther Strange, whom he very publicly supported, came in second.

41. On Wednesday, Pence cut his international trip to Central and South America short to come home. The stated reason was to join a national security meeting on Friday, although rumors flew with other theories.

42. On Wednesday, Fox News's Shep Smith said his show had "reached out to Republicans of all stripes across the country today" and couldn't find a single one willing to come on to discuss Trump's Tuesday comments.

43. In a letter, former CIA director Brennan told CNN's Wolf Blitzer that Trump's comments on Charlottesville were "despicable" and that Trump "is putting our national security and our collective futures at grave risk."

44. On Wednesday, the heads of the army, navy, air force, marines, and National Guard tweeted to condemn the racist violence in Charlottesville, declaring that the nation's armed forces stand unequivocally against hatred.

45. Senator Bob Corker, one of Trump's first Senate supporters, who had been under consideration for vice president, said Trump "has not yet been able to demonstrate the stability nor some of the competence" to be a successful leader.

46. European leaders, including Merkel and May, denounced Trump's comments on Charlottesville. Martin Schulz, leader of Germany's Social Democratic party, said Trump "is betraying our Western values."

47. Representative Steve Cohen of Tennessee, a ranking member of the House Judiciary Subcommittee on the Constitution and Civil Justice, introduced articles of impeachment in response to Trump's comments on Charlottesville.

48. On Wednesday, Sessions told NBC News that the Charlottesville car attack may be considered a "hate crime."

49. The *USA Today* editorial board called on Congress to censure Trump for his "shocking equivocations about the white-supremacist mayhem in Charlottesville," challenging Republicans to "stand up for American values" or be Trump enablers.

50. On Thursday, the Cleveland Clinic pulled its 2018 Florida gala from Mar-a-Lago. Cleveland Clinic had held its event there for eight years.

51. By Friday evening, sixteen charities had pulled their events from Mar-a-Lago, costing the Trump Organization hundreds of thousands, or possibly millions, in lost revenues.

52. Citing violence at Charlottesville, Texas A&M and the University of Florida canceled scheduled speaking appearances by white supremacist Richard Spencer, both citing safety concerns.

53. On Thursday, Michigan State University denied a request by Spencer to rent space on the campus for a September event.

54. Students and graduates of Lehigh University petitioned trustees to revoke Trump's honorary degree, citing Trump's "both sides" remarks.

55. Thousands gathered at UVA on Wednesday night for an unannounced candlelight vigil. They chanted, "Love wins," and sang "We Shall Overcome" and "Amazing Grace."

56. At a funeral for Heather Heyer, her mother, Susan Bro, said, "They tried to kill my child to shut her up. Well, guess what? You just magnified her." Bro told NBC Thursday that she has received death threats from hate groups.

57. Bro said she will not meet with Trump after he blamed "both sides" for violence in Charlottesville. She also has not answered his phone calls.

58. Trump continued to tweet about Confederate statues after his news conference: "can't change history, but you can learn from it. Robert E Lee, Stonewall Jackson—who's next, Washington, Jefferson? So foolish!"

59. The great-great grandchildren of Robert E. Lee, Jefferson Davis, and Stonewall Jackson called for Confederate statues to be removed. They also condemned the white supremacist violence in Charlottesville.

60. They also suggested statues be moved to museums. Bertram Hayes-Davis, great-great-grandson of Jefferson Davis, suggested, "In a public place, if it is offensive and people are taking issue with it, let's move it."

61. In the days following the Charlottesville alt-right rally, thirteen U.S. cities and Duke University said they would remove Confederate monuments. Several other cities are considering the same.

62. After a terrorist attack in Spain, Trump tweeted about what General Pershing did in the Philippines in 1911 when terrorists were caught: "There was no more Radical Islamic Terror for 35 years!" PolitiFact rated Trump's claim "Pants on Fire."

63. Trump continued to do battle with Republicans, targeting Flake, whom he called "toxic" and "WEAK on borders, crime and a non-factor in Senate," and Graham, whom he said "can't forget his election trouncing."

64. Countering Trump, McConnell offered his "full support" for Flake.

65. James Murdoch, son of Trump ally Rupert Murdoch, the owner of Fox News, donated one million dollars to the Anti-Defamation League in the wake of Charlottesville. As many on social media noted, Fox News played a major role in stoking the hate of far-right extremists.

66. According to government documents published by one of Murdoch's newspapers Tuesday, Australian authorities denied a bid by Trump to build a casino in 1988 due to his ties to the Mafia and organized crime.

67. The *Huffington Post* reported on Trump aide (and Sebastian Gorka's wife) Katharine Gorka's role in helping to pull DHS funding from Life After Hate, a group dedicated to countering neo-Nazis and white supremacists, as noted in Week 33. Of note: also in Week 33, the State Department's anti-Semitism monitoring office was shuttered.

68. In an interview Thursday, former vice president Al Gore said if he could give Trump one piece of advice, it would be to resign.

69. On Friday, the seventeen remaining members of Trump's presidential arts and humanities panel resigned in protest over his Charlottesville comments.

70. Trump's White House responded late Friday, saying Trump was going to disband the arts and humanities panel anyway.

71. Trump and Melania said they will not attend this year's Kennedy Center Honors in December. According to Sanders, the decision is meant to allow "honorees to celebrate without any political distraction."

72. The decision was made after numerous honorees announced their intentions to skip or protest if Trump attended. After Trump's cancellation, event organizers said, "We are grateful for this gesture."

73. NBC called this week Trump's "worst week yet," and said he was more isolated than ever.

74. Hope Hicks took over as the interim White House communications director, as Trump continued his search to replace Scaramucci. Hicks is the fourth person in that role.

75. Trump's personal lawyer John Dowd forwarded an e-mail containing secessionist Civil War propaganda. The e-mail also stated that the group Black Lives Matter "has been totally infiltrated by terrorist groups."

76. Trump's DoJ issued a warrant to DreamHost, demanding the company turn over all IP addresses related to DisruptJ20.org, a website used in planning actions to interrupt Trump's inauguration.

77. A week after the inauguration, the DoJ had asked for information such as people's physical and e-mail addresses, and DreamHost had complied. DreamHost's lawyers called the latest request a "complete overreach."

78. The *NYT* reported that Mueller, for the first time, is seeking to interview past and current members of Trump's White House beyond Manafort, including members of the communications team.

79. Mueller is interested in interviewing Priebus about what occurred during the campaign and in the White House, especially as it relates to the June 2016 Trump Tower meeting and the Comey firing.

80. During a press conference on his visit to Colombia, Pence told reporters that he "never witnessed" any evidence of Russian collusion with the Trump campaign and that he was "not aware" of it ever having occurred.

81. *WaPo* reported that Trump aide George Papadopoulos, starting in March 2016 with an e-mail headed "Meeting with Russian Leadership—Including Putin," repeatedly tried to get Trump aides to meet with Russians.

82. Experts on Russian intelligence speculated that his e-mail chain offers further evidence that Russians were looking for entry points into the Trump campaign. Papadopoulos said he was acting as a Russian intermediary.

83. The *NYT* reported on an investigation by Ukrainian investigators and the FBI of a Ukrainian malware expert named "Profexer," for his part in a network of hackers allegedly engaged by Russia to hack the U.S. election.

84. Also under investigation is a Russian government hacking group, Advanced Persistent Threat 28, or Fancy Bear, believed to be involved in the DNC hacking. Much of the hacking work was outsourced to private vendors.

85. In the first known hitch, Mueller's team lost a top FBI investigator, Peter Strzok. It is unclear why Strzok stepped away.

86. A U.S. District Court judge ruled that as part of a libel suit brought by Webzilla CEO Aleksej Gubarev against *BuzzFeed*, Steele could be questioned about the funding and sourcing of the dossier.

87. Representative Dana Rohrabacher, an advocate for the Kremlin, said he plans to brief Trump on his meeting with Assange. Assange told Rohrabacher that he was not behind the DNC hack and that the Russians were not involved.

88. Assange is trying to strike a deal so he can stop living in asylum at the Ecuadorian embassy in London. In Week 23, Sessions said the DoJ was preparing charges against Assange, whose "arrest is a priority."

89. The National Parks Service reversed a ban on plastic water bottles at national parks. The move came after confirmation of Trump's deputy interior

secretary, a former lobbyist who previously represented Deer Park, the bottled-water brand.

90. In a tweet, the Trump Organization featured a photo with the caption "From our Presidential Ballroom to intimate historic rooms," to advertise meeting and event space.

91. Raising ethical concerns, Justice Neil Gorsuch is scheduled to address conservative groups at the Trump International Hotel in D.C. in September, less than two weeks before the court will hear arguments on Trump's Muslim ban.

92. Mattis's Department of Defense parted ways with senior media adviser Steve Warren. Pentagon reporters have complained about lack of access to Mattis, and some were recently kicked off Mattis's Middle East trip at the last minute.

93. On Friday, Trump friend and ally Carl Icahn resigned as a special adviser to Trump, although Icahn had done nothing in that role. The White House said on Monday that Icahn had been fired.

94. Icahn resigned hours before the *New Yorker* published a piece on his conflicts of interest (see Week 20). The head of a watchdog group said, "This kind of self-enrichment and influence" was "unprecedented."

95. Trump tweeted photos from Camp David of him signing the Global War on Terrorism War Memorial Act. Of the fourteen people at the signing, there was only one woman and not a single person of color.

96. In an interview with the *American Prospect* on Wednesday, a venting Bannon referred to white supremacists as "clowns" and "losers."

97. Contradicting Trump, Bannon said of North Korea, "There's no military solution here, they got us," and added, "It's just a sideshow."

98. In new interviews, Bannon said he viewed the post-Charlottesville racial strife and turmoil as a political winner for Trump.

99. On Friday, Trump fired Bannon. According to Bannon allies, he submitted his intention to leave the White House on August 7.

100. *Axios* reported that Bannon met with the billionaire Mercer family for five hours Friday in New York, saying that "together they will be a well-funded force on the outside."

101. Bannon told Bloomberg that he would be returning to run *Breitbart* and that he would be "going to war for Trump against his opponents—on Capitol Hill, in the media, and in corporate America."

102. Bannon told the *Weekly Standard*, "The Trump presidency that we fought for, and won, is over," saying Trump will not achieve his campaign promises. Bannon vowed to continue the fight from the outside.

103. In a *NYT* op-ed titled "I Voted for Trump. And I Sorely Regret It," past avid supporter Julius Krein wrote of his disillusionment with Trump and the realization that Trump would not achieve his stated goals.

104. Right-wing radio host Rush Limbaugh backed white nationalists and told his twenty-six million listeners that America is on the "cusp of a second civil war," blaming international financiers who are trying to bring down America.

105. On Saturday, Boston hosted a free speech rally organized by conservatives and libertarians at Boston Commons. Friday, Mayor Marty Walsh said five hundred police officers would be there, and urged people to stay away.

106. Thousands of counterprotesters marched through downtown Boston to condemn white supremacists and neo-Nazis. Police estimated more than forty thousand counterprotesters peacefully marched against roughly forty rally participants.

Week 41

AUGUST 20–26, 2017

Week 41 is full of content about Trump-Russia and signs that the Mueller probe is closing in on Trump and his regime. News stories indicate that despite Trump's public indifference and belittlement of the probe, he is privately consumed by it and acting in ways that could well be construed as, and lead to charges for, obstruction of justice.

In the two weeks since Charlottesville, our country is consumed in flames of hate, and Trump is fanning those flames. As well, he continues his unimpeded march to authoritarian power, neutralizing the judicial branch with an unethical pardon and attacking members of his own party in an effort to silence them. So far, the latter is largely working, and as this week comes to a close, remaining checks and balances to save our democracy are eroding and Trump appears to feel fully in power.

1. Following the counterprotest march of over forty thousand in Boston, Trump tweeted the country needs "to heel." Trump used the misspelled word four times in two consecutive deleted tweets, before correcting it to "heal."

2. Reverend A. R. Bernard, pastor of a megachurch in Brooklyn, became the first member of Trump's Evangelical Advisory Board to resign over Charlottesville.

3. No White House officials were made available for Sunday political talk shows.

4. Sunday on CNN, Carl Bernstein urged reporters to interview Republicans on or off the record about whether Trump is mentally fit to lead.

5. An NBC News/Marist poll found that Trump's approval in three key battleground states has eroded: in Michigan, 36 percent approve and 55 percent disapprove; in Pennsylvania, the ratio is 35–54; and in Wisconsin it is 34–56.

6. NPR reported that some Liberty University graduates are returning their diplomas to protest school President Jerry Falwell Jr.'s ongoing support of Trump, which continued even after Trump's remarks on Charlottesville.

7. Former HHS secretaries from both parties urged Republicans to move quickly to stabilize Obamacare as Trump threatened to continue withholding key payments to insurers.

8. Sunday night, when asked by reporters for his reaction to five sailors injured and ten missing after the USS *John S. McCain* collided with a merchant ship, Trump responded, "That's too bad."

9. *USA Today* reported that Secret Service agents have already hit the federally mandated pay caps meant to last the entire year for protecting Trump. Under the Trump regime, an unprecedented forty-two people have protection.

10. The Secret Service cited Trump's frequent weekend trips to his properties and his family's extensive business and vacation travel. The Secret Service spent sixty thousand dollars on golf carts, revenues that go to the Trump Organization.

11. Trump disbanded a federal advisory panel for the National Climate Assessment, which helped policymakers and private-sector officials incorporate the government's climate analysis into long-term planning.

12. Since being established in 1990, the National Climate Assessment is supposed to release reports every four years. The next assessment would have been due in 2018.

13. Trump's Interior Department ordered the National Academy of Sciences to halt its study of health risks and harm caused by mountaintop-removal coal mining in Appalachia.

14. The *New Yorker* reported on the dismantling of HUD under a thoroughly uninformed secretary, Ben Carson. There are still no nominees for major parts of HUD, including the Federal Housing Administration and many other agencies.

15. Carson's team removed online training materials meant to help homeless shelters provide equal access to transgender people and pulled back a survey focused on projects in Houston and Cincinnati to reduce LGBT homelessness.

16. The Interior Department's Office of the Inspector General confirmed in a letter that it is investigating Secretary Zinke's pressure on Senator Murkowski to vote yes on the Obamacare repeal.

17. An ABC News/*WaPo* poll found that 9 percent of Americans say it's acceptable to hold neo-Nazi or white supremacist views. This meshes with the 10 percent who say they support the alt-right movement.

18. The Anne Frank Center tweeted in alarm, "1 in 10 adults in U.S. say neo-Nazi views acceptable—22 million Americans. Evil epidemic of hatred."

19. The poll also found that three in ten Trump supporters accept or are indifferent to white supremacists.

20. Singer Billy Joel wore a Star of David during the encore of his sold-out show in New York City.

21. Brandeis University was closed and evacuated Wednesday after the school received a bomb threat.

22. The *Huffington Post* reported a spike in anti-Semitism in the two weeks since Charlottesville. ADL provided a list of more than two dozen incidents involving swastikas, broken glass, and neo-Nazi propaganda.

23. A coalition of major rabbinical groups canceled their annual High Holidays call with the president, saying Trump's "words have given succor to those who advocate anti-Semitism."

24. The UN Committee on the Elimination of Racial Discrimination urged the U.S. government to reject racial hatred and violence. The statement was released online after Trump's mixed messages on Charlottesville.

25. The Girl Scouts' CEO wrote a letter to families, providing resources to talk to girls about what they are hearing in the news and about hate and violence, adding that lying about what really happened can "undermine her trust."

26. Twenty organizations have pulled their charity events from Mar-a-Lago in response to Trump's comments on Charlottesville.

27. Daniel Kammer, the State Department science envoy, resigned in an open letter, citing Trump's "attacks on core values of the United States." The first letters of the seven paragraphs spell the word "IMPEACH."

28. On his radio show, Trump's nominee for Department of Agriculture, Sam Clovis, said that "LGBT behavior" is a choice and that legalizing gay marriage could lead to the legalization of pedophilia.

29. Liz MacKean, the BBC journalist who broke the news of the torture of gay men in Russia, died of a stroke at the age of fifty-two.

30. Trump signaled he is likely to end DACA, the Obama program that allows young people who came to the U.S. illegally as children to remain here. As many as one million immigrants could be affected.

31. The DHS announced it will require holders of employment-based visas to be interviewed in order to update their status. More than one hundred thousand visa holders could be impacted.

32. The Brennan Center and Protect Democracy Project filed a lawsuit for info on communication between government agencies and the Election Integrity Commission. The agencies did not respond to a FOIA request.

33. On Tuesday, the DoJ dropped its request for IP addresses from DreamHost for the anti-Trump site DisruptJ20.org, but still requested information that related to the planning and participation of the January 20 riot.

34. On Thursday, a court ordered DreamHost to turn over the data requested. The court asked the DoJ to disclose its method for searching the data to minimize the exposure of data on third-party visitors to the site.

35. In a *WaPo* op-ed, activist Melissa Byrne described being grabbed, cuffed, and questioned, and having her banner confiscated by the Secret Service without having been read her rights at a Starbucks in Trump Tower.

36. On Monday, Trump delivered his second address to the nation. Reading from a teleprompter, he asked the American people to trust him in sending thousands more troops to Afghanistan.

37. Trump opened the speech with a call for unity. Historian Michael Beschloss noted that this was the first time a leader "had to start a speech on war and peace by vowing that he opposed bigotry and prejudice."

38. Trump's speech was full of his typical bellicose terms, like "overwhelming force," but offered little in the way of strategy or substance.

39. Of note, three generals now seem to have Trump's ear: Kelly, McMaster, and Mattis. As recently as Week 38, Trump had scoffed at increasing the number of troops in Afghanistan. He also compared the war in Afghanistan to a 21 Club renovation.

40. There is not yet a confirmed U.S. ambassador to Afghanistan.

41. Twenty-four hours after his address to the nation, Trump headed to a campaign rally in Phoenix, despite pleas from the mayor of Phoenix in an op-ed and on air that it was not a good time for Trump to visit.

42. Despite his calls for unity Monday, Trump delivered a seventy-two-minute dystopian speech in which he repeatedly attacked the media and "others"—again targeting marginalized communities.

43. Trump referred to the media as the enemy of the American people, saying, "They don't like our country." After the speech, many in the media expressed concern about their safety.

44. Trump also threatened to shut down the government in the fall if Congress did not approve funding for his wall.

45. Despite his advance promises not to, Trump attacked McCain and Flake, the two senators of Arizona, in his speech without using their names.

46. Also, despite promising not to do so, Trump insinuated he would pardon Sheriff Joe Arpaio, saying that the legal system had not treated him fairly.

47. During his speech, Trump did not mention the accident involving the USS *John S. McCain* or the continuing search for missing sailors.

48. *WaPo* reported that as Trump ranted and rambled, "hundreds left early." The room was only partially filled when Trump began to speak.

49. Police used tear gas to disperse crowds of thousands of protesters after Trump's speech. Police helicopters circled downtown Phoenix.

50. In a likely violation of the Hatch Act, Ben Carson appeared onstage in Phoenix after being introduced as the secretary of HUD.

51. NPR fact-checked Trump's speech and found numerous false and misleading statements.

52. Ahead of the rally Tuesday, Trump met with potential Republican challengers to Senator Flake in the 2018 primaries. During the brief meeting, Trump referred to the senator as "the flake."

53. After Trump's Phoenix speech, former DNI Clapper told CNN he questioned Trump's "fitness to be in this office."

54. Clapper said that, understanding the levers of power available to a president, he found the speech "downright scary and disturbing."

55. Clapper also said Trump could be a threat to national security. He worries about Trump's access to nuclear codes, noting that in a fit of pique, "there's actually very little to stop him."

56. Trump tweeted, asking if Clapper, "who famously got caught lying to Congress," would share "his beautiful letter to me"? Clapper said he had handwritten almost identical notes to both candidates for Election Day.

57. CNN reported Wednesday that the White House was preparing paperwork and talking points for surrogates in preparation for Trump to pardon Arpaio.

58. On Monday, in a later-deleted Instagram post, Mnuchin's wife, Louise Linton, bragged about traveling on a chartered government plane and about the lavish fashion brands she was wearing.

59. On Wednesday, CREW requested information on authorization of the chartered airplane. Typically, secretaries fly on commercial flights for domestic travel.

60. Ethics groups also filed requests to learn if the trip to Fort Knox, Kentucky, was planned so Mnuchin and his wife could view the solar eclipse near the path of totality.

61. On a sudden, unannounced trip to the Middle East, Kushner was snubbed by the Egyptian foreign minister, who canceled their meeting without officially citing a reason. The meeting did later take place.

62. NPR reported that Trump's approval with women is at a historically low 29 percent. Trump's approval with men is much higher (43 percent).

63. The *NYT* reported on a brewing war between Trump and McConnell, as the two haven't spoken for weeks. McConnell questioned whether Trump can salvage his presidency.

64. McConnell also questioned Trump's understanding of the presidency and claimed that Trump was "entirely unwilling to learn the basics of governing."

65. The *NYT* also reported on an August 9 call that Trump made to McConnell. Trump brought up health care, but was "even more animated" about McConnell's refusal to protect him from the Russia investigation.

66. After the *NYT* story broke, another Republican senator called the reporter to say Trump is "consumed with Russia."

67. *Politico* reported on more clashes between Trump and Republican senators over Russia. In additional to Trump's public admonishments of McConnell, McCain, and Flake, Trump also targeted Corker and Tillis.

68. Trump tried to convince Corker that the Russian sanctions bill wasn't good policy, saying it was unconstitutional and would damage him. Trump berated Tillis for his bipartisan bill to protect Mueller from being fired.

69. Including these contacts, *WaPo* counted seven times so far Trump has attempted to influence actions related to the Russia investigation.

70. On Tuesday, Glenn Simpson, the founder of private research firm Fusion GPS, who hired Steele to produce the Trump dossier, testified for ten hours in front of the Senate Judiciary Committee. He also provided forty thousand pages of documents.

71. The Senate Judiciary Committee will vote on releasing the testimony to the public. Rachel Maddow said Simpson's lawyer has given the okay to release the testimony and documents publicly.

72. *WaPo* reported that CIA director Pompeo, Trump's close ally, required the Counterintelligence Mission Center, which is investigating possible collusion between Trump and Russia, to report directly to him.

73. Current and former agents expressed apprehension about conflicts of interest. There is "real concern for interference and politicization," and that Pompeo may bring newly discovered information to the White House.

74. Pompeo spends more time at the White House than his predecessors. He also defended Trump's comments on Charlottesville, saying Trump's condemnation of bigotry was "frankly pretty unambiguous."

75. Pompeo has also shown a willingness to handle political assignments for the White House: for example, calling news agencies, speaking on condition of anonymity, at the White House's behest to dispute a *NYT* article on Trump-Russia.

76. In an internal CIA memo released under the FOIA, former CIA director Brennan wrote that some in Congress don't get the "gravity" of Russian election meddling.

77. Kushner Companies, the real estate company of Kushner's family, switched to a public relations firm with crisis management expertise.

78. The *NYT* reported on Rinat Akhmetshin, one of the attendees of the June 9 meeting at Trump Tower, and his extensive and deep ties to Russian intelligence, government, and oligarchs.

79. Akhmetshin has worked on behalf of several Russian oligarchs to hack adversaries' e-mails and documents in order to buffer their case. Mueller is interested in why Akhmetshin attended the June 9 meeting.

80. CNN reported that congressional investigators unearthed an e-mail from Rick Dearborn, a top campaign aide who is now Trump's deputy chief of staff, about an individual seeking to connect top Trump officials with Putin.

81. The *WSJ* reported that Mueller is looking into Flynn's role in seeking Hillary's e-mails from Russian hackers, along with now deceased GOP operative Peter W. Smith.

82. Investigators have examined intelligence reports that detail Russian hackers discussing how to obtain e-mails from Hillary's server and then transmit them to Flynn via an intermediary.

83. NBC reported that Mueller issued the first grand jury subpoenas to executives who worked on an international campaign organized by Manafort, a significant step in the inquiry, which also focuses on Trump and Kushner.

84. Mueller's team is examining lobbying done by Manafort for a Russia-backed Ukrainian political party from 2012 to 2014. According to recent financial disclosures, Manafort was paid seventeen million dollars between 2013 and 2014.

85. *USA Today* reported on a Russian propaganda network on Twitter aimed at American audiences that consistently spreads links from alt-right media including *Breitbart*, *True Pundit*, and *Gateway Pundit*.

86. Roger Stone told *TMZ* that if Trump is impeached the country will break out into civil war, saying, "You will have a spasm of violence in this country, and insurrection, like you've never seen."

87. The *NYT* reported on the Trump International Hotel in D.C., the now highly profitable meeting place for Trump family members, surrogates, lobbyists, and journalists. Trump continues to profit from the hotel's operations.

88. The hotel is also described as a "safe zone for Trump supporters." Richard Spencer stayed at the hotel and met there with white nationalist Evan McClare as he planned the Charlottesville rally.

89. *WaPo*'s fact-checker reported that Trump's list of false and misleading claims had topped one thousand items early in the week. By week's end, the list approached eleven hundred items, one of the busiest weeks of lying yet.

90. After Icahn resigned in Week 40 ahead of a story on his influencing regulations to his financial benefit, the Trump regime stated that unlike a government employee, Icahn had "no official role or duties."

91. Icahn financially benefited from his 82 percent stake in CVR Energy. The company had accumulated a large short position in biofuels blending credits, called RINs, the price of which fell when Icahn's proposal on the biofuels regulation was reported in February, netting him a huge return.

92. On Friday, Trump attacked another Republican, saying Corker is constantly asking if he should run in 2018, and "Tennessee not happy!" Corker had questioned Trump's fitness to serve in Week 40.

93. In an interview with the *Financial Times*, Cohn was openly critical of Trump's Charlottesville response, saying Trump "must do better" in condemning neo-Nazis and white supremacists.

94. Federal Reserve Board chair Janet Yellen spoke out openly against the Trump regime's efforts to roll back banking regulations enacted after the 2008 financial crisis, saying these regulations have made the banking system safer.

95. Changing course, Bloomberg reported that the White House no longer plans to work with Congress to produce a joint tax plan, instead relying on the House and Senate to hash it out. Trump said he will rally the public instead.

96. The White House rapid response director, Andy Hemming, is leaving. Hemming had worked from 5:30 A.M. to 11 P.M. every weekday blasting out stories favorable to the Trump regime.

97. The RNC passed a resolution to condemn neo-Nazis, the KKK, and white supremacists, despite pushback from several Republican members. The resolution did not, however, mention Trump.

98. A Quinnipiac poll found that 62 percent of Americans believe Trump is dividing the country.

99. As Trump left the White House Friday afternoon, while a hurricane was nearing Texas, a reporter asked, "Do you have a message for the people of Texas?" Trump responded, "Good luck to everybody."

100. Hours before Hurricane Harvey, thought by weather researchers to be the worst hurricane in twelve years, hit landfall in Texas, with the country anxiously watching, Trump issued an unrelated directive and pardon.

101. Late Friday, Trump signed a directive that precludes transgender individuals from joining the military. Mattis has six months to develop a plan to implement the order, and has discretion over those already serving.

102. Trump's directive also bans DoD from paying for medical treatment regimens for transgender individuals currently serving in the military.

103. Late Friday, Trump pardoned former sheriff Joe Arpaio, an elected official who defied a federal court's order to stop violating people's constitutional rights. Arpaio had been found in contempt of court in his ongoing case but had not yet been sentenced.

104. The *NYT* editorial board had noted that with a pardon of Arpaio, Trump would show "his contempt for the American court system" and also send a "message to other officials that they may flout court orders also."

105. Legal experts raised questions about whether Trump's pardon of Arpaio was testing the waters and sending a signal to those under investigation by Mueller.

106. Late Friday, Trump adviser Sebastian Gorka left his post as deputy assistant in the White House. In a letter, Gorka said he resigned. Trump aides said he was fired.

107. Shortly after 11 P.M. EST, Hurricane Harvey made landfall as a Category 4 storm. The National Hurricane Center said it expects "catastrophic and life-threatening" flash flooding and fifteen to thirty inches of rain.

108. The Trump regime imposed sanctions on Venezuela; however, Citgo was exempted. As cited in Week 25, Citgo donated five hundred thousand dollars to Trump's inauguration, and that money may have come indirectly from Russia.

Week 42

AUGUST 27–SEPTEMBER 2, 2017

Despite being a summer week heading into Labor Day weekend, Week 42 is the longest list so far, with the most items relating to Trump-Russia. News reports indicate that the

Mueller probe is moving ahead on many fronts and uncovering damaging evidence about the Trump regime.

This week Trump was unable to control the narrative. Media accounts paint a disturbing picture of a leader who is stormy, depressed, angry, unsteady, and increasingly isolated. Resignations and firings continue en masse, as Trump's White House is filled with drama, showcasing his inability to work with others and hire talent.

Stories less covered continue to detail bigotry toward, and the stripping away of rights and protections of, marginalized communities and women. Another continuing theme is the dismantling of government programs and initiatives, alongside instituting authoritarian measures.

1. *WaPo* reported that before Trump pardoned Arpaio, he had asked Sessions to have the Justice Department drop its case.

2. Ten days before Hurricane Harvey, Trump revoked the Federal Flood Risk Management Standard, an Obama-era set of regulations designed to make federally funded infrastructure less vulnerable to flooding.

3. On Sunday morning, as Houston was flooding, Trump promoted a book by Sheriff David Clarke on Twitter: "great book by a great guy, highly recommended!"

4. Former Office of Government Ethics director Shaub noted that it is a government ethics violation to use public office to endorse any product, service, or enterprise.

5. Clarke, who has been the subject of repeated allegations of mistreating inmates in his jails, abruptly resigned as sheriff on Thursday. Speculation grew that he would be taking a position in the Trump regime.

6. On Sunday, when asked by reporter Chris Wallace about Charlottesville, Tillerson said, "I don't believe anyone doubts the American people's values"—and when asked about Trump's response, said, "The president speaks for himself."

7. Also on Sunday, a video emerged on Facebook of Mattis telling troops, "You just hold the line until our country gets back to understanding and respecting each other and showing it."

8. On Tuesday, again going against Trump, Mattis announced that transgender troops will be allowed to remain in the military pending the results of a study by experts.

9. On Wednesday, shortly after Trump tweeted about North Korea "Talking is not the answer!" Mattis contradicted Trump's statement and told reporters, "We're never out of diplomatic solutions."

10. *BuzzFeed* reported that ICE left fifty immigrant women and children stranded at a bus station in San Antonio as Hurricane Harvey approached.

11. On Monday, Trump reversed an Obama-era policy allowing police to receive surplus military gear.

12. Buried in a bill that Trump signed into law is a provision that allows police warrantless searches in parts of Virginia, Maryland, and D.C. There was almost no media coverage.

13. In Salt Lake City, a nurse was forcibly arrested after she followed hospital protocol and refused to let the police draw blood from an unconscious patient who was not a suspect and faced no charges.

14. Televangelist Jim Bakker said Christians would start a civil war if Trump is impeached. Roger Stone expressed a similar sentiment in Week 41.

15. A group of evangelical leaders in Tennessee released the "Nashville Statement," which denounced gay marriage and condemned acceptance of "homosexual immorality or transgenderism."

16. Reuters reported that Confederate flag sales have boomed since Charlottesville. One company said their orders quadrupled.

17. A federal judge in San Antonio temporarily blocked a Texas ban on sanctuary cities from going into effect on Friday.

18. Trump's HHS cut the advertising budget for Obamacare by 90 percent. Lowering enrollment is a way to compromise the ACA.

19. The ACLU said it is deeply concerned about reports of abuse and retaliation by ICE against ACLU clients who are participating in a class action suit to stop the immediate deportation of any Iraqi nationals.

20. A decorated marine, George Ybarra, who served in the Persian Gulf War, was transferred to an immigration center in Arizona. Although a federal judge ruled that Ybarra is a citizen, ICE continues to work to deport him to Mexico.

21. The Trump regime said women's rights will not be part of its demands in negotiations with the Taliban in Afghanistan.

22. Mnuchin said the Treasury Department may scrap plans finalized under Obama to put Harriet Tubman on the twenty-dollar bill to replace Andrew Jackson.

23. The Trump White House removed a list from the White House website of more than 250 schools under investigation by the Obama administration for violating Title IX by mishandling campus sexual assault, signaling an end of enforcement and accountability.

24. Trump ended an Obama-era rule that required companies to collect pay data for workers of different genders, races, and ethnic groups.

25. The Trump regime's Transportation Department abandoned an Obama-era plan of local hiring for public workers. The program was meant to help offset longstanding racial and gender imbalances in the construction industry.

26. Sessions's DoJ will retry the woman whom prosecutors say disrupted Sessions's Senate confirmation hearing by laughing.

27. *USA Today* reported that anti-protester bills are gaining traction in Republican-controlled statehouses. So far, twenty states have proposed bills with restrictions on the right to assemble and protest, and six have approved legislation that targets protesters.

28. The Interior Department's watchdog group dropped its investigation of the threat by Secretary Zinke to Senator Lisa Murkowski over her vote to repeal Obamacare, after the two senators from Alaska declined to be interviewed.

29. The GSA's Office of the Inspector General (OIG) is undertaking a formal review of how the agency has handled the lease of Trump Hotel D.C.

30. Trump's Election Integrity Commission apologized after being chastised by a district judge for its failure to disclose documents publicly as required.

31. In addition to his position as vice chair of Trump's Election Integrity Commission, Kris Kobach will become a regular columnist at *Breitbart*.

32. On Monday, in a press conference with Finnish president Sauli Niinistö, Trump defended his decision to pardon Arpaio. When asked about the timing, Trump said, "In the middle of a hurricane, even though it was Friday evening, I assumed the ratings would be far higher than they would be normally."

33. Trump confused two Finnish women journalists with dirty-blond hair as being the same person, saying, "Again. You're going to give her—the same one?" Niinistö responded, "No, they are not the same lady."

34. Trump also falsely claimed that Finland is buying Boeing fighter jets. Niinistö pushed back in a tweet Monday, calling this "ankka," which translates to a falsehood or fake news.

35. On Tuesday, Trump visited Austin. He did not tour areas heavily hit by Hurricane Harvey or meet with any victims. By Tuesday, Harvey had dumped more rain than any storm in history in parts of Texas.

36. Trump praised Federal Emergency Management Agency (FEMA) administrator Brock Long, saying that he "has really become very famous on television over the last couple of days."

37. Trump acknowledged the crowd, "What a crowd, what a turnout!"—but failed to mention or acknowledge the fifteen deaths, tens of thousands of displaced, or irreversible damage caused by Harvey.

38. Trump wore a USA hat during the visit with a "45" on the side. This merchandise is for sale on Trump's website for forty dollars.

39. Ari Fleischer, press secretary for George W. Bush, said of the visit that there was "something missing," and that was "empathy for the people who suffer."

40. As Hurricane Harvey continued to devastate, the AP reported that the Republicans are considering cutting one billion dollars from disaster accounts to help finance Trump's wall.

41. The *NYT* reported on voting irregularities in the 2016 election: voters falsely being told they were ineligible to vote, or turned away from polls, or sent to other polling places in several blue counties in swing states.

42. Little digital forensic investigation has been done to examine the impact in at least twenty-one states whose election systems were targeted by Russia.

43. Academic and private election security experts warn that future elections, including next year's midterms, could be subject to hacking, since nothing has been done to improve election procedures or build an effective defense.

44. Moyers & Company reported that pro-Russian bots have been taking up right-wing causes after Charlottesville. A behavioral scientist published a case study on Medium focusing on their impact on the narrative around Berkeley.

45. Bloomberg reported on the growing sophistication of pro-Russian bots, which are already taking a role in sowing seeds of discord in the U.S. and taking on Trump critics like Senator McCain.

46. Experts say the Russian bots never left after the 2016 election and are sharpening their attacks for upcoming elections in 2018 and 2020. The bots are learning to mimic human behavior.

47. *WaPo* reported that during his run for president, in late 2015 and early 2016, Trump was seeking a deal for a Trump Tower in Moscow. Lawyer Michael Cohen took the lead for Trump. The deal was never publicly disclosed.

48. Felix Sater urged Trump to come to Moscow and said he could get Putin to say "great things" about Trump. In late 2015, Trump started to publicly praise Putin. Shortly after, Putin offered praise of Trump in return.

49. Sater said that at Trump's request, he traveled to Russia with Ivanka and Donald Jr. A lawyer for the Trump Organization said they happened to be there at the same time.

50. The *NYT* reported on e-mails between Cohen and Sater that were turned over Monday to the House Intelligence Committee. Sater e-mailed Cohen, "Our boy can become president of the USA and we can engineer it."

51. Sater said he lined up financing for Trump for the Trump Tower in Moscow through VTB Bank, a bank under U.S. sanctions for its involvement in Russia's efforts to undermine democracy in Ukraine.

52. VTB is also majority-owned by the Russian government, as are other banks including VEB, Alfa Bank, and Sberbank—all of which have ties to Trump and his aides.

53. In an e-mail, Sater bragged about his Russia connections, saying, "I arranged for Ivanka to sit in Putin's private chair at his desk."

54. Ivanka told *WaPo* that she did not recall sitting in Putin's chair. She also said she was not involved with Cohen's discussion on the project, except to recommend architects.

55. ABC reported that in October 2015, four months into his presidential campaign, Trump signed a letter of intent for Trump Tower Moscow.

56. Rachel Maddow noted that the day Trump signed the term sheet for Trump Tower Moscow was the same day as the third Republican primary debate. Trump seemed off and had a poor performance that night.

57. *WaPo* reported that in mid-January 2016, Cohen e-mailed Putin press secretary Dmitry Peskov to ask for his assistance with the stalled Moscow project and to arrange "meetings with the appropriate individuals."

58. The e-mail is the first known direct outreach by a senior Trump aide to a senior member of Putin's government. Cohen told congressional investigators that he did not receive a response.

59. Peskov confirmed Wednesday that he received Cohen's e-mail asking for his help in getting the stalled Trump Tower Moscow project moving again, but said he did not respond or share it with Putin.

60. In Week 15, Sater and Cohen were involved in a back-channel plan to get U.S. sanctions against Russia lifted. In Week 17, Alex Orono, a Russian working with them on this plan, died suddenly.

61. Sater has cooperated with U.S. authorities in the past, signing a plea deal with Andrew Weissmann, who is now part of Mueller's special counsel.

62. *Yahoo News* reported that Eric Swalwell, a Democrat on the House Intelligence Committee, said the panel may call Trump to testify on the Trump Tower Moscow deal to clear up past conflicting statements.

63. Trump has publicly said of Sater, if he was sitting in the same room, "I really wouldn't know what he looked like." It is believed Sater was conducting business for Trump through 2016.

64. The *NYT* reported on an eight-page letter from Cohen's attorney to the House Intelligence Committee giving a point-by-point rebuttal to the Steele dossier and "vehemently" denying Russian collusion.

65. CNN reported that Rick Clay of West Virginia tried through Trump aide Dearborn to make contact with Russians, allegedly to discuss their "shared Christian values."

66. NBC reported that Mueller's team is investigating Trump's role in crafting Donald Jr.'s response to the June 9 meeting, and whether Trump knew about the meeting and tried to conceal its purposes.

67. The *Financial Times* reported that Akhmetshin gave testimony under oath for several hours on August 11, another sign Mueller is looking closely at the June 9 meeting.

68. The *Guardian* reported that after learning that the Senate Judiciary Committee would interview Donald Jr. about the June 9 meeting, Trump called the committee chair, Grassley, to offer Iowa federal support for the ethanol industry.

69. Grassley tweeted about Trump's phone call offering support. Also of note, the Senate Judiciary Branch will shortly vote on whether to make the Fusion GPS testimony on the Steele dossier public.

70. CNN reported that Mueller has issued subpoenas to Manafort's former attorney, Melissa Laurenza of Akin Gump, and to his current spokesperson, Jason Maloni.

71. *Politico* reported that Mueller is teaming up with New York attorney general Schneiderman on its investigation into Manafort and his financial transactions. The two teams have shared evidence and talked frequently in recent weeks.

72. Mueller and Schneiderman have pressured Manafort by approaching his family and former business partners. Several people and firms who have worked with Manafort have been subpoenaed.

73. Trump has privately discussed his pardon powers with aides. State and federal investigators believe the potential of a pardon has influenced Manafort's decision on cooperating. Trump cannot pardon state crimes.

74. The *WSJ* reported on Manafort's close relationship with Russian oligarch Deripaska. The two worked together from 2004 to 2015 in countries with Russian political interests, including Ukraine, Georgia, and Montenegro.

75. As noted in Week 28, Deripaska has offered to give testimony to congressional investigators in exchange for immunity. That offer is still being rejected, to avoid interference with Mueller's probe.

76. NBC reported that Manafort turned over notes taken during the June 9 meeting to congressional investigators and Mueller. The words "donor" and "RNC" appear in close proximity. It is illegal for foreigners to donate to American elections.

77. The *Daily Beast* reported Mueller enlisted help from the IRS's Criminal Investigation (CI) unit, an elite investigative entity that focuses exclusively on financial crime, including tax evasion and money laundering.

78. One of Mueller's top deputies, Andy Weissmann, has worked with the CI unit extensively. The CI unit would have access to Trump's tax returns.

79. Bloomberg detailed the massive debt Kushner has outstanding against his family's real estate investment in 666 Fifth Avenue. To pay off looming debt, the family has sold off properties and forgone new deals.

80. Kushner Companies bought the building near a market high and has tried to get China and sovereign funds to buy the property or refinance part of the debt. These efforts may be influencing U.S. foreign policy, as noted in Week 35.

81. Source speculated the rationale for Kushner's meeting with Sergey Gorkov, head of the Kremlin-controlled VEB bank, and Kislyak in late December could have been in his capacity as head of his family's real estate business and this transaction.

82. The *WSJ* reported that lawyers for Trump have met with Mueller and submitted memos arguing that Trump didn't obstruct justice by firing Comey. They also claim Comey is not a reliable witness. Experts say this is highly unusual.

83. *Axios* reported that Russian diplomats continue to die unexpectedly. Russia's ambassador to Sudan was the seventh diplomat to die since November.

84. Representative Ron DeSantis floated an amendment to end the Mueller probe and stop Mueller from looking into activities prior to June 2015. DeSantis is a Trump loyalist and is considering running for governor of Florida in 2018.

85. *WaPo* reported on Trump's White House during a "summer of crisis," citing Trump's "dark mood." Trump is fighting with Kelly, Tillerson, and Cohn, and friends say, "He's turning on people that are very close to him."

86. *WaPo* reported that Kelly refused to join Trump onstage in Phoenix after Trump prompted, "Where's General Kelly? Get him out here. He's great."

87. *WaPo* also reported that Trump continues to call friends and outside advisers, including Bannon, from his personal phone when Kelly isn't around.

88. *Politico* reported on the shrinking West Wing, citing three factors: (1) Kelly's careful review process, (2) five open-ended Russia investigations making it hard to hire, and (3) Trump's dark mood over the summer.

89. Eight of the twenty-eight members of the National Infrastructure Advisory Council resigned. In a letter, the cybersecurity experts said that Trump "threatened the security of the homeland," citing Charlottesville and withdrawal from the Paris agreement.

90. Trump lashed out at, then fired, longtime aide George Gigicos because of the small crowd size at his Phoenix rally last week.

91. Responding to criticism about unfilled key roles in the executive branch, Trump tweeted to @foxandfriends: "We are not looking to fill all of those positions. Don't need many of them—reduce size of government."

92. *ProPublica* reported that while Trump continues to leave key executive branch positions that require Senate confirmation unfilled, he has quietly installed more than one thousand political staffers.

93. Many of these hires are regulating industries they used to work in. Most names are kept secret. These employees working in the shadows face less scrutiny than those appointments requiring Senate approval and answer to no one but the White House.

94. The RNC chief of staff, Sara Armstrong, resigned. Armstrong is the sixth RNC staffer to leave in the past month.

95. *Foreign Policy* reported that two top State Department officials resigned in what was called "Black Friday." One State Department official said, "Dissatisfaction is a big factor" for why diplomats continue to take early retirement or new jobs.

96. Longtime Trump aide Keith Schiller, best known for hand-delivering the letter to Comey about his firing, is leaving the White House.

97. Indictments were issued for fifteen security guards of Turkey's Erdogan who in Week 31 had attacked protesters outside the Turkish embassy in D.C.

98. The UN human rights chief, Zeid Ra'ad al-Hussein, slammed Trump's attacks on the media, warning that Trump's rhetoric could provoke violence: "ultimately the sequence is a dangerous one."

99. Zeid also raised concern about Trump's "worrying remarks" about women, Mexicans, Muslims, and issues like immigration.

100. NBC reported on a focus group in Pittsburgh, where voters, including those who voted for Trump, expressed "abject disappointment" in his tone and leadership. Also noted was Trump's lack of empathy.

101. A Pew Research poll found just 16 percent of Americans like the way Trump conducts himself. The poll also noted a deterioration in Republican support: a third agree with Trump on only a few or no issues.

102. The Gallup daily tracking poll found that Trump matched his biggest net disapproval of –27 (34 percent approval, 61 percent disapproval), with the trend continuing lower.

103. A Fox News poll found that voter satisfaction with the direction of the country declined to just 35 percent, and 56 percent think Trump is tearing the country apart.

104. On Friday, the *NYT* reported that Mueller has obtained an early draft of a letter written by Trump and a political aide giving Trump's reasons for firing Comey.

105. The *WSJ* paraphrased Trump's thoughts as conveyed in the draft of his letter to Comey: "You've told me three times I'm not under investigation but you won't tell the world, and it's hampering the country."

106. *Politico* reported that the decision to fire Comey was made in Bedminster, where Trump huddled with Kushner and Stephen Miller. McGahn, Priebus, and Bannon warned Trump against it, saying it would trigger a firestorm.

107. The *NYT* reported that Trump was supposed to golf that weekend, but it rained, so instead he stewed inside about Comey and the Russia investigation. Trump ordered Miller to draft the letter.

108. After returning from Bedminster on Monday, May 8, Trump handed copies of the letter to senior officials including McGahn and Pence in the Oval Office. McGahn was alarmed and tried to stop Trump from sending the letter.

109. On May 8, Rosenstein got a copy of Trump's letter and agreed to write a separate memo. On May 9, Trump's letter was replaced with Rosenstein's public letter, which offered a simpler rationale for firing Comey: his handling of the Clinton e-mail investigation.

110. In an op-ed, McCain blasted Trump, saying Congress doesn't answer to him despite his recent attacks: "We must, where we can, cooperate with him. But we are not his subordinates."

111. On Thursday, Press Secretary Sanders said Trump promised to donate one million dollars of his "personal money" to Hurricane Harvey victims. On Friday, when pressed on where the money was coming from, Sanders said she wasn't sure.

112. At a signing ceremony in the Oval Office Friday, religious leaders took turns praising and thanking Trump for his response to Hurricane Harvey.

113. The *NYT* reported on Kelly's unhappiness serving under Trump, telling an associate it was "by far the hardest job he had ever had." Trump likes to surround himself with former military men from "central casting."

114. Trump berated Kelly after the Phoenix campaign rally. Kelly told White House staff members that "he had never been spoken to like that during thirty-five years of serving his country," and that he would not let it happen again.

115. Kelly has not been able to get Trump to stop binge-watching Fox News, Trump's primary source of information. Trump does not have a web browser on his phone, despite his frequent retweets of story links.

116. In a radio interview, Eric Trump said the negative media coverage was impacting his father: "It important to keep in context. Otherwise, quite frankly, you'd probably end up killing yourself out of depression."

117. On Friday, a day after Trump ordered Russia to close three U.S. outposts, a fire was reported at Russia's D.C. diplomatic annex, and smoke was coming out of the chimney at the consulate in San Francisco on a one-hundred-degree day.

Week 43

SEPTEMBER 3-9, 2017

This week the Mueller probe edged toward engulfing Trump's entire inner circle. Also of great import, Facebook finally admitted to the company's role in allowing Russian bots to infiltrate our election. Speculation grew that Russia influenced our election and that the Trump campaign was complicit.

This week the Trump regime continued its assault on marginalized communities and women, rescinding DACA and taking away protections for victims of campus sexual assault. A second major hurricane illuminated the extent to which the Trump regime has already deconstructed federal agencies like the EPA and State Department.

1. Late on the Friday night of Labor Day weekend, the DoJ unceremoniously announced that there is no evidence Obama wiretapped Trump Tower. Trump did not apologize to Obama for this frequently repeated false claim.

2. Trump visited Hurricane Harvey survivors in Houston seeking shelter at the NRG Center. While preparing to serve lunch, Trump said his hands were "too big" to fit in the plastic serving gloves.

3. As he left the shelter, Trump told survivors, "Have a good time, everybody."

4. The Pentagon miscalculated the number of troops deployed after Harvey: command said 6,300 were deployed, but the actual number was 1,638.

5. On Saturday afternoon, the AP reported that while many ultrapolluted Superfund sites in Houston were flooded and there was concern about toxins spreading, the EPA was not on scene.

6. The EPA responded with a statement on Sunday, in which the agency personally attacked the credibility of the AP reporter: "Michael Biesecker has a history of not letting the facts get in the way of his story."

7. The EPA said the Superfund sites were inaccessible, but they had used aerial imaging in their assessments. The AP reported its staff had used a boat and vehicles and gone on foot to reach seven of the sites.

8. *WaPo* reported that the EPA has taken the unusual step of putting a Trump political operative, John Konkus, who has little environmental policy experience, in charge of doling out hundreds of millions of EPA grants.

9. The GAO will investigate hiring practices by the EPA. Agencies are not supposed to hire industry lobbyists for two years after they have stopped working as lobbyists, but the EPA allegedly skirted those orders using a provision of the Safe Drinking Water Act.

10. Trump nominated David Zatezalo, a former chief executive of Rhino Resources, a company that repeatedly clashed with federal regulators over safety, to run the Mine Safety and Health Administration.

11. Trump nominated Jim Bridenstine, a congressman from Oklahoma who has denied climate change and has no science credentials, to lead the National Aeronautics and Space Administration (NASA). This is the longest in its history that NASA has been without a leader.

12. CNN reported ahead of his Senate confirmation that parts of Bridenstine's online presence were scrubbed, including radio and video interviews, and Facebook, Twitter, and YouTube accounts belonging to his campaign.

13. Following a nuclear test by North Korea that unleashed a 6.3-magnitude tremor Saturday, Trump was openly critical of South Korea, tweeting, "their talk of appeasement with North Korea will not work."

14. The *NYT* reported that Trump's antagonistic comments recently have made South Korea question its alliance with the U.S., which stretches over sixty-seven years.

15. Later that day, Mattis addressed the press and said, "Our commitments among the allies are iron-clad." Mattis repeated that commitment in a statement on Wednesday.

16. This marked the third time in a week that Mattis's message has differed from Trump's (see Week 42), in addition to his statement to troops in Week 42 about upholding American values in the era of Trump.

17. The *WSJ* reported that nearly four hundred EPA employees have left in recent days, leaving the agency with its lowest staffing in almost thirty years.

18. The Pentagon dramatically scaled back the number of reporters traveling with Mattis overseas to just six: one wire service, one newspaper, a radio pool reporter, and a three-person pool television crew.

19. The AP, the oldest and largest American wire service, which provides news to thousands of print and broadcast clients and has traveled with the defense secretary for decades, will not be included on all trips.

20. The Ninth Circuit Court of Appeals narrowed the scope of Trump's second Muslim ban, ruling that extended family members of legal U.S. residents are exempt from the ban.

21. The Trump regime filed papers with the Supreme Court in support of a Christian baker in Colorado, whom a state court ruled against for refusing to make a wedding cake for a gay couple.

22. The U.S. Commission on Civil Rights issued a letter denouncing Trump's pardon of Arpaio, citing Arpaio's repeated violation of the civil rights of Latinos and defying a federal court order, among other violations.

23. Trump's DHS planned massive nationwide raids to target eighty-four hundred undocumented immigrants, described as "the largest operation of its kind in the history of ICE," for later this month.

24. NBC reported that the "massive roundup" plan was canceled late Thursday due to Hurricane Irma and damage caused by Hurricane Harvey.

25. Sessions announced that nonsanctuary jurisdictions would get "priority consideration" in a grant program called Community Oriented Policing Services (COPS). While Obama had used the program to promote trust between police officers and community members, Sessions and Trump are using it to crack down on immigrants.

26. On Thursday, at the same time as Donald Jr.'s Senate testimony, DeVos said in a speech at George Mason University that she will roll back an Obama-era directive on campus sexual assault. She did not take any questions.

27. DeVos said she would develop a replacement that she said would do a better job of "balancing the rights of victims and the accused." Men's rights advocates applauded DeVos for listening to their side.

28. On a call with survivor advocates Friday, former vice president Biden said DeVos "does not speak for the American people" and called on advocates to meet with college and university administrators and "demand they step up."

29. CBC News reported on a spike in international undergraduate and graduate applications to Canadian universities in the wake of Trump.

30. As part of the NAFTA negotiations, Canada demanded that the U.S. end its "right to work" laws in place in some states. Canadian officials say these laws gut unions by starving them of money.

31. The ACLU reported that ICE has asked the National Archives and Record Administration for permission to begin destroying eleven types of records, including those related to sexual assaults and solitary confinement.

32. A Republican in the House referred to a female colleague who was challenging his amendment as "young lady" and said that she "doesn't know a damn thing what she's talking about." He later apologized.

33. The FBI will probe the brutal arrest by Utah cops of a nurse who followed hospital policy and refused to draw blood from a patient, as reported in Week 42.

34. In Iowa, a photo of five high school boys wearing KKK hoods and burning a cross circulated on social media. The boys were suspended from school for nine days.

35. Rachel Maddow ran a segment on how Trump has given white nationalists like Bannon and the alt-right a path to power.

36. An *Atlantic* piece, "Donald Trump Is the First White President," spoke of Trump's white support, the undertones of racism successfully harnessed in his campaign, and his obsession with the negation of Obama's legacy.

37. *USA Today* investigated membership in Trump's clubs and traced forty-five hundred members. For the first time in U.S. history, wealthy people have close access to a president as a result of payments that enrich him personally.

38. *USA Today* found that membership includes more than fifty executives whose companies hold federal contracts and twenty-one lobbyists and trade group officials. Two-thirds played on a Trump course on one of the fifty-eight days he was there so far this year.

39. Republican leaders prevented a vote on a bill in the House that would have banned federal spending at Trump businesses.

40. Representative Bill Pascrell's motion to demand that Trump release his tax returns was voted down 21–14 in the House Ways and Means Committee, helping Republicans avoid a more public vote in the full House. This breaks a forty-year precedent of presidents making their tax returns public.

41. The GAO will investigate Zinke's threat to withhold support for Alaska over Murkowski's Obamacare repeal vote. In Week 42, the OIG closed its investigation after the two Alaska senators refused to participate.

42. A lawsuit filed against Trump's Election Integrity Commission alleges that at least two members are using personal e-mails for office business.

43. Kobach authored an article at *Breitbart* claiming out-of-state voters changed the outcome of the New Hampshire Senate race in 2016. This claim is false.

44. Kobach and the Election Integrity Commission will arrive in New Hampshire next week to discuss, among other things, "election integrity issues affecting public confidence."

45. New Hampshire senators Jeanne Shaheen and Maggie Hassan issued a statement condemning Trump's Election Integrity Commission for misleading the public. They also called on New Hampshire's secretary of state to resign from the commission.

46. As Congress returned from its summer recess, the *WSJ* reported on the unusually strained relations between Trump and Republicans, saying Trump had invited leaders to Bedminster, "but they were unable to coordinate schedules."

47. Trump ended the Deferred Action for Childhood Arrivals program, which gives certain legal protections to those who arrived in the country illegally as children (within a specific time frame).

48. The *NYT* reported that as late as an hour before the DACA decision was announced on Tuesday, administration officials expressed concern that Trump didn't fully grasp the details of rescinding DACA or its impact.

49. Instead of facing the public, Trump sent Sessions to speak to the press on Tuesday to announce that the government was ending DACA. Sessions claimed that DACA was "deemed illegal by, I think, just about every legal expert."

50. Javier Palomares, the CEO of the Hispanic Chamber of Commerce, resigned from Trump's National Diversity Coalition over Trump's decision to end DACA.

51. A *Politico*/Morning Consult poll found just 15 percent of Americans believe DACA should be rescinded, while 76 percent believe Dreamers should be allowed to stay.

52. On Tuesday, in a nighttime tweet, Trump signaled that he may be open to changing his mind on DACA, saying if Congress can't pass something in six months, "I will revisit this issue!"

53. The U.S. Conference of Catholic Bishops issued a statement denouncing-Trump's decision to end DACA.

54. Bannon told CBS's *60 Minutes* that he disagrees with Trump on ending DACA, but blasted the U.S. Conference of Catholic Bishops, saying they are opposed to DACA because "they need illegal aliens to fill the churches."

55. *Vox* noted despite that Trump's tweet, the government is already winding down DACA, as the Trump regime is no longer accepting new applications from young immigrants.

56. On Thursday, Trump again tweeted his assurance to Dreamers, falsely claiming that if you "are concerned about your status during the 6 month period, you have nothing to worry about—No action!"

57. CNN estimated 983 undocumented immigrants per day will lose protection they previously enjoyed under DACA, as the two-year tenure of their status expires.

58. At an Oval Office meeting on Wednesday, after Republican leaders and Mnuchin advocated for an eighteen-month hike for the debt ceiling, Trump unexpectedly sided with "Chuck and Nancy" (Schumer and Pelosi) for a three-month hike.

59. Later, at a rally in North Dakota, Trump called Democratic senator Heidi Heitkamp, who is running for reelection, a "good woman," and said, "These are great people. They work hard. They're for you 100 percent."

60. On Wednesday, after months of denying that Russia had purchased advertisements there, Facebook issued a bland headline, "An Update on Information Operations on Facebook," admitting this wasn't true.

61. Facebook told congressional investigators Wednesday that the company sold one hundred thousand dollars' worth of advertisement to Internet Research Agency, a "troll farm" in St. Petersburg with a history of pushing pro-Kremlin propaganda.

62. Facebook reported that roughly a quarter of the ads were "geographically targeted." The ads' focus was to amplify divisive issues like LGBT matters, race issues, immigration, and gun rights.

63. The *Daily Beast* calculated that one hundred thousand dollars in Facebook ads could have reached as many as seventy million users if shared in a sophisticated manner.

64. The *NYT* reported on the sophisticated ways "troll farms" manipulated and disseminated news on Facebook and Twitter during the 2016 election. Former FBI agent Clint Watts called it a "bot cancer eroding trust."

65. The *NYT* also found that some of the most aggressive and misogynistic Bernie Sanders supporters on Twitter were actually Russian bots and trolls.

66. A *WaPo* columnist speculated that Trump would not have won without the help of an organized Russian attack on Facebook. A *NYT* op-ed decreed: "Facebook Wins, Democracy Loses."

67. Reuters reported that Facebook turned over data to Mueller about Russian involvement, including copies of advertisements and data about buyers.

68. Mark Warner, the ranking Democrat on the Senate Intelligence Committee, said Facebook's Russia disclosure is the "tip of the iceberg" on election interference through social media.

69. McClatchy reported that Facebook, Twitter, and other social media companies may be subpoenaed. A former prosecutor said that Facebook ad buys suggest "numerous crimes, including conspiracy to defraud" the U.S.

70. *USA Today* reported that Russia has interfered in at least twenty-seven European and North American countries' elections since 2004.

71. Nunes, who had recused himself from the Russia investigation as chair of the House Intelligence Committee, lashed out at Sessions in a letter for not sharing FBI and DoJ documents related to the Steele dossier. Nunes also threatened Sessions and FBI director Wray with a public hearing.

72. *Vanity Fair* reported that Representative Trey Gowdy is also waging a war to discredit the Steele dossier. Gowdy claims subpoenas are necessary because the FBI and DoJ haven't supplied the documents underlying the dossier.

73. Trump attorney Michael Carvin filed a brief asking a federal judge to toss out a lawsuit that accuses the Trump campaign of conspiring with Russian operatives to publish stolen DNC information on WikiLeaks.

74. In Week 23, the DoJ said it was preparing charges against Assange, with Sessions saying that Assange's arrest was a priority. Strangely, this never happened, and now the Trump regime is defending WikiLeaks.

75. At a news conference in China, Putin said, Trump is "not my bride, and I am not his groom."

76. On Thursday, Donald Jr. met with the Senate Judiciary Committee behind closed doors. Only one Senate Republican attended the hearing, and stayed for only about five minutes.

77. Feinstein, the ranking Democrat, said Donald Jr. has agreed to public testimony, and if he doesn't follow through he will be subpoenaed. Grassley, to whom Trump offered federal support for the ethanol industry in Week 42, said no final decision has been made.

78. Donald Jr. claimed he took the meeting with Veselnitskaya and others because she might have damaging information "concerning the fitness, character, or qualifications" of Hillary.

79. NPR obtained a copy of Donald Jr.'s four-page statement in which he said that Veselnitskaya "provided no meaningful information" and that the meeting was "primarily focused on Russian adoptions" and the Magnitsky Act.

80. Donald Jr. disclosed, for the first time, three phone calls with Agalarov before the June 9 meeting, the content of which he couldn't recall. He said he had no recollection of any documents left by Russian visitors.

81. Donald Jr. also said he did "not collude with any foreign government and do not know of anyone who did," and that he hoped the interview had fully satisfied the Senate inquiry.

82. *Newsweek* compiled a list of Donald Jr.'s rationales for taking the meeting. Thursday's testimony was his fifth version so far.

83. After Donald Jr.'s testimony, Democratic senator Coons issued a memo citing statute 18 U.S.C. 1001(a) and (c)(2), which outlines the punishments for lying to Congress.

84. CNN reported that Mueller will seek to interview the staff aboard Air Force One present as Trump helped craft the misleading statement issued by Donald Jr. about the June 9 meeting at Trump Tower.

85. Mueller wants to know how the statement was put together, whether information was intentionally left out, and who was involved. Mueller considers the aides who helped craft the statement to be witnesses.

86. In Donald Jr.'s Senate testimony, he claimed he was not aware of what role, if any, his father might have played in drafting the statement.

87. *WaPo* reported that Mueller has alerted the White House that his team will seek to speak with six Trump insiders, including Hicks, Priebus, Spicer, McGahn, and one of McGahn's deputies, James Burnham.

88. Each of the six was privy to internal discussions in areas being investigated by Mueller, including the Comey firing, Trump's inaction on Flynn, and possible coordination with Russia.

89. Mueller also expects to question Josh Raffel, a White House spokesperson who works closely with Kushner, as well as possibly Trump family members, including Kushner.

90. The *Daily Beast* reported that Mueller wants to speak with Hicks about what happened on Air Force One as Trump crafted Donald Jr.'s statement.

91. The *Daily Beast* also reported that efforts are under way to organize a legal defense fund for White House staffers. Legal fees related to the Mueller probe are expected to be high, with lawyers likely billing five hundred to one thousand dollars per hour.

92. Late Friday, *Politico* reported that Hicks hired Robert Trout, a highly regarded attorney, to represent her in the Mueller probe.

93. CNN obtained the seventeen-page Trump Tower Moscow letter of intent, signed by Trump in October 2015, the day of a Republican primary debate. The property would be named Trump World Tower Moscow.

94. The deal would have given Trump perks including a four-million-dollar up-front fee, no up-front costs, a percentage of the sales, and the opportunity to name the hotel spa after his daughter Ivanka.

95. During the campaign, Trump said he had "nothing to do with Russia."

96. On Friday, Trump hosted Russia's new U.S. ambassador, Anatoly Antonov, in D.C. Russian media reported that Antonov described the meeting as "warm." U.S. media was not informed of the meeting.

97. Antonov said Russia did not interfere in the U.S. election. Two years ago, the EU put Antonov on its list of officials subject to sanctions, citing his involvement in supporting the deployment of Russian troops to Ukraine.

98. Dmitry Firtash, a Ukrainian industrialist and top-tier Russian mob associate with ties to Manafort, is fighting U.S. prosecutors' efforts to bring him to Chicago for a trial; he is charged with bribery. He remains in Vienna on $174 million bail.

99. Asked for comment on the second major hurricane in two weeks, Irma, Pruitt said that now isn't the right time to talk about climate change.

100. On Thursday, by a 31–0 vote, the Senate Appropriations Committee allocated fifty-one billion dollars for the State Department and foreign operations, nearly eleven billion more than requested by the Trump regime.

101. On Friday, the committee blasted the Trump regime in its report, saying its approach to foreign policy weakens U.S. standing in the world.

102. On Friday, the State Department was criticized for its response to Hurricane Irma, which has already affected thousands of Americans in the Caribbean islands. A task force was set up Friday, after the storm hit.

103. State Department employees point out that there is currently no undersecretary of state for management, who would typically be in charge of State's response to a storm of Irma's magnitude.

104. In another move toward what Bannon had called the "deconstruction of the administrative state," the OMB issued a memo directing "a net reduction in total incremental regulatory costs" for agencies.

105. The *WSJ* reported that Trump is unlikely to nominate Cohn as Federal Reserve chair when Yellen's term comes up in February, citing Cohn's criticism of Trump's Charlottesville response in a *Financial Times* interview (noted in Week 41).

106. The *NYT* reported that Kelly is trying to be welcoming to Cohn, but White House aides say Trump is freezing Cohn out by employing a familiar tactic: refusing to make eye contact with him.

107. Bannon told CBS's *60 Minutes* that Chris Christie didn't get a position in Trump's cabinet because Christie wasn't loyal after the release of the *Access Hollywood* tape.

108. Bloomberg reported that key Trump aides said Trump is rattled by the pending departure of longtime bodyguard Schiller. Aides described Schiller as the "emotional anchor" for Trump in the White House turmoil.

Week 44

SEPTEMBER 10–16, 2017

Front and center this week were reports on Russia's use of social media to influence the U.S. election, possibly with help from the Trump regime. As well, a slew of reporting continued to build the evolving mosaic of connections and quid pro quo between members of the Trump regime and Putin allies.

Trump's short-lived pivot ended abruptly late in the week when he again evoked "both sides" on Charlottesville, then started an embarrassing tweet storm about a tragic bombing in London. An interview by Rachel Maddow of Hillary Clinton about her new book provided a momentary pause and wake-up call for how much our country has changed—both our global standing and government competency—under a leader who admires authoritarian leaders and aspires to authoritarianism.

1. When asked about Hurricane Irma, Trump took the opportunity to compliment the Coast Guard's branding: "If you talk about branding? No brand has improved more than the United States Coast Guard."

2. *Axios* reported that according to an adviser, Trump finally realized: "People really f@&@ing hate me." The adviser noted that Trump's need for affirmation may have led to his sudden embrace of Senator Chuck Schumer and Representative Nancy Pelosi.

3. White House social media director Dan Scavino Jr. tweeted, then deleted, a video that he incorrectly described as showing Miami airport during Hurricane Irma.

4. *Foreign Policy* reported on growing concerns within the CIA that because of his personal beliefs, Trump ally Pompeo is rolling back the agency's diversity mandate.

5. In June, senior CIA management abruptly canceled an event with the Matthew Shepard Foundation. The foundation was created by the Shepard family in honor of their late gay son. Shepard's death led to some of the country's first federal hate crime laws.

6. On Sunday, Trump announced his sixth wave of U.S. attorney nominations: forty-one of the forty-two were men.

7. On Monday, Trump nominated six more people to become U.S. attorneys. All six were white men.

8. Trump's NASA nominee, Jim Bridenstine, was quoted as saying the agency should be reorganized, and "expansion of human knowledge" about space and Earth should be removed from NASA's objectives.

9. The University of North Carolina's board of governors approved a ban on litigation, which effectively ended the UNC law school's civil rights center's work benefiting low-income and minority groups.

10. ICE arrested a thirty-four-year-old father of two in Santa Fe, using his younger brother, who was in HHS custody, as bait.

11. The *Phoenix New Times* reviewed ICE arrest records and found that employees at two Motel 6 locations in predominantly Latino neighborhoods were alerting ICE about undocumented guests.

12. After an outcry on social media, Motel 6 said it would stop sharing guest lists, but has yet to acknowledge if this was done only at the local level or to explain why employees were collaborating with ICE.

13. The *NYT* reported that the Trump regime is considering lowering the refugee quota to below 50,000, the lowest level since 1980 and less than half the 110,000 admitted by Obama in 2016.

14. An ABC News affiliate reported that DACA recipients are being detained for hours at Texas border checkpoints, with no explanation as to why. The U.S. Border Patrol claims it's new protocol.

15. A federal judge in Chicago blocked DoJ rules under Sessions that require sanctuary cities to cooperate with immigration agents in order to get public safety grants, like the COPS program (noted in Week 43).

16. In the wake of Charlottesville, the Senate unanimously passed a resolution condemning white supremacists, neo-Nazis, and other hate groups. The resolution called Heather Heyer's murder a "domestic terrorist act."

17. The resolution urges Trump and his regime to speak out against hate groups, and it called on the DoJ and federal agencies to use all resources to improve data on hate crimes and address the growth of hate groups.

18. On Tuesday, the House unanimously approved the resolution, and on Wednesday, Press Secretary Sanders said Trump "looks forward" to signing the resolution.

19. Instead, on Thursday, Trump claimed that both sides were to blame in Charlottesville, repeating his charge that those who resisted the neo-Nazis and white supremacists were as much to blame as the alt-right crowds.

20. *WaPo* reported that *Politico*'s editors warned staff about covering topics like physical attacks on journalists and white supremacy: "Try to stay away from those things because some of them are partisan."

21. Trump nominated Eric Dreiband to lead the DoJ's Civil Rights Division. Dreiband testified against the Lilly Ledbetter Fair Pay Act and represented UNC in banning transgender people from using the bathroom corresponding to their gender identity.

22. In her book *Unbelievable: My Front-Row Seat to the Craziest Campaign in American History*, reporter Katy Tur detailed an unwanted kiss from Trump while covering his campaign. Tur said she was "mortified."

23. *Axios* reported that according to an internal memo, the CDC is cracking down on employees' communications with the press. The memo instructs staffers not to speak to reporters, "even for a simple data-related question."

24. On Monday, Trump's DoJ said in a court filing that a judge should erase her finding that Arpaio violated a court order and was guilty of criminal contempt—a symbol of vindication.

25. Two legal advocacy groups filed challenges to Trump's pardon of Arpaio, saying it was unconstitutional because it undermines the power of the judicial branch.

26. *Salon* reported that Trump has formed at least forty-nine new businesses since he announced his run for the presidency and continuing since he took office. He has done almost nothing to separate himself from his businesses.

27. McClatchy reported that despite Trump's pledge not to work with foreign entities, a construction company owned by the Chinese government was hired to work on Trump's new golf club development in Dubai.

28. *BuzzFeed* reported that Trump International Beach Resort in Florida has asked the government for permission to hire more temporary foreign workers. Trump has sought more than 380 H-2 visas since June 2015.

29. Florida attorney general Pam Bondi will start next week on Trump's commission to combat the opioid crisis. In April, an ethics commission cleared Bondi of accepting a twenty-five-thousand-dollar donation from Trump at the same time she received a complaint on Trump University for fraud, which her office dismissed.

30. In a September report on executive branch agency waivers and authorizations, the Office of Government Ethics noted that the White House has refused to provide information requested and to answer follow-up questions on secret White House waivers.

31. The Secret Service released just twenty-two of the visitor names to Mar-a-Lago in response to an April FOIA filing by CREW and two other groups. All twenty-two names were related to Japanese prime minister Abe's February visit.

32. The limited disclosure violated a federal judge's order to turn over all visitor names from January 20 to March 8, 2017. Trump has spent twenty-five days at Mar-a-Lago. CREW promised to head back to court.

33. *WaPo* shared a receipt sent to "National Security Council" from Mar-a-Lago, showing that taxpayers were billed the "rack rate" of $1,092 for a two-night stay. Mar-a-Lago is 99 percent owned by Trump's revocable trust.

34. Derek Harvey, the controversial former Mideast chief for the NSC who was fired by McMaster, is going to work for Nunes.

35. At Trump's behest, McConnell is considering making the blue slip, a way for individual senators to block a nominee from their home states, advisory instead of dispositive when it comes to appeals court nominees.

36. *Politico* reported that, in a reversal of internal policy, OGE told White House staffers that they may accept anonymous donations from lobbyists to legal defense funds.

37. Late Friday, after publication of the *Politico* story, OGE clarified its rules, saying contributions to legal defense funds from anonymous donors, as well as those from lobbyists and foreign governments, are unacceptable.

38. ABC reported that Mnuchin requested use of a government jet to take him and his wife to their honeymoon in Europe, prompting an "inquiry" by the Treasury Department's Office of the Inspector General.

39. CREW sued the Treasury Department for documents relating to Mnuchin's use of a government plane to travel to Kentucky with his wife, Louise Linton. The Treasury Department failed to respond to a prior request for disclosure.

40. Trump's Election Integrity Commission convened its second meeting in New Hampshire. Of note, the list of witnesses included no people of color or women, but did include allies of Kris Kobach and tarnished academics such as John Lott Jr.

41. *Gizmodo* reported on a document obtained from the DoJ showing that Sessions was lobbied by the Heritage Foundation to exclude Democrats, mainstream Republicans, and academics from the Election Integrity Commission.

42. The author of the letter from Heritage, Hans von Spakovsky, participated on a panel during Kobach's New Hampshire meeting. Spakovsky has led the charge for strict voter ID laws for more than a decade.

43. In a statement, Alan King, a Democratic judge from Alabama on Trump's Election Integrity Commission, criticized the commission for overzealous efforts to purge less affluent people from voter rolls.

44. *ProPublica* investigated the Election Integrity Commission's use of e-mails and found that no instruction or training has been given. Some commission members are using private e-mail accounts, which violates federal law.

45. On Monday, Mexico withdrew its offer of aid to help Hurricane Harvey victims, noting that Trump failed to send condolences to Mexico after a magnitude 8.1 earthquake and a hurricane.

46. The *NYT* reported that in a White House meeting, Kelly likened Mexico to Venezuela under the leadership of the Chávez regime and suggested it was on the verge of a collapse, which would have repercussions for the U.S.

47. Despite an ongoing DoJ investigation into Malaysian prime minister Najib Razak for misappropriating billions of dollars from a government fund he controlled, Trump invited him to the White House for a friendly visit.

48. Najib has also been criticized for human rights violations under his leadership. He and his entourage stayed at the Trump International Hotel in D.C.

49. Yahoo reported that Russian news agency Sputnik is under investigation by the FBI into whether it is acting as an undeclared propaganda arm of the Kremlin in violation of the Foreign Agents Registration Act (FARA).

50. Andrew Feinberg, Sputnik's former White House correspondent, turned over e-mails to the FBI. Feinberg said supervisors regularly "would say, 'Moscow wants this or Moscow wants that.'"

51. Feinberg also told MSNBC that many of the popular articles from right-wing media outlets like *Breitbart News*, *InfoWars*, and *Gateway Pundit* were prominently featured on Sputnik's website.

52. RT, the Russian state-owned news outlet, said it will be required by the FBI to register as a foreign agent in the U.S., signaling that its content will be viewed as propaganda of Moscow.

53. Russian journalist Yulia Latynina fled Russia with her family following a series of attacks. Latynina writes for an independent newspaper and Friday received a prize for defending human rights and freedom of the press.

54. Priebus and McGahn both hired lawyer William Burck to represent them in the Mueller Russia probe.

55. *Politico* reported that lawyers for former and current Trump aides are advising clients not to lie for Trump. Lawyers are also warning clients that being connected to Trump won't protect them from criminal charges.

56. The *WSJ* reported that some of Trump's lawyers concluded earlier this summer that Kushner should step down. Among their concerns were undisclosed meetings with Russians and mentioning the Mueller probe to other White House staff.

57. Also, knowing that the June 9 meeting was yet to come out publicly, lawyers had prepared talking points for Kushner's resignation, blaming the toxic political environment and his being used as a weapon against Trump.

58. Russian politician Vyacheslav Nikonov, a member of the Duma, said on live TV that Russia stole the U.S. presidency. The TV show focused on the U.S.'s diminishing power on the world stage.

59. The *Daily Beast* reported that Russia used Facebook's event-management tool to remotely organize and promote political protests, including an August 2016 anti-immigrant, anti-Muslim rally in Idaho.

60. The event was hosted by "SecuredBorders," outed as a Russian front in March. When its Facebook page was taken down last month, the group had 133,000 followers.

61. Former FBI agent Clint Watts noted that this group is an example of the next step in Russian influence: "The second part of behavior influence is when you can get people to physically do something."

62. In the months leading up to the Idaho rally, there were dozens of stories on right-wing websites like *InfoWars* and *Breitbart* implying that immigrants were taking over Twin Falls.

63. *Business Insider* reported on another Russian-linked Facebook group, "Heart of Texas," which had over 225,000 followers and was taken down by Facebook last week.

64. The group started by posting anti-Hillary memes, then shifted as Election Day neared. Starting in November, "Heart of Texas" organized a series of anti-immigrant, anti-Hillary rallies across Texas.

65. *ProPublica* reported that Facebook enabled advertisers to target ads toward users who expressed interest in categories like "Jew hater" and "how to burn Jews." After *ProPublica* contacted Facebook, Facebook took these down.

66. Bloomberg reported that Russia's effort to influence U.S. voters through Facebook and other social media is a "red-hot" focus of Mueller, as well as possible links in that effort to the Trump campaign.

67. The *WSJ* reported that Facebook has given Mueller more details on Russian ad buys, including copies of the ads and details about the accounts that bought them and the targeting criteria they used.

68. While Congress has the power to subpoena Facebook for "basic subscriber records" and to call witnesses, Mueller's search warrant compels Facebook to disclose much more detailed information.

69. *Vanity Fair* reported that congressional investigators and Mueller are focused on whether any Americans helped Russia target social media to impact crucial swing districts and wavering voter demographics.

70. In an interview with *Forbes* after the election, Kushner bragged about the Trump campaign's online efforts and said he had a technology expert "give me a tutorial on how to use Facebook micro-targeting."

71. *Vanity Fair* questioned possible ties between Kushner and Parscale to data-mining firm Cambridge Analytica, whose major investor is Robert Mercer, a patron of Bannon.

72. Senate Intelligence Committee ranking members Burr and Warner said they are likely to ask representatives from Facebook to publicly testify about Russia's activity on their platform during the 2016 election.

73. Senator Warner tweeted that groups linked to Russia that used Facebook to meddle in the 2016 election paid in rubles.

74. A campaign finance reform group, headed by former FEC chair Trevor Potter, said Facebook was an "accomplice" in a Russian influence scheme and called on the company to publicly release Russian ads.

75. *BuzzFeed* obtained a proposal delivered by a Putin diplomat to Trump three months after taking office detailing a wholesale restoration of diplomatic, military, and intelligence channels between Russia and the U.S.

76. Members of the White House and State Department did not dispute the authenticity of the proposal. Sources believe the fact that delivering the proposal meant Russia believed Trump would not hold alleged 2016 election interference against it.

77. The *Daily Beast* reported that the Trump campaign has begun turning over documents to Mueller. The Mueller probe is broad, and it is treating the White House, transition team, and campaign as separate legal entities.

78. At a press briefing Tuesday, Sanders said the DoJ "should certainly look at" prosecuting Comey, claiming he had leaked privileged information to the media and offered false testimony to Congress.

79. On Wednesday, Sanders again said Comey, essentially a political opponent, should face criminal charges for leaking a memo to the *NYT*.

80. Sanders also said ESPN reporter Jemele Hill should be fired for her Monday tweet referring to Trump as "a white supremacist who has largely surrounded himself w/ other white supremacists."

81. The *NYT* reported that after Trump was told that Mueller was appointed, he berated Sessions in the Oval Office. Trump called Sessions an "idiot," and said picking him for AG was "one of the worst decisions he had made."

82. Trump blamed the Mueller appointment on Sessions's decision to recuse himself from the DoJ Russia investigation and said Sessions should resign. Sessions said he would quit and sent a resignation letter.

83. Sessions later told associates that the way Trump demeaned him was his most humiliating experience in decades of public life.

84. Flynn refused a new request to appear in front of the Senate Intelligence Committee. Flynn has offered to testify before both the Senate and House Intelligence Committees in exchange for immunity, but neither committee accepted the offer.

85. Top Democrats on the House Intelligence and Foreign Relations Committees wrote in a letter that Flynn concealed more than a dozen foreign contacts and overseas trips during the process of renewing his security clearances in 2016.

86. The foreign contact information came from three private companies advised by Flynn that were pursuing a joint venture with Russia in 2015 and 2016 to bring nuclear power to several Middle Eastern countries.

87. The *WSJ* reported that Flynn continued promoting the project after he took the position of national security adviser in the Trump regime, even after NSC ethics advisers directed Flynn to remove himself from the project.

88. Even after Flynn was fired by Trump, he continued to lobby members of Trump's inner circle on the project, including Cohn and outside adviser Thomas Barrack, ahead of their May trip to Saudi Arabia.

89. NBC reported that Flynn's son, Michael G. Flynn, is a subject of the federal investigation into Russian meddling in the 2016 election. The inquiry is based at least in part on his work with Flynn Intel Group.

90. CNN reported that the DoJ refused the Senate Judiciary Committee's request to interview two top FBI officials, Carl Ghattas and James Rybicki, on the firing of Comey, citing Mueller's ongoing investigation.

91. The *NYT* reported that Senate Judiciary Committee ranking members Grassley and Feinstein are considering subpoenaing members of the DoJ in their inquiry on Trump's firing of Comey.

92. CNN reported that Susan Rice privately told the House Intelligence Committee that she unmasked the identities of senior Trump officials to understand why the crown prince of the UAE came to New York late last year.

93. The New York meeting (reported in Week 21) took place last December, and was attended by Flynn, Kushner, and Bannon. In an unusual breach of protocol, the UAE did not advise the Obama administration in advance.

94. Shortly after, in January, Erik Prince, brother of Betsy DeVos, attended a secret meeting in Seychelles, arranged by the UAE, with a Russian close to Putin, allegedly to set up a back channel for communications.

95. *WaPo* reported that DHS ordered all federal agencies to ban the use of Kaspersky security software. Cofounder Eugene Kaspersky graduated from a KGB-supported school and worked in Russian military intelligence.

96. The move comes after the GSA removed the company from its approved-vendor list, suggesting a vulnerability exists with Kaspersky that could give the Kremlin backdoor access to the systems the company protects.

97. *BuzzFeed* reported that Flynn, Bannon, and Kushner met with Jordan's King Abdullah II in New York days before Trump was inaugurated to push a deal on which Flynn was advising, concerning nuclear power plants in the Middle East.

98. An eyewitness said at least half a dozen other people were with the trio at the Four Seasons bar. Flynn failed to disclose the meeting in security clearance forms, and Kushner disclosed it only in his amended forms.

99. As part of the for-profit deal, reactors would be built by U.S. companies and security would be provided by the Russian state-owned firm Rosoboron. Congressional approval would have been needed.

100. In February, Abdullah visited the White House and met with Trump, Kelly, and Mattis. A statement afterward underscored that the U.S. "is committed to strengthening the security and economic partnership with Jordan."

101. Bloomberg reported that at the time Veselnitskaya met with Donald Jr. at Trump Tower, she also represented real estate company Prevezon, which was under criminal investigation for a money-laundering case.

102. In 2013, Bharara filed a civil suit against Prevezon. Sessions abruptly settled the case two days before trial in May for just $5.9 million. There was no mention of the ongoing criminal investigation.

103. Democratic lawmakers want to know if Trump team members put pressure on Sessions to settle the case after Bharara was fired.

104. Bloomberg said that in the criminal case, several countries, and banks including Citigroup, Deutsche Bank, UBS, and TD, have supplied documents to the U.S. to track more than two hundred million dollars that left Russia after a massive fraud.

105. *Business Insider* reported that in the Prevezon criminal case, grand jury testimonies are at a key stage. Prevezon is owned by the son of a powerful Russian government official.

106. *Politico* reported that Kyle Freeny, an attorney working on the DoJ's highest-profile money-laundering case, is joining Mueller's team.

107. Democrats flipped two very pro-Trump districts in special elections: there was a twenty-eight-point swing in New Hampshire and a thirty-one-point swing in Oklahoma.

108. Benevity tracked a shift in donations made by U.S. employees of *Fortune* 1000 companies: the ACLU went from number 87 in 2015 to the top spot in 2017. SPLC went from number 230 in 2015 to number 17 in 2017.

109. Early Friday morning, Trump took to Twitter after a bombing in London: "Another attack in London by a loser terrorist," and "Loser terrorists must be dealt with in a much tougher manner."

110. UK prime minister May publicly alluded to Trump's tweet, saying she never thinks it's helpful to "speculate" on "an ongoing investigation." On Friday, McMaster tried to clarify the tweets, saying Trump was speaking "generally."

111. Bloomberg reported that May complained directly to Trump, saying she was unhappy with his response when he called to offer condolences.

112. Joining his classmates at Yale, 185 of Mnuchin's high school classmates from Riverdale Country School called on him to resign.

113. The *WSJ* reported that Representative Dana Rohrabacher contacted the White House trying to broker a "deal" that would end Assange's U.S. legal troubles, in exchange for a computer drive or other data-storage device that he said would exonerate Russia.

114. Kelly intercepted the call and advised Rohrabacher the deal "was best directed to the intelligence community." Kelly did not make Trump aware of Rohrabacher's message.

115. The AP reported that despite a pledge by the Trump inaugural committee to give leftover funds to charities, nothing has been donated. The group has helped pay for redecorating the White House and the Pences' residence in D.C.

116. Trump's inaugural committee raised $107 million, a record amount and double what Obama raised for his well-attended first inauguration. The amount of time to close out the books is also unusual.

117. Pence's press secretary, Marc Lotter, resigned. It was unclear what his next move will be. Pence recently replaced his chief of staff.

118. In an *Atlantic* article, "How Trump Is Ending the American Era," Eliot Cohen described the damage Trump has done and continues to do to America's global standing.

119. On Friday, the Pentagon issued new guidance clarifying that transgender troops currently in the military can reenlist in the next several months. This is yet another example in the past weeks of Mattis going against Trump.

Week 45

SEPTEMBER 17-23, 2017

Week 45 is the week of Paul Manafort—who now, in retrospect, seems an even odder choice by Trump for campaign manager. As Mueller zeroes in on Manafort and Flynn, almost every Trump campaign and White House staffer, past and present, is being drawn into the expanding Russia probe. This week several regime members drew heat for unrepentant kleptocracy.

This week DHS informed twenty-one states that their election systems were targeted by Russia, strangely nearly a year after the election and late on a Friday afternoon. Trump, who benefited from a slight approval-rating reprieve courtesy of positive media coverage of his UN speech read off a teleprompter, continues to deny Russian involvement and to act erratically and unbefitting of the office on both foreign policy and domestic issues. Trump also continues to ignore what is shaping up to be a humanitarian crisis in Puerto Rico.

1. In a series of bizarre Sunday morning tweets, Trump referred to Kim Jong-un as "Rocket Man," retweeted a criticism of a *NYT* story, and retweeted two of his own tweets.

2. Trump also retweeted a GIF of him hitting Hillary in the head with a golf ball, sparking criticism for the violent imagery against a female political opponent. Elected Republicans remained silent.

3. The original account of the golf GIF was @Fuctupmind, whose Twitter feed is full of racist, anti-Semitic, and anti-LGBTQ tweets.

4. Trump began his first UN remarks by mentioning Trump World Tower: "I actually saw great potential right across the street, to be honest with you."

5. Trump threatened to "totally destroy" North Korea and, using his new nickname for Kim Jong-un, said, "Rocket Man is on a suicide mission." North Korea's ambassador walked out before Trump's speech started.

6. Trump also said, "I will always put America first," and urged other leaders to put their own countries first. Several analysts compared Trump's speech to the rhetoric of the 1920s, when traditionalists reacted to changing times by stoking hate of others.

7. *WaPo*'s Asia Pacific reporter noted that Kim Jong-un's regime tells North Korean people every day that the U.S. "wants to destroy them and their country. Now, they will hear it from another source"—Trump.

8. On Wednesday, in an escalating war of words, North Korea's foreign minister likened Trump to a "dog barking."

9. On Thursday, while threatening escalation, Kim Jong-un called Trump a "mentally deranged U.S. dotard." North Korea analysts noted that it is unprecedented to have Kim Jong-un himself directly attack a U.S. leader.

10. On Friday, the *Los Angeles Times* reported that aides repeatedly warned Trump not to deliver a personal attack on Kim Jong-un at his UN speech, saying insults could irreparably escalate tensions.

11. Pew Research reported America's image has suffered since Trump took office. In a survey spanning thirty-seven nations, just 22 percent have confidence Trump is doing the right thing in international affairs, versus 64 percent for Obama.

12. As tensions rise with North Korea, 76 percent of South Koreans and 72 percent of Japanese say they have no confidence in Trump to do the right thing in world affairs.

13. Trump also blasted Iranian leaders as a "corrupt dictatorship behind the false guise of a democracy," and said that "the Iran deal was one of the worst and most one-sided transactions," and an "embarrassment" to the U.S.

14. On Friday, Iran showed off its new ballistic missile at a military parade in Tehran. President Rouhani said, "When it comes to defending our country, we will ask nobody for their permission."

15. At a bilateral meeting, Trump praised Turkey's authoritarian leader Erdogan, saying, "We have a great friendship." Erdogan is the subject of international condemnation for his brutal crackdown on dissidents.

16. State authorities in New Hampshire are investigating the wounding of an eight-year-old biracial boy as a possible hate crime. Teenagers pushed the boy off a picnic table with a rope around his neck.

17. U.S. Army recruiters are canceling contracts with hundreds of immigrant recruits, exposing some to deportation. Recruiters claim the move is to eliminate onerous background investigations during the enlistment process.

18. *Newsweek* reported white supremacists are recruiting on college campuses. At the University of Houston, flyers reading "Beware the International Jew" and "Imagine a Muslim-Free America" were hung around campus.

19. McClatchy reported that the Trump regime is considering a policy that would fast-track the deportation of thousands of unaccompanied Central American teenagers who arrived at the southern border.

20. More than 150,000 children who crossed the southern border into the U.S., escaping violence and poverty in El Salvador, Honduras, and Guatemala, would be sent back when they turn eighteen, without seeing an immigration judge first.

21. NPR reported that parents in Texas who traveled to a hospital to get their two-month-old a lifesaving operation were arrested and put into deportation proceedings. A hospital nurse may have tipped off border patrol.

22. Under Obama, immigration agents avoided enforcement actions at hospitals, schools, and churches. The Trump regime rounds up people in the country illegally at those places, even if they have no criminal record.

23. The *Guardian* reported that Trump has assembled the most male-dominated government in decades, with 80 percent of nominations for top jobs in the Trump regime going to men.

24. On Friday, DeVos formally rescinded Obama-era policies on campus sexual assault meant to protect victims, instead siding with men's rights advocates. No formal policy was put in place, just a higher burden of proof.

25. The *WSJ* reported that as Trump's temporary travel ban expired Friday, DHS may replace it with a targeted approach that will impact nine countries, only one of which is not majority Muslim. Trump has no business interests in the six already on the list; his involvement in the additional three is uncertain.

26. A triathlon scheduled to take place at Trump National Golf Club in North Carolina, originally named "Tri at the Trump," then rebranded "Tri for

Good," was canceled amid controversy. This would have been the race's fourth year.

27. WJAR-TV, one of Rhode Island's most-watched television stations, said it is being forced by its owner, Sinclair Broadcast Group, to broadcast multiple programs favorable to Trump.

28. The AP reported that the Republican Governors Association quietly set up a news site, the *Free Telegraph*. Critics called the website, which makes no mention of a being sponsored by an official party committee, propaganda.

29. On Monday, Trump said he was looking into staging a military parade down Pennsylvania Avenue for next July 4.

30. On Wednesday, in a speech at a lunch with African leaders, Trump praised the health care of "Nambia," a nonexistent African country.

31. Nicaragua announced that it will sign on to the Paris climate accord—leaving only Syria and the U.S. the only countries opposed.

32. Trump blocked a woman with stage 4 Hodgkin's lymphoma on Twitter. Laura Packard had tweeted that the proposed health care repeal bill, known as Graham-Cassidy, would jeopardize the lives of people like her who rely on Obamacare exchanges for coverage.

33. The AP reported that lawmakers across the country introduced dozens of bills this year that would close or limit public access to a wide range of government records and meetings.

34. The Trump regime has removed links to taxpayer-funded climate data on the U.S. Geological Survey website. A search for "Effects of Climate Change" returned 2,825 items in December; today it returns zero items.

35. *WaPo* reported that in a memo to Trump, Interior Secretary Zinke is recommending modifying ten national monuments created by Obama, including shrinking the boundaries of at least four.

36. Supreme Court justice Neil Gorsuch campaigned for McConnell in a speech in McConnell's hometown on Thursday. In Week 21, McConnell passed the filibuster-ending "nuclear option" that allowed Gorsuch to get confirmed.

37. *WaPo* reported that Democrats are introducing the Hotel Act, legislation that would ban federal officials from using taxpayer funds for travel expenses at Trump-owned properties or locales.

38. *Politico* reported that HHS Secretary Tom Price used a private jet for travel, breaking precedent. Price has been an outspoken critic of federal spending and has developed a plan for department-wide savings at HHS.

39. *Politico* also reported that Price traveled by private plane at least twenty-four times since early May, costing taxpayers more than three hundred thousand dollars. Many flights were to conferences, so dates were known well in advance.

40. The most frequent justification for chartered flights is lack of comparable options. *Politico* found several commercial flight options at comparable times for five chartered flights Price took last week.

41. *WaPo* reported that according to a senior administration official, the White House did not approve Price's travel on chartered planes.

42. On Friday, *WaPo* reported that the HHS inspector general is investigating Price's use of two dozen chartered flights in recent months.

43. ABC reported that Treasury Department investigators are also looking into a charter flight Steven Mnuchin took from New York to D.C. on August 15 at a cost to taxpayers of twenty-five thousand dollars. There are ample flight and rail alternatives available for this route.

44. For a third time, Republicans in the Senate tried to pass health care legislation without using regular order or trying for any bipartisan support. McCain's vote against these tactics will likely cause the bill to fail.

45. The Trump regime continued to sabotage Obamacare: HHS announced it will shut down the @HHSgov website for twelve hours during all but one Sunday in the remaining six weeks of open enrollment season.

46. Jeff Mateer, Trump's nominee for a federal judgeship in Texas, in two 2015 speeches, described transgender children as evidence of "Satan's plan" and lamented that states were banning conversion therapy.

47. *WaPo* reported that the EPA has spent $833,000 on Scott Pruitt's round-the-clock personal security detail over the past three months, doubling what was spent by his predecessors, amid massive cost cutting for the agency.

48. According to a copy of his schedule obtained by *WaPo*, Pruitt met regularly with executives from the auto, mining, and fossil fuel industries—in some cases shortly before making decisions favorable to them.

49. *Politico* reported that a review of Trump's picks for USDA hires reveals that the agency is full of campaign staff and volunteers, many of whom have little or no federal policy experience or knowledge about agriculture.

50. Trump's picks are also being paid above their pay scale. One former truck driver is being paid at one of the highest level on the federal government's pay scale, a GS-12, earning eighty thousand dollars annually, although he has no college degree.

51. Former Trump campaign adviser Michael Caputo said he will need to liquidate part of his children's college fund to pay for specialized legal representation in the Mueller Russia probe.

52. Flynn's siblings launched a legal defense fund to help defray the costs of the Russia probe. The family will not disclose the identity of donors, raising concerns from ethics experts.

53. Reuters reported that Trump is using money donated to his reelection campaign and the RNC to pay for his legal fees related to the Russia probe.

54. CNN reported that the RNC spent $231,000 in August to cover Trump's personal legal fees, paying Jay Sekulow $131,000 and John Dowd $100,000.

55. The RNC has also payed nearly two hundred thousand dollars for Donald Jr.'s legal fees related to the Russia probe in August.

56. The *WSJ* reported that the Republican Party is funding Trump's legal defense in the Russia probe with help from a handful of wealthy individuals, including Len Blavatnik, a Ukrainian-born American with close business ties to Russian oligarchs.

57. The *NYT* reported that Donald Jr. has decided to forgo his Secret Service protection, saying he wants more privacy.

58. Jody Hunt, Sessions's chief of staff and Trump's pick to be assistant attorney general in charge of the DoJ's Civil Division, was present at a key meeting between Sessions, Comey, and Trump, at which Trump asked all but Comey to leave.

59. Sessions's new chief of staff, Matthew Whitaker, said that Mueller's Russia probe is turning into a "witch hunt" and that Rosenstein should "order Mueller to limit the scope of his investigation."

60. On Tuesday, Senate investigators canceled a meeting with Michael Cohen, saying he broke an agreement by releasing a statement and speaking to the media. NBC reports the committee will subpoena Cohen instead.

61. The *Guardian* reported on the eighth person at the June 9 Trump Tower meeting, Ike Kaveladze, saying he is an associate of some of Russia's richest and most powerful people.

62. Kaveladze was involved in the 2013 takeover of Stillwater Mining by Norilsk Nickel, a Russian mining firm owned by an associate of Putin—the first Russian company to take a majority stake in a U.S. company. Kaveladze served on the new company's board.

63. *NYT* reporters overheard two Trump lawyers, Cobb and Dowd, discussing over lunch a clash within Trump's legal team over how much to cooperate with Mueller.

64. According to the overheard conversation, White House officials fear that their colleagues are wearing wires for Mueller. The *NYT* reported that in the aftermath McGahn erupted at Cobb, and Kelly reprimanded Cobb.

65. CBS reported that FBI surveillance of Manafort during 2016 picked up conversations between Manafort and Russians about the campaign. The surveillance may also have picked up conversations between Manafort and Trump.

66. The *WSJ* reported that Mueller's team interviewed Deputy Attorney General Rosenstein in June or July about Trump's firing of Comey. Mueller has independent authority over his investigation, but ultimately answers to Rosenstein.

67. Rosenstein said that Trump shrugged off any potential consequences for firing Comey. Rosenstein also turned over to Mueller's team the May 8 memo from Trump that outlined his rationale for firing Comey.

68. CNN reported that Manafort was wiretapped by the U.S. government. The wiretap was first authorized by the special court that handles FISA warrants in 2014, when Manafort was the subject of an FBI investigation.

69. The surveillance was discontinued late last year for lack of evidence, then restarted by the FBI under a new FISA warrant for ties between the Trump campaign and Russia, which extended into early 2017.

70. The *NYT* reported on aggressive tactics being employed by Mueller's investigators against Manafort, including prosecutors telling him as they searched his Virginia home that they planned to indict him.

71. To get the search warrant, Mueller's team had to show probable cause that Manafort's home contained evidence of a crime. To pick the lock, prosecutors had to persuade a judge that Manafort was likely to destroy evidence if given advance warning of the search.

72. Also of note: Mueller's team first learned of the e-mails between Donald Jr. and Russians to set up the June 9 meeting through *NYT* reporting.

73. *WaPo* reported Mueller has requested extensive records and e-mail correspondence from the White House for thirteen categories that investigators for the special counsel have identified as critical to their probe.

74. Mueller's agents have zeroed in on Manafort and Flynn. Their past associates are being questioned on whether they tried to conceal consulting work that could have benefited foreign governments.

75. The *NYT* reported that Mueller's latest requests relate to the areas of Flynn's hiring and firing, Comey's firing, and Trump's Oval Office meeting with Lavrov and Kislyak at which he said the Comey firing has relieved "great pressure" on him.

76. Documents are also sought that record internal White House communications with Manafort, as well as with Trump's campaign foreign policy team: Carter Page, J. D. Gordon, Keith Kellogg, George Papadopoulos, Walid Phares, and Joseph E. Schmitz.

77. Other subjects on which Mueller is requesting records include Flynn's conversations with Kislyak, Spicer's statements on Comey's firing, the June 9 Trump Tower meeting, and the White House response to that meeting.

78. *Axios* reported that Spicer's colleagues say he filled "notebook after notebook" at meetings during the campaign and then at the White House.

79. When *Axios*'s Mike Allen texted Spicer for a comment, Spicer responded, "From a legal standpoint I want to be clear: Do not email or text me again. Should you do again I will report to the appropriate authorities."

80. *WaPo* reported that less than two weeks before the Republican National Convention, Manafort made an offer, in an e-mail through an intermediary, to give Russian oligarch Oleg Deripaska a private briefing.

81. Manafort and Deripaska had a business relationship in which Manafort was paid as an investment consultant. Deripaska is one of Russia's richest men and someone Putin "turns to on a regular basis," according to a U.S. diplomatic cable released by WikiLeaks.

82. Per documents shared with *WaPo*, Manafort e-mails indicate that he may have been looking to get paid money owed by past clients using his role and influence as Trump's campaign manager. An e-mail in April asked, "How do we use to get whole?"

83. Also of note, Deripaska claimed that Manafort siphoned off nineteen million dollars of funds intended for investments—for which Deripaska sued in U.S. court. It is possible Manafort was looking to wipe that debt away.

84. In another e-mail, Manafort communicated with Konstantin Kilimnik, his longtime employee in Kiev who attended Soviet military school, using code terms like "OVD" for Deripaska and "black caviar" for possible payments.

85. The *NYT* reported that in order to help defray his legal expenses, Manafort is working for allies of the leader of Iraq's Kurdish region on a referendum on Kurdish independence from Iraq. The U.S. opposes the referendum.

86. As part of that work, Manafort may leave the country and return to the region in the coming days for the vote.

87. The *NYT* reported that New York–based law firm Skadden, Arps has been asked by the DoJ for documentation related to work arranged by Manafort for Viktor Yanukovych, the Russia-aligned former prime minister of Ukraine.

88. The work was part of an effort to shield Yanukovych from international condemnation for his government's prosecution and conviction of former Ukrainian prime minister Yulia Tymoshenko without evidence and for political reasons.

89. Skadden, Arps has returned half of the $1.1 million in fees the firm received. It is unclear if the document request relates to Mueller's Russia probe and its focus on Manafort.

90. Former Trump campaign manager Lewandowski, while defending Trump, said he hopes Manafort, Stone, or any others on the campaign who colluded with Russia in 2016 "go to jail for the rest of their lives."

91. Mueller brought in Stephen Kelly, former congressional affairs chief for the FBI, to act as a liaison to Capitol Hill. Kelly will be a point of contact and keep congressional investigators up to date on the special counsel's probe.

92. Twitter will meet with the Senate Intelligence Committee next week relating to the committee's investigation into Russian interference in the U.S. election.

93. Bowing to pressure from lawmakers and the public, Facebook will release three thousand ads bought by a Russian agency to congressional investigators. Facebook also vowed to be more "transparent."

94. The *Daily Beast* reported that Russians used Facebook to organize more than a dozen pro-Trump rallies in Florida during the 2016 election. The page for one such group, "Being Patriotic," was closed by Facebook in August 2017.

95. On Friday morning, Trump described Russia's purchase of Facebook ads as a "Russia hoax" while attacking Hillary, tweeting that the greatest influence on the election was "the Fake News Media 'screaming' for Crooked Hillary Clinton."

96. *USA Today* reported that according to the FBI, as many as thirty-nine states had their election systems scanned or targeted by Russia. Several states are now considering switching back to paper ballots.

97. On Friday, DHS contacted election officials in twenty-one states to notify them that they had been targeted by Russian government hackers during the 2016 election. This was the first time government officials contacted the states.

98. DHS did not make the names of the twenty-one states public, citing privacy. *BuzzFeed* reported that state officials are outraged and want to know why it took DHS a year to inform them. Senator Warner called the delay "unacceptable."

99. Pennsylvania and Wisconsin, states with odd voting patterns that were the subject of recounts, were among the twenty one disclosed as of Friday night. Officials in Florida, another surprise on Election Night, said they were also a target of Russia.

100. On Friday night, former DNI Clapper said U.S. intelligence's findings on Russia's election interference "did serve to cast doubt on the legitimacy" of Trump's victory and expressed concern that Russian interference will continue.

101. On Friday night in Alabama, at what was supposed to be a campaign rally for Senator Luther Strange, Trump said of his support of Strange, "I'll be honest, I might have made a mistake."

102. The campaign rally turned out to be a ninety-minute rant, during which Trump again derided Kim Jong-un, calling him "Little Rocket Man."

103. Trump also said of Colin Kaepernick, who knelt during the national anthem at football games in the 2016 season in protest against American racism, that NFL owners should respond by saying, "Get that son of a bitch off the field."

104. The next morning, Trump tweeted about Stephen Curry, a member of the NBA champion Golden State Warriors who had expressed reservations about going to the White House: "Stephen Curry is hesitating, therefore invitation is withdrawn!"

105. A *WaPo* opinion writer described how Trump is making Americans sick: including rising blood pressure, a surge in mouth guards for nighttime teeth clenching and grinding, and unusually busy psychotherapists.

106. Hurricane Maria hit Puerto Rico, decimating the island and leaving 3.5 million without electricity. On Friday, seventy thousand were evacuated over concern that a dam might fail. Trump did little to mention or address this crisis.

107. The Trump regime plans to roll back Obama-era limitations on drone strikes and commando raids outside conventional battlefields.

Week 46

SEPTEMBER 24–30, 2017

This week the country turned to a humanitarian crisis in Puerto Rico, where 3.5 million Americans lack basics like water, food, medicine, and electricity. At least sixteen have already died. Trump seemed split between denying the crisis altogether and blaming Puerto Rico, its officials, and the media. The regime's late and inadequate response to Hurricane Maria is the clearest fallout of Trump's unstaffed federal agencies.

This week Trump's regime came under increased scrutiny for blatant and irreverent kleptocracy. HHS Secretary Price was the first casualty from unfolding scandals of several regime members involving millions spent on chartered and military flights, and other wasted taxpayer money. Social media giants Facebook and Twitter also took center stage in the probe of Russia's involvement with the 2016 election and possible Trump campaign complicity.

1. At his UN speech on Saturday, North Korea's foreign minister warned that a strike against the U.S. mainland is "inevitable" following Trump's mocking Kim Jong-un with the nickname "Little Rocket Man."

2. An ABC/*WaPo* poll found that 66 percent see Trump as doing more to divide than unite the country. Just 37 percent trust Trump on his handling of North Korea.

3. Eight months in, the ABC/*WaPo* poll found Trump's approval at 39 percent (57 percent disapprove), the lowest approval level eight months into office since Truman's presidency.

4. The *St. Louis Post–Dispatch* reported that more than 120 people were forcibly arrested in downtown St. Louis by police cracking down on protests against the acquittal of police officer Jason Stockley in the shooting death of Anthony Lamar Smith, an African American man. Numerous innocent bystanders were swept up by police.

5. *BuzzFeed* reported that the DHS published new requirements for immigration files, including social media handles, aliases, associated identifiable information, and search results. The rules take effect October 18.

6. The new policy will cover not only new immigrants, but also green card holders and naturalized citizens. The policy will also affect U.S. citizens who communicate with immigrants.

7. In February, the DHS Office of Inspector General reported that the DHS pilot program for using social media to screen applicants for immigration lacked criteria to determine if the practice is effective.

8. NBC reported that the Trump regime wants to lower the number of refugees allowed into the U.S. to 45,000 in 2018, down significantly from the 110,000 Obama had aimed for in fiscal year 2017, and lower than even the State Department's recommended cap of 50,000 in the travel ban.

9. The *Boston Globe* reported that fifty immigrants were arrested in Massachusetts as part of nearly five hundred rounded up nationwide in sanctuary cities. As a state, Massachusetts did not fall in line with Trump's aggressive deportation policies.

10. Reuters reported that the number of immigrants without criminal histories arrested by ICE is up by more than 200 percent since Trump took office.

11. Trump's DoJ is demanding private account information for thousands of Facebook users in three separate search warrants targeting anti-administration activists. Three activist leaders are named.

12. One leader, Emmelia Talarico, operated the DisruptJ20.org page where Inauguration Day protests were organized and discussed. The page was visited by roughly six thousand users.

13. The *Daily Beast* reported that documents obtained under a FOIA request strongly suggest ICE agents are using private information obtained by NSA surveillance in their investigations.

14. *Politico* reported immigration judges sent to the U.S.-Mexico border to speed deportations by Trump are finding their caseloads nearly empty, while full caseloads back home are left unattended to.

15. Ten Confederate flags posters with cotton branches attached to them were found at American University Tuesday night.

16. Franklin Township in Ohio, a state that wasn't part of the Confederacy, will reinstall a confederate monument taken down in the wake of Charlottesville.

17. At the Air Force Academy, after racial slurs were found scrawled outside black students' doors, Lieutenant General Jay Silveria gathered all four thousand cadets and told them, "You should be outraged not only as an airman, but as a human being."

18. House Republican Mark Walker referred to his female colleagues as "eye candy." After public condemnation, he said he regretted his "flippant remark meant to be lighthearted."

19. An article in the *Columbia Journalism Review* argued that "given the surfeit of evidence," including most recently Trump's "castigation of NFL players," it is appropriate to use the term "racist" about Trump.

20. At a private dinner Monday night, Trump sounded satisfied with his NFL feud, telling guests, "It's really caught on."

21. David McCraw of the Palmetto Restaurant and Ale House in Greenville, South Carolina, said his restaurant will ban all NFL games until protests end.

22. In a letter to students and parents, the principal of Parkway High School in Los Angeles said athletes must "stand in a respectful manner" during the national anthem, or risk losing playing time or being removed from their team.

23. Trump's DoJ argued that employers can fire people because of their sexual orientation. The DoJ inserted itself into a case opposing the Equal Employment Opportunity Commission (EEOC) brought by Donald Zarda, who was fired by Altitude Express for being gay.

24. *BuzzFeed* reported that, for the first time, HHS's ten regional representatives will not help states with planning for the upcoming open enrollment period of Obamacare.

25. In a letter, Oklahoma officials blamed the Trump regime for rising insurance premiums after the regime missed a deadline to approve a waiver that would have reduced premiums by 30 percent for 130,000 residents.

26. Starting Wednesday and continuing for days, Trump repeatedly blamed the failure of the latest GOP Obamacare repeal attempt on a U.S. senator being in the hospital, confounding his own aides. No senator is in the hospital.

27. On Monday, at a rally in Alabama for Strange that Pence also attended, campaign staffers informed reporters that they couldn't leave the pen to interview voters.

28. On Tuesday, at a speech at Georgetown Law, Sessions criticized U.S. universities for being "politically correct" and infringing on students' free-speech rights.

29. Students and faculty protested Sessions's speech by kneeling outside the auditorium where the speech was held, but ironically, many were not allowed inside.

30. Chuck Rosenberg, the acting head of the DEA, resigned Tuesday, saying Trump has little respect for the law. Rosenberg has served under both George W. Bush and Obama, and served twice as Comey's chief of staff.

31. *Politico* reported that even after departures of many Trump aides this summer, many who remain are reaching out to headhunters, lobbyists, and GOP operatives for help in finding new jobs.

32. *USA Today* reported that information on Ivanka's China supply chain has disappeared since she took a senior role in the Trump regime, according to companies that track shipping data. Tracking data has vanished, leaving the identity of 90 percent of shipments' origins a mystery.

33. Ivanka's business secrecy obscures whether China is using business ties to try to influence the White House—and whether Ivanka could profit from Chinese government subsidies while destroying American jobs.

34. On Monday, in a speech to an oil industry group, Zinke said nearly one-third of Interior's employees are not loyal to Trump. He also said he is working to make the department's culture more business friendly.

35. Zinke also added, without explanation, "Fracking is proof that God's got a good sense of humor and he loves us."

36. After campaigning for McConnell in Kentucky in Week 45, Gorsuch addressed a conservative group at the Trump International Hotel in D.C., prompting protests and criticism for speaking at a venue that is the subject of several lawsuits against Trump.

37. Sunlight Foundation reported that the Trump National Golf Club in D.C. hosted the Turkish Airlines World Golf Cup in September, again raising Emoluments Clause concerns. The Turkish government owns 49 percent of Turkish Airlines.

38. *WaPo* reported that at a private dinner Tuesday, Trump told attendees he thought his calling Kim Jong-un "Rocket Man" at his address to the UN would be seen as a compliment, not an insult.

39. *Politico* reported that Kushner used a private e-mail set up last December to communicate with transition team members about government business.

40. Kushner's lawyer said fewer than one hundred e-mails were sent to or received from that private account from January through August, but failed to address December, a month when Kushner had undisclosed meetings with Russians.

41. On Monday, the *NYT* reported that six White House advisers (Kushner, Ivanka, Cohn, Bannon, Miller, and Priebus) used private e-mail accounts to discuss White House matters, sparking charges of hypocrisy.

42. While four advisers used commercial e-mail services like Gmail, Kushner created a domain, IJKFamily.com, in December 2016 for himself and Ivanka.

43. On Monday, Representative Cummings, the top Democrat on the House Oversight Committee, announced he is investigating Kushner's use of personal e-mails.

44. CNN reported that Kushner didn't inform the Senate Intelligence Committee about the existence of his personal e-mail account during his recent closed interview.

45. Burr and Warner wrote a letter to Kushner's attorney instructing him to double-check that he has turned over every relevant document, including those from his personal e-mail account, as well as any other e-mail accounts.

46. *Politico* reported the White House launched an internal probe of private e-mail use following *Politico*'s Sunday report. Of particular interest are Kushner and Ivanka's use of a private e-mail domain.

47. The *WSJ* reported that McGahn considered resigning last summer over lack of protocols for meetings between Trump and Kushner, and concern that the meetings would be construed by Mueller as an effort to coordinate stories.

48. Reuters reported in a letter, Senators John McCain and Ben Cardin noted that two months after signing it, Trump has not begun enforcing a law imposing new sanctions on Russia, Iran, and North Korea.

49. The letter also noted that the Trump regime has not yet provided information related to Russia's defense and intelligence sectors required under the measure. That information is due tomorrow.

50. *WaPo* reported that Obama met privately with Facebook CEO Mark Zuckerberg at a world leaders meeting in Peru on November 19 to warn him that if Russian interference wasn't addressed, it would get worse in the next presidential election.

51. Facebook contacted the FBI in June 2016 over concerns of Russian espionage after tracking a hacking group, but failed to recognize that Russian operatives were pumping propaganda using ad microtargeting.

52. *WaPo* reported that Russian operatives used targeted ads on Facebook to exploit racism and anti-Muslim and anti-immigrant sentiments, and to sow chaos among Americans during the 2016 election.

53. The divisive themes promulgated by Russian operatives on Facebook mirrored those used by Trump and his supporters on social media and on right-wing websites. Investigators are looking into the possibility of coordination.

54. *BuzzFeed* reported that Bannon plotted to infiltrate Facebook by getting a spy through the company's hiring process. The idea came from Chris Gacek, a former congressional staffer who now works at the Family Research Council.

55. *Politico* reported that in addition to Trump, Russian-funded Facebook ads also backed Stein and Sanders.

56. The *Daily Beast* reported that Russian operatives impersonated real American Muslims in a Facebook group called United Muslims of America named after a real nonprofit, and shared fake memes about Hillary, McCain, and more.

57. CNN reported that Russian operatives bought ads on Facebook that referenced Black Lives Matters and targeted residents of Ferguson and Baltimore. The ads were meant to sow discord among Americans.

58. Congressional investigators are examining the sophisticated targeting by the Russian operatives, and whether they knew how to target their ads because of collusion with the Trump campaign.

59. Paul Horner, a leading purveyor of fake news during the 2016 election, was found dead of an apparent drug overdose. He was thirty-eight. Horner told *WaPo* in 2016 that he thought Trump won the White House because of him.

60. *Mother Jones* reported on a new study that found Russia concentrated millions of fake news tweets to twenty-seven states, twelve of which were swing states, including Pennsylvania, Michigan, and Florida, where Trump narrowly won.

61. In a Facebook post, Zuckerberg said he was wrong to dismiss the notion of fake news and its impact on the election: "Calling that crazy was dismissive and I regret it. This is too important an issue to be dismissive."

62. In explaining why Trump hasn't been suspended from Twitter despite violating the company's guidelines relating to threats of violence (against North Korea), the company cited his tweets' "newsworthiness."

63. The *NYT* reported that Russian operatives relied heavily on Twitter to influence the 2016 election. The platform was used for large-scale automated messaging using "bot" accounts to spread false stories and promote news articles.

64. Russian operatives' use of Twitter continues: this week a network of accounts activated around Trump's admonishment of the NFL. These accounts continue to identify divisive issues and fan the flames.

65. Twitter executives met with House and Senate investigators who are probing Russian interference. The company found roughly two hundred accounts believed to be tied to the same Russian operatives who bought ads on Facebook.

66. Twitter handed over copies of all sponsored tweets purchased by Kremlin-backed news agency RT. Twitter said RT spent $274,000 on ads in 2016.

67. Warner said he wasn't satisfied with Twitter's Senate Intelligence Committee briefing, saying it was "frankly inadequate on almost every level."

68. The *WSJ* reported that Google is conducting a broad internal investigation to assess whether Russian operatives used its ads or services to try to manipulate voters. The company is also talking with congressional investigators.

69. On Tuesday, the Trump regime denied a request by Puerto Rico to waive the Jones Act in order to ease shipping restrictions and help get fuel and supplies to the island. Trump had waived the act during Harvey and Irma.

70. On Tuesday, McCain asked the Trump regime to reverse course and waive the Jones Act to help the Puerto Rican people.

71. On Wednesday, amid uproar, Trump said he was reluctant to waive the Jones Act, saying that "we have a lot of shippers and a lot of people that work in the shipping industry" who are opposed to lifting the act.

72. Bowing to public pressure, Trump finally waived the Jones Act on Thursday, announced through a tweet by Press Secretary Sanders.

73. Lawmakers said Trump's ten-day Jones Act waiver is not enough for Puerto Rico. Several members of Congress are pushing for a one-year period.

74. On Thursday, the AP reported that despite acting DHS secretary Elaine Duke saying "the relief effort is under control," Puerto Ricans say relief is failing them. A young mother of two said, "I have not received any help, and we ran out of food yesterday."

75. On Friday, while speaking about his tax plan, Trump said Puerto Rico relief is hampered by its being surrounded by water: "This is an island, surrounded by water. Big water. Ocean water."

76. Cummings, the ranking Democrat on the House Oversight Committee, and Stacey Plaskett, the nonvoting representative in the House for the U.S. Virgin Islands, called for an emergency hearing on Trump's hurricane response to Puerto Rico and the Virgin Islands. The Katrina hearing was cited as precedent.

77. On Friday, the general in charge of relief in Puerto Rico said there are "not enough" troops or equipment in place to help.

78. On Friday, in a tear-filled plea to the media, San Juan mayor Carmen Yulín Cruz said, "I will do what I never thought I was going to do. I am begging, begging anyone who can hear us to save us from dying."

79. On Saturday, in a series of tweets, Trump attacked the mayor of San Juan for "poor leadership" and being "nasty." Mayor Cruz tweeted asking people to focus on "saving lives" and not to be "distracted by anything else."

80. Trump also sent a series of tweets before and after his golf game Saturday blaming the "Fake News Media," working in conjunction with Democrats, for spreading disinformation and "doing their best to take the spirit away from our soldiers."

81. Trump also tweeted blame at the people of Puerto Rico during the week, saying they "want everything to be done for them" and that they were "already suffering from broken infrastructure & massive debt."

82. Ironically, Trump's golf club in Puerto Rico filed for bankruptcy, listing assets of nine million dollars and liabilities of seventy-eight million dollars. The Puerto Rican government's thirty-three-million-dollar investment in Trump's Coco Beach club was completely wiped out.

83. *WaPo* reported on Trump's "lost weekend"—after Maria hit Puerto Rico on September 20, Trump spent a long weekend (September 21–24) in New Jersey, during which he and his top aides effectively went dark on Puerto Rico.

84. It wasn't until the following Tuesday, September 26, that Trump addressed the situation in Puerto Rico, after senior officials said on Monday that Trump "was becoming frustrated by the coverage he was seeing on TV."

85. *Politico* reported that Price combined business travel on government-funded private jets with personal travel, including a trip to St. Simons Island, where he and his wife own property, and a lunch with his son.

86. On Thursday, *Politico* reported that Price also took military jets to Europe, Asia, and Africa with his wife, costing taxpayers over five hundred thousand dollars.

87. In total, Price's travel costs exceeded one million dollars since May. On Thursday, Price said he'd pay for "his seat" on the flights and wrote a check for fifty-two thousand dollars.

88. Trump said Price is a "fine man" but that he "didn't like the optics." Price resigned late Friday, joining an unusually long list of Trump regime firings and resignations.

89. *WaPo* reported that the EPA is spending almost twenty-five thousand dollars to construct a secure, soundproof communications booth for Pruitt. No previous EPA head had a similar setup.

90. Pruitt and his deputies have taken other steps to heighten security, including having EPA staff members surrender their cell phones and other digital devices before entering meetings with Pruitt.

91. *WaPo* also reported that Pruitt took charter and military flights that cost taxpayers more than fifty-eight thousand dollars. The EPA's inspector general announced a preliminary probe into Pruitt's travels to Oklahoma at taxpayer expense.

92. *Politico* reported that Interior Secretary Zinke has taken several flights on private or military aircraft, including a twelve-thousand-dollar charter plane to his hometown in Montana, and two chartered flights for Zinke and his staff to the U.S. Virgin Islands in March.

93. *WaPo* reported that Zinke charged taxpayers twelve thousand dollars for a flight on a private plane owned by oil executives.

94. *WaPo* reported that Veterans Affairs Secretary David Shulkin took a ten-day, taxpayer-funded trip to Europe in July with his wife. Shulkin had four days of meetings, and the rest was spent on vacation, including attending Wimbledon, taking a cruise, and sightseeing.

95. CBS reported that the Trump kids' ski vacation to Aspen in March cost taxpayers more than half a million dollars, including $330,000 in security costs, $196,000 in lodging, and tens of thousands in other expenses.

96. On Wednesday, Trump launched his tax plan, saying, "I don't benefit. I don't benefit." The *NYT* reported, based on the two pages of his 2005 return that are the only personal Trump tax documents to have been made public, that Trump could save more than $1.1 billion under his new plan.

97. The *WSJ* reported that the Treasury Department took down a 2012 economic analysis that contradicts Mnuchin's take on who benefits from a corporate tax cut.

98. CNN reported that after months of being at odds, the IRS Criminal Investigation division is now sharing years of Manafort's and Flynn's tax returns with Mueller. It is not clear whether Mueller has Trump's tax returns.

99. CNN also reported that the IRS Criminal Investigation division has been working with the FBI to investigate Manafort since before the election, in probes that center on possible money laundering and tax fraud issues.

100. ABC reported that Mueller is investigating Russian-American money that flowed into the Trump campaign during the election. Three Americans with significant Russian business connections contributed almost two million dollars.

101. *Politico* reported that Pence sent his lawyer to meet with Mueller over the summer to express his willingness to cooperate in the Russia probe.

102. CNN reported that Mueller could start interviewing White House staff this week or possibly next.

103. Spicer hired criminal defense attorney Chris Mead to represent him in Mueller's Russia probe.

104. *BuzzFeed* reported that Tillerson and Lavrov had a forty-five-minute private meeting. Undersecretary of State Tom Shannon, Deputy Assistant Secretary of State Elisabeth Millard, and other U.S. officials were excluded, and a full readout was not provided.

105. After the candidate he backed in Alabama, Luther Strange, lost the Senate primary Tuesday, Trump deleted his tweets supporting Strange.

106. Roy Moore, the winner in Alabama who was backed by Bannon, is so extremist in his racism, xenophobia, and homophobia that many Republicans, when asked, simply claimed they had never heard of him.

107. Senator Bob Corker, a Trump ally during the 2016 campaign, became the second Republican to unexpectedly announce he will not seek reelection in 2018.

108. A Quinnipiac poll found that 69 percent of Americans think Trump should stop tweeting from his personal account, and 57 percent think he is not fit to serve.

109. Trump waited four days to call Merkel and congratulate her on winning reelection as chancellor of Germany. Merkel had called Trump on November 9, one day later.

110. Fifty days after Trump announced he was going to declare the opioid crisis a national emergency, he still has not made it official.

San Juan mayor Carmen Yulín Cruz comforts a victim of Hurricane Maria. (THAIS LLORCA/EPA-EFE/SHUTTERSTOCK)

Week 47

OCTOBER 1-7, 2017

This was a dark week for our country, with the unfolding humanitarian crises in Puerto Rico and the U.S. Virgin Islands and the deadliest mass shooting in modern history in Las Vegas. Trump's tin ear and lack of empathy to victims of these events were conspicuous in his ominous "calm before the storm" statement Thursday.

Major stories broke on Kushner and Ivanka's use of personal e-mail accounts, all of which were surreptitiously moved to a Trump Organization server. Mueller's Russia probe continued full steam, and news of a meeting between Mueller's team and Christopher Steele indicated the dossier is likely being used as a road map. As in every weekly list, this week rights and protections were taken away from women and marginalized communities.

1. Despite the humanitarian crisis in Puerto Rico, for a second weekend since Maria hit, Trump golfed Saturday and Sunday at Trump properties. DoD reported Saturday that just 45 percent of Puerto Ricans have drinking water and 5 percent have electricity.

2. Late Saturday, the White House sent flattering readouts of Trump's conversations with a former governor of Puerto Rico, and the governors of Puerto Rico and the U.S. Virgin Islands. Readouts are typically reserved for calls with foreign leaders.

3. On Saturday, Trump sent twenty-five tweets, his highest number of tweets in a day since taking office, continuing his manufactured battle with the NFL and his attacks on "fake news" and the mayor of San Juan.

4. On Saturday, after his first tour of Puerto Rico, the DoD's primary military liaison with FEMA, top general Jeffrey Buchanan, said the damage there is "the worst I've ever seen."

5. Fourteen Democrats on the House Natural Resources Committee called for an oversight hearing on the Trump regime's handling of the Puerto Rico and U.S. Virgin Islands relief efforts.

6. On Sunday night, in the deadliest mass shooting in modern U.S. history, one man who owned forty-seven guns killed fifty-eight people in Las Vegas and wounded hundreds. Trump said the quick response of law enforcement was "in many ways, a miracle."

7. In the aftermath of the shooting, top trending stories on Facebook and Google promoted politicized fake news from unreliable sources like 4chan that claimed the shooter was a Democrat opposed to Trump.

8. While refusing to call the white male shooter a terrorist, Trump referred to him as "a very sick man" and "demented." The first bill Trump signed revoked an Obama-era gun check regulation that added to the national background check database people who received disability checks for mental illness and people found unable to handle their financial affairs.

9. NBC obtained the Trump White House talking points distributed for the Las Vegas shooting. They include "thoughts and prayers," "gather facts before making policy arguments," and comparisons to Baltimore and Chicago murders.

10. On Saturday, funding for the Children's Health Insurance Program (CHIP), which provides health care for nine million children and pregnant women in low-income households, expired. No action was taken by Congress to renew it.

11. Two high school football players in Crosby, Texas, were kicked off their high school football team for protesting during the national anthem—one knelt and one raised his fist.

12. According to Shaun King, at least two NFL teams are bowing to pressure by Trump and plan to create policies requiring their players to stand during the national anthem.

13. Joining Saudi Arabia, Iraq, and the UAE, the U.S. voted against a UN Human Rights Council resolution that condemns the death penalty for consensual same-sex sexual acts. The resolution passed by a 27–13 margin.

14. A judge in Texas ruled that state officials would be violating state privacy laws if they handed over voters' personal information to Trump's Election Integrity Commission. The judge issued a temporary restraining order.

15. Trump's DoJ is investigating affirmative action at Harvard. The revelation came to light after watchdog group American Oversight filed a FOIA request for information on affirmative action investigations at two schools.

16. Brownsville, Texas, city commissioner Cesar De Leon apologized after the release of a recording of his racist rant using the "n-word" about county and city officials. After initially refusing to, he resigned under pressure.

17. *BuzzFeed* reported that Trump regime lawyers asked a court to dismiss a lawsuit filed to halt Trump's transgender military ban, saying the Pentagon hasn't finalized the details of the ban yet.

18. Six transgender soldiers who are part of the lawsuit say they have already suffered—their medical treatments have been canceled and their careers are being derailed—and hence they need immediate relief.

19. On Wednesday, Sessions rolled back an Obama-era policy that protected transgender workers from discrimination, saying, "Title VII does not prohibit discrimination based on gender identity per se."

20. On Friday, Trump rolled back Obamacare's birth control mandate, allowing any employer to cite religious or moral objections to covering the cost of birth control for employees under its health care plan.

21. On Friday, Sessions issued new guidelines that instructed federal agencies and attorneys to protect religious liberty. The policy provides broad exemptions to discriminate against women and LGBTQ people.

22. ABC reported that Sessions consulted with Alliance Defending Freedom, a Christian legal advocacy group that champions conservative causes, ahead of issuing the new guidelines.

23. After Governor Jerry Brown signed a law limiting cooperation between local police and ICE in California, the Trump regime said it will go after undocumented immigrants and likely pick up "collateral" they were not initially targeting.

24. *Mother Jones* reported that according to documents released by a federal court, Kris Kobach tried to urge Trump to roll back voter protection by amending the National Voter Registration Act, adding requirements to make it harder to register to vote.

25. On Tuesday, fourteen days after Hurricane Maria decimated the island, Trump visited Puerto Rico. He praised federal and local officials for the response, but purposefully excluded the mayor of San Juan.

26. Trump complained about the costs of helping Americans in Puerto Rico, saying, "You've thrown our budget a little out of whack because we've spent a lot of money." Similar statements were not made about Texas or Florida.

27. Trump hailed the relief response as "incredible" and "great," and bragged that "only sixteen people are known to have died," many less than Katrina. Hours later, the death count rose to thirty.

28. In an image that became symbolic of his trip to Puerto Rico and his lack of empathy for the people, Trump went to a supply distribution point dressed in a dark suit and tossed rolls of paper towels into a crowd.

29. Oxfam took the unusual step of criticizing the U.S. government. Oxfam said it is "outraged at the slow and inadequate response" by the Trump regime in Puerto Rico.

30. Oxfam also announced it would be taking the rare step of intervening in an American disaster, pursuing its own two-pronged approach in Puerto Rico.

31. CNN's Dr. Sanjay Gupta, who is in Puerto Rico, warned that tens of thousands could die for want of insulin, blood pressure medications, and antibiotics, as well as sweltering heat and lack of food and water.

32. By Friday, the official death count in Puerto Rico reached thirty-six, but as NPR reported, the actual toll is expected to be much higher, with uncounted bodies piling up in places that have no way to communicate.

33. Representative Luis Gutiérrez, who traveled to Puerto Rico at his own expense, said the media reports are correct: the island is a humanitarian crisis. Gutiérrez said the Trump regime doesn't "want you to know the truth."

34. *WaPo* reported that FEMA removed statistics about drinking water access and electricity in Puerto Rico from its website on Thursday morning.

35. Following a social media outcry, the statistics were restored on Friday afternoon. They reveal that the progress is extremely slow.

36. On Wednesday morning, Trump said he would wipe out Puerto Rico's debt, causing trading prices of Puerto Rico municipal bonds to plummet. Director of the Office of Management and Budget Mick Mulvaney dialed back: "I wouldn't take it word for word with that."

37. *Politico* reported on a third, previously undisclosed e-mail account on Kushner and Ivanka's private domain. The three accounts raise concern about the security of sensitive government documents.

38. The third account has hundreds of e-mails from White House addresses. In addition to Kushner and Ivanka, personal household staff had access to the account for scheduling purposes.

39. *USA Today* reported that Kushner and Ivanka's personal e-mails were redirected to a Trump Organization server within three days after public disclosure about the existence of personal e-mails.

40. The move also comes shortly after Mueller asked the White House to turn over records related to his investigation of Russia's interference in the election.

41. Representative Elijah Cummings asked the FBI to investigate whether Kushner and Ivanka exposed classified information through their use of personal e-mail and its transfer to Trump Organization servers.

42. The U.S. Office of Special Counsel found Ambassador Haley violated the Hatch Act by promoting a House candidate on Twitter. Haley was given a warning. The investigation followed a complaint filed by CREW in June.

43. *WaPo* reported that, back in August, Trump saw an article about Republican-controlled Iowa requesting federal permission to fix its Obamacare markets. Trump's instruction was, "Tell Iowa no."

44. Trump's HHS has taken many steps to suppress sign-ups for Obamacare, including slashing grants for groups that help consumers, cutting the enrollment period in half, and reducing the advertising budget by 90 percent.

45. McClatchy reported that Kushner and Ivanka were both fined two hundred dollars for missing deadlines to submit financial reports required by government ethics rules. This is Kushner's second time being fined for late filings.

46. After receiving an eighteen-day filing extension, Kushner has made changes to his financial disclosure forms thirty-nine times. In many cases, those changes were in response to questions from the OGE.

47. Eli Miller, Treasury Secretary Mnuchin's chief of staff, flew in hedge fund billionaire Nelson Peltz's private jet to Palm Beach. The Treasury Department's inspector general office has launched an inquiry.

48. *BuzzFeed* reported that the U.S. intelligence unit of Mnuchin's Treasury Department has been violating domestic surveillance laws by spying on financial records of U.S. citizens and companies.

49. The Interior Department's inspector general opened an investigation into Secretary Zinke's travel, including his use of taxpayer-funded charter and military planes, and his mixing of official trips with political appearances.

50. The *NYT* reported on EPA chief Pruitt's schedule: almost every day he has multiple meetings, sessions, or speaking engagements with top corporate executives and lobbyists of the industries the EPA regulates, but rarely does he meet with environmental groups or consumer or public health advocates.

51. *Politico* reported that in a closed-door meeting with wealthy donors, Pence's chief of staff, Nick Ayers, floated the idea of a "purge" of anti-Trump Republicans, saying they are blocking Trump's legislative agenda.

52. A federal judge in Phoenix dismissed the criminal case against Arpaio and accepted Trump's pardon. In her fourteen-page ruling, she held off on ruling on Arpaio's request to throw out all orders in the case that would completely clear his record.

53. *Mother Jones* reported that ten months in, Trump still hasn't appointed someone to head the DHS's National Protection and Programs Directorate, an agency charged with protecting our elections from cyberattacks.

54. In a letter to the White House, Cummings, the top Democrat on the House Oversight Committee, asked Kellyanne Conway, known to have traveled with Price, to provide documentation related to all her noncommercial flights.

55. Reuters reported that Energy Secretary Perry took a charter flight from Pennsylvania to Ohio the day before Price resigned. Commercial alternatives were available.

56. *WaPo* reported that Transportation Secretary Chao used government planes seven times, including day trips to cities within an hour of D.C., as well as for trips to France and Italy, which cost taxpayers tens of thousands of dollars.

57. The *NYT* reported that Mnuchin traveled on military jets seven times at a cost of more than eight hundred thousand dollars. The investigation by the OMB found that while he broke no laws, Mnuchin gave loose justifications for the costly flights.

58. Donald Jr. has delivered several speeches, earning as much as one hundred thousand dollars per speech. His speeches raise ethics and conflict-of-interest concerns, especially as related to access to the White House.

59. Trump's Interior Department rejected twenty-five petitions to list a variety of animal species as endangered or threatened, including several whose decline is linked to climate change. Trump has yet to nominate a director of the Fish and Wildlife Service.

60. In response to a FOIA lawsuit, the Secret Service said it does not have a complete Mar-a-Lago visitor log. As noted in Week 44, all the Secret Service has turned over so far is a one-page listing of twenty-two Japanese officials.

61. Joel Clement, an Interior Department executive turned whistleblower who claimed that the Trump regime retaliated against him for disclosing how climate change affects Alaska Native communities, resigned Wednesday.

62. The *Guardian* reported that, in what may be a watershed case, U.S. professor David Carroll is suing Cambridge Analytica in British court to ask for his personal data back. UK law allows for such requests, unlike U.S. law.

63. On Monday, Facebook shared in a blog post that Russia purchased one hundred thousand dollars' worth of political ads, which reached about ten million Americans. More than half the ads were seen after the election, indicating that Russia continues to meddle in U.S. politics.

64. *WaPo* reported on research by social media analyst Jonathan Albright, who found that Russian propaganda on Facebook may have been viewed by hundreds of millions of people, perhaps billions.

65. The *WSJ* reported that after internal debate, Facebook decided to scrap mention of Russia in a public report released on April 27 about manipulation of its platform during the 2016 election.

66. Instead, in a significantly shortened report, Facebook blamed "malicious actors." It is unclear how much Facebook knew at the time. Not until September 6 did Facebook identify Russia as the source of interference.

67. *Fast Company* reported that after it found accounts suspected of being Russian-sponsored on Instagram (which is owned by Facebook) and called Facebook to confirm, Facebook updated its blog post to clarify that about 150 political ads sold to Russia showed up on Instagram.

68. CNN reported that Russian operatives targeted Michigan and Wisconsin with Facebook ads. Some of the ads were highly sophisticated in their targeting of key demographic groups in areas of the states that turned out to be pivotal.

69. Trump won both states by under 1 percent: Michigan by 10,700 of 4.8 million votes cast and Wisconsin by 22,700 votes. Congressional investigators want to know if the Russian operatives advertising on Facebook had any assistance from the Trump campaign.

70. The *WSJ* reported on the most significant security breaches in years: in 2015 Russian hackers stole NSA data. The breach could enable Russia to evade NSA cybersurveillance and infiltrate U.S. networks.

71. The breach is the first confirmed time Kaspersky software was exploited by Russian hackers. As noted in Week 34, Eugene Kaspersky was trained at a KGB-sponsored technical school and worked in Russian military intelligence.

72. *Politico* reported that Trump loyalists are losing patience with the congressional Russia probes, saying they have distracted from his agenda and allowed Democrats to question the legitimacy of his win.

73. *WaPo* said these loyalists are pushing Republican committee chairs to wrap up their investigations and make the scandal disappear. An interim press briefing by Senators Richard Burr and Mark Warner, ranking members of the Intelligence Committee, on Wednesday was cited as an example, after Burr proposed issuing an interim report and Democrats on the committee objected, fearing that Burr was feeling pressure to conclude the investigation prematurely.

74. Burr and Warner said they concurred with U.S. intelligence's assessment that Russia interfered in the 2016 election. They also said the issue of collusion is still open.

75. Burr and Warner also detailed some threads of investigations including Russian efforts on social media, the April 2016 meeting at the Mayflower Hotel, and changes to the Republican Party platform.

76. Burr said they had "hit a wall" with the Steele dossier because the author would not meet with them. On Thursday, Rachel Maddow, however, reported that Christopher Steele is open to meeting with the Senate Intelligence Committee, contradicting Burr's claims.

77. On Wednesday, Reuters reported that Mueller has taken over FBI inquiries into the Steele dossier as part of the special counsel's Russia probe.

78. On Thursday, CNN reported that Mueller's team met with Steele this past summer. The broad assertion of the dossier, that Russia waged a campaign to interfere in the election, is now accepted by U.S. intelligence.

79. The CIA and FBI took Steele's research seriously enough that they chose not to include it in the publicly released January report on Russian interference to avoid divulging the parts of the dossier they had corroborated and how.

80. Three Russian owners of Alfa Bank, Mikhail Fridman, Petr Aven, and German Khan, sued Fusion GPS and its founder, claiming their reputations were unfairly tattered by the dossier. The three sued *BuzzFeed* in Week 28.

81. *Mother Jones* reported that Senator Ron Wyden, a member of the Senate Intelligence Committee, does not concur with Burr's statement that he can say certifiably there was no voter tampering. Wyden also questioned Burr's handling of the investigation.

82. The *Daily Beast* reported that the Senate Judiciary Committee is not investigating Russian interference, but engaging in routine oversight of the DoJ. Sources include a staffer for Grassley, Republican chair of the committee.

83. *WaPo* reported that Trump lawyer Michael Cohen turned over documents to congressional investigators and Mueller related to two previously undisclosed contacts with Russians. These contacts are not related to Trump Tower Moscow.

84. Cohen and a business associate e-mailed weeks before the Republican National Convention about whether Cohen would travel to an economic conference in Russia attended by Putin and his top financial and government leaders.

85. Cohen also received a proposal in late 2015 for a Moscow residential project from a company founded by a Russian billionaire who once served in the Russian parliament. Cohen maintains he never traveled to Russia.

86. *Foreign Policy* reported a previously undisclosed meeting: Representative Rohrabacher met with Veselnitskaya in Moscow two months prior to the infamous June 9 meeting with Donald Jr.

87. *Politico* reported that Trump lawyer Ty Cobb is putting the finishing touches on launching a legal defense fund to help midlevel White House staffers cover their legal costs related to Mueller's Russia probe.

88. *Newsweek* reported that Robert Mercer, Bannon ally and part owner of Cambridge Analytica, donated two hundred thousand dollars to the Republican Party legal defense fund the day Trump fired Comey.

89. The *Atlantic* revealed e-mails between Manafort and Kilimnik referenced in the *WaPo* story in Week 45. The e-mails suggest that Manafort was extremely eager to please Russian oligarch Deripaska and to get paid for past debts.

90. Kilimnik met Manafort on August 2 in New York City. E-mails sent by Kilimnik before the meeting made a point about the "future of his country." Days before, Trump said "Wouldn't it be a great thing if we could get along with Russia?"

91. After Tillerson said Saturday he was reaching out to Pyongyang in hopes of starting a new dialogue, Trump undercut him Sunday, tweeting, "I told [Rex] he is wasting his time trying to negotiate with Little Rocket Man."

92. NBC reported that Tillerson almost resigned this past summer after Trump's Boy Scout speech. Days before that speech, Tillerson referred to Trump as a "moron" in a meeting with national security and cabinet officials.

93. After the report, Tillerson pulled together an impromptu news conference to publicly praise Trump. CBS's Bob Schieffer described it as "not like a news conference, it was more like a hostage tape."

94. Senator Bob Corker, a Trump ally during the campaign who is retiring, in a harsh rebuke of Trump, said Kelly, Mattis, and Tillerson are the "people that help separate our country from chaos."

95. The *New Yorker* reported that shortly after Tillerson was confirmed, he met Trump at the White House, and Trump "began fulminating about federal laws that prohibit American businesses from bribing officials overseas."

96. On Friday, for the first time in seven years, the U.S. economy lost jobs. Expectations for September were to add eighty thousand jobs; however, thirty-three thousand jobs were lost. Job totals from July and August were also downwardly revised.

97. On Thursday, at a dinner surrounded by military leaders and their spouses at the White House, Trump warned that this is "the calm before the storm." What he meant was unknown by even members of his staff.

98. The mystery around his pronouncement continued on Friday when he was asked about the statement and responded, "You'll find out," then winked.

99. A September AP-NORC poll showed Trump reaching his lowest approval yet: 32 percent approve, 67 percent disapprove. Trump's approval among Republicans fell to 67 percent.

100. The poll also found that just 24 percent think the country is headed in the right direction, 26 percent believe Trump is a strong leader, 23 percent view him as honest, and 16 percent say he is level-headed.

101. One year after the infamous *Access Hollywood* tape went public, women's advocacy group UltraViolet played the footage, looping it again and again, on a large screen on the Mall in D.C. for twelve hours straight.

102. *ProPublica* reported that Ivanka and Donald Jr. were close to being charged for felony fraud in 2012 for misleading prospective buyers of units in the Trump SoHo. Their partners were Felix Sater and Tevfik Arif.

103. Trump lawyer Kasowitz contributed twenty-five thousand dollars to Manhattan district attorney Vance before a sit-down, and later donated thirty-two thousand dollars. The case against Ivanka, Donald Jr., Sater, and Arif was dropped. Felix Sater is a frequent subject of the *Weekly List*, including involvement with Trump Tower Moscow.

104. Breaking from the advice of Tillerson and Mattis, Trump is expected to decertify the landmark deal curbing Iran's nuclear program. Iran has not breached the accord, but instead, Trump claims, has breached the "spirit" of the deal.

105. The *Huffington Post* reported that the Trump regime is preparing to repeal the Clean Power Plan, an Obama-era climate change policy which limits greenhouse gas emissions from power plants. Trump has called the policy "stupid."

106. Almost three weeks after Hurricane Maria, when just 12 percent of the population of Puerto Rico had electricity and 55 percent had drinking water, on Saturday morning, Trump made his sixty-ninth trip to a Trump golf course during his 260 days in office.

Week 48

OCTOBER 8-14, 2017

This week numerous accounts leaked to the media by Trump aides and Republican insiders, starting with ominous statements by Senator Bob Corker, described a White House in peril. Increasingly, Trump seems isolated, erratic, unmoored, and unfit for office.

The humanitarian crisis in Puerto Rico worsened with the inadequate response by the federal government. Amid criticism, Trump threatened to pull out, but later backed off. Although the death count officially stands at forty-five, reporting revealed possibly hundreds more preventable deaths related to Hurricane Maria.

Trump remains silent on both California's deadliest wildfires and the deadliest combat incident since he took office. He continues to focus on undoing Obama's legacy, piece by piece. The Mueller investigation hit Trump's inner circle, and social media's role in aiding Russia continues to unfold.

1. On Saturday night, Richard Spencer led another white supremacist torch-lit rally at the University of Virginia. The rally lasted ten minutes and forty to fifty people attended. Spencer vowed, "We will keep coming back."
2. On Sunday, Trump attacked former ally Corker in a series of incendiary tweets, saying "Corker 'begged' me to endorse him for re-election" and "wanted to be Secretary of State." Trump claimed to have said no to both.
3. Corker responded, tweeting that it's a shame the White House has become an "adult day care center" and that someone "missed their shift this morning."
4. On Sunday, Pence left a Colts game after a protest during the national anthem. Pence later issued a full statement opposing the protests. The Colts were playing the 49ers, a team known to protest.
5. Before the game, Pence tweeted a photo of himself and his wife wearing Colts gear. The photo was one he originally tweeted in 2014.
6. Shortly after, Trump tweeted that he had asked Pence to leave the game "if any players kneeled," and said he was proud of the Pences.
7. The pool of journalists covering Pence were not allowed into the stadium and were told, "There may be an early departure from the game." ABC estimated that Pence's flight cost taxpayers nearly $250,000.

8. Bowing to pressure from Trump, the Cowboys' Jerry Jones, after kneeling with players in week 3 of the season, changed course, saying any player who "disrespects the flag" by kneeling will not be allowed to play.

9. On Tuesday, Trump threatened the NFL over protests, saying the league is "getting massive tax breaks" and the law should be changed. This claim is false: the NFL gave up its 501(c)(6) tax-exempt status in 2015.

10. On Tuesday, bowing to pressure from Trump and fans, NFL commissioner Roger Goodell, who previously had said players had the right to voice their opinions, sided with owners who are opposed to letting players demonstrate.

11. On Monday, Pence headlined a fund-raiser in California for Republicans including controversial Kremlin ally Rohrabacher. Rohrabacher had a previously undisclosed meeting in Russia with Veselnitskaya, described in Week 47.

12. The University of Wisconsin approved a policy that calls for suspending or expelling students who disrupt campus speeches and presentations. The policy mirrors Republican legislation passed by the state assembly.

13. On Columbus Day, unlike Obama, Trump celebrated the "arrival of Europeans," but did not mention the suffering of Native Americans.

14. On Sunday, Trump's DHS allowed the Jones Act waiver, which helped speed relief to Puerto Rico, to expire. No explanation was given.

15. Trump's EPA announced it would repeal the Clean Power Plan, Obama's signature policy to curb greenhouse gas emissions from power plants. The statement described the regulation as the "so-called Clean Power Plan."

16. On Friday, Trump addressed the Values Voters Summit hosted by the Family Research Council, which has been classified by SPLC as an antigay hate group. Trump is the first U.S. leader to address the group.

17. Reuters reported that the Trump regime has been quietly cutting support for halfway houses for federal prisoners, severing contracts with as many as sixteen facilities, forcing some inmates to stay behind bars longer.

18. ABC reported that the Treasury Department's inspector general is looking into allegations reported by *BuzzFeed* in Week 47 that agency officials have been illegally looking at private financial records of U.S. citizens.

19. A report compiled by the Government Accountability Office, at House and Senate Democrats' request, found that the Trump transition team ignored ethics officials and refused to cooperate with the GAO.

20. Trump named Kathleen Hartnett White to the White House's Council on Environmental Quality. Hartnett White, a climate science denier, once said, "Fossil fuels dissolved the economic justification for slavery."

21. In response to a filing by CREW, Trump's DoJ told a court in D.C. that Trump can destroy records without judicial review, including tweets.

22. Brian Brooks became the second candidate under consideration for deputy treasury secretary to withdraw from consideration. Mnuchin said he has no plans to fill the number two slot in his agency.

23. *WaPo* reported that at the Interior Department, when Zinke enters the building a staffer takes the elevator to the seventh floor, climbs the stairs to the roof, and puts up a special flag. The flag comes down when he leaves.

24. On Wednesday, NBC reported that Tillerson's calling Trump a "moron" was provoked by Trump's suggesting a tenfold increase in the U.S. nuclear arsenal during a July 20 meeting with high-ranking national security leaders.

25. In response to the story, which he called "Fake News," Trump tweeted a threat to revoke the broadcasting licenses of "NBC and the Networks."

26. Later that afternoon, at a news conference, Trump again lashed out at the independent news media, saying it's "frankly disgusting the press is able to write whatever it wants to write."

27. In a statement Wednesday night, Republican senator Ben Sasse asked Trump if he was "recanting" his oath to protect the First Amendment.

28. Indiana Republican lawmaker Jim Lucas drafted a bill that would require professional journalists to be licensed by state police.

29. Under pressure to confirm Trump's judicial nominees, McConnell will no longer allow "blue slips," used by senators to deny a nominee from their state a Senate Judiciary Committee hearing and vote on confirmation.

30. The Trump regime withdrew from the United Nations Educational, Scientific and Cultural Organization (UNESCO), citing anti-Israel bias and the organization's being in arrears on a $550 million payment. Israel remains part of UNESCO.

31. The *NYT* published an interview with Corker in which he said Trump is treating his office like a "reality show" with reckless threats to other countries that could put our country "on the path to World War III."

32. Corker said he is concerned about Trump and that Trump's behavior should concern "anyone who cares about our nation." He added that there is no "good cop, bad cop" strategy with Tillerson—Trump is undermining diplomacy.

33. Corker said nearly all Senate Republican share his concerns: "the vast majority of our caucus understands what we're dealing with here."

34. *WaPo* reported that Trump is frustrated by his cabinet and that he is not getting enough credit for his handling of three hurricanes. Trump is lashing out and rupturing alliances with both Republicans and Democrats.

35. One confidant said Trump is like a whistling teapot, saying when he does not blow off steam, he can turn into a pressure cooker and explode: "I think we are in pressure cooker territory."

36. *Politico* quoted ten current and former White House aides who employed strategies like delays and distractions as "guardrails" in trying to manage Trump's impulsivity.

37. *Vanity Fair* reported that sources say Trump is "unstable," "losing a step," and "unraveling." They say the White House is in crisis as advisers struggle to contain Trump, who is increasingly unfocused and consumed by dark moods.

38. Trump allegedly told his former bodyguard Schiller, "I hate everyone in the White House!" Kelly is allegedly miserable in the job, and is staying on in a sense of duty and to keep Trump from making disastrous decisions.

39. One former official speculated that Kelly and Mattis have discussed what they would do if Trump ordered a nuclear strike: "Would they tackle him?"

40. According to sources, Bannon said the risk to Trump's presidency wasn't impeachment, but the Twenty-fifth Amendment. Bannon thinks Trump has only a 30 percent chance of making it through a full term.

41. In a column titled "What Bob Corker Sees in Trump," conservative columnist Peggy Noonan urged Republicans that they have a duty to speak on the record about what they see happening with Trump.

42. On Thursday, at a signing ceremony for his health care executive order, Trump nearly walked out of the room without signing the order. Pence pulled him back in.

43. On Tuesday, Trump said in an interview with *Forbes* that he could beat Tillerson in an IQ test. Trump met with Tillerson later that day at the White House.

44. On Friday, Corker called out Trump for his effort to disempower Tillerson, saying: "You cannot publicly castrate your own secretary of state without giving yourself that binary choice."

45. CNN's Fareed Zakaria said, "It's very clear now that we essentially have no diplomacy going on in the United States," adding that the way Trump has treated Tillerson is "the most dramatic example of it."

46. On *60 Minutes*, Parscale, the Trump campaign's digital director, claimed he fine-tuned ads on Facebook to directly reach voters with the exact messages they cared most about. He also claimed he handpicked Republican Facebook employees to help.

47. The *Daily Beast* reported that the Kremlin recruited two black video bloggers, Williams and Kalvin Johnson, to produce incendiary YouTube videos calling Hillary a racist. The videos were spread on social media platforms.

48. *WaPo* reported that Google has uncovered evidence of about one hundred thousand dollars' worth of ads purchased by Russian agents to spread disinformation across the company's many products, including YouTube, during the 2016 election.

49. Google said the ads do not appear to be from the same Kremlin-linked troll farm that bought ads on Facebook. Some ads touted Trump, Bernie Sanders, and Jill Stein, while others aimed to fan the flames of divisive issues.

50. Representative Devin Nunes, who recused himself from the Russia probe as chair of the House Intelligence Committee, unilaterally signed off on subpoenas to Fusion GPS, the research firm that produced the Steele dossier. Democrats were not consulted.

51. Reuters reported that Chuck Grassley, the Republican chair of the Senate Judiciary Committee, is also taking steps to discredit the dossier, according to Democrats on the committee.

52. Carter Page, who earlier said he was eager to testify, told the Senate Intelligence Committee that he will not cooperate with any requests to appear before the panel on Russia and will plead the Fifth.

53. The *Daily Beast* reported that the House Permanent Select Committee on Intelligence is looking at Cambridge Analytica's work from the Trump campaign as part of its Russia probe.

54. Cambridge Analytica, which has ownership ties to the Mercers and Bannon, was brought in to help the campaign by Kushner. The company is also under investigation in the UK for its role in Brexit.

55. The *NYT* reported that Israel caught Kaspersky Lab working with the Russian government to search the world for U.S. secrets, using Kaspersky software to scan for classified words. Kaspersky software is used by four hundred million people.

56. The *WSJ* reported that Russia's use of the Kaspersky program to spy on the U.S. is broader and more pervasive than the operation against one individual noted in Week 47. Trump continues to deny Russian meddling in the U.S. election.

57. *Politico* reported that as part of their posture to show cooperation, Trump's attorneys may offer Mueller a meeting with Trump. If Mueller doesn't ask by Thanksgiving, attorneys may force the issue by volunteering his time.

58. Legal experts were surprised by Trump's lawyers' strategy, noting that Trump would be speaking under oath, that he routinely distorts facts, and that he would be interviewed in connection with a criminal investigation.

59. CNN reported that Russian operatives used YouTube, Tumblr, and even Pokémon Go as part of their effort to interfere in the election, using a campaign titled "Don't Shoot Us" to spread a divisive message.

60. NBC reported that Manafort had a previously undisclosed twenty-six-million-dollar loan from Deripaska through a series of transactions. It is unclear if the twenty-six million dollars is a loan or an indirect payment from the Russian oligarch.

61. The loan brings the total financial relationship between Manafort and Deripaska to sixty million dollars over the past decade, according to financial documents filed in Cyprus and the Cayman Islands.

62. Manafort's spokesman, Jason Maloni, initially responded to NBC with a statement including the sentence: "Mr. Manafort is not indebted to former clients today, nor was he at the time he began working for the Trump campaign."

63. Maloni's statement was later revised and that sentence was removed. Both Manafort and Maloni have received subpoenas to supply documents and testimony in the Mueller probe.

64. Yahoo reported that Andrew Feinberg, former correspondent for Sputnik, provided a style guide he was given the day he started at Sputnik and e-mails to FBI investigators looking into possible violations of the law that requires agents of foreign nations to register with the DOJ.

65. Further, the Senate Select Committee on Intelligence is investigating RT and Sputnik as possible parts of the Russian state-run propaganda machine in the broader probe into Russia's election meddling.

66. On Friday, Mueller's team interviewed Trump's former chief of staff, Priebus. Priebus's lawyer said he voluntarily met with investigators and "was happy to answer all of their questions."

67. Priebus was present during Trump's efforts to limit the Russia probe and for discussions that led to the firing of Comey. He was also asked to leave the Oval Office before the infamous Trump-Comey conversation.

68. *Politico* reported that Twitter deleted tweets and other user data of potentially irreplaceable value to investigators in the Russia probe.

69. Federal investigators believe Twitter was one of Russia's most potent weapons. Bots and fake accounts launched recurring waves of pro-Trump, anti-Clinton story lines that were either false or greatly exaggerated.

70. The AP reported that Twitter has turned over 201 accounts linked to Russian attempts at influencing the 2016 election to Senate investigators. It is unclear if the posts associated with these accounts have been deleted.

71. CNN reported that an attorney for Roger Stone said he has complied with the House Intelligence Committee request to provide the identity of his intermediary to WikiLeaks' Assange.

72. The *WSJ* reported that congressional investigators are homing in on connections between the Trump campaign and social media companies such as Facebook and Twitter. Digital director Parscale was paid eighty-eight million dollars during the campaign, making him the highest-paid vendor.

73. Every vendor that worked with Parscale on the Trump campaign signed a nondisclosure agreement, and there are no federal disclosure requirements for online ads.

74. Both Congress and Mueller are investigating the role that activity on Facebook and Twitter played in the 2016 election, and whether the Russian social-media activity was in any way connected to the Trump campaign.

75. A Morning Consult poll found Trump's approval has fallen in every state since he took office. The swings were as high as 30 percentage points in blue states Illinois and California, to 11 points in red state Louisiana.

76. A Reuters/Ipsos poll found that Trump's popularity is eroding in small towns and rural communities: in September, 47 percent approved and 47 percent disapproved, down from 55/39 in his first four weeks in office.

77. *WaPo* reported that as of October 10, after 263 days in office, Trump has made 1,318 false or misleading claims.

78. The Brookings Institute released a 108-page report that concluded Trump "likely obstructed justice" in his firing of Comey. If Mueller agrees, there are legitimate articles of impeachment that could be drawn up.

79. In a letter to Mattis, over one hundred Democrats are demanding proof that Trump did indeed consult with the Pentagon, as he claimed in a tweet, prior to announcing his ban of transgender individuals from military service.

80. A Kaiser Foundation poll found that 62 percent of Americans say Puerto Ricans aren't getting the help they need. Just 76 percent were aware that Puerto Ricans are U.S. citizens.

81. On Thursday, in a series of tweets, Trump threatened to abandon Puerto Rico's recovery effort, blaming the island for its infrastructure problems and saying relief workers would not stay "in P.R. forever."

82. The tweets follow harsh criticism from Puerto Rico of the Trump regime's response to Hurricane Maria. One Puerto Rican said, "He doesn't think of us as Americans."

83. Trump also quoted Sharyl Attkisson, a television journalist with Sinclair Broadcasting, who said that while Puerto Rico survived Hurricane Maria, now "a financial crisis looms largely of their own making."

84. Later Thursday, the White House issued a statement committing "the full force of the U.S. government" for now, but adding, "successful recoveries do not last forever."

85. At a House Energy and Commerce hearing about efforts to rebuild the island's energy grid, Energy Secretary Rick Perry referred to Puerto Rico as a country.

86. The next day, Trump referred to the Virgin Islands' governor as a president.

87. *Vox* reported that although the official death count in Puerto Rico is 45, they found 81 deaths linked to Hurricane Maria, as well as 450 more reported deaths, most of causes still unknown, and 69 still missing.

88. Puerto Rico's governor said four deaths are being investigated as cases of leptospirosis, a disease spread by animals' urine through contaminated water. A total of ten people have come down with the disease.

89. Rachel Maddow reported that a doctor resigned from the disaster response team in Puerto Rico after seeing medical workers getting manicures and pedicures from residents of the island in medical triage tents.

90. The *NYT* reported that Puerto Rico's health care system is in dire condition and continues to suffer from mismanagement. Getting patients to health care resources is also a problem. The USNS *Comfort* ship, which carries 800 medical personnel and can serve 250 patients at a time, has seen 82 patients in six days.

91. CNN reported that Puerto Ricans are drinking water from a hazardous-waste site, having no other options for water.

92. A *Politico*/Morning Consult poll found that just 32 percent of registered voters think the federal government has done enough to help Puerto Rico.

93. Bloomberg revealed that one of its reporters was inadvertently included on the Pentagon's internal e-mail message that detailed how to spin Hurricane Maria to convince the public that the government response was going well.

94. On Thursday, Trump signed an executive order ending Obamacare subsidies for the poor. Not paying the subsidies could boost premiums for millions and send the health insurance exchanges into turmoil.

95. NPR estimated that consumers who earn 400 percent of the federal poverty level—$48,000 for individuals or $98,400 for a family of four—will see their cost of their plans rise by, on average, 20 percent nationwide.

96. Doctors, hospitals, insurers, state insurance commissioners, and patient advocates denounced Trump's move. Trump's action puts pressure on Congress to protect consumers from soaring premiums.

97. The *WSJ* reported that if Congress doesn't succeed in producing health care legislation, White House aides said Trump "will claim victory" for ending the Iran deal, cutting billions in payments to health insurers, and deporting hundreds of thousands of immigrants.

98. On Friday, a coalition of attorneys general from eighteen states and D.C. filed a lawsuit to block Trump's halt to subsidy payments under Obamacare.

99. The *NYT* reported that as of Friday, Trump has taken twelve actions which could weaken Obamacare and curtail enrollment, including spreading negative news releases and posting infographics criticizing the health law.

100. On Saturday, Trump boasted on Twitter that health insurance companies' stocks "plunged yesterday" after his steps to dismantle Obamacare.

101. A Kaiser Health poll found that 71 percent of Americans say the Trump regime should work to improve Obamacare, while just 21 percent say they should make it fail.

102. On Friday, Trump slammed Iran as a "menace" and called for "decertification" of the nuclear deal, the Joint Comprehensive Plan of Action (JCPoA), saying Iran is "not living up to the spirit of the deal."

103. Trump sent the deal back to Congress with a sixty-day window to address its "many serious flaws" or see it "terminated."

104. Top officials on Trump's national security team, including Mattis and Tillerson, said Iran has technically complied with JCPoA's restrictions. The International Atomic Energy Association also confirmed compliance.

105. The *Daily Beast* reported while McMaster also wanted to save the Iran deal, Trump consulted Fox News's Sean Hannity and former UN ambassador John Bolton, two neoconservatives who pushed for decertification.

106. The leaders of Britain, Germany, and France declared their commitment to stand by JCPoA. The deal was the culmination of sixteen years of diplomacy.

107. After being added to Trump's travel ban, Chad pulled its troops from the fight against Boko Haram in Niger. U.S. officials had warned Trump his decision would have major consequences for the fight against terrorism.

108. California's deadliest wildfires charred more than 221,754 acres of land in Northern California and left at least thirty-five dead and hundreds more missing. Trump has yet to publicly comment or tweet about the wildfires.

109. Nor has Trump publicly commented on the deadliest combat incident since he took office, which took place in Niger last Saturday while Trump was golfing. The ambush by ISIS left four soldiers dead and two wounded.

110. As the week ended, twenty-four days after Hurricane Maria, just 64 percent of Puerto Ricans had access to drinking water, and only 14.6 percent had electricity.

111. Trump spent his fourth weekend since Hurricane Maria golfing. On Saturday, he visited Trump National Golf Club in Virginia, his seventy-second day of golf since taking office.

Week 49

OCTOBER 15–21, 2017

This was one of the worst weeks, if not the worst, for our country since Trump took office. As the length of the list reveals, this was a week of complete chaos and eroding norms. There was an observable sense of exhaustion, anger, sadness, fear, and loss among Americans.

With Trump effectively driving the narrative around his response to the death of a soldier, there was little coverage or focus on most items on this list. Many of these news stories would in normal times be front-page coverage for months. Investigations of Russian interference quietly progressed on several fronts, and alarmingly, Trump and some prominent regime members continue to deny the existence of, and refuse to take steps to protect against, Russian involvement in our elections.

1. At the Values Voter Summit, Trump ally and former adviser Sebastian Gorka told the crowd, "The left has no idea how much more damage we can do to them as private citizens."
2. *BuzzFeed* reported that a subpoena was issued in March by Summer Zervos's lawyer to Trump's campaign for documents about "any woman alleging" Trump touched her inappropriately. Zervos is suing Trump for defamation after he called her accusation that he assaulted her a lie.
3. Larry Flynt took out a full-page ad in the Sunday edition of *WaPo* offering to pay ten million dollars for "information leading to the impeachment and removal from office" of Trump.
4. The *New Yorker* reported on "Duty to Warn," a group of psychiatrists mobilizing behind the Twenty-fifth Amendment who claim Trump "suffers from an incurable malignant narcissism" that makes him unfit to serve and dangerous.
5. The editorial board of the *San Francisco Chronicle* published an op-ed, "California Burns: Where's the President?" as Trump for a second week was silent on California's deadliest wildfire.
6. The *New Yorker* reported on Pence's extremism on social issues. In a meeting, when the discussion turned to LGBT rights, Trump pointed at Pence and said: "Don't ask that guy—he wants to hang them all!"

7. The media company of Trump ally Anthony Scaramucci ran a Twitter poll asking people to vote on the number of Jews killed in the Holocaust. Before it was taken down, one in five responded "less than one million."

8. *Mic* reported that army recruiters have been instructed by Gregory C. Williamson, chief of the Accessions Suitability Office Guard Strength Division, to stop enlisting green card holders "until further notice." Barring green card holders from enlisting is against federal law.

9. A federal judge in Hawaii blocked Trump's revised travel ban, saying it "suffers from precisely the same maladies as its predecessor."

10. A federal judge in Maryland granted a nationwide preliminary injunction, saying the Trump regime has "not shown that national security cannot be maintained without an unprecedented eight-country travel ban."

11. White supremacist Richard Spencer spoke at the University of Florida in his first campus speech since the "Unite the Right" rally in Charlottesville. His appearance was met with mass protests inside and outside the auditorium.

12. Florida governor Rick Scott declared a state of emergency for Alachua County. The University of Florida banned torches, masks, weapons, and athletic equipment that could be used as a weapon.

13. Police announced that three white nationalists were charged with attempted homicide after they argued with and fired a shot at a group of protesters following Spencer's speech.

14. A federal judge in Kansas denied bond for one of three men in a militia group called the Crusaders, a group of Trump supporters who had plotted an attack against Muslims one day after the 2016 election to "wake people up."

15. On Friday, *Mashable* reported that the EPA climate change website, which was taken down in April, reappeared in part, but with all references to climate change removed.

16. *Forbes* reported that during the transition period, Wilbur Ross moved assets into family trusts, leaving more than two billion dollars off his financial disclosure report. *Forbes* discovered the discrepancy based on the magazine's records from its list of the four hundred richest people in America.

17. Ross's moving of assets raises concerns of violating federal rules, and also, given his role as secretary of commerce, potential for conflicts of interest.

18. Representative Elijah Cummings said "several" Trump aides have admitted to using private e-mails for government business and "confessed" that they failed to forward official records, in violation of federal record-keeping law.

19. Representative Trey Gowdy had joined Cummings in Week 46 to request details on private e-mail use, with an initial deadline of October 10. The White House did not fully respond. Now Cummings is concerned that Gowdy is letting the White House slide.

20. Trump will meet Philippine president Duterte on his upcoming trip to Asia. Duterte has come under international criticism for his brutal crackdown on drug trafficking, including thousands of extrajudicial killings.

21. In a speech at the Heritage Foundation, Pruitt said the Trump regime plans to restrict scientists who get EPA grants from serving on the agency's scientific advisory committees.

22. Earlier this year, Pruitt failed to renew half of the membership of the eighteen-person Board of Scientific Counselors. He is considering more than 130 candidates who reject mainstream science on climate change.

23. Trump's nominee for drug czar, Tom Marino, withdrew from consideration after a *WaPo/60 Minutes* investigation detailed how he helped steer legislation that weakened the DEA's ability to go after drug distributors.

24. Anthony Alexis, the Consumer Financial Protection Bureau's enforcement chief, announced he is stepping down. Alexis is the highest-profile official to leave the agency since Trump took office.

25. A federal judge ruled that Trump's pardon of Arpaio will not wipe out the guilty verdict she returned or any other rulings in the case. The court had found Arpaio guilty of criminal contempt. Arpaio's lawyer will likely appeal.

26. *Politico* reported that Trump personally interviewed at least two candidates for U.S. attorney positions in New York. The U.S. attorney would have jurisdiction over Trump Tower and could investigate the Trump regime.

27. CNN reported that Trump also met with Jessie Liu, whom he tapped to be the next U.S. attorney for the District of Columbia, where Trump now resides.

28. On Monday, Trump had a pair of Q&A sessions, first in the Cabinet Room and then in the Rose Garden with Senator Mitch McConnell. The sessions covered a variety of topics and were filled with false statements.

29. Trump bragged about his performance in office in all areas. Trump noted that James Lee Witt, a FEMA administrator under Bill Clinton, gave him an "A-plus" for handling the hurricanes, including Puerto Rico. This is false.

30. At the Cabinet Room Q&A, Trump bragged that his moves had ended Obamacare: "There is no such thing as Obamacare anymore."

31. A Yale Law School professor detailed how Trump's admission that he is trying to kill Obamacare is illegal: "Modern American history has never seen as full-scale an effort to sabotage a valid law," upheld twice by the Supreme Court.

32. Also Monday, Trump said he and McConnell are "closer than ever before." Bannon is waging a war on the GOP establishment and has suggested opposition to McConnell as a litmus test for his support.

33. When asked about his twelve-day silence on U.S. soldiers killed in an ambush in Niger, Trump claimed Obama and past presidents "didn't make calls" to families of soldiers killed in duty. This is a false statement.

34. On Tuesday, Trump evoked his chief of staff's son to attack Obama, saying Obama "did not call General Kelly after the death of his son." The *Daily Beast* confirmed that White House officials signed off on this line of attack.

35. CNN reported that Kelly did not know Trump would use the death of his son publicly. Kelly and much of the White House were caught off guard.

36. The AP contacted the families of all forty-three people who have died in military service since Trump took office and made contact with about twenty of them. More than half said they had not heard from Trump.

37. Trump also complained how hard it was on him to make these calls: "It is a very difficult thing . . . it is a very, very tough day." He failed to mention, however, the hardship on the families of fallen soldiers.

38. Trump also claimed "absolutely no collusion" between his campaign and Russia, and said the Russia story is an excuse by Democrats for losing. He also referenced Hillary repeatedly, saying he hoped she would run again.

39. *WaPo* reported that the Trump campaign spent $1.1 million in legal fees for the Mueller probe during the quarter ended in September. In a sign of increased activity, $927,000 was spent during the first six months of the year.

40. The Trump campaign and RNC continue to pay for lawyers working on behalf of Trump and Donald Jr., but not for lawyers for Trump campaign or White House staffers.

41. *Business Insider* reported that Veselnitskaya was acting as an agent for the Kremlin when she delivered a memo at the Trump Tower meeting. The same memo was given to Rohrabacher during his Moscow visit in April 2016.

42. CNN reported that Senate investigators have spoken with some of the Russians present at the Trump Tower meeting. Senator Burr said he is "sequencing" interviews "before we know exactly what we want from Don Jr."

43. Yahoo reported on a Russian TV interview of an agent who worked in the English language department of a Russian troll farm. He was instructed: "We had a goal to set up the Americans against their own government."

44. The agents watched *House of Cards* to better understand American politics, and were instructed to repetitively post anti-Hillary comments about her wealth, her private e-mail server, and Bill Clinton's administration.

45. CNN reported that House and Senate investigators are interviewing Matt Tait, a cybersecurity expert recruited by Republican operative Peter W. Smith, about Smith's interactions with the Trump campaign.

46. Tait has in the past said he believes Smith had connections with Flynn, Bannon, and Conway during the campaign. The Senate Intelligence Committee has also reached out to Eric York, another security expert enlisted by Smith.

47. *Business Insider* reported that Mueller has also interviewed Tait as part of the probe into the relationship between Smith and Flynn, and their possible collusion with Russia to get Hillary's deleted e-mails.

48. *Business Insider* reported on tools used by a Cambridge Analytica intern that aid in targeting U.S. voters on divisive issues. The tools were left unprotected online for a year, including the eight months before the election.

49. CNN reported that based on internal company documents, Yevgeny Prigozhin, a Russian oligarch in Putin's inner circle, is thought to be behind the Russian troll farm in St. Petersburg called Internet Research Agency.

50. On Monday, Alabama Republican Roy Moore's Senate campaign said it does not know why more than a thousand fake Twitter accounts originating from Russia started following Moore's account, causing a spike in his following.

51. In a letter, the lawyer for the founders of Fusion GPS said they are refusing to comply with Nunes's subpoena. Fusion GPS lawyers argued that Nunes signed the subpoena "with no authority to sign it, as part of personal mission."

52. On Thursday, citing Fusion GPS's refusal, Trump tweeted suggesting the FBI, Democrats, and Russians as coconspirators behind the "Fake dossier."

53. NBC News reported that the Senate Intelligence Committee subpoenaed Carter Page for documents and testimony as part of its Russia investigation. Page will likely evoke the Fifth Amendment, according to an unnamed source with knowledge of the matter.

54. *Politico* reported that Spicer was interviewed by Mueller's team on Tuesday. Reportedly he was grilled on the firing of Comey and his statements, as well as about Trump's meetings with Lavrov and Kislyak in the Oval Office.

55. Mueller's team is actively interviewing Trump's former and current aides. Priebus and Keith Kellogg, interim national security adviser after Flynn, have been interviewed. Hicks and McGahn are expected to be interviewed shortly.

56. Mikhail Khodorkovsky, a prominent exiled Russian oligarch, told MSNBC: "I am almost convinced that Putin's people have tried to influence the U.S. election in some way."

57. Khodorkovsky also said of Kushner's meeting with VEB's Gorkov last December that Gorkov was acting on behalf of the Kremlin. Kushner has said the meeting was to discuss business.

58. Kushner added Charles Harder to his legal team. *Vanity Fair* speculated that the addition may have come out of concern about Priebus's testimony in Week 48, as it relates to Kushner's proximity to Trump's decision to fire Comey.

59. NYU journalism professor Jay Rosen noted Harder's expertise: "defamation, reputation protection, privacy, media law, entertainment, intellectual property and business litigation."

60. The *Daily Beast* reported that Donald Jr. and Conway pushed tweets by the Russian troll farm Internet Research Agency, including allegations of voter fraud, the week before Election Day.

61. Trump aides and allies Flynn, his son Michael Flynn Jr., Roger Stone, Sebastian Gorka, Brad Parscale, and Ann Coulter tweeted Russian troll farm content. Clint Watts told the *Daily Beast* that Russia can declare success: Americans using content against Americans.

62. *Politico* reported that the Senate Intelligence Committee interviewed Trump's former campaign manager Corey Lewandowski on Wednesday. Lewandowski signed off on Page's July 2016 trip to Moscow.

63. The Senate Intelligence Committee announced it will postpone and reschedule its open hearing of Michael Cohen scheduled for October 25. In Week 45, the committee abruptly canceled their interview after Cohen breached its terms.

64. *Politico* reported that a federal judge has tossed out a libel suit filed by Russian oligarch Deripaska alleging that the AP falsely implied he was paying Manafort to advance the goals of the Russian government and Putin.

65. CNN reported that RT is resisting the DoJ's request that its American arm register under the Foreign Agents Registration Act. The DoJ deadline was October 17, but RT has not yet registered.

66. McCain said the White House blocked its cyber czar, Rob Joyce, from testifying before the Senate Armed Services Committee about U.S. efforts to defend against cyberattacks. McCain signaled that Joyce could be subpoenaed.

67. During a panel hosted by the George W. Bush Institute, UN ambassador Nikki Haley called Russia's interference in the 2016 election "warfare," and added, "We've got to fix it."

68. On Thursday, at a security conference in Washington, CIA director Pompeo made a false statement on Russian election interference: "The intelligence community's assessment is that the Russian meddling that took place did not affect the outcome of the election."

69. The CIA quickly issued a statement clarifying Pompeo's remarks: "The intelligence assessment with regard to Russian election meddling has not changed." Pompeo has a record of statements minimizing the Russia issue.

70. Putin entered American politics again, saying in an interview that Americans should not "disrespect" Trump. Putin also defended Trump's voters and his nontraditional ways, and criticized the U.S. media.

71. The acting commissioner of Pennsylvania's Obamacare exchange said premiums are expected to spike by 31 percent for 2018 because of Trump's decision to stop paying key subsidies.

72. On Tuesday, at a news conference in the Rose Garden, Trump said he would support the Alexander-Murray deal, which would stabilize Obamacare insurance markets by restoring subsidies cut by Trump.

73. On Wednesday, in an early morning tweet, Trump changed his position: "can never support bailing out ins co's who have made a fortune w/ O'Care." He repeated his new position later in a tax reform meeting.

74. On Wednesday, Senator Lamar Alexander told reporters, "The president called me ten days ago and asked me to work with Senator Murray to do this."

75. Gallup found that in the third quarter, likely as a result of actions by Trump and Congress, the uninsured rate rose to 12.3 percent. This reverses the trend of the past three years, in which the rate of U.S. uninsured declined from 18 percent to 10.9 percent.

76. In a speech Monday, McCain repudiated Trump: "Spurious nationalism cooked up by people who would rather find scapegoats than solve problems is as unpatriotic as an attachment to any other tired dogma."

77. On Tuesday, Trump threatened McCain, telling a radio host, "You know, I'm being very nice. I'm being very, very nice. But at some point I fight back, and it won't be pretty."

78. On Thursday, George W. Bush delivered a rebuke of Trump in a speech at the Bush Institute, without mentioning Trump by name. Bush called on America to "reject bigotry and white supremacy."

79. Bush added, "We've seen nationalism distorted into nativism. Bigotry seems emboldened. Our politics seems more vulnerable to conspiracy theories and outright fabrication."

80. After the speech, McCain tweeted his support of Bush: "Important speech by my friend, President George W. Bush today, reminding U.S. of the values that have made America a beacon of hope for all."

81. McCain became the first Republican to sign onto a bill drafted by Senators Amy Klobuchar and Mark Warner, the Honest Ads Act, which would increase the transparency of political advertisements on social media platforms.

82. NPR revealed that the Trump National Golf Club in Los Angeles claims to have donated $5 million to charitable causes and lists about two hundred recipients. Many contacted said they never received the money, and only $800,000 was accounted for.

83. *WaPo* reported that in a June call, Trump offered a grieving military father twenty-five thousand dollars from his personal account and said his staff would establish an online fund-raiser for the family. The father said neither happened.

84. Shortly after the *WaPo* story, the White House said Trump had sent the twenty-five-thousand-dollar check he had promised to the father. Military families are privately concerned about a commander in chief writing checks to parents of fallen soldiers.

85. On Wednesday, in a series of tweets, Trump suggested that Comey exonerated Hillary "long before investigation was complete." Trump threatened, "Where is Justice Department?"

86. On Wednesday, Sessions testified in front of the Senate Judiciary Committee during a highly contentious five-hour oversight hearing. Sessions repeatedly said his discussions with Trump were off-limits to lawmakers.

87. When asked about his conversations with Russians during the campaign, he said he "could not recall" the specifics of conversations, but "I don't think there was any discussions about the details of the campaign."

88. Sessions acknowledged he discussed Comey with Trump before writing the letter that was used to justify the firing, but refused in questioning to share what Trump said to him about Comey.

89. Sessions says he can't "make a blanket commitment" not to jail journalists, and that he reserves the right to jail journalists "if we have to."

90. On Tuesday night, Representative Frederica Wilson told CNN she had overheard Trump's condolence call to army sergeant La David T. Johnson's widow, Myeshia Johnson. Wilson said Myeshia "broke down" during the call.

91. Wilson said when Myeshia hung up, she said, "He didn't even remember his name." Wilson also said Trump basically told Myeshia, "I guess he knew what he signed up for, but I guess it still hurt."

92. Wednesday morning, Trump tweeted that Wilson had fabricated what he said, adding, "(and I have proof). Sad!" No proof has been given.

93. Trump repeated his claim later when asked by a reporter about his statement: "I didn't say what that congresswoman said; didn't say it all. She knows it." The White House did not confirm or deny Wilson's account.

94. Sergeant La David Johnson's mother, Cowanda Jones-Johnson, who also heard the call, told *WaPo* that Wilson's account was accurate and that Trump did tell Myeshia her husband "must have known what he signed up for."

95. Chuck Hagel, former Republican senator and secretary of defense under Obama, told *USA Today* that Trump's talk about the fallen troops "sickens" him and was "beneath the dignity of the presidency."

96. Sergeant Johnson's body wasn't found until two days after he was killed in Niger. Johnson was one of four Green Berets killed in an ambush.

97. Rachel Maddow speculated that Trump's behavior may have been a diversion away from explaining what happened in Niger. Two weeks later there still has not been an explanation of the mission or the ambush.

98. *Politico* reported that staffers at the NSC drafted a Niger sympathy statement for Trump on October 5. Trump never released the statement.

99. On Thursday, McCain, chairman of the Senate Armed Services Committee, said the Trump regime has not been forthcoming about the attack in Niger, and that he may issue subpoenas to get access to information he wants.

100. The *Los Angeles Times* reported that General Waldhauser, commander of U.S. Africa Command, asked for more military resources in March. CNN reported that Sergeant Johnson's body was found nearly a mile from the site of the ambush.

101. On Thursday, the Pentagon announced it has sent a team to Niger to conduct a "review of the facts" of what happened on October 4. It is still not known with certainty what group carried out the attack.

102. On Thursday, Kelly delivered an impassioned defense of Trump and his call to Johnson's widow, evoking his own experience with the loss of his son and his experience in the military as a four-star general.

103. Kelly drew ire for stating that in his day women were "sacred, looked upon with great honor," given Trump's record with women; and for saying that Gold Star families should be off-limits, given Trump's attacks on the Khans.

104. Kelly attacked Wilson, saying he was "stunned" by her account and that she exhibited "selfish behavior." Kelly chastised Wilson as being "in a long tradition of empty barrels making the most noise" for allegedly saying she helped get funding for a building.

105. Late Thursday, Trump attacked Wilson on Twitter, calling her "wacky Congresswoman Wilson(D)," and said she "gave a total lie on content!"

106. The *Miami Herald* reported that Kelly got his facts wrong when attacking Wilson. Kelly claimed Wilson said "she got the money" for a new building during a 2015 ceremony. Wilson was not in Congress when the money was secured.

107. On Friday, the *Sun Sentinel* released a full video of Wilson's remarks. Wilson took credit for securing approval for the naming of the building. She did not take credit for funding.

108. On Friday afternoon, the White House stood by Kelly, issuing a statement repeating the "empty barrel" assertion and attacking Wilson even though the video showed his claim was false.

109. On Friday afternoon at the press briefing, Press Secretary Sanders said it's "highly inappropriate" to get into a debate with a four-star general. *WaPo* listed several four-star generals Trump has publicly bashed.

110. On Friday, Trump signed an executive order allowing the air force to recall as many as one thousand retired pilots to active duty. The order could also be used to call up more officers in other branches.

111. Bennie Thompson, the ranking Democrat on the House Homeland Security Committee, called for an investigation of drinking water in Puerto Rico. As noted in Week 48, Puerto Ricans are drinking from a Superfund site.

112. CNN reported that only thirty-three of the 250 beds (16 percent) on the USNS *Comfort* are being used, nearly two weeks after the ship arrived.

113. CNN reported that one month after Hurricane Maria, one million Americans are still without drinking water and three million without electricity. One Puerto Rican commented, "Much of the island feels like it was hit by a storm yesterday."

114. On Thursday, at a press conference with Puerto Rico's governor, Trump rated his handling of disaster relief as 10 out of 10. Recent polls show Americans give him a rating of 4 out of 10.

115. Trump repeated his warning that FEMA could not stay forever. At some point, Trump said, "FEMA has to leave" and "the people have to take over."

116. The official death toll remains at forty-eight, but as *Vox* reported in Week 48, the actual count could be hundreds more. Senators Ed Markey and Elizabeth Warren and Representatives Nydia Velázquez and Mike Thompson have asked for an audit of the death count.

117. On Thursday, Oxfam issued a statement saying that one month in, "Without reliable water supply, electricity, phone service and other basic amenities, life in Puerto Rico is untenable."

118. On Wednesday, courtroom proceedings began in CREW's case against Trump in the Southern District of New York. CREW alleges he violated the Emoluments Clause of the Constitution by continuing to own and profit from his businesses.

119. Jacksonville Jaguars owner Shad Khan said Trump's recent grudge against the NFL is because Trump's bid to buy the Buffalo Bills in 2014 failed.

120. On Thursday, former CIA director John Brennan said that Trump has escalated tensions with North Korea to a dangerous level, and that cabinet members and senior officials may need to step in as "governors" to prevent war.

121. A federal judge on Wednesday barred the Trump regime from blocking an undocumented immigrant teen "Jane Doe" from getting an abortion. The judge said she was "astounded" the regime was trying to block the teen.

122. A federal appeals court on Friday said that Jane Doe could get an abortion but would need a sponsor. Trump's HHS in March announced that federally funded shelters are prohibited from providing access to abortions to unaccompanied minors.

123. *Politico* reported that Trump officials were blindsided and are scrambling to come up with an opioid plan after Trump's off-script statement Monday in which he promised to deliver an emergency declaration next week.

124. *Newsweek* reported that Senator Ben Cardin, ranking member of the Senate Foreign Relations Committee, joined House Democrats in demanding that Ivanka's security clearance be reviewed given her failure to divest from her business empire.

125. The *Daily Beast* reported that at the end of a tumultuous week, White House aides say Trump shows zero remorse, and he "loved Kelly's performance" and "considers the issue won." Kelly, however, is looking more and more dispirited.

126. On Friday in a tweet, Trump falsely blamed a 13 percent rise in UK crime on "Radical Islamic terror." A report by the UK's Office of National Statistics out Thursday said the increase was due to knife crime and sexual offenses.

127. *Forbes*'s 2017 list of the four hundred richest Americans list showed that Trump's wealth fell by $600 million, to $3.1 billion. Trump fell from number 156 to number 248.

128. *Smithsonian* reported on a survey that found a spike in fear. In 2017, the majority American survey respondents claimed they were afraid of five given items, up from one in prior years. Americans also have "a great fear of some of the things happening in this presidency." The most feared item is corruption of government officials (74 percent).

129. As the week drew to a close, thirty-two days after Hurricane Maria hit Puerto Rico, just 16.6 percent of the island's population has electricity, and 71.7 percent have drinking water.

Myeshia Johnson, the widow of fallen Miami Gardens soldier Sgt. La David T. Johnson, who was killed in an ambush in Niger, in west Africa, earlier this month, cries atop the casket with his body at Miami International Airport, October 17, 2017. (WFOR–CBS Miami)

Week 50

OCTOBER 22–28, 2017

The feelings of anxiety and fear amid continued chaos and eroding norms were palpable in this second-consecutive record-setting week. The Trump regime continued their attacks on rights and protections, while the Republican Party split deepened after a historic anti-Trump/save our country speech by Senator Jeff Flake.

The week closed with the unexpected news that the Mueller probe has produced its first results: charges filed in federal court. The news provided the first relief, and possible accountability, after unending news of corruption, incompetence, and kleptocracy. The humanitarian crisis in Puerto Rico worsened amid news of an insider deal and cover-ups, as Trump continued to turn a blind eye of indifference.

1. *Axios* reported that Trump pledged to spend at least $430,000 of his own money to pay some of the legal bills for White House staff due to the Russia investigation. The RNC has paid roughly $430,000 to cover Trump's and Donald Jr.'s lawyers.

2. Reuters reported that Canada is granting asylum to people who fear being deported by Trump. More than fifteen thousand people crossed the U.S.-Canadian border to claim refugee status this year. Many had been in the U.S. legally.

3. The U.S. Air Force responded to Trump's executive order in Week 49 that allows the service to recall retired pilots, saying the air force did not know about it in advance and does not "currently intend to recall retired pilots."

4. *Defense One* reported that the air force is preparing to put nuclear-armed bombers back on twenty-four-hour ready alert, a status not seen since the Cold War ended in 1991.

5. On Sunday, on the same day the Kremlin issued an arrest warrant for him through Interpol, the State Department revoked a visa for British citizen Bill Browder, a hedge fund manager turned human rights activist responsible for the Magnitsky Act.

6. On Monday night, the U.S. cleared Browder to enter. The explanation given anonymously by a Trump regime member is that the initial action had been taken automatically in response to an Interpol notice filed by Russia.

7. Veselnitskaya detailed the Kremlin's gripes with Browder in a memo she brought to the June 9 meeting with Donald Jr., Kushner, and Manafort.

8. *Politico* reported that four officials at three different federal agencies are doing substantially similar work to the positions for which they have been nominated, despite not having been confirmed yet.

9. The *Atlantic* reported that Trump is rush-shipping condolences to Gold Star families following his false claim he had called "virtually all" of the families. Four families received next-day UPS letters from Trump.

10. McCain took a swipe at Trump on C-SPAN3, saying those "at the highest income level" avoided the Vietnam-era draft by finding a doctor who "would say that they had a bone spur." Trump took a medical deferment because of a bone spur and avoided the draft.

11. The women of the Congressional Black Caucus demanded that Kelly apologize to Representative Frederica Wilson, citing the *Sun Sentinel* video showing that Kelly's public statement in Week 49 was false.

12. On Monday, Myeshia Johnson told *Good Morning America* that Trump "made me cry even worse." She also said she didn't like Trump's tone and that she broke down when Trump fumbled her husband's name.

13. Trump tweeted immediately after her interview, refuting Myeshia: "I had a very respectful conversation with the widow of Sgt. La David Johnson, and spoke his name from beginning, without hesitation!"

14. On Wednesday, Trump again said Myeshia's recollection is incorrect, telling reporters he did say La David Johnson's name, and he has "one of the great memories of all time."

15. DeVos's Education Department rescinded seventy-two special education policy documents that outline the rights of students with disabilities, saying the guidelines were "outdated, unnecessary or ineffective."

16. Anti-Semitic posters that read JUST SAY NO TO JEWISH LIES! and JOIN THE WHITE GANG, adorned with swastikas, were found on Cornell University's campus and Collegetown.

17. The NAACP issued a travel advisory for African Americans who fly on American Airlines. The group cited a disturbing pattern of black passengers being removed from flights and other troublesome conduct.

18. Georgia representative Betty Price, wife of former HHS secretary Tom Price, asked in a study committee if the government could "quarantine" people with HIV.

19. In a meeting of NFL owners and league executives regarding player protests, Texans owner Robert McNair said of the players, "We can't have the inmates running the prison." He later apologized.

20. A Post-it that read JEWS WILL BURN was left on the locker of a Jewish sixth-grade student at Middlebrook School in Wilton, Connecticut, one of several recent anti-Semitic incidents at the school.

21. White supremacist group Identity Evropa hung flyers across Rutgers University campuses that read OUR GENERATION. OUR FUTURE. OUR LAST CHANCE. The group's founder has close ties to Richard Spencer.

22. Mahwah, New Jersey, proposed rules aimed at barring Orthodox Jews from moving in. A complaint by the state attorney general compared the Mahwah lawmakers to "1950s-era white flight suburbanites who sought to keep African-Americans" out from their communities.

23. Viviana Andazola Marquez, a senior at Yale, wrote that while bringing her father, who works and has raised four children, for a final interview with Immigration Services, he was detained and faces deportation proceedings.

24. Rosa Maria Hernandez, a ten-year-old Mexican girl with cerebral palsy, is potentially facing deportation after going through a Border Patrol checkpoint in South Texas to get emergency gallbladder surgery.

25. On Wednesday, the immigrant teen known as Jane Doe was able to terminate her pregnancy. The ACLU said Jane's battle to seek an abortion is part of the Trump regime's efforts to drastically restrict abortion access for minors in their custody.

26. Scott Lloyd, head of the Office of Refugee Resettlement, has tried to block abortions for teens in custody. The *WSJ* reported that his work is part of a broader push by the Trump regime "to deliver socially conservative policies."

27. At a House hearing Thursday, Lloyd refused to answer many questions posed by Democrats who charged that he had overstepped his expertise and authority in his dealing with female detainees.

28. In the wake of numerous men in high-profile positions being accused of sexual misconduct, when asked about Trump at a press briefing, Press Secretary Sanders said all the women who accused Trump of sexual harassment are lying.

29. Trump's EPA canceled a speaking appearance by three agency scientists scheduled to discuss climate change at a conference in Rhode Island. The cancellations highlight concern that the EPA will silence government scientists.

30. CBC reported that Kelly Craft, the new U.S. ambassador to Canada, says she believes "both sides" of the climate change science.

31. Trump's FCC chairman, Ajit Pai, announced a vote in November to roll back regulations passed in 1975 that ban media cross-ownership of newspaper, radio, and television at the local level to protect consumers.

32. Pai's move comes as Trump ally Sinclair Broadcasting seeks to acquire Tribune Media. The combined company would reach 72 percent of U.S. households.

33. The AP reported that a computer server crucial to a lawsuit against Georgia election officials in Week 34 was quietly wiped clean by the Center for Elections Systems at Kennesaw State University just after the suit was filed.

34. Representative Elijah Cummings again called on Representative Trey Gowdy to sign on to a request for documents from Kushner and Ivanka on their use of private e-mail accounts, saying if he doesn't, the House Oversight Committee should vote on issuing subpoenas.

35. *WaPo* reported that GEO Group, a giant private-prison company, switched the venue for its annual leadership conference to Trump National Doral Miami.

36. GEO Group gave $250,000 to a Trump super PAC and hired two former aides of Sessions and a Trump fund-raiser as outside lobbyists. The company's stock has tripled since Obama said he would phase out private prisons.

37. Donald Jr. tweeted a photo of him onstage with his father: "Great time with @realDonaldTrump in Texas." The two are supposed to maintain a firewall between them as Donald Jr. comanages the family businesses.

38. The Government Accountability Office will probe the Election Integrity Commission's funding, internal operations, and methods for protecting and sorting voter files. The probe comes as three Democratic senators said the commission had ignored their requests.

39. On Thursday, at a speech at the Heritage Foundation, Sessions scolded federal judges who have ruled against or criticized the Trump regime, saying that "coequal branches of government ought to respect one another."

40. Sessions also said that religious expression overrides civil rights laws, saying the First Amendment guarantees include "the freedom not to create expression for ceremonies that violate one's religious beliefs."

41. *FiveThirtyEight* reported that under Trump and Sessions, 70 percent of the tables from the FBI's "Crime in the United States," a report considered the gold standard for tracking crime statistics, have been taken offline.

42. Former Trump White House aide Sebastian Gorka told Fox News that Trump's former political opponent Hillary Clinton should be tried for treason and executed, saying Uranium One is the equivalent of the espionage of the Rosenbergs in 1951.

43. CNN reported that Trump made it clear to the State Department that he wants to accelerate the release of any remaining Hillary e-mails in its possession.

44. Trump has also called on the DOJ to lift the gag order on an undercover FBI informant who played a critical role in an FBI investigation into Russian efforts to gain influence in the U.S. uranium industry.

45. Trump has yet to implement Russian sanctions from legislation signed August 2, after being approved by an overwhelming majority in the House and Senate. The deadline to implement them was October 1.

46. *Foreign Policy* reported that Tillerson shuttered the State Department's Coordinator for Sanctions Policy office, which oversees sanctions policy, as part of an overhaul of the department.

47. On Friday, the Trump regime, facing vociferous public criticism, started to roll out Russian sanctions on a very limited basis: the State Department listed thirty-nine Russian companies and government organizations to be sanctioned.

48. The *NYT* reported that China's Xi has succeeded in positioning China as a responsible power by stepping up when Trump has failed, citing speaking up for globalization at Davos and signing the Paris climate accord.

49. The *WSJ* reported that Trump almost deported fugitive businessman Guo Wengui after receiving a letter from the Chinese government that was hand-delivered by Steve Wynn, the Republican National Committee finance chairman.

50. Trump allegedly said to his secretary: "Where's the letter that Steve brought? We need to get this criminal out of the country." Wynn's Macau casino empire cannot operate without a license from the Chinese territory.

51. The *Washington Times* reported that at a meeting this spring, Sessions threatened to resign if the Trump regime deported Guo Wengui.

52. On Wednesday, Trump called to congratulate China's Xi after Xi asserted his absolute supremacy over China's one-party state, calling it an "extraordinary elevation" and comparing Xi to a "king."

53. Reuters reported that after Trump's abrupt decision to decertify the Iran nuclear deal, European leaders are nervous. No longer is there confidence that Europe can muddle through three more years without disruptions.

54. On Wednesday, Trump blamed the generals for the Niger ambush. In Week 16, Trump also blamed the generals for a SEAL killed in the failed Yemen raid.

55. Trump repeatedly referred to "my generals" and "my military." This reference has angered many in the military who believe the reference suggests Trump's sense of ownership over the country's armed forces.

56. In an interview with Fox Business Network, Trump relished his ability to diminish the press, saying, "I really started this whole fake news thing," adding, "I'm so proud that I have been able to convince people how fake it is."

57. *WaPo* reported that lawmakers in both parties are expressing frustration about the inability to accomplish anything with Trump. Lawmakers consider him "untrustworthy, chronically inconsistent and easily distracted."

58. A Fox News poll showed Trump's approval falling to a new low of 38 percent. Trump is losing support from white men without a college degree (from 68 percent last month to 56 percent this month) and white evangelical Christians (from 74 percent to 66 percent).

59. The *NYT* listed the 382 people, places, and things Trump has insulted on Twitter since he declared his candidacy (this list is continuously updated).

60. On Wednesday, the *Daily Beast* reported that Alexander Nix, head of Cambridge Analytica, had reached out to WikiLeaks founder Julian Assange during the election campaign for help finding and then publicly releasing Hillary's thirty-three thousand deleted e-mails.

61. In response to the *Daily Beast*'s reporting, Assange provided this statement: "We can confirm an approach by Cambridge Analytica and can confirm that it was rejected by WikiLeaks."

62. Late Wednesday, Michael Glassner, Trump campaign executive director, issued a statement seeking to distance the campaign from Cambridge Analytica. The Trump campaign paid Cambridge Analytica $5.9 million.

63. On Friday, the *WSJ* reported that Trump donor Rebekah Mercer reached out to Nix on August 26, 2016, to ask whether Cambridge Analytica could better organize the Hillary-related e-mails being released by WikiLeaks.

64. The *WSJ* reported that Nix's outreach to Assange came before his company began working for the Trump campaign in July. U.S. intelligence determined that the e-mails were stolen by Russian intelligence and given to WikiLeaks.

65. The Senate Intelligence Committee sought and received materials from the estate of Peter W. Smith that could help determine whether Smith was working with members of the Trump campaign to obtain Hillary's missing e-mails.

66. *BuzzFeed* reported that Russian troll farm the Internet Research Agency used Instagram to exploit divisions and social movements.

67. Michael Cohen met privately with House and Senate intelligence panels as part of their investigation into Russian interference in the 2016 election. Cohen is still expected to testify publicly later this year.

68. The *Daily Beast* reported that due to concern over Rohrabacher's ties to Russia, the House Committee on Foreign Affairs placed heightened restrictions on his trips abroad, committee money for travel, and hearings he can hold.

69. Tatyana Felgenhauer, a Russian radio journalist, was stabbed in the throat by an attacker who burst into her studio. There has been a string of attacks against journalists and opposition activists in Moscow.

70. British lawmakers asked Facebook to provide information on any ads purchased by Russian-linked accounts before June's general election and last year's Brexit referendum.

71. The Senate Judiciary Committee ended its bipartisan investigation into whether Trump obstructed justice or colluded with Russia. Republicans and Democrats say they will now conduct separate probes.

72. The *Daily Beast* reported that just three of the thirteen Republican members of the House Intelligence Committee regularly attend when Trump-Russia witnesses are grilled behind closed doors. The three participate in a very limited way.

73. Republicans on the committee are instead focused on other issues. Nunes is working with Representatives Ron DeSantis and Peter King, who are not on the committee, to probe an Obama-era uranium deal that Trump has repeatedly promoted.

74. Former U.S. ambassador to Russia Michael McFaul compared the recycling of the uranium deal to classic whataboutism, perfected by the Kremlin.

75. Nunes said he "would prefer" that reporters stop saying he recused himself from the Russia probe, even though, in Week 21, he recused himself from the Russia probe.

76. Twitter banned ads from Russian-state-owned news outlets RT and Sputnik. The Kremlin said it would respond, saying the move flouted international and domestic laws on free speech.

77. The *WSJ* reported that the Manhattan U.S. attorney's office is pursuing an investigation of Manafort for possible money laundering. The investigation is being conducted in collaboration with Mueller's probe.

78. At the same time, the Brooklyn U.S. attorney's office is pursuing an inquiry involving Kushner Companies. Trump has interviewed, and is said to be close to nominating, candidates to lead both the Manhattan and Brooklyn offices.

79. Among those interviewed are Geoffrey Berman, who is a law partner of Rudy Giuliani at Greenberg Traurig LLP, and Edward McNally, a law partner of Marc Kasowitz at Kasowitz Benson Torres & Friedman LLP.

80. *Politico* reported that the Realtor who helped Manafort buy the Alexandria apartment recently raided by the FBI testified before a grand jury in Mueller's Russia probe, after efforts by the Realtor to quash the subpoena.

81. The *NYT* reported that records show that Veselnitskaya was working on behalf of the Kremlin when she met with Donald Jr. and others on June 9. This undercuts her account that she was working as an independent actor.

82. On Friday, Carter Page met with the Senate Intelligence Committee for more than five hours in a closed session. Asked by NBC News whether he answered all the committee's questions, Page responded, "Thanks, have a great day."

83. Dana Boente, a thirty-three-year veteran of the DoJ, abruptly announced his resignation as U.S. attorney for the Eastern District of Virginia on Thursday. Boente is serving as acting assistant attorney general of the National Security Division of the DoJ.

84. In a statement, former CIA director James Woolsey said he and his wife have been in communication with the FBI regarding his knowledge of former national security adviser Flynn. Woolsey also claims he is getting smeared by Flynn.

85. Late Friday, CNN reported that the first charges have been filed in the Mueller investigation. The charges are sealed. Plans were made Friday for anyone charged to be taken into custody as soon as Monday. Reuters confirmed the report.

86. *WaPo* reported that Whitefish Energy, a two-year-old company with two full-time employees, signed a three-hundred-million-dollar no-bid contract, the biggest yet in Puerto Rico, to repair and reconstruct the island's electrical infrastructure.

87. Whitefish Energy is located in Whitefish, Montana, and its owner, Andy Techmanski, is friends with Interior Secretary Zinke. One of Zinke's sons had a summer job with Techmanski. Zinke said he played no role in the contract.

88. On Wednesday, Puerto Rico installed an emergency manager at the island's utility. Senator Lisa Murkowski said her Committee on Energy and Natural Resources will hold hearings. House committees are investigating too.

89. Five weeks after Maria hit, just 25 percent of Puerto Rico has electricity. San Juan mayor Cruz expressed her frustration on CNN about the Whitefish contract and lack of progress. She also tweeted to request transparency.

90. In response, Whitefish Energy tweeted to the mayor with a threat to halt work: "We've got 44 linemen rebuilding power lines in your city & 40 more men just arrived. Do you want us to send them back or keep working?"

91. Later Wednesday, Whitefish Energy tweeted an apology to Mayor Cruz and everyone in Puerto Rico.

92. A copy of the Whitefish Energy deal documents surfaced Friday, revealing that as part of the contract, the government is not allowed to "audit or review the cost and profit elements" for how the company spends the three hundred million dollars.

93. On Friday, Zinke and the White House sought to distance themselves from Whitefish Energy. Press Secretary Sanders said Trump had personally asked Zinke about the deal, which he claimed to know nothing about.

94. Zinke claimed Whitefish Energy contacted him at the Interior Department, but in a statement, he said the contact occurred only after the company had won the contract with Puerto Rico. The contract was no-bid.

95. Puerto Rico reported at least seventy-six cases of suspected and confirmed leptospirosis, including a handful of deaths, caused by contaminated water. Almost a quarter of Puerto Ricans are still without drinking water.

96. *Vox* reported that the nation's largest nurses' union condemned the federal government's emergency response in Puerto Rico, saying millions are suffering and accusing the government of leaving people to die.

97. Nurses cited perilous conditions: doctors performing surgery with light from their cell phones, children screaming from hunger, elderly residents suffering severe dehydration, black mold throughout entire communities.

98. *BuzzFeed* reported that crematoriums in Puerto Rico are burning the dead. Communication between the central institute certifying official hurricane deaths and the territory's funeral homes and crematoriums is broken, so these deaths are not being counted.

99. *BuzzFeed* later reported the Puerto Rican government allowed 911 bodies to be cremated without first conducting medical examinations to determine if they should be included in the official death toll.

100. On Tuesday morning, Corker and Trump escalated their battle. Corker said Trump was "debasing" the country with his "untruths," "name-calling," and "attempted bullying."

101. Trump responded in a series of tweets, calling Corker a "lightweight" who "couldn't get elected dog catcher in Tennessee." Trump also falsely claimed that Corker helped Obama "give U.S. the bad Iran Deal."

102. Corker responded in a tweet of his own: "Same untruths from an utterly untruthful president. #AlertTheDaycareStaff."

103. Trump responded again on Twitter, calling Corker an "incompetent head of the Foreign Relations Committee," and saying people like "liddle' Bob Corker have set the U.S. way back."

104. Corker responded, telling CNN about his previous support of Trump that he "would not do that again," and said Trump has "great difficulty with the truth."

105. The same day, Trump attended a lunch with Republican senators and tweeted how well it went, claiming he received "multiple standing ovations!"

106. As Trump entered the Republican lunch, a protester threw Russian flags at him and yelled, "Trump is treason!" The protester was arrested.

107. On Tuesday afternoon, Senator Jeff Flake gave an impassioned, historic speech on the Senate floor, saying that he would not be seeking reelection. He also wrote an op-ed titled "Enough," saying it is time to stand up to Trump.

108. Flake cautioned against "the new normal" and said, "We must never adjust to the present coarseness of our national dialogue" set by Trump, including "the regular and casual undermining of our democratic norms and ideals."

109. On foreign policy, Flake said that "the efficacy of American leadership around the globe has come into question" and cautioned, "Despotism loves a vacuum. And our allies are now looking elsewhere for leadership."

110. Flake also criticized Trump for normalizing lies, "calling fake things true and true things fake," and called Trump's behavior "reckless, outrageous, and undignified," and "dangerous to our democracy."

111. Flake appealed to his fellow Republicans, saying the pivot to governing by Trump is not coming, and "when the next generation asks us, why didn't you do something? Why didn't you speak up? What are we going to say?"

112. After Flake's speech, his fellow Arizona senator, McCain, took the Senate floor to honor his friend: "When Flake's service to the Senate is reviewed it will be one of honor, of brilliance, of patriotism, of love of country."

113. On Wednesday, Trump continued his attacks on Corker and Flake on Twitter. He also tweeted two more times about the standing ovations.

114. In a 51–50 vote with Pence as tiebreaker, the Senate voted to end consumers' right to file class-action suits against financial firms, a major step toward dismantling the Consumer Financial Protection Bureau, the watchdog agency conceived and established by Senator Elizabeth Warren.

115. Trump's USDA withdrew an Obama-era rule that would have made it easier for independent farmers to bring lawsuits against big food companies, on the day before it was set to take effect.

116. U.S. ambassador to New Zealand Scott Brown is under investigation by the State Department for making inappropriate comments during a Peace Corps event in Samoa. Brown blamed his comments on people at the event not liking Trump.

117. Bloomberg reported that at least a quarter of the pipes used in the Keystone XL pipeline came from a Russian steel company whose biggest shareholder is a Russian oligarch and Trump family friend, Roman Abramovich.

118. Foreign steel imports are up 24 percent in 2017. More than sixty steelworkers met with Congress in September to tell them of their growing frustration with the White House delays. Commerce Secretary Wilbur Ross said the regime is focused on tax reform.

119. On Friday, Trump tweeted an attack on Tom Steyer, calling him "Wacky & totally unhinged." Steyer, a California billionaire activist, launched a ten-million-dollar national ad campaign calling for Trump's impeachment.

120. After pledging to release the remaining classified records about the JFK assassination as required early Thursday, and Trump's bragging about it on Twitter, the Trump regime flubbed the release, resulting in only a partial release of records late Thursday.

121. A federal judge who oversaw the collection of government documents on JFK's assassination called Trump's handling of the release "disappointing" because so many of the records have been held back for review.

122. On Thursday, Trump declared the U.S. opioid abuse a national public health emergency in a speech. The formal declaration came more than two months after Trump initially said he would do so on August 10 (Week 39).

123. Trump pledged no new money to combat opioid abuse, but offered instead an advertising campaign with a slogan, "Just Say No"—a concept that has had little success in the past.

124. Information on the Niger ambush continued to slowly trickle out. Democrats on the House and Senate Armed Services Committees complained that the Pentagon has not been forthcoming.

125. McClatchy reported that Michael Cohen netted close to twenty million dollars by selling real estate properties well above market value to mysterious buyers. Experts say such deals are red flags of money laundering.

126. In 2014, a buyer using an LLC bought a property from Cohen for ten million dollars in cash that Cohen had paid just two million dollars for three years prior. Three other properties in the same time frame followed a similar pattern.

127. On Friday, Trump gave Halloween candy to kids at the White House. Trump told one young girl: "Well, you have no weight problems, that's the good news, right? So you take out whatever you need."

128. Anna Wintour, chair of the Metropolitan Museum of Art's annual gala, said that Trump won't be invited back. Trump has been a regular at the fund-raiser since the 1980s.

129. On Friday, Trump released a promotional video—"Big announcement next week!"—on Instagram, ahead of his announcement of a new Federal Reserve chair.

130. On Saturday, two hundred white nationalists carried a Confederate flag and chanted for closed borders and deportations in Shelbyville, Tennessee. The rally is one of two expected in Tennessee on Saturday. The rally also drew counterprotesters.

Week 51

OCTOBER 29-NOVEMBER 4, 2017

"It's like Christmas Eve," said one person on Twitter Sunday night, as the country braced for the first indictments from the Mueller probe on Monday. The indictment of Paul Manafort was expected, of his business associate Rick Gates, less so. But what riveted the country were the court documents and e-mails of Trump adviser George Papadopoulos, who is cooperating in the Mueller probe. Bedlam in the Trump regime ensued. As one aide put it, "It's every man for himself!"

This week Trump made his most aggressive statements against the DoJ, FBI, and court system for not doing what he thinks they should do. Alarm bells of authoritarianism and not-normal were ringing, as were warnings from even some Republicans not to interfere with the Mueller investigation.

1. *WaPo* reported that Donald Jr. and Eric are set to launch two real estate projects in India, despite vows early on that there would be no new foreign deals while Trump was in office to avoid potential conflicts of interest.

2. NBC reported that U.S Attorney Dana Boente, who submitted his resignation in Week 50, did so at the behest of Sessions, who said Boente should clear the way so Trump could name his successor.

3. In an NBC News/*WSJ* poll, Trump's approval dropped to the lowest level yet: 38 percent approve, 58 percent disapprove. The drop came from independents (from 41 percent in September to 34 percent) and whites without a college degree (58 percent to 51 percent).

4. On Monday, Trump hit his lowest approval and largest net gap on Gallup Daily: 33 percent approve, 62 percent disapprove, for a net score of –29.

5. *Politico* reported that Kushner took an unannounced trip to Saudi Arabia, his third this year. Days later, *Fortune* reported that Kushner's plans to save his overleveraged 666 Fifth Avenue property were found to be "not feasible."

6. On Sunday, ahead of news coming Monday from the Mueller probe, in a series of tweets, Trump assailed Obamacare, Democrats, Hillary, and the "Fake Dossier," and implored: "DO SOMETHING!"

7. In a seemingly coordinated effort, Murdoch-owned outlets bashed Mueller and called for his firing, including the *WSJ* editorial board and a Sunday op-ed, a *New York Post* op-ed, and continuing coverage on Fox News.

8. CNN reported that several Fox News employees said they were embarrassed and humiliated by the network's coverage of the Mueller investigation. One said, "Fox feels like an extension of the Trump White House."

9. *Politico* reported on fears that Obamacare is about to have its worst open-enrollment season ever, citing numerous steps by the Trump regime to create confusion and end public promotions to raise consumer awareness.

10. In Edison, New Jersey, an unknown group sent out flyers ahead of the November 7 election that read MAKE EDISON GREAT AGAIN and called for the deportation of two Asian school board candidates.

11. A student at the University of Hartford was charged with criminal mischief and expelled after an Instagram post in which she bragged about harassing her black American roommate: "I can finally say goodbye to Jamaican Barbie."

12. A federal judge temporarily blocked parts of Trump's memo banning transgender people from the military, ruling it was based on "disapproval of transgender people generally."

13. The judge also blasted Trump's abrupt announcement on Twitter "without any of the formality or deliberative processes" to come up with policy. She ruled the status quo should stay in place for now.

14. On Tuesday, Trump's lawyer again sought the dismissal of Summer Zervos's defamation lawsuit against him, arguing that Trump's expression of his political opinion is protected by the First Amendment.

15. The AP reported that Betsy DeVos is considering only partially forgiving federal loans for students defrauded by for-profit colleges, reversing an Obama-era policy that entirely erased such debt.

16. Sessions told *Fox News Sunday* he is "disturbed" that Jane Doe, the seventeen-year-old undocumented immigrant, was able to get a legal abortion in Week 50, saying, "I think it's a serious problem, it should not have happened."

17. On Friday, Sessions's DoJ took the unusual step of accusing the ACLU of misconduct for helping "Jane Doe" get a safe and legal abortion.

18. On Friday, federal officials released Rosa Maria Hernandez, the ten-year-old undocumented immigrant girl with cerebral palsy who was detained in Week 50 after undergoing surgery in Texas.

19. In an op-ed, Senator Elizabeth Warren argued that the Supreme Court needs to adopt an ethics code, citing the conflict of Neil Gorsuch's keynoting an event at the Trump International Hotel in D.C. on the same day the Supreme Court took on a case related to the hotel.

20. Papa John's CEO, John Schnatter, blamed the company's poor third-quarter performance on NFL anthem protests, telling ESPN: "We are disappointed the NFL and its leadership did not resolve this."

21. Trump judicial nominee Leonard Steven Grasz, who was nominated in August to the Eighth Circuit Court of Appeals, became the second Trump nominee to be deemed "not qualified" by the American Bar Association.

22. On Tuesday, at an EPA event with Trump by his side, Scott Pruitt announced a new policy barring scientists who receive EPA grants from serving on the agency's advisory boards. Critics called it a move to silence scientists.

23. Pruitt also named the chairmen of each of the three most high-profile panels: Michael Honeycutt, Tony Cox, and Paul Gilman—all of whom disagree with the scientific basis of major Obama administration policies.

24. On Friday, Pruitt overhauled the EPA's external advisory boards. Among the new advisers selected are industry players, including one who believes air quality is too clean for children and multiple climate change skeptics.

25. On Thursday, speaking during an energy policy discussion, Rick Perry linked fossil fuel development to preventing sexual assault in a comment about the lack of electricity in Africa, saying "when the lights are on, when you have a light that shines, the righteousness, if you will on those types of acts."

26. The Sierra Club called on Perry to resign over his comments. The Department of Energy said Perry's comments were meant to highlight the way electricity will improve the lives of people in Africa.

27. On Thursday, the U.S. withdrew from the Extractive Industries Transparency Initiative (EITI), an international effort to fight corruption in revenues from oil, gas, and mineral extraction.

28. *USA Today* reported Trump has appointed at least five people who are members of his clubs to senior roles in his administration. He has also given donors and allies prized diplomatic postings in European capitals.

29. This marks the first time in history that a president has awarded government posts to people who pay money to his own companies.

30. On Monday, Mueller's office announced that Paul Manafort and his business partner Rick Gates were indicted by a federal grand jury on twelve charges, including conspiracy against the United States, over the years 2006–2016.

31. Other charges include money laundering, failing to register as a foreign agent, and seven counts of failure to file reports of foreign bank accounts.

32. The indictments say both Manafort and Gates generated tens of millions from their lobbying work in Ukraine from 2006 to 2016 and hid the payments by laundering money. Manafort laundered more than eighteen million dollars.

33. Manafort was Trump's campaign manager from April to August 2016. Gates was a top campaign deputy, played a key role in planning Trump's inauguration, and was in and out of the White House during Trump's early days.

34. Both were put under house arrest, and bail was set at ten million dollars for Manafort and five million for Gates. Reports showed that Manafort's wealth fluctuated wildly, and he kept three passports, after submitting ten passport applications.

35. Bloomberg reported that on Monday Gates was fired from Colony NorthStar, where he had been a consultant to Tom Barrack, a longtime friend of Trump. Barrack also was the chairman of Trump's inaugural committee.

36. Also revealed on Monday, former Trump foreign policy adviser George Papadopoulos pleaded guilty to making a false statement to FBI investigators about his contacts with high-level Russian connections.

37. Papadopoulos's plea agreement describes his extensive efforts to broker connections between Russian officials and the Trump campaign. He has also turned over months of e-mails.

38. On April 25, he wrote, "The Russian government has an open invitation by Putin for Mr. Trump to meet him when he is ready." Sam Clovis, Papadopoulos's supervisor, as well as Corey Lewandowski and Manafort, received his e-mails.

39. Court documents quote one unidentified campaign "supervisor" telling Papadopoulos in an August 2016 e-mail that "I would encourage you" to make a trip to Moscow to arrange such a meeting. Yahoo reported that this is Clovis.

40. On Monday, the *Daily Beast* reported that Bannon encouraged Trump to bring in new lawyers and to take a much more aggressive approach, including considering the possibility of defunding the Mueller probe.

41. *WaPo* reported on Trump's Monday, saying he spent the morning upstairs watching TV separated from his White House staff and was visibly angry the entire day. The mood in the White House was described as weariness and fear of the unknown.

42. *Vanity Fair* reported that the West Wing is on edge, and for the first time impeachment is being considered as a realistic outcome. Trump advisers Dina Powell and Gary Cohn have been leaving rooms when the subject of Russia comes up.

43. Steve Bannon and Roger Stone are urging Trump to take steps to counter Mueller—Bannon citing Trump's slipping grasp on power. Stone advised appointing a special prosecutor to investigate Hillary's role in Uranium One.

44. Reportedly, Trump blames Kushner for his decision to fire Michael Flynn and James Comey, which led to Mueller's appointment. Allegedly Trump said, "Jared is the worst political adviser in the White House in modern history."

45. CNN reported that Kushner's team has turned over documents to Mueller in the special counsel's investigation of Kushner's role in the firing of Comey. Sources say Kushner is not a target of the investigation.

46. On Monday night, John Kelly reignited his feud with Representative Frederica Wilson, telling Fox News of his criticism of her, "I stand by my comments." In Week 48, a video released by the *Sun Sentinel* showed that Kelly's accusations were false.

47. Kelly also sparked controversy with factually incorrect and divisive claims that the Civil War was caused by "the lack of an ability to compromise" and that Confederate leader Robert E. Lee "was an honorable man."

48. On Tuesday, several Senate Republicans, including Jeff Flake, Roy Blunt, John McCain, Mitch McConnell, Richard Shelby, and John Kennedy, separately said they would not support any moves to crack down on the Mueller investigation.

49. Bloomberg reported that Papadopoulos's e-mails show that top Trump campaign officials agreed to a preelection meeting with representatives of Putin. The e-mail is cited in an FBI agent's affidavit supporting the charges against Papadopoulos.

50. The Trump regime tried to distance itself from Papadopoulos. Press Secretary Sarah Huckabee Sanders said he was a mere volunteer. Mike Caputo said Papadopoulos was just a "coffee boy." Trump called him a "low level volunteer."

51. In a March 21 interview with the *WaPo* editorial board, Trump had named Papadopoulos among people advising him on matters of national security, referring to Papadopoulos as "an energy and oil consultant. Excellent guy."

52. On Thursday, the *NYT* reported on court documents describing a March 31, 2016, meeting between Trump and his foreign policy team. According to campaign adviser J. D. Gordon, Papadopoulos pitched his Russia idea at that meeting.

53. Gordon said Trump listened with interest, but Sessions vehemently opposed the idea. Gordon said Sessions also said no one should talk about Papadopoulos's idea because it might leak.

54. On Tuesday, NBC reported that former top Trump campaign official Sam Clovis, who supervised Papadopoulos, was questioned last week by Mueller's team.

55. On Tuesday, *Politico* reported that Clovis has been a cooperating witness in the Senate Intelligence Committee's Russia probe. Clovis is Trump's controversial nominee for the top scientific job at the Department of Agriculture.

56. On Thursday, Clovis withdrew from consideration for the Department of Agriculture post, citing "the political climate inside Washington." CNN reported that sources say the withdrawal was related to the Russia probe.

57. On Thursday, Carter Page told CNN that during more than six hours of closed-door testimony to the House Intelligence Committee, Page testified he had told Sessions during the 2016 presidential campaign that he was traveling to Russia.

58. NBC reported that Sessions rejected Papadopoulos's plan to use his Russian contacts to set up a meeting between Trump and Putin. Sessions testified to Congress that he had no knowledge of any communication from any campaign officials about election interference by Russia. Congressional investigators want to question Sessions about this interaction with Papadopoulos.

59. In June, Sessions had told his Senate colleagues under oath that he had "no knowledge" of any conversations by anyone on the Trump campaign about "any type of interference with any campaign" by Russians.

60. On Friday, NBC reported that contrary to the Trump regime's efforts to downplay Papadopoulos's role in the campaign, records show he was a prominent figure and frequently acted as a surrogate.

61. Papadopoulos was at the Republican National Convention and was invited by the American Jewish Committee to speak on a panel there along with two Republicans on the House Foreign Affairs Committee and Senator Bob Corker.

62. Papadopoulos also acted as a surrogate six weeks before the election, giving an interview to the Russian Interfax News Agency in which he said that Trump will "restore the trust" between the U.S. and Russia.

63. The *NYT* reported that Page told the House Intelligence Committee on Thursday that after his July 2016 trip to Moscow to meet with Russian government officials, he sent an e-mail to at least one Trump campaign aide describing the trip.

64. Details came out during sharp questioning by Representative Adam Schiff. Page's e-mail detailed his meetings with government officials, legislators, and business executives in Moscow. The recipient(s) of the e-mail has not been made public.

65. On Thursday, Manafort and Gates were back in court. Both will be confined to their homes and are subject to electronic monitoring devices due to flight risk. The judge is also considering imposing a gag order on attorneys.

66. A *WaPo*/ABC poll found that 58 percent of Americans approve of Mueller's handling of the Trump-Russia investigation; just 28 percent disapprove. Roughly half say it's likely Trump committed a crime.

67. The American Psychological Association Stress in America Survey found that 59 percent of Americans say this is the lowest point in U.S. history. Two-thirds say the future of the nation is a very or somewhat significant source of stress.

68. *Business Insider* reported that a federal judge in New York has denied Veselnitskaya's request to enter the U.S. to represent her client, Prevezon, which has not paid the $5.9 million settlement it reached with Sessions's DoJ in May.

69. The settlement was a fraction of the $230 million Preet Bharara had been seeking before he was fired. If Prevezon does not pay the settlement amount, the judge says Prevezon will need to go to court without Veselnitskaya.

70. On Wednesday, after the terrorist attack in New York City by a Muslim American, Trump bemoaned our justice system, calling it "a joke" and "a laughingstock," and saying "no wonder so much of this stuff takes place."

71. Trump made his comments during a cabinet meeting. Sessions was in the room. Trump also threatened to send the terror suspect to Guantánamo.

72. On Wednesday, in a series of tweets, Trump blamed Senator Schumer for the October 31 NYC terror attack, tweeting "Diversity Visa Lottery Program" is a "Chuck Schumer beauty."

73. Trump's claim is false: the program was passed with bipartisan support in 1990 and signed into law by George H. W. Bush. Trump's invented claim came from a segment running that morning on Fox News.

74. On Wednesday night, Trump tweeted that the suspect had asked to hang the ISIS flag in his hospital room and that he "SHOULD GET DEATH PENALTY!"

75. On Thursday, in tweets, Trump backed away from his threat to send the suspect to Guantánamo, saying the process there takes longer, and again called for the death penalty: "Should move fast. DEATH PENALTY!"

76. Legal experts say Trump's tweets and statements will actually hurt the prosecution, pointing out that defense attorneys will claim that the jury pool has been poisoned by the publicity surrounding Trump's expression of opinion.

77. Trump also told Fox News that he was unsure if Rex Tillerson will remain secretary of state for the balance of his term. Trump said the White House was "not happy" that some State Department staffers were not supporting his agenda.

78. When pressed about filling vacant high-profile roles in the State Department such as assistant secretary of state, Trump said, "I'm the only one that matters," adding, "We don't need all the people that they want."

79. Reuters reported that at a recent meeting, former secretary of state Colin Powell told H. R. McMaster that the regime was gutting State. McMaster reportedly replied that there were people who did not support Trump's agenda.

80. On Friday, Trump criticized a military court for giving Bowe Bergdahl, the soldier who deserted his unit in Afghanistan in 2009 and was held by the Taliban for five years, a dishonorable discharge but no jail time, calling the decision "a complete and total disgrace to our Country and to our Military."

81. Ironically, Trump's speaking out may have, in part, led to the decision. Last week the judge said he would consider Trump's past comments as evidence for a lighter sentence.

82. On Thursday, on a radio show, Trump expressed frustration with not being able to direct the DoJ to investigate his former rival Hillary for the dossier, saying he is "very unhappy" with the DoJ and "very frustrated by it."

83. On Friday, in a series of tweets, Trump continued, saying that "everybody is asking" why the DoJ and FBI aren't investigating Hillary and the Democrats. He tweeted, "At some point the Justice Department, and the FBI, must do what is right and proper. The American public deserves it!"

84. On Friday, Trump also left open—for the fourth time—the possibility that he may fire Sessions if the DoJ does not investigate Trump's political rivals, saying "a lot of people are disappointed in the Justice Department, including me."

85. The *NYT* noted that in the past four decades, no president has sought to publicly pressure law enforcement as much as Trump.

86. The *WSJ* reported that the FBI is investigating the decision by Puerto Rico's power authority (PREPA) to award a three-hundred-million-dollar contract to Whitefish Energy.

87. On Sunday, Puerto Rico governor Ricardo Rosselló petitioned the board of PREPA to invoke the cancellation clause for the territory's contract with Whitefish Energy after FEMA flagged "significant concerns."

88. *Business Insider* reported that the USNS *Comfort* was anchored off Puerto Rico until last Friday. Now that the *Comfort* has docked, medical staff attended seven hundred patients over the weekend, up from nine a day prior.

89. Six weeks after Hurricane Maria, doctors and nurses say Puerto Ricans still face widespread symptoms related to unclean water, including vomiting, diarrhea, and asthma, as well as seventy-four suspected cases of leptospirosis.

90. Rachel Maddow reported that Puerto Rican officials refuse to answer how many of the suspected seventy-four cases of leptospirosis, a disease transmitted by contact with water contaminated by animal urine, have led to death.

91. The *Atlantic* reported that as Puerto Rico ended its contract with Whitefish, there are several investigations into PREPA's two-hundred-million-dollar contract with Mammoth Energy Services' Cobra Acquisitions, which was awarded on October 19.

92. A letter from the House Energy and Commerce Committee said the Cobra contract "would appear to have the effect of preventing government oversight of the agreement." Questions are also raised about the bidding process.

93. On Friday, San Juan mayor Carmen Yulín Cruz told CNN that the actual death toll from Maria is closer to five hundred, not fifty-four.

94. On Thursday, Trump's Twitter account was "inadvertently deactivated" by a Twitter employee for eleven minutes at just after 7 P.M. EST. The employee, still unidentified, did this on their last day of work.

95. As of Tuesday, Tom Steyer's online petition asking Congress to impeach Trump had garnered more than 1.1 million signatures in its first week.

96. A Public Policy Polling survey found a record level of support for impeaching Trump: 49 percent support impeachment, while 41 percent oppose it.

97. On Tuesday, ahead of congressional testimony, Facebook admitted that Russian influence on their platform had reached 126 million Americans, far greater than what the company had previously disclosed.

98. Lawmakers released three thousand Russian ads spread on Facebook. The ads were highly sophisticated and targeted candidates as well as issues like illegal immigration and gun ownership, and groups like Black Lives Matter and Muslims.

99. On Tuesday and Wednesday, general counsel for social media companies Facebook, Twitter, and Google testified before a Senate Judiciary subcommittee and the Senate and House Intelligence Committees.

100. Senator Al Franken blasted Facebook for accepting payments in rubles for U.S. election ads. Senator Dianne Feinstein said, "You've created these platforms, and now, they're being misused," adding, "Do something about it. Or we will."

101. Senator Mark Warner chastised the companies for being unresponsive and slow to investigate. He asked, "Do you believe that any of your companies have identified the full scope of Russian active measures?" Facebook said no.

102. Warner said the Facebook ads "are just the tip of a very large iceberg," and the real story is "the amount of misinformation and divisive content" pushed on Russian-backed pages.

103. Senator Amy Klobuchar pushed executives to weigh in on legislation that would require the companies to report who funds political ads online. In Week 49, Klobuchar and Warner gained bipartisan support of their Honest Ads Act.

104. Twitter identified 2,752 accounts controlled by Russian operatives and more than 36,000 bots that tweeted 1.4 million times during the election. Weeks ago, Twitter had said it found just 201 accounts linked to Russia.

105. Bloomberg reported that Twitter was warned in 2015 by company executive Leslie Miley about a vast number of accounts with IP addresses in Russia and Ukraine. Miley, the only black engineer in leadership, was dismissed later that year.

106. On Thursday, Robert Mercer resigned as CEO of his giant hedge fund, Renaissance Technologies. In a letter to employees, Mercer said he is under "scrutiny from the press" and has been unfairly linked to Bannon.

107. Robert Mercer also sold his stake in *Breitbart* to his daughter Rebekah. In a statement, Mercer tried to distance himself from Milo Yiannopoulos, who, according to *BuzzFeed*, had cultivated white nationalists while at *Breitbart*.

108. On Friday, three conservative House Republicans—Matt Gaetz, Andy Biggs, and Louie Gohmert—said they plan to file a resolution calling on Mueller to recuse himself from his probe of Russian meddling, over conflicts of interest.

109. On Wednesday, the Georgia attorney general's office announced it will no longer represent the state's top elections official in an elections integrity lawsuit filed days before a crucial computer server was quietly wiped clean, as noted in Week 50.

110. Georgia secretary of state Brian Kemp, the main defendant, is running for governor in 2018. The server in question made headlines in June when a security expert disclosed a gaping security hole that wasn't fixed.

111. The erased hard drives are central to the lawsuit filed in Week 34 because they could have revealed whether the Ossoff-Handel House race in Georgia was compromised by hackers. It is not clear who ordered the data erased.

112. The AP obtained Russian hackers' unpublished digital hit list, which had targets around the world: in addition to Hillary's e-mails, it includes e-mails of Ukrainian officers, Russian opposition figures, and U.S. defense contractors.

113. The list came from a database of nineteen thousand malicious links collected by cybersecurity firm SecureWorks after hacking group Fancy Bear accidentally exposed part of its phishing operation to the Internet.

114. The list also provides the most detailed forensic evidence yet of the close alignment between Russian hackers and the Kremlin.

115. On Friday, the AP reported on how Russia hacked into Hillary's campaign starting on March 10, 2016. Through a malicious link, hacker group Fancy Bear was able to enter John Podesta's e-mail account.

116. On April 26, before the DNC knew it had been hacked, court documents show that Papadopoulos says he was told about the hacking by a professor closely connected to the Russian government: "They have dirt on her. They have thousands of emails."

117. According to the AP, Guccifer 2.0 acted as a kind of master of ceremonies during a summer of leaks. He also coordinated with WikiLeaks and wrote, "Together with Assange we'll make america great again."

118. The AP also reported that Guccifer 2.0 had doctored at least one of Podesta's e-mails to get media attention: the word "CONFIDENTIAL" was not in the original document.

119. CNN reported that Trump's longtime bodyguard and close confidant Keith Schiller will testify to the House Intelligence Committee next week, as will Glenn Simpson of Fusion GPS.

120. *WaPo* reported that Schiller is expected to be questioned about Trump's 2013 Moscow trip, which is behind some of the most salacious allegations in the dossier, as well as Trump's firing of Comey.

121. This week the committee interviewed Carter Page and Ike Kaveladze, one of the people at the June 9 Trump Tower meeting, as well as a former assistant attorney general in the National Security Division of the DoJ, Mary McCord, and Sally Yates.

122. Rachel Maddow noted that the sudden rush of witnesses, some of whom are central figures and Trump insiders, may indicate that Republicans on the House Intelligence Committee are trying to bring its investigation to a close.

123. On Friday, CBS News reported that Trump campaign officials in legal jeopardy may be rushing to offer their cooperation to get a better deal from Mueller. One official who is being investigated said, "It's every man for himself."

124. *USA Today* reported that Trump's Election Integrity Commission may have gone dark. Its last public meeting was on September 12, and it's unclear, even to commission members, when the next meeting will be held.

125. The commission has held two meetings since it was set up in May, and has been sued by numerous civil rights and voting rights groups for lack of transparency and governance.

126. With Election Day coming next Tuesday, Twitter bots swarmed an important governor's race in Virginia. As in the 2016 election, the bots are focused on fanning racial strife.

127. Joe Ricketts, a Trump supporter, shuttered both *DNAinfo* and *Gothamist*, two of NYC's leading sources of local news, which he purchased in March, after employees voted to join a union. Ricketts made no attempt to sell.

128. *ProPublica* reported that two former CIA employees say Christopher Sharpley, Trump's nominee for CIA inspector general, "deliberately misled Congress" by saying he didn't know about a pending complaint filed against him.

129. *Mother Jones* reported that the Trump Organization experienced a major cyber breach in 2013, likely by Russian hackers. Until this week, the penetration had gone undetected. Information could be compromised.

130. As reported in Week 47, Kushner and Ivanka's personal e-mail accounts used for White House business were redirected to Trump Organization servers.

131. On Saturday, Trump solicited the Saudi Arabian government, tweeting to ask it to list its IPO of Aramco on the New York Stock Exchange.

132. On Saturday, stopping in Hawaii en route to Asia, Trump visited his Trump-branded Hawaii resort. This marks Trump's ninety-seventh trip to a Trump-owned property during his time in office.

133. As Trump heads to Asia, there is a sense that he has accelerated China's rise by being an unsteady leader. The Communist Party–owned Chinese paper *People's Daily* says Beijing is the "new role model," and Trump needs to prove he can be "constructive."

Week 52

NOVEMBER 5–11, 2017

This week started and ended in chaos, with a respite in between as Trump traveled to Asia and stayed on script. The length of this week's list is a testament to how broad-based the attacks on our democracy and the erosion of norms have become—well beyond Trump as the sole actor.

The Resistance that started as Trump took office has grown in both impact and power, as evidenced by Tuesday's elections, which were a wipeout for Republicans and an amazing display of diversity. A revolution around sexual assault and harassment is gathering steam, with offenders being outed daily.

All the while, the Mueller probe progresses. This week more ties between the Trump campaign and Russia were exposed, and questions surfaced as to the knowledge and engagement of senior people on the campaign, including Trump.

1. *WaPo* reported that as the winter tourism season kicks in, Trump has secured seventy H-2B visas from the Labor Department to hire cooks, maids, and servers to work at Mar-a-Lago, despite urging the country to hire American.

2. The *Dallas Morning News* reported that GOP campaigns for Trump, Mitch McConnell, Marco Rubio, Scott Walker, Lindsey Graham, John Kasich, and John McCain took in $7.35 million in donations from Leonard Blavatnik, a Ukrainian oligarch with ties to Putin.

3. Blavatnik donated one million dollars to Trump's inaugural committee. Blavatnik also has a close relationship with Oleg Deripaska, the Russian oligarch who has had ties to Paul Manafort for over a decade and appears frequently in the *Weekly List.*

4. Saudi Arabia arrested eleven princes, four ministers, and tens of former ministers. Trump tweeted his approval, saying he had "great confidence" in Mohammed bin Salman and his father, King Salman.

5. In Week 51, Jared Kushner returned from a previously undisclosed trip to Saudi Arabia, and Trump tweeted that he would appreciate it if Saudi Arabia would list the IPO of Aramco on the New York Stock Exchange.

6. Juli Briskman, the cyclist who flipped off Trump as his motorcade drove by, was fired from Akima LLC, a government contracting firm, under a social media policy, although she wasn't wearing anything company related.

7. Ironically, Briskman oversaw the firm's social media presence and had flagged a middle-aged executive man for a violation after he wrote on Facebook in a discussion with an employee on Black Lives Matter, "You're a f------ Libtard a------." He cleaned up the comment and was not fired.

8. Sessions's DoJ dropped its case against Desiree Fairooz, a retired children's librarian affiliated with Code Pink, who laughed at Sessions during his Senate confirmation hearing.

9. Republican representative Rob Bishop moved closer to his goal of invalidating the Endangered Species Act. Bishop has shepherded five bills out of the House Natural Resources Committee he chairs that would dismantle the law piece by piece.

10. In his most aggressive step yet to reverse Obama's "war on coal," Energy Secretary Rick Perry announced a proposal to alter electricity markets, which would provide a huge windfall for coal magnate Bob Murray, a big Trump donor.

11. On Tuesday, Syria joined the Paris climate accord, leaving the U.S. as the sole country rejecting the global pact.

12. On Thursday, Trump's EPA proposed reversing an Obama-era regulation that tightened emissions standards for heavy-duty trucks with older engines, part of Obama's efforts to reduce soot and other pollutants.

13. Carrier Corp., the plant Trump promised to save, announced less than four months after it laid off 340 employees at its Indianapolis factory that the company will terminate an additional 215 employees in January.

14. Representative Scott Allen, a lawmaker in Wisconsin, said women should be forced to give birth to grow the labor force: "Labor force shortages are tied to population declines. Labor force shortages are a limiting factor in economic growth."

15. On Monday, Trump's DHS announced it would not renew temporary protections that expire on January 5 for fifty-three hundred Nicaraguans. The regime gave a six-month reprieve to eighty-six thousand Hondurans covered by the program.

16. *WaPo* reported that John Kelly tried to pressure acting DHS secretary Elaine Duke to expel Hondurans. In a call while traveling in Japan, Kelly was "irritated" and admonished her not to "kick the can down the road."

17. Despite Trump's efforts to derail Obamacare by starving the exchange of sign-ups, ACA registration spiked at open enrollment's start: over two hundred thousand people chose a plan on November 1, more than doubling last year's first-day enrollment.

18. *WaPo* reported that Betsy DeVos has shrunk the Education Department, shedding 350 workers since December, with buyouts offered to an additional 255 employees. Only eight of the fifteen key roles requiring Senate confirmation have nominees.

19. *WaPo* reported that the U.S. Agency for International Development (USAID) sent letters to seventy applicants for jobs in the foreign service, saying the positions had been canceled. This comes amid a State Department hiring freeze.

20. *Foreign Policy* reported that scores of senior diplomats, including 60 percent of career ambassadors, have left the State Department since Trump took office. There are seventy-four key roles at State that are vacant and have no nominee.

21. A top U.S. diplomat, American Foreign Service Association president and former ambassador Barbara Stephenson, blasted the Trump regime in an open letter, "Time to Ask Why," pointing out that the problem is not just top leadership leaving, but recruitment falling dramatically, too.

22. *Newsweek* reported that Lara Trump, Eric's wife, has taken on White House duties, hosting high-level meetings on domestic policy initiatives with cabinet members, lawmakers, and Trump advisers.

23. Leaked documents, the "Paradise Papers," reveal that Commerce Secretary Wilbur Ross failed to disclose his interest in Navigator Holdings, a shipping company with significant ties to Russia, during his confirmation hearing.

24. Navigator's most important business relationship is with SIBUR, an energy company controlled by Putin's son-in-law and Russian oligarchs Timchenko and Michelson, both of whom are on the Treasury Department's sanction list.

25. Penny Young Nance, Trump's likely nominee for ambassador for global women's issues, is a strong opponent of abortion and gay rights, and said the movie *Frozen* sends a harmful message about the role of men.

26. Kyle Yunasaka, the brother of Lara Trump, was named chief of staff at the Energy Department's Office of Energy Policy. Yunasaka has no education or work experience in energy.

27. Trump's nominee William Wehrum was confirmed to a key post in the EPA despite oil industry ties. As an attorney, Wehrum represented the American Petroleum Institute, the American Fuel & Petrochemical Manufacturers, and the American Chemistry Council.

28. In a filing with the Securities and Exchange Commission, Icahn Enterprises announced that the U.S. attorney for the Southern District of New York has issued a subpoena seeking information related to activities while Carl Icahn was an adviser to Trump. In Week 40, Icahn benefited from actions taken as adviser relating to his 82 percent stake in CVR Energy.

29. The *Daily Beast* reported that Trump appointed David Kautter to become the interim IRS commissioner. Kautter's firm had to pay $123 million to the U.S. Treasury in 2013 as part of a settlement for a tax shelter scheme.

30. Brett Talley, a blogger nominated by Trump for federal judge in Alabama, has never tried a case and was unanimously rated "not qualified" by the American Bar Association. It is highly atypical to have a nominee be deemed not qualified, let alone four already.

31. Brett Talley's nomination passed the Senate Judiciary Committee on a party-line vote.

32. *Politico* reported that the House Rules Committee, which is controlled by Speaker Paul Ryan, set a record for the most closed rules in a session. Ryan has yet to allow a single piece of legislation to be governed by an open rule. Under open rule, lawmakers are allowed to propose amendments for a bill on the floor.

33. The *NYT* reported that there has been a spike in deaths in Puerto Rico, but few are being attributed to Maria. Puerto Rican officials acknowledged that 472 more people died this September compared with the same month last year.

34. On Tuesday, Natalie Jaresko, executive director of the Financial Oversight and Management Board for Puerto Rico, told Congress nearly 60 percent of Puerto Rico is without electricity and thousands remain in shelters.

35. NPR reported that federal troops have started to leave Puerto Rico, while many are still without a steady supply of food and running water, and while schools remain closed.

36. On Friday, three-star army general Jeffrey Buchanan, who coordinated the federal military response in Puerto Rico following Hurricane Maria, said in a news conference, "We're out of the crisis," and is leaving next week.

37. Tuesday's election was a trouncing for the Republican Party, including governor seats in New Jersey and Virginia, and fifteen legislative seats shifting hands in Virginia (three are still undecided), and a key race in Westchester County, New York.

38. History was made in many races nationwide as women, people of color, and LGBTQ individuals won their races, including numerous "firsts."

39. In the Virginia legislature, eleven of the fifteen Democrats who won were women—including two who are the first Hispanic women to serve in the state's legislature. Women candidates racked up victories around the country.

40. Danica Roem was elected in Virginia as the first openly transgender legislator, defeating Bob Marshall, an outspoken opponent of transgender rights who introduced the controversial transgender "bathroom bill."

41. Republican John Carman, a New Jersey politician who joked about the Women's March, asking if it would be "over in time for them to cook dinner," was defeated by a thirty-two-year-old woman, Ashley Bennett, a first-time candidate.

42. More than two dozen House Republicans have announced they won't be running again in 2018, well above the average number of House retirements per election cycle. More announcements are expected.

43. Starting with accusations against Harvey Weinstein and the #MeToo campaign, scores of women and men have come forward to share their stories of sexual assault, harassment, and rape as adults and children.

44. Accusations have come against men in Hollywood, academia, sports, corporate America, politics, and more. On Thursday, CNN hosted a prime-time town hall, "Tipping Point: Sexual Harassment in America."

45. On Thursday, a Senate resolution introduced by Senators Amy Klobuchar and Chuck Grassley requiring mandatory harassment training for all senators, officers, employees, and interns in the Senate unanimously passed.

46. On Thursday, *WaPo* reported that Alabama senate candidate Roy Moore sexually assaulted a fourteen-year-old girl when he was in his early thirties. Moore denied the allegations, employing a Trump distraction: blame the liberal, fake media.

47. The *WSJ* reported that, based on an examination of 159,000 deleted tweets, Kremlin-backed support for Trump on Twitter started as early as June 2015. Russian accounts attacked Hillary and Jeb Bush, the GOP frontrunner at the time.

48. In the two weeks ahead the November 2016 election, Russian account activity escalated. Trump campaign insiders like Flynn and conservative pundits like Sean Hannity followed and retweeted these accounts.

49. The *NYT* reported that Russian billionaire investor Yuri Milner made major investments in U.S. social media companies Twitter and Facebook using money from state-owned Russian banks VTB and Gazprom Investholding.

50. Milner ultimately owned more than 8 percent of Facebook and 5 percent of Twitter, and later sold these stakes, but retains large U.S. technology holdings. He also has investments in real estate partly owned by Kushner.

51. NBC reported that Mueller has enough evidence to bring charges against Flynn and his son. Mueller is applying pressure on Flynn after the Manafort indictment and speaking to witnesses about his lobbying work.

52. Mueller is looking into whether Flynn was behind a request to the FBI in the weeks after Trump's inauguration to conduct a new review of Turkey's 2016 request to extradite Fethullah Gulen, an elderly Muslim cleric.

53. CNN reported that Michael Flynn and his wife, Lori, are concerned about their son's legal exposure in the Mueller probe, and this could factor into Flynn's decision on how to respond to Mueller.

54. On Sunday, Senator Lindsey Graham said Sessions needs to return to the Senate Judiciary Committee and answer questions about Trump campaign ties to Russia, after revelations in Week 51 showed that Sessions's previous statements were false.

55. Sessions is set to face questions about Russia from the House Judiciary Committee in an open hearing next week as part of DoJ oversight. Sessions will also likely speak to the House Intelligence Committee in a closed setting.

56. *WaPo* reported that, based on a review of court documents and interviews, at least nine members of the Trump regime had meetings with Russians during the campaign and transition.

57. The nine are George Papadopoulos, Paul Manafort, Jeff Sessions, Donald Trump Jr., Michael Cohen, Jared Kushner, Michael Flynn, Carter Page, and J. D. Gordon. Questions arose as to whether the Kremlin sought to infiltrate the Trump campaign, or if their separate communications with Russians are a coincidence.

58. On Monday, a transcript of Page's six and a half hours of testimony to the House Intelligence Committee was released. The testimony disputes Page's initial claims that his visit to Moscow in July 2016 was in a private capacity.

59. Page testified that he sent an e-mail in advance of his trip to Corey Lewandowski, Hope Hicks, and Gordon. Page said Lewandowski gave him the okay to go. Page said he also mentioned his trip to Sessions.

60. Gordon told CNN that he "discouraged Carter from taking the trip to Moscow because it was a bad idea," but Page ignored him: "He eventually went around me directly to campaign leadership."

61. Page met with Russian deputy prime minister Arkady Dvorkovich. Page reported to the campaign after his trip that Dvorkovich "expressed strong support for Mr. Trump and a desire to work together."

62. Page also acknowledged meeting with other high-level Russian officials and said they discussed the U.S. presidential election "in general terms."

63. Page acknowledged he met with Andrey Baranov, head of investor relations at Rosneft, a Russian state-owned oil company. He also met with an investor-relations official at energy company Gazprom.

64. Representative Adam Schiff asked if there was a discussion about the 19 percent stake in Rosneft in exchange for the lifting of U.S. sanctions on Russia. Page said that "he may have briefly mentioned it," but the quid pro quo was not discussed directly. Igor Sechin, the CEO of Rosneft, offered Page the stake if he could assist in getting the sanctions lifted.

65. Page again met with Baranov in Moscow a month after the election. The Russian government owns a majority stake in Rosneft. The Treasury Depart sanctioned Rosneft after Russia annexed Crimea in 2014.

66. Page acknowledged that he has met with the FBI several times and answered questions about events described in the Steele dossier. Page said Mueller has not made any indication he will indict him.

67. After the trip, Page offered the Trump campaign a readout. He also spoke to national cochairman Sam Clovis, who Page said separately asked him to sign a nondisclosure agreement.

68. Page acknowledged that he praised Gordon and five others on the Trump policy team in an e-mail for changing the Republican Party platform on Ukraine: "As for the Ukraine amendment, excellent work."

69. Page received a text, then a call, from Steve Bannon in January advising him not to appear on MSNBC. He also received a letter from Trump campaign law firm Jones Day imploring him not to say he is part of the campaign.

70. In an interview with Bloomberg, Veselnitskaya said Donald Jr. hinted the Magnitsky Act would be reexamined if Trump won, in exchange for written evidence that illegal proceeds went to Hillary's campaign.

71. The *Intercept* reported that CIA director Mike Pompeo met with William Binney, an advocate for a fringe DNC hack theory, on October 24. Binney has accused intelligence of subverting the Constitution and violating civil rights.

72. Binney argues that the DNC data was "leaked," not hacked, "by a person with physical access" to the DNC's computer system. U.S. intelligence's official assessment is that Russian intelligence was behind the DNC hack.

73. NBC reported that according to Binney, Pompeo took the meeting at the behest of Trump. It is extremely unusual for a CIA director to meet with someone like Binney, who also makes frequent appearances on RT's English-language television network.

74. On Wednesday, U.S. district judge Berman Jackson issued a gag order in the Manafort and Rick Gates criminal cases, directing prosecutors and defense to refrain from making statements to the media or in public settings.

75. CNN reported that Joseph Mifsud, the academic suspected of being a link between Papadopoulos and the Russian officials in discussions about Hillary's e-mails, has vanished. In court documents, Mifsud is referred to as "Foreign Contact 1."

76. *Politico* reported that congressional investigators are also probing the GOP platform fight as part of the Russia investigation. Gordon acknowledged being interviewed by lawmakers, but wouldn't say if he has met with Mueller.

77. Papadopoulos, Manafort, and Gates were also involved in the convention. Without naming names, Gordon said others in the Trump campaign involved in pushing the platform change are also being interviewed.

78. The AP reported that Russian Twitter trolls organized to deflect public attention from Trump's *Access Hollywood* tapes, instead touting damaging e-mails hacked and leaked from John Podesta.

79. The AP reported on Russia's cyber-meddling strategy: swiftly react, distort, and distract attention from any negative Trump news. There were spikes in Twitter activity on September 16, October 6, and November 8.

80. Mueller interviewed Stephen Miller, bringing the Russia investigation into Trump's inner circle. Miller is the highest-level aide still working at the White House known to have talked to Mueller's team.

81. CNN reported that Miller was questioned on his role in the firing of James Comey and about the March 2016 meeting where Papadopoulos said he could arrange a meeting between Trump and Putin through his connections.

82. *Business Insider* reported that many Trump advisers are facing sky-high legal bills. Roger Stone blasted out a statement asking for help paying the nearly $460,000 in legal fees he has incurred in the Russia probe.

83. Gordon told *Business Insider* that the RNC is taking care of Trump and Donald Jr., and "the rest of us who aren't billionaires must fend for ourselves." Gordon said he has incurred an almost five-figure legal bill.

84. On Thursday, RT said the DoJ has ordered the broadcaster to register as a foreign agent by Monday. RT's editor in chief Margarita Simonyan called the timing a "cannibalistic deadline" and an attempt to "drive [RT] out of the country."

85. On Friday, the *WSJ* reported that Cambridge Analytica's outreach to Julian Assange happened as the company was in advanced stages of contract negotiations with the Trump campaign, and had already dispatched employees to work on the campaign.

86. In addition to the previously disclosed nine million dollars paid by the Trump campaign for providing data, polling, and research services, Cambridge Analytica was also paid an additional six million dollars that was routed through Parscale.

87. Cambridge Analytica is partly owned by Rebekah and Robert Mercer, who made his first donation to Trump on June 21, 2016. Bannon served on Cambridge Analytica's board and holds a stake in the company.

88. According to a person with knowledge of the investigation, Papadopoulos initially misled FBI agents out of what he claimed was loyalty to Trump: he didn't want to contradict Trump's statement that he had had no contact with Russians.

89. *Business Insider* reported that Devin Nunes, who was then chair of the House Intelligence Committee, attended a breakfast on January 18 that Flynn and the Turkish foreign minister also attended. Press was excluded.

90. NBC reported that Mueller is probing a meeting on September 20 in D.C. between Flynn and Representative Dana Rohrabacher, set up by Flynn's lobbying firm, the Flynn Intel Group. Two of Flynn's business partners and his son also attended.

91. Mueller is reviewing e-mails sent from Flynn Intel Group to Rohrabacher's congressional staff thanking them for the meeting.

92. On Friday, the *NYT* reported on a meeting in London on March 24, 2016, between Papadopoulos, Mifsud, and Olga Polonskaya, a thirty-year-old Russian who was introduced as Putin's niece. Putin has no niece.

93. Mueller is interested in interactions between the three and a fourth man with contacts inside Russia's foreign ministry as a central part of the investigation into the Kremlin's role in the 2016 election.

94. Papadopoulos met Mifsud for breakfast in April. As noted in Week 51, Mifsud bragged about having "dirt" on Hillary: "thousands of e-mails." Mifsud's outreach began after Papadopoulos joined the Trump campaign.

95. The day before his breakfast, Papadopoulos e-mailed Stephen Miller, saying that Trump has an "open invitation" from Putin to visit Russia. The day after, he wrote, "some interesting messages coming in from Moscow."

96. Together with items involving Page, there is increasing evidence not only of contact between the Trump campaign and Russians, but also that senior campaign officials were aware of the contacts.

97. NBC reported that Mueller is probing a possible quid pro quo between Flynn and Turkey during the presidential transition. Flynn met with senior Turkish officials in December 2016 at the 21 Club restaurant, near Trump Tower.

98. Mueller is looking into whether they discussed orchestrating the return of Turkish cleric Fethullah Gulen, who lives in Pennsylvania, as well as freeing Turkish-Iranian gold trader Reza Zarrab, who is jailed in the U.S.

99. Flynn was allegedly offered a fifteen-million-dollar payment if he could orchestrate the deal. Flynn's son may have also been involved. Trump campaign senior adviser Rudy Giuliani is part of Zarrab's defense team.

100. Reuters reported that Mueller questioned Clovis this week on whether Trump or top aides knew of the extent of the campaign's contacts with Russia, and who approved and directed the contacts.

101. A *WaPo*/ABC News survey found just 37 percent approve and 59 percent disapprove of the job Trump is doing, lower than any leader in the last seven decades, nine months in. Fifty-five percent think Trump is not keeping his campaign promises.

102. The poll found that just one-third believe Trump is honest and trustworthy, and 65 percent say he has accomplished "not much" or "little or nothing."

103. On Thursday, Tom Steyer said he would spend an additional ten million dollars on his campaign to impeach Trump. Nearly two million people have signed his online petition to demand Trump be impeached.

104. On Monday, Trump's DoJ told AT&T that in order for the planned takeover of Time Warner to go through, the company must sell off CNN. As detailed in the *Weekly List*, Trump has a long-running feud with CNN.

105. On Wednesday, AT&T's CFO said on a conference call that this type of merger hasn't been blocked for over forty years. AT&T has signaled that it intends to challenge the regime in court over the requirement.

106. On Thursday, AT&T's CEO told CNBC, "I have never been told that the price of getting the [Time Warner] deal done was selling CNN," and that he has never offered to sell it, either.

107. On Friday, Reuters reported that Trump ally Rupert Murdoch called AT&T's CEO on May 16 and August 8 to ask if CNN was for sale.

108. On Friday, a federal judge dismissed, for a second time, a pair of lawsuits seeking to force the State Department to do more to recover Hillary's e-mails. As noted in Week 51, Trump has been tweeting and speaking out about the need to find them.

109. The judge cited the FBI's use of grand jury subpoenas sent not only to Hillary's provider and accounts, but ones used by people she corresponded with, as satisfying the State Department's obligation to take reasonable steps.

110. On Wednesday, Senator Bob Corker announced that as chair of the Senate Foreign Relations Committee, he will hold hearings on Trump's ability to use nuclear weapons. Corker said it has been four decades since Congress looked at the issue.

111. An NBC/*WSJ* poll found that in counties that voted for Trump, a plurality—41 percent—say the country is worse off now than it was when Trump took office. Thirty-two percent believe the country is better off, and 26 percent believe it's the same.

112. After repeatedly bashing China for unfair trade and saying the country was "raping" the U.S. economy during his campaign, while visiting Beijing, Trump praised Xi, saying, "I don't blame China." The crowd of business leaders applauded.

113. The two leaders did not take questions from the press, a victory for Xi, who oversees an authoritarian system that limits press freedom. Former Democratic and Republican aides called it an "embarrassing capitulation."

114. Chinese state media approved of the summit, saying that Trump "respects our head of state and has repeatedly praised" Xi publicly.

115. On Friday, Press Secretary Sarah Huckabee Sanders said there would be no formal meeting between Trump and Putin in Vietnam, but that they might "bump into each other."

116. After staying mostly on script during his Asia trip, on Saturday, Trump reverted to lies and dangerous statements in a twenty-six-minute question-and-answer session with reporters aboard Air Force One.

117. On Saturday, Trump had his second private, "sideline" meeting with Putin (in Week 36 it was revealed that Trump had a clandestine meeting with Putin at the G20 summit) without media access.

118. Trump told reporters of his conversation with Putin, "He said he didn't meddle—I asked him again," adding Putin "means it." Trump also said, "I think he is very insulted by it, which is not a good thing for our country."

119. Trump dismissed the Russia probe as an "artificial Democratic hit job" and said it would put American lives at risk, saying it "gets in the way and that's a shame because people will die because of it."

120. Trump attacked U.S. intelligence, saying, "I mean, give me a break, they are political hacks . . . I mean, you have Brennan, you have Clapper, and you have Comey." Trump sided instead with "President Putin, very strong."

121. Following that statement, former NSA director General Michael Hayden tweeted, "CIA just told me: The Dir stands by and has always stood by the January 2017 Intelligence Community Assessment," and went on to question which side Trump is on.

ACKNOWLEDGMENTS

The List was started as a way to keep us informed and grew thanks to the grassroots support of my fellow Americans. It was truly a gift for me that each week The List was read and shared and used as a source of activism and revitalization.

I want to thank my amazing children, Amanda and Jackson, for their understanding and support, and for sharing me every night as I sat at my computer to chronicle our failing democracy. Our family grew through this process, and I'm pretty sure we have a greater appreciation for our fragile freedoms and the need for civil activism. And of course, my loyal and patient furry children, Shep and Arleen (so pretty).

Thank you to my friends and community who knew when to take me to dinner or for a glass of wine. For stopping at the gas station, the gym, the coffee shop to thank me—or for sending me flowers, or chocolate, or books, or bourbon. To my social media followers who were the fuel that kept me going on the days it was relentless and heartbreaking and difficult to cope.

Thank you to my agent, Mollie at CAA, for walking me through the process of my first book, and to Anton and Nancy and all the fabulous folks at Bloomsbury for their patience and professionalism, and for having a vision for this project before I even had one myself.

NOTES

GLOSSARY

AP:	Associated Press
BF:	*BuzzFeed*
BI:	*Business Insider*
CT:	*Chicago Tribune*
DB:	*Daily Beast*
DI:	*Daily Intelligencer (New York Magazine* blog)
DK:	*Daily Kos*
FP:	*Foreign Policy*
FT:	*Financial Times*
IBT:	*International Business Times*
IJR:	*Independent Journal Review*
LAT:	*Los Angeles Times*
MJ:	*Mother Jones*
NLJ:	*National Law Journal*
NR:	*New Republic*
NYDN:	*New York Daily News*
NYer:	*New Yorker*
NYP:	*New York Post*
NYT:	*New York Times*
TPM:	*Talking Points Memo*
USAT:	*USA Today*
USN:	*U.S. News & World Report*
VF:	*Vanity Fair*
WSJ:	*Wall Street Journal*
WE:	*Washington Examiner*
WaPo:	*Washington Post*
YN:	*Yahoo News*

WEEK 1

1. Chris Sommerfeldt, "More than 700 'Hateful Harassment' Attacks Reported Since Donald Trump's Election," *NYDN*, 11/19/16.

2. Nick Fox (@NickFoxNYT), "A @nytimes editor should explain why the Hamilton story is top of the homepage and Trump's $25M fraud settlement is a small line at the bottom" Twitter, 11/19/16, 8:39 p.m.

4. Daniel Lombroso and Yoni Applebaum, "'Hail Trump!': White Nationalists Salute the President-Elect," *Atlantic*, 11/21/16.

6. Brent Budowsky, "Secretary of State Romney Would Be a Smart Move," *The Hill*, 11/18/16.

9. Abigail Tracy, "Trump Responds to Amorous Neo-Nazi Supporters: Nothing to See Here," *VF*, 11/22/16.

WEEK 2

1. Isabel Vincent, "Melania and Barron Trump Won't Be Moving to the White House," *NYP*, 11/20/16.

2. *Wikipedia*, s.v. "Melania Trump," last edited 12/1/17, 10:55, en.wikipedia.org/wiki/Melania_Trump.

3. Jay Solomon, "Donald Trump Jr. Held Talks on Syria with Russia Supporters," *WSJ*, 11/23/16.

4. "U.N. Syria Expert: Aleppo Is in Freefall," NBCNews.com, 11/25/16; Will Kirby, "Russia Threatens Washington to 'STOP Getting in the Way' in Syria amid Escalating Tensions," *Express*, 11/25/16.

5. Tucker Reals, "Russia Responds to NATO Advance with Missiles in Its Europe Enclave," CBS News, 11/21/16.

6. Craig Timberg, "Russian Propaganda Effort Helped Spread 'Fake News' During Election, Experts Say," *WaPo*, 11/24/16.

7. Emily Smith and Daniel Halper, "Donald Trump's Media Summit Was a 'F—ing Firing Squad,'" *NYP*, 11/21/16.

8. Michael D. Shear, Julie Hirschfeld Davis, and Maggie Haberman, "Trump, in Interview, Moderates Views but Defies Conventions," *NYT*, 11/22/16.

9. Philip Bump, "A Running List of How Donald Trump's New Position May Be Helping His Business Interests," *WaPo*, 11/21/16; updated 1/3/17.

10. Nadia Prupis, "Nepotism Strikes Again: Ivanka Trump Joined Call with Argentina President," *Common Dreams*, 11/22/16; Cristiano Lima, "Ivanka Trump Sits in on Meeting with Japanese Prime Minister," *Politico*, 11/17/16.

11. Isaac Arnsdorf, "Trump: 'The President Can't Have a Conflict of Interest,'" *Politico*, 11/22/16.

12. David A. Fahrenthold, "Trump Foundation Admits to Violating Ban on 'Self-dealing,' New Filing to IRS Shows," *WaPo*, 11/22/16.

13. Wisconsin Elections Commission, "Wisconsin Elections Commission Receives Two Presidential Election Recount Petitions," 11/25/16.

14. Harper Neidig, "Report: Trump Team Wants Romney to Apologize," *The Hill*, 11/25/16.

15. Reuters, "Donald Trump Souvenirs: Are People Still Buying 'Make America Great Again' Merchandise?" *IBT*, 11/24/16; "Trump Make America Great Again Red Cap Collectible Ornament," www.amazon.com/Trump-America-Great-Collectible-Ornament/dp/B01N67D8HO.

16. Sammy Nickalls, "'Are Jews People' Was an Actual, Real Discussion Topic on CNN," Esquire.com, 11/21/16.

17. Sarah Larimer, "This Airline Passenger's Pro-Trump Rant Was Caught on Video. Now He's Banned from Delta," *WaPo*, 11/28/16.

18. Robert O'Harrow Jr., "Trump Adviser Received Salary from Charity While Steering Breitbart News," *WaPo*, 11/23/16.

WEEK 3

1. Maureen B. Costello, "The Trump Effect: The Impact of the 2016 Presidential Election on Our Nation's Schools," 11/28/16, www.splcenter.org/20161128/trump-effect-impact-2016-presidential-election-our-nations-schools; Cassie Miller and Alexandra Werner-Winslow, "Ten Days After: Harassment and Intimidation in the Aftermath of the Election," 11/29/16, www.splcenter.org/20161129/ten-days-after-harassment-and-intimidation-aftermath-election; "Hate Map," www.splcenter.org/hate-map.

3. Steve Benen, "Offered Daily Intelligence Briefings, Trump Takes a Pass," *MaddowBlog*, 11/28/16.

5. Donald Trump (@realDonaldTrump), "The Green Party just dropped its recount suit in Pennsylvania and is losing votes in Wisconsin recount. Just a Stein scam to raise money!" Twitter, 12/4/16, 10:58 a.m.; Laura Dimon, "Drunk Men Screaming Trump's Name Try to Rip off Muslim Student's Hijab as Straphangers Stand Idly by on East Side Subway, Cops Say," *NYDN*, 12/3/16.

6. Donald Trump (@realDonaldTrump), "In addition to winning the Electoral College in a landslide, I won the popular vote if you deduct the millions of people who voted illegally" Twitter, 11/27/16, 12:30 p.m.; Danielle Kurtzleben, "Here Are the Problems with the Trump Team's Voter Fraud

Evidence," NPR.org, 11/28/16; Harper Neidig, "Conway: Trump Has Been 'Receiving Information' of Voter Fraud," *The Hill*, 12/2/16.

7. Chad Livengood and Jennifer Chambers, "Stein Suit Follows Trump's in Michigan Recount Bid," *Detroit News*, 12/2/16; David Eggert and Scott Bauer, "Michigan Board to Hear Trump's Challenge to Recount Effort," AP, 12/2/16.

8. Paulina Firozi, "Teen: Trump Edited My Tweet about CNN," *The Hill*, 11/29/16.

9. Claire Landsbaum, "Kellyanne Conway Scolded a High-School Student for Asking Her about Donald Trump's History of Sexual Assault," *The Cut*, 11/30/16.

10. Donald Trump (@realDonald Trump), "Nobody should be allowed to burn the American flag—if they do, there must be consequences—perhaps loss of citizenship or year in jail!" Twitter, 11/29/16, 3:55 a.m.

11. Jordain Carney, "McConnell Pushes Back at Trump on Flag-burning Comments," *The Hill*, 11/29/16; Nolan D. McCaskill, "Paul Ryan: I've Discussed Constitution 'Extensively' with Trump," *Politico*, 12/2/16.

12. Mark Hensch, "Trump Campaign Promotes Cyber Monday Sale," *The Hill*, 11/28/16.

13. David Filipov and James McAuley, "Russia Has Been in Contact with Trump Team over Syria, Senior Diplomat Says," *WaPo*, 11/30/16.

14. Dylan Stableford, "Petraeus Would Need to Inform His Probation Officer if He Joins Trump's Cabinet," *YN*, 12/1/16.

15. Henry C. Jackson and Alex Isenstadt, "Romney Gushes over Trump after Posh Dinner," 11/29/16; "ExxonMobil Execs among Trump Cabinet Considerations," *Rachel Maddow Show*, MSNBC, 12/1/16.

16. Drew Harwell, "Trump Announces He Will Leave Business 'In Total'—Leaving Open How He Will Avoid Conflicts of Interest," *WaPo*, 11/30/16.

17. Spencer Ackerman, "Senators Call for Declassification of Files on Russia's Role in US Election," *Guardian*, 12/1/16; Eliza Collins, "Yes, 17 Intelligence Agencies Really Did Say Russia Was Behind Hacking," *USAT*, 10/21/16.

18. Nick Gass, "Clinton Faces Late Summer Scandal Wave," *Politico*, 8/22/16; Nolan D. McCaskill and Madeline Conway, "Bahrain to Host Event at Trump's D.C. Hotel, Raising Ethical Concerns," *Politico*, 11/29/16.

19. Ben White, "Goldman Sachs Poised for Return to Power in Trump White House," *Politico*, 11/30/16.

20. Sean Colarossi, "Trump's Self-Congratulatory Tour Kicks Off with Half-Empty Rally in Cincinnati," *Politicus USA*, 12/1/16.

21. Stephen Collinson, "New Trump, Same as the Old Trump," CNN.com, 12/2/16; Jonathan Chait, "Trump Camp Thinking of Locking Up *New York Times* Editor, Too," *DI*, 12/2/16.

22. Bill McGurn, "Trump's Carrier Shakedown," *WSJ*, 12/1/16.

23-24. Mark Landler, "Trump's Breezy Calls to World Leaders Leave Diplomats Aghast," *NYT*, 12/1/16.

25. Ananya Roy, "Trump Backs Philippines' Drug War and Believes It Is the Right Way to Handle the Issue, Duterte Says," *IBT*, 12/8/16.

26. Ben Blanchard, "China Lodges Protest after Trump Call with Taiwan President," Reuters, 12/2/16.

WEEK 4

1. Jessica Contrera, "Trump Says 'SNL' Is 'Unwatchable.' Then Why Can't He Stop Watching?" *WaPo*, 12/4/16; Jonathan Lemire, "Trump on New Boeing Air Force One: 'Cancel Order!'" AP, 12/6/16; Jacob Pramuk, "Union Leader Who Called Out Donald Trump Says He's Getting Threats from Trump Supporters," CNBC.com, 12/8/16; Christina Cauterucci, "Getting the Women's March on Washington on the Road," *Slate*, 11/23/16.

2. Cynthia Littleton, "Donald Trump to Remain Executive Producer on 'Celebrity Apprentice,'" *Variety*, 12/8/16.

3. Asawin Suebsaeng and Gideon Resnick, "Mark Burnett Clamps Down on 'The Apprentice' Staff over Donald Trump Leaks," *DB*, 11/2/16.

4. Adam Entous, Ellen Nakashima, and Greg Miller, "Secret CIA Assessment Says Russia Was Trying to Help Trump Win White House," *WaPo*, 12/9/16.

5. Daniel Politi, "How Mitch McConnell Prevented Stronger Action Against Russian Election Meddling," *The Slatest*, 12/10/16.

6. Steven Mufson, Philip Rucker, and Karoun Demirjian, "Trump Picks ExxonMobil CEO Rex Tillerson to Be Secretary of State," *WaPo*, 12/13/16.

7. Rebecca Savransky, "Trump on Intelligence Briefings: 'I Get It When I Need It,'" *The Hill*, 12/11/16.

8. Reuters, "Somali-American Minnesota State Representative Says Harassed by DC Cabbie," 12/8/16.

9. Daniel J. Solomon, "David Duke Says Jews Aren't White—and Jews Clap Back," *Forward*, 12/6/16.

10. Gabby Morrongiello, "Trump Exploring Legal Options to Give Ivanka, Kushner Roles in His Administration," *WE*, 12/11/16.

11. David A. Graham, "All the President-Elect's Generals," *Atlantic*, 12/8/16.

12. Ben Walsh, "Donald Trump Picks Another Goldman Sachs Exec to Join His Administration," *HuffPost*, 12/9/16; Peter Schroeder, "Goldman Sachs Accounts for a Quarter of Dow Jones Gains Since Election," *The Hill*, 12/20/16.

13. Oliver Milman and the AP, "Leonardo DiCaprio Meets Trump as Climate Sceptic Nominated," *Guardian*, 12/8/16.

14. Sam Stein, "The RNC Is Hosting Its Christmas Party This Year at Donald Trump's Hotel," *HuffPost*, 12/19/16.

15. Maggie Haberman and Jo Becker, "Donald Trump Is Said to Intend to Keep a Stake in His Business," *NYT*, 12/7/16.

16. Jim Tankersley and Jose A. DelReal, "Trump's Economic Team Has Six Men Named Steve but No Women," *WaPo*, 8/5/16.

17. Erik Hayden, "Mark Burnett Meets with Trump over Inauguration Plans," *Hollywood Reporter*, 12/8/16.

18. Josh Dawsey and Shane Goldmacher, "Giuliani Pulls Name from Contention for Secretary of State," *Politico*, 12/9/16; Eitan Arom, "L.A.-based Holocaust Claims Lawyer Sues FBI over Clinton Warrant," *Jewish Journal*, 12/7/16.

19. Rebecca Savransky, "Trump Selling 'Official' Presidential Hat for $40," *The Hill*, 12/5/16.

20. Donald J. Trump, Facebook post, 12/4/16, www.facebook.com /DonaldTrump/posts /10158226484895725.

22. Kate Abbey-Lambertz, "Jill Stein Condemns Premature End to the Michigan Recount," *HuffPost*, 12/10/16.

WEEK 5

1. Spencer Ackerman, "Intelligence Figures Fear Trump Reprisals over Assessment of Russia Election Role," *Guardian*, 12/11/16.

2. Olivia Nuzzi, "Here's What Trump Should Have Told Us at That Dec. 15 Press Conference," *DB*, 12/15/16.

3. Katie Little, "Trump Reportedly Not Planning to Divest from His Businesses," CNBC.com, 12/16/16.

4. Tina Nguyen, "Trump Grill Could Be the Worst Restaurant in America," *VF*, 12/14/16.

5. Alex Griswold, "Reince Priebus Hints President Trump Could Do Away with White House Press Briefings," *Mediaite*, 12/14/16.

6. "Is Ivanka Trump Getting the White House Office Usually Reserved for the First Lady?" *US Weekly*, 12/15/16.

7. Walter Einenkel, "Kellyanne Conway Just Explained the 'Loophole' Trump Will Be Using to Get around Anti-Nepotism Law," *DK*, 12/15/16.

8. David E. Sanger, "Trump, Mocking Claim That Russia Hacked Election, at Odds with G.O.P.," *NYT*, 12/10/16.

9. Jeremy Diamond, "Russian Hacking and the 2016 Election," CNN, 12/16/16.

10. Julia Manchester, "Conway: Obama Could Shut Down Trump Feud if He Loved 'the Country Enough,'" CNN .com, 12/16/16.

11. Kevin Johnson, "FBI Accepts CIA Conclusion That Russians Hacked to Help Trump," *USAT*, 12/16/16.

12. Jacob Pramuk, "Democrats Hit Trump on DC Hotel Lease, but Federal Agency Pushes Back on Their Claims," CNBC.com, 12/14/16.

13. Lolita Baldor, "Flynn Investigated by Army for Wrongly Sharing Intelligence," AP, 12/14/16; Kimberly Ricci, "Michael Flynn Quietly Deleted a Tweet Promoting the Insane Pizzagate Conspiracy Theory," *Uproxx*, 12/14/16.

14. Eric Lipton and Maggie Haberman, "Available to the Highest Bidder: Coffee with Ivanka Trump," *NYT*, 12/15/16.

15. Steven Mufson and Juliet Eilperin, "Trump Transition Team for Energy Department Seeks Names of Employees Involved in Climate Meetings," *WaPo*, 12/9/16.

16. Lisa Hagen and Ben Kamisar, "Trump Basks in Victory on 'Thank You Tour,'" *The Hill*, 12/1/16.

17. Jen Wieczner, "When Donald Trump Hate-Tweeted Lockheed Martin, Hedge Funds Were Ready," *Fortune*, 12/14/16.

18. Gregory Krieg and Eugene Scott, "White Males Dominate Trump's Top Cabinet Posts," CNN.com, updated 1/19/17.

19. Dominique Fortes, "Trump Team 'Bounced' Twitter from Tech Summit over 'Crooked Hillary' Emoji Flap," CNBC.com, 12/14/16.

20. Nate Raymond, "Clinton Aide Huma Abedin Seeks to Review FBI's Email Search Warrant," AOL.com, 12/16/16.

WEEK 6

1. Kenneth P. Vogel, "Trump Private Security Force 'Playing with Fire,'" *Politico*, 12/19/16.

2. David Badash, "Trump Statement on Winning Electoral College Vote Is Filled with Lies," New Civil Rights Movement, 12/19/16.

3. Rachel Stockman, "Legal Experts: 'Meritless' FBI Warrant Used to Obtain Clinton Emails Violates Fourth Amendment," *Law & Crime*, 12/20/16; Dan Hopkins, "Voters Really Did Switch to Trump at the Last Minute," *FiveThirtyEight*, 12/20/16.

4. Rachel Bade, "Trump Posse Browbeats Hill Republicans," *Politico*, 12/21/16.

5. Bianca Padró Ocasio, "O'Reilly: Left Wants 'Power Taken Away from the White Establishment,'" *Politico*, 12/20/16.

6. Colby Itkowitz, "Jewish Family Falsely Blamed for Cancellation of a School's Christmas Play," *WaPo*, 12/22/16.

7. De Elizabeth, "Donald Trump's National Security Advisor Met with 'Alt-Right' Freedom Party Leader," *Teen Vogue*, 12/20/16.

8. Donald Trump (@realDonaldTrump), "The so-called 'A' list celebrities are all wanting tixs to the inauguration, but look what they did for Hillary, NOTHING. I want the PEOPLE!" Twitter, 12/22/16, 5:59 p.m.; Tahirah Hairston, "The Rockettes Are Performing at Trump's Inauguration—and Some of Them Are Mad as Hell," *Splinter*, 12/23/16.

9. Jessie Hellmann, "Gingrich suggests Trump pardon advisers who break the law," *The Hill*, 12/19/16.

10. Paulina Firozi, "Gingrich: Trump Doesn't Want to 'Drain the Swamp' Anymore," *The Hill*, 12/21/16; Oliver Darcy, "'I Goofed': Newt Gingrich Says He Made 'Boo Boo' When He Claimed Trump Softened on His 'Drain the Swamp' Promise," *BI*, 12/22/16.

11. Judd Legum and Kira Lerner, "Under Political Pressure, Kuwait Cancels Major Event at Four Seasons, Switches to Trump's D.C. Hotel," *ThinkProgress*, 12/19/16.

12. Doug Cameron and Damian Paletta, "Donald Trump Meets with Boeing, Lockheed CEOs," *WSJ*, 12/21/16.

13. Olivia Solon, "Oracle Executive Publicly Resigns after CEO Joins Trump's Transition Team," *Guardian*, 12/21/16.

14. "Trophy Donors," Snopes, 12/21/16, www.snopes.com/trump-sons-fundraiser/.

15. Josh Rogin, "Trump Team Asked State Department for Info on Women's Issues Programs, Sparking Fears of Another Witch Hunt," *WaPo*, 12/22/16.

16. Donald Trump (@realDonald Trump), "The United States must greatly strengthen and expand its nuclear capability until such time as the world comes to its senses regarding nukes" Twitter, 12/22/16, 8:50 a.m.

17. Harper Neidig, "Trump Shares Letter from Putin: 'His Thoughts Are So Correct,'" *The Hill*, 12/23/16; Donald Trump (@realDonaldTrump), "Vladimir Putin said today about Hillary and Dems: 'In my opinion, it is humiliating. One must be able to lose with dignity.' So true!" Twitter, 12/23/16, 4:13 p.m.

WEEK 7

1. Nelson D. Schwartz and Michael J. de la Merced, "Trump Takes Credit for

Sprint Plan to Add 5,000 Jobs in U.S.," *NYT*, 12/28/16.

2. Donald Trump (@realDonaldTrump), "Great move on delay (by V. Putin)—I always knew he was very smart!" Twitter, 12/30/16, 11:41 a.m.

3. Juliet Eilperin and Adam Entous, "Russian Operation Hacked a Vermont Utility, Showing Risk to U.S. Electrical Grid Security, Officials Say," *WaPo*, 12/31/16.

4. John Wagner, "Trump on Alleged Election Interference by Russia: 'Get On with Our Lives,'" *WaPo*, 12/29/16.

5. Tamara Keith, "President-Elect Trump Breaks with Long History of Press Conferences," *Morning Edition*, NPR, 12/15/16.

6. Donald Trump (@realDonaldTrump), "The U.S. Consumer Confidence Index for December surged nearly four points to 113.7, THE HIGHEST LEVEL IN MORE THAN 15 YEARS! Thanks Donald!" Twitter, 12/27/16, 7:10 p.m.

7. Charley Lanyon, "Paul Ryan Introduces New Rules Banning Lawmaker Livestreaming," *DI*, 12/27/16.

8. Mark Berman and David A. Fahrenthold, "Donald Trump Plans to Shut Down His Charitable Foundation, Which Has Been under Scrutiny for Months," *WaPo*, 12/24/16; Maggie Penman, "Trump Plans to Dissolve His Foundation; N.Y. Attorney General Pushes Back," *The Two-Way* (blog), NPR, 12/24/16.

9. Madeline Conway and Kenneth P. Vogel, "Mar-a-Lago Sold Tickets to New Year's Eve Party with Trump," *Politico*, 12/30/16.

10. Erik Wemple, "Facebook Scrubs—Then Restores—Post That Called Trump Supporters 'Fascists,'" *WaPo*, 12/30/16.

11. Maggie Penman, "Simon & Schuster Will Publish Book by Breitbart Editor, Despite Criticism," *The Two-Way* (blog), NPR, 12/30/16.

12. GOP, "RNC Message Celebrating Christmas," press release, 12/25/16, gop.com/rnc-message-celebrating-christmas-2016/.

13. Nikita Vladimirov, "McCain Schedules Hearing on Foreign Cyber Threats to US," *The Hill*, 12/30/16.

14. Katie Bo Williams, "Second FOIA Lawsuit Targets Details on Election Interference," *The Hill*, 12/30/16.

15. Osita Nwanevu, "Neo-Nazis Are Planning an Armed March against Jews in Richard Spencer's Hometown," *Slate*, 12/27/16.

16. Donald Trump (@realDonald Trump), "Happy New Year to all, including to my many enemies and those who have fought me and lost so badly they just don't know what to do. Love!" Twitter, 12/31/16, 5:17 a.m.

17. Donald Trump (@realDonaldTrump), "Doing my best to disregard the many inflammatory President O statements and roadblocks.Thought it was going to be a smooth transition—NOT!" Twitter, 12/28/16, 6:07 a.m.

WEEK 8

1. Adam Edelman, "Trump Will Use Twitter for Major Policy Announcements after Taking Office: 'When He Tweets He Gets Results,'" *NYDN*, 1/1/17.

2. Jennifer Calfas, "Trump's Executive Producer Credit Appears in 'Apprentice' Premiere," *The Hill*, 1/2/17.

3. Donald Trump (@realDonaldTrump), "Happy New Year to all, including to my many enemies and those who have fought me and lost so badly they just don't know what to do. Love!" Twitter, 12/31/16, 5:17 a.m.; Barack Obama, (@POTUS44), "It's been the privilege of my life to serve as your President. I look forward to standing with you as a citizen. Happy New Year everybody." Twitter, 1/1/17, 9:00 a.m.

4. Maggie Haberman, "Trump Promises a Revelation on Hacking," *NYT*, 12/31/16.

5. Jennifer Calfas, "Joe Scarborough Attacks Report He Partied with Trump," *The Hill*, 1/1/17; Margaret Sullivan, "Joe Scarborough Defends Schmoozing with Trump as 'the Washington Way,'" *WaPo*, 1/4/17.

6. Matthew Yglesias, "Trump Adds Goldman Sachs Lawyer to His Wall Street Dream Team," *Vox*, 1/4/17.

7. Kate Sheppard, "Wall Street Journal Editor Says His Newspaper Won't Call Donald Trump's Lies 'Lies,'" *HuffPost*, 1/3/17.

8. Donald Trump (@realDonaldTrump), "Julian Assange said 'a 14 year old could have hacked Podesta'—why was DNC so careless? Also said Russians did not give him the info!" Twitter, 1/4/17, 4:22 a.m.; Donald Trump (@realDonald Trump), "The dishonest media likes saying that I am in Agreement with Julian Assange—wrong. I simply state what he states, it is for the people. . . ." Twitter, 1/5/17, 5:25 a.m.; "Assange in 'Hannity' Exclusive: Russian Gov't Was Not Source for Hacked Emails," *Hannity*, 1/3/17, FoxNews.com.

9. Donald Trump (@realDonaldTrump), "The 'Intelligence' briefing on so-called 'Russian hacking' was delayed until Friday, perhaps more time needed to build a case. Very strange!" Twitter, 1/3/17, 5:14 p.m.

10. Matthew Rozsa, "Donald Trump Is Going to Appoint Pam Bondi, Who Got an Illegal Payment from the Trump Foundation, to a White House Spot," *Salon*, 1/5/17.

11. Nolan D. McCaskill, "Key Moments from the Senate's Russian Hacking Hearing," *Politico*, 1/5/17.

12. Burgess Everett, "Senate Push for New Russia Hacking Probe Fizzles," *Politico*, 1/3/17.

13. Donald Trump (@realDonald Trump), "General Motors is sending Mexican made model of Chevy Cruze to U.S. car dealers-tax free across border. Make in U.S.A.or pay big border tax!" Twitter, 1/3/17, 4:30 a.m.; Donald Trump (@realDonaldTrump), "Toyota Motor said will build a new plant in Baja, Mexico, to build Corolla cars for U.S. NO WAY! Build plant in U.S. or pay big border tax." Twitter, 1/5/17, 10:14 a.m.; Ylan Q. Mui, "Donald Trump Just Threatened Toyota—but It Looks Like He Got the Facts Wrong," *WaPo*, 1/5/17.

14. Danielle Paquette, "The Real Reason Ford Abandoned Its Plant in Mexico Has Little to Do with Trump," *WaPo*, 1/4/17.

15. Michelle Ye Hee Lee, "What Trump Got Wrong on Twitter This Week," *WaPo*, 1/6/17.

16. Eric Lipton, "With No Warning, House Republicans Vote to Gut Independent Ethics Office," *NYT*, 1/2/17; Rachael Bade, "House GOP Reverses Course on Gutting Ethics Panel," *Politico*, 1/3/17; Donald Trump (@realDonaldTrump), "With all that Congress has to work on, do they really have to make the weakening of the Independent Ethics Watchdog, as unfair as it" Twitter, 1/3/17, 7:03 a.m.

17. Meg Wagner, "President-elect Donald Trump Calls Chuck Schumer 'Clown,' Blasts Obamacare in Typo-Filled Tweets," *NYDN*, 1/5/17.

18. Jenna Portnoy and Lisa Rein, "House Republicans Revive Obscure Rule That Allows Them to Slash the Pay of Individual Federal Workers to $1," *WaPo*, 1/5/17.

19. Mike Murphy, "U.S. Taxpayers May End Up Paying for Trump's Border Wall with Mexico," *MarketWatch*, 1/5/17.

20. Damian Paletta and Julian E. Barnes, "Donald Trump Plans Revamp of Top U.S. Spy Agency," *WSJ*, 1/4/17.

21. Philip Rucker, "Former CIA Director James Woolsey Quits Trump Transition Team," *WaPo*, 1/5/17.

22. Julia Hirschfeld Davis, "In Break with Precedent, Obama Envoys Are Denied Extensions Past Inauguration Day," *NYT*, 1/5/17.

23. Donald Trump (@realDonaldTrump), "Wow, the ratings are in and Arnold Schwarzenegger got "swamped" (or destroyed) by comparison to the ratings machine, DJT. So much for. . . ." Twitter, 1/6/17, 4:34 a.m.

24. Tom Boggioni, "Bombshell Report Claims at Least 50 Trump Electors Are Illegitimate—and Should Not Have Voted," *Raw Story*, 1/4/17.

25. Donald Trump (@realDonaldTrump), "I am asking the chairs of the House and Senate committees to investigate top secret intelligence shared with NBC prior to me seeing it." Twitter, 1/6/17, 8:51 a.m.; Donald Trump (@realDonald Trump), "Intelligence stated very strongly there was absolutely no evidence that hacking affected the election results. Voting machines not touched!" Twitter, 1/7/17, 3:56 a.m.

26. Spencer Ackerman, Sam Thielman, and David Smith, "US Intelligence Report: Vladimir Putin 'Ordered' Operation to Get Trump Elected," *Guardian*, 1/6/17.

27. Donald Trump (@realDonaldTrump), "Only reason the hacking of the poorly defended DNC is discussed is that the loss by the Dems was so big that they are totally embarrassed!" Twitter, 1/7/17, 4:03 a.m.

28. Jim Sciutto, Dierdre Walsh, and Eugene Scott, "Donald Trump on Russia hacking allegations: 'This Is a Political Witch Hunt,'" CNN.com 1/6/17; Donald Trump (@realDonald Trump), "Having a good relationship with Russia is a good thing, not a bad thing. Only 'stupid' people, or fools, would think that it is bad! We. . . . ." Twitter, 1/7/17, 7:02 a.m.

WEEK 9

1. "US Ethics Office Struggled to Gain Access to Trump Team, Emails Show," CNBC.com, 1/7/17.

2. Jonathan O'Connell, "Third Lien on Trump Hotel Brings Alleged Unpaid Bills to over $5 Million," *WaPo*, 1/6/17.

3. Jessica Taylor, "Ethics Office Warns Confirmations for Trump Nominees Are Moving Too Fast," NPR.org, 1/7/17; Rebecca Savransky, "McConnell: Dems Need to 'Grow Up,' Work with GOP on Speedy Confirmations," *The Hill*, 1/8/17.

4. Mallory Shelbourne, "Hannity Deletes 'Make Russia Great Again' Endorsement," *The Hill*, 1/8/17.

5. "Watch (and Read) All of Meryl Streep's Provocative Golden Globes Acceptance Speech," *LAT*, 1/8/17.

6. Donald Trump (@realDonaldTrump), "Meryl Streep, one of the most over-rated actresses in Hollywood, doesn't know me but attacked last night at the Golden Globes. She is a. . . . ." Twitter, 1/9/17, 3:27 a.m.

7. Donald Trump (@realDonaldTrump), "It's finally happening—Fiat Chrysler just announced plans to invest $1BILLION in Michigan and Ohio plants, adding 2000 jobs. This after . . ." Twitter, 1/9/17, 6:14 a.m.; Bryce Covert, "Fiat Chrysler Says Trump Had Nothing to Do with Its Jobs Announcement," *ThinkProgress*, 1/9/17.

8. John Wagner and Ashley Parker, "Trump's Son-in-Law, Jared Kushner, to Join White House as Senior Advisor; No Formal Role for Ivanka Trump," *WaPo*, 1/9/17.

9. Emily Heil, "Donald Trump Says D.C. Dress Shops Are Sold Out of Inauguration Gowns. Wrong!" *WaPo*, 1/9/17.

10. Ashley Feinberg, "Trump Is Letting Go the People in Charge of Maintaining Our Nuclear Arsenal," *Gizmodo*, 1/9/17; Peter Hermann and Aaron C. Davis, "Head of D.C. National Guard to Be Removed from Post in Middle of Inauguration," *WaPo*, 1/13/17.

11. Dave Weigel, "Booker Becomes First Senator to Testify Against Colleague," *WaPo*, 1/11/17.

12. Evan Perez, Jim Sciutto, Jake Tapper, and Carl Bernstein, "Intel Chiefs Presented Trump with Claims of Russian Efforts to Compromise Him," CNN.com, 1/12/17.

13. Ken Bensinger, Miriam Elder, and Mark Schoofs, "These Reports Allege Trump Has Deep Ties to Russia," *BF*, 1/10/17.

14. Donald Trump (@realDonaldTrump), "James Clapper called me yesterday to denounce the false and fictitious report that was illegally circulated. Made up, phony facts.Too bad!" Twitter, 1/12/17, 4:23 a.m.; Office of the Director of National Intelligence, "DNI Clapper Statement on Conversation with President-elect Trump," press release, 1/11/17, www.dni.gov/index.php/newsroom/press-releases/item/1736-dni-clapper-statement-on-conversation-with-president-elect-trump; Max Greenwood, "FBI Director Briefed Trump on Dossier: Reports," *The Hill*, 1/12/17.

15. Chris Sanchez, "Paid Staffers Were on Hand to Cheer for Trump at His Press Conference," *BI*, 1/11/17.

16. Libby Nelson, "Trump Finally Announced His Plan to Avoid Business Conflicts. It's a Sham," *Vox*, 1/11/17.

17. Steven Perlberg, "CMO Today: Trump Clashes with CNN, *BuzzFeed* at Press Conference," *WSJ*, 1/12/17.

18. "Remarks of Walter M. Shaub, Jr., Director, U.S. Office of Government Ethics . . ." www.oge.gov/web/OGE.nsf/0/DCC328BD6DB515CC852580A50079449D/$FILE/Remarks%20of%20W%20M%20Shaub%20Jr.pdf; Darren Samuelsohn and Josh Gerstein, "Chaffetz Threatens to Subpoena Federal Ethics Watchdog over Trump Criticism," *Politico*, 1/12/17.

19. Reuters, "Trump and AT&T CEO Meet amid Planned Time Warner Acquisition," 1/12/17; Donald Trump (@realDonaldTrump), ".@CNN is in a total meltdown with their FAKE NEWS because their ratings are tanking since election and their credibility will soon be gone!" Twitter, 1/12/17, 6:22 a.m.

20. Heather Caygle and John Bresnahan, "Numerous House Democrats to Skip Trump's Inauguration," *Politico*, 1/13/17.

21. Brooke Seipel, "Trump's L.L. Bean Tweet Would Break WH Policy: Report," *The Hill*, 1/12/17.

22. Josh Gerstein, "DOJ Watchdog Opens Review of Comey's Clinton Email Investigation," *Politico*, 1/12/17.

23. Jonah Engel Bromwich, "C-Span Online Broadcast Interrupted by Russian Network," *NYT*, 1/12/17.

24. David Ignatius, "Why Did Obama Dawdle on Russia's Hacking?" *WaPo*, 1/12/17; Jonathan Landay and Arshad Mohammed, "Trump Adviser Had Five Calls with Russian Envoy on Day of Sanctions: Sources," Reuters, 1/13/17.

25. Donald Trump (@realDonald Trump), "released by 'Intelligence' even knowing there is no proof, and never will be. My people will have a full report on hacking within 90 days!" Twitter, 1/13/17, 3:16 a.m.

26. Michael D. Shear, "Rudy Giuliani's Cybersecurity Role Reflects Diminished Place in Trump World," *NYT*, 1/12/17; Christopher Brennan, "Tech Experts Slam Vulnerable Giuliani Website after He Is Picked to Be Cybersecurity Czar," *NYDN*, 1/13/17.

27. Ben Kamisar, "Scaramucci Lands White House Job," *The Hill*, 1/12/17.

28. Chuck Todd, Sally Bronston, and Matt Rivera, "Rep. John Lewis: 'I Don't See Trump as a Legitimate President,'" NBCNews.com, 1/14/17.

29. Donald Trump (@realDonald Trump), "mention crime infested) rather than falsely complaining about the election results. All talk, talk, talk—no action or results. Sad!" Twitter, 1/14/17, 5:07 a.m.

30. Mike Lillis and Katie Bo Williams, "Dems 'Outraged' with Comey after House Briefing," *The Hill*, 1/13/17.

31. Kim Sengupta, "Former MI6 Agent Christopher Steele's Frustration as FBI Sat on Donald Trump Russia File for Months," *Independent* (UK), 1/13/17.

32. Elana Schor, "Intelligence Committee Will Investigate Possible Russia-Trump Links," *Politico*, 1/13/17.

33. Christina Wilkie (@christinawilkie), "The @FEC just sent Trump a 250 page letter listing what appear to be illegal campaign contributions. Read it here: http://docquery.fec.gov/pdf/964/201701100300074964/201701100300074964.pdf . . ." Twitter, 1/12/17, 9:11 p.m.

34. Emily Tamkin, "Head of FSB Cyber Unit May Soon Be Dismissed," *FP*, 1/13/17.

35. Mark Landler, "Human Rights Group Portrays U.S. as Major Threat, Citing Trump," *NYT*, 1/12/17.

36. David M. Jackson, "New Poll Has Trump Approval Rating at 37%, Obama at 55%," *USAT*, 1/10/17.

WEEK 10

1. Tim Shipman, Toby Harnden, Richard Kerbaj, and Tom Harper, "Trump Wants Putin Summit in Reykjavik," *Sunday Times* (UK), 1/15/17.

2. Rainer Buergin and Toluse Olorunnipa, "Trump Slams NATO, Floats Russia Nuke Deal in European Interview," Bloomberg.com, 1/15/17.

3. Rachel Donadio (@RachelDonadio), "Front page of today's Le Monde. Trump Against Europe." Twitter, 1/17/17, 2:14 p.m.

4. Peter J. Boyer, "Exclusive: The Trump Administration May Evict the Press from the White House," *Esquire*, 1/14/17; Ken Meyer, "Trump: I Won't Evict Press from White House Briefing Room, but I'll Pick Who Comes In," *Mediaite*, 1/18/17.

6. Jason Silverstein, "Donald Trump Cancels Martin Luther King Day Visit to National African American History Museum," *NYDN*, 1/15/17; Brian Stelter (@brianstelter), "Conway on Friday: 'The President-elect expects to go to Washington, D.C. on Monday.' Spicer today: 'He was never going to Washington.' ???" Twitter, 1/16/17, 8:14 a.m.

7. Natasha Bertrand, "Explosive Memos Suggest That a Trump-Russia Quid Pro Quo Was at the Heart of the GOP's Dramatic Shift on Ukraine," *BI*, 1/15/17.

8. Joe Davidson, "New Feds Could Be Fired for 'No Cause at All' by Trump Under Planned Legislation," *WaPo*, 1/12/17.

9. Eli Watkins, "Donald Trump Slams CIA Director Brennan over Plea for 'Appreciation' of Intel Community," CNN.com, 1/16/17; Shane Harris, "CIA Director John Brennan Rejects Donald Trump's Criticism," *WSJ*, 1/16/17.

10. Gary Langer, "Public Splits on Trump's Ethics Compliance; Three-Quarters Want Tax Returns Released (POLL)," ABCNews.com, 1/16/17.

11. Andrew Kaczynski, "Before Presidential Run, Trump Called Russia the 'Biggest Problem' and Geopolitical Foe of U.S.," CNN.com, 1/17/17.

12. Abby Phillip, "Trump Aide Reince Priebus Warns Ethics Chief to "Be Careful,'" *WaPo*, 1/15/17.

13. Tuckers Reals, "Putin: Spreaders of 'Fake' Trump News 'Worse Than Prostitutes," CBS, 1/17/17.

14. Jake Tapper (@jaketapper), "There are 23 Cabinet and Cabinet level positions. 18 out of 23 PEOTUS Trump picks are white men." Twitter, 1/19/17, 7:34 a.m.; Rep. Barbara Lee (@RepBarbaraLee), "Trump has appointed ZERO Latinos to serve in his administration. But he has selected at least 1 white nationalist. We know where he stands." Twitter, 1/19/17, 7:48 a.m.; Justin Baragona, "Donald Trump: 'We Have, by Far, the Highest IQ of Any Cabinet Ever,'" *Mediaite*, 1/19/17.

15. Thierry Meyssan, "General Flynn's Proposals to Reform Intelligence," *Voltaire Network*, 12/1/16.

16. Ashley Parker and Philip Rucker, "Donald Trump Waits in His Tower—Accessible Yet Isolated," *WaPo*, 1/17/17.

17. Paul A. Eisenstein, "GM's $1B Investment Is Not Driven by Trump and Likely Dates Back to 2014," NBCNews.com, 1/17/17; Jacob Bunge and Christopher Alessi, "Bayer Will Keep Monsanto Jobs in U.S., Trump Team Says," *WSJ*, 1/18/17.

18. Ben Guarino, "Police: Conn. Politician Said He No Longer Has to Be 'Politically Correct,' Pinched Woman's Groin," *WaPo*, 1/17/17.

19. Nick Penzenstadler, "Trump Accuser Sues for Defamation," *USAT*, 1/17/17; Charlotte Alter, "Former *Apprentice* Contestant Sues Donald Trump for Defamation over Sexual Harassment Accusations," *Time*, 1/18/17.

20. Rebecca Leber (@rebleber), "another reminder that Tillerson only intends to stay away from State decisions benefiting Exxon for *one year* http://pfds.opensecrets.org.s3.amazonaws.com/N99999876_2016_nom_A.pdf . . ." Twitter, 1/17/17, 10:25 a.m.

21. Daniel Lippman, "Trump's D.C. Hotel Bans Press During Inauguration Week," *Politico*, 1/18/17; Ashley Parker (@AshleyRParker), "From The Podium: @seanspicer lauds the 'stunning' Trump Hotel in DC: 'I encourage you to go there, if you haven't been.'" Twitter, 1/19/17, 7:33 a.m.

22. Mike Smith, "Trump 'Cyber Tsar' Giuliani Among Swathes of Hacked Top Appointees," Channel4.com (UK), 1/18/17.

23. Sarah Dutton, Jennifer De Pinto, Fred Backus, Kabir Khanna, and Anthony Salvanto "More Americans Disapprove than Approve Trump's Handling of Transition," CBS News, 1/18/17; Dana Blanton, "Fox News Poll: A Divided, Yet Optimistic Country Awaits Trump," FoxNews.com, 1/19/17.

24. Karen Tumulty, "How Donald Trump Came Up with 'Make America Great Again,'" *WaPo*, 1/18/17.

25. Brooke Seipel, "Trump Team Wanted Tanks, Missile Launchers in Parade: Report," *The Hill*, 1/19/17.

26. Peter Stone and Greg Gordon, "FBI, 5 Other Agencies Probe Possible Covert Kremlin Aid to Trump," McClatchy, 1/18/17.

27. Elise Viebeck, "Nearly 70 Democratic Lawmakers Now Skipping Trump's Inauguration," *WaPo*, 1/19/17.

28. Eugene Scott, "Cummings: I'm Attending Inauguration to Witness History," CNN.com, 1/19/17.

29. Burgess Everett and Josh Dawsey, "Trump Set to Take Office Without Most of His Cabinet," *Politico*, 1/17/17; Charles P. Pierce (@CharlesPPierce), "Stats: 690 Senate-confirmable jobs. New administration has noiminated . . . 28. As of 12:15 Fri. there won't be an Executive branch. Seems odd." Twitter, 1/18/17, 3:34 p.m.

30. Jordan Fabian and Ben Kamisar, "Trump Keeping 50 Obama Administration Officials," *The Hill*, 1/19/17.

31. John Hudson (@John_Hudson), "State Dept still has gotten no guidance from Trump team on whether the US should attend upcoming Syria peace talks in Kazakhstan" Twitter, 1/19/17, 11:31 a.m.

32. Erik Wemple, "In Retraction Request to CNN, Trump Team Confirms CNN Story," *WaPo*, 1/18/17.

33. Abigail Tracy, "Joe Biden Is Worried Donald Trump Might Destroy Western Civilization," *VF*, 1/18/17.

34. Michael S. Schmidt, Matthew Rosenberg, Adam Goldman, and Matt Apuzzo, "Intercepted Russian Communications Part of Inquiry into Trump Associates," *NYT*, 1/19/17.

35. Claudia Koerner, "Trump's Inaugural Concert Didn't Fill the National Mall," *BF*, 1/19/17.

36. "The *Guardian* View on Donald Trump's Inauguration: A Declaration of Political War," *Guardian*, 1/20/17.

37. Katy Tur (@KatyTurNBC), "Parade route from Capital to WH. Entire stands empty. Crowd thin." Twitter, 1/20/17, 10:56 a.m.

38. Lisa Rein, "Interior Department Reactivates Twitter Accounts After Shutdown Following Inauguration," *WaPo*, 1/21/17.

39. George Takei (@GeorgeTakei), "The White House removed its climate change web page. And the healthcare, civil rights and LGBT sections. Just thought you should know." Twitter, 1/20/17, 10:40 a.m.

40. Eric Lipton and Susanne Craig, "A Trump Hotel in Washington Champagne Toasts in an Ethical 'Minefield,'" *NYT*, 1/19/17.

41. Esther Yu Hsi Lee, "More than 2 Million People Are in the Streets Resisting Trump," *ThinkProgress*, 1/21/17; AP (@AP), "Latest: Washington city official estimates turnout for Women's March at 500K—double the initial predictions. http://apne.ws/2j7iAqB " Twitter, 1/21/17, 7:00 a.m.

WEEK 11

Introduction. Adam Gopnik, "Orwell's '1984' and Trump's America," *NYer*, 1/27/17; Jennifer Rubin, "Trump's Authoritarian Tendencies Are Revealed Once Again," *WaPo*, 1/27/17; Jeet Heer, "Donald Trump Is Becoming an Authoritarian Leader Before Our Very Eyes," *NR*, 1/23/17; Christina Manduley, "McMullin: Trump Team's Media Attacks Are Authoritarian-like," CNN.com, 1/26/17; David Moscrop, "Donald Trump Invites Authoritarianism to America," *Maclean's* (Canada), 1/25/17.

1. Sarah Frostenson, "The Women's Marches May Have Been the Largest Demonstration in US History," *Vox*, 1/31/17.

2. "Protesters from Canada, UK, 'Turned Away at US Border,'" BBC News, 1/21/17.

3. Bradd Jaffy (@BraddJaffy), "'This was the largest audience to ever witness an inauguration—period,' Trump White House press secretary claims" Twitter, 1/21/17, 2:48 p.m.; Eric Bradner, "Conway: Trump White House Offered 'Alternative Facts' on Crowd Size," CNN.com, 1/23/17.

4. Jon Swaine, "Four More Journalists Get Felony Charges After Covering Inauguration Unrest," *Guardian*, 1/24/17; Tim Pool (@Timcast), "Article fails to mention that two NBC reporters and I were released without charge shortly after being arrested." Twitter, 1/25/17, 5:41 a.m.

5. Christine Wang, "Trump Declares National Day of Patriotic Devotion . . . but You Already Missed It," CNBC.com, 1/23/17.

6. Eric Lipton and Adam Liptak, "Foreign Payments to Trump Firms Violate Constitution, Suit Will Claim," *NYT*, 1/22/17.

7. Bonnie Honig, "The President's House Is Empty," *Boston Review*, 1/19/17.

8. Carol E. Lee, Devlin Barrett, and Shane Harris, "U.S. Eyes Michael Flynn's Links to Russia," *WSJ*, 1/22/17.

9. Jeff Brady, "Trump Reportedly Called National Park Service over Inauguration Crowd Photos," *The Two-Way* (blog), NPR, 1/27/17.

10. Jim Zarroli, "Trump Has Yet to Sever Ties with Businesses, Despite Promises, Report Says," *The Two-Way* (blog), NPR, 1/22/17; Jackie Northam, "Trump Files Documents to Shift Management of Businesses to His Sons," *The Two-Way* (blog), NPR, 1/23/17.

11. Janko Roettgers, "White House Comment Line Shut Down, Tells Callers to Use Non-existent Facebook Messenger Account Instead," *Variety*, 1/23/17.

12. Eric Bradner, "Conway: Trump Will Not Release Tax Returns," CNN.com, 1/22/17.

13. Donald Trump (@realDonald Trump), "Had a great meeting at CIA Headquarters yesterday, packed house, paid great respect to Wall, long standing ovations, amazing people. WIN!" Twitter, 1/22/17, 4:35 a.m.; Jeff Pegues, "Sources Say Trump's CIA Visit Made Relations with Intel Community Worse," CBS News, 1/23/17.

14. Greg Buestein and Jim Galloway, "CDC Cancels Next Month's 'Climate and Health' Summit in Atlanta," *Atlanta Journal Constitution*, 1/23/17.

15. Karen Tumulty, "Trump's Disregard for the Truth Threatens His Ability to Govern," *WaPo*, 1/24/17; Christopher Ingraham, "The Trump Administration Just Told a Whopper About the Size of the Federal Workforce," *WaPo*, 1/23/17.

16. Chris Cillizza, "The Leaks Coming Out of the Trump White House Cast the President as a Clueless Child," *WaPo*, 1/26/17.

17. Gabriella Lacombe, "Updated: State Department's Apology for Decades of Anti-LGBTQ Discrimination Removed from Official Website," GayRVA.com, 1/23/17.

18. Emily Crockett, "Trump Reinstated the Global Gag Rule. It Won't Stop Abortion, but It Will Make It Less Safe," *Vox*, 1/25/17.

19. Abby Phillip and Mike DeBonis, "Without Evidence, Trump Tells Lawmakers 3 Million to 5 Million Illegal Ballots Cost Him the Popular Vote," *WaPo*, 1/23/17; Bradd Jaffy (@BraddJaffy), "White House press secretary says President Trump believes millions voted illegally 'based on studies & evidence,'" Twitter, 1/24/17, 10:58 a.m.

20. Kate Sheppard, "EPA Freezes Grants, Tells Employees Not to Talk About It, Sources Say," *HuffPost*, 1/25/17.

21. AP (@AP), "BREAKING: Trump bans EPA employees from providing updates on social media or to reporters, bars awarding new contracts or grants." Twitter, 1/24/17, 9:42 a.m.

22. Sam Stein and Kate Sheppard, "Federal Workers Told to Halt External Communication in First Week Under Trump," *HuffPost*, 1/25/17.

23. Theodore Schleifer and Joshua Berlinger, "Trump Says He'll Send in Feds if Chicago Doesn't Fix 'Horrible Carnage Going On,'" CNN.com, 1/25/17.

24. Gina Mei, "Republican Legislators Around the Country Proposed Bills That Would Criminalize Peaceful Protests," *Esquire*, 1/23/17.

25. Mike Eckel, "Reports: Second FSB Agent Arrested; Possible Links to U.S. Election Hacking," Radio Free Europe/ Radio Liberty, 1/26/17; Robert Mendick and Robert Verkaik, "Mystery Death of Ex-KGB Chief Linked to MI6 Spy's Dossier on Donald Trump," *Telegraph* (UK), 1/27/17.

26. Matthew Miller (@matthewamiller), "DOJ rules clearly require him to recuse from the campaign probe. Not following them is a huge breakdown in the rule of law." Twitter, 1/24/17, 5:09 a.m.

27. The Spectator Index (@ spectatorindex), "GERMANY: Merkel's advisors say they're struggling to open communication channels with Trump and have 'given up' on him acting 'presidential,'" Twitter, 1/23/17, 2:10 p.m.

28. Mark Murray (@mmurraypolitics), "So the White House just released this email" Twitter, 1/25/17, 6:37 a.m.

29. Max Fisher, "Trump Prepares Orders Aiming at Global Funding and Treaties," *NYT*, 1/25/17.

30. Russ Choma, "Donald Trump's Foreign Business Partners Got VIP Treatment During the Inauguration," *MJ*, 1/25/17.

31. AP (@AP), "BREAKING: Trump administration mandating EPA scientific studies, data undergo review by political staff before public release." Twitter, 1/25/17, 1:53 p.m.

32. David Jackson and Gregory Korte, "Trump Delays Signing Order to Investigate Unfounded Voter Fraud Claims," *USAT*, 1/26/17; Matea Gold and Alice Crites, "It Turns Out Jared Kushner and Sean Spicer Are Also Registered to Vote in Two States," *WaPo*, 1/26/17.

33. James Masters, "Donald Trump Says Torture 'Absolutely Works'—but Does It?" CNN.com, 1/26/17; Amir Tibon, "Top Trump Officials Find Themselves at Odds with President over Draft Torture Order," *Haaretz* (Israel), 1/26/17; "Trump: Mattis Can Override Me on Torture," *DB*, undated.

34. Steve Benen, "Trump Creates New Dangers with Provocative Comments About Iraqi Oil," *MaddowBlog*, 1/26/17.

35. Robert Moran (@RobertMoran215), "'I've seen better cabinets at Ikea'—Anti-Trump protest outside Loews hotel in Center City tonight" Twitter, 1/25/17, 5:29 p.m.; Azmat Khan (@AzmatZahra), "In anticipation of a Muslim travel ban, civil rights groups are organizing an emergency rally in NYC's Washington Square Park today at 5pm." Twitter, 1/25/17, 5:50 a.m.

36. Arlette Saenz, "President Trump Tells ABC News' David Muir Alleged Voter Fraud Probe Has 'a Lot to Look Into,'" ABCNews.com, 1/25/17; Political Capital (@PoliticalCapital), "Trump: 'You can see the crowd goes all the way back people over there . . . just lots of people' Muir: 'Sir, the question was about Medicare'" Twitter, 1/26/17, 8:33 a.m.; ABC News (@ABC), "Pres. Trump 'won't allow' anyone to demean people in Inauguration crowd: 'We had the biggest audience in the history of inaugural speeches.'" Twitter, 1/25/17, 7:17 p.m.

37. Thomas Goetz (@tgoetz), "Good lord: @TheEconomist just downgraded the US on the democracy scale: Now rated a "flawed democracy" http://econ .st/2kuBnhw " Twitter, 1/25/17, 3:05 p.m.

38. Josh Rogin, "The State Department's Entire Senior Administrative Team Just Resigned," *WaPo*, 1/26/17.

39. Merrit Kennedy, "Mexico's President Cancels Planned D.C. Trip to Meet with Trump," *The Two-Way* (blog), NPR, 1/26/17.

40. "Trump's Little Mexican War," *WSJ*, 1/27/17.

41. Michael M. Grynbaum, "Trump Strategist Stephen Bannon Says Media Should 'Keep Its Mouth Shut,'" *NYT*, 1/26/17.

42. Tamara Keith, "Trump Signs a Record Number of Executive Actions—but Nothing About Ethics," NPR.org, 1/28/17.

43. Isaac Arnsdorf, "Trump Picks Leader for Federal Agency Overseeing His D.C. Hotel," *Politico*, 1/26/17.

44. Natasha Bertrand, "Memos: CEO of Russia's State Oil Company Offered Trump Adviser, Allies a Cut of Huge Deal if Sanctions Were Lifted," *BI*, 1/27/17.

45. David Gibson, Religion News Service, "Trump Fails to Mention Jews in Holocaust Remembrance Statement," *USAT*, 1/27/17.

46. Michael D. Shear and Helene Cooper, "Trump Bars Refugees and Citizens of 7 Muslim Countries," *NYT*, 1/27/17.

47. Reuters, "Trump Says Syrian Christians Will Be Given Priority When Applying for Refugee Status in the US," *BI*, 1/27/17.

48. Caleb Melby, Blacki Migliozzi, and Michael Keller, "Trump Immigration Ban Excludes Countries with Business Ties," Bloomberg.com, 3/6/17 (updated).

49. Elana Schor, "Republicans Warn Trump Against Lifting Russia Sanctions," *Politico*, 1/27/17.

WEEK 12

1. Adrienne Mahsa Varkiani, "Here's Your List of All the Protests Happening Against the Muslim Ban," *ThinkProgress*, 1/28/17; Connor Gillies (@Connor Gillies), "This is the scene here in #Glasgow as thousands turn out for #Trump ban protest. A sea of placards, chanting and speeches." Twitter, 1/30/17, 9:38 a.m.

2. Richard Pérez-Peña, "Trump's Immigration Ban Draws Deep Anger and Muted Praise," *NYT*, 1/28/17; Laura Goodstein, "Christian Leaders Denounce Trump's Plan to Favor Christian Refugees," *NYT*, 1/29/17.

3. Mark Hensch, "598 Colleges Have 'Concerns' on Trump Travel Ban," *The Hill*, 2/3/17.

4. Philip Rucker and David Filipov, "Trump Orders ISIS Plan, Talks with Putin and Gives Bannon National Security Role," *NYT*, 1/28/17; Cristina Marcos, "Dem Offers Bill to Remove Bannon from National Security Council," *The Hill*, 2/1/17.

5. Michael D. Shear, Nicholas Kulish, and Alan Feuer, "Judge Blocks Trump Order on Refugees amid Chaos and Outcry Worldwide," *NYT*, 1/28/17; Dept. of Homeland Security, "Department of Homeland Security Response to Recent Litigation," press release, 1/29/17, www.dhs.gov/news/2017/01/29/department-homeland-security-response-recent-litigation.

6. Paul Soulellis (@soulellis), "judicial branch missing from whitehouse.gov" Twitter, 1/29/17, 5:21 p.m.; Matt Shuham, "Judicial Branch Page Restored to White House Site After Social Media Outcry," *TPM Livewire*, 1/30/17.

7. Yonatan Zunger, "Trial Balloon for a Coup?" *Medium*, 1/29/17.

8. Matt Dathan and Joseph Curtis, "More than 900,000 Sign Petition to Cancel Donald Trump's State Visit to Britain in Just Twelve Hours—Meaning It HAS to Be Debated in Parliament," *Daily Mail* (UK), 1/29/17.

9. Sam Jones and Philip Oltermann, "Merkel 'Explains' Refugee Convention to Trump in Phone Call," *Guardian*, 1/29/17.

10. AP, "White House's 'Alternative Facts' Send Sales of '1984' Soaring," 1/25/17.

11. Amy B. Wang, "Trump Asked for a 'Muslim Ban,' Giuliani Says—and Ordered a Commission to Do It 'Legally,'" *WaPo*, 1/29/17.

12. Tim Mak (@timkmak), "Rubio: The State Department has told my office they've been specifically instructed not to talk to Congress about Trump's immigration ban" Twitter, 1/30/17, 3:35 p.m.

13. Glenn Thrush and Maggie Haberman, "Bannon Is Given Security Role Usually Held for Generals," *NYT*, 1/29/17.

14. Garance Burke, "AP: Trump's Voter Fraud Expert Registered in 3 States," AP, 1/31/17.

15. Rachael Bade, Jake Sherman, and Josh Dawsey, "Hill Staffers Secretly Worked on Trump's Immigration Order," *Politico*, 1/30/17.

16. Julie Pace and Eric Tucker, "Trump Fires Dept. Head over Executive Order Defiance," AP, 1/31/17.

17. Reuters, "Trump Fires Acting US Attorney General Yates, White House Says She 'Betrayed' DOJ," CNBC.com, 1/31/17; Wikipedia, s.v. "Sally Yates," last modified 12/11/17, en.wikipedia.org/wiki/Sally_Yates#Dismissal.

18. Jean Eaglesham and Lisa Schwartz, "Trump's Tax Plan Could Preserve Millions in Savings for His Businesses," *WSJ*, 1/29/17.

19. Roman Olearchyk and Kathrin Hille, "Fighting Escalates in Eastern Ukraine," *FT*, 1/30/17.

20. Chiara Palazzo and James Rothwell, "Quebec Mosque Shooting: Student Charged with Six Counts of Murder over Gun Attack in Mosque," *Telegraph* (UK), 1/31/17; Adam Taylor, "Donald Trump Often Tweets About Terror and Violence, but Said Nothing About an Attack on Muslims in Quebec City," *WaPo*, 2/2/17.

21. Mark Landler, "State Dept. Officials Should Quit if They Disagree with Trump, White House Warns," *NYT*, 1/31/17.

22. Joan Biskupic, Aaron Kessler, and Ryan Struyk, "Trump Judicial Picks Lack Decades-long Diversity Drive," CNN, 11/30/17.

23. Hadas Gold, "White House Ices Out CNN," *Politico*, 1/31/17.

24. Frank Bruni, "The Supreme Court Meets Reality TV," *NYT*, 1/31/17.

25. Shane Goldmacher, Josh Gerstein, and Matthew Nussbaum, "Trump Picks Gorsuch for Supreme Court," *Politico*, 1/31/17; Kate Nocera (@KateNocera), "Sen. Hatch, Don Jr. and Eric" Twitter, 1/31/17, 5:38 p.m.

26. Amy Brittain and Drew Harwell, "Eric Trump's Business Trip to Uruguay Cost Taxpayers $97,830 in Hotel Bills," *WaPo*, 2/3/17.

27. Donald Trump (@realDonald Trump), "Nancy Pelosi and Fake Tears Chuck Schumer held a rally at the steps of The Supreme Court and mic did not work (a mess)-just like Dem party!" Twitter, 1/31/17, 3:21 a.m.

28. "Trump Cancels Planned Milwaukee Economic Speech," *CT*, 2/1/17.

29. Elise Viebeck, "'Please Press 1' to Leave a Message About Donald Trump, Says House Oversight Voice Mail," *WaPo*, 1/31/17.

30. Cleve R. Wootson Jr., "Trump Implied Frederick Douglass Was Alive. The Abolitionist's Family Offered a 'History Lesson.'" *WaPo*, 2/2/17; Lilly Workneh, "Mike Pence Recognized Black History Month by Honoring a White Man," *HuffPost*, 2/3/17.

31. Thomas Gibbons-Neff and Missy Ryan, "In Deadly Yemen Raid, a Lesson for Trump's National Security Team," *WaPo*, 1/31/17; Tom Bowman, "Security Roundup: Yemen Raid; National Security Council Shakeup," *Morning Edition*, NPR, 1/30/17.

32. Ayesha Rascoe, "U.S. Military Probing More Possible Civilian Deaths in Yemen Raid," Reuters, 2/1/17.

33. Mark Sumner, "Trump Didn't Bother to Show Up in Situation Room for Botched Yemen Raid," *DK*, 2/2/17; Tommy Christopher, "White House Reveals Trump Was Not in the Situation Room During His First Military Raid," Shareblue Media, 2/2/17.

34. "At Least 17 Bomb Threats Called In to JCCs Nationwide in Third Wave of Harassment," Jewish Telegraphic Agency, 1/31/17.

35. "First Lady Melania Trump May Stay in NYC Permanently and Never Move into the White House," *Us Weekly*, 2/1/17.

36. "Covering Trump the Reuters Way," Reuters, 1/31/17.

37. Brad Plumer, "On the Same Day Rex Tillerson Is Confirmed, the House Votes to Kill a Transparency Rule for Oil Companies," *Vox*, 2/1/17.

38. Linette Lopez (@lopezlinette), "GOP wants to ditch this transparency rule for oil/gas companies just after mystery person bought 19% of Rosneft & confirming Tillerson" Twitter, 2/1/17, 1:38 p.m.; Natasha Bertrand, "Memos: CEO of Russia's State Oil Company Offered Trump Adviser, Allies a Cut of Huge Deal if Sanctions Were Lifted," *BI*, 1/27/17.

39. Vivian Salama, "Trump to Mexico: Take Care of 'Bad Hombres' or US Might," AP, 2/2/17; AP (@AP), "BREAKING: US official: Trump remark about having military deal with 'hombres' in Mexico was 'lighthearted,' part of security talks." Twitter, 2/2/17, 5:44 a.m.

40. Greg Miller and Philip Rucker, "'This Was the Worst Call by Far': Trump Badgered, Bragged and Abruptly Ended Phone Call with Australian Leader," *WaPo*, 2/2/17; Sky News Australia (@SkyNewsAust), "#BREAKING Sky News sources say Donald Trump was 'yelling' during his phone conversation with PM Turnbull and hung up after 25 minutes" Twitter, 2/1/17, 7:33 p.m.

41. Donald Trump (@realDonald Trump), "Do you believe it? The Obama Administration agreed to take thousands of illegal immigrants from Australia. Why? I will study this dumb deal!" Twitter, 2/1/17, 7:55 p.m.; Jordain Carney, "McCain Calls Australian Ambassador to Express Support After Trump Exchange," *The Hill*, 2/2/17; Kyle Griffin (@kylegriffin1), "House Dem Whip Steny Hoyer spoke with Australia's Ambassador to the US today 'to reiterate the importance of our nations' strong ties'." Twitter, 2/2/17, 10:54 a.m.

42. Libby Hill, "'Pray for Arnold': Trump Keeps Trashing 'Apprentice' Ratings, but Are They Really That Bad?" *LAT*, 2/2/17.

43. Mark Lander and Laurie Goodstein, "Trump Vows to 'Destroy' Law Banning Political Endorsements by Churches," *NYT*, 2/2/17.

44. U.S. Dept. of the Treasury, "Publication of Cyber-Related General License," Treasury.gov, 2/2/17; TASS, "Former FSB Head Says Easing of US Sanctions Paves Way for Setting up Anti-terror Coalition," 2/12/17.

45. Nick Baumann and Matt Ferner, "Virginia Just Filed a Contempt Motion Against Trump over Immigration Order," *HuffPost*, 2/2/17.

46. Justin Jouvenal, Rachel Weiner, and Ann E. Marimow, "Justice Dept. Lawyer Says 100,000 Visas Revoked Under Travel Ban; State Dept. Says About 60,000," *WaPo*, 2/3/17.

47. Ari Melber, "Officials Warned Trump Against 'Unprecedented' Plan to Staff Cabinet Without Ethics Vetting," NBCNews.com, 2/2/17.

48. Josh Dawsey, Isaac Arnsdorf, Nahal Toosi, and Michael Crowley, "White House Nixed Holocaust Statement Naming Jews," *Politico*, 2/2/17.

49. Brooke Seipel, "Nordstrom to Reduce Stock of Ivanka Trump Merchandise: Report," *The Hill*, 2/2/17; Reuters, "Nieman Marcus Pulls Ivanka Trump's Jewelry Line from Website," *YN*, 2/3/17.

50. Public Policy Polling, "After 2 Weeks, Voters Yearn for Obama," 2/2/17, http://www.publicpolicypolling.com/wp-content/uploads/2017/09/PPP_Release_National_2217.pdf; Kevin M. Kruse (@KevinMKruse), "Polls asking about impeachment for Nixon didn't reach this level until sixteen months into Watergate scandal." Twitter, 2/2/17, 5:11 p.m.

51. Nadia Khomami, "Former Norway PM Held at Washington Airport over 2014 Visit to Iran," *Guardian*, 2/3/17.

52. Sherley Boursiquot, "Donald Trump White House Dress Code Policy? Female Staffers Must 'Dress Like Women,' President Says," *IBT*, 2/2/17.

53. Samantha Schmidt and Lindsey Bever, "Kellyanne Conway Cites 'Bowling Green Massacre' That Never Happened to Defend Travel Ban," *WaPo*, 2/3/17.

54. Christina Wilkie (@christinawilkie), "Trump: 'We expect to be cutting a lot of Dodd Frank. Friends of mine with nice businesses can't borrow money . . . bc of the rules in Dodd Frank.'" Twitter, 2/3/17, 9:54 a.m.

55. Joel Rose, "After 2 Weeks in Office, Trump Faces More than 50 Lawsuits," *All Things Considered*, NPR, 2/2/17.

56. Michael M. Grynbaum and Katie Rogers, "*New Yorker* and *Vanity Fair* Pull Out of Correspondents' Dinner Parties," *NYT*, 2/3/17.

57. Brooke Seipel, "Bush-Appointed Judge Halts Trump Travel Ban Nationwide," *The Hill*, 2/3/17.

WEEK 13

1. Abby Phillip, "O'Reilly Told Trump That Putin Is a Killer. Trump's Reply: 'You Think Our Country Is So Innocent?" *WaPo*, 2/4/17.

2. Taylor Link, "'I Have No Words': Conservatives Are Shocked by Trump's 'Disgusting' Moral Relativism with Vladimir Putin," *Salon*, 2/6/17; "Kremlin Demands Apology from Fox News Host Bill O'Reilly for Calling Putin 'a Killer,'" *Moscow Times*, 12/5/17.

3. Glenn Thrush and Maggie Haberman, "Trump and Staff Rethink Tactics After Stumbles," *NYT*, 2/5/17.

4. Ibid.; Donald Trump (@realDonald Trump), "I call my own shots, largely based on an accumulation of data, and everyone knows it. Some FAKE NEWS media, in order to marginalize, lies!" Twitter, 2/6/17, 4:07 a.m.

5. Nathan Hodge, Olga Razumovskaya, and Shane Harris, "Russian Arrests Spur Questions over Links to U.S. Hacking," *WSJ*, 2/5/17.

6. Isaac Arnsdorf, "Pelosi Calls for Probe of Possible Russian Blackmail for Trump," *Politico*, 2/5/17.

7. Paulina Firozi, "Sixth New England Patriot Announces He Will Skip White House Visit," *The Hill*, 2/10/17.

8. Anita Kumar, "Trump White House Is Leaving the Public in the Dark. Is It Growing Pains—or a Plan?" McClatchy, 2/3/17.

9. Saturday Night Live, "Sean Spicer Press Conference (Melissa McCarthy)," YouTube, posted 2/5/17, www.youtube.com/watch?v=UWuc18xISwI&feature=youtu.be; Annie Karni, Josh Dawsey, and Tara Palmeri, "White House Rattled by McCarthy's Spoof of Spicer," *Politico*, 2/6/17.

10. Steven Swinford and Ben Farmer, "Donald Trump Petition: MPs to Debate Whether UK State Visit Should Go Ahead as More than 1.5M Call for It to be Cancelled," *Telegraph* (UK), 1/31/17; Jon Stone, "Donald Trump Will Not Be Allowed to Address Parliament on UK State Visit, Says Speaker John Bercow," *Independent* (UK), 2/6/17.

11. *Washington Post* and Partnership for Public Service, "Tracking How Many Key Positions Trump Has Filled So Far," *WaPo*, 12/8/16 (last updated).

12. Aaron Blake, "InfoWars Is Behind President Trump's Idea That the Media Is Covering Up Terrorist Attacks," *WaPo*, 2/6/17.

13. David Jackson, "More than Two Weeks In, Trump's White House Is Still Not Open for Tourists," *USAT*, 2/7/17.

14. Julia Marsh, "Melania Sues *Mail Online* a Third Time for Claiming She Was an Escort," *NYP*, 2/6/17.

15. Ari Berman, "House Republicans Just Voted to Eliminate the Only Federal Agency That Makes Sure Voting Machines Can't Be Hacked," *The Nation*, 2/7/17.

16. Karin Brulliard, "USDA Abruptly Purges Animal Welfare Information from Its Website," *WaPo*, 2/3/17.

17. Jay Michaelson, "President Trump to Judges: Drop Dead," *DB*, 2/8/17; Donald Trump (@realDonaldTrump), "Just cannot believe a judge would put our country in such peril. If something happens blame him and court system. People pouring in. Bad!" Twitter, 2/5/17, 12:39 p.m.

18. Rob Tornoe, "President Trump Lashes Out at 'So-Called Judge' on Twitter for Blocking Travel Ban," Philly.com, 2/4/17.

19. Arnie Seipel and Ted Robbins, "Trump Slams Senator Who Revealed Gorsuch's Criticism of Remarks on Judges," NPR.org, 2/8/17; Tom Kutsch, Jordyn Phelps, and Katherine Faulders, "Trump Suggests That SCOTUS Nominee Neil Gorsuch's Criticism Was Misrepresented," ABCNews.com, 2/9/17; Rebecca Savransky, "Trump Contradicts Gorsuch Spokesman, Accuses Blumenthal of Misrepresenting Comments," *The Hill*, 2/9/17.

20. Daniel Victor, "'Nevertheless, She Persisted': How Senate's Silencing of Warren Became a Meme," *NYT*, 2/8/17.

21. S. V. Date and Christina Wilkie, "Leaks Suggest Trump's Own Team Is Alarmed by His Conduct," *HuffPost*, 2/8/17.

22. David E. Sanger and Eric Schmitt, "Yemen Withdraws Permission for U.S. Antiterror Ground Missions," *NYT*, 2/7/17; Domenico Montanaro, Tom Bowman, and Danielle Kurtzleben, "FACT CHECK: Trump's Yemen Raid—'Winning Mission' or 'Failure'? It's Not So Simple," NPR.org, 2/10/17.

23. Andrew Ackerman, "GOP-Led SEC Considers Easing Pay-Gap Disclosure Rule of Dodd-Frank," *WSJ*, 2/6/17.

24. Donald Trump (@realDonald Trump), "My daughter Ivanka has been treated so unfairly by @Nordstrom. She is a great person—always pushing me to do the right thing! Terrible!" Twitter, 2/8/17; Jennifer Calfas, "Nordstrom Stock Gains Over 4 Percent After Trump Tweet," *The Hill*, 2/8/17.

25. Richard W. Painter, "The Lesson of Nordstrom: Do Business with the Trumps or Else," *NYT*, 2/9/17.

26. Richard Pérez-Peña and Rachel Abrams, "Kellyanne Conway Promotes Ivanka Trump Brand, Raising Ethics Concerns," *NYT*, 2/9/17; Jill Disis and Jackie Wattles, "Kellyanne Conway Unrepentant for Ivanka Trump Plug," CNN.com, 2/9/17.

27. Eric Levitz, "GOP Oversight Chair Calls Conway Promoting Ivanka's Brand 'Unacceptable,'" *DI*, 2/9/17.

28. Emily Tamkin, "French Intelligence Agency Braces for Russian Bots to Back Le Pen," *FP*, 2/8/17; John Walsh, "French Candidate Marine Le Pen: Jews Will Have to Leave if They Don't Give Up Israeli Citizenship," *IBT*, 2/10/17.

29. Jordain Carney, "Senators Move to Limit Trump on Russia Sanctions," *The Hill*, 2/8/17.

30. Lindsey Bever, "University Apologizes 'with Heavy Hearts and Great Embarrassment' for Hitler Valentine's Day Card," *WaPo*, 2/10/17.

31. Jonathan Landay and David Rohde, "Exclusive: In Call with Putin, Trump Denounced Obama-era Nuclear Arms Treaty—Sources," Reuters, 2/9/17.

32. Josh Zumbrun, "Donald Trump's Cabinet Won't Include Chairman of CEA," *WSJ*, 2/9/17.

33. Mike DeBois, "Democrat Moves to Force House Debate on Trump's Alleged Business Conflicts and Russia Ties," *WaPo*, 2/9/17.

34. "In SC Business, Trump Claims No Relationship to Son He Bailed Out," *Rachel Maddow Show*, MSNBC, 1/13/17, http://www.msnbc.com/rachel-maddow/watch/trump-tries-to-stick-sc-tax payers-with-bill-for-trump-jr-s-mess-854853699850.

35. Kelsey Snell, Paul Schwartzman, Steve Friess, and David Weigel, "Swarming Crowds and Hostile Questions Are the New Normal at GOP Town Halls," *WaPo*, 2/10/17.

36. Anna Swartz, "51% of Trump Voters Think the "Bowling Green Massacre" Justifies Trump's Muslim Ban," *Mic*, 2/10/17.

37. Reuters, "US Court Upholds Obama-era Retirement Advice Rule," CNBC.com, 2/9/17.

38. Kate Bennett, "Without Melania Trump, Mrs. Abe Rolls Solo in Washington," CNN.com, 2/10/17.

39. Matthew Rosenberg and Matt Apuzzo, "Flynn Is Said to Have Talked to Russians About Sanctions Before Trump Took Office," *NYT*, 2/9/17.

40. Matthew Nussbaum and Kyle Cheney, "Pence Was Told Flynn Didn't Discuss Sanctions, Aides Say," *Politico*, 2/10/17; Kevin Liptak, Jeff Zeleny, and Elizabeth Landers, "Trump Says He's Unaware of Reports Flynn Discussed Sanctions with Russian Ambassador," CNN.com, 2/10/17.

41. Eli Stokols, "Trump Brings Up Vote Fraud Again, This Time in Meeting with Senators," *Politico*, 2/10/17.

42. Jonathan O'Connell, "Feds, Trump Attorneys Wrangle over President's D.C. Hotel Lease," *WaPo*, 2/10/17.

43. "Trump Agrees to Honour 'One China' Policy Despite Threats," BBC News, 2/10/17.

44. Lisa Rein, Abigail Hauslohner, and Sandhya Somashekhar, "Federal Agents Conduct Immigration Enforcement Raids in at Least Six States," *WaPo*, 2/11/17.

45. Jim Sciutto and Evan Perez, "US Investigators Corroborate Some Aspects of the Russia Dossier," CNN.com, 2/10/17; Mark Hensch, "Spicer: White House 'Disgusted by CNN's Fake News,'" *The Hill*, 2/10/17.

46. Matthew Yglesias, "Only 29% of Americans Think Trump Is Respected in the World," *Vox*, 2/10/17.

47. Katelyn Marmon and Victoria Fleischer, "WATCH: 19 Lies the Trump Administration Told This Week," *ThinkProgress*, 2/10/17.

WEEK 14

1. Kevin Liptak, "At Mar-a-Lago, Trump Tackles Crisis Diplomacy at Close Range," CNN.com, 2/13/17; "Beware Downloading Some Apps or Risk 'Being Spied On,'" CBSNews.com, 7/4/16.

2. Amy Siskind (@Amy_Siskind), "What an embarrassment! Posted on FB: a citizen snapped photos of Trump getting notified about N. Korea & conferring w/Abe (not our experts)" Twitter, 2/13/17, 8:17 a.m.

3. Terence Burlij (@burlij), "Conway at 4:07: 'Gen. Flynn does enjoy the full confidence of the president.' Spicer at 5:11: 'The president is evaluating the situation.'" Twitter, 2/13/17.

5. Donald Trump (@realDonaldTrump), "The real scandal here is that classified information is illegally given out by 'intelligence' like candy. Very un-American!" Twitter, 2/15/17, 5:13.

6. Michael S. Schmidt, Mark Mazzetti, and Matt Apuzzo, "Trump Campaign Aides Had Repeated Contacts with Russian Intelligence," *NYT*, 2/14/17; Pamela Brown, Jim Sciutto, and Evan Perez, "Trump Aides Were in Constant Touch with Senior Russian Officials During Campaign," CNN.com, 2/15/17.

7. Dana Milbank, "While Trump Scandals Mount, Chaffetz Decides to Investigate . . . a Cartoon Character," *WaPo*, 2/13/17.

8. Eric Lichtblau, "Jeff Sessions Resists Pressure to Remove Himself in Russia Inquiries," *NYT*, 2/14/17.

9. James Risen and Matthew Rosenberg, "White House Plans to Have Trump Ally Review Intelligence Agencies," *NYT*, 2/15/17.

10. Josh Gerstein, "FBI Releases Files on Trump Apartments' Race Discrimination Probe in '70s," *Politico*, 2/15/17.

11. Paul Sonne, "Pentagon Finds It Has No Records Approving Mike Flynn's Russian-TV Pay," *WSJ*, 2/16/17.

12. Ashley Parker and Philip Rucker, "Upheaval Is Now Standard Operating Procedure Inside the White House," *WaPo*, 2/13/17.

13. David Ferguson, "Democratic Senators Demand to Know Why Betsy DeVos Took Down Website for Disabled Students," *Raw Story*, 2/11/17.

14. Art Swift, "Americans See U.S. World Standing as Worst in a Decade," Gallup News, 2/10/17.

15. Canadian Press, "Ontario School Board Cancels Trips to U.S., Cites 'Safety and Equity' Concerns," *Toronto Star*, 2/12/17.

16. Caroline Hallemann, "Trump Reportedly Picked Patrick Park for Austrian Ambassador," *Town & Country*, 2/13/17.

17. Kyle Balluck, "Franken: GOP Colleagues Question Trump's Mental Health," *The Hill*, 2/12/17; Lance Dodes and Joseph Schachter, "Mental Health Professionals Warn About Trump," letter to the editor, *NYT*, 2/13/17.

18. Glenn Kessler, Stephen Miller's Bushels of Pinocchios for Fales Voter-Fraud Claims," *WaPo*, 2/12/17.

19. Josh Gerstein, "Feds Drop Request to Rein in Ban on Obama Transgender Policy," *Politico*, 2/11/17.

20. Claire Landsbaum, "Here Are All the Stores Distancing Themselves from Trump Brands," *The Cut*, 2/13/17.

21. Ben Kamisar, "Trump Presser Takes Questions Exclusively from Conservative Media," *The Hill*, 2/15/17.

22. Anthony Capaccio, "Trump's F-35 Calls Came with a Surprise: Rival CEO Was Listening," Bloomberg.com, 2/16/17.

23. Nick Wadhams, Patrick Donahue, and Ilya Arkhipov, "Tillerson Has Awkward First Encounter with Lavrov at G-20," Bloomberg.com, 2/16/17.

24. James Hill, Lauren Pearle, Meghan Keneally, and Julia Jacobo, "Court Blocks Trump's Immigration Order Indefinitely," ABCNews.com, 2/13/17.

25. Ariane de Vogue, "'Dreamer Arrest a Wake-up Call for Immigrant Rights Groups," CNN.com, 2/15/17; Katie Mettler, "'This Is Really Unprecedented': ICE Detains Woman Seeking Domestic Abuse Protection at Texas Courthouse.

26. Barbara Starr, "Pentagon Might Propose Sending Ground Troops to Syria," CNN.com, 2/15/17.

27. Emre Peker, "Trudeau Urges Deeper EU-Canadian Ties," *WSJ*, 2/16/17.

28. Andrew Rafferty, "Office of Government Ethics: 'Strong Reason' to Think Conway Violated Rules," NBCNews.com, 2/14/17.

29. Timothy Cama, "Trump Signs Repeal of Transparency Rule for Oil Companies," *The Hill*, 2/14/17.

30. snipe, mother of assets (@snipeyhead), "Here are the folks who voted against releasing Trumps tax returns" Twitter, Twitter Moments, 2/14/17.

31. Kurt Eichenwald (@kurteichenwald), "Details: SSV-175 Viktor Leonov is outfitted with spying equipment to intercept signals intelligence. It's 30 miles off Connecticut coast." Twitter, 2/15/17, 11:28 a.m.; Michael R. Gordon, "Russia Deploys Missile, Violating Treaty and Challenging Trump," *NYT*, 2/14/17; Ivan Watson and Sebastian Shukla, "Russian Fighter Jets 'Buzz' US Warship in Black Sea, Photos Show," CNN.com, 2/16/17.

32. Nick Robins-Early, "Rising Violence in Ukraine Puts the Spotlight on U.S. Relations with Russia," *HuffPost*, 2/16/17.

33. Michael McFaul (@McFaul), "Is Kremlin already losing faith in Trump?" Twitter, 2/12/17, 3:20 p.m.

34. Jean Eaglesham and Lisa Schwartz, "Commerce Nominee Wilbur Ross

Will Keep His State in Chinese-Government-Backed Company," *WSJ*, 2/13/17.

35. AP, "China Awards Trump Valuable New Trademark," ABCNews.com, 2/15/17.

36. Daniel Burke, "More Bomb Threats Target Jewish Community. Trump Finally Responds," CNN.com, 2/27/17; Feliks Garcia, "Donald Trump Brags About Electoral College Victory While Answering Question on Anti-Semitism," *Independent* (UK), 2/15/17.

37. Shane Harris and Carol E. Lee, "Spies Keep Intelligence from Donald Trump on Leak Concerns," *WSJ*, 2/16/17.

38. Gardiner Harris, "Where Is Rex Tillerson? Top Envoy Keeps Head Down and Travels Light," *NYT*, 2/15/17.

39. Eli Stokols and Josh Dawsey, "Trump Ignores 'the Grown-ups' in His Cabinet," *Politico*, 02/17/2017.

40. Margaret Brennan and Kylie Atwood, "State Dept. Carries Out Layoffs Under Rex Tillerson," CBSNews.com, 2/17/17.

41. Ashley Dejean, "Exclusive: Classified Memo Tells Intelligence Analysts to Keep Trump's Daily Brief Short," *MJ*, 2/16/17.

42. Des Bieler, "Jared Kushner's Family Says It Won't Buy Marlins if Jeffrey Loria Becomes Ambassador to France," *WaPo*, 2/15/17.

43. "In First Month, Views of Trump Are Already Strongly Felt, Deeply Polarized," 2/16/17, Pew Research Center; "Gallup Daily: Trump Job Approval," Gallup News, news.gallup.com/poll/201617/gallup-daily-trump-job-approval.aspx.

44. Elizabeth Elizalde, "White House Removes Six Staffers After Failing FBI Background Checks: Report," *NYDN*, 2/16/17.

45. Kurt Eichenwald, "U.S. Allies Conduct Intelligence Operation Against Trump Staff and Associates, Intercepted Communications," *Newsweek*, 2/15/17.

46. Traci G. Lee, "10 Resign from President's Advisory Commission on Asian American and Pacific Islanders," NBCNews.com, 2/16/17.

47. Olivia Beavers, "GOP Senator Suggests Trump Consult Therapist in Text to CNN," *The Hill*, 2/16/17.

48. Inae Oh, "Trump Asks African-American Reporter to Arrange Meeting with Congressional Black Caucus," *MJ*, 2/16/17.

49. Eli Watkins, "Trump Tells Jewish Magazine's Reporter to 'Sit Down,' Blames Anti-Semitism on 'the Other Side,'" CNN.com, 2/16/17.

50. Sari Horwitz and Adam Entous, "Flynn in FBI Interview Denied Discussing Sanctions with Russian Ambassador," *WaPo*, 2/16/17.

51. Jim Sciutto, Ryan Browne, and Jake Tapper, "Harward Says No to National Security Adviser Role," CNN.com, 2/17/17; Jake Tapper (@jaketapper), "A friend of Harward's says he was reluctant to take NSA job bc the WH seems so chaotic; says Harward called the offer a 'shit sandwich.'" Twitter, 2/16/17, 4:22 p.m.

52. Julian E. Barnes, Shane Harris, and Paul Sonne, "Trump and Candidates for National Security Adviser Spar over Staffing," *WSJ*, 2/17/17.

53. Keach Hagey and Damian Paletta, "Jared Kushner Delivers Critique of CNN to Time Warner Executive," *WSJ*, 2/17/17.

54. Justine Medina (@jnmedina8989), "So, @realDonaldTrump and Co are paying ppl to attend their Tampa rally this weekend. Craigslist ad has been taken down, but:" Twitter, 2/16/17, 1:18 p.m.

55. Garance Burke, "AP Exclusive: DHS Weighed Nat Guard for Immigration Roundups," AP, 2/18/17; John Kelly to Kevin McAleenan et al., "Implementing the President's Border Security and Immigration Enforcement Improvements Policies," memorandum, 1/25/17, www.documentcloud.org/documents/3467508-Trump-National-Guard-Draft-Memo.html?utm_campaign=SocialFlow&utm_source=Twitter&utm_medium=AP.

56. Hui Min Neo, Michelle Fitzpatrick, and Bryan McManus, "Europe Warns US Against Hurting Cohesion, Favouring Russia," *YN*, 2/17/17.

57. Jenna Johnson and Matea Gold, "Trump Calls the Media 'the Enemy of the American People,'" *WaPo*, 2/17/17; John Schindler (@20committee), "'Enemy of the people' was the term used by Lenin, Stalin, etc to justify the murder of millions of innocent people." Twitter, 2/17/17, 1:59 p.m.

58. Ted Barrett, Tom LoBianco, and Ashley Killough, "Comey Talks Russia with Senators in Closed-Door Briefing," CNN.com, 2/17/17; Marco Rubio (@marcorubio), "I am now very confident Senate Intel Comm I serve on will conduct thorough bipartisan investigation of #Putin interference and influence" Twitter, 2/17/17, 2:59 p.m.

59. Drew Harwell, Amy Brittain, and Jonathan O'Connell, "Trump Family's Elaborate Lifestyle Is a 'Logistical Nightmare'—at Taxpayer Expense," 2/16/17.

60. Kyle Griffin (@kylegriffin1), "Rep. Barbara Lee has led 70+ Democrats in introducing legislation urging the removal of Steve Bannon from the National Security Council." Twitter, 2/17/17, 4:15 p.m.

61. Sharon LaFraniere and Alan Rappeport, "Popular Domestic Programs Face Ax Under First Trump Budget," *NYT*, 2/17/17.

WEEK 15

1. Reuters, "Trump Sons Open Dubai Golf Course, Praise U.S. Ally," *HuffPost*, 2/18/17.

2. Sewell Chan "'Last Night in Sweden'? Trump's Remark Baffles a Nation," *NYT*, 2/19/17.

3. Donald Trump (@realDonaldTrump), "My statement as to what's happening in Sweden was in reference to a story that was broadcast on @FoxNews concerning immigrants & Sweden." Twitter, 2/19/17, 1:57 p.m.

4. John Kelly to Kevin McAleenan et al., "Enforcement of the Immigration Laws to Serve the National Interest," memorandum, 2/17/17, www.mcclatchydc.com/news/politics-government/white-house/article133607784.ece/BINARY/DHS%20enforcement%20of%20immigration%20laws.

5. Megan Twohey and Scott Shane, "A Back-Channel Plan for Ukraine and Russia, Courtesy of Trump Associates," *NYT*, 2/19/17.

6. Michael Schwirtz, "Ukraine Lawmaker Who Worked with Trump Associates Faces Treason Inquiry," *NYT*, 2/21/17.

7. Josh Marshall, "A Big Shoe Just Dropped," *TPM Editor's Blog*, 2/19/17.

8. Harry Siegel, "Stephen Miller Called Brooklyn U.S. Attorney at Home and Told Him How to Defend Travel Ban in Court," *NYDN*, 2/18/17.

9. Nick Timiraos, "Trump Team's Growth Forecasts Far Rosier than Those of CBO, Private Economists," *WSJ*, 2/17/17.

10. William Maudin and Devlin Barrett, "Trump Administration Considers Change in Calculating U.S. Trade Deficit," *WSJ*, 2/19/17.

11. David Leonhardt, "The Struggle Inside the *Wall Street Journal*," *NYT*, 2/14/17.

12. Bill Neely, "Russia Compiles Psychological Dossier on Trump for Putin," NBCNews.com, 2/20/17.

13. Michael Rothfeld and Craig Karmin, "Trump's Former Campaign Chairman Paul Manafort Thrust Back into Focus," *WSJ*, 2/20/17.

14. Eric Bradner and Manu Raju, "Senators Want Russia-related Materials Preserved," CNN, 2/20/17.

15. Camila Domonoske, "Another Wave of Bomb Threats Targets Jewish Community Centers," *The Two-Way* (blog), NPR, 2/21/17; Fred Barbash and Ben Guarino, "More than 170 Gravestones Vandalized at Jewish Cemetery in Mo.; Centers Threatened," *Pittsburgh Post-Gazette*, 2/21/17.

16. Julie Hirschfeld Davis, "In First, Trump Condemns Rise in Anti-Semitism, Calling It 'Horrible,'" *NYT*, 2/21/17.

17. Sarah Larimer, "Anne Frank Center Slams Trump: 'Do Not Make Us Jews Settle for Crumbs of Condescension,'" *WaPo*, 2/21/17.

18. Hayley Miller, "National Security Council Spokesman Resigns over Donald Trump's 'Disturbing' Actions," *HuffPost*, 2/21/17.

19. Trip Gabriel, Thomas Kaplan, Lizette Alvarez, and Emmarie Huetteman, "At Town Hall, Doses of Fury and a Bottle of Tums," *NYT*, 2/21/17.

20. Brenna Williams and Paul P. Murphy, "Constituents Search for 'Missing' Representatives," CNN.com, 2/23/17; Laura Clawson, "Gabby Giffords to Louie Gohmert: 'Have Some Courage. Face Your Constituents.'" *DK*, 2/23/17.

21. Shivani Vora, "After Travel Ban, Interest in Trips to U.S. Declines," *NYT*, 2/20/17.

22. Mallory Shelbourne, "Poll: Majority of Americans Fear US Will Become Involved in Another Major War," *The Hill*, 2/22/17.

23. David Nakamura, "Trump Administration Issues New Immigration Enforcement Policies, Says Goal Is Not 'Mass Deportations,'" *WaPo*, 2/21/17.

24. Jim Roberts (@nycjim), "New DHS deportation rules make no distinction between being charged with a crime and being convicted." Twitter, 2/21/17, 2:15 p.m.

24. Editorial Board, "Mr. Trump's 'Deportation Force' Prepares an Assault on American Values," *NYT*, 2/21/17.

25. Rafael Bernal, "Lawyers: ICE Detainee with Brain Tumor Removed from Hospital," *The Hill*, 2/22/17.

26. Philip Bump, "Trump's Deputy National Security Adviser Was Once Accused of Violating Voter Registration Laws," *WaPo*, 2/21/17.

27. Garance Franke-Ruta, "Resistance Report: More than 1 Million Sign White House Petition for Trump's Tax Returns, Breaking Record," *YN*, 2/21/17.

28. Paulina Firozi, "Trudeau: Canada Will Continue to Accept Asylum Seekers from US," *The Hill*, 2/21/17.

29. Anthony Capaccio, "Air Force Stumped by Trump's Claim of $1Billion Savings on Jet," Bloomberg.com, 2/22/17.

30. Marcelo Rochabrun, "Mexican Official Says Deporting Non-Mexicans to Mexico Is a 'Non-Starter,'" *ProPublica*, 2/22/17.

31. Philip Rucker, "Trump Touts Recent Immigration Raids, Calls Them a 'Military Operation,'" *WaPo*, 2/23/17; Steve Benen, "Trump's 'Military Operation' Apparently Isn't a Military Operation," *MaddowBlog*, 2/23/17.

32. "Mexico Foreign Minister Vents 'Irritation' at Rex Tillerson," BBC News, 2/23/17; Azam Ahmed, Gardiner Harris, and Ron Nixon, "As Kelly and Tillerson Visit Mexico, Their Reassurances Differ from Trump's Stance," *NYT*, 2/23/17.

33. Carol Morello and Anne Gearan, "In First Month of Trump Presidency, State Department Has Been Sidelined," *WaPo*, 2/22/17.

34. Michele Kelemen (@michelekele men), "The daily advisory from State. . . . no briefing." Twitter, 2/22/17, 6:29 a.m.

35. Max Greenwood, "State Department Memo—on Dangers of Leaks—Leaks to Media," *The Hill*, 2/24/17.

36. Jeremy W. Peters, Jo Becker, and Julie Hirschfeld Davis, "Trump Rescinds Rules on Bathrooms for Transgender Students," *NYT*, 2/22/17.

37. Steven Thrasher (@thrasherxy), "2. I went to the US Interagency Council on Homelessness's page on LGBT youth homelessness. It is a DEAD URL http://ln.is/www.usich.gov/issue/IhQUR . . ." Twitter, 2/22/17, 3:51 p.m.

38. S. V. Date, "As SEALs Fought for Their Lives, Trump's Account Sent and Deleted a TV Tweet," *HuffPost*, 2/23/17.

39. Timothy Cama, "Eric Trump's Brother-in-Law Working at Energy Dept.," *The Hill*, 2/23/17.

40. Kenneth P. Vogel, David Stern, and Josh Meyer, "Manafort Faced Blackmail Attempt, Hacks Suggest," *Politico*, 2/23/17.

41. Peter Baker, "McMaster May Reorganize Trump's Foreign Policy Team Once Again," *NYT*, 2/22/17.

42. Tom Kludt, "Bannon Rips 'Corporatist, Globalist Media' at CPAC," CNN.com, 2/23/17.

43. Tal Kopan, "Trump Administration Lags in Filling Key Posts," CNN.com, 2/17/17.

44. Jake Tapper and Pamela Brown, "White House Effort to Justify Travel Ban Causes Growing Concern for Some Intelligence Officials," CNN.com, 2/25/17.

45. Vivian Salama and Alicia A. Caldwell, "AP Exclusive: DHS Report Disputes Threat from Banned Nations," AP, 2/24/17.

46. Chris Cillizza, "Donald Trump's Streak of Falsehoods Now Stands at 33 Days," *WaPo*, 2/21/17.

47. Rumana Ahmed, "I Was a Muslim in Trump's White House," *Atlantic*, 2/23/17.

48. Alan Taylor, "Dakota Access Pipeline Protesters Burn Their Camp Ahead of Evacuation," *Atlantic*, 2/22/17.

49. Jim Sciutto, Evan Perez, Shimon Prokupecz, Manu Raja, and Pamela Brown, "FBI Refused White House Request to Knock Down Recent Trump-Russia Stories," CNN.com, 2/24/17.

50. Spencer Ackerman, "White House Confirms Conversation with FBI About Trump and Russia," *Guardian*, 2/24/17.

51. Julie Hirschfeld Davis, "Trump Denounces F.B.I. over Leaks, Demanding Investigation," *NYT*, 2/24/17.

52. "Vitaly I. Churkin, Russian Ambassador to the U.N., Dies at 64," *WaPo*, 2/20/17; Rickey Gevers (@UID_), "Russian Ambassadors that died last 3 months: Vitaly Churkin, Andrei Malanin, Alexander Kadakin, Andrei Karlov and Mikhail Lesin." Twitter, 2/23/17, 12:31 p.m.

53. Sari Horwitz, "Law Professors File Misconduct Complaint Against Kellyanne Conway," *WaPo*, 2/23/17.

54. Tim Dickinson, "Border Patrol Agents Stop Domestic Travelers at New York Airport," *Rolling Stone*, 2/23/17.

55. Julie Hirschfeld Davis and Michael M. Grynbaum, "Trump Intensifies His Attacks on Journalists and Condemns F.B.I. 'Leakers,'" *WaPo*, 2/24/17; Sabrina Siddiqui, "Trump Press Ban: BBC, CNN and *Guardian* Denied Access to Briefing," *Guardian*, 2/25/17.

56. Hadas Gold (@Hadas_Gold), "WSJ says they would not have participated in gaggle had they known of the blocking of others and said they won't in future" Twitter, 2/24/17, 12:41 p.m.

57. Tim Alberta (@TimAlberta), "A section of people in the back of #CPAC2017 waving Russian flags—a staffer just came and demanded they all be handed over." Twitter, 2/24/17, 7:27 a.m.

58. Samantha Schmidt, "Suspect in Kansas Bar Shooting of Indians Apparently Thought They Were Iranians," *WaPo*, 2/28/17.

59. Annie Gowen and Rama Lakshmi, "'I Appeal to All the Parents in India Not to Send Their children' to the U.S., Distraught Father Says After Shooting," *WaPo*, 2/24/17.

60. Greg Miller and Adam Entous, "Trump Administration Sought to Enlist Intelligence Officials, Key Lawmakers to Counter Russia Stories," *WaPo*, 2/24/17.

61. Carrie Dann, "Majority of American Say Congress Should Probe Contact Between Trump, Russia: Poll," NBCNews.com, 2/24/17.

62. Mark Landler and Eric Schmitt, "H.R. McMaster Breaks with Administration on Views of Islam," *NYT*, 2/24/17.

WEEK 16

1. Max Greenwood and Jordan Fabian, "Trump: I Won't Attend White House Correspondents' Dinner," *The Hill*, 2/25/17.

2. Mike Allen, "Exclusive: Spicer Arranged CIA, GOP Intelligence Push-back," *Axios*, 2/27/17.

3. Karoun Demirjian, "House Intelligence Chairman Says He Hasn't Found Evidence of Trump Team's Ties to Russian," *WaPo*, 2/27/17.

4. Citizens for Responsibility and Ethics in Washington to FBI, "Federal Bureau of Investigation—Chief of Staff Reince Priebus & FBI Deputy Andrew McCabe" FOIA request, 2/27/17, https://s3.amazonaws.com/storage.citizensforethics.org/wp-content/uploads/2017/02/28230157/FBI-2017-2-27-Commun.-with-WH-re.-invest.-1.pdf

5. "Trump Accuses Obama of Being Behind Town Hall Protests," *Politico*, 2/28/17.

6. Allan Smith, "TRUMP: 'I Haven't Called Russia in 10 Years," *BI*, 2/27/17.

7. Olivia Beavers, "George W. Bush: We Need Answers on Trump Team Ties to Russia," *The Hill*, 2/27/17.

8. David Cay Johnson, "Wilbur Ross Is Another Trump Cabinet Pick with Underexamined Russian Ties," *DB*, 2/27/17.

9. "New Commerce Secretary at Nexus of Lucrative Trump Russian Deal," *Rachel Maddow Show*, MSNBC, 2/27/17.

10. Nikita Vladimirov, "Swedish 'National Security Advisor' Interviewed by Fox News Not Known to Swedish Officials: Report," *The Hill*, 2/25/17; Liam Stack and Christina Anderson, "Fox News Distances Itself from Controversial Swedish Guest," *NYT*, 2/27/17.

11. "Dozens of Gravestones Toppled at Philadelphia Jewish Cemetery," *Times of Israel*, 2/26/17; John Bacon, "Jewish Sites Reported 31 Threats Monday; More than 100 in '17," *USAT*, 2/27/17.

12. Mark Berman, "Trump Questions Who Is Really Behind Anti-Semitic Threats and Vandalism," *WaPo*, 3/1/17.

13. Albert Samaha and Talal Ansari, "Four Mosques Burned in Seven Weeks—Leaving Many Muslims and Advocates Stunned," *BF*, 2/28/17.

14. Tom Hamburger and Rosalind S. Helderman, "FBI Once Planned to Pay Former British Spy Who Authored Controversial Trump Dossier," *WaPo*, 2/28/17.

15. Kim Sengupta, "US Senate Calls on British Spy Christopher Steele to Give Evidence on Explosive Trump-Russia Dossier," *Independent* (UK), 3/2/17.

16. Julie K. Brown, "Slain SEAL's Dad Wants Answers: 'Don't Hide Behind My Son's Death,'" *Miami Herald*, 2/26/17.

17. Rebecca Kheel, "Trump Appears to Blame Generals for SEAL's Death in Yemen Raid," *The Hill*, 2/28/17.

18. Maxwell Tani, "'This Was a Mission That Was Started Before I Got Here'. Trump Suggests Obama Is to Blame for the Raid That Lost a Navy SEAL," *BI*, 2/28/17; Andrea Mitchell (@mitchellreports), "Fmr Deputy CIA Dir David Cohen on Yemen raid: It was not approved by the Obama administration. I was there, I was in all of those meetings." Twitter, 3/3/17, 9:47 a.m.

19. Mark Hensch, "Yemen SEAL Raid Yielded No Significant Intel: Report," *The Hill*, 2/27/17.

20. Austin Wright, "Top Democrats Demand Answers on Trump's China Trademark," *Politico*, 2/24/17.

21. Benjamin Siegel and Alexander Mallin, "White House: Conway 'Inadvertently' Promoted Ivanka Trump Brand on Fox News," ABCNews.com, 3/1/17.

22. Cristina Alesci, "Ethics Concerns Shadow New Trump Hotel in Vancouver," CNN.com, 3/1/17.

23. Jennifer Gould Keil, "$16M Trump Penthouse Sells to Exec with Ties to China," *NYP*, 2/28/17.

24. Brooke Seipel, "Muhammad Ali Jr. Detained by Immigration at Florida Airport," *The Hill*, 2/24/17; Erin McCann, "French Historian Says He Was Threatened with Deportation at Houston Airport," *NYT*, 2/26/17.

25. Julia Ioffe, "The State of Trump's Department," *Atlantic*, 3/1/17; Nick Wadhams, "Top Asia Diplomat at State Department Joins Wave of Departures," Bloomberg.com, 3/2/17; Conor Finnegan, "What Slashing the State Department Budget by One-Third Would Really Mean," ABCNews.com, 3/1/17.

26. Yeganeh Torbati, "State Department to Resume Briefings in March after Six-week Hiatus," Reuters, 2/24/17.

27. Paulina Firozi, "State Department Tweets Then Deletes Kudos to Iranian Director for Oscar Win," *The Hill*, 2/27/17.

28. Matthew Boyle, "Exclusive—President Trump: *New York Times* 'Intent Is So Evil and So Bad,' 'They Write Lies,'" *Breitbart*, 2/27/17.

29. "Donald Trump Made 61 Statements in His Speech. 51 Were False," indy100, *Independent* (UK).

30. Inimai M. Chettiar, Ames Grawert, "Crime Isn't Out of Control. But the White House Wants You to Think It Is," 3/1/17; James Cullen, "Just Facts: Crime in Context—the Lessons of History," 10/7/16; "Preliminary Analysis of 2015 FBI Uniform Crime Report," 9/26/16. All available at www.brennancenter.org.

31. Ariel Zilber, "Justice Ruth Bader Ginsburg Skipped Trump's Address Before Congress—Months After Calling the President 'a Faker,'" *Daily Mail* (UK), 3/1/17.

32. Caroline Kenny, "Democratic Women Wear White to Trump's Address," CNN, 3/1/17.

33. Brooke Seipel, "CNN: Trump Misled Reporters on Immigration to Get Good Coverage Pre-speech," *The Hill*, 3/1/17.

34–35. Matthew Rosenberg, Adam Goldman, and Michael S. Schmidt, "Obama Administration Rushed to Preserve Intelligence of Russian Election Hacking," *NYT*, 3/1/17.

36. Adam Entous, Ellen Nakashima, and Greg Miller, "Sessions Met with Russian Envoy Twice Last Year, Encounters He Later Did Not Disclose," *WaPo*, 3/1/17.

37. Matthew Yglesias, "A Timeline of Jeff Sessions and Michael Flynn's Talks with the Russian Ambassador," *Vox*, 3/3/17; Josh Rogin, "Trump Campaign Guts GOP's Anti-Russia Stance on Ukraine," *WaPo*, 7/18/16.

38. Paul Sonne, Rebecca Ballhaus, and Carol E. Lee, "Jeff Sessions Used Political Funds for Republican Convention Expenses," *WSJ*, 3/2/17.

39. Mark Landler and Eric Lichtblau, "Jeff Sessions Recuses Himself from Russia Inquiry," *NYT*, 3/2/17.

40. Jon Schuppe, "Sessions Will Submit Amended Testimony, Address Senators' Questions," NBCNews.com, 3/3/17.

41. Josh Meyer, "Former Trump Adviser Carter Page Also Met with Russian Envoy," *Politico*, 3/2/17.

42. "Carter Page: 'I Don't Deny' Meeting with Russian Ambassador," *All In with Chris Hayes*, MSNBC, 3/2/17; CNN (@CNN), "Former Trump aide backtracks after admitting to Russia contact: I never spoke with him for more than 10 seconds" Twitter, 3/3/17, 5:38 p.m.

43. Michael S. Schmidt, Matthew Rosenberg, and Matt Apuzzo, "Kushner and Flynn Met with Russian Envoy in December, White House Says," *WaPo*, 3/2/17.

44. Evan Perez, Shimon Prokupecz, and Eli Watkins, "Sessions Did Not Disclose Meetings with Russian Ambassador," CNN.com, 3/2/17.

45. Allan Smith, "Russian Ambassador at Center of Sessions Firestorm Did Not Attend Corresponding Democratic Convention Event," *BI*, 3/3/17.

46. Susan B. Glasser, "Trump Takes on the Blob," *Politico*, March/April 2017.

47. Tony Cook, "Pence Used Personal Email for State Business—and Was Hacked," *USAT*, 3/2/17.

48. Tony Cook, "Pence Turns Over to State 13 Boxes of Emails amid Controversy," *IndyStar*, 3/4/17.

49. Paulina Firozi, "Trump Transition Team Canceled Plan for Ethics Training for Staff: Report," *The Hill*, 3/2/17.

50. "*TRMS* Exclusive: DHS Document Undermines Trump Case for Travel Ban," *MaddowBlog*, 3/3/17.

51. Julia Wick, "This Is What It's Like When a Father of 4 Is Detained by ICE While Dropping His Daughters Off at School" *LAist*, 3/2/17.

52. Sarah Fowler, "Immigrant Detained After Press Conference," *Clarion-Ledger* (Jackson, MS), 3/1/17.

53. Colin Daileda, "Sean Spicer Really Wants His Office to Stop Leaking Everything He Does," *Mashable*, 2/27/17.

54. Arshad Mohammed, Jonathan Landay, and Warren Strobel, "Exclusive: Trump Aides' Bid to Plug Leaks Creates Unease Among Some Civil Servants," Reuters, 3/3/17.

55. Reuters, "Top Talent Leaves NSA amid Trump Fears and Morale Slump," *Newsweek*, 2/28/17.

56. Elias Groll, "Trump White House Shopping for Technology to Plug Leaks," *FP*, 3/3/17.

57. Chelsea Bailey, "Schwarzenegger Quits 'The Celebrity Apprentice,' Citing Too Much 'Baggage,'" NBCNews.com, 3/3/17.

58. Arnold (@Schwarzenegger), "You should think about hiring a new joke writer and a fact checker." Twitter, 3/4/17, 5:57 a.m.

59. Jordyn Phelps, "Obama Denies Trump's Unsubstantiated Claim That He Wiretapped Phones in Trump Tower," ABCNews.com, 3/4/17.

WEEK 17

1. Kyle Balluck, "White House Calls on Congress to Investigate Trump's Wiretap Claims," *The Hill*, 3/5/17.

2. Kailani Koenig, "Former DNI James Clapper: 'I Can Deny' Wiretap of Trump Tower," NBCNews.com, 3/5/17.

3. Michael S. Schmidt and Michael D. Shear, "Comey Asks Justice Dept. to Reject Trump's Wiretapping Claim," *NYT*, 3/5/17.

4. Michael S. Schmidt, "White House Rejects Comey's Assertion That Wiretapping Claim Is False," *NYT*, 3/6/17.

5. Philip Rucker, Robert Costa, and Ashley Parker, "Inside Trump's Fury: The President Rages at Leaks, Setbacks and Accusations," *WaPo*, 3/5/17; Robert Costa (@costareports), "Trump woke up in good spirits, per his confidants. Read the papers and watched early cable shows, liked that they covered his allegations." Twitter, 3/5/17, 3:40 p.m.

6. Amanda Wills (@AmandaWills), "Today is the first weekday that Trump's schedule is entirely closed press http://www.cnn.com/2017/03/06/politics/trump-latest/index.html . . ." Twitter, 3/6/17, 8:16 a.m.

7. David Ferguson, "Trump Ally Roger Stone Suspended from Twitter After Misogynist Meltdown—and He's Still Whining About It," *Raw Story*, 3/9/17; Brooke Seipel, "Trump Adviser Admits to Contact with DNC Hacker," *The Hill*, 3/10/17.

8. David Smith, "Ex-Trump Adviser Says Phone May Have Been Tapped, Without Offering Evidence," *Guardian*, 3/9/17.

9. Glenn Kessler, "Trump's 'Evidence' for Obama Wiretap Claims Relies on Sketchy, Anonymously Sourced Reports," *WaPo*, 3/5/17.

10. Alicia A. Caldwell and Jill Colvin, "Trump Signs Anti-Terror Travel Ban—Without New Fanfare," AP, 3/6/17.

11. Reid Wilson, "Four States Suing to Block Trump's New Travel Ban," *The Hill*, 3/9/17; Ed Kilgore, "Trump's Team's Words Could Sabotage the Second Travel Ban, Just like the First," *DI*, 3/8/17.

12. Josh Marshall, "New Development on the Michael Cohen 'Peace Plan' Meeting," *TPM Editor's Blog*, 3/4/17.

13. Caitlyn Stulpin, "First Import of Russian Steel Arrives at New Paulsboro Port," NJ.com, 3/2/17.

14. "Keystone XL Builders Can Use Non-U.S. Steel, White House Says Now," Reuters, 3/3/17.

15. Julie Bykowicz, "Trump Hotel May Be Political Capital of the Nation's Capital," AP, 3/5/17.

16. Jonathan O'Connell, "Top Official Overseeing Trump's D.C. Hotel Is Out at GSA as Democrats Call for Investigation of Lease," *WaPo*, 3/8/17.

17. Rich Gardella and Tracy Connor, "Wine Bar Sues Donald Trump for Unfair Competition over D.C. Hotel," NBCNews.com, 3/9/17.

18. Emma Löfgren, "Rinkeby Teens Say Russian TV Crew Tried to Bribe Them," *The Local* (Sweden), 3/6/17.

19. Kevin G. Hall, Adam Bell, Rick Rothacker, and Greg Gordon, "Trump, Russian Billionaire Say They've Never Met, but Their Jets Did—in Charlotte," McClatchy, 3/7/17.

20. Andrew Kaczynski, "Russian Ambassador Denied Meeting with Trump or Campaign Officials in October Speech," CNN.com, 3/9/17.

21. Andrew Beatty (@AndrewBeatty), "Five hours after DPRK missile launch, Abe has addressed parliament, South Korea MoD has briefed. Not a peep from the White House." Twitter, 3/5/17, 7:18 p.m.

22. Felicia Schwartz (@felschwartz), "1:35 pm Trump/Tillerson scheduled to have lunch 3:43 pm @realDonald Trump issues statement congratulating Exxon Mobil on $20 billion program" Twitter, 3/6/17, 12:49 p.m.

23. Amy Siskind, "What Trump and Tillerson did today after lunch. I just can't! https://www.whitehouse.gov/the-press-office/2017/03/06/president-trump-congratulates-exxon-mobil-job-creating-investment http://news.exxonmobil.com/press-release/exxonmobil-plans-investments-20-billion-expand-manufacturing-us-gulf-region" Facebook post, 3/6/17.

24. Benjamin Mullin, "Bureau Chiefs 'Deeply Concerned' That Rex Tillerson Is Ditching the Press on Asia Trip," Poynter Institute, 3/9/17; Cameron Joseph (@cam_joseph), ".@PressSec on why Tillerson not allowing press on his Asia trip plane: 'There's an element of cost savings . . . the sec. is trying to achieve'" Twitter, 3/10/17, 11:29 a.m.

25. Caleb R. Newton, "State Department Kicks MSNBC's Andrea Mitchell Out of Press Briefing," *Bipartisan Report*, 3/7/17.

26. Tracy Wilkinson, "Mexican Foreign Secretary Goes Straight to the White House, Skips Usual Channels," *LAT*, 3/9/17; *ProPublica* (@ProPublica), "Mexican foreign minister met with Kushner and other WH officials, who didn't even tell the State Dept about it." Twitter, 3/9/17, 6:59 p.m.

27. Michael M. Grynbaum (@grynbaum), "State Dept asked NYC Medical Examiner not to disclose cause of death of Russian UN ambassador who died last month" Twitter, 3/10/17, 8:43 a.m.

28. Andrea Mitchell (@mitchellreports), "Fmr. Ambassador Chris Hill: Vacuum of leadership at State Dept. is 'unprecedented'" Twitter, 3/10/17, 11:49 a.m.

29. Justin Elliott, Al Shaw, and Derek Kravitz, "Meet the Hundreds of Officials Trump Has Quietly Installed Across the Government," *ProPublica*, 3/8/17.

30. *Washington Post* and Partnership for Public Service, "Tracking How Many Key Positions Trump Has Filled So Far," *WaPo*, 12/8/16 (last updated).

31. Iona Craig, "Death in Al Ghayil," *The Intercept*, 3/9/17.

32. Paul D. Shinkman, "Top General: I'm Responsible for Fatal Yemen Raid," *USN*, 3/9/17.

33. Edgar Sandoval and Thomas Tracy, "Bomb Threat Prompts Evacuation of Jewish Children's Museum in Brooklyn; Coast Clear After 3-Hour Search," *NYDN*, 3/9/17; Victoria Brownworth (@VABVOX), "The largest synagogue in the Pacific Northwest has been vandalized. On shabbat. h/t @hanamkim " Twitter, 3/10/17, 1:11 p.m.; Donna St. George, "Anti-Semitic Incidents Under Investigation in Two Md. Schools," *WaPo*, 3/9/17.

34. Max Boot, "WikiLeaks Has Joined the Trump Administration," *FP*, 3/8/17.

35. Simon Rosenberg, "Why the Return of WikiLeaks Is a Problem for Trump," *USN*, 3/9/17.

36. Max Greenwood, "Trump Ally Farage Visits Embassy Where Julian Assange Lives," *The Hill*, 3/9/17.

37. Ron Charles, "Costco—Yes, Costco—Now Stocks Orwell's '1984,'" *WaPo*, 3/8/17.

38. Gina Cherelus, "Father of Slain Soldier Who Criticized Trump Says Travel Rights Reviewed," Reuters, 3/6/17; Clare Foran, "The Curious Case of Khizr Khan's 'Travel Privileges,'" *Atlantic*, 3/7/17.

39. Chris Geidner, "ACLU Lawyer Files Ethics Complaint Against Jeff Sessions over Russia Testimony," *BF*, 3/9/17.

40. Meera Jagannathan, "Ethics Office Scolds White House for Not Disciplining Kellyanne Conway over Ivanka Trump Plug," *NYDN*, 3/9/17.

41. Alana Abramson, "President Trump's Allies Keep Talking About the

'Deep State.' What's That?" *Time*, 3/8/17.

42. Sean Hannity (@seanhannity), "It's time for the Trump administration to purge the deep state saboteurs from the government . . . hear more at 10pm #Hannity" Twitter, 3/9/17, 6:45 p.m.

43. Joy Reid (@JoyAnnReid), "To be clear, during an interview with my friend and colleague @KatyTurNBC, congressman @SteveKingIA called for a purge of federal staff." Twitter, 3/10/17, 12:52 p.m.

44. Kevin Liptak and Hunter Schwarz, "Spicer Doesn't Reject Concept of 'Deep State,'" CNN.com, 3/11/7.

45. Del Quentin Wilber, "Jeff Sessions Asks 46 Obama-Appointed U.S. Attorneys to Resign," *LAT*, 3/10/17.

46. Tom Hamburger, "Watchdogs Ask U.S. Attorney to Investigate Trump over Foreign Business Deals," *WaPo*, 3/8/17.

47. Benjamin Weiser and Nick Corasaniti, "Preet Bharara Says He Will Stay On as U.S. Attorney Under Trump," *NYT*, 11/30/16; Brooke Seipel, "US Attorney Bharara Won't Resign Despite Trump Demand: Reports," *The Hill*, 3/11/17.

48. Michael Crowley, "The Man Who Wants to Unmake the West," *Politico*, March/April 2017.

49. Eric Lipton and Susanne Craig, "With Trump in White House, His Golf Properties Prosper," *NYT*, 3/9/17.

50. Adam Davidson, "Donald Trump's Worst Deal," *NYer*, 3/13/17.

51. Michael R. Gordon, "Russia Has Deployed Missile Barred by Treaty, U.S. General Tells Congress," *NYT*, 3/8/17.

52. Errin Haines Whack, "Muhammad Ali's Son Says He Was Detained Again at Airport," AP, 3/11/17.

53. Chad Day and Stephen Braun, "Flynn Admits to Turkey Lobbying Before the Election That May Have Benefited the Country," *TPM*, 3/8/17.

54. southpaw (@nycsouthpaw), "During the transition, Flynn held up approval of a Kurdish plan to seize Raqqa that Turkey wouldn't like. washingtonpost .com/world/national- . . ." Twitter, 3/10/17, 11:59 a.m.; Adam Entous, Greg Jaffe, and Missy Ryan, "Obama's White House Worked for Months on a Plan to Seize Raqqa. Trump's Team Took a Brief Look and Decided Not to Pull the Trigger," *WaPo*, 2/2/17.

55. Erik Wemple, "*The Hill* Publishes Editor's Note on Michael Flynn Op-Ed Regarding Turkey," *WaPo*, 3/10/17.

56. Laura Rozen (@lrozen), "Flynn paid ex FBI official McCauley who claimed quid pro quo w/State's Patrick Kennedy on Clinton email marking" Twitter, 3/10/17, 12:40 p.m.

57. "White House Says Trump Did Not Know Flynn Was Representing Turkey," Reuters, 3/10/17.

58. Rogelio Garcia Lawyer (@LawyerRogelio), "Fmr. Trump transition official this AM on @MSNBC: The Trump transition 'was aware' of Mike Flynn's lobbying work." Twitter, 3/10/17, 12:20 p.m.

59. Natasha Bertrand (@NatashaBertrand), "Pence says he didn't know about Flynn's lobbying work for Turkey. Rep. Cummings sent him a letter about it in Nov http://read.bi/2nmsgge" Twitter, 3/10/17, 5:31 a.m.; Josh Feldman, "Pence on New Flynn Revelations: 'Affirmation' of Trump's Decision to Ask for Resignation," *Mediaite*, 3/9/17.

60. Pamela Brown and Jose Pagliery, "Sources: FBI Investigation Continues into 'Odd' Computer Link Between Russian Bank and Trump Organization," CNN.com, 3/10/17.

61. Simon Ostrovsky, "Ukraine Lawyer Seeks Probe of Alleged Hacked Texts of Manafort's Daughter," CNN.com, 3/11/17.

62. Matthew Rozsa, "Sean Spicer Tries to Laugh Off Trump's Previous Dismissal of Job Reports Accuracy," *Salon*, 3/10/17; Michelle Ye Hee Lee, "Trump Keeps Claiming He's Created U.S. Jobs Since Election Day. Not so," *WaPo*, 3/10/17.

63. "50 Days of 'Facts,'" *All In with Chris Hayes*, MSNBC, 3/10/17.

64. Julia La Roche, "The White House May Have Broken a Rule When It Tweeted About the Jobs Report," *Yahoo Finance*, 3/10/17.

WEEK 18

1. AP, "Kellyanne Conway: 'Microwaves That Turn into Cameras' Can Spy on Us," *Guardian*, 3/13/17; Jeremy Diamond, "Spicer: Trump Didn't Mean Wiretapping When He Tweeted About Wiretapping," CNN.com, 3/14/17.

2. Jill Disis, "Trump's Budget Director Claims Obama Was 'Manipulating' Jobs Data," CNN.com, 3/12/17.

3. Christopher M. Matthews and Erin Ailworth, "Rex Tillerson Used Email Alias at Exxon to Discuss Climate Change, New York Says," *WSJ*, 3/13/17.

4. David Kocieniewski and Caleb Melby, "Kushners May Get $400 Million from Chinese on Tower," Bloomberg.com, 3/13/17.

5. Jamie Feldman, "Ivanka Trump Imported, 53 Metric Tons of Chinese Goods During Her Dad's 'Buy American' Speech," *HuffPost*, 3/20/17.

6. Andy Kroll and Russ Choma, "Businesswoman Who Bought Trump Penthouse Is Connected to Chinese Intelligence Front Group," *MJ*, 3/15/17.

7. Ben Blanchard and Steve Holland, "Trump Changes Tack, Backs 'One China' Policy in Call with Xi," Reuters, 2/9/17.

8. Julie Pace, "Trump's Allies Melting Away on Wiretapping Claims," AP, 3/16/17.

9. Lachlan Markay, "Monica Crowley Lost White House Job, Now She's Got One with Pro-Russian Oligarch," *DB*, 3/14/17.

10. Reuters Top News (@Reuters), "Special Report: $98.4 million worth of Trump luxury property bought by those with Russian passports or addresses. http://reut.rs/2mDwQXL" Twitter, 3/17/17, 11:51 a.m.

11. John Pacenti, "Yachts of Trump Financial Backer, Russian Oligarch Seen Close Together," *Palm Beach Post*, 3/17/17.

12. Matea Gold, "The Mercers and Stephen Bannon: How a Populist Power Base Was Funded and Built," *WaPo*, 3/17/17.

13. Rosalind S. Helderman and Tom Hamburger, "Trump Adviser Flynn Paid by Multiple Russia-related Entities, New Records Show," *WaPo*, 3/16/17.

14. Carol E. Lee, Rob Barry, Shane Harris, and Christopher S. Stewart, "Mike Flynn Didn't Report 2014 Interaction with Russian-British National," *WSJ*, 3/18/17.

15. "Russian Spy Ship Returns off U.S. Coast, near Sub Base," CBSNews.com, 3/15/17.

16. Vindu Goel and Eric Lichtblau, "Russian Agents Were Behind Yahoo Hack, U.S. Says," *NYT*, 3/15/17.

17. "John McCain Says Rand Paul Is 'Working for Vladimir Putin,'" CBSNews.com, 3/15/17.

18. Charles P. Pierce, "The Executive Branch Is About to Be 'Reorganized' into Oblivion," *Esquire*, 3/14/17.

19. Alex Isenstadt and Kenneth P. Vogel, "'People Are Scared': Paranoia Seizes Trump's White House," *Politico*, 3/15/17.

20. Christian Datoc, "Tillerson: 'I'm Confident' Budget Cuts Will Make State Dept. 'Much More Efficient,'" *Daily Caller*, 3/16/17.

21. Matt Gertz, "State Department Rewards Reporter Who Wrote Tillerson Puff Piece with Sole Seat on His Plane to Asia," *Media Matters*, 3/15/17.

22. Anne Gearan and Anna Fifield, "Tillerson Says 'All Options Are on the Table' When It Comes to North Korea," *WaPo*, 3/19/17; Nikita Vladimirov, "Report: Tillerson Cuts Short South Korean Visit, Citing 'Fatigue,' *The Hill*, 3/17/17.

23. Elliot Smilowitz, "Tillerson: 'I'm Not a Big Media Press Access Person,'" *The Hill*, 3/18/17.

24. Brent Kendall and Ian Lovett, "Trump's Revised Travel Ban Is Blocked by Two Federal Judges," *WSJ*, 3/16/17.

25. Lydia Wheeler, "Judge Cites Trump Allies' Own Remark in Block of Travel Ban," *The Hill*, 3/15/17.

26. Hadas Gold, "Reporter Quits News Site over Obama Conspiracy Story," *Politico*, 3/16/17.

27. Steven Perlberg, "A Top Adviser to Mike Pence Is an Investor in Favored Media Outlet," *BF*, 3/19/17.

28. AP, "After Judge Blocks Trump's Revised Travel Ban, President Vows to 'Fight This Terrible Ruling,'" CNBC.com, 3/15/17.

29. Jacob Pramuk, "Trump May Have Just Dealt a Blow to His Own Executive Order," CNBC.com, 3/15/17.

30. Devlin Barrett, Abigail Hauslohner, and David Nakamura, "Internal Trump Administration Data Undercuts Travel Ban," *WaPo*, 3/16/17.

31. Amy Siskind (@Amy_Siskind), "Wow, Trump sure packed 'em in, in Nashville tonight 😂😂😂😂😂😂 Twitter, 3/15/17, 6:39 p.m.; Megan Seling (@mseling), "Protesters shutting down a Trump supporter by chanting "Bless your heart." Only in Nashville." Twitter, 3/15/17, 4:30 p.m.

32. Lili Bayer and Larry Cohler-Esses, "EXCLUSIVE: Nazi-Allied Group Claims Top Trump Aide Sebastian Gorka as Sworn Member," *Forward*, 3/16/17.

33. Mallory Shelbourne, "Dutch Exit Polls: Surprisingly Poor Showing for Far-Right Wilders," *The Hill*, 3/15/17.

34. Bradd Jaffy (@BraddJaffy), "Trump tells Michigan governor: Come take a photo 'even though you didn't endorse me . . . I never forget.'" Twitter, 3/16/17, 6:13 a.m.

35. David Fahrenthold (@Fahrenthold), "After Nov 8, we got 3 big, new promises abt charitable donations from @realDonaldTrump & those around him. Today, here's what we know: (1/4)" Twitter, 3/16/17, 8:09 a.m.

36. Darren Samuelsohn, "Trump Organization: First Treasury Donation on Hotel Stays to Come in 2018," *Politico*, 3/17/17.

37. Eric Leveson, "This Map Shows Just How Widespread the Jewish Center Bomb Threats Are," CNN.com, 3/13/17.

38. Alan Gomez, "Trump Travel Ban Dealt Another Blow by Maryland Judge," *USAT*, 3/16/17.

39. Louis Nelson, "Mulvaney: Proposed Cuts to Meals on Wheels Are Compassionate to Taxpayers," *Politico*, 3/16/17.

40. Richard Rubin, "One Beneficiary of GOP's Tax Bill: President Trump," *WSJ*, 3/17/17.

41. Michael D. Shear, "Trump Calls 2005 Tax Return Release 'Fake News,'" *NYT*, 3/15/17; Joe Concha, "Maddow: Trump Tax Return Leak like 'a Drop of Water' in the Desert," *The Hill*, 3/16/17.

42. Reuters, "Citing Trump, New Jersey Legislature Passes Tax Disclosure Bill," 3/16/17.

43. Saleha Mohsin, "Trump Nominates Goldman's Donovan as Deputy Treasury Secretary," Bloomberg.com, 3/14/17.

44. Peter Overby, "Ethics Documents Suggest Conflict of Interest by Trump Adviser," *The Two-Way* (blog), NPR, 3/14/17.

45. Arnie Seipel and Brian Naylor, "As Senate Investigators Push Back, White House Defends Trump Surveillance Claims," NPR.org, 3/15/17; Manu Raju, Tom LoBianco, and Theodore Schleifer, "Ryan, Senate Intel Committee See No Evidence of Trump Wiretap," CNN.com, 3/16/17.

46. Amy Siskind (@Amy_Siskind), "Senate Intel Com. statement Now what @GOP? Trump gets to call a past pres a 'Bad (or sick) guy' and no consequences?" Twitter, 3/16/17, 11:09 a.m.

47. Philip Rucker and Abby Phillip, "Spicer Says Trump 'Stands By' Unproved Allegation That Obama Ordered Wiretapping of Trump Tower," *WaPo*, 3/16/17.

48. Barney Henderson, "GCHQ Slaps Down White House Claims of Trump Tower Wiretapping Claims as 'Utterly Ridiculous,'" *Telegraph* (UK), 3/17/17.

49. Steven Swinford, "Donald Trump Fuels Diplomatic Row with Britain After Apology from US Officials over GCHQ Wiretapping Claims," *Telegraph* (UK), 3/18/17.

50. Lisa Hagen, "Spicer: We Don't Regret Repeating Claim That UK Spied on Trump," *The Hill*, 3/17/17.

51. David Mack (@davidmackau), "Photographers: Can we get a handshake? Merkel (to Trump): Do you want to have a handshake? Trump: *no response* Merkel: *makes awkward face*" Twitter, 3/17/17.

52. Eric Lipton (@EricLiptonNYT), "Ivanka at meeting with German Chancellor. Why?" Twitter, 3/17/17, 3:56 p.m.

53. Elyse Wanshel, "Donald Trump Misspeaks, Calls U.S. a Company Instead of a Country," *HuffPost*, 3/17/17.

54. Peter Baker and Steven Erlanger, "Trump Offers No Apology for Claim on British Spying," *NYT*, 3/17/17.

55. Amy Siskind, "Distancing themselves from Trump's lies about Obama wiretap: * House Intel Com ✅ * Senate Intel Com ✅ * fmr DNI Clapper ✅ * FBI's Comey ✅ * Jeff fucking Sessions ✅ * FoxNews ✅" Facebook post, 3/17/17.

56. Madeline Conway, "GOP Rep. Tom Cole: Trump Owes Obama an Apology for Wiretapping Claim," *Politico*, 3/17/17.

57. Julia Edwards Ainsley, "Exclusive: Immigration Judges headed to 12 U.S. Cities to Speed Deportations," Reuters, 3/17/17.

58. Katie Mettler, "Francisca Lino, Mom of Six, Is About to Be Deported. Her Congressman Protested and Was Handcuffed," *WaPo*, 3/14/17.

59. AJ Willingham, "Canadian Girl Guides Won't Come to the US Anymore," CNN.com, 3/14/17.

60. Chris Massie, "Steve King: Blacks and Hispanics 'Will Be Fighting Each Other' Before Overtaking Whites in Population," CNN.com, 3/14/17.

61. Barbara Campbell, "Trump Administration Files Motion Aimed at Controlling Consumer Protection Agency," *The Two-Way* (blog), NPR, 3/17/17.

62. Alexandra Petri, "Trump's Budget Makes Perfect Sense and Will Fix America, and I Will Tell You Why," *WaPo*, 3/16/17.

63. Devlin Barrett, "Kellyanne Conway's Spouse Headed for Senior Justice Department Post," *WaPo*, 3/17/17.

64. Jason Noble (@jasonnobleDMR), "Make no mistake: this is a tough crowd for @joniernst. Many of her talking points on health, climate change are being met with loud boos." Twitter, 3/17/17, 10:15 a.m.

65. "House Intel Leaders Ask FBI, CIA, NSA for Answers on Mike Flynn," *Rachel Maddow Show*, MSNBC, 3/15/17.

66. Nolan D. McCaskill, "McCain on Trump-Russia Probes: 'Lot of Shoes to Drop from This Centipede," *Politico*, 3/12/17.

WEEK 19

2. "Gallup Daily: Trump Job Approval," Gallup News, news.gallup.com /poll/201617/gallup-daily-trump-job -approval.aspx.

3. Euan McKirdy, "Germany's Defense Minister to Trump: No, We Don't Owe NATO Money," CNN.com, 3/20/17.

4. Erica Orden, "New York Attorney General Steps Up Scrutiny of White House," *WSJ*, 3/19/17.

5. Norman L. Eisen and Richard W. Painter, "Trump's Unprecedented War on Ethics: Eisen and Painter," *USAT*, 3/20/17.

6. Lisa Rein and Juliet Eilperin, "White House Installs Political Aides at Cabinet Agencies to Be Trump's Eyes and Ears," *WaPo*, 3/19/17; *Washington Post* and Partnership for Public Service, "Tracking How Many Key Positions Trump Has Filled So Far," *WaPo*, 12/8/16 (last updated).

7. Nahal Toosi and Andrew Restuccia, "Federal Staffers Panicked by Conservative Media Attacks," *Politico*, 3/22/17.

8. Matt Apuzzo, Matthew Rosenberg, and Emmarie Huetteman, "F.B.I. Is Investigating Trump's Russia Ties, Comey Confirms" *NYT*, 3/20/17.

9. Ken Dilanian, "Comey: 'No Information' to Back Trump's Claim Obama Wiretapped Him," NBCNews.com, 3/20/17.

10. President Trump (@POTUS), "FBI Director Comey refuses to deny he briefed President Obama on calls made by Michael Flynn to Russia." Twitter, 3/20/17, 11:33 a.m.

11. Reuters, "Rep. Himes Asks Comey, Rogers about Trump's Tweets," 3/20/17; Calvin Woodward and Jim Drinkard, "AP FACT CHECK: Trump Tweets vs. FBI Testimony on Russia," AP, 3/20/17.

12. Peter Stone and Greg Gordon, "FBI's Russian-Influence Probe Includes a Look at *Breitbart*, *InfoWars* News Sites," McClatchy, 3/20/17.

13. Jackie Northam and Marilyn Geewax, "Ivanka Trump's Move to the White House Raises Questions About Ethics," *The Two-Way* (blog), NPR, 3/21/17.

14. Mark Hensch, "Government Watchdogs: Give Ivanka Trump Official Title," *The Hill*, 3/24/17.

15. AP, "Trump Winery Seeks More Foreign Workers This Season," *Denver Post*, 3/20/17.

16. Stephanie Chan, "Ivanka Trump's Brand Sued over 'Unfair Competition,'" *Hollywood Reporter*, 3/20/17.

17. Peter Grant, "Jared Kushner's White House Role Complicates Skyscraper Deal," *WSJ*, 3/21/17.

18. Marilyn Geewax and Jackie Northam, "At Trump's D.C. Hotel, a U.S.-Turkey Relations Conference Stirs Up Ethics Questions," NPR.org, 3/21/17.

19. James V. Grimaldi, Dion Nissenbaum, and Margaret Coker, "Ex-CIA Director: Mike Flynn and Turkish Officials Discussed Removal of Erdogan Foe from U.S.," *WSJ*, 3/24/17.

20. Steve Eder and Ben Protess, "'Turkish Trump,' a Hotel Plan and a Tangle of Foreign Ties," *NYT*, 3/22/17.

21. Mike DeBonis, Kelsey Snell, and Robert Costa, "Trump to GOP Critics of Health-Care Bill: 'I'm Gonna Come After You,'" *WaPo*, 3/21/17.

22. Anna R. Schecter, "Trump's Business Is in Violation of New York City Law," NBCNews.com, 3/21/17.

23. Luke Harding and Nick Hopkins, "Bank That Lent $300M to Trump Linked to Russian Money Laundering Scam," *Guardian*, 3/21/17.

24. "A Dire Period of Scandal for Trump in Turmoil" *Rachel Maddow Show*, MSNBC, 3/24/17.

25. Bernard Condon and David Koenig, "New Trump Hotels Face Political Fights, Ethics Questions," AP, 3/21/17.

26. Jon Levine, "Report: 'Obsessive' Trump Records 'Basically All of the Cable News,'" *Mediaite*, 3/22/17.

27. Rich Calder, "Exxon Says It Lost Emails from Tillerson's Alias Account," *NYP*, 3/22/17.

28. Jackie Northam, Marilyn Geewax, "GSA Says Trump D.C. Hotel Lease Is Valid, Despite Ban on Elected Officials," *The Two-Way* (blog), NPR, 3/23/17.

29. Traci G. Lee, "Hawaii Republican Leader Rep. Beth Fukumoto Officially Resigns from GOP," NBC News, 3/22/17.

30. Jeff Horwitz and Chad Day, "AP Exclusive: Before Trump Job, Manafort Worked to Aid Putin," AP, 3/22/17.

31. AP (@AP), "BREAKING: White House: Trump not aware of Manafort's work for Russian billionaire when Manafort worked on presidential campaign." Twitter, 3/22/17.

32. Jack Gillum, Menalaos Hadjicostis, and Eric Tucker, AP, "AP Exclusive: US Probe of Ex-Trump Aide Extends to Cyprus," *YN*, 3/23/17.

33. "A Dire Period of Scandal for Trump in Turmoil" *Rachel Maddow Show*, MSNBC, 3/24/17.

34. Office of Cory Booker, "Booker, Markey, Blumental, Udall, Baldwin Urge Secretary Ross to Respond to Unanswered Questions on Russian Banking Ties," press release, 3/10/17, www.booker.senate .gov/?p=press_release&id=558.

35. Andrew Roth, "New Documents Show Trump Aide Laundered Payments from Party with Moscow Ties, Lawmaker Alleges," *WaPo*, 3/21/17.

36. Pamela Brown, Evan Perez, Shimon Prokupecz, and Jim Sciutto, "US Officials: Info Suggests Trump Associates May Have Coordinated with Russians," CNN.com, 3/23/17.

37. Erin McPike, "Trump's Diplomat," *IJR*, 3/22/17.

38. Manu Raju and Theodore Schleifer, "Schiff: New Evidence Shows Possible Trump-Russia Collusion," CNN.com, 3/24/17.

39. Andrew Higgins, "Lawyer for Family of Sergei Magnitsky, Dead Russian Whistle-Blower, Is Seriously Injured," *NYT*, 3/21/17.

40. Mike Hayes, "A Russian Lawyer Involved in a US Prosecution Mysteriously Plunged from His Apartment Window," *BF*, 3/21/17.

41. Bill Chappell, "Former Russian Lawmaker Is Shot to Death Outside Hotel in Kiev," *The Two-Way* (blog), NPR, 3/23/17.

42. Austin Wright, "Nunes Claims Some Trump Transition Messages Were Intercepted," *Politico*, 3/22/17.

43. Jacob Pramuk, "Trump Transition Members Had Information 'Incidentally Collected,' House Intelligence Chair Says," CNBC.com, 3/22/17.

44. Mike Levine, "Intel Chair Devin Nunes Unsure if Trump Associates Were Directly Surveilled," ABCNews .com, 3/23/17.

45. Adam K. Raymond, "Republican Leading Russia Investigation Admits 'Duty and Obligation' to Trump," *DI*, 3/24/17.

46. Ken Dilanian and Ali Vitali, "Nunes Backs Down from Assertion Trump Was Monitored," NBCNews.com, 3/24/17.

47. Judd Legum, "House Intelligence Committee Chairman Abruptly Cancels Open Hearing on Russia," *ThinkProgress*, 3/24/17.

48. Tim Mak, "Devin Nunes Vanished the Night Before He Made Trump Surveillance Claims," *DB*, 3/24/17.

49. Editorial Board, "Nunes's Grandstanding Proves He Can't Lead the Russia Investigation," *WaPo*, 3/23/17.

50. Kelsey Sutton, "Poll: Majority of Americans Want Independent Commission to Investigate Trump-Russia-Ties," *Politico*, 3/24/17.

51. Reuters Top News (@Reuters), "BREAKING: House Oversight Committee requests documents from White House, FBI on any communications, payments between Flynn and Russia" Twitter, 3/22/17, 9:43 a.m.

52. Maggie Haberman, "Senators Ask Trump Adviser to Preserve Any Russia-Related Documents," *NYT*, 3/18/17.

53. Richard W. Painter (@RWPUSA), "I testified before the US House Oversight Committee at the hearing today. In a nutshell I told them 'treason is an oversight issue.'" Twitter, 3/23/17, 12:50 p.m.

54. Kenneth P. Vogel and Eli Stokols, "RNC Paid Intel Firm for Clinton Dirt," *Politico*, 3/23/17,

55. Natalie Thongrit, "JUST IN: Trump Administration Caught 'Purging' Cell Phones to Erase Russian Data—Busted!" *Bipartisan Report*, 3/25/17.

56. Taylor Link, "Sean Spicer Compares Ex-campaign Chairman Paul Manafort to Someone Trump Sat Next to on a Plane," *Salon*, 3/23/17; Jason Linkins, "Hey, Why Is the *National Enquirer* Saying That Michael Flynn Is a Russian Spy?" *HuffPost*, 3/24/17.

57. Brian Ross and Matthew Mosk, "Russian Mafia Boss Still at Large After FBI Wiretap at Trump Tower," ABCNews.com, 3/21/17.

58. "A President's Credibility," *WSJ*, 3/21/17.

59. Derek Hawkins, "Worried About Trump's Travel Ban, Canada's Largest School District Calls Off U.S. Trips," *WaPo*, 3/24/17.

60. Cleve R. Wootson Jr., "A California Waiter Refused to Serve 4 Latina Customers Until He Saw 'Proof of Residency,'" *WaPo*, 3/19/17.

61. Michael Matza, "Fearing Raid on Immigrants, Organizers Cancel Cinco de Mayo Festival," Philly.com, 3/20/17.

62. Christopher Matthews, "Trump Claims Credit for 2016 Charter Jobs Pledge," *Axios*, 3/24/17.

63. Max Greenwood, "Judge Who Blocked Second Travel Ban Getting Death Threats," *The Hill*, 3/24/17.

65. Robert Pear, Thomas Kaplan, and Maggie Haberman, "In Major Defeat for Trump, Push to Repeal Health Law Fails," *NYT*, 3/24/17.

66. Tim Hains, "Trump on Obamacare: 'Losers' Are Chuck Schumer and Nancy Pelosi, 'Let It Explode,'" *RealClearPolitics*, 3/24/17; "The ObamaCare Republicans," *WSJ*, 3/24/17.

67. Tim Arango and Helene Cooper, "U.S. Investigating Mosul Strikes Said to Have Killed Up to 200 Civilians," *NYT*, 3/24/17.

WEEK 20

2. Bojan Pancevski, "Germany Slams 'Intimidating' £300Bn White House Bill," *Sunday Times* (UK), 3/26/17.

3. Ashley Parker and Philip Rucker, "Trump Taps Kushner to Lead a SWAT Team to Fix Government with Business Ideas," *WaPo*, 3/26/17.

4. Jo Becker, Matthew Rosenberg, and Maggie Haberman, "Senate Committee to Question Jared Kushner over Meetings with Russia," *NYT*, 3/27/17.

5. Thomas Frank and Marshall Cohen, "Russian Banker Who Met with Jared Kushner Has Ties to Putin," CNN.com, 3/28/17.

6. "Russian Bank VEB Says Executives Had Talks with Trump Son-in-Law," Reuters, 3/27/17.

7. Scott Glover, "Bank Kushner Met with Paid Russian Intelligence Agent's Legal Tab," CNN.com, 3/30/17.

8. David Edwards, "Jared Kushner Flew to Aspen Same Day as 'One of Putin's Closest Confidants' Whose Wife Is Pals with Ivanka," *Raw Story*, 3/27/17.

9. Rob Schmitz, "Kushner Family, China's Anbang End Talks over Manhattan Real Estate Deal," *The Two-Way* (blog), NPR, 3/29/17.

10. "Ivanka Trump to Be Assistant to US President," BBC News, 3/30/17; Michael McFaul (@McFaul), "As is the National Security Advisor . She has the same rank as General McMaster (3 stars)" Twitter, 3/29/17, 4:15 p.m.

11. Steve Reilly (@BySteveReilly), "Trump attorneys in January said Ivanka Trump would resign her business positions. She remains listed as CEO of this NY-based corporation:" Twitter, 3/29/17, 3:16 p.m.

12-13. Jesse Drucker, Eric Lipton, and Maggie Haberman, "Ivanka Trump and Jared Kushner Still Benefiting from Business Empire, Filings Show," *NYT*, 3/31/17.

14. Matea Gold, Drew Harwell, and Jenna Johnson, "Trump's Closest Aides Hail from Ranks of Financial Elite," *WaPo*, 4/1/17.

15. Paul A. Eisenstein "As Trump Flaunts Ford's $1.2B Investment, Ford Says It Was Planned in 2015," NBCNews.com, 3/28/17.

16. Michelle Ye Hee Lee, "Trump Keeps Claiming He's Created U.S. Jobs Since Election Day. Not So," *WaPo*, 3/10/17.

17. Annie Lowrey, "Trump's Anti-immigrant Policies Are Scaring Eligible Families Away from the Safety Net," *Atlantic*, 3/24/17.

18. Shannon Dooling, "ICE Arrests Green Card Applicants in Lawrence, Signaling Shift in Priorities," WBUR.org, 3/30/17.

19. Phil Helsel, "Hawaii Judge Extends Order Blocking Trump 'Travel Ban,'" NBCNews.com, 3/29/17.

20. Vivian Yee, "Meet the Everyday People Who Have Sued Trump. So Far, They've Won," *NYT*, 3/29/17.

21. Mary Emily O'Hara, "LGBTQ Advocates Say Trump's New Executive Order Makes Them Vulnerable to Discrimination," NBC News, 3/29/17.

22. Kyle Fitzpatrick, "BREAKING: The Trump Administration Has Removed LGBT People from the US Census," ATTN:.com, 3/30/17.

23. Christina Wilkie (@christinawilkie), "'If I weren't president, [women's empowerment] would be a very scary statement. We can't compete!' Trump says at women's event." Twitter, 3/29/17, 1:01 p.m.

24. Jeremy Binckes, "Donald Trump's Lawyers Say a Sexual Harassment Lawsuit Will 'Distract the President from His Duties," *Salon*, 3/29/17.

25. Charlie Savage and Eric Schmitt, "Trump Eases Combat Rules in Somalia Intended to Protect Civilians" *NYT*, 3/30/17.

26. Loveday Morris and Liz Sly, "Panic Spreads in Iraq, Syria as Record Numbers of Civilians Are Reported Killed in U.S. Strikes," *WaPo*, 3/28/17.

27. Ron Allen, "Survey Finds Foreign Students Aren't Applying to American Colleges," NBCNews.com, 3/25/17.

28. Lydia Saad, "Trump's Approval Rating Unusually Low, Unusually Early," Gallup News, 3/29/17.

29. Aidan Quigley, "Trump Won't Throw First Pitch on Nationals Opening Day," *Politico*, 3/28/17.

30. Oren Dorell, "Trump's Business Network Reached Alleged Russian Mobster," *USAT*, 3/28/17.

31. Ilya Marritz and Andrea Bernstein, "Paul Manafort's Puzzling New York Real Estate Purchases," WNYC.org, 3/28/17.

32. Erik Wemple, "Russian Billionaire Attempts to Stifle AP Scoop," *WaPo*, 3/28/17.

33. Marina Fang, "Devin Nunes Cancels House Intelligence Committee Meetings amid Growing Questions," *HuffPost*, 3/28/17.

34-35. Devlin Barrett and Adam Entous, "Trump Administration Sought to Block Sally Yates from Testifying to Congress on Russia," *WaPo*, 3/28/17.

36. Matthew Rosenberg, Maggie Haberman, and Adam Goldman, "2 White House Officials Helped Give Nunes Intelligence Reports," *NYT*, 3/30/17.

37. Greg Miller and Karen DeYoung, "Three White House Officials Tied to Files Shared with House Intelligence Chairman," *WaPo*, 3/30/17.

38. E. Randol Schoenberg, "News Drives Genealogy, and Vice-versa," Schoenblog.com, 3/31/17.

39. Barton Gellman, "Is the Trump White House Spying on the FBI?" Century Foundation, 3/30/17.

40. Adam Schiff (@RepAdamSchiff), "Viewed docs today at White House invitation. Here are my thoughts:" Twitter, 3/31/17.

41. Kyle Griffin (@kylegriffin1), ".@CREWcrew and Democracy 21 request an OCE inquiry into whether Devin Nunes violated House ethics rules." Twitter, 3/31/17, 6:07 p.m.

42. Matea Gold, "A Former Trump Administration Appointee Who Left Without Signing Ethics Pledge Is Now a Lobbyist," *WaPo*, 3/29/17.

43. Justin Elliott, "How the Trump Administration Responds to Democrats' Demands for Information: It Doesn't," *ProPublica*, 3/30/17.

44. Bethania Palma, "Is the #Calexit Campaign Supported by Russia?" Snopes, 1/31/17, https://www.snopes.com/2017/01/30/calexit-campaign-supported-russia.

45-46. Paul Wood, "Trump Russia Dossier Key Claim 'Verified,'" BBC News, 3/30/17.

47. Rosalind S. Helderman and Tom Hamburger, "Who Is 'Source D'? The Man Said to Be Behind the Trump-Russia Dossier's Most Salacious Claim," *WaPo*, 3/29/17.

48. Matthew Campbell, "FBI Visits Office of Saipan Casino Run by Trump Protege," Bloomberg.com, 3/31/17.

49. Shane Harris, Carol E. Lee, and Julian E. Barnes, "Mike Flynn Offers to Testify in Exchange for Immunity," *WSJ*, 3/30/17.

50. Donald Trump (@realDonaldTrump), "Mike Flynn should ask for immunity in that this is a witch hunt (excuse for big election loss), by media & Dems, of historic proportion!" Twitter, 3/31/17, 4:04 a.m.

51. Robert Kelner (@robkelner), "A prediction: Donald Trump will make novel and unusual use of the President's pardon power. An under-utilized tool of political power." Twitter, 11/12/16, 8:20 p.m.

52. Travis Gettys, "Ex-intel Official: There's Only One Person Mike Flynn Could Give Up to Get Immunity—Donald Trump," *Raw Story*, 3/31/17.

53. Camila Domonoske, "Judge Approves $25 Million Settlement of Trump University Lawsuit," *The Two-Way* (blog), NPR, 3/31/17.

54. Richard Greenberg, "Obama Officials Made List of Secret Russia Probe Documents to Protect Them," NBCNews.com, 3/31/17.

55. CBS Evening News (@CBSEveningNews), "Intel chairman says Russia hired more than 1000 hackers to create fake, anti-Clinton news in key states, won by Trump. @jeffpeguescbs, now"

Twitter, 3/29/17, 3:31 p.m.; Emily Schultheis, "Richard Burr: Senate Russia Probe Has Seven Full-time Staffers," CBSNews.com, 3/29/17.

56-57. Veronica Stracqualursi and Adam Kelsey, "Trump's Campaign Tactics, Trolls Strengthened Russia's Election Meddling, Expert Says," ABCNews .com, 3/30/17.

58. Jason Le Miere, "Did Russia Help Trump Win the Primary? Marco Rubio Deliberately 'Sidelined,' Senate Investigation Told," *Newsweek*, 3/30/17.

59. Tom LoBianco, "Senate Russia Hearing: Rubio Divulges Hack Attempts," CNN.com, 3/31/17.

60. Jeff Pegues, "FBI Probing Whether Trump Aides Helped Russian Intel in Early 2016," CBSNews.com, 3/31/17.

61. Anthony Cormier, Jeremy Singer-Vine, and John Templon, "Trump's Longtime Lawyer Is Defending Russia's Biggest Bank," *BF*, 3/23/17.

62. Philip Bump, "Nearly 1 out of Every 3 Days He Has Been President, Trump Has Visited a Trump Property," *WaPo*, 3/28/17.

63. Carrie Levine and Chris Zubak-Skees, "Wilbur Ross Will Shepherd Trump's Trade Policy. Should He Also Own a Shipping Firm?" Center for Public Integrity, 3/23/17.

64. Tom Winter, "Judge: Why Is Giuliani Defending Alleged Iranian Money Launderer?" NBCNews.com, 3/28/17.

65. Tom Winter, "Did Giuliani Try to Cut Deal Between U.S. and Turkey for Iranian?" NBCNews.com, 3/31/17.

66. Sylvan Lane, "Senate Dem Calls for Ethics Probe of Treasury Secretary," *The Hill*, 3/27/17; Ali Vitali, "Mnuchin: 'Not My Intention' to Promote *Lego Batman* Movie," NBCNews.com, 3/31/17.

67. Robert Faturechi, "Tom Price Intervened on Rule That Would Hurt Drug Profits, the Same Day He Acquired Drug Stock," *ProPublica*, 3/31/17.

68. Nadia Prupis, "Oklahoma Bar Launches Investigation to Determine if Trump's EPA Chief Lied Under Oath," *Common Dreams*, 3/30/17.

69. Felicia Schwartz, "State Department Press Room Goes Dark—at Least for Now," *WSJ*, 3/27/17; Erin McPike, "Trump's Diplomat," *IJR*, 3/21/17.

70. Anne Gearan and Carol Morello, "Secretary of State Rex Tillerson Spends His First Weeks of Isolated from an Anxious Bureaucracy," *WaPo*, 3/30/17.

71. Ellen Mitchell, "House Lawmakers Urge Trump to Fill Pentagon Positions," *The Hill*, 3/31/17.

72. Josh Voorhees, "Carl Icahn Is Apparently Profiting Enormously from His Role as an Adviser to Donald Trump," *The Slatest*, 3/27/17.

73. Josh Saul and Max Kutner, "FBI Director James Comey Tried to Reveal Russian Tampering Months Before Election," *Newsweek*, 3/29/17.

74. Brooke Seipel, "Trump Leaves Photo Op Before Signing Executive Orders," *The Hill*, 3/31/17.

75. Danielle Kurtzleben, "Trump Embraces One of Russia's Favorite Propaganda Tactics—Whataboutism," 3/17/17.

WEEK 21

2. Peter Baker and Matthew Rosenberg, "Trump Tries to Deflect Russia Scrutiny, Citing 'Crooked Scheme' by Obama," *NYT*, 4/3/17.

3. Maggie Haberman, Matthew Rosenberg, and Glenn Thrush, "Trump, Citing No Evidence, Suggests Susan Rice Committed Crime," *NYT*, 4/5/17.

4. Editorial Board, "Our Dishonest President," *LAT*, 4/2/17.

5. "100 Days of Trump Claims," *WaPo*, undated.

6. "Judge to Trump: No Protection for Speech Inciting Violence," AP, 4/2/17.

7. Tim Marcin, "Donald Trump's Latest Approval Rating Plunges as White Male Supporters Flee the President," *Newsweek*, 4/4/17.

8. Josh Sanburn, "Less than Half of White Men Now Support President Trump, Polls Find," *Time*, 4/6/17.

9. Ana Swanson, "U.S. Hiring Slumped in March as Employers Added Only 98,000 Jobs," *WaPo*, 4/7/17.

10. Derek Kravitz and Al Shaw, "Trump Lawyer Confirms President Can Pull Money from His Businesses Whenever He Wants," *ProPublica*, 4/4/17.

11. Jacob Gardenswartz, "Sean Spicer Called *ProPublica* a 'Left-Wing Blog.' ProPublica Came Back with the Receipts," *Vox*, 4/4/17.

12. Max Abelson and Zachary Mider, "Billionaire Feinberg Might Keep Cerberus Stake in New Trump Role," Bloomberg.com, 4/3/17.

13. Theodoric Meyer, Kenneth P. Vogel, and Josh Dawsey, "Former Trump Staffers Hunt for Foreign Lobbying Work," *Politico*, 4/3/17.

14. Cecilia Kang and Michael D. Shear, "Trump Leaves Science Jobs Vacant, Troubling Critics," *NYT*, 3/30/17.

15. Victoria Herrmann, "I Am an Arctic Researcher. Donald Trump Is Deleting My Citations," *Guardian*, 3/28/17; Kurt Eichenwald (@kurteichenwald), "'It's a bloodbath.' A scientist on rampant deletion of scientific data collected by govment agencies. We're in China's Cultural Revolution." Twitter, 4/4/17, 10:22 a.m.

16. Darren Samuelsohn and Rebecca Morin, "Trump Aide Accused of Hatch Act Violation After Urging Amash Primary Challenge," *Politico*, 4/1/17; Dan Scavino Jr. (@DanScavino), https://twitter.com/DanScavino.

17. White House, Office of the Press Secretary, "Presidential Executive Order on Providing an Order of Succession Within the Department of Justice," 3/31/17, www.whitehouse.gov/the-press -office/2017/03/31/presidential-executive -order-providing-order-succession-within.

18. Harper Neidig, "Twitter Alleges Trump Administration Tried to Unmask Critical Account," *The Hill*, 4/6/17.

19. Anick Jesdanun, "Twitter: US Backs Down on Seeking Anti-Trump User Records," AP, 4/7/17.

20. Blake Hounshell (@blakehounshell), "U.S. Strategic Command, which controls America's nuclear strike forces, is linking to Breitbart." Twitter, 4/5/17, 8:16 p.m.

21. Adam Weinstein, "Jared Goes to Iraq! A Picture Story," *Task & Purpose*, 4/6/17.

22. Ashley Parker and Dan Lamothe, "White House Violated Protocol by Confirming Jared Kushner's Trip before He Landed in Iraq, *WaPo*, 4/3/17.

23. "Jared Kushner as the De Facto Secretary of State," *Morning Joe*, MSNBC, 4/3/17.

24. Paulina Firozi, "Cambridge Passes Resolution Calling for Trump Impeachment Investigation," *The Hill*, 4/3/17.

25. Josh Meyer, "Relatives of U.S. Prisoners in Egypt Chide Trump," *Politico*, 4/3/17.

26. Mary Emily O'Hara, "Trump Pulls Back Obama-Era Protections for Women Workers," NBCNews, 4/3/17.

27. Jina Moore, "The Trump Administration Just Cut All Funding for the UN's Family Planning Agency," *BF*, 4/3/17.

28. Michael M. Grynbaum and Jjm Rutenberg, "Trump, Asked About Accusations Against Bill O'Reilly, Calls Him a 'Good Person,'" *NYT*, 4/5/17; National Sexual Violence Resource Center, Sexual Assault Awareness Month, www.nsvrc.org.

29. Alison Fox, "Hate Crimes, Subway Incidents Spike in First 3 Months of 2017," *AM New York*, 4/4/17.

30. Jillian Jorgensen, "Judge Rules New York City Can Dump Personal Info Obtained for Municipal ID Cards as It Moves to Protect Immigrants," *NYDN*, 4/7/17.

31. Barbara Brosher, "Indiana Restaurant Owner Deported Despite Pending Legal Action," Indiana Public Media, 4/5/17; NPR (@NPR), "An attorney for Roberto Beristain says none of his client's lawyers was notified of his deportation." Twitter, 4/5/17, 5:15 p.m.

32. David J. Lynch, "FBI Plans to Create Special Unit to Co-ordinate Russia Probe," *FT*, 4/2/17.

33. Matea Gold, Rosalind S. Helderman, and Sari Horwitz, "Michael Flynn Did Not Initially Reveal Income from Russia-Related Entities on His Personal Financial Disclosures," *WaPo*, 4/1/17.

34. Michael Isikoff, "White House Pulled Out of Meet and Greet with 'Conservatives' Favorite Russian' over Suspected Mob Ties," *YN*, 4/2/17.

35. U.S. Immigration and Customs Enforcement, "ICE Deports Convicted Russian Spy," news release, 4/5/17, www.ice.gov/news/releases/ice-deports-convicted-russian-spy.

36. Ali Watkins, "A Former Trump Adviser Met with a Russian Spy," *BF*, 4/3/17.

37–38. Adam Entous, Greg Miller, Kevin Sieff, and Karen DeYoung, "Blackwater Founder Held Secret Seychelles Meeting to Establish Trump-Putin Back Channel," *WaPo*, 4/3/17.

39. Lauren Werner (@LaurenWern), FBI is probing link between Alfa Bank + Trump Org servers. 80% of pings from Alfa. 19% pings from Spectrum Health (tied to Devos' hubby)" Twitter, 4/3/17, 2:31 p.m.

40. Jo Becker and Matthew Rosenberg, "Kushner Omitted Meeting with Russians on Security Clearance Forms," *NYT*, 4/6/17.

41. Lili Bayer, "EXCLUSIVE: Controversial Trump Aide Sebastian Gorka Backed Violent Anti-Semitic Militia," *Forward*, 4/3/17.

42. Bradd Jaffy (@BraddJaffy), "Devin Nunes to step aside from House Intel Russia investigation after ethics complaint" Twitter, 4/6/17, 6:41 a.m.

43. Caroline O. (@RVAwonk), "GOP Chair of House Ethics Cmte announces they are investigating House Intel Chair Devin Nunes for unauthorized release of classified intel." Twitter, 4/6/17, 10:34 a.m.

44. Nancy A. Youssef, "Trump May Have Changed His Syria Policy and the Pentagon Is Confused," *BF*, 4/5/17.

45. Jennifer Jacobs, "Bannon Taken Off Trump National Security Council in Shake-up," Bloomberg.com, 4/5/17.

46. Eliana Johnson, Kenneth P. Vogel, and Josh Dawsey, "Megadonor Urged Bannon Not to Resign," *Politico*, 4/5/17; Jane Mayer, "The Reclusive Hedge-Fund Tycoon Behind the Trump Presidency," *NYer*, 3/27/17.

47. National Security Council homepage, www.whitehouse.gov/nsc.

48–49. Eric Lichtblau, "C.I.A. Had Evidence of Russian Effort to Help Trump Earlier than Believed," *NYT*, 4/6/17.

52. Dana Milbank, "Mitch McConnell, the Man Who Broke America," *WaPo*, 4/7/17.

53. Sarah Kendzior (@sarahkendzior), "They will continue to rewrite major rules and disregard norms. Once installed, autocrats always rewrite laws to preserve their own power." Twitter, 4/6/17, 9:04 a.m.

54. Asawin Suebsaeng, "Steve Bannon Calls Jared Kushner a 'Cuck' and 'Globalist' Behind His Back," *DB*, 4/6/17; Mike Allen, "Exclusive: Trump Eyes New Chief of Staff; House Leader on Short List," *Axios*, 4/7/17.

55. *Washington Post* and Partnership for Public Service, "Tracking How Many Key Positions Trump Has Filled So Far," *WaPo*, 12/8/16 (last updated).

56. Scott Horsley, "Trump Donates Salary to National Parks Even as He Tries to Cut Interior Department," NPR.org, 4/4/17.

57. Sue-Lin Wong and David Brunnstrom, "North Korea Warns of Nuclear Strike if Provoked; Trump 'Armada' Steams On," Reuters, 4/10/17.

58. Tom Phillips, "Trump Told Xi of Syria Strikes over 'Beautiful Piece of Chocolate Cake,'" *Guardian*, 4/12/17.

59. Everett Rosenfeld, "The US Warned the Russians Ahead of Syria Missile Strikes," CNBC.com, 4/6/17.

60. PolitiFact (@PolitiFact), "On the campaign trail, @realDonaldTrump promised to remove existing Syrian refugees from the US http://www.politifact.com/truth-o-meter/ . . ." Twitter, 4/7/17, 10:25 a.m.

61. Lizzie Dearden, "Survivors of Donald Trump's Yemen Raid Reveal Horror of 'Women and Children Being Gunned Down,'" *Independent*, 3/9/17.

62. German Lopez, "The Pentagon Just Released Video of the US Attack on Syria," *Vox*, 4/6/17.

63. Jason Le Miere, "Trump's Attack on Syria Killed Four Children, State News Agency Claims," *Newsweek*, 4/17/17.

64. Jim Sciutto (@jimsciutto), "New: Airstrikes again target Syrian city of Khan Sheikhoun in rebel-held Idlib, site of last week's horrific suspected chemical attack" Twitter, 4/8/17, 5:17 a.m.

65. Margaret Sullivan, "The Media Loved Trump's Show of Military Might. Are We Really Doing This Again?" *WaPo*, 4/8/17.

66. "Trump Confident U.S. Military Strike on Syria Wiped Out Russian Scandal," *The Onion*, 4/7/17; "The Trump-Putin Theory on Syria That Can't Be Ruled Out," *Last Word with Lawrence O'Donnell*, MSNBC, 4/7/17.

WEEK 22

2. Linda Qiu, "Trump Says He Didn't Know Bannon Until Campaign, but They Met in 2011," *NYT*, 4/12/17.

3. Spencer Ackerman, "What's Trump's Plan for Syria? Five Different Policies in Two Weeks," *Guardian*, 4/11/17.

4. "Syrian Governor Confirms Air Base Operating Again," Reuters, 4/8/17.

5. "Syria War: G7 Fails to Agree Sanctions on Russia After 'Chemical Attack,'" BBC News, 4/11/17; Nick Wadhams and John Follain, "Tillerson Asks Why U.S. Taxpayers Should Care About Ukraine," Bloomberg.com, 4/11/17.

6. Nikita Vladimirov, "Tillerson Leaves Press Pool Behind to Meet Putin," *The Hill*, 4/12/17; David E. Sanger, "At Meeting, Putin and Tillerson Find Very Little to Agree On," *NYT*, 4/12/17.

7. Francesca Chambers, "Trump Says Relations with Russia Are 'at an All-time Low'—Then Warns Vladimir Putin: The U.S. Is Very, Very Strong," *Daily Mail* (UK), 4/12/17.

8. Donald Trump (@realDonaldTrump), "Things will work out fine between the U.S.A. and Russia. At the right time everyone will come to their senses & there will be lasting peace!" Twitter, 4/13/17, 6:16 a.m.

9. Sheera Frenkel, "This Russian Hacker's Wife Says He Was Arrested for Being 'Linked to Trump's Win,'" *BF*, 4/10/17.

10-11. Ellen Nakashima, Devlin Barrett, and Adam Entous, "FBI Obtained FISA Warrant to Monitor Trump Adviser Carter Page," *WaPo*, 4/11/17.

12. Morgan Winsor, "Carter Page: 'Something May Have Come Up in a Conversation' with Russians About US Sanctions," ABCNews.com, 4/13/17.

13. Natasha Bertrand, "Memos: CEO of Russia's State Oil Company Offered Trump Adviser, Allies a Cut of Huge Deal if Sanctions Were Lifted," *BI*, 1/27/17.

14. Jim Sciutto, Manu Raju, and Eric Bradner, "CNN Exclusive: Classified Docs Contradict Nunes Surveillance Claims, GOP and Dem Sources Say," CNN.com, 4/12/17.

15. Jack Gillum, Chad Day, and Jeff Horwitz, "AP Exclusive: Manafort Firm Received Ukraine Ledger Payout," AP, 4/12/17.

16. Tom Winter, "Paul Manafort May Register as a Foreign Agent," NBCNews.com, 4/12/17.

17-18. "The Latest: Manafort Registering with US as Foreign Agent," AP, 4/12/17.

19. Mike McIntire, "After Campaign Exit, Manafort Borrowed from Businesses with Trump Ties," *NYT*, 4/12/17.

20. Anthony Cormier, "Why Trump's Lawyer Was Sued over $350,000 He Says He Doesn't Remember Cashing," *BF*, 4/14/17.

21. Tom Newton Dunn, "MOSCOW MONEY: Ex-MI6 Chief Accuses Donald Trump of Secretly Borrowing from Russia to Keep His Property Empire Afloat During the Financial Crisis," *Sun* (UK), 4/13/17.

22-24. Luke Harding, Stephanie Kirchgaessner, and Nick Hopkins, "British Spies Were First to Spot Trump Team's Links with Russia," *Guardian*, 4/13/17.

25. Jim Sciutto, Pamela Brown, and Eric Bradner, "British Intelligence Passed Trump Associates' Communications with Russians on to US Counterparts," CNN.com, 4/14/17.

26-27. Richard Gonzales, "CIA Director Pompeo Denounces WikiLeaks as 'Hostile Intelligence Service,'" *The Two-Way* (blog), NPR, 4/13/17.

28. Mike Pompeo (@RepMikePompeo), "Need further proof that the fix was in from Pres. Obama on down? BUSTED: 19,252 Emails from DNC Leaked by Wikileaks" Twitter, 7/24/16, 9:36 a.m.

29. Michael Grunwald and Kenneth P. Vogel, "Roger Stone Convinced Obama Administration Got FISA Warrant to Monitor Him," *Politico*, 4/12/17.

30. "British Intel Agency Reported Trump Campaign Russia Ties: Report," *Rachel Maddow Show*, MSNBC, 4/13/17.

31. Tim Mak, "Congressman Investigating Trump Goes to Russia's Money Laundromat, Cyprus," *DB*, 4/14/17.

32. Ruben Major (@rubenkmajor), "Breaking—#VoteHacking? @TheJusticeDept confirms 90 pages of swing state machine flaws in #FOIA answer. #NAVO. https://navo-us.org/" Twitter, 4/12/17, 6:32 p.m.

33. Shane Goldmacher, "White House on Edge as 100-Day Judgment Nears," *Politico*, 4/10/17.

34. Jeffrey Sonnenfeld, "Trump's White House Is a Family Business. That's Not a Bad Thing," *Politico*, 4/8/17.

35. Philip Rucker, Ashley Parker, and Robert Costa, "Inside Bannon's Struggle: From 'Shadow President' to Trump's Marked Man," *WaPo*, 4/12/17.

36. Alice Ollstein, "The GOP's Existential Crisis: If They Can't Pass Tax Cuts, What Can They Do?" *TPM*, 4/12/17.

37. Beth Reinhard and Rebecca Ballhaus, "Impact of Federal Hiring Freeze Seen at Veterans Affairs, Prisons, Social Security," *WSJ*, 4/9/17.

38. Brian Naylor "Trump Lifting Federal Hiring Freeze," NPR.org, 4/12/17.

39. Rene Marsh and Gregory Wallace, "More than 350 Jobs at EPA Unfilled During Trump Hiring Freeze," CNN.com, 4/13/17; John W. Schoen, "Trump Administration Hasn't Even Named Candidates for Hundreds of Key Positions," CNBC.com, 4/13/17.

40. Benjamin Siegel, "Trump Threatens to Undermine Obamacare to Get Democrats to Negotiate," ABCNews.com, 4/12/17.

41. Kelsey Sutton, "GAO Says It's Investigating Trump Transition Team," *Politico*, 4/12/17.

42. Josh Mitchell, "Trump Administration Scraps Obama Plan for Student-Loan Servicing," *WSJ*, 4/12/17; Danielle Douglas-Gabriel, "Dems Raise Concern About Possible Links Between DeVos and Student Debt Collection Agency," *WaPo*, 1/17/17.

43. Christina Wilkie, "Trump Taps Salesman to Run Military Draft," *HuffPost*, 4/13/17.

44. Edward-Isaac Dovere, "Prediction Prof: Trump Will Be Impeached," *Politico*, 4/13/17.

45. Tim Mak (@timkmak), "CREW, the National Security Archive, and the Knight First Amendment Institue sue for White House, Mar-a-Lago, Trump Tower visitor logs" Twitter, 4/10/17, 9:51 a.m.

46. Jordan Fabian, "Trump Administration Won't Release White House Visitor Logs," *The Hill*, 4/14/17.

47. Ibid.; AP, "How Much Do Trump's Mar-a-Lago Trips Cost?" *Denver Post*, 4/13/17.

48. Drew Schwartz, "Trump's on Track to Spend More on Travel in One Year than Obama Ever Did," Vice.com, 4/11/17.

49. Hui-yong Yu, "Trump's Washington Hotel Seen Facing New Set of Legal Challenges," Bloomberg.com, 4/12/17.

50. Miles Moffeit and Sue Ambrose, "Deal over Trump-Branded Dallas Hotel Is Dead," *Dallas Morning News*, 4/12/17.

51. Polly Mosendz "The Seven Types of People Who Tweet at Trump," *Bloomberg Businessweek*, 4/10/17.

52. Ronn Blitzer, "Judge Orders Trump to Pay $300K for Stiffing Paint Company on Golf Resort Renovation," *Law & Crime*, 4/14/17.

53. Jill Colvin and Ken Thomas, "Trump Reverses Himself on NATO, China, Russia and More," AP, 4/13/17.

54. Samuel Osborne, "Donald Trump Admits Xi Jinping Gave Him a History Lesson on North Korea," *Independent* (UK), 4/13/17; Eli Stokols and Michael C. Bender, "Donald Trump's Recent Policy Reversals Reflect Business Influence," *WSJ*, 4/13/17; Fredreka Schouten, "Boeing Pledges $1 Million for Donald Trump's Inaugural Events," *USAT*, 12/8/16; Sui-Lee Wee, "In China, Trump Wins a Trove of New Trademarks," *NYT*, 3/8/17.

55. Steve Kopack (@SteveKopack), "Treasury just announced that China, Japan, S. Korea, Taiwan, Germany & Switzerland are on its new special currency 'monitoring list'" Twitter, 4/14/17, 2:13 p.m.

56. Angelo Young, "Donald Trump Recounts Eating 'the Most Beautiful Piece of Chocolate Cake' with Xi Jinping While Launching Missiles 'Heading to Iraq," *Salon*, 4/12/17.

57. Jessica Estepa and David Jackson, "Sean Spicer: Adolf Hitler Remark 'Was a Mistake,'" *USAT*, 4/11/17.

58. Rebecca Savransky, "Anne Frank Center Calls for Spicer to Be Fired," *The Hill*, 4/11/17; Alan Yuhas, "White House Defends Trump Holocaust Statement That Didn't Mention Jews," *Guardian*, 2/28/17.

59. Jose Gabriel Montelongo-Mendez (@flyinthebottle), "Obama went to the Passover Seders In the WH. No one from Trump's family showed up, even though Jared + Ivanka are Jewish." Twitter, 4/11/17, 11:41 a.m.

60. Alexander Smith and Vladimir Banic, "Sebastian Gorka Made Nazi-Linked Vitezi Rend 'Proud' by Wearing Its Medal," NBCNews.com, 4/8/17.

61. Paula Reid, "Sessions Orders Prosecutors to Crack Down on Illegal Immigration," CBSNews.com, 4/11/17.

62. Jorge Rivas, "ICE Quietly Confirms 367 Immigrants Were Detained in Raids Across the Country," *Splinter*, 4/10/17.

63. AP, "Mom of 4 U.S.-Born Children to Be Deported After Court Blocks Stay," CBSNews.com, 4/11/17.

64. Thomas Gibbons-Neff and Erin Cunningham, "U.S. Military Drops 22,000-Pound Bomb on Islamic State Forces in Afghanistan," *WaPo*, 4/13/17.

65. Shane Savitsky, "Trump Says He's Given Full Authorization to 'My Military,'" *Axios*, 4/13/17.

66. "Gallup Daily: Trump Job Approval," Gallup News, news.gallup.com/poll/201617/gallup-daily-trump-job-approval.aspx.

67. Chris Sommerfeldt and Terence Cullen, "Video Shows 'Mother of All Bombs' Hitting ISIS Base in Afghanistan, Killing 36 Militants," *NYDN*, 4/14/17.

68. William M. Arkin, Cynthia McFadden, and Kenzi Abou-Sabe, "U.S. May Launch Strike if North Korea Reaches for Nuclear Trigger," NBCNews.com, 4/13/17; AP (@AP), "BREAKING: North Korea's vice foreign minister says President Trump is 'making trouble' with 'aggressive' tweets." Twitter, 4/13/17, 8:26 p.m.

69. Karen Yourish and K. K. Rebecca Lai, "Trump Tops Obama, Bush and Clinton in Golfing and Private Getaways So Far," *NYT*, 4/9/17; updated 4/28/17.

70. Perry Stein, "Thousands Expected for Tax Day March Calling for Trump to Release His Returns," *WaPo*, 4/13/17.

WEEK 23

2. Peter Overby, "Trump's Wiretap Tweets Bring Lawsuit Seeking Proof," NPR.org, 4/19/17.

4. Ryan Lizza, "The Continuing Fallout from Trump and Nunes's Fake Scandal," *NYer*, 4/18/17.

5. *This Week* (@ThisWeekABC), "Pres. Trump at White House Easter Egg Roll: 'We will be stronger and bigger and better as a nation than ever before. We're right on track.'" Twitter, 4/17/17, 7:32 a.m.; Daniella Diaz (@Daniella Micaela), "That's a subtle nudge from Melania to remind Trump to lift his hand during the national anthem . . ." Twitter, 4/17/17, 7:41 a.m.

6–7. Eric Lipton, Ben Protess, and Andrew W. Lehren, "With Trump Appointees, a Raft of Potential Conflicts and 'No Transparency,'" *NYT*, 4/15/17.

8. Juliet Eilperin, "EPA Emerges as Major Target After Trump Solicits Policy Advice from Industry," *WaPo*, 4/16/17.

10. Rebecca Ballhaus, "Donald Trump's Companies Benefit from Campaign Funds," *WSJ*, 4/15/17.

11. Danielle Kurtzleben, "We Now Know Trump's Inauguration Donors. Where the Money Went Is Another Story," NPR, 4/19/17.

12. Anna Swartz, "Trump Inauguration Donor's Son Was Involved in NSC Meetings on Venezueala Exposed by 'Mic,'" *Mic*, 4/21/17.

13. Matthew Yglesias, "After Meeting with Pharma Lobbyists, Trump Drops Promise to Negotiate Drug Prices," *Vox*, 1/31/17.

14. Neil Connor and AP, "Ivanka Trump 'Won China Trademarks as She Dined with President Xi Jinping,'" *Telegraph* (UK), 4/19/17.

15. Lionel Barber, Gabriel Wildau, and Yuan Yang, "Former Trump Aide Advises Chines Tycoon on Building Contracts," *FT*, 4/17/17.

16. Cristian Farias, "'Emoluments' Challenge to Donald Trump's Ethics Conflicts Gets a Big Boost," *HuffPost*, 4/18/17.

17. Bess Levin, "Dow Chemical Donates $1 Million to Trump, Asks Administration to Ignore Pesticide Study," *VF*, 4/20/17.

18. Isaac Arnsdorf and Josh Dawsey, "Trump's Billionaire Adviser Stands to Gain from Policies He Helped Shape," *Politico*, 4/18/17.

19–20. Nick Penzenstadler, Steve Reilly, and John Kelly, "Trump Condos Worth $250 Million Pose Potential Conflict," *USAT*, 4/20/17.

21. Brooke Seipel, "Oversight Asks Trump for Details on Foreign Profit Donations," *The Hill*, 4/21/17.

22. Lauren Fox and Deirdre Walsh, "Rep. Jason Chaffetz Is Not Running for Re-election," CNN.com, 4/19/17.

23. Keri Geiger and Michael Riley, "Blackwater Founder Said to Have Advised Trump Team," Bloomberg .com, 4/18/17.

25. AP, "Top National Security Official Leaving Justice Department in Middle of Trump-Russia Investigation," NBCNews.com, 4/20/17.

26. Evan Perez, Shimon Prokupecz, and Manu Raju, "FBI Used Dossier Allegations to Bolster Trump-Russia Investigation," CNN .com, 4/18/17.

27. Pamela Brown, Shimon Prokupecz, Jim Sciutto, and Marshall Cohen, "Sources: Russia Tried to Use Trump Advisers to Infiltrate Campaign," CNN .com, 4/21/17.

28. Evan Perez, Pamela Brown, Shimon Prokupecz, and Eric Bradner, "Sources: US Prepares Charges to Seek Arrest of WikiLeaks' Julian Assange," CNN .com, 4/20/17.

29. Michael Calderone and Ryan J. Reilly, "Sessions Leaves Door Open to Prosecuting News Organizations over Leaks," *HuffPost*, 4/21/17.

30. Corky Siemaszko, "InfoWars' Alex Jones Is a 'Performance Artist,' His Lawyer Says in Divorce Hearing," NBCNews.com, 4/17/17.

31. Robert Windrem, "Guess Who Came to Dinner with Flynn and Putin," NBCNews.com, 4/18/17.

32. Matthew Schofield, "Let's Try This Again: House Panel Issues New Invitations in Its Russia Investigation," McClatchy, 4/21/17.

33. Jon Sharman, "Russian Journalist and Putin Critic Dies After Being Beaten Up by Strangers," *Independent* (UK), 4/19/17.

34. Andrew Rettman, "Russian-Lined Fake News Floods French Social Media," *EU Observer*, 4/20/17.

35. Ned Parker, Jonathan Landay, and John Walcott, "Putin-Linked Think Tank Drew Up Plan to Sway 2016 US Election—Documents," Reuters, 4/19/17.

36. Jay Solomon and Bradley Olson, "Exxon Seeks U.S. Waiver to Resume Russia Oil Venture," *WSJ*, 4/19/17.

37. Holly Watt, "Leave.EU Under Investigation over EU Referendum Spending," *Independent*, 4/21/17.

38. Andrew Kaczynski, "AG Sessions Says He's 'Amazed' a Judge 'on an Island in the Pacific' Can Block Trump's Immigration Order," CNN.com, 4/21/17.

39. Devlin Barrett and Matt Zapotosky, "New York Officials Blast Sessions for Calling City 'Soft on Crime,'" *WaPo*, 4/21/17.

40. Maria Sacchetti, "ICE Immigration Arrests of Noncriminals Double Under Trump," *WaPo*, 4/16/17.

41. Alan Gomez and David Agren, "First Protected DREAMer Is Deported Under Trump," *USAT*, 4/18/17.

42. Steve King (@SteveKingIA), "First non-valedictorian DREAMer deported. Border Patrol, this one's for you. http://usat.ly/2pyZriQ" Twitter, 4/18/17, 3:42 p.m.

43. Phil Helsel, "Judge Curiel, Once Criticized by Trump, Gets Deported 'Dreamer' Case," NBCNews.com, 4/20/17.

44. Tony Romm, "Trump Signed an Executive Order to Review High-Skilled H-1B Immigration Visas," *Recode*, 4/19/17.

45. Tal Kopan and Curt Devine, "The Trump Family's Long History with Immigration," CNN.com, 4/20/17.

46. Zachary Cohen and Ryan Browne, "4 Times in 4 Days: Russian Military Aircraft Fly off US Coast," CNN.com, 4/21/17.

47. Andrew E. Kramer, "'They Starve You. They Shock You': Inside the Anti-gay Pogrom in Chechnya," *NYT*, 4/21/17; Jason Slotkin, "Top Russian Court Bans Jehovah's Witnesses, Claiming 'Extremist Activities,'" *The Two-Way* (blog), NPR.

48. Dave Lawler, "Report: Trump Called Erdogan to Offer Congratulation," *Axios*, 4/17/17; Shane Savitsky, "International Monitors: Turkish Referendum Not 'Genuinely Democratic,'" *Axios*, 4/17/17.

49. Franco Ordoñez and Anita Kumar, "Secret Meeting at Mar-a-Lago Raises Questions About Colombia Peace and Trump," *Miami Herald*, 4/20/17.

50. Rick Newman, "Trump's Latest Target: Canada?" *Yahoo Finance*, 4/21/17.

51. Euan McKirdy, "Mockery, Anger in South Korea over USS Carl Vinson 'Bluffing,'" CNN.com, 4/20/17.

52. Mark Landler and Eric Schmitt, "Aircraft Carrier Wasn't Sailing to Deter North Korea, as U.S. Suggested," *NYT*, 4/18/17; Louis Nelson, "Pence: Misstatements About U.S. Aircraft Carrier Location Not Intentional," *Politico*, 4/19/17.

53. Lesley Wroughton, "U.S. Says Iran Complies with Nuke Deal but Orders Review on Lifting Sanctions," Reuters, 4/18/17.

54. Michelle Ye Hee Lee, "Trump's Claim That Korea 'Actually Used to Be a Part of China,'" *WaPo*, 4/19/17.

55. Terence Cullen, "White House Demands Carriage Ride with the Queen When Trump Visits the UK," *NYDN*, 4/15/17.

56. *Washington Post* and Partnership for Public Service, "Tracking How Many Key Positions Trump Has Filled So Far," *WaPo*, 12/8/16 (last updated).

57. Brooke Seipel, "State Dept. Official Reassigned After Conservative Media Criticism: Report," *The Hill*, 4/21/17.

58. Melanie Eversley, "Surgeon General Dismissed, Replaced by Trump Administration," *USAT*, 4/21/17.

59. Annie Waldman, "DeVos Pick to Head Civil Rights Office Once Said She Faced Discrimination for Being White," *ProPublica*, 4/14/17.

60. "100 Days of Trump Claims," *WaPo*, www.washingtonpost.com/graphics/politics/trump-claims/?tid=ss_tw&utm_term=.a34415f9ee27.

61. Jeffrey M. Jones, "Trump's Job Approval in First Quarter Lowest by 14 Points," Gallup News, 4/20/17.

62. Emily Peck, "Donald Trump's Rise Laid the Groundwork for Bill O'Reilly's Fall," *HuffPost*, 4/19/17.

63. Laura Smith-Spark and Jason Hanna, "March for Science: Protesters Gather Worldwide to Support 'Evidence,'" CNN, 4/22/17.

WEEK 24

1. Max Greenwood, "Ryan: Russian Meddling Probes Can Help US Allies," *The Hill*, 4/22/17.

2. Max Boot, "Putin's Propaganda Machine Targets Europe," *Commentary*, 4/25/17.

3. Jeff Pegues, "WikiLeaks Releases More Top-Secret CIA Docs as U.S. Considers Charges," CBSNews.com, 4/21/17.

4. Gail Sheehy, "At Yale, Psychiatrists Cite Their 'Duty to Warn' About an Unfit President," *DI*, 4/23/17.

5. Donald J. Trump for President, Inc., "Donald Trump's Contract with the American Voter," assets.donaldjtrump.com/_landings/contract/O-TRU-102316-Contractv02.pdf.

6. Darren Samuelsohn, "State Department, U.S. Embassies Promoted Trump's Mar-a-Lago," *Politico*, 4/24/17; Jessica Estepa, "State Dept. Removes Post Promoting Mar-a-Lago from Embassy Site," *USAT*, 4/24/17.

7. Gardiner Harris, "Tillerson in No Rush to Fill Nearly 200 State Department Posts," *NYT*, 4/27/17.

8. Matthew Yglesias, "Trump's Treasury Department Hasn't Filled Any Tax Policy Jobs," *Vox*, 4/24/17.

9. "The 1-Page White House Handout on Trump's Tax Proposal," CNN.com, 4/26/17.

10. Greg Sargent, "Democrats have a New Strategy to Keep Up the Pressure on Trump. It Might Work," *WaPo*, 4/10/17.

11. Lisa Rein, "Slow Pace of Trump Nominations Leaves Cabinet Agencies 'Stuck' in Staffing Limbo," *WaPo*, 4/25/17.

12. Curtis M. Wong, "Nikki Haley Condemns Alleged Abuse, Killings of Gay Men in Chechnya," *HuffPost*, 4/20/17; Somini Sengupta and Gardiner Harris, "State Department Wants to Clear Nikki Haley's Remarks Before She Speaks," *NYT*, 4/27/17.

13. "Top UN Diplomats Invited to White House Luncheon Ahead of Federal Budget Showdown," CBS New York; Abigail Tracy, "Donald Trump Just Took a Weird Shot at Nikki Haley," *VF*, 4/24/17.

14. James Hohmann, "The Daily 202: 15 Trumpists Who Did Not Survive the First 100 Days," *WaPo*, 4/24/17.

15. Daniel Chaitin, "Carl Bernstein: 'Serious Belief' in FBI and Congress That There Is an 'Active Cover-up' on Russia," *WE*, 4/22/17.

16. Michael Isikoff, "Senate Russia Probe Flounders amid Partisan Bickering," *YN*, 4/24/17.

17. Natasha Bertrand, "A Former Top NSA Lawyer Is Joining the Senate's Trump-Russia Probe," *BI*, 4/26/17; Jessica Schulberg, "Senate Intelligence Committee Divided on Whether It Has Enough Staff to Pull Off Russia Investigation," *HuffPost*, 4/27/17.

18. Josh Gerstein, "New Chief Named for Justice Department Unit Probing Trump-Russia Ties," *Politico*, 4/28/17.

19. Isaac Arnsdorf, "Flynn's Turkish Lobbying Linked to Russia," *Politico*, 4/25/17.

20. Katie Bo Williams, "White House Rejects Oversight Request for Flynn Documents," *The Hill*, 4/25/17.

21. Tom LoBianco and Manu Raju, "House Oversight Committee: Flynn Might Have Broken the Law," CNN.com, 4/25/17.

22. Margaret Hartmann, "Chaffetz Takes Weeks-Long Leave from Congress Owing to Foot Surgery," *DI*, 4/27/17.

23. Katie Bo Williams, "Cummings: White House 'Covering Up' for Flynn," *The Hill*, 4/27/17; CBS News (@CBSNews), "'The evidence . . . is powerful, mounting, incontrovertible evidence that there has been a violation of criminal law,' Rep. Blumenthal says" Twitter, 4/27/17, 7:30 a.m.

24–25. Byron Tau, "Pentagon Opens Probe into Michael Flynn's Foreign Payments," *WSJ*, 4/27/17.

26. Ben Kamisar and Jordan Fabian, "Spicer Blames Obama for Flynn's Security Clearance," *The Hill*, 4/27/17.

27. Brooke Seipel, "Trump Team Did Background Check on Flynn, Knew of Turkey Ties: Report," *The Hill*, 4/28/17.

28. Rowan Scarborough, "Trump's Lawyer Launches Legal Action Against *BuzzFeed* for Publishing 'Completely Fabricated' Dossier," *Washington Times*, 4/24/17.

29–30. Julian Borger, "UK Was Given Details of Alleged Contacts Between Trump Campaign and Moscow," *Guardian*, 4/28/17.

31. U.S. Dept. of Justice Office of Public Affairs, "Russian National Indicted with Multiple Offenses in Connection with Kelihos Botnet," press release, 4/21/17, www.justice.gov/opa/pr/russian-national-indicted-multiple-offenses-connection-kelihos-botnet.

32. Office of David Cicilline, "Cicilline Asks DOJ Inspector General to Investigate Yates, Bharara Firings," press release, 4/25/17, https://cicilline.house.gov/press-release/cicilline-asks-doj-inspector-general-investigate-yates-bharara-firings.

33. Daniel Dale (@ddale8), "Trump made 16 false claims in his bonkers AP interview, the most of any interview of his presidency or his campaign. #TrumpCheck " Twitter, 4/25/17, 12:30 p.m.; "Transcript of AP Interview with Trump," AP, 4/23/17; Tina Nguyen, "The 11 Most Jaw-Dropping Moments from Trump's A.P. Interview," *VF*, 4/24/17.

34. William Steakin, "President Trump Brags About Getting Highest Ratings Since 9/11 Coverage," AOL.com, 4/24/17.

35. Brandon Carter, "Report: Trump Won't Fire Spicer Because 'the Guy Gets Great Ratings,'" *The Hill*, 4/23/17.

36. Sarah Westwood, "Exclusive Interview: Trump 'Absolutely' Looking at Breaking Up 9th Circuit," *WE*, 4/26/17; Elliot Hannon, "Trump Floats Idea of 'Breaking Up' the Court Ruling Against Him Like an Old Fashioned Dictator," *The Slatest*, 4/26/17.

37. Christine Datoc, "Trump's VOICE Hotline Allegedly Flooded with Calls Reported Space Aliens," *Daily Caller*, 4/27/17.

38. Vivian Yee, "Judge Blocks Trump Effort to Withhold Money from Sanctuary Cities," *NYT*, 4/25/17.

39. Maria Sacchetti and Ed O'Keefe, "ICE Data Shows Half of Immigrants Arrested in Raids Had Traffic Convictions or No Record," *WaPo*, 4/28/17.

40. Lawrence Hurley, "U.S. Chief Justice Alarmed at Trump Administration Immigration Case Stance," Reuters, 4/26/17.

41. Nikita Vladimirov, "9th Circuit Denies Wider Court Review of Trump's Travel Ban," *The Hill*, 4/21/17.

42. Doug Criss and Carma Hassan, "Anti-Semitic Incidents Rose a Whopping 86% in the First 3 Months of 2017," CNN.com, 4/24/17.

43. Jon Sharman, "Donald Trump to Strip All Funding from State Department Team Promoting Women's Rights Around the World," *Independent* (UK), 4/25/17.

44. David Mack, "A Trump Supporter Allegedly Attacked Students at a Kentucky University with a Machete," *BF*, 4/28/17.

45. Lydia Wheeler, "USDA to Ease School Meal Standards," *The Hill*, 4/28/17.

46. NBC News (@NBCNews), "Mnuchin says Trump won't release tax returns. The president 'has given more financial disclosure than anybody else' http://snpy.tv/2oJQMZe" Twitter, 4/26/17, 11:02 a.m.

47. Jesse Drucker, "Bribe Cases, a Jared Kushner Partner and Potential Conflicts," *NYT*, 4/26/17.

48. Scott Maxwell, "I Think I Did More Investigating on Bondi-Trump U than State 'Investigators' Did," *Orlando Sentinel*, 4/6/17.

49. Kenneth P. Vogel and Josh Dawsey, "Lewandowski's Firm Appears to Offer Trump Meetings," *Politico*, 4/28/17.

50. Christina Wilkie (@christinawilkie), "Here's the public spreadsheet we're using to verify the records of Trump's inaugural donors. Help us! #CitizenSleuth" Twitter, 4/22/17, 5:18 p.m.

51. Alison Smale, "Ivanka Trump Is Jeered in Berlin After Defending Her Father," *NYT*, 4/25/17.

52. Drew Harwell, "Workers Endured Long Hours, Low Pay at Chinese Factory Used by Ivanka Trump's Clothing-Maker," *WaPo*, 4/25/17.

53. Michelle Castillo, "Facebook Found Fake Accounts Leaking Stolen Info to Sway Presidential Election," CNBC .com, 4/27/17.

54. Reuters, "US to Impose 20% Tariffs on Canadian Softwood Lumber: Ross," CNBC.com, 4/24/17.

55. Binyamin Appelbaum and Glenn Thrush, "Trump's Day of Hardball and Confusion on Nafta," *NYT*, 4/27/17.

56. David Nakamura and Ed O'Keefe, "Trump Administration Talks Tough on North Korea, but Frustrated Lawmakers Want Details," *WaPo*, 4/26/17.

57. Stephen J. Adler, Steve Holland, and Jeff Mason, "Exclusive: Trump Says 'Major, Major' Conflict with North Korea Possible, but Seeks Diplomacy," Reuters, 4/27/17.

58. Stephen J. Adler, Jeff Mason, and Steve Holland, "Exclusive: Trump Says He Thought Being President Would Be Easier than His Old Life," Reuters, 4/27/17.

59. Kyle Griffin (@kylegriffin1), "This happened. Trump brought printed map handouts showing his electoral college win to his Reuters interview." Twitter, 4/28/17, 7:02 a.m.

60. Natasha Bertrand (@Natasha Bertrand), ".@PhilipRucker tells @chrislhayes that Trump asked him during their 100-day interview to run the election map on the front page of WashPo." Twitter, 4/28/17, 5:10 p.m.

61. Patrick Gillespie, "Trump's 1st Economic Report Card: Slowest Growth in 3 Years," CNN.com, 4/28/17.

63. Brian Stelter, "Exclusive: Federal Probe of Fox News Expands," CNN .com, 4/27/17.

64. Brian Stelter (@brianstelter), "New CNN/ORC POLL Is Trump Honest and Trustworthy? Yes: 37% No: 61%" Twitter, 4/26/17, 6:04 p.m.

65. Chris Crowley, "Koi, in the Trump Soho, Will Close, Citing a Sharp Drop in Business," *Grub Street*, 4/26/17.

66. Chris Mooney and Juliet Eilperin, "EPA Website Removes Climate Science Site from Public View After Two Decades," *WaPo*, 4/29/17.

67. Phil McCausland, "Trump Will Hold Rally Instead of Attending White House Correspondents' Dinner," NBCNews.com, 4/22/17.

WEEK 25

1. Michael Gerson, "Trump's 100th-Day Speech May Have Been the Most Hate-Filled in Modern History," *WaPo*, 5/1/17.

2. Aaron Blake, "Trump Wants More Power and Fewer Checks and Balances—Again," *WaPo*, 5/2/17.

3. Ed Kilgore, "Trump Calls for Government Shutdown in September," *DI*, 5/2/17.

4. Julian Borger, "Donald Trump Blames Constitution for Chaos of His First 100 Days," *Guardian*, 4/30/17.

5. Christine Wang, "Trump Repeats That He's Open to Meeting Kim Jong Un, Says He 'Would be Honored to Do It," CNBC.com, 5/1/17.

6. Humeyra Pamuk, Ercan Gurses, "Turkey Fires 3,900 in Second Post-referendum Purge," Reuters, 4/29/17; *Washington Post* and Partnership for Public Service, "Tracking How Many Key Positions Trump Has Filled So Far," *WaPo*, 12/8/16 (last updated).

7. Matthew Lee and Josh Lederman, "Tillerson Surveys State Department Workers Ahead of Overhaul," AP, 5/2/17.

8. John Dickerson, "FULL TRANSCRIPT: President Donald Trump's Interview with 'Face the Nation,'" CBSNews.com, 4/30/17.

9. Eric Auchard, Bate Felix, "French Candidate Macron Claims Massive Hack as Emails Leaked," Reuters, 5/5/17.

10. Philippe Sotto, John Leicester, Raphael Satter and AP, "Macron Hit by Hack, 'Significant Amount' of Data Leaked ahead of French Election, Watchdog Says," *CT*, 5/6/17.

11. Reuters, "German Intel Chief Accuses Russia of Cyberattacks in Run Up to Election," *Haaretz*, 5/4/17.

12. Mark Landler, "Trump's 'Very Friendly' Talk with Duterte Stuns Aides and Critics Alike," *NYT*, 4/30/17.

13. Reuters, "Donald Trump Tells Duterte: 'You're Doing a Great Job', Philippines Claims," *Guardian*, 5/3/17.

14. Carol Morello and Anne Gearan, "Tillerson Says Putting Pressure on North Korea Is Just the Beginning," *WaPo*, 5/3/17.

15. Drew Harwell and Matea Gold, "While in White House, Trumps Remained Selling Points for 'Very

Special' Philippines Project," *WaPo*, 5/2/17.

16. Matthew Kupfer, "Someone Is Blinding Russian Opposition Activists with Chemicals," *Moscow Times*, 5/1/17.

17. Oren Dorell, "Mysterious Rash of Russian Deaths Casts Suspicion on Vladimir Putin," *USAT*, 5/2/17.

18. Jordain Carney and Joe Uchill, "McCain 'Looking at Other Options' to Pass Russia Sanctions," *The Hill*, 5/2/17.

19. Matt McDermott (@mattmfm), "Both this tweet (from official WH staffer) and the act it's depicting (cabinet secretary electioneering) are obvious Hatch Act violations." Twitter, 4/30/17, 3:45 p.m.; Sarah H. Sanders (@SHSanders45), ".@SecretaryRoss talks to supporters and signs autographs in PA. Glad to have him helping @POTUS #maga." Twitter, 4/29/17, 8:30 p.m.

20. Ken Meyer, "Press Corps Erupts in Cries of 'SEAN!' After Spicer Walks Out Without Taking Questions," *Mediaite*, 5/2/17.

21. Alexander Mallin, "Office of Government Ethics Wants to Know About Any Ethics Waivers for Trump Appointees," ABCNews.com, 4/29/17.

22. Jill Disis, "Ethics Office Says It Wasn't Consulted About Ivanka Trump Job," CNN.com, 5/1/17.

23. John Bowden, "Voice of America Posts Story About Ivanka Trump's New Book," *The Hill*, 5/2/17.

24. Laura Bassett, "State Department Promotes Ivanka Trump's Book in Another Ethics Blunder," *HuffPost*, 5/4/17.

25. Michael Grunwald, Andrew Restuccia, and Josh Dawsey, "Trump Starts Dismantling His Shadow Cabinet," *Politico*, 5/1/17.

26. Scott Christianson and Greg Gordon, "Billionaire Robert Mercer Did Trump a Huge Favor. Will He Get a Payback?" McClatchy, 5/1/17 (updated 11/6/17).

27. Nicholas Fandos, "Congress Allocates $120 Million for Trump Family's Security Costs," *NYT*, 5/1/17.

28. Jean Eaglesham, Juliet Chung, and Lisa Schwartz, "Trump Adviser Kushner's Undisclosed Partners Include Goldman and Soros," *WSJ*, 5/3/17.

29. Theodoric Meyer and Michael Stratford, "Trump Transition Staffers Head to K Street Despite Lobbying Ban," *Politico*, 5/3/17.

30. Gene Maddaus, "Wilbur Ross Says Syria Missile Strike Was 'After-Dinner Entertainment' at Mar-a-Lago," *Variety*, 5/1/17.

31. Paulina Firozi, "Trump Chief of Staff: 'We've Looked At' Changing Libel Laws," *The Hill*, 4/30/17.

32. Christopher Mele, "A Code Pink Protester Laughs Over a Trump Nominee and Is *Convicted*," *NYT*, 5/3/17.

33. Mark Hensch, "FCC to Investigate, 'Take Appropriate Action' on Colbert's Trump Rant," *The Hill*, 5/5/17.

34. Max Greenwood, "GOP Chairman Tells Agencies to Exclude Info from FOIA Requests," *The Hill*, 5/5/17.

35. Alana Abramson, "President Trump Was 'Directly Involved' in Hunt for Tweeter of Inauguration Crowd Photo," *Time*, 5/2/17.

36. Philip Bump, "On More than a Third of the Days Since Nov. 8, Trump Has Mentioned the Election Results," *WaPo*, 5/3/17.

37. "Trump's Fitness to Serve Is 'Officially Part of the Discussion in Congress,'" *Fresh Air*, NPR, 5/4/17.

38. Susan Kelleher, "Kent School District Halts International Field Trips over Border Concerns," *Seattle Times*, 4/29/17 (updated 5/8/17).

39. Rafael Bernal, "Trump Won't Hold White House Cinco de Mayo Celebration: Report," *The Hill*, 5/3/17.

40. Ben Kamisar, "Dem Senator Blasts Trump over Deportation of Honduran Mother," *The Hill*, 5/3/17.

41. Rafael Bernal, "Texas Police Chiefs Slam Sanctuary City Bill," *The Hill*, 5/5/17.

42. Ashley Parker and Krissah Thompson, "White House Fires Its Chief Usher—the First Woman in That Job," *WaPo*, 5/5/17.

43. Michael Stratford, "Trump Suggests Financing for Historically Black Colleges May Be Unconstitutional," *Politico*, 5/5/17.

44. Olivia Beavers, "CNN: Trump Ending Michelle Obama's Girls Education Program," *The Hill*, 5/1/17.

45. Alan Rappeport, "White House Proposes Cutting Drug Control Office Funding by 95%," *NYT*, 5/5/17.

46. *WaPo* (@washingtonpost), "Rape charges to be dropped against immigrant teens in Md. case that drew a White House rebuke" Twitter, 5/5/17, 7:27 a.m.; Brian Stelter (@brianstelter), "Fox News devoted days of coverage to this. Tied it to Trump's immigration agenda. But now police say they can't substantiate the rape claims" Twitter, 5/5/17, 9:11 a.m.

47. Sarah Westwood, "Sebastian Gorka to Accept Role Outside White House," *WE*, 4/30/17; Mitch Prothero, "The Hungarian Rise and Fall of Sebastian Gorka," *BF*, 4/26/17; Nikita Vladimiro, "Gorka: Reports About Leaving White House 'Very Fake News,'" *The Hill*, 5/4/17.

48. Lachlan Markay and Asawin Suebsaeng, "Trump and Bannon 'Personally Intervened' to Save Seb Gorka," *DB*, 5/5/17.

49. Kenneth P. Vogel, "Lewandowski's Firm Quietly Inked Deal with Venezuela-Owned Company," *Politico*, 5/3/17.

50. Vanessa Neumann, "Russia Gave to Citgo, Then Citgo Gave to Trump," *Politico*, 4/27/17.

51. Natasha Bertrand, "Memos: CEO of Russia's State Oil Company Offered Trump Adviser, Allies a Cut of Huge Deal if Sanctions Were Lifted," *BI*, 1/27/17.

52. Damien Sharkov, "Donald Trump Urged to Block Russian U.S. Oil Firm Deal," *Newsweek*, 5/4/17.

53. Jennifer Jacobs and Ben Brody, "Lewandowski Exits Lobby Firm amid Reports of Foreign Clients," Bloomberg .com, 5/4/17.

54. Aric Jenkins, "Mark Green Withdraws as Nominee for Army Secretary," *Time*, 5/5/17.

55. *MaddowBlog* (@MaddowBlog), "Trump's failure to fill key defense positions is worse than ridiculous." Twitter, 5/5/17, 6:51 p.m.

56. Aidan McLaughlin, "President Trump Reportedly Speaks to Fox News Chief Rupert Murdoch 'Almost Every Day," *Mediaite*, 5/5/17; Gabriel Sherman, "The Big Winner in Donald Trump's

Decision to Fire Preet Bharara Might Be Rupert Murdoch," *DI*, 3/12/17.

57. Matthew Rosenberg and Maggie Haberman, "Senate Asks Trump Associates for Records of Communication with Russians," *NYT*, 5/5/17.

58. Ken Dilanian, "Senate Committee Asks Carter Page to Reveal Russian Contacts," NBCNews.com, 5/5/17.

59-60. Greg Miller and Adam Entous, "Flynn Was Warned by Trump Transition Officials About Contacts with Russian Ambassador," *NYT*, 5/5/17.

61-62. Julie Pace, "Trump Transition Raised Flags About Flynn Russia Contacts," AP, 5/5/17.

63. *MaddowBlog* (@MaddowBlog), "Obama team gave Trump camp only hours notice of Russia retaliation: NBC News" Twitter, 5/5/17, 6:31 p.m.

64. Julie Pace, "Trump Transition Raised Flags About Flynn Russia Contacts," AP, 5/5/17.

65. Jim Sciutto, Manu Raju, and Pamela Brown, "Sources: Former Acting AG Yates to Contradict Administration About Flynn at Hearing," CNN.com, 5/2/17.

66. Jeremy Diamond, "Trump on Obama Wiretapping Claim: It Has 'Been Proven Very Strongly,'" CNN .com, 5/1/17.

67. Dell Cameron, "Trump 'Wiretap' Truther Rand Paul Now Thinks Obama Spied on Him, Too," *Gizmodo*, 5/5/17; Senator Rand Paul (@RandPaul), "I have formally requested from the WH and the Intel Committees info on whether I was surveilled by Obama admin and or the Intel community!" Twitter, 5/5/17, 6:12 a.m.

68. Bradd Jaffy (@BraddJaffy), "FBI Director Comey says Sally Yates did tell him about her concerns regarding Mike Flynn; also reiterates there was no spying on Trump Tower" Twitter, 5/3/17, 8:32 a.m.

69. "Annotated: Trump's Executive Order on Religious Liberty," NPR.org, 5/4/17.

70. Dave Quinn, "Cases of Beer Rolling Into U.S. Capitol Were Just One Thing That Had People Howling About Health-Care Vote," *People*, 5/5/17.

71. Mark Hensch, "GOP Rep Unaware of Health Bill's Impact on His State Despite Voting for It," *The Hill*, 5/5/17; First Amendment, "Turn On Your Phones Rep. John Faso. Face the FURY of American You Betrayed on Health Care," *DK*, 5/5/17.

72. Lindsey Ellefson, "Not Even a Preexisting Condition Kept Jason Chaffetz from Voting on the AHCA Today," *Mediaite*, 5/4/17.

73. Nikita Vladimirov, "Cook Political Report Moves 20 Districts toward Dems after ObamaCare Repeal Vote," *The Hill*, 5/5/17.

WEEK 26

1. Jon Henley and Jennifer Rankin, "Macron Defeats Le Pen in French Election," *Brexit Means* (podcast), *Guardian*, 5/10/17.

2-3. Carole Cadwalladr, "The Great British Brexit Robbery: How Our Democracy Was Hijacked," *Guardian*, 5/7/17.

4. Javier C. Hernández, Cao Li, and Jesse Drucker, "Jared Kushner's Sister Highlights Family Ties in Pitch to Chinese Investors," *NYT*, 5/6/17.

5. Cristina Alesci and Jill Disis, "Kushner Family Apologized for Mentioning White House Adviser Jared Kushner," CNN.com, 5/8/17.

6. Congcong Zhang (@daphnewelkin5), "I was threatened, harassed and forced to delete recordings and photos of The Kushner family recruiting Chinese investors in US Green cards." Twitter, 5/6/17, 8:34 a.m.

7. Natasha Bertrand, "'Outrageous' and 'Groundless': It Looks like Carter Page Is Not Going to Give the Senate What It Wants," *BI*, 5/8/17.

8. Bill Littlefield, "A Day (and a Cheeseburger) with President Trump," *Only a Game* (blog), WBUR.org, 5/5/17.

9. Leah McElrath, "House Intel Dem: Trump Family's Russian Money 'Consistent with Trump Russia Pattern,'" Shareblue Media, 5/8/17.

10. Tarini Parti, "Trump-Connected Lobbyists Are Making Millions, Even as Some Come Under Scrutiny," *BF*, 5/8/17.

11. John Bowden, "Goldman Sachs Hires Trump Campaign Official as Lobbyist: Report," *The Hill*, 5/10/17.

12. Reuters, "Democratic Senators Ask US Regulators to Look into Whether Carl Icahn Violated 'Insider Trading' Laws in Biofuels Market," CNBC.com.

13. Rebecca Morin, "Commerce Secretary Warns Canada Against 'Retaliatory Action' on Lumber Tariff," *Politico*, 5/6/17.

14. Nikki Haley (@nikkihaley), "Our statement on the humanitarian and human rights situation in Venezuela:" Twitter, 5/6/17, 7:34 a.m.

15. U.S. Dept. of State, "May 2017 Department Press Briefings (DPB) and Policy Briefings," www.state.gov/r/pa /prs/dpb/2017/05.

16. Rebecca Savransky, "Rahm Emanuel Revives Deleted EPA Climate Change Webpage," *The Hill*, 5/6/17; U.S. Environmental Protection Agency, "Climate Change," climatechange .cityofchicago.org.

17. Mallory Shelbourne, "Trump Call for Muslim Ban Deleted from Site After Reporter's Question," *The Hill*, 5/8/17.

18. NBC *Nightly News* with Lester Holt (@NBCNightlyNews), "WATCH: This Indiana company, Rexnord, is shipping jobs to Mexico, despite Pres. Trump's tweet." Twitter, 5/7/17, 5:13 p.m.; Donald Trump (@realDonaldTrump), "Rexnord of Indiana made a deal during the Obama Administration to move to Mexico. Fired their employees. Tax product big that's sold in U.S." Twitter, 5/7/17, 3:58 p.m.

19. Cyra Master, "Trump Voters Lament Deportation of Their Neighbor," *The Hill*, 5/7/17.

20. Alicia A. Caldwell, "AP Exclusive: US Digs for Evidence of Haiti Immigrant Crimes," AP, 5/9/17.

21. Liam Stack, "Texas Bill Would Let Adoption Agencies Reject Families on Religion Grounds," *NYT*, 5/11/17.

22. Christopher Mele, "Reporter Arrested in West Virginia After Persistently Asking Questions of Tom Price," *NYT*, 5/10/17.

23. Andrew Joseph, "Tom Price Commends West Virginia Officers Who Arrested Journalist Asking Questions," *STAT*, 5/10/17.

24. Coral Davenport, "E.P.A. Dismisses Members of Major Scientific Review Board," *NYT*, 5/7/17.

25. Devin Henry, "Two EPA Science Board Members Resign in Protest," *The Hill*, 5/12/17.

26. Katherine Faulders and Alexander Mallin, "President Trump Launches Commission on 'Election Integrity,'" ABCNews.com, 5/11/17.

27. Jesse Lehrich (@JesseLehrich), "'It's only been 54 years since we were jailed, beaten, & killed for trying to cast a vote.'—@repjohnlewis on new 'voter fraud' commission." Twitter, 5/12/17, 10:43 a.m.

28. Sari Horwitz and Matt Zapotosky, "Sessions Issues Sweeping New Criminal Charging Policy," *WaPo*, 5/12/17.

29. Brooke Singman, "ICE Arrests 1,378 Suspected Gang Members in Largest Sweep to Date," FoxNews.com, 5/11/17.

30. Donald Trump (@realDonaldTrump), "China just agreed that the U.S. will be allowed to sell beef, and other major products, into China once again. This is REAL news!" Twitter, 5/12/17, 6:20 a.m.; U.S. Dept. of Agriculture, "China Moves to Reopen Market to U.S. Beef," press release, 9/22/16, www.usda.gov/media/press-releases/2016/09/22/china-moves-reopen-market-us-beef.

31. Kate Brannen, "The Knives Are Out for Lt. Gen. H.R. McMaster," *FP*, 5/9/17.

32. Alayna Treene, "'A Lot of What We Do . . . Is Trying to Keep Up with the President,'" *Axios*, 5/12/17.

34. Joe Concha, "CNN Anchors Liken Trump's Yates Tweets to 'Witness Intimidation,'" *The Hill*, 5/8/17.

35. Amber Phillips, "5 Things We Learned from Sally Yates's Testimony on What the White House Knew About Michael Flynn," *WaPo*, 5/8/17.

36–37. Riley Beggin and Veronica Stracqualursi, "A Timeline of Sally Yates' Warnings to the White House About Mike Flynn," ABCNews.com, 5/8/17.

38. John Bowden, "Graham Wants Panel to Look into Trump's Business Dealings: Report," *The Hill*, 5/9/17.

39. Emily Tillett, "Trump's Claim Flynn's Security Clearance Was from Obama Administration," CBSNews.com, 5/9/17; Peter Alexander (@PeterAlexander), "NEW: Flynn never received broader security clearance needed to serve as Natl Security Advisor before his firing. via @KenDilanianNBC" Twitter, 5/8/17, 11:07 a.m.

40. Amy Siskind (@Amy_Siskind), "7 tweets on #SallyYates and Russia today—AND a new Twitter cover. @realDonaldTrump thou doth protest too much! #PutinPuppet" Twitter, 5/8/17, 6:46 p.m.; Donald Trump (@realDonaldTrump), "China just agreed that the U.S. will be allowed to sell beef, and other major products, into China once again. This is REAL news!" Twitter, 5/12/17, 6:20 a.m.

41. Alex Ward, "Trump: James Clapper Said I Have No Russia Connections. Clapper: No I Didn't," *Vox*, 5/12/17.

42. Peter Elkind, "James Comey's Testimony on Huma Abedin Forwarding Emails Was Inaccurate," *ProPublica*, 5/8/17.

43. Tom LoBianco, "First on CNN: Senate Russia Investigators Ask Treasury for Trump Team Financial Information," CNN.com, 5/10/17.

44. Shane Harris and Carol E. Lee, "Financial-Crimes Monitor to Share Records in Trump-Russia Probe," *WSJ*, 5/12/17.

45. Chris Smith, "Inside Trump's Coming War with the F.B.I.," *VF*, 5/11/17.

46. US Attorney SDNY (@SDNYnews), "Acting USAtty Kim: We will not allow the US financial system to be used to launder proceeds of crimes committed anywhere-here or in Russia" Twitter, 5/12/17, 6:51 p.m.

47. Gene Sperling (@genebsperling), "Wow. 178 Former US Attorneys & Asst US Attorneys of SDNY just wrote a bipartisan letter today to Deputy AG calling for a Special Prosecutor" Twitter, 5/12/17, 7:21 p.m.

48. Pete Madden and Matthew Mosk, "Donald Trump's Tax Law Firm Has 'Deep' Ties to Russia," ABCNews.com, 5/12/17.

49. Pamela Engel, "The Deputy Attorney General Laid Out Why James Comey Was Fired," *BI*, 5/9/17.

50. Euan McKirdy, "Preet Bharara, Sally Yates and James Comey: Fired While Investigating Donald Trump," CNN.com, 5/10/17; Laura Jarrett, "Longtime DOJ Official Overseeing Trump-Russia Probe to Step Down," CNN.com, 4/21/17.

51. Evan Perez, Shimon Prokupecz, and Pamela Brown, "CNN Exclusive: Grand Jury Subpoenas Issued in FBI's Russia Investigation," CNN.com, 5/10/17.

52. Phil McCausland, "Senate Intel Committee Subpoenas Michael Flynn," NBCNews.com, 5/11/17.

53. Quinnipiac Poll, 5/10/17, https://poll.qu.edu/national/release-detail?ReleaseID=2456.

54. Ali Vitali, Abigail Williams, and Halimah Abdullah, "Trump and Lavrov Meet amid Scrutiny of Campaign, Russia Ties," NBCNews.com, 5/10/17.

55. Mark Hensch, "Russia Diplomat Appears to Scold NBC News's Andrea Mitchell," *The Hill*, 4/12/17.

56. Matt Novak (@paleofuture), "Photos of Trump's meeting with Lavrov and Kislyak just hit the Getty wire and they're all credited to Russian news agency TASS" Twitter, 5/10/17, 8:37 a.m.

57. Jim Sciutto (@jimsciutto), "WH readout of Lavrov meeting does not mention Kislyak. W/o Russian MFA photos, would not know he was there. Convos w/him got Flynn fired." Twitter, 5/11/17, 9:22 a.m.

58. Susan B. Glasser, "Russia's Oval Office Victory Dance," *Politico*, 5/10/17.

59. Jo Uchill, "Senate Intel Committee Invites Comey to Testify Next Week," *The Hill*, 5/10/17.

60. Matthew Rosenberg and Matt Apuzzo, "Days Before Firing, Comey Asked for More Resources for Russia Inquiry," *NYT*, 5/10/17.

61. Michael Hayden, "When Trump's Washington Starts to Resemble Nicaragua," *The Hill*, 5/10/17.

62. Edward Luce, "Comey Falls Victim to Trump's Tuesday Night Massacre," *FT*, 5/9/17.

63. "Rod Rosenstein's Letter Recommending Comey Be Fired," BBC News, 5/10/17.

64. Elizabeth Landers (@ElizLanders), "@VP said 7 times yesterday during presser on the hill that @POTUS fired Comey b/c of 'recommendation of deputy attorney general.'" Twitter, 5/11/17, 10:15 a.m.

65. Philip Rucker, Ashley Parker, Sari Horwitz, and Robert Costa, "Inside Trump's Anger and Impatience—and His Sudden Decision to Fire Comey," *WaPo*, 5/10/17.

66. Devlin Barrett and Philip Rucker, "Trump Said He Was Thinking of

Russia Controversy When He Decided to Fire Comey," *WaPo*, 5/11/17.

67. Philip Rucker, Ashley Parker, Sari Horwitz, and Robert Costa, "Inside Trump's Anger and Impatience—and His Sudden Decision to Fire Comey," *WaPo*, 5/10/17.

68. "Comey Infuriated Trump with Refusal to Preview Senate Testimony: Aides," Reuters, 5/10/17.

69. Maggie Haberman, Glenn Thrush, Michael S. Schmidt, and Peter Baker, "'Enough Was Enough': How Festering Anger at Comey Ended in His Firing," *NYT*, 5/10/17.

70–71. Shane Harris and Carol E. Lee, "Comey's Firing Came as Investigators Stepped Up Russia Probe," *WSJ*, 5/10/17.

72. Mallory Shelbourne, "20 Attorneys General Call for Independent Investigation on Russia," *The Hill*, 5/11/17.

73. Mark Hensch, "Trump Scraps Visit to FBI Headquarters: Report," *The Hill*, 5/11/17.

74. Tim Johnson, Peter Stone, and David Goldstein, "Sources: Comey Sought to Expand Trump-Russia Probe of Former Campaign Officials," McClatchy, 5/11/17.

75. *Rachel Maddow Show*, 5/11/17.

76–77. Michael Rothfeld, Mark Maremont, and Rebecca Davis O'Brien, "Former Trump Adviser Paul Manafort's Bank Records Sought in Probe," *WSJ*, 5/12/17.

78. Steve Kopack (@SteveKopack), "WASHINGTON (AP)—Acting FBI Director Andrew McCabe tells Senate panel he will not update the White House on the Russia investigation." Twitter, 5/11/17, 8:27 a.m.

79. Phil Mattingly (@Phil_Mattingly), "McCabe blows up central WH talking point/rationale: 'The vast majority of employees enjoyed a deep, positive connection to Director Comey.'" Twitter, 5/11/17, 8:33 a.m.

80. AP Politics (@AP_Politics), "BREAKING: Acting FBI director calls Trump-Russia investigation 'highly significant,' contradicting White House claim" Twitter, 5/11/17, 8:46 a.m.

81. Alexandra Wilts, "Donald Trump Claims James Comey Assured Him 'Three Times' That He Was Not Under FBI Investigation," *Independent* (UK), 5/11/17; Kyle Griffin (@kylegriffin1), "COLLINS: Is it standard practice to inform someone that they're NOT the subject of a probe? McCABE: 'It is not.' —via @MSNBC" Twitter, 5/11/17, 8:46 a.m.

82. Ali Watkins, "Rosenstein Meets with Senate Intel Leaders After Comey Firing," *Politico*, 5/11/17.

83. Betsy Woodruff (@woodruffbets), "Sarah Flores, DOJ spox, says Burr asked for this meeting w Rosenstein before Comey's firing and is 'nothing unusual'" Twitter, 5/11/17, 9:28 a.m.

84. Michael S. Schmidt, "In a Private Dinner, Trump Demanded Loyalty. Comey Demurred," *NYT*, 5/11/17.

85. Ken Dilanian and Pete Williams, "My Dinner with Comey: Clapper, Others Dispute Trump Account of Meeting with FBI Director," NBCNews.com, 5/12/17.

86. Kartikay Mehrotra, "Trump Ordered to Turn Over Giuliani Memo in Travel Ban Suit," Bloomberg.com, 5/11/17.

87. Donald Trump (@realDonald Trump), "James Comey better hope that there are no 'tapes' of our conversations before he starts leaking to the press!" Twitter, 5/12/17, 5:26 a.m.

88. Pamela Brown, "Source: Comey Is 'Not Worried About Any Tapes,'" CNN.com, 5/12/17.

89. Michael Beschloss (@BeschlossDC), "Presidents are supposed to have stopped routinely taping visitors without their knowledge when Nixon's taping system was revealed in 1973." Twitter, 5/12/17, 5:59 a.m.

90. Rebecca Shabad, "Top Democrats Demand Any 'Tapes,' All Communications Between Trump and James Comey," CBSNews.com, 5/12/17.

91. Max Greenwood, "Chaffetz Asks Justice Department to Investigate Comey Firing," *The Hill*, 5/10/17.

92. Saba Hamedy, "Feinstein, Durbin Call on Rosenstein to Resign if No Special Prosecutor Is Named," CNN, 5/12/17.

93. CNBC (@CNBC), "JUST IN: Trump to welcome President Erdogan of Turkey to Washington on May 16, White House says. http://cnbc.com" Twitter, 5/10/17, 4:30 p.m.

WEEK 27

1. Alexandra Berzon, "Former Employees of Donald Trump Say They Saw Him Tape Conversations," *WSJ*, 5/13/17.

2. "Cooking Up an Economic Policy," *Economist*, 5/13/17.

3. Alexandra King, "Gen. Hayden: I've Changed My Mind About Special Prosecutors," CNN.com, 5/15/17.

4. Olivia Beavers, "Torch-Carrying White Nationalists Protest Removal of Confederate Statue," *The Hill*, 5/14/17.

5. "Angela Merkel's CDU 'Seizes Key State from Rivals," BBC News, 5/14/17.

6. Mark Murray, "NBC/*WSJ*: Just 29 Percent Approve of Trump's Firing of James Comey," NBCNews.com, 5/14/17.

7. Martha Ross, "Melania Trump Celebrated Mother's Day with Barron While Donald Trump Went Golfing," *Mercury News*, 5/15/17.

8. Daniel Dale (@ddale8), "An unusual Trump administration statement on North Korea—it begins with a Russian perspective." Twitter, 5/13/17, 7:50 p.m.

9. Chas Danner, "Comey Declines Invitation to Testify, Several Candidates Are Being Considered to Replace Him," *DI*, 5/13/17.

10. Drew Harwell and David A. Fahrenthold, "At Mar-a-Lago, the Star Power of the Presidency Helps Charities—and Trump—Make More Money," *WaPo*, 5/13/17.

11. Mike Allen, "Scoop: Trump, Irked at Cabinet and Staff, Mulls Sweeping Shake-up," *Axios*, 5/14/17.

12. Juliet Eilperin, "Under Trump, Inconvenient Data Is Being Sidelined," *WaPo*, 5/14/17.

13. Daniella Silva, "James Clapper: Our Institutions 'Are Under Assault' Both Externally and Internally," NBCNews .com, 5/14/17.

14. Nancy Solomon, "GOP Congressman Frelinghuysen Targets Activist in Letter to Her Employer," WNYC.org, 5/15/17.

15. Natasha Bertrand (@Natasha Bertrand), "Carter Page's latest letter is addressed to Rosenstein and includes Maroon 5 lyrics. Which he cites in the footnotes." Twitter, 5/15/17, 7:11 a.m.

16. Rachel Manteuffel, "When President Trump's Bodyguard Revealed Jim

Mattis's Private Cellphone Number," WaPo, 5/15/17.

17. Josh Gerstein, "Russian Oligarch Deripaska Sues AP for Libel," *Politico*, 5/16/17.

18. Tom Philpott, "Trump's EPA Greenlights a Nasty Chemical. A Month Later, It Poisons a Bunch of Farmworkers," *MJ*, 5/15/17.

19. Vivian Salama and AP, "Trump Meets with UAE Crown Prince Ahead of Overseas Trip," *USN*, 5/15/17.

20–21. Greg Miller and Greg Jaffe, "Trump Revealed Highly Classified Information to Russian Foreign Minister and Ambassador," *WaPo*, 5/15/17.

22. Jim Dalrymple II and Jason Leopold, "Trump Revealed Highly Classified Information to Russians during White House Visit," *BF*, 5/15/17.

23. Matthew Rosenberg and Eric Schmitt, "Trump Revealed Highly Classified Intelligence to Russia, in Break with Ally, Officials Say," *NYT*, 5/15/17; "White House Denies Reports of Classified Leaks to Russia," *Nightly News*, NBCNews.com, 5/15/17.

24. Donald Trump (@realDonaldTrump), "As President I wanted to share with Russia (at an openly scheduled W.H. meeting) which I have the absolute right to do, facts pertaining. . . ." Twitter, 5/16/17, 4:03 a.m.; Donald Trump (@realDonaldTrump), ". . . to terrorism and airline flight safety. Humanitarian reasons, plus I want Russia to greatly step up their fight against ISIS & terrorism." Twitter, 5/16/17, 4:13 a.m.; Donald Trump (@realDonaldTrump), "I have been asking Director Comey & others, from the beginning of my administration, to find the LEAKERS in the intelligence community. . . . ." Twitter, 5/16/17, 5:10 a.m.

25. Donald Trump (@realDonald Trump), "As President I wanted to share with Russia (at an openly scheduled W.H. meeting) which I have the absolute right to do, facts pertaining. . . ." Twitter, 5/16/17, 4:03 a.m.; Michael McFaul (@McFaul), "You do not have the right to leak classified information obtained from other countries, without their permission." Twitter, 5/16/17, 6:44 a.m.

26. AP (@AP), "BREAKING: European official to AP: Country might stop sharing intel with US if Trump gave classified info to Russian diplomats." Twitter, 5/16/17, 6:21 a.m.

27. Michael Beschloss (@BeschlossDC), "McMaster confirms that Trump made decision to give highly classified intelligence to the Russians on spur of moment." Twitter, 5/16/17, 9:01 a.m.; Josh Rogin (@joshrogin), "McMaster: "The president wasn't even aware of where this information came from. #facepalm" Twitter, 5/16/17, 9:05 a.m.

28. Adam Goldman, Eric Schmitt, and Peter Baker, "Israel Said to Be Source of Secret Intelligence Trump Gave to Russians," *NYT*, 5/16/17.

29. Sheera Frenkel, "Israeli Official: Trump Sharing Intelligence with Russia Is 'Worst Fears Confirmed,'" *BF*, 5/16/17.

30. Brian Ross, James Gordon Meek, and Randy Kreider, "Trump's Disclosure Endangered Spy Placed Inside ISIS by Israel, Officials Say," ABCNews.com, 5/16/17.

31. Shane Harris, Carol E. Lee, and Paul Sonne, "Israel Provided Intelligence Trump Shared with Russia, Officials Say," *WSJ*, 5/16/17.

32. Emily Shugerman, "More Americans Support Trump's Impeachment than Oppose It for First Time, Poll Finds," *Independent* (UK), 5/16/17.

33. Adam Edelman, "Trump Meets Turkish President Recep Erdogan at White House," *NYDN*, 5/17/17.

34. Amerika'nın Sesi (@VOATurkish), "#Erdoğan'ın korumaları kavgaya karıştı http://ow.ly/U23u30b MRLv#amerikaninsesi" Twitter, 5/16/17, 5:00 p.m.; Julia Manchester, "Video Shows Turkey's Erdogan Watched His Guards Clash with Protesters," *The Hill*, 5/18/17.

35. Stephen Gutowski, "D.C. Police Chief Says Diplomatic Immunity Could Hinder Pursuit of Turkish Officials Involved in Attack on Protesters," *Washington Free Beacon*, 5/17/17.

36. Amanda Holpuch, "John McCain: Turkish Ambassador Should Be 'Thrown Out' for Violence," *Guardian*, 5/18/17.

37. Ceren Borazan (@CerenBorazan), "Dear @POTUS I'm being attackd in this photo. I was assaulted by this man, strangled for protesting. Please help me find & prosecute this man" Twitter, 5/18/17, 4:21 p.m.

38. Mark Hensch, "State Dept Summons Turkish Ambassador over DC Brawl," *The Hill*, 5/19/17.

39. Peter W. Singer (@peterwsinger), "The @VP account tweeted this, then deleted it, after @DionNissenbaum reported how it showed Erdogan + @POTUS son in laws in govt positions" Twitter, 5/16/17, 4:06 p.m.

40–42. Michael S. Schmidt, "Comey Memo Says Trump Asked Him to End Flynn Investigation," *NYT*, 5/16/17.

43. Devlin Barrett, Ellen Nakashima, and Matt Zapotosky, "Notes Made by FBI Director Comey Say Trump Pressured Him to End Flynn Probe," *WaPo*, 5/16/17.

44. Joe Concha, "Fox Host: No Republicans 'Willing to Go on Camera' After Comey Memo," *The Hill*, 5/16/17; Ed O'Keefe (@edatpost), "Wow: @CBSThisMorning says it asked 20 GOP lawmakers to be a guest this AM to talk about Trump. And asked the WH for someone. ALL declined." Twitter, 5/17/17, 4:16 a.m.

45. Joe Concha, "Russia on Trump Leak Reports: Don't Read American Newspapers," *The Hill*, 5/16/17.

46. Reuters Top News (@Reuters), "LATEST: Russia's Putin says he can give record of Trump and Lavrov conversation to U.S. congress and senate http://reut.rs/2reyeFv" Twitter, 5/17/17, 4:27 a.m.

47. Tom Winter and Kenzi Abou-Sabe, "Feds Subpoena Records for $3.5M Mystery Mortgage on Manafort's Home," NBCNews.com, 5/16/17.

48. Kyle Griffin (@kylegriffin1), "New: Democratic Senators incl. Heinrich and Warren are calling for an investigation into Attorney General Jeff Sessions" Twitter, 5/17/17, 6:50 a.m.

49. Benjamin Haddad (@benjaminhad dad), "The French Prime Minister, economics minister and national security adviser are experts on Germany. Tells you something." Twitter, 5/17/17, 8:33 a.m.

50. Gabe Ortiz, "An Immigrant Committed Suicide While in Detention This Week—or According to ICE, 'Passed Away,'" *DK*, 5/16/17.

51. Ryan Devereaux (@rdevro), "New data on ICE arrests just released. 41,000 arrests in Trump's first 100 days, increase of 37.6 percent over the same period in 2016." Twitter, 5/17/17, 8:21 a.m.

52. John Harwood, "Trump's Favorite Tools—Hyperbole and Exaggeration—Turn into Traps," CNBC.com, 5/17/17.

53. Rob Barry, Christopher S. Stewart, and Brett Forrest, "Russian State-Run Bank Financed Deal Involving Trump Hotel Partner," *WSJ*, 5/17/17.

54. Charlie May, "Trump's Coast Guard Commencement Speech: 'No Politician in History' Has Been Treated So 'Unfairly,'" *Salon*, 5/17/17.

55. Jeremy Diamond and Laura Jarrett, "Special Counsel Appointed in Russia Probe," CNN.com, 5/18/17.

56. Sari Horwitz, Karoun Demirjian, and Elise Viebeck, "Rosenstein Defends His Controversial Memo Used to Justify Trump's Firing of Comey," *WaPo*, 5/19/17.

57. Jonathan Karl (@jonkarl), "The White House was blinded by the Special Counsel announcement—given only about a 30-minute heads up" Twitter, 5/17/17, 3:10 p.m.

58. Brian Stelter, "White House PR Strategy in Chaos: Conway Interview Offered to Fox, then Canceled," CNN .com, 5/18/17.

59–60. Adam Entous, "House Majority Leader to Colleagues in 2016: 'I Think Putin Pays' Trump," *WaPo*, 5/17/17.

61. Ibid.; Josh Dawsey (@jdawsey1), "Spokespeople for Ryan and McCarthy denied this happened. Post told them they had audio. They changed their tunes!" Twitter, 5/17/17, 3:04 p.m.

62. Bill Allison, "Pence Takes Steps to Build War Chest as White House Stumbles," Bloomberg.com, 5/17/17.

63. Matthew Rosenberg and Mark Mazzetti, "Trump Team Knew Flynn Was Under Investigation Before He Came to White House," *NYT*, 5/17/17.

64. Matthew Nussbaum, "Pence Stands by Claim He Didn't Know About Flynn Lobbying Investigation," *Politico*, 5/18/17; Dr. Dena Grayson (@DrDenaGrayson), "Pence lied saying he didn't know #Flynn lobbied for foreign govt/paid by #Russia. Yet Rep Cummings told Pence about BOTH in NOVEMBER." Twitter, 5/4/17, 8:24 a.m.

65–67. Matthew Rosenberg and Mark Mazzetti, "Trump Team Knew Flynn Was Under Investigation Before He Came to White House," *NYT*, 5/17/17.

68–69. Tom Winter and Ken Dilanian, "Flynn, Manafort Are Key Figures in Russia Probe Mueller Will Lead," NBCNews.com, 5/17/17.

70. Vera Bergengruen, "Flynn Stopped Military Plan Turkey Opposed—after Being Paid as Its Agent," McClatchy, 5/17/17.

71–73. Ned Parker, Jonathan Landay, and Warren Strobel, "Exclusive: Trump Campaign Had at Least 18 Undisclosed Contacts with Russians; Sources," Reuters, 5/18/17.

74. Michael Isikoff, "As Investigators Circled Flynn, He Got a Message from Trump: Stay Strong," *YN*, 5/18/17.

75. Ali Rogin and Veronica Stracqualursi, "Senate Intel Chair Backtracks on Claim Flynn Won't Honor Subpoena," ABCNews.com, 5/18/17.

76. Maggie Haberman and Glenn Thrush, "Advisers Urge Trump to Hire Outside Lawyer in Russia Inquiry," *NYT*, 5/18/17.

77. Massimo Calabresi, "Inside Russia's Social Media War on America," *Time*, 5/18/17.

78. Jake Sherman and Rachael Bade, "Chaffetz to Announce Early Departure from Congress," *Politico*, 5/19/17.

79. Chris Riotta, "Will Trump Be Removed from Office? White House Aides Begin Looking for New Jobs During Russia Scandal," *Newsweek*, 5/18/17.

80. Austin Wright, Elana Schor, Seung Min Kim, and Burgess Everett, "Senators: Rosenstein Knew Comey Would Be Fired before Writing Memo," *Politico*, 5/18/17.

81. Donald Trump (@realDonald Trump), "This is the single greatest witch hunt of a politician in American history!" Twitter, 5/18/17.

82. Julian Borger, Lauren Gambino, Ben Jacobs, and Lois Beckett, "Trump Denies Collusion with Russia but Says He 'Speaks for Himself,'" *Guardian*, 5/19/17.

83. Kyle Griffin (@kylegriffin1), "Rosenstein releases opening remarks from briefings—says: 'My memorandum is not a statement of reasons to justify a for-cause termination.'" Twitter, 5/19/17, 8:46 a.m.

84. Kyle Griffin (@kylegriffin1), "Powerful final message from Elijah Cummings: 'This is about the fight for the soul of our democracy. We cannot afford to lose this one.'" Twitter, 5/19/17, 9:32 a.m.

85–86. Michael S. Schmidt, "Comey, Unsettled by Trump, Is Said to Have Wanted Him Kept at a Distance," *NYT*, 5/18/17.

87. Devlin Barrett, Ellen Nakashima, and Adam Entous, "Comey Prepared Extensively for His Conversations with Trump," *WaPo*, 5/18/17.

88. Michael S. Schmidt, "Comey, Unsettled by Trump, Is Said to Have Wanted Him Kept at a Distance," *NYT*, 5/18/17.

89. Mark Landler, Eric Scmitt, and Matt Apuzzo, "$110 Billion Weapons Sale to Saudis Has Jared Kushner's Personal Touch," *NYT*, 5/18/17.

90. Tom LoBianco, "First on CNN: Devin Nunes Continues Reviewing Russia Intelligence, Despite Recusal," CNN.com, 5/18/17.

91. Vaughn Hillyard, "VP Mike Pence Was Never Informed About Flynn: Source," NBCNews.com, 5/19/17; Elizabeth Landers, "Pence Is a Loyal Soldier, but News Cycle Is Wearing on Him," CNN.com, 5/19/17.

92. "In 298 Days, President Trump Has Made 1,628 False and Misleading Claims," *WaPo*, updated 11/13/17.

93. Lachlan Markay (@lachlan), "Someone edited Wikipedia to remove Trump from Joe Lieberman's law firm's list of clients. Check out the same acct's last edit, 1 of 2 others" Twitter, 5/18/17, 7:42 p.m.

94. Ana Marie Cox (@anamariecox), "How is this real life?" Twitter, 5/19/17, 7:05 a.m.

95. Cristina Marcos, "First Republicans Talk Possibility of Impeachment for Trump," *The Hill*, 5/17/17.

96. Mark Murray (@mmurraypolitics), "Spicer responds to NYT/Comey/Russia story in stmt to @PeterAlexander—accuses Comey of 'grandstanding' and 'politicizing' Russia probe" Twitter, 5/19/17, 12:21 p.m.

97-98. Matt Apuzzo, Maggie Haberman, and Matthew Rosenberg, "Trump Told Russians That Firing 'Nut Job' Comey Eased Pressure from Investigation," *NYT*, 5/19/17.

99. Devlin Barrett and Matt Zapotosky, "Russia Probe Reaches Current White House Official, People Familiar with the Case Say," *NYT*, 5/19/17.

100. Julia Edwards Ainsley, "White House Looking at Ethics Rule to Weaken Special Investigation: Sources," Reuters, 5/19/17.

101. Andrew Buncombe and Mythili Sampathkumar, "Donald Trump's Son-in-Law Jared Kushner 'Person of Interest in Russia Investigation,'" *Independent* (UK), 5/19/17.

102. Gloria Borger, Pamela Brown, Jim Sciutto, Marshall Cohen, and Eric Lichtblau, "First on CNN: Russian Officials Bragged They Could Use Flynn to Influence Trump, Sources Say," CNN.com, 5/19/17.

103. Damian Paletta, "Trump's Pick for Treasury Second-in-Command Withdraws from Consideration," *WaPo*, 5/19/17.

104. Jim Acosta (@Acosta), "Talked to a former Trump campaign staffer who has hired attorney in Russia probe and feels Trump himself should help pay for legal costs . . ." Twitter, 5/19/17, 7:52 p.m.

105. Laura Rozen (@lrozen), Twitter, 5/19/17, 12:07 p.m.

WEEK 28

1. Julie Bykowicz, "Trump Attorney Didn't Want Him to Sign Financial Disclosure," AP, 5/19/17.

2. Eric Lipton, "White House Moves to Block Ethics Inquiry into Ex-lobbyists on Payroll," *NYT*, 5/22/17; Eric Lipton, "White House Backs Down on Keeping Ethics Waivers Secret," *NYT*, 5/26/17.

3/4. Lydia Wheeler, "GOP Talks of Narrowing 'Blue-Ship' Rule for Judges," *The Hill*, 5/20/17.

5. Tovia Smith, "As White Supremacists Push onto Campuses, Schools Wrestle with Response" *All Things Considered*, NPR, 5/12/17.

6. Mallory Shelbourne, "Chaffetz: Jail Individuals Leaking Information," *The Hill*, 5/21/17.

7. Jonathan Swan, "Trump Wanted to Veto Bill to Keep Government Open," *Axios*, 5/21/17.

8. Ryan Dezember, "Saudi Arabia's $20 Billion Wager with Blackstone Is Record-Sized Bet on U.S. Infrastructure," *MarketWatch*, 5/21/17.

9. Kate Bennett, "Saudis, UAE Pledged $100 Million to Ivanka Trump-Proposed Fund," CNN.com, 5/21/17.

10. Barak Ravid, "Trump Tells Netanyahu He 'Never Mentioned' Israel in Intel Leak to Russians," *Haaretz*, 5/22/17.

11. Robbie Gramer, "Israel Changed Intelligence Sharing with U.S. After Trump Comments to Russia," *FP*, 5/24/17.

12. Reuters, "Turkey Summons US Envoy over Washington Street Brawl," CNBC.com, 5/23/17.

13. Marc Caputo, "Amid Complicated Relations with U.S., Turkey Hires Longtime Trump Lobbyist Brian Ballard," *Politico*, 5/22/17.

14. Dave Lawler, "Trump Praised Duterte for 'Great Job' on Drugs, Per Transcript," *Axios*, 5/23/17.

15. AP, "Trump Reveals Location of 2 Nuclear Submarines to Philippines' President," *LAT*, 5/24/17.

16. David Smith and Ewen MacAskill, "US Leak of Manchester Attacker's Name Strikes New Blow to Intelligence Sharing," *Guardian*, 5/23/17.

17. "Manchester Attack: Police Not Sharing Information with US," BBC News, 5/25/17; BBC Breaking News (@BBCBreaking), "UK police investigating Manchester attack to resume sharing intelligence with the US, BBC understands http://bbc.in/2rVku08" Twitter, 5/25/17, 1:11 p.m.

18. Manu Raju and Jeremy Herb, "Senate Intel Leaders: Door Open to Holding Flynn in Contempt After Invoking Fifth Amendment," CNN.com, 5/22/17.

19. Shane Savitsky, "Christie Says He Warned Trump Not to Hire Flynn," *Axios*, 5/22/17.

20. Seung Min Kim, "Sessions' Senate Testimony Canceled This Week," *Politico*, 5/22/17.

21. Alex Moe, Courtney Kube, Ken Dilanian, and Kasie Hunt, "Flynn 'Lied to Investigators' About Russia Trip, Says Top House Dem," NBCNews.com, 5/23/17.

22. Pamela Brown and Shimon Prokupecz, "First on CNN: Mueller Briefed on Secret Comey Memos, Source Says," CNN.com, 5/22/17.

23-25. Adam Entous and Ellen Nakashima, "Trump Asked Intelligence Chiefs to Push Back Against FBI Collusion Probe After Comey Revealed Its Existence," *WaPo*, 5/22/17.

26. Shane Harris, "Democratic Senator Asks NSA for Security Details on Trump's Russia Meeting," *WSJ*, 5/22/17.

27. Kenneth P. Vogel, "FEC Member Urges Escalated Trump-Russia Inquiry," *Politico*, 5/23/17.

28. Matthew Rosenberg, Adam Goldman, and Matt Apuzzo, "Top Russian Officials Discussed How to Influence Trump Aides Last Summer," *NYT*, 5/24/17.

29-30. Greg Miller, "CIA Director Alerted FBI to Pattern of Contacts Between Russian Officials and Trump Campaign Associates," *WaPo*, 5/23/17.

30-31. Matt Zapotosky and Matea Gold, "Justice Department Ethics Experts Clear Mueller to Lead Russia Probe," *WaPo*, 5/23/17.

32. Katie Bo Williams, "Senate Intel Panel Issues Subpoenas to Flynn Businesses," *The Hill*, 5/23/17.

33. Natasha Bertrand (@Natasha Bertrand), "Senate Intel Committee votes to give Burr and Warner blanket authority to issue subpoenas in Russia probe as they deem necessary." Twitter, 5/25/17, 1:23 p.m.

34. Robert Costa, "Senate Intelligence Committee Requests Trump Campaign Documents," *WaPo*, 5/26/17.

35. Sharon Begley, "Trump Wasn't Always So Linguistically Challenged. What Could Explain the Change?" *STAT*, 5/23/17.

36. Jerome Corsi (@jerome_corsi), "Jerome Corsi, Washington Bureau Chief, http://Infowars.com. We have WH PRESS CREDENTIALS. I'm in WH May 22, 2017" Twitter, 5/22/17, 7:41 a.m.

37. Jacqueline Thomsen, "National Endowment for the Humanities Chairman Announces Resignation," *The Hill*, 5/22/17.

38. Michael Stratford and Kimberly Hefling, "Top Education Dept. Official Resigns After Clash with DeVos," *Politico*, 5/24/17.

39. Lawrence H. Summers, "Trump Budget Is Simply Ludicrous," *WaPo*, 5/23/17.

40. Matea Gold, "Trumps 'Huuuuuuge' Caribbean Estate Is on the Market for $28 Million, Prompting Questions," *WaPo*, 5/21/17.

41. Eric Lipton, Steve Eder, and Ben Protess, "With a Presidential Boost, the P.G.A. Comes to Trump National," *NYT*, 5/26/17.

42. Mario Parker, "Icahn Guides Trump's Policy and Scores $60 Million," Bloomberg.com, 5/24/17.

43. Nicole Hensley, "Rudy Giuliani Tries Covering Up His Role in Crafting Trump's 'Muslim Ban,'" *NYDN*, 5/24/17.

44. Jennifer Bendery, "Betsy DeVos: If States Discriminate Against LGBTQ Students, It's Cool by Me," *HuffPost*, 5/24/17.

45. Ari Melber, Meredith Mandell, and Diana Marinaccio, "Trump Failing to Track Foreign Cash at His Hotels," NBCNews.com, 5/24/17; Ari Melber (@AriMelber), "Important because: Constitution bans foreign gov gifts Courts will rule on how that impacts Trump Trump Org not even tracking all foreign $" Twitter, 5/24/17, 9:29 a.m.; Ari Melber, Meredith Mandell, and Diana Marinaccio, "Trump Failing to Track Foreign Cash at His Hotels," NBC News, 5/24/17.

46. *Washington Post* and Partnership for Public Service, "Tracking How Many Key Positions Trump Has Filled So Far," *WaPo*, 12/8/16 (last updated).

47. Tarini Parti, "A Top Mar-a-Lago Employee Is Quietly Doing Government Work for Trump's Foreign Trip," *BF*, 5/24/17.

48. Harriet Baskas, "Tourism to the U.S. Has Been in Decline Since Trump Took Office," NBCNews.com, 5/24/17.

49. Harriet Sinclair, "Remember the Carrier Jobs Trump 'Saved'? Company Announces 600 Layoffs Before Christmas," *Newsweek*, 5/23/17.

50. Robbie Gramer, "NATO Frantically Tries to Trump-Proof President's First Visit," *FP*, 5/15/17.

51. CNN Politics (@CNNPolitics), "Watch President Trump push Prime Minister Markovic of Montenegro aside at the NATO summit http://cnn.it/2qnTmVn" Twitter, 5/25/17, 1:10 p.m.; Zack Beauchamp, "Trump Lectured NATO Leaders About Defense Spending. It Was Awkward to Watch," *Vox*, 5/25/17.

52. Julian E. Barnes and Carol E. Lee, "Trump Declines to Back Core NATO Tenet, to Dismay of European Allies," *WSJ*, 5/25/17.

53. Anthony Faiola, "'The Germans Are Bad, Very Bad': Trump's Alleged Slight Generates Confusion, Backlash," *WaPo*, 5/26/17.

54. *PBS NewsHour* (@NewsHour), "WATCH: Aya Hijazi, who spent 3 years in Egyptian jail, tells @JudyWoodruff about her conversation with Pres. Trump after returning to the US" Twitter, 5/26/17, 1:54 p.m.

55. Alicia Acuna, "Greg Gianforte: Fox News Team Witnesses GOP House Candidate 'Body Slam' Reporter," FoxNews.com, 5/24/17; Jonathan Martin and Alexander Burns, "Greg Gianforte, Montana Republican, Captures House Seat Despite Assault Charge," *NYT*, 5/25/17.

56. Ben Jacobs, "GOP Candidate Greg Gianforte Has Financial Ties to US-Sanctioned Russian Companies," *Guardian*, 5/25/17.

57. Paul Farhi, "Press Advocates See Trump's Words Behind Physical Attacks on Journalists," *WaPo*, 5/25/17.

58. Eliana Johnson and Josh Dawsey, "Trump Eyeing Lewandowski, Bossie as Crisis Managers," *Politico*, 5/22/17.

59. Rebecca Ballhaus and Michael C. Bender, "Donald Trump Retains Marc Kasowitz as Private Lawyer in Russia Probe," *WSJ*, 5/23/17.

60. Jim Acosta, "Trump Team Preps 'War Room' to Defend Against Russia Probe," CNN.com, 5/25/17.

61. Joe Concha, "Gingrich: Abolish 'Totally Destructive' CBO," *The Hill*, 5/25/17.

62. Julie Hirschfeld Davis and Ron Nixon, "Trump Budget Takes Broad Aim at Undocumented Immigrants," *NYT*, 5/25/17.

63. Tara Palmeri, "Trump Team Keeps U.S. Reporters in the Dark Overseas," *Politico*, 5/25/17.

64. Daniel Bice, "Sheriff Clarke Directed Staff to Hassle Plane Passenger After Brief Exchange," *Milwaukee Journal Sentinel*, 5/25/17.

65. Mark Joseph Stern, "Fourth Circuit Upholds Travel Ban Injunction, Saying It 'Drips with Religious Intolerance,'" *The Slatest*, 5/25/17.

66. P. R. Lockhart, "DHS Public Database Includes Personal Information of Abuse Victims," *MJ*, 5/26/17.

67. Yeganeh Torbati, "Exclusive: Tillerson Declines to Host Ramadan Event at State Department," Reuters, 5/26/17.

68. "PPB: Suspect Hurled Insults at Muslim Women, Slashed Throats of Men Who Tried to Stop Him," KATU.com, 5/26/17.

69. Manu Raju and Evan Perez, "First on CNN: AG Sessions Did Not Disclose Russia Meetings in Security Clearance Form, DOJ Says," CNN.com, 5/25/17.

71. Greg Farrell, "Democrats Ask Deutsche Bank to Produce Documents on Trump Family Loans," Bloomberg.com, 5/24/17.

72. Matthew Rosenberg, Adam Goldman, and Matt Apuzzo, "Top Russian Officials Discussed How to Influence Trump Aides Last Summer," *NYT*, 5/24/17.

73. Kenneth P. Vogel, "Manafort Advised Trump Team on Russia Scandal," *Politico*, 5/25/17.

74–75. Karoun Demirjian and Devlin Barrett, "How a Dubious Russian Document Influenced the FBI's Handling of the Clinton Probe," *WaPo*, 5/24/17.

76. Andy Greenberg, "Russian Hackers Are Using 'Tainted Leaks' to Sow Disinformation," *Wired*, 5/25/17.

77. Alexandra Berzon and Rob Barry, "How Alleged Russian Hacker Teamed Up with Florida GOP Operative," *WSJ*, 5/25/17.

78–79. Matt Zapotosky, Sari Horwitz, Devlin Barrett, and Adam Entous, "Jared Kushner Now a Focus in Russia Investigation," *WaPo*, 5/25/17.

80. Matthew Miller (@matthewamiller), "Interesting. Not a clear sign yet he's decided, but a signal Mueller is considering whether to investigate obstruction." Twitter, 5/25/17, 2:35 p.m.

81. Josh Gerstein, "Lieberman Withdraws from FBI Director Search," *Politico*, 5/25/17.

82. Matthew Nussbaum, "Cohn: White House Won't Roll Back Russia Sanctions," *Politico*, 5/26/17.

83. Quinnipiac Poll, 5/24/17, https://poll.qu.edu/national/release-detail?ReleaseID=2460.

84-86. Ellen Nakashima, Adam Entous, and Greg Miller, "Russian Ambassador Told Moscow That Kushner Wanted Secret Communications Channel with Kremlin," *WaPo*, 5/26/17.

88-89. Ned Parker and Jonathan Landay, "Exclusive: Trump Son-in-Law Had Undisclosed Contacts with Russian Envoy—Sources," Reuters, 5/26/17.

90. Ryan Lizza (@RyanLizza), "Below is the statement from Jamie Gorelick, Kushner's lawyer, regarding the Reuters piece http://mobile.reuters.com/article/amp/idUSKBN18N018 . . ." Twitter, 5/26/17, 6:43 p.m.

91. Barry Meier and Jesse Drucker, "Russian Once Tied to Trump Aide Seeks Immunity to Cooperate with Congress," *NYT*, 5/26/17.

92. Josh Gerstein, "Russian Bank Owners Sue *BuzzFeed* over Trump Dossier Publication," *Politico*, 5/26/17.

93. Brandon Carter, "Trump Cancels Iowa Campaign Rally," *The Hill*, 5/27/17.

WEEK 29

1. Robert Costa, "Trump Family Members Met with GOP Leaders to Discuss Strategy," *WaPo*, 5/27/17.

2. Steve Horn, "Tillerson Present as Exxon Signed Major Deal with Saudi Arabia," *DeSmogBlog*, 5/30/17.

3. Nicolas Fandos, "Gun Deal in Jeopardy for Turkish Guards Who Beat Protesters," *NYT*, 6/1/17.

4. Julia Manchester, "Trump Complained of Trouble Setting Up Golf Courses in EU During Brussels Visit: Report," *The Hill*, 5/27/17.

5. Brooke Seipel, "Trump Is Only G7 Leader Not to Hold Press Conference After Summit," *The Hill*, 5/27/17.

6. Martin Pengelly, "White House Photo Caption Omits Husband of Luxembourg's Gay PM," *Guardian*, 5/27/17.

7. Agence France-Presse, "Merkel Warns US, Britain No Longer Reliable Partners," *YN*, 5/28/17.

8. Mary Bowerman, "French President Emmanuel Macron Says Trump Handshake Was 'Not Innocent,'" *USAT*, 5/29/17.

9. Jacob Pramuk, "Putin: It Would Be Nice for Russia if NATO Were 'Falling Apart,'" CNBC.com, 6/2/17.

10. Niv Ellis, "Macron Labels Russian Media Outlets as 'Propaganda,'" *The Hill*, 5/29/17; Gasta (@VictorCahat), "BREAKING France takes in #LGBT refugees from #Chechnya same day #Putin visits Versailles. Proud of my President ! #Macron" Twitter, 5/29/17, 7:53 a.m.

11. Mallory Shelbourne, "McCain Tells Australians: Trump Has Unsettled Americans Too," *The Hill*, 5/30/17.

12. Gloria Borger, "Trump, Home All Alone," CNN.com, 5/30/17.

13. Michael C. Bender and Peter Nicholas, "Trump Pushing Big White House Changes as Russia Crisis Grows," *WSJ*, 5/27/17; Henry J. Gomez, Tarini Parti, Adrian Carrasquillo, and Steven Perlberg, "No One Wants the Big White House Job That Just Opened Up," *BF*, 5/30/17.

14. Graham Lanktree, "Trump's Communications Director, Mike Dubke, Quits as Shake-up Looms," *Newsweek*, 5/30/17.

15. David Lat, "Wachtell Lipton Partner George Conway Withdraws from Justice Department Consideration," *Above the Law*, 6/2/17.

16. Julia Edwards Ainsley, "Trump's Continued Search for New FBI Chief Seen as Chaotic: Sources," Reuters, 6/2/17.

17. Graham Lanktree, "Trump Gives Out His Cell Number, Worrying Security Experts," *Newsweek*, 5/31/17.

18. Craig Timberg, "'Something Fishy' Is Going On with Trump's Twitter Account, Researchers Say," *WaPo*, 5/31/17.

19-20. Juliet Eilperin, Emma Brown, and Darryl Fears, "Trump Administration Plans to Minimize Civil Rights Efforts in Agencies," *WaPo*, 5/29/17.

21. Jason Wilson, "Portland Republican Says Party Should Use Militia Groups After Racial Attack," *Guardian*, 5/29/17.

22. Mark Hensch, "Trump: Portland Attacks 'Unacceptable,'" *The Hill*, 5/29/17.

23. Elizabeth Preza, "'I Don't Want to Be Associated with Him': 100 Eighth Graders Refuse to Pose with Paul Ryan During DC Trip," *Raw Story*, 5/27/17.

24. Ilya Marritz and Andrea Bernstein, "Trump SoHo Plans Layoffs," WNYC.org, 5/24/17.

25. Nicole Gaouette and Laura Jarrett, "Trump Admin Gives Embassies Broad New Discretion to Limit Travelers," CNN.com, 5/26/17.

26. "Windows Shattered at *Herald-Leader* Building; Suspected Bullet Damage Found," *Lexington Herald-Leader* (KY), 5/29/17.

27. Julianne Hing, "Texas's SB 4 Is the Most Dramatic State Crackdown Yet on Sanctuary Cities," *The Nation*, 6/1/17.

28. Gus Bova, Sam DeGrave, and Kolten Parker, "Texas Republican Called ICE on SB 4 Protesters, Threatened to Shoot Colleague," *Texas Observer*, 5/29/17.

29. Matt Steves, "Man Faces Deportation After Failing to Pay Fare on Minneapolis Light Rail," *NYT*, 5/30/17.

30. AP, "ICE Agents Eat Breakfast, Compliment Chef, Then Arrest 3 Workers at Michigan Restaurant," *CT*, 5/26/17.

31. Trevor Timm, "ICE Agents Are Out of Control. And They Are Only Getting Worse," *Guardian*, 5/31/17.

32. Bill Chappell, "Trump Asks Supreme Court to Reinstate Travel Ban on 6 Majority-Muslim Nations," *The Two-Way* (blog), NPR, 6/2/17.

33. "Noose Found Inside National Museum of African American History and Culture," NBCWashington.com, 6/1/17.

34. Nick Fugallo and Max Jaeger, "Pissed-off Artist Adds Statue of Urinating Dog Next to 'Fearless Girl,'" *NYP*, 5/29/17.

35. Donald Trump (@realDonaldTrump), "The U.S. Senate should switch to 51 votes, immediately, and get Healthcare and TAX CUTS approved, fast and easy. Dems would do it, no doubt!" Twitter, 5/30/17, 6:59 a.m.

36. Anthony Kuhn, "China Detains Activist Investigating Factory Making

Ivanka Trump Shoes," NPR.org, 5/31/17.

37. Brandon Carter, "Grassley Calls for Investigation into Chinese Promotion of Kushner Family Company Deal," *The Hill*, 5/29/17.

38. Mark Moore, "McCain Says Russia Is a Bigger Threat than ISIS," *NYP*, 5/29/17.

39. Darren Samuelsohn, "Trump Aides Facing Perilous Stage of Russia Probe," *Politico*, 5/27/17.

40. Cristiano Lima, "Clapper on Kushner-Russia Reports: My 'Warning Light Was Clearly On,'" *Politico*, 5/28/17.

41. Matthew Rosenberg, Mark Mazzetti, and Maggie Haberman, "Investigation Turns to Kushner's Motives in Meeting with a Putin Ally," *NYT*, 5/29/17.

42. Pamela Brown, Jim Sciutto, and Dana Bash, "Sources: Russians Discussed Potentially 'Derogatory' Information About Trump and Associates During Campaign," CNN .com, 5/30/17.

43. Tony Romm, "Hillary Clinton Says the Russians Had to Be Guided by Americans," *Recode*, 5/31/17.

44. Brian Ross and Matthew Mosk, "Congress Expands Russia Investigation to Include Trump's Personal Attorney," ABCNews.com, 5/30/17.

45. Hallie Jackson, "House Russia Probers Contact Former Trump Aide Boris Epshteyn," NBCNews.com, 5/30/17.

46. Ryan Lizza, "Trump's 'Good Job' Call to Roger Stone," *NYer*, 5/31/17.

47. Jim Sciutto, Jamie Gangel, Shimon Prokupecz, and Marshall Cohen, "First on CNN: Sources: Congress Investigating Another Possible Sessions-Kislyak Meeting," CNN.com. 5/31/17.

48. Byron Tau and Shane Harris, "House Intelligence Panel Issues Seven Subpoenas as Russia Probe Ramps Up," *WSJ*, 6/1/17.

49. Alice Ollstein, "House Intel Sends Unmasking Subpoenas as Russia Probe Escalates," *TPM*, 6/1/17; Joe Uchill, "Top Dem: Nunes Violating Russia Recusal with Subpoenas," *The Hill*, 6/1/17.

50. Matthew Yglesias, "Trump Has Granted More Lobbyist Waivers in 4 Months than Obama Did in 8 Years," *The Hill*, 6/1/17.

51. Steve Eder and Eric Lipton, "White House Waivers May Have Violated Ethics Rules," *NYT*, 6/1/17.

52. Philip Klein, "Mick Mulvaney: The Day of the CBO 'Has Probably Come and Gone,'" *WE*, 5/31/17.

53. Benjamin Lord (@benjalord), "Reminder: It has been 36 days since @StateDept has held a "daily" press briefing. What have they to hide? This is unacceptable." Twitter, 6/2/17, 5:40 p.m.

54. Burgess Everett and Josh Dawsey, "White House Orders Agencies to Ignore Democrats' Oversight Requests," *Politico*, 6/2/17.

55. Matt Flegenheimer, "What's a 'Covfefe'? Trump Tweet Unites a Bewildered Nation," *NYT*, 5/31/17.

56. Jordan Fabian, "Spicer Offers Cryptic Explanation for Trump 'Covfefe' Tweet," *The Hill*, 5/31/17.

57. Tina Dupuy (@Tinadupuy), "Only 28 percent of trump voters wanted to end the Paris Agreement. 😃" Twitter, 6/1/17, 8:31 p.m.

58. Alex Johnson, Erik Ortiz, and Becky Bratu, "Casino Robbery Ends with Dozens Dead at Resort in Philippines," NBCNews.com, 6/2/17.

59. Heather Long, "Trump Takes Credit for 1 Million Jobs. Not True," NBCMontana.com, 6/2/17.

60. Jeff Cox, "May Nonfarm Payrolls Total 138,000 vs 185,000 Expected," CNBC.com, 6/2/17.

61. Ivanka Trump (@IvankaTrump), "I am proud to support my LGBTQ friends and the LGBTQ Americans who have made immense contributions to our society and economy." Twitter, 6/1/17, 6:22 p.m.; Maeve Reston and Betsy Klein, "Ivanka Trump: America's Most Powerful Jewish Woman," CNN, June 2017.

62. Steven Shepard, "Poll: Support for Trump Impeachment Rises," *Politico*, 5/31/17.

63. Karen DeYoung and Adam Entous, "Trump Administration Moves to Return Russian Compounds in Maryland and New York," *WaPo*, 5/31/17.

64–65. Michael Isikoff, "How the Trump Administration's Secret Efforts to Ease Russia Sanctions Fell Short," *YN*, 6/1/17.

66. David Filipov, Amy Brittain, Rosalind S. Helderman, and Tom Hamburger, "Explanations for Kushner's Meeting with Head of Kremlin-Linked Bank Don't Match Up," *WaPo*, 6/1/17.

67. Brian Ross and Matthew Mosk, "Lawmakers Ask Whether Looming Debt Left Jared Kushner Vulnerable to Russian Influence," ABCNews.com, 6/2/17.

68. Shawn Boburg, "How Jared Kushner Built a Luxury Skyscraper Using Loans Meant for Job-Starved Area," *WaPo*, 5/31/17.

69. Ken Dilanian, "Did Trump, Kushner, Sessions Have an Undisclosed Meeting with Russian?" NBCNews .com, 6/1/17.

70. Stephanie Kirchgaessner, Nick Hopkins, and Luke Harding, "Nigel Farage Is 'Person of Interest' in FBI Investigation into Trump and Russia," *Guardian*, 6/2/17.

71. Del Quentin Wilber, "Comey to Testify That Trump Asked Him to Back Off Flynn Investigation," *WSJ*, 5/31/17.

72. Mike Levine, "DOJ Never Told Comey of Concerns Before Axing Him and Now He's 'Angry,' Sources Say," ABCNews.com, 6/2/17.

73. Matt Apuzzo and Michael S. Schmidt, "Comey Expected to Testify Before Senate, if He Isn't Blocked," *NYT*, 5/31/17; Susan Heavey, "Will Trump Block Comey Testimony? White House Does Not Know Yet," Reuters, 6/2/17.

74. Andrew Higgins, "Maybe Private Russian Hackers Meddled in Election, Putin Says," *NYT*, 6/1/17.

75. Tom Schoenberg, "DOJ's Weissmann, Joining Mueller's Russia Investigation Team, Sources Say," Bloomberg.com, 6/1/17.

76–77. Sadie Gurman, Eric Tucker, and Jeff Horwitz, "Special Counsel's Trump Investigation Includes Manafort Case," AP, 6/3/17.

78. Nathan Layne, Mark Hosenball, and Julia Edwards Ainsley, "Exclusive: Special Counsel Mueller to Probe Ex-Trump Aide Flynn's Turkey Ties," Reuters, 6/2/17.

79. Josh Dawsey, "Trump Needs Quick Wins, but Congress Not Poised to Deliver," *Politico*, 6/2/17.

80. Joshua Holland, "Americans Are Taking to the Streets to Demand the Truth on Trump and Russian," *The Nation*, 5/31/17.

Closing Note. Amy Siskind (@Amy_Siskind), "Remember when we were outraged by Tillerson's and Pence's email scandals a few months ago? We've normalized those too in the chaos. #resist" Twitter, 6/2/17, 7:40 p.m.

WEEK 30

1. Donald Trump (@realDonaldTrump), "At least 7 dead and 48 wounded in terror attack and Mayor of London says there is 'no reason to be alarmed!'" Twitter, 6/4/17, 4:31 a.m.

2. Dave Lawler, "U.S. Ambassador Contradicts Trump over Criticism of London Mayor," *Axios*, 6/4/17.

3. Donald Trump (@realDonald Trump), "People, the lawyers and the courts can call it whatever they want, but I am calling it what we need and what it is, a TRAVEL BAN!" Twitter, 6/5/17, 3:25 a.m.

4. Donald Trump (@realDonaldTrump), "The Justice Dept. should have stayed with the original Travel Ban, not the watered down, politically correct version they submitted to S.C." Twitter, 6/5/17, 3:29 a.m.

5. Matt Zapotosky, "Trump's Latest Tweets Will Probably Hurt Effort to Restore Travel Ban," *WaPo*, 6/5/17.

6. Peter Baker and Maggie Haberman, "Trump Grows Discontented with Attorney General Jeff Sessions," *NYT*, 6/5/17.

7. Michael R. Gordon, "Mattis Beseeches Officials at Singapore Conference to 'Bear with Us,'" *NYT*, 6/2/17.

8. Susan B. Glasser, "Trump National Security Team Blindsided by NATO Speech," *Politico*, 6/5/17.

9. Max Greenwood, "Third Noose This Week Found at DC Construction Site," *The Hill*, 6/3/17.

10. Michael E. Miller, "The Ku Klux Klan Wants to Rally in Charlottesville. Now This College Town Is on Edge Again," *WaPo*, 6/6/17.

11. Mica Rosenberg and Reade Levinson, "Exclusive: Trump Targets Illegal Immigrants Who Were Given Reprieves from Deportation by Obama," Reuters, 6/9/17.

12. Albert Samaha, Mike Hayes, and Talal Ansari, "The Kids Are Alt-Right," *BF*, 6/6/17.

13. David Ferguson, "Fearing for Her Life, Iowa Democrat Abandons Race to Unseat GOP Rep. Steve King," *Raw Story*, 6/3/17.

14. Eliana Johnson and Michael Crowley, "The Bottleneck in Rex Tillerson's State Department," *Politico*, 6/4/17.

15. Mallory Shelbourne, "LA Mayor: Immigration Arrests Could Cause a 'Tinderbox,'" *The Hill*, 6/4/17.

16. Jen St. Denis, "Canadian Searches for U.S. Flights Drop 43% After Trump Travel Ban," *Metro* (Canada), 1/30/17.

17. Brian Stelter (@brianstelter), "'WHY I DISAGREE WITH MY DAD' is the cover of this week's @USWeekly" Twitter, 6/7/17, 6:59 a.m.

18. Mike Snider, "Is Trump's Blocking of Some Twitter Users Unconstitutional?" *USAT*, 6/6/17.

19. Don Merica and Miranda Green, "Trump Has Filed for an Extension of His 2016 Tax Return," CNN.com, 6/3/17.

20. Byron Tau and Rebecca Ballhaus, "Trump Hotel Received $270,000 from Lobbying Campaign Tied to Saudis," *WSJ*, 6/6/17.

21. Brandon Carter, "DOJ: Trump Can Accept Payments from Foreign Governments," *The Hill*, 6/9/17.

22. Sarah Mulholland and Caleb Melby, "Kushners Hunting Hard for a Loan to Pay Back Chinese Investors," Bloomberg.com, 6/5/17.

23. Andrea Bernstein, "Kushner Family's Jersey City Project Set to Lose $6.5 Million Annual Tax Credit," WNYC.org, 6/9/17.

24. Elise Labott, Zachary Cohen, and Michelle Kosinski, "Sources: Acting US Ambassador to China Quit over Trump Climate Decision," CNN.com, 6/6/17.

25. Ali Breland, "Michelle Lee Resigns from Top Spot at Patent Office," *The Hill*, 6/6/17.

26. Chris Mooney, "85 Percent of the Top Science Jobs in Trump's Government Don't Even Have a Nominee," *WaPo*, 6/6/17.

27. David Smith, "Newseum Chief Fears for Future of Journalism Under Trump," *Guardian*, 6/5/17.

28. Hadas Gold (@Hadas_Gold), "BREAK: New Rep. Gianforte to pay $50,000 to the Commitee to Protect Journalists in civil settlement for assaulting @Bencjacobs" Twitter, 6/7/17, 6:27 p.m.

29. Darren Samuelsohn, "Everything We Know About the Mueller Probe So Far," *Politico*, 6/6/17; Tony Mauro, "Mueller Enlists Top Criminal Law Expert for Russia Probe," *NLJ*, 6/9/17.

30. Michael Isikoff, "Four Top Law Firms Turned Down Requests to Represent Trump," *YN*, 6/6/17.

31-32. Dan Alexander, "How Donald Trump Shifted Kids-Cancer Charity Money into His Business," *Forbes*, 6/6/17.

33. Ian Simpson, "New York Attorney General Looking at Eric Trump Charity's Payouts," Reuters, 6/9/17.

34. Manu Raju and Jeremy Herb, "Michael Flynn Turns Over 600 Pages of Documents to Senate Intel," CNN .com, 6/6/17.

35. Matthew Cole, Richard Esposito, Sam Biddle, and Ryan Grim, "Top-Secret NSA Report Details Russian Hacking Effort Days Before 2016 Election," *The Intercept*, 6/5/17.

36. U.S. Dept. of Justice Office of Public Affairs, "Federal Government Contractor in Georgia Charged with Removing and Mailing Classified Materials to a News Outlet," press release, 6/5/17, https://www.justice.gov/opa/pr/federal-government-contractor-georgia-charged-removing-and-mailing-classified-materials-news; Gideon Resnick, "WikiLeaks Declares War on *The Intercept*," *DB*, 6/6/17.

37. Susan Page, "Sen. Mark Warner: More State Election Systems Were Targeted by Russians," *USAT*, 6/6/17.

38. Maya Rao, "Sen. Amy Klobuchar Wants Senate Briefing on Russian Vote Hacking Attempts," *Star Tribune* (MN), 6/6/17.

39. "Deutsche Bank Ignores U.S. Trump/Russia Query: Democratic Staffer," Reuters, 6/4/17.

40. Karen Freifeld and Patrick Rucker, "Exclusive: Deutsche Bank Says Privacy Laws Prevent Trump Financial Disclosures," Reuters, 6/8/17.

41. Jennifer Rubin, "Intelligence Officials' Outrageous Contempt of Congress," *WaPo*, 6/7/17.

42. Tom Porter, "Pro–Donald Trump Group Slams FBI's James Comey as 'Showboat' and Failure in Attack Ads to Coincide with Testimony," *Newsweek*, 6/7/17.

43–44. Adam Entous, "Top Intelligence Official Told Associates Trump Asked Him if He Could Intervene with Comey on FBI Russia Probe," *WaPo*, 6/6/17.

45. Michael S. Schmidt and Matt Apuzzo, "Comey Told Sessions: Don't Leave Me Alone with Trump," *NYT*, 6/6/17.

46. ABC News Politics (@ABCPolitics), "MORE: Sources say Trump lashed out repeatedly at Sessions in private meetings, blaming his recusal for expansion of Russian investigation." Twitter, 6/6/17, 3:34 p.m.; Jonathan Karl, "Attorney General Jeff Sessions Suggested He Could Resign amid Rising Tension with President Trump," ABCNews.com, 6/6/17.

47. Tom LoBianco and Manu Raju, "Nunes Won't Say if He Stepped Aside in Russia Probe," CNN.com, 6/6/17.

48. Murray Waas, "3 Senior FBI Officials Can Vouch for Comey's Story About Trump," *Vox*, 6/7/17.

49. Quinnipiac Poll, 6/7/17, https://poll.qu.edu/national/release-detail?ReleaseID=2462.

50. Conor Finnegan, "Senior State Dept. Official Heading to Russia to Talk 'Irritants,'" ABCNews.com, 6/7/17.

51. Damien Sharkov, "Putin Vows Military Response to 'Eliminate NATO Threat' if Sweden Joins U.S.-Led Alliance," *Newsweek*, 6/2/17.

52. "Trump-Russia Probe 'Bigger than Watergate' Says Clapper," BBC News, 6/8/17.

53. Senate Select Committee on Intelligence, Statement for the Record, James B. Comey, June 8, 2017, https://www.intelligence.senate.gov/sites/default/files/documents/os-jcomey-060817.pdf.

54. Christopher Wilson and Gabby Kaufman, "Trump Asked FBI Head for 'Loyalty' and a Halt to Flynn Probe: 10 Takeaways from Comey's Prepared Testimony," *YN*, 6/7/17.

55. Kenneth F. McCallion, "Donald Trump's New FBI Director Pick Has Russian Ties of His Own," *USAT*, 6/9/17.

56. Katie Rogers and Emily Cochrane, "Gripped by Comey Fever, Washington Plays Hooky," *NYT*, 6/8/17.

57. Eric Levitz, "Recap: James Comey Testifies on Trump to the Senate," *DI*, 6/8/17.

58. Mark Berman, "Comey Testimony," *WaPo*, live updates, 6/8/17, 10:41 a.m.

59. Sean Rossman, "Comey's, 'Lordy, I Hope There Are Tapes' Gives Internet the Vapors," *USAT*, 6/8/17; Jordain Carney, "Schumer to Trump: Play Comey Tapes or Admit They Don't Exist," *The Hill*, 6/8/17.

60. Mark Berman, "Comey Testimony," *WaPo*, live updates, 6/8/17, 10:52 a.m.

61. "Comey Testimony: Highlights of the Hearing," *NYT*, 6/8/17.

62. Jason Le Miere, "Trump Under Investigation for Obstruction of Justice, James Comey Says in Testimony," *Newsweek*, 6/8/17.

63. Matthew Schofield, "Did Russia Interfere in the 2016 Elections? No Doubt, Comey Says," *News & Observer* (NC), 6/8/17.

64. Ben Mathis-Lilley, "First Sentence of Trump Lawyer's Response to Comey Misspells the Word *President*," *The Slatest*, 6/8/17; Alana Abramson, "President Trump's Lawyer Made a Mistake in Describing James Comey's Testimony," *Time*, 6/9/17; Abigail Tracy, "Trump's Official Response to Comey Doesn't Add Up," *VF*, 6/8/17.

65. Sam Stein, "Top Dem Donor Calls on Lawmakers to Take Up Trump Impeachment," *HuffPost*, 6/9/17.

66. Jessica Estepa, "Trump Surrogates Go on the Attack," *USAT*, 6/8/17.

67. Kyle Griffin (@kylegriffin1), "Of note: NBC reports this 3rd meeting is the Sessions-Mayflower event that's been previously reported but DOJ denies http://nbcnews.to/2rYAOQn" Twitter, 6/8/17, 4:11 p.m.

68. Steven Erlanger and Stephen Castle, "Theresa May Loses Overall Majority in U.K. Parliament," *NYT*, 6/8/17.

69. David Chalian (@DavidChalian), "Sen. Angus King on @AC360: 'Our staff is going to interview Jared Kushner next week.'" Twitter, 6/8/17, 5:24 p.m.; Alice Ollstein, "NBC: Congress Wants to Ask if Kushner Sought Russian Funding for NYC Tower," *TPM*, 6/5/17.

70–71. "Pelosi: I'm Concerned About Trump's 'Fitness for Office,'" *Morning Joe*, MSNBC, 6/9/17.

72. Elizabeth Preza, "'Insanity': Internet Stunned as Trump Sides with Saudis Instead of His Own Secretary of State in Qatar Dispute," *Raw Story*, 6/9/17.

73. Joe Johns and Dan Merica, "Trump's Lawyer to File Complaint Against Comey over Memos," CNN.com, 6/9/17.

74. "Trump Social Media Director Violated Law with Call to Oust Congressman: Agency," Reuters, 6/9/17.

75. Reuters, "After Sowing Doubts, Trump Backs NATO Mutual Defense under Charter," 6/9/17.

76–77. Julie Hirschfeld Davis and Glenn Thrush, "Calling Comey a Liar, Trump Says He Will Testify Under Oath," *NYT*, 6/9/17.

78. Sam Stein, "Top Dem Donor Calls on Lawmakers to Take Up Trump Impeachment," *HuffPost*, 6/9/17.

WEEK 31

1. Patrick Wintour, "Trump's State Visit to Britain Put on Hold," *Guardian*, 6/12/17.

2. Laura M. Holson, "At the 'Summer White House,' You Are Never Far from a Trump Photo," *NYT*, 6/3/17; Amy B. Wang and Ana Swanson, "President Trump Can't Stop Crashing Parties at His Golf Clubs," *WaPo*, 6/11/17.

3. Philip Bump (@pbump), "Every 3.5 days, he's at one of his private properties. Every 6.2 days, he golfs." Twitter, 6/10/17, 9:34 a.m.

4. Victoria Guida, "Trump Attorney Won't Rule Out Firing Mueller," *Politico*, 6/11/17.

5. Niall Stanage, "The Memo: Trump Allies Turn Fire on Mueller," *The Hill*, 6/12/17.

6. Newt Gingrich (@newtgingrich), "Muelleris now clearly the ti[p of the deep state spear aimed at destroying or at a minimum undermining and crippling the Trump presidency." Twitter, 6/15/17, 4:28 a.m.

7. Mallory Shelbourne, "NY Attorney: 'Very Weird and Peculiar' That Trump Called Me 3 Times Before I Was Fired," *The Hill*, 6/11/17.

8. Eli Watkins, "Preet Bharara Opens Up About His Interactions with Trump," CNN.com, 6/12/17.

9. Jesse Eisinger and Justin Elliott, "Trump's Personal Lawyer Boasted That He Got Preet Bharara Fired," *ProPublica*, 6/13/17.

10. Louise Radnofsky, "Secret Service Has No Audio or Transcripts of Any Tapes Made in Trump White House," *WSJ*, 6/12/17.

11. James Marson, "Hundred, Including Kremlin Critic Alexei Navalny, Detained amid Russia Protests," *WSJ*, 6/12/17.

12. "The Latest: Moscow Court Jails Opposition Leader for 30 Days," AP, 6/12/17.

13. Rebecca Savransky, "Gianforte Sentenced to Complete Community Service After Assaulting Reporter," *The Hill*, 6/12/17.

14. State of Hawai'i; Ismail Elshikh v. Donald J. Trump, No. 1:17-cv-00050, 9th Cir., filed June 12, 2017, http://cdn.ca9.uscourts.gov/datastore/opinions/2017/06/12/17-15589.pdf; Laura Jarrett and Ariane de Vogue, "9th Circuit Deals Trump Travel Ban Another Defeat," CNN.com, 6/13/17.

15. Jordan Fabian, "Trump Changes Travel Ban Expiration Date Ahead of High Court Decision," *The Hill*, 6/14/17.

16. John Harwood, "Trump Makes Bizarre Claims at Press Event as Cabinet Members Take Turns Praising Him," CNBC.com, 6/13/17.

17. Julia Ioffe (@juliaioffe), "Putin televises the beginnings of his cabinet meetings." Twitter, 6/12/17, 2:15 p.m.

18. Dylan Stafford, "Congressman Introduces 'COVFEFE Act' to Make Social Media a Presidential Record," CNN.com, 6/12/17.

19. Ashley Feinberg, "A Running List of People Donald Trump Has Blocked on Twitter," *Wired*, 6/14/17.

20. Darlene Superville and Emily Swanson, "Poll Shows Most Doubt Trump's Respect for Institutions," AP, 6/14/17.

21. Josh Lederman and Emily Swanson, "AP-NORC Poll: Just 1 in 5 Support Trump's Move to Fire Comey," AP, 6/15/17.

22. Matt Egan, "CEOs to Trump: You're Failing," CNN.com, 6/15/17.

23. Michael Riley and Jordan Robertson, "Russian Cyber Hacks on U.S. Electoral System Far Wider than Previously Known," Bloomberg.com, 6/13/17.

24. Rick Pearson, "Rep. Quigley Says Russian Operatives Hacked Illinois Elections Board Last Year," *CT*, 6/5/17.

25. Lachlan Markay and Asawin Suebsaeng, "Trump 'Aggressively Courted' Cindy McCain for State Dept Job," *DB*, 6/12/17.

26. Zachary Cohen, "US Ambassador to Qatar to Step Down amid Diplomatic Crisis," CNN.com, 6/13/17.

27. Nick Visser, "Scott Pruitt Leaves G7 Climate Meeting More than a Day Early," *HuffPost*, 6/11/17.

28. Brad Plumer, "Energy Department Closes Office Working on Climate Change Abroad," *NYT*, 6/15/17.

29. Ivo Daalder (@IvoHDaalder), "Tillerson won't begin staffing State Dept till next year. This is insane." Twitter, 6/14/17, 6:22 a.m.

30. David Mack, "Commerce Department Removes Sexual Orientation and Gender Identity from Equal Employment Policy," *BF*, 6/16/17.

31. Greg B. Smith, "President Trump Chooses Inexperienced Woman Who Planned His Son Eric's Wedding to Run N.Y. Federal Housing Programs," *NYDN*, 6/15/17.

32. Russ Choma, "Federal Ethics Czar: Steve Bannon Violated White House Ethics Rules," *MJ*, 6/14/17.

33. Nick Penzenstadler, Steve Reilly, and John Kelly, "Most Trump Real Estate Now Sold to Secretive Buyers," *USAT*, 6/13/17.

34. AP, "China Approves Nine Trump Trademarks It Had Previously Rejected," *Guardian*, 6/14/17.

35. Bernard Condon, "Trump Partner Said in Running to Build FBI Headquarters," AP, 6/14/17.

36. Krithika Varagur, "Revealed: Reality of Life Working in an Ivanka Trump Clothing Factory," *Guardian*, 6/13/17.

37. Karoun Demirjian, "Sessions at the Senate," *WaPo*, live updates, 6/13/17, 11:25 a.m.

38. Kasie Hunt (@kasie), "ALERT: Reporters at Capitol have been told they are not allow to film interviews with senators in hallways, contrary to years of precedent" Twitter, 6/13/17, 8:30 a.m.

39. Karen Tumulty (@ktumulty), "Everything old is new again. Letter to my bureau chief, after Capitol cops expelled me from hallway for doing my job:" Twitter, 6/13/17, 10:09 a.m.

40. Alexander Bolton, "Senate Republicans Back Off Proposed Restrictions on Media," *The Hill*, 6/13/17.

41. "The Latest: DC Police to Charge 12 Turkish Security Agents," AP, 6/14/17.

42–43. Eli Watkins, "Judge Orders DOJ to Produce Sessions' Clearance Form," CNN.com, 6/13/17.

44. Allan Smith, "The Most Important Takeaway from Jeff Sessions' Testimony Was What He Refused to Say—and Legal Experts Say Congress Should Subpoena Him for Answers," *BI*, 6/14/17.

45–47. Stephanie Kirchgaessner, "Lobbyist for Russian Interests Says He Attended Dinners Hosted by Sessions," *Guardian*, 6/15/17.

48. Jane C. Timm and Chandelis R. Duster, "Sen. Kamala Harris Again Interrupted by Male Colleagues," NBCNews.com, 6/13/17; Jeremy Herb, "Senators Try to Quiet Harris, but She Doesn't Back Down," CNN.com, 6/7/17.

49. Leigh Ann Caldwell, "Senate Passes New Russian Sanctions Bill That Would Curb Trump's Power," NBCNews.com, 6/15/17.

50. Garrett M. Graff, "Robert Mueller Chooses His Investigatory Dream Team," *Wired*, 6/14/17.

51. Matt Pearce and Joseph Tanfani, "Virginia Gunman Hated Republicans, and 'Was Always in His Own Little World,'" *LAT*, 6/14/17.

52. David Jackson and Michael Collins, "Trump Keeps Policy on Dreamers, Eliminates Protection for Older Immigrants," *USAT*, 6/16/17.

53. Lanning Taliaferro, "UPDATE: ICE Says Ossining High School Senior Was Ordered Deported in November," *Ossining Patch*, 6/9/17.

54–55. Devlin Barrett, Adam Entous, Ellen Nakashima, and Sari Horwitz, "Special Counsel Is Investigating Trump for Possible Obstruction of Justice, Officials Say," *WaPo*, 6/14/17.

56. NBC *Nightly News* with Lester Holt (@NBCNightlyNews), "'@NBCNews has learned the president of the United States is now under criminal investigation,' @LesterHoltNBC reports on @NBCNightlyNews." Twitter, 6/15/17, 3:50 p.m.

57. Darren Samuelsohn, "Rosenstein Prods Media for 'Anonymous Allegations' on Russia Probe," *Politico*, 6/15/17.

58. Heather Caygle and John Bresnahan, "Pelosi Predicts Trump Will 'Self-Impeach,'" *Politico*, 6/13/17.

59. Donald Trump (@realDonald Trump), "I am being investigated for firing the FBI Director by the man who told me to fire the FBI Director! Witch Hunt" Twitter, 6/16/17, 6:07 a.m.

60. Sari Horwitz, Devlin Barrett, and Lynh Bui, "Trump Takes a Twitter Swipe at Deputy Attorney General, a Key Figure in Russia Probe," *WaPo*, 6/16/17.

61. Sarah D. Wire, "Feinstein Says She's Increasingly Concerned Trump Will Try to Fire Mueller, Rosenstein," *LAT*, 6/16/17.

62. Julie Pace, "Trump Acknowledges for First Time He's Under Investigation," AP, 6/16/17.

63. Rebeca R. Ruiz and Sharon LaFraniere, "Role of Trump's Personal Lawyer Blurs Public and Private Lines," *NYT*, 6/11/17.

64. Joe Patrice, ". . . And Now the Inevitable Ethics Complaint Against Trump's Lawyer," *Above the Law*, 6/15/17.

65–66. Sari Horwitz, Matt Zapotosky, and Adam Entous, "Special Counsel Is Investigating Jared Kushner's Business Dealings," *WaPo*, 6/15/17.

67–68. Tom LoBianco, "First on CNN: House Russia Investigators Want to Bring in Trump Digital Director," CNN.com, 6/16/17.

69. Ashley Parker, "Pence Hires Outside Counsel to Deal with Russia Probe Inquiries," *WaPo*, 6/15/17.

70. "Pence Hires Lawyer with Relevant Experience; Mueller Builds Team," *Rachel Maddow Show*, MSNBC, 6/15/17.

71. Katy Tur (@KatyTurNBC), "Exclusive: Trump personal lawyer, Michael Cohen, has hired his own counsel: Stephen Ryan, of McDermott, Will & Emery.- source w knowledge" Twitter, 6/16/17, 9:28 a.m.

72. Rosalind S. Helderman and Philip Rucker, "Trump's Personal Lawyer, Michael Cohen, Hires His Own Lawyer in Russia Probe," *WaPo*, 6/16/17.

73. Angelica LaVito, "NBC: Trump's Lawyer Has Hired His Own Lawyer," CNBC.com, 6/16/17.

74. Tom DiChristopher, "The New Coal Jobs the Trump Team Is Touting Might Not Actually Exist," CNBC.com, 6/15/17.

75. Aida Chavez, "Putin Offers Political Asylum to Comey," *The Hill*, 6/15/17.

76. Heidi Blake, Tom Warren, Richard Holmes, Jason Leopold, Jane Bradley, and Alex Campbell, "From Russia with Blood," *BF*, 6/15/17.

77. Dan Merica and Lauren Fox, "Trump Calls GOP Health Care Bill 'Mean' and Democrats Pounce, Republicans Worry," CNN.com, 6/20/17.

78. Sara Kliff (@sarakliff), "Per @NoamLevey, McConnells office is refusing meetings with major patient advocacy groups." Twitter, 6/16/17, 12:52 p.m.

79. U.S. Office of Govt. Ethics, "Trump, Donald J 2017 Financial Disclosure Report," https://oge.app.box.com/s/kz4qvbdsbcfrzq16msuo4zmth6rerh1c; Phil McCausland, "Trump Reports Hundreds of Millions in Financial Liabilities," NBCNews.com, 6/16/17.

80. Matt Ford, "Donald Trump Reports He's Getting Rich as President," *Atlantic*, 6/16/17.

81. Phil McCausland, "Trump Reports Hundreds of Millions in Financial Liabilities," NBCNews.com, 6/16/17.

82. Aaron C. Davis, "D.C. and Maryland Sue President Trump, Alleging Breach of Constitutional Oath," *WaPo*, 6/12/17.

83. Tom Hamburger and Karen Tumulty, "Congressional Democrats to File Emoluments Lawsuit Against Trump," *WaPo*, 6/14/17.

84. Sara Trefethen, Elizabeth Rosner, and Ruth Brown, "Rich Oil Tycoon Pulls Jackass Move with His Yacht," *NYP*, 6/15/17.

85. Justin McCurry, "USS Fitzgerald Collison: Trump Criticised for Leaving Key Posts Unfilled," *Guardian*, 6/17/17.

WEEK 32

1. Kenneth T. Walsh, "Trump Enjoys Camp David," *USN*, 6/19/17.

2. Mike McIntire, "Russia Renewed Unused Trump Trademarks in 2016," *NYT*, 6/18/17.

3. Erica L. Green, "Education Dept. Says It Will Scale Back Civil Rights Investigations," *NYT*, 6/16/17.

4. Scott A. Schoettes, "Trump Doesn't Care About HIV. We're Outta Here," *Newsweek*, 6/16/17.

5. Steven Mufson, "Rick Perry Just Denied That Humans Are the Main Cause of Climate Change" *NYT*, 6/19/17.

6. Laura Meckler, "Justice Department Explores Court Challenges to 'Sanctuary Cities,'" *WSJ*, 6/23/17.

7. Julie Zauzmer, "Funeral, Vigil for Muslim Teen Killed in Attack Near Mosque Draws Throngs," *WaPo*, 6/21/17.

8. Amy Brittain and Abigail Hauslohner, "Anti-sharia Group Offers Donors a Private Tour and Cocktails at Trump Hotel," *WaPo*, 6/20/17.

9. AP, "Attorney to Challenge Law Used in Gorilla Mask Case," NBCNews.com, 6/23/17.

10. Hansi Lo Wang, "Collecting LGBT Census Data Is 'Essential' to Federal Agency, Document Shows," NPR.org, 6/20/17.

11. Claire Shaffer, "Trump's White House Won't Acknowledge June as LGBT Pride Month, Even as Everyone Else Does," *Newsweek*, 6/5/17.

12. Sarah Binder, "Yes, Mitch McConnell's Secretive Lawmaking Is Really Unusual—in These 4 Ways," *WaPo*, 6/19/17.

13. Ben Protess, Jessica Silver-Greenberg, and Sharon LaFraniere, "Kushner Is Said to Be Reconsidering His Legal Team," *NYT*, 6/18/17.

14. NBC Politics (@NBCPolitics), "JUST IN: Republican litigator Chuck Cooper is representing Attorney General Jeff Sessions on matters pertaining to the Russia investigation" Twitter, 6/20/17, 1:15 p.m.

15. Graham Lanktree, "Mike Pence's Private Email Account Is Costing Indiana $100,000 in Lawyers' Fees," *Newsweek*, 6/18/17.

16. Samantha Michaels, "Lawsuit Accuses Private Prison Company of Illegally Funding a Trump Super-PAC," *MJ*, 6/15/17.

17. Karen Freifeld, "Mueller Team Lawyer Brings Witness-Flipping Expertise to Trump Probes," Reuters, 6/19/17.

18. *Situation Room* (@CNNSitRoom), "Sen. Whitehouse: Signals show that Michael Flynn could already be cooperating with the FBI" Twitter, 6/19/17, 2:32 p.m.

19. Matthew Mosk, Brian Ross, and Pete Madden, "Flynn Failed to Report Foreign Trip to Broker US-Russia Nuclear Deal, House Democrats Say," ABCNews.com, 6/19/17.

20–21. Matt Apuzzo, Matthew Rosenberg, and Adam Goldman, "Despite Concerns About Blackmail, Flynn Heard C.I.A. Secrets," *NYT*, 6/20/17.

22–24. Matthew Mosk and Brian Ross, "Lawmakers Intensify Negotiations in Pursuit of Key Trump-Related Banking Records," ABCNews.com, 6/20/17.

25. Gary Silverman, "Trump's Russian Riddle," *FT*, 8/14/16.

26. Timothy L. O'Brien, "Trump, Russia and a Shadowy Business Partnership," Bloomberg.com, 6/21/17.

27. Jennifer de Pinto, Fred Backus, Kabir Khanna, and Anthony Salvanto, "Trump's Handling of Russia Investigations Weighs on Approval Ratings," CBSNews.com, 6/20/17.

28. Tony Mauro, "Mueller Recruits Another Lawyer from Solicitor General's Office to Russia Probe," *NLJ*, 6/19/17.

29. Tom Kludt, "Off-Camera, No Audio Broadcast: White House Keeps Undermining Press Briefing," CNN .com, 6/19/17.

30. Alayna Treene, "Spicer Doesn't Know if Trump Has Seen the Senate Health Bill," *Axios*, 6/20/17.

31. Maggie Haberman and Glenn Thrush, "'I'm Right Here!' Sean Spicer Says While Toiling to Find Successor," *NYT*, 6/20/17.

32. Tom LoBianco, "Jeh Johnson Hearing: House Russia Probe Digs into DNC Cyberfailings, Voter Roll Hacks," CNN.com, 6/22/17.

33. Byron Tau and Erica Orden, "Russia Targeted 21 States for Election Hacking, Official Says," *WSJ*, 6/21/17.

34. Kevin Collier, "DHS Never Ran Audit to See if Votes Were Hacked," *DB*, 6/20/17.

35. "In 298 Days, President Trump Has Made 1,628 False and Misleading Claims," *WaPo*, updated 11/13/17.

36. David Leonhardt and Stuart A. Thompson, "Trump's Lies," *NYT*, updated 7/21/17.

37. Robert Farley, Brooks Jackson, and Lori Robertson, "Fact Check: Trump Makes Misleading Claims at Iowa Rally," *USAT*, 6/23/17; Maggie Haberman, "Trump Turns an Iowa Rally into a Venting Session," *NYT*, 6/21/17.

38. Bradd Jaffy (@BraddJaffy), "Trump on the wealth of his economic cabinet picks: 'In those particular positions, I just don't want a poor person'" Twitter, 6/21/17, 5:49 p.m.

39. Ellen Mitchell, "Layoffs Announced at Boeing Plant Trump Visited," *The Hill*, 6/22/17.

40. Harriet Sinclair, "Trump's 2020 Re-election Campaign to Kick Off with $35,000-per-Ticket Dinner at Own Hotel in Washington, D.C.," *Newsweek*, 6/21/17.

41. Donald Trump (@realDonald Trump), "Mexico was just ranked the second deadliest country in the world, after only Syria. Drug trade is largely the cause. We will BUILD THE WALL!" Twitter, 6/22/17, 3:15 p.m.

42. Ragıp Soylu (@ragipsoylu), "Trump calls new Saudi Crown Prince Mohammed bin Salman to congratulate him for his new role" Twitter, 6/21/17, 10:32 a.m.

43. Dexter Filkins, "Are Russian Operatives Attacking Putin Critics in the U.S.?" *NYer*, 6/19/17.

44. Greg Price, "Rex Tillerson to Work with Russia on Cybersecurity (Even After Hacking)," *Newsweek*, 6/19/17.

45. Julie Hirschfeld Davis and Matt Flegenheimer, "White House Tries to Get G.O.P. to Water Down Russia Sanctions Bill," *NYT*, 6/21/17.

46. Jordain Carney, "House Republicans Block Russia Sanctions Bill," *The Hill*, 6/20/17.

47. Alex Moe and Ken Dilanian, "Democrats Ask Why Jared Kushner Still Has a Security Clearance," NBCNews.com, 6/21/17.

48. U.S. Senate, Committee on the Judiciary to Director of White House Management and Office of Administration and FBI, 6/22/17, https://www.judiciary.senate.gov/imo/media/doc/2017-06-22%20CG%20DF%20LG%20SW%20to%20White%20House%20FBI%20%28Kushner%20Clearance%29.pdf.

49. Jason Leopold and Claudia Koerner, "Memo Shows Preet Bharara Was Concerned After Phone Call from White House," *BF*, 6/23/17.

50. Nancy Cook and Josh Dawsey, "Trump Loses Patience with His White House Counsel," *Politico*, 6/23/17.

51. Dana Bash, Evan Perez, and Manu Raju, "Intel Chiefs Tell Investigators Trump Suggested They Refute Collusion with Russians," *Politico*, 6/22/17.

52. Ken Dilanian, "Coats Tells House Investigators President Trump Seemed Obsessed with Russia Probe," NBCNews.com, 6/22/17.

53. Stephen Collinson, "Trump Ends His Self-Made Crisis Where It Started: Twitter," CNN.com, 6/23/17.

54. Donald Trump (@realDonald Trump), "By the way, if Russia was working so hard on the 2016 Election, it all took place during the Obama Admin. Why didn't they stop them?" Twitter, 6/22/17.

55. "US Election Officials Still Assessing Russian 2016 Cyber Attack," *Rachel Maddow Show*, MSNBC, 6/21/17.

56. Shane Harris and Kate Fazzini, "Computer-Security Firm Says Voter Data Set Left Unprotected Online," *WSJ*, 6/9/17.

57–59. Dell Cameron and Kate Conger, "GOP Data Firm Accidentally Leaks Personal Details of Nearly 200 Million American Voters," *Gizmodo*, 6/19/17.

60-61. Naomi Martin, "Russian Hackers Targeted Dallas County Servers Before Presidential Election," *Dallas Morning News*, 6/14/17.

62. "US Election Officials Still Assessing Russian 2016 Cyber Attack," *Rachel Maddow Show*, MSNBC, 6/21/17.

63-64. Rebecca Ballhaus, Erica Orden, and Valerie Bauerlein, "State Officials to Testify on Possible Russian Involvement in 2016 Election, "*WSJ*, 6/18/17.

65. Massimo Calabresi, "Election Hackers Altered Voter Rolls, Stole Private Data, Officials Say," *Time*, 6/22/17.

66. Jeff Pegues, "Investigators Probe Whether Trump Associates Got Info from Hacked Voter Databases," CBSNews.com, 6/22/17.

67-68. Natasha Bertrand, "A Long-Overlooked Player Is Emerging as a Key Figure in the Trump-Russia Investigation," *BI*, 6/23/17.

69. Scott Wong, "Gowdy Won't Use Oversight Gavel to Probe Russia," *The Hill*, 6/23/17.

70. Mark Murray, "Poll: More Americans Believe Comey over Trump," NBCNews.com, 6/23/17.

71. Michael A. Memoli, "Trump Says He Tweeted about Tapes to Influence Comey's Account of Their Private Conversations," *LAT*, 6/23/17.

72. "Trump Says Comey-Mueller Friendship 'Bothersome,'" FoxNews .com, 6/23/17.

73-76. Greg Miller, Ellen Nakashima, and Adam Entous, "Obama's Secret Struggles to Punish Russia for Putin's Election Assault," *WaPo*, 6/23/17.

77. Donald Trump (@realDonald Trump), "Just out: The Obama Administration knew far in advance of November 8th about election meddling by Russia. Did nothing about it. WHY?" Twitter, 6/23/17, 5:43 p.m.

78. Dan Merica, "Spokeswoman: Trump Thinks Election Hacking 'Probably Was Russia,'" CNN.com, 6/22/17.

79. Ken Dilanian, Hallie Jackson, Likhitha Butchireddygari, and Gabriela Martinez, "Trump White House Has Taken Action to Stop Next Election Hack," NBCNews.com, 6/24/17.

80. Timothy Egan, "Our Fake Democracy," *NYT*, 6/23/17.

WEEK 33

1. Carma Hassan, "California Adds 4 States to Travel Ban for Laws It Says Discriminate Against LGBTQ Community," CNN.com, 6/23/17.

2. Jason Szep and Matt Spetalnick, "Exclusive: Overruling Diplomats, U.S. to Drop Iraq, Myanmar from Child Soldiers' List," Reuters, 6/23/17.

3. Josh Harkinson, "The Trump Administration Is Pulling a Grant from a Group That Combats Neo-Nazis," *MJ*, 6/23/17.

4. Ron Kampeas, "State Dept.'s Anti-Semitism Monitoring Office to Be Unstaffed as of July 1," Jewish Telegraphic Agency, 6/22/17; Anti-Defamation League, "U.S. Anti-Semitic Incidents Spike 86 Percent So Far in 2017 After Surging Last Year, ADL Finds," ADL.org.

5. Richard Fausset, "Federal Court Lifts Injunction on Mississippi Anti-gay Law," *NYT*, 6/22/17.

6. Emily Shugerman, "In North Carolina You Can't Legally Withdraw Consent After Sex Begins, Letting Rapists Escape Unpunished," *Independent* (UK), 6/22/17.

7. Amy B. Wang, "President Trump Just Ended a Long Tradition of Celebrating Ramadan at the White House," *WaPo*, 6/25/17.

8. Hilary Brueck, "Denied: Afghanistan's All-Girl Robotics Team Can't Get Visas to the US," *Forbes*, 6/29/17.

9. AP, "Historical Marker of Civil-Rights Icon Emmett Till Vandalized in Mississippi," NBCNews .com, 6/26/17.

10. Brett Murphy, "Rigged," part 1, *USAT*, 6/16/17; Brett Murphy, "Morgan Southern Fires Trucker Who Spoke About 20-Hour Workdays," *USAT*, 7/11/17.

11. Ariane de Vogue, "Supreme Court Allows Parts of Travel Ban to Take Effect," CNN.com, 6/27/17.

12. Suzanne Gamboa, "Texas AG, Others Demand Trump Stop New DACA Permits, End Renewals," NBCNews.com, 6/29/17.

13. Jordan Fabian, "White House: Chicago Gun Violence 'Driven by Morality,'" *The Hill*, 6/30/17.

14. Ali Vitali, "Trump Highlights Crimes by Undocumented Immigrants," NBCNews.com, 6/28/17.

15. Tara Palmeri, "White House Council for Women and Girls Goes Dark Under Trump," *Politico*, 6/30/17.

16. Jeremy Herb, "Pentagon Delays Decision on Transgender Recruits," CNN.com, 6/30/17.

17-19. Michael Kranish, "Kushner Firm's $285 Million Deutsche Bank Loan Came Just Before Election Day," *WaPo*, 6/25/17.

20. Christian Berthelsen and Greg Farrell, "Deutsche Bank Said Near Fed Deal on Russia; DOJ Probe Looms," Bloomberg.com, 5/24/17.

21. Max Seddon, "Kushner Meeting Shines Spotlight on Russian Bank," *FT*, 6/25/17.

22. Josh Dawsey, "Kushner Adds Powerhouse Lawyer Abbe Lowell to Legal Team," *Politico*, 6/26/17.

23-24. Tom Hamburger and Rosalind S. Helderman, "Former Trump Campaign Chairman Paul Manafort Files as Foreign Agent for Ukraine Work," *WaPo*, 6/27/17.

25. Eric Garcia, "Report: Manafort Donated to Rohrabacher After Meeting," *Roll Call*, 6/28/17.

26. Cecilia Vega and Benjamin Siegel, "Trump's Longtime Bodyguard Turned White House Aide Keith Schiller Eyed in House's Russia Probe, Sources Say," ABCNews.com, 6/29/17.

27. Lily Dobrovolskaya and Nicholas Nehamas, "Russian Official Linked to South Florida Biker Club Spent Millions on Trump Condos," *Miami Herald*, 6/22/17.

28-30. Sara Murray and Dana Bash, "Officials Struggle to Convince Trump That Russia Remains a Threat," CNN .com, 6/28/17.

31. Ali Watkins, "Intelligence Officials Worry State Dept. Going Easy on Russian Diplomats," *Politico*, 6/23/17.

32. Donald Trump (@realDonald Trump), "Hillary Clinton colluded with the Democratic Party in order to beat Crazy Bernie Sanders. Is she allowed to so collude? Unfair to Bernie!" Twitter, 6/25/17, 5:00 a.m.

33. Nada Bakos, "This Is What Foreign Spies See When They Read President Trump's Tweets," *WaPo*, 6/23/17.

34. John Hudson, "Moscow Is Recalling Russia's Ambassador to the US amid Election Controversy," *BF*, 6/26/17.

35. Devlin Barrett, "FBI Has Questioned Trump Campaign Adviser Carter Page at Length in Russia Probe," *WaPo*, 6/26/17.

36. Julia Manchester, "Ivanka Ordered to Testify in Dispute over Shoe Design," *The Hill*, 6/24/17.

37. Gerry Shih, "China Frees 3 Activists Who Probed Ivanka Trump Shoe Supplier," NBCWashington.com, 6/28/17.

38. Jon Swaine, "Authorities to Investigate Jay Sekulow Nonprofit After 'Troubling' Revelations," *Guardian*, 6/28/17.

39. Sahil Kapur (@sahilkapur), "The White House statement on the Senate Trumpcare score attacks the CBO, but doesn't defend the bill itself." Twitter, 6/26/17, 3:35 p.m.

40. German Lopez, "The Senate Health Care Bill Polls Even Worse than the Wildly Unpopular House Bill," *Vox*, 6/28/17.

41. Elizabeth Landers, Jim Acosta, and Dana Bash, "Pro-Trump Group Pulls Ad Against Fellow GOP Senator," CNN.com, 6/27/17.

42. Robert Costa, Sean Sullivan, Juliet Eilperin, and Kelsey Snell, "How the Push for a Senate Health-Care Vote Fell Apart amid GOP Tensions," *WaPo*, 6/28/17.

43–44. Courtney Kube and Alex Johnson, "White House Warns Syria Against Chemical Attack 'Preparations,'" NBCNews.com, 6/27/17.

45. Richard Wike, Bruce Stokes, Jacob Poushter, and Janell Fetterolf, "2. Worldwide, Few Confident in Trump or His Policies," Pew Research Center, 6/26/17.

46. AP, "Poll: Little Global Confidence in President Trump on Foreign Affairs," NBCNews.com, 6/27/17.

47. Daniel Dale, "Under Trump, a Majority of Canadians Dislike the U.S. for the First Time in 35 Years, Likely Much Longer," *Toronto Star*, 6/26/17.

48. Daniel Dale, "Donald Trump Makes 21 False Claims in Missouri Speech About Tax Plan," *Toronto Star*, updated 12/7/17.

49. Coral Davenport, "E.P.A. Official Pressured Scientist on Congressional Testimony, Emails Show," *NYT*, 6/26/17.

50. Daniel Lippman and John F. Harris, "'It's the End of Small Talk in Washington,'" *Politico*, July–August 2017.

51. Kevin Liptak and Allie Malloy, "White House Disinvites Press from Fundraiser," CNN.com, 6/29/17.

52. David A. Fahrenthold, "A *Time* magazine with Trump on the Cover Hangs in His Golf Clubs. It's Fake," *WaPo*, 6/27/17.

53. Niall Stanage, "Trump Praises Female Reporter's 'Nice Smile' on Call to Irish PM," *The Hill*, 6/27/17; Samantha Schmidt, "'I Bet She Treats You Well': Trump Calls Over Irish Reporter, Compliments Her 'Nice Smile,'" *WaPo*, 6/28/17.

54. Kyle Griffin (@kylegriffin1), "Trump today to Ireland's PM: 'We have so many people from Ireland in this country. I know so many of them, too. I feel I know all of them.'" Twitter, 6/27/17, 5:27 p.m.

55. "Republicans Already Working to Discredit Trump Russia Probe," *Rachel Maddow Show*, MSNBC, 6/28/17.

56. "Deutsche Bank Adds Lawyer with Financial Crime Background," *Rachel Maddow Show*, MSNBC, 6/27/17.

57. Jenny Strasburg, "Deutsche Bank Again Rebuffs Democratic Lawmakers' Requests for Trump Accounts," *WSJ*, 6/29/17.

58. Benjamin Siegel, "Graham, Grassley Ask FBI for Russia Investigation Surveillance Warrants," ABCNews.com, 6/28/17.

59. Brandon Carter, "Trump Election Panel Asks All 50 States for Voter Roll Data," *The Hill*, 6/29/17.

60. Dartunorro Clark, "Backlash at Trump Commission Request for 'Confidential' Voter Data," NBCNews .com, 7/1/17.

61. Dartunorro Clark, "Backlash at Trump Commission Request for 'Confidential' Voter Data," NBCNews .com, 7/1/17; Elliot Smilowitz, "Ind. Official Won't Turn Over Voter Data Despite Being on Trump's Voter Fraud Panel," *The Hill*, 6/30/17; Adam Ganucheau, "Hosemann on Trump Voter ID Request: 'Go Jump in the Gulf,'" *Mississippi Today*, 6/30/17.

62. Donald Trump (@realDonald Trump), "Numerous states are refusing to give information to the very distinguished VOTER FRAUD PANEL. What are they trying to hide?" Twitter, 7/1/17, 6:07 a.m.

63–64. "Correction: EPA-Dow Chemical Story," AP, 7/3/17.

65. David Choi, "'What the Heck Is This Thing': Sally Yates Describes How She Found Out About Trump's Travel Ban," *BI*, 6/29/17.

66. Max Greenwood, "Sally Yates: Trump Administration Behavior 'Should Be Alarming to Us as a Country,'" *The Hill*, 6/27/17.

67. Mike Levine, "At Least 1 US Nuclear Plant's Computer System Was Hacked," ABCNews.com, 6/28/17.

68. Josh Dawsey, Eliana Johnson, and Alex Isenstadt, "Tillerson Blows Up at Top White House Aide," *Politico*, 6/28/17.

70. Michael Isikoff, "Trump's Lawyers Fail to Follow Through on Threats to Comey," *YN*, 6/28/17.

71. Donald Trump (@realDonald Trump), "So they caught Fake News CNN cold, but what about NBC, CBS & ABC? What about the failing @nytimes & @washingtonpost? They are all Fake News!" Twitter, 6/27/17, 5:47 a.m.

72. Joe Concha, "Trump Posts O'Keefe Videos on Instagram," *The Hill*, 6/28/17.

73. Brian Stelter (@brianstelter), "3 fresh examples of press access being rolled back—at the White House, Pentagon, and Justice Department http://bit.ly/2trdBrr" Twitter, 6/28/17, 8:46 p.m.

74. Josh Delk, "Senate Panel to Get Comey Memos: Report," *The Hill*, 6/28/17.

75. Donald Trump (@realDonald Trump), "I heard poorly rated @Morning_Joe speaks badly of me (don't watch anymore). Then how come low I.Q. Crazy Mika, along with Psycho Joe, came.." Twitter, 6/29/17, 5:52 a.m.

76. "Krauthammer on Trump's Tweets: This Is What It's like in a Banana Republic," FoxNews.com, 6/29/17.

77. Julie Hirschfeld Davis, "Trump to Meet with Putin at G-20 Gathering Next Week," *NYT*, 6/29/17.

78. Yochi Dreazen, "Trump and Putin Are Meeting Tomorrow. Guess Which One Has an Agenda?" *Vox*, updated 7/6/17.

80–82. Shane Harris, "GOP Operative Sought Clinton Emails from Hackers, Implied a Connection to Flynn," *WSJ*, 6/29/17.

83. Shane Harris, Michael C. Bender, and Peter Nicholas, "GOP Activist Who Sought Clinton Emails Cited Trump Campaign Officials," *WSJ*, 7/1/17.

84. Gabriel Sherman, "What Really Happened Between Donald Trump, the Hosts of *Morning Joe*, and the *National Enquirer*," *DI*, 6/30/17.

85. Rachel Stockman, "Impeachable Offense? The Major Legal Concerns if Trump Blackmailed MSNBC's Mika and Joe," *Law & Crime*, 6/30/17.

86. Alex Sherman and Anousha Sakoui, "Jared Kushner Almost Bought the *National Enquirer* Three Years Ago," Bloomberg.com, 6/30/17; Jeffrey Toobin, "The *National Enquirer*'s Fervor for Trump," *NYer*, 7/3/17.

87. Tami Luhby, "32 Million People Would Lose Coverage if Obamacare Was Repealed," CNN.com, 6/30/17.

88. Michael Isikoff, "Bill to Create Panel That Could Remove Trump from Office Quietly Picks Up Democratic Support," *YN*, 6/30/17.

WEEK 34

Introduction. MoveOn.org, Facebook post, 7/4/17, https://www.facebook.com/moveon/videos/10154551772655493/?pnref=story.

1. Donald Trump (@realDonaldTrump), "Numerous states are refusing to give information to the very distinguished VOTER FRAUD PANEL. What are they trying to hide?" Twitter, 7/1/17, 6:07 a.m.

2. Liz Stark and Grace Hauck, "Forty-Four States and DC Have Refused to Give Certain Voter Information to Trump Commission," CNN.com, 7/5/17.

3. Pema Levy, "These Three Lawyers Are Quietly Purging Voter Rolls Across the Country," *MJ*, 7/7/17.

4. Anna Massoglia (@annalecta), "Hatch Act complaint against Kobach filed by @LawyersComm for using Trump's Election Integrity Commission to solicit political campaign money" Twitter, 7/3/17, 1:29 p.m.

5. Luke Broadwater, "Maryland Official Resigns from Trump Voter Fraud Panel," *Baltimore Sun*, 7/3/17.

6. Lydia Wheeler and Mike Lillis, "Voter Fraud Commission May Have Violated Law," *The Hill*, 7/5/17.

7. Sam Levine, "This DOJ Letter May Be More Alarming than Trump Commission's Request for Voter Data," *HuffPost*, 7/5/17; "Justice Department Pushes States on Voter Roll Purge," *Rachel Maddow Show*, MSNBC, 7/6/17.

8. Michael D. Shear, "'I'm President and They're Not': Trump Attacks Media at Faith Rally," *NYT*, 7/1/17.

9. Donald Trump (@realDonaldTrump) and President Trump (@POTUS), "#FraudNewsCNN #FNN" Twitter, 7/2/17, 6:21 a.m.

10. Avi Selk, "A Reddit User Who Wrote About Stabbing Muslims Is Claiming Credit for Trump's CNN Video," *WaPo*, 7/2/17.

11. Abby Ohlheiser, "The Reddit User Behind Trump's CNN Meme Apologized. But #CNNBlackmail Is the Story Taking Hold," *WaPo*, 7/5/17; Lloyd Grove, "High Anxiety at CNN amid Attacks from Trump and His Trolls," *DB*, 7/6/17; Joe Pompeo, "CNN Clamor Grows—NYT Copy-Editor Culling in Progress—Farewell for Now, Dear Reader," *Politico*, 7/7/17.

12. Lloyd Grove, "High Anxiety at CNN amid Attacks from Trump and His Trolls," *DB*, 7/6/17.

13. Hadas Gold, "Free-Press Groups Warn of Violence Against Media," *Politico*, 7/4/17.

14. Kelsey Tamborrino, "Maine's LePage Suggests He Makes Up Stories to Mislead Press," *Politico*, 7/6/17.

15. Michael M. Grynbaum, "The Network Against the Leader of the Free World," *NYT*, 7/5/17.

16. Alex Pfeiffer, "Source: Trump Doesn't Back the Time Warner and AT&T Merger if Zucker Still Heads CNN," *Daily Caller*, 7/6/17.

17. Matt Shuham, "Report: Trump Patron's Fund Bought Millions Worth of Shares in Time, Inc." *TPM*, 7/5/17.

18–19. "Maddow to News Orgs: Beware of Forged Trump Russia Documents!" *Rachel Maddow Show*, MSNBC, 7/6/17.

20. Ali Watkins and Josh Dawsey, "Trump's Leaks Crackdown Sends Chills Through National Security World," *Politico*, 7/7/17.

21. Tim Stelloh and Daniella Silva, "Protesters Rally in Dozens of Cities to Call for Trump's Impeachment," NBCNews.com, 7/2/17.

22. Liz Johnstone, "Tracking President Trump's Visits to Trump Properties," NBCNews.com, 8/10/17.

23. Coral Davenport, "Counseled by Industry, Not Staff, E.P.A. Chief Is off to a Blazing Start," *NYT*, 7/1/17.

24. Michael Biesecker, "States Sue over EPA's Decision to Keep Pesticide on Market," AP, 7/6/17.

25. Lillian Price and Jason Stein, "Wisconsin Assembly Passes Campus Free Speech Bill," *Milwaukee Journal Sentinel*, 6/23/17.

26. Caitlin Dickerson, "Trump Administration Targets Parents in New Immigration Crackdown," *NYT*, 7/1/17.

27. Josh Dawsey and Eliana Johnson, "Tillerson Argued with a Second White House Aide," *Politico*, 6/30/17.

28. Sarah Kaplan, "New Florida Law Lets Any Resident Challenge What's Taught in Science Classes," *WaPo*, 7/1/17.

29. Molly Hensley-Clancy, "18 States Are Suing Betsy DeVos over For-Profit College Rules," *BF*, 7/6/17.

30. Benjamin Wermund, "Title IX List Going Out of Print?" *Politico*, 6/29/17.

31. Christopher Ingraham, "White House Gender Pay Gap More than Triples Under Trump," *WaPo*, 7/5/17.

32. Rebecca Shabad, "Are Sleeveless Dresses 'Appropriate Attire'? Congress Doesn't Think So," CBSNews.com, 7/6/17.

33. Josh Delk, "Trump Lawyers Push Dismissal of Sexual Harassment Lawsuit," *The Hill*, 7/8/17.

34. "Auschwitz Memorial Condemns Congressman's Gas Chamber Video," AP, 7/4/17.

35. Mollie Reilly, "Disability Advocates Arrested at Rob Portman's Columbus Office," *HuffPost*, 7/7/17.

36. Joe Heim, "KKK Marchers Say They Will Be Armed Saturday at Charlottesville Rally," *WaPo*, 7/7/17.

37. Shawn Musgrave, "Pro-Trump Twitter Operatives Market Paid Tweets," *Politico*, 7/2/17.

38. Julian Borger, "Investigators Explore if Russia Colluded with Pro-Trump Sites During US Election," *Guardian*, 7/5/17.

39. Jordan Pearson, "The Same Twitter Bots That Helped Trump Tried to Sink Macron, Researcher Says," *Motherboard*, 7/6/17.

40. Amy B. Wang, "Some Trump Supporters Thought NPR Tweeted 'Propaganda.' It Was the Declaration of Independence," *WaPo*, 7/5/17.

41. Jessica Taylor, "Trump Fails to Reach Beyond Base as Independents' Disapproval Grows," NPR.org, 6/28/17.

42. Jessica Taylor, "Majority of Americans Believe Trump Acted Either Illegally or Unethically with Russia," NPR.org, 7/6/17.

43. Olivia Beavers, "McCain, Warren, Graham Visit Troops in Afghanistan for Fourth of July," *The Hill*, 7/4/17.

44. Josh Gerstein, "Despite Recusal, Sessions Offers Advice on Trump-Russia Probe," *Politico*, 7/1/17.

45. Rebecca Ballhaus, "Ethics Office to Release Two Dozen More Trump Waivers," *WSJ*, 6/2/17.

46. John Bowden, "Watchdog Says State Dept. Failing to Adequately Track Foreign Aid," *The Hill*, 7/1/17.

47. Felicia Schwartz, "State Department Workers Vent Grievances over Trump, Tillerson, Cite Longer-Term Issues," *WSJ*, 7/4/17.

48. Danielle Paquette and *WaPo*, "Trump Struck the Carrier Deal in the Dark. An Indiana Group Is Suing to Learn Details," *LAT*, 7/6/17.

49. German Lopez, "Trump's Pick to Lead Federal Civil Rights Efforts Defended Companies Accused of Discrimination," *Vox*, 6/30/17.

50. David Sirota, "Justice Department's Corporate Crime Watchdog Resigns, Saying Trump Makes It Impossible to Do Job," *IBT*, 7/2/17.

51. Rosalind S. Helderman and Matea Gold, "Federal Ethics Chief Who Clashed with White House Announces He Will Step Down," *WaPo*, 7/6/17.

52. Brooke Seipel, "Outgoing Ethics Director: Ethics Program 'a Very Serious Disappointment in the WH,'" *The Hill*, 7/7/17.

53. Citizens for Responsibility and Ethics in Washington, "CREW Files Ethics Complaint Against Jared Kushner," press release, 7/6/17, www.citizensforethics.org/press-release/crew-files-ethics-complaint-jared-kushner.

54. Natasha Bertrand, "House Republican Leader Balks at Russia Sanctions Bill over Concerns It Would Harm Texas Energy Companies," *BI*, 7/3/17.

55. Bradley Olson and Peter Nicholas, "Oil Giants Lobby Against Bill to Toughen Russia Sanctions," *WSJ*, 7/3/17.

56. Madeline Conway and Tyler Fisher, "Trump Organization Renews Rights to TrumpTowerMoscow.com," *Politico*, 7/5/17.

57. Dave Lawler, "Russia's Sputnik News Coming to D.C. Airwaves," *Axios*, 7/3/17.

58–60. Matt Tait, "The Time I Got Recruited to Collude with the Russians," *Lawfare*, 6/30/17.

61–62. David Goldstein and Greg Gordo, "Kremlin Documents Suggest Link between Cyber Giant and Russia Spy Agency," McClatchy, 7/3/17.

63–65. Pamela Brown, Shimon Prokupecz, and Evan Perez, "Russia Steps Up Spying Efforts After Election," CNN.com, 7/18/17.

66. AP, "Lawsuit Seeks to Void Georgia Congressional Election Results," *USN*, 7/4/17.

67–68. Brian Kemp, "States Keep Our Elections Secure," *USAT*, 7/2/17.

69. Del Quentin Wilber and Aruna Viswanatha, "Special Counsel Robert Mueller Taps Broad Range of Talent for Russia Probe," *WSJ*, 7/6/17.

70. Tom Burgis, "Russia-Born Dealmaker Linked to Trump Assists Laundering Probe," *FT*, 7/6/17.

71. Noah Barkin, "Merkel's Party No Longer Describing U.S. as a 'Friend,'" *HuffPost*, 7/3/17.

72. Marc Champion, Peter Martin, and Brian Parkin, "China, Germany Step Up as U.S. Retires from World Leadership," Bloomberg.com, 7/4/17.

73. Jacob Poushter, "On World Affairs, Most G20 Countries More Confident in Merkel than Trump," Pew Research Center, 7/5/17.

74. Heather Stewart, Patrick Greenfield, and Lisa O'Carroll, "White House Says Donald Trump Will Not Make Snap Visit to UK," *Guardian*, 7/3/17.

75. Glenn Thrush and Julie Hirschfeld Davis, "Trump, in Poland, Asks if West Has the 'Will to Survive,'" *NYT*, 7/6/17.

76. Darlene Superville and Ken Thomas, "Correction: Trump Story," AP, 7/6/17.

77. Glenn Thrush and Julie Hirschfeld Davis, "Trump, in Poland, Asks if West Has the 'Will to Survive,'" *NYT*, 7/6/17.

78. Dan Merica, "Trump Says Election Meddling 'Could Be Russia' but 'Nobody Really Knows for Sure,'" CNN.com, 7/6/17.

79. Karine Jean-Pierre (@K_JeanPierre), "This is what Donald Trump said today, out loud in public on a foreign trip in Poland: 'Do we even have seventeen intelligence agencies?'" Twitter, 7/6/17, 8:46 a.m.

80. "Russian Embassy Accuses Washington of Kidnapping," *Moscow Times*, 7/6/17.

81. Kyle Griffin (@kylegriffin1), "Top Senate Dems have sent a letter to Trump saying it'd 'be a severe dereliction of the duty' not to bring up election meddling with Putin." Twitter, 7/6/17, 8:11 a.m.

82. Brian Bennett, "Stakes Are High for Trump's Meeting with Putin. Here's What to Expect," *LAT*, 7/4/17.

83. Noa Yadidi and Allie Malloy, "Mexican Foreign Minister: 'Wall Was Not Discussed' in Bilateral Meeting," CNN.com, 7/7/17.

84. Donald Trump (@realDonald Trump), "Everyone here is talking about why John Podesta refused to give the DNC server to the FBI and the CIA. Disgraceful!" Twitter, 7/7/17, 12:40 a.m.

85. Victoria Craw, "Putin and Trump Talk Election Meddling, Syria and Ukraine in Two Hour Meeting at Hamburg G20," news.com.au, 7/18/17.

86. Jonathan Swan, "Inside the Trump-Putin Meeting," *Axios*, 7/6/17.

87. Steve Rosenberg (@BBCSteveR), "According to Lavrov, Trump told Putin some circles in America were 'exaggerating' allegations of Russian interference in the US election." Twitter, 7/7/17, 10:39 a.m.

88. Sally Yates (@SallyQYates), "POTUS' inexplicable refusal to confirm Russian election interference insults career intel pros & hinders our ability to prevent in future." Twitter, 7/7/17, 7:01 a.m.

89. Ken Gude (@KenGude), "Tillerson confirms U.S. surrender to Russia on election interference. This is a huge green light for future Russian influence operations." Twitter, 7/7/17, 11:55 a.m.; Caitlin Huey-Burns (@CHueyBurns), "'There was not a lot of re-litigating of the past,' Tillerson says re Putin meeting. 'This is a really important relationship.'" Twitter, 7/7/17, 11:04 a.m.

90. AP, "No Deal on Seized Russian Compounds in US After Trump-Putin Talks," NBCWashington.com, 7/8/17.

91. Stephen F. Hayes, "Trump Caves to Putin," *Weekly Standard*, 7/7/17.

92. AP (@AP), "BREAKING: Putin says he thinks Trump believes his denial of Russian meddling in US vote, but better to ask Trump himself." Twitter, 7/8/17, 7:34 a.m.

93. Abby Phillip, "Ivanka Trump Takes Father's Seat at G-20 Leaders' Table in Break from Diplomatic Protocol," *WaPo*, 7/8/17.

94. Michael Birnbaum and Damian Paletta, "At G-20, World Aligns Against Trump Policies Ranging from Free Trade to Climate Change," *WaPo*, 7/7/17.

95. Kevin Dolak, "US Stands Alone at G-20 Summit with Position on Climate Change," ABCNews.com, 7/8/17.

96. Michael Birnbaum and Damian Paletta, "Trump Leaves Leaders Fearing the Future as G-20 Summit Closes," *WaPo*, 7/8/17.

WEEK 35

1. "Pope Warns G20 Against 'Dangerous Alliances' Damaging Poor, Migrants: Paper," Reuters, 7/8/17.

2. Marina Fang, "Trump Proposes 'Cyber Security Unit' with Russia, Downplays Election Interference," *HuffPost*, 7/9/17.

3. Donald Trump (@realDonaldTrump), "The fact that President Putin and I discussed a Cyber Security unit doesn't mean I think it can happen. It can't-but a ceasefire can,& did!" Twitter, 7/9/17, 5:45 p.m.

4. Ellen Nakashima, "U.S. Officials Say Russian Government Hackers Have Penetrated Energy and Nuclear Company Business Networks," *WaPo*, 7/8/17.

5. Mark Hosenball, "Foreign Hackers Probe European Critical Infrastructure Networks: Sources," Reuters, 7/10/17.

6. Nicole Einbinder, "This Arkansas Bill Would Force Rape Survivors to Notify Their Attacker if They Need an Abortion," *Bustle*, 7/6/17.

7. Kyle Griffin (@kylegriffin1), "Capitol police are arresting health care protesters outside of GOP senate offices (via @MSNBC)." Twitter, 7/10/17, 11:34 a.m.

8. "Correction: Immigration Arrests Story," AP, 7/12/17.

9. Saeed Kamali Dehghan, "Iranian Cancer Researcher Detained at Boston Airport Despite Valid Visa," *Guardian*, 7/11/17.

10. Phillip Connor and Jens Manuel Krogstad, "In First Months of Trump Presidency, Christians Account for Growing Share of U.S. Refugee Arrivals," Pew Research Center, 7/12/17.

11. Jennifer Sinco Kelleher, "Judge in Hawaii Hands Trump Latest Defeat on Travel Ban," *PBS NewsHour*, 7/14/17.

12. Pete Kasperowicz, "Steve King: Use Planned Parenthood, Food Stamp Money to Fund Border Wall," *WE*, 7/12/17.

13. Eliana Johnson and Josh Dawsey, "Trump Crafting Plan to Slash Legal Immigration," *Politico*, 7/12/17.

14. Abigail Hauslohner and David Nakamura, "In Memo, Trump Administration Weighs Expanding the Expedited Deportation Powers of DHS," *WaPo*, 7/14/17.

15. Christina Cauterucci, "Betsy DeVos Plans to Consult Men's Rights Trolls About Campus Sexual Assault," *Slate*, 7/11/17.

16. Robert Silverman, "Betsy DeVos to Meet with Accused Rapists," *DB*, 7/12/17.

17. Katie Mettler, "Trump Official Apologizes for Saying Most Campus Sexual Assault Accusations Come After Drunken Sex, Breakups," *WaPo*, 7/13/17.

18. Pete Madden and Erin Galloway, "Jeff Sessions Addresses 'Anti-LBGB Hate Group,' but DOJ Won't Release His Remarks," ABCNews.com, 7/12/17.

19. Rebecca Shabad, "Female Lawmaker Violates Alleged House Dress Code," CBSNews.com, 7/12/17.

20. Josh Delk, "Female Lawmakers 'Bare Arms' in Sleeveless Attire to Support New House Dress Code," *The Hill*, 7/14/17.

21. Jane Kay, "Trump Administration Suddenly Pulls Plug on Teen Pregnancy Programs," *Reveal*, 7/14/17.

22. Scott Neuman, "ACLU Files Suit Against White House Election Fraud Commission," *The Two-Way* (blog), NPR, 7/10/17.

23. Michael Sheetz, "White House Publishes Voter-Fraud Feedback, Exposes Personal Information," CNBC .com, 7/14/17.

24. Brian Eason, "More than 3,000 Colorado Voters Have Canceled Their Registrations Since Trump Election Integrity Commission Request," *Denver Post*, 7/13/17.

25. Michelle Hackman, "Group Alleges Tom Price Improperly Spent Campaign Funds During Confirmation Fight," *WSJ*, 7/7/17.

26. Christina Wilkie and Chris Zubak-Skees, "Steve Bannon Misreports $2 Million Debt in Financial Disclosure," Center for Public Integrity," 7/13/17.

27. Will Evans, "Trump's Pick for Wage Chief Sued for Stiffing House Cleaners," *Reveal*, 7/12/17.

28. Matea Gold, Drew Harwell, Maher Sattar, and Simon Denyer, "Ivanka Inc.," *WaPo*, 7/14/17.

29. Christopher Matthews, "Indiana Lost 5,000 Manufacturing Jobs Under Trump," *Axios*, 7/11/17.

30. Jean Eaglesham and Lisa Schwartz, "Startup That Got a Seat at White House Roundtable Is Part-Owned by Kushner Family," *WSJ*, 7/14/17.

31. Hadas Gold, "Sinclair Increases 'Must-Run' Boris Epshteyn Segments," *Politico*, 7/11/17.

32. Justin Wm. Moyer, "From the Kremlin to K Street: Russia-Funded Radio Broadcasts Blocks from the White House," *WaPo*, 7/12/17.

33. "Zakharova Praises Russia Ambassador to US Efforts to Improve Bilateral Relations," Sputniknews.com; "'Intense Russophobia': US Activist Advises Companies Not to Insure Russian Ambassador's Life," RT.com, 7/11/17; Adam Garrie, "Radicalised Lesbian Threatens Russia Ambassador to USA," *The Duran*, 7/11/17.

34. Kenneth P. Vogel, "At Private Dinners, Pence Quietly Courts Big Donors and Corporate Executives," *NYT*, 7/9/17.

35. Danielle Ivory and Robert Faturechi, "The Deep Industry Ties of Trump's Deregulation Teams," *NYT*, 7/11/17.

36. Ben Walsh, Ryan Grim, and Clayton Swisher, "Jared Kushner Tried and Failed to Get a Half-Billion-Dollar Bailout from Qatar," *The Intercept*, 7/10/17.

37. Christine Brennan, "Donald Trump Said to Have Threatened USGA with Lawsuit if It Moved Women's Open," *USAT*, 7/11/17.

38. Donald Trump (@realDonald Trump), "I will be at the @USGA #USWomensOpen in Bedminster, NJ tomorrow. Big crowds expected & the women are playing great-should be very exciting!" Twitter, 7/14/17.

39. Amy Brittain, "State Department Spent More than $15,000 for Rooms at New Trump Hotel in Vancouver," *WaPo*, 7/12/17.

40. Mark Landler, Eric Schmitt, and Michael R. Gordon, "Trump Aides Recruited Businessmen to Devise Options for Afghanistan," *NYT*, 7/10/17.

41. Matt Ferner, "Twitter Users Who Were Blocked by Trump Take Him to Court," *HuffPost*, 7/12/17.

42. Ken Dilanian, "Comey Friend Responds to Trump Tweet About 'Illegal' Leaks," NBCNews.com, 7/10/17.

43-44. Jo Becker, Matt Apuzzo, and Adam Goldman, "Trump Team Met with Lawyer Linked to Kremlin During Campaign," *NYT*, 7/8/17.

45-47. Jo Becker, Matt Apuzzo, and Adam Goldman, "Trump's Son Met with Russian Lawyer After Being Promised Damaging Information on Clinton," *NYT*, 7/9/17.

48. Derek Hawkins, "Donald Trump Jr.'s Lawyer Is a Juilliard-Trained Trombonist Who Plays in a Symphony and Defends Mobsters," *WaPo*, 7/11/17; Philip Bump, "The Galaxy of Lawyers Defending Team Trump on the Russia Probe Gets Another Star," *WaPo*, 7/10/17.

49. Rosalind S. Helderman and Tom Hamburger, "Donald Trump Jr. Met with Russian Lawyer During Presidential Campaign After Being Promised Information Helpful to Father's Effort," *WaPo*, 7/9/17.

50. "Russia's Lavrov Threatens US over Seized Diplomatic Mansions," BBC News, 7/11/17.

51. Donald Trump Jr. (@Donald JTrumpJr), "Here's my statement and the full email chain" Twitter, 7/11/17, 8:00 a.m.; Brian Stelter (@brianstelter), "Confirmed from an NYT source: 'We were preparing to publish' story—Don Jr. camp 'asked for more time' to comment 'and then pre-empted us'" Twitter, 7/11/17, 2017.

52-54. Jo Becker, Adam Goldman, and Matt Apuzzo, "Russian Dirt on Clinton? 'I Love It,' Donald Trump Jr. Said," *NYT*, 7/11/17.

55. "Read the Emails on Donald Trump Jr.'s Russia Meeting," *NYT*, 7/11/17.

56-57. Jo Becker, Adam Goldman, and Matt Apuzzo, "Russian Dirt on Clinton? 'I Love It,' Donald Trump Jr. Said," *NYT*, 7/11/17.

58. Donald Trump (@realDonaldTrump), "How long did it take your staff of 823 people to think that up—and where are your 33,000 emails that you deleted?" Twitter, 6/9/16, 1:40 p.m.

59. Julian Assange (@JulianAssange), "Contacted Trump Jr this morning on why he should publish his emails (i.e with us). Two hours later, does it himself:" Twitter, 7/11/17, 12:14 p.m.

60. Callum Borchers, "The 4 Times Donald Trump Jr. Has Changed His Story About Meeting with a Russian Lawyer," *WaPo*, 7/11/17.

61. Peter Baker and Maggie Haberman, "Rancor at White House as Russia Story Refuses to Let the Page Turn," *NYT*, 7/11/17.

62. Samuel Chamberlain, "Donald Trump Jr. Tells Sean Hannity: 'In Retrospect I Probably Would Have Done Things a Little Differently,'" FoxNews.com, 7/12/17.

63-65. Michael Isikoff, "New Details Emerge on Moscow Real Estate Deal That Led to the Trump-Kremlin Alliance," *YN*, 7/11/17.

66. Michael Birnbaum, "Here's What the Businessmen Who Brokered the Russia Meeting with Trump Jr. Said in an Interview Last year," *WaPo*, 7/11/17.

67. Shimon Prokupecz, Evan Perez, and Pamela Brown, "Source: Justice Dept. Probe Will Look at Trump Jr.'s Disclosed Emails, Meeting," CNN.com, 7/11/17.

68. Kathryn Watson, "Joe Scarborough Announces He's Leaving the Republican Party," CBSNews.com, 7/12/17.

69. Peter Baker and Maggie Haberman, "Rancor at White House as Russia Story Refuses to Let the Page Turn," *NYT*, 7/11/17.

70. Justin Elliott and Jesse Eisinger, "Trump's Russia Lawyer Isn't Seeking Security Clearance, and May Have Trouble Getting One," *ProPublica*, 7/11/17.

71. Justin Elliott, "Trump Lawyer Marc Kasowitz Threatens Stranger in Emails: 'Watch Your Back, Bitch,'" *ProPublica*, 7/13/17.

72-74. Peter Stone and Greg Gordon, "Trump-Russia Investigators Probe Jared Kushner-run Digital Operation," McClatchy, 7/12/17.

75. Shane Harris, "Russian Officials Overheard Discussing Trump Associates Before Campaign Began," *WSJ*, 7/12/17.

76. "Rep. Brad Sherman Introduces Articles of Impeachment against Trump," *LAT*, 7/12/17.

77. Vivian Salama, "Trump in Paris: The Curious Case of His Friend Jim," AP, 7/12/17.

78. Jon Henley, "'You're in Such Good Shape': Trump Criticised for 'Creepy' Comment to Brigitte Macron," *Guardian*, 7/13/17.

79-80. Natasha Bertrand, "House Democrats Want to Know Why a Major Russian Money-Laundering Case Was Abruptly Settled," *BI*, 7/12/17.

81–82. Jose Pagliery, "Russian Money-Laundering Details Remain in the Dark as US Settles Fraud Case," CNN.com, 5/13/17.

83. Jonathan Swan, "Scoop: Trump Lawyers Want Wall Between Kushner, President," *Axios*, 7/12/17.

84–85. Mark Katkov and James Doubek, "Justice Department Releases Sessions' Disclosure Form, a Day Late," *The Two-Way* (blog), NPR, 7/13/17.

86. Craig Unger, "Trump's Russian Laundromat," *NR*, 7/13/17.

87. *The Lead* CNN (@TheLeadCNN), "Gorka says WH is considering giving back compounds to Russia because 'we want to give collaboration' a chance" Twitter, 7/13/17, 1:15 p.m.; Jim Sciutto (@jimsciutto), "As CNN has reported, US Intel found evidence the compounds were used for spying on the US" Twitter, 7/13/17, 1:30 p.m.

88. Dana Farrington, "Trump Says He Would Invite Putin to White House 'at the Right Time,'" NPR.org, 7/13/17.

89. Marl Landler and Maggie Haberman, "With Glare on Trump Children, Political Gets Personal for President," *NYT*, 7/12/17.

90–91. Katherine Skiba, David Heinzmann, and Todd Lighty, "Peter W. Smith, GOP Operative Who Sought Clinton's Emails from Russian Hackers, Committed Suicide, Records Show," *CT*, 7/13/17.

92. Ibid.; Shane Harris (@shaneharris), "When I spoke to Peter Smith I had no indication that he was ill or planning to take his own life." Twitter, 7/13/17, 4:15 p.m.

93. Ken Dilanian, Natasha Lebedeva, and Hallie Jackson, "Former Soviet Counterintelligence Officer at Meeting with Donald Trump Jr. and Russian Lawyer," NBCNews.com, 7/14/17.

94. Desmond Butler and Chad Day, "Russian-American Lobbyist Joined Trump's Son's Meeting, Too," AP, 7/15/17.

95. Katie Zavadski, Nico Hines, and Kevin Poulsen, "Trump Team Met Russian Accused of International Hacking Conspiracy," *DB*, 7/14/17.

96. AP, "Chuck Grassley Wants Donald Trump Jr. to Testify, Willing to Subpoena Him," *Des Moines Register*, 7/13/17.

97. Office of Chuck Grassley, "Complaint: Firm Behind Dossier & Former Russian Intel Officer Joined Lobbying Effort to Kill Pro-Whistleblower Sanctions for Kremlin," 3/31/17, news release, www.grassley.senate.gov/news/news-releases/complaint-firm-behind-dossier-former-russian-intel-officer-joined-lobbying-effort.

98. Jenna McLaughlin, Robbie Gramer, and Jana Winter, "Private Email of Top U.S. Russia Intelligence Official Hacked," *FP*, 7/14/17.

99. Michael Isikoff, "Sources: Trump Lawyers Knew of Russia Emails Three Weeks Ago," *YN*, 7/13/17.

100. "Trump Tower Russia Meeting: At Least Eight People in the Room," CNN.com, 7/15/17.

101. Aaron Blake, "'Lie After Lie After Lie': Fox News's Shepard Smith Has a Cronkite Moment on Russia," *WaPo*, 7/14/17; Leanne Naramore (@LeanneNaramore), "Shep Smith: 'The deception, Chris, is mind-boggling . . . why are we getting told all these lies?'" Twitter, 7/14/17.

102. Brett Forrest and Paul Sonne, "Russian Lawyer Whom Trump Jr. Met Says She Was in Contact with Top Russian Prosecutor," *WSJ*, 7/14/17; Philip Bump, "Who's Who in the Stunning Russia-Conspiracy Emails Released by Donald Trump Jr.," *WaPo*, 7/11/17.

103. Michael Isikoff, "White House Shakes Up Legal Team as Probe Gathers Steam," *YN*, 7/14/17.

104. "Trump Role in Publishing Hacked Material Draws Lawsuit," *Rachel Maddow Show*, MSNBC, 7/13/17; United to Protect Democracy v. Donald J. Trump for President, Inc., No. 1:17-cv-1370, U.S. District Court for the District of Columbia, filed 7/12/17, www.documentcloud.org/documents/3893506-Invasion-of-Privacy-lawsuit-complaint-Trump.html.

105. Christopher Mele, "Retrial Ordered for Activist Who Laughed During Sessions Confirmation," *NYT*, 7/14/17.

106. Alan Gomez, "First DREAMer Deported Under Trump Files Court Documents Disputing Administration's Account," *USAT*, 7/14/17.

WEEK 36

1. Marshall Cohen, "Trump Re-election Campaign Paid $50,000 to Law Firm Now Representing Donald Trump Jr.," CNN.com, 7/16/17.

2. Ashley Feinberg, "Trump's 2020 Campaign Has Already Paid Out $600K—to Trump," *Wired*, 7/20/17.

3. Maxwell Tani, "'I Ask the Questions and You Answer Them': Anchors Grill Trump's Lawyer in Blistering Interviews over Trump Jr.'s Meeting with a Russian Lawyer," *BI*, 7/16/17.

4. Arshad Mohammed and Howard Schneider, "U.S. Secret Service Rejects Suggestion It Vetted Trump's Son's Meeting," Reuters, 7/16/17.

5. Paulsen, "Record-Low Ratings for U.S. Women's Open," *Sports Media Watch*, 7/18/17.

6. Alexa Corse, "South Carolina May Prove a Microcosm of U.S. Election Hacking Efforts," *WSJ*, 7/16/17.

7–9. Massimo Calabresi, "Inside the Secret Plan to Stop Vladimir Putin's U.S. Election Plot," *Time*, 7/20/17.

10. Scott Clement and Dan Balz, "Poll Finds Trump's Standing Weakened Since Springtime," *WaPo*, 7/16/17.

11. Monmouth University Polling Institute, "Trump Ratings Hold Steady Despite Campaign's 2016 Russia Meeting," 7/17/17, www.monmouth.edu/polling-institute/reports/MonmouthPoll_NJ_071717.

12. Tom Jensen, "Health Care a Mine Field for Republicans; Many Trump Voters in Denial on Russia," Public Policy Polling, 7/18/17.

13. Gregory Krieg, "President Trump's First Six Months: By the Numbers," CNN.com, 7/20/17.

14. Jennifer Rubin, "Kobach Is a 'Useful Idiot' for Russia," *WaPo*, 7/20/17; Vanita Gupta, "The Voter Purges Are Coming," *NYT*, 7/19/17.

15. Jennifer Rubin, "Kobach Is a 'Useful Idiot' for Russia," *WaPo*, 7/20/17.

16. Samuel Oakford, "Trump's Air War Has Already Killed More than 2,000 Civilians," *DB*, 7/17/17.

17. Brian Naylor, "Mar-a-Lago Visitor Logs to Become Public, if They Exist," NPR.org, 7/17/17.

18. Eric Lipton and Nicholas Fandos, "Departing Ethics Chief: U.S. Is 'Close to a Laughingstock,'" *NYT*, 7/17/17.

19. Tracy Jan, "Trump Officials Open Border to 15,000 More Foreign Workers," *WaPo*, 7/17/17.

20. AP, "Dozens of Foreign Workers Sought for Trump's Florida Clubs," *Washington Times*, 7/21/17.

21. Jacqueline Thomsen, "White House Silent on Producing Ivanka Trump's Products in US," *The Hill*, 7/16/17.

22. Nina Totenberg, "Conservative Political Blogger Confirmed for Seat on Federal Appeals Court," NPR.org, 7/20/17.

23. Daniel Boffey and Christian Davies, "Poland May Be Stripped of EU Voting Rights over Judicial Independence," *Guardian*, 7/19/17.

24. Reuters, "Diplomats to Tillerson: Don't Eliminate State Department's Refugee Office," *Guardian*, 7/17/17.

25. Colum Lynch, "Tillerson to Shutter State Department War Crimes Office," *FP*, 7/17/17.

26. Tim Starks, "Top State Cyber Official to Exit, Leaving Myriad Questions," *Politico*, 7/18/17.

27. Abigail Williams and AP, "Under Tillerson, Exxon Showed 'Reckless Disregard' for Russia Sanctions, Says Treasury," NBCNews .com, 7/20/17.

28–29. Erica Orden and Byron Tau, "GOP Seeks to Close Federal Election Agency," *WSJ*, 7/17/17.

30. Andrew E. Kramer, "Huge Manafort Payment Reflects Murky Ukraine Politics," *NYT*, 7/15/17.

31–32. Michael Rothfeld, "New York Seeks Bank Records of Former Trump Associate Paul Manafort," *WSJ*, 7/17/17.

33. Jim Sciutto (@jimsciutto), "Just in: Russian Dep Foreign Minister Rybakov says Russian government 'almost' at a deal on getting back property seized by the US" Twitter, 7/17/17, 3:05 p.m.

34. Donald Trump (@realDonald Trump), "The Senate must go to a 51 vote majority instead of current 60 votes. Even parts of full Repeal need 60. 8 Dems control Senate. Crazy!" Twitter, 7/18/17, 6:26 a.m.

35. Hadas Gold, "Sinclair Executive Defends Company from 'Biased' Media in Internal Memo," *Politico*, 7/18/17.

36. Christopher Ingraham, "Jeff Sessions Wants Police to Take More Cash from American Citizens," *WaPo*, 7/17/17.

37. Senator Rand Paul (@RandPaul), "Asset forfeiture is an unconstitutional taking of property without trial. It's wrong and I call on the AG and the Adminsitraion to stop." Twitter, 7/20/17, 5:21 a.m.

38. Bradd Jaffy (@BraddJaffy), "WASHINGTON (AP)—Trump says Republicans should 'let Obamacare fail,' says, 'I'm not going to own it'" Twitter, 7/18/17, 9:46 a.m.

39. Evan Perez and Sara Murray, "WH Aides Exposed to Scrutiny over Russia Meeting Response," CNN.com, 7/14/17.

40. Desmond Butler and Chad Day, "Russian-American Lobbyist Joined Trump's Son's Meeting, Too," AP, 7/15/17.

41–42. Rosalind S. Helderman and Tom Hamburger, "Eighth Person in Trump Tower Meeting Is Identified," *WaPo*, 7/18/17.

43. Kyle Cheney, Darren Samuelsohn, and Ryan Hutchins, "Eighth Person in Trump Tower Meeting Was Linked to Money Laundering," *Politico*, 7/18/17.

44. "Ian Bremmer on Trump-Putin Meeting: Charlie Rose," *Charlie Rose*, PBS, 7/17/17.

45. Julie Hirschfeld Davis, "Trump and Putin Held a Second, Undisclosed, Private Conversation," *NYT*, 7/18/17.

46. Hallie Jackson (@HallieJackson), "NEW: White House offers expanded explanation of that second Trump/ Putin talk, via pool. Says they spoke 'briefly.' Key grafs —>" Twitter, 7/18/17, 4:09 p.m.; Julie Hirschfeld Davis, "Trump and Putin Held a Second, Undisclosed, Private Conversation," *NYT*, 7/18/17.

47. Nico Hines, "GOP Lawmaker Got Direction from Moscow, Took It Back to D.C.," *DB*, 7/19/17.

48. Greg Jaffe and Adam Entous, "Trump Ends Covert CIA Program to Arm Anti-Assad Rebels in Syria, a Move Sought by Moscow," *NYT*, 7/19/17.

49. Office of John McCain, "Statement by SASC Chairman John McCain on Reports Regarding Program to Assist the Syrian Opposition," press release, 7/20/17, www.mccain.senate.gov/public /index.cfm?p=press-releases&id=99F39 35E-EC3A-48DB-8C73-4C623D8 C9709.

50. "Russia Says in Talks with U.S. to Create Cyber Security Working Group: RIA," Reuters, 7/20/17.

51. "Excerpts from the *Times*'s Interview with Trump," *NYT*, 7/19/17.

52. Peter Baker, Michael S. Schmidt, and Maggie Haberman, "Citing Recusal, Trump Says He Wouldn't Have Hired Sessions," *NYT*, 7/19/17.

53–54. "Excerpts from the *Times*'s Interview with Trump," *NYT*, 7/19/17.

55. Ibid.; "Did Japan's First Lady Pretend Not to Speak English to Snub Trump," *Guardian*, 7/21/17.

56. Everett Rosenfeld and Angelica LaVito, "Mueller Reportedly Looking into Trump's Family Business as Part of Russia Probe," CNBC.com, 7/20/17.

57–58. Greg Farrell and Christian Berthelsen, "Mueller Expands Probe to Trump Business Transactions," Bloomberg.com, 7/20/17.

59–60. Erica Orden, "Special Counsel Investigating Possible Money Laundering by Paul Manafort," *WSJ*, 7/20/17.

61–65. Ben Protess, Jessica Silver-Greenberg, and Jesse Drucker, "Big German Bank, Key to Trump's Finances, Faces New Scrutiny," *NYT*, 7/19/17.

67–68. Vivian Salama, "Trump's Embrace of Russia Making Top Advisers Wary," AP, 7/20/17.

69. John Santucci and David Caplan, "What We Know About the Trump Legal Team Shakeup," ABCNews.com, 7/21/17.

70. Glenn Thrush and Maggie Haberman, "Sean Spicer Resigns as Press Secretary," *NYT*, 7/21/17.

71. Natasha Bertrand, "The White House's New Communications Director Has Been in Senators' Crosshairs," *BI*, 7/21/17.

72. Meg Wagner, "White House Press Briefing: Live Updates," CNN.com, 7/21/17.

73. Kevin Johnson, "In Break with Trump, Top Intelligence and Homeland Security Officials Affirm Russia's Election Meddling," *USAT*, 7/21/17.

74. Maria Tsvetkova and Jack Stubbs, "Exclusive: Moscow Lawyer Who Met Trump Jr. Had Russian Spy Agency as Client," Reuters, 7/21/17.

75. Allegra Kirkland, "Senate Intel Chair: 'The Unmasking Thing Was All Created by Devin Nunes,'" *TPM*, 7/21/17.

76. Michelle R. Smith, "Former Trump Adviser Flynn Consulting Again, Says Brother," AP, 7/21/17.

77. Matea Gold and Lisa Rein, "White House Taps New Acting Ethics Chief, Elevating General Counsel over Chief of Staff," *WaPo*, 7/21/17.

78–80. Carol D. Leonnig, Ashley Parker, Rosalind S. Helderman, and Tom Hamburger, "Trump Team Seeks to Control, Block Mueller's Russia Investigation," *WaPo*, 7/21/17.

81. John Bowden, "Dem Senator: Pardoning Targets of Russia Probe Would Be 'Crossing a Fundamental Line,'" *The Hill*, 7/20/17.

82. Fox News (@FoxNews), ".@newtgingrich: 'The Mueller investigation has so many conflicts of interests, it's almost an absurdity.' #Hannity" Twitter, 7/20/17, 7:33 p.m.

83. Brian Beutler, "We're on the Brink of an Authoritarian Crisis," *NR*, 7/20/17.

84–86. Adam Entous, Ellen Nakashima, and Greg Miller, "Sessions Discussed Trump Campaign–Related Matters with Russian Ambassador, U.S. Intelligence Intercepts Show," *WaPo*, 7/21/17.

87. John Santucci, Benjamin Siegel, and Justin Fishel, "Jared Kushner Agrees to Appear Before House Intelligence Committee," ABCNews.com, 7/21/17.

88. Jana Winter, Robbie Gramer, and Dan De Luce, "Trump Assigns White House Team to Target Iran Nuclear Deal, Sidelining State Department," *FP*, 7/21/17.

89–91. Jonathan O'Connell, Matea Gold, Drew Harwell, and Steven Rich, "In Revised Filing, Kushner Reveals Dozens of Previously Undisclosed Assets," *WaPo*, 7/21/17.

92. Miranda Green and Manu Raju, "Trump Jr. and Manafort Reach Deal with Senate Panel to Avoid Pubic Hearing," CNN.com, 7/21/17.

93. Ashley Parker and David Nakamura, "In Tweet Storm, Trump Decries 'Illegal Leaks' and Asserts 'All Agree' He Has Complete Power to Pardon," *WaPo*, 7/22/17.

94. Jessica Estepa, "Poll: Two-Thirds of Americans Disapprove of President Trump's Twitter Habit," *USAT*, 7/17/17.

95. Matt Flegenheimer and David E. Sanger, "Congress Reaches Deal on Russia Sanctions, Setting Up Tough Choice for Trump," *NYT*, 7/22/17.

WEEK 37

1. Eli Watkins, "Scaramucci: Trump Still Doesn't Accept Intelligence Conclusion on Russia," CNN.com, 7/23/17.

2. "Former CIA Director: Elected Officials Need to 'Stand Up' if Mueller Is Fired," NBCNews.com, 7/22/17.

3. Stephen Collinson, "Trump: 'We'll Let Obamacare Fail,'" CNN.com, 7/18/17; Paul Krugman, "Health Care in a Time of Sabotage," *NYT*, 7/21/17.

4. Liz Johnstone, "Tracking President Trump's Visits to Trump Properties," NBCNews.com, 8/10/17.

5. Fred Imbert, "Investors Have Dumped Majority of 'Trump Trade,' No Longer Banking on President's Agenda," CNBC.com, 7/24/17.

6–7. Jonathan Blitzer, "A Veteran ICE Agent, Disillusioned with the Trump Era, Speaks Out," *NYer*, 7/24/17.

8. Mana Yegani (@Law_Mana), "Breaking: Several people were arrested by ICE at the Houston USCIS (INS) office when they went for their marriage interviews for green cards" Twitter, 7/25/17, 5:22 p.m.

9. "U.S. Muslims Concerned About Their Place in Society, but Continue to Believe in the American Dream," Pew Research Center, 7/26/17.

10. Jan Cienski, "Protests in Warsaw as Government Moves on Courts," *Politico*, 7/21/17.

11. Donald Trump (@realDonald Trump), "So why aren't the Committees and investigators, and of course our beleaguered A.G., looking into Crooked Hillarys crimes & Russia relations?" Twitter, 7/24/17, 5:49 a.m.

12. Mike Allen, "Exclusive: Trump Ponders Rudy Giuliani for Attorney General," *Axios*, 7/24/17; Sari Horwitz, Matt Zapotosky, and Robert Costa, "Trump Leaves Sessions Twisting in the Wind While Berating Him Publicly," *WaPo*, 7/25/17.

13. Donald Trump (@realDonald Trump), "Attorney General Jeff Sessions has taken a VERY weak position on Hillary Clinton crimes (where are E-mails & DNC server) & Intel leakers!" Twitter, 7/25/17, 3:12 a.m.; Mike Allen, "Trump in Phone Call: 'What Would Happen if I Fired Sessions?'" *Axios*, 7/25/17.

14. Donald Trump (@realDonald Trump), "Why didn't A.G. Sessions replace Acting FBI Director Andrew McCabe, a Comey friend who was in charge of Clinton investigation but got. . . ." Twitter, 7/26/17, 6:48 a.m.

15. Carol D. Leonnig, Ashley Parker, and Philip Rucker, "Trump Talks Privately About the Idea of a Recess Appointment to Replace Sessions," *WaPo*, 7/26/17.

16. ChuckGrassley (@ChuckGrassley), "Everybody in D.C. Shld b warned that the agenda for the judiciary Comm is set for rest of 2017. Judges first subcabinet 2nd / AG no way" Twitter, 7/26/17, 5:18 p.m.; Jordain Carney, "Senate Dems Warn They Will Block Recess Appointments," *The Hill*, 7/25/17.

17. Paul Kane, "Senate Republicans Have Tolerated Trump's Controversies. His Treatment of Sessions Is Different." *WaPo*, 7/26/17.

18. NBC *Nightly News* with Lester Holt (@NBCNightlyNews), "President's criticisms 'kind of hurtful,' AG Sessions tell Fox News, but 'he wants all of us to do our job, and that's what I intend to do.'" Twitter, 7/27/17, 12:39 p.m.

19–20. Sally Q. Yates, "Sally Yates: Protect the Justice Department from President Trump," *NYT*, 7/28/17.

21. Eric Lipton, "New Ethics Chief Has Fought to Roll Back Restrictions," *NYT*, 7/26/17.

22. Christina Wilkie, "Steve Bannon Has a Shadow Press Office. It May Violate Federal Law." Center for Public Integrity, 7/27/17 (updated 8/4/17).

23. Christopher Ingraham, "Federal Judge Upholds Fine Against Kris

Kobach for 'Pattern' of 'Misleading the Court' in Voter-ID Cases," *WaPo*, 7/26/17.

24. Jane Musgrave, "West Palm Suit Says Trump Defying U.S. Constitution Emoluments Clause," *Palm Beach Post*, 7/28/17.

25. Ryan Struyk, "Trump's Approval is Underwater in 11 States He Won in November," CNN.com, 7/26/17.

26. Daniel Dale, "The 17 Most Jaw-dropping Moments of Donald Trump's Speech to Boy Scouts," *Toronto Star*, 7/24/17.

27. Alan Blinder and Mitch Smith, "After Trump Injects Politics into Speech, Boy Scouts Face Blowback," *NYT*, 7/25/17.

28. Jena McGregor, "How Trump's Speech to the Boy Scouts Could Put AT&T's CEO in a Tricky Spot," *WaPo*, 7/26/17.

29. Alana Abramson, "The Head of the Boy Scouts Just Apologized After Trump's National Jamboree Speech," *Time*, 7/27/17.

30. Sean Gallagher, "Tillerson Cuts High-Profile Cyberdiplomacy Office in State Dept. Reorg," *Ars Technica*, 7/20/17.

31. Josh Rogin, "State Department Head of Diplomatic Security Resigns," *WaPo*, 7/26/17.

32. John King, "A Chill Emanating from the White House Reaches State Department," CNN.com, 7/24/17; Graham Lanktree, "Rex Tillerson Debates Quitting After 'Unprofessional' Trump Bashes Jeff Sessions," *Newsweek*, 7/24/17.

33. Michelle Kosinski, Zachary Cohen, and Elise Labott, "Tillerson Takes Time Off as State Dept. Refuses to Say He Is Happy in His Role," CNN.com, 7/25/17.

34. Michelle Kosinski, Zachary Cohen, and Elise Labott, "Tillerson Takes Time Off as State Dept. Refuses to Say He Is Happy in His Role," CNN.com, 7/25/17.

35. A.J. Katz, "Andrea Mitchell Wants More Transparency From Pres. Trump's State Department," TVNewser, 7/29/17.

36. John Gizzi, "White House Won't Rule Out More Departures After Spicer," *Newsmax*, 7/22/17; Susan B. Glasser, "The Trump White House's War Within," *Politico*, 7/24/17; "Trump's 'America First' Policy Is Dividing the WH," *Axios*, 7/25/17.

37. Philip Rucker and Ashley Parker, "New Communications Director Moves Toward Possible Staff Purge at White House," *WaPo*, 7/24/17; "Scaramucci's First Firing at the White House," *Axios*, 7/25/17.

38-40. Charlie Savage and Adam Goldman, "Justice Dept. Nominee Says He Once Represented Russian Bank," *NYT*, 7/24/17.

41. Natasha Bertrand, "A Pro-Putin California Congressman Has Been Accused of Violating US Sanctions on Russia," *BI*, 7/24/17.

42. "READ: Jared Kushner's Statement on Russia to Congressional Committees," CNN.com, 7/24/17.

43. Peter Baker (@peterbakernyt), "Unusual: White House sets up a podium with the White House seal on the driveway for Jared Kushner to make his statement." Twitter, 7/24/17, 9:39 a.m.

44-46. Matt Apuzzo and Maggie Haberman, "'I Did Not Collude,' Kushner Says After Meeting Senate Investigators," *NYT*, 7/24/17.

47. Benjamin Siegel, "Jared Kushner Faced Second Day of Questioning on the Hill in Russia Probe," ABCNews .com, 7/25/17.

48-51. Wendy Dent, Ed Pilkington, and Shaun Walker, "Jared Kushner Sealed Real Estate Deal with Oligarch's Firm Cited in Money-Laundering Case," *Guardian*, 7/24/17.

52-53. Russ Choma and Dan Friedman, "Firm of Oligarch Behind Trump Jr. Meeting Was 'Primary Client' of Co. Probed for Money Laundering," *MJ*, 7/25/17.

54. Josh Delk, "WH Says Ivanka Will Not Retain Kushner's Russia Probe Lawyer," *The Hill*, 7/25/17; "Donald Trump Jr. Adds Washington Lawyer to Legal Team," Reuters, 7/23/17.

55. Eileen Sullivan and Adam Goldman, "Manafort Talks with Senate Investigators About Meeting with Russians," *NYT*, 7/25/17.

56. Morgan Chalfant, "House Intel Lawmakers Question Kushner for Three Hours as Part of Russia Probe," *The Hill*, 7/25/17.

57-58. Charles P. Pierce, "This Is How the Russian Kleptocracy Operates," *Esquire*, 7/27/17.

59. Manu Raju (@mkraju), "'I can tell you with 100% certainty that [Russian intelligence] knew about' Trump Tower meeting with Don Jr 'IN ADVANCE,' Browder testifies" Twitter, 7/27/17, 6:57 a.m.; Manu Raju (@mkraju), "Browder says that Fusion GPS—the firm behind the Russian dossier to get dirt on Trump—was hired by the Russians" Twitter, 7/27/17, 6:54 a.m.

60. John Parkinson and John Verhovek, "House Approves Russia Sanctions, Curbing Trump's Power," ABCNews. com, 7/25/17.

61. Stepan Kravchenko, "Russia Warns of 'Painful' Response if Trump Backs U.S. Sanctions," Bloomberg.com, 6/26/17.

62. Benjamin Parker, "The Other Russia: Poisonings, 'Accidents,' and Assassinations," *Weekly Standard*, 7/24/17.

63. Jason Leopold, Ken Bensinger, Anthony Cormier, Heidi Blake, Alex Campbell, Tom Warren, Jane Bradley, and Richard Holmes, "'Everyone Thinks He Was Whacked,'" *BF*, 7/28/17.

64. Sean Sullivan, Juliet Eilperin, and Kelsey Snell, "GOP Bill Is Voted Down as Divided Senate Dives into Health-Care Debate," *WaPo*, 7/26/17; Rebecca Savransky, "Poll: Support for ObamaCare Repeal-only Plan at 13 Percent," *The Hill*, 7/19/17.

65. "Protesters Disrupt Senate Floor," CNN.com, 7/25/17.

66. Jennifer Bendery (@jbendery), "Reporters blocked from Senate halls where protesters being arrested, shouting, 'Kill the bill!' Being told, 'no photos. Delete your photos.'" Twitter, 7/25/17, 11:36 a.m.

67. Philip Bump, "Senators on Hot Mic: Trump Is 'Crazy,' 'I'm Worried,'" *WaPo*, 7/25/17.

68. Sophie Tatum and Kyung Lah, "Political Chemistry: Scientists Running for Office in Age of Trump," CNN.com, 7/24/17.

69. Rebecca Shapiro, "Trump Ranks Himself Just Behind Lincoln.

Seriously." *HuffPost*, 7/26/17; Lee Moran, "Donald Trump's Mount Rushmore 'Joke' Goes Down as You'd Expect," *HuffPost*, 7/26/17.

70. Daniel Dale (@ddale8), "Tonight, the president told a graphic tale about sadistic illegal immigrants torturing beautiful teen girls:" Twitter, 7/25/17, 5:24 p.m.

71. Glenn Kessler and Michelle Ye Hee Lee, "26 Hours, 29 Trumpian False or Misleading Claims," *WaPo*, 7/26/17.

72. Donald Trump (@realDonald Trump), "After consultation with my Generals and military experts, please be advised that the United States Government will not accept or allow . . ." Twitter, 7/26/17, 5:55 a.m.; Donald Trump (@realDonaldTrump), ". . . . Transgender individuals to serve in any capacity in the U.S. Military. Our military must be focused on decisive and overwhelming. . . . ." Twitter, 7/26/17, 6:04 a.m.

73. Tom Vanden Brook, David Jackson, and Emma Kinery, "Trump's Ban Leaves Transgender Troops in Limbo, and His White House and Pentagon Scrambling," *USAT*, 7/26/17.

74-75. Helene Cooper, "Transgender People Can Still Server for Now, U.S. Military Says," *NYT*, 7/27/17.

76. Julie Hirschfeld Davis and Helene Cooper, "Trump Says Transgender People Will Not Be Allowed in the Military," *NYT*, 7/26/17.

77. Jessica Estepa, "Sen. Orrin Hatch: 'Transgender People Are People and Deserve the Best We Can Do for Them,'" *USAT*, 7/26/17.

78. Andrew Restuccia and Kyle Cheney, "Candidate for DHS Job Withdraws Because of Transgender Ban," *Politico*, 7/27/17.

79. Diana Ruggiero and Madison Park, "DOJ Files Amicus Brief That Says Title VII Does Not Protect Sexual Orientation," CNN.com, 7/27/17.

80. AP, "Lawmaker Blames Female Senators for Failed Health Care Bill," NBCNews.com, 7/24/17.

81. Donald Trump (@realDonald Trump), "Senator @lisamurkowski of the Great State of Alaska really let the Republicans, and our country, down yesterday. Too bad!" Twitter, 7/26/17, 4:13 a.m.

82. Erica Martinson, "Trump Administration Threatens Retribution Against Alaska over Murkowski Health Votes," *Anchorage Daily News*, 7/26/17 (updated 12/2/17).

83. Elise Viebeck, "Female Senators Are Increasingly on Receiving End of Insults from Male Officials," *WaPo*, 7/27/17.

84. Jacob Pramuk, "Lindsey Graham: 'There Will Be Holy Hell to Pay' if Trump Fires Sessions," CNBC.com, 7/27/17.

85. Jacqueline Thomsen, "Graham, Booker Writing Bill to Prevent Trump from Firing Special Counsel," *The Hill*, 7/27/17.

86. Colleen Shalby, "Scaramucci Tweets, Then Deletes, Confusing Statement That Referred to Information in Politico Report as a 'Leak,'" *LAT*, 7/26/17.

87-88. Ryan Lizza, "Anthony Scaramucci Called Me to Unload About White House Leakers, Reince Priebus, and Steve Bannon," *NYer*, 7/27/17.

89. Jon Levine, "Ryan Lizza: Scaramucci Told Me He Knew the Conversation Was '100% on the Record,'" *Mediaite*, 7/28/17.

90. Matt Flegenheimer, "With New Sanctions, Senate Forces Trump's Hand on Russia," *NYT*, 7/27/17.

91-92. Anne Gearan and Andrew Roth, "Trump Plans to Sign New Russia Sanctions Bill, White House Says," *WaPo*, 7/28/17.

93-94. Philip Bump, "Trump's Speech Encouraging Police to be 'Rough,' Annotated," *WaPo*, 7/28/17.

95. Suffolk County PD (@SCPDHq), "As a department, we do not and will not tolerate roughing up of prisoners." Twitter, 7/28/17, 1:53 p.m.

96. Gainesville Police (@GainesvillePD), "The @POTUS made remarks today that endorsed and condoned police brutality. GPD rejects these remarks and continues to serve with respect." Twitter, 7/28/17, 5:02 p.m.

97. "Statement from the International Association of Chiefs of Police on Police Use of Force," theiacpblog.org, 7/28/17.

98. "How the 'Skinny' Repeal Bill Was Defeated, Play by Play," *Roll Call*, 7/27/17.

99. Eric Levitz, "It's an Abomination That 49 GOP Senators Voted for 'Skinny Repeal,'" *DI*, 7/28/17.

100. "Enzi to Murray: 'Perhaps Your Time Might Be Better Spent Taking a Look at the Bill,' " *WaPo*, 7/27/17.

101. Ali Rogin, "How the GOP 'Skinny Repeal' Bill Tanked," ABCNews.com, 7/28/17.

102. Donald Trump (@realDonald Trump), "3 Republicans and 48 Democrats let the American people down. As I said from the beginning, let ObamaCare implode, then deal. Watch!" Twitter, 7/27/17, 11:25 p.m.

103. Donald Trump (@realDonald Trump), "If Republicans are going to pass great future legislation in the Senate, they must immediately go to a 51 vote majority, not senseless 60 . . ." Twitter, 7/28/17, 6:46 a.m.

104. Peter Nicholas and Michael C. Bender, "Trump Names Homeland Security Secretary John Kelly as New Chief of Staff," *WSJ*, 7/28/17.

105. Domenico Montanaro, "Trump Chief of Staff Priebus Is Out—in Biggest White House Staff Shake-up Yet," NPR.org, 7/28/17.

106. Editorial Board, "Priebus Wasn't the Problem," *WSJ*, 7/28/17.

107. Philip Bump, "An Overview of the Firings, Resignations and Withdrawn Nominations of the Trump White House," *WaPo*, updated 8/18/17.

108. Philip Rucker, Abby Phillip, Robert Costa, and Ashley Parker, "Trump Names Homeland Security Secretary John Kelly as White House Chief of Staff, Ousting Reince Priebus," *WaPo*, 7/28/17; John Harwood (@JohnJHarwood), "Ryan-Priebus ally to me: next phase of Trump presidency will be warfare against GOP Congress" Twitter, 7/28/17, 2:23 p.m.

109. Donald Trump (@realDonald Trump), "Republicans in the Senate will NEVER win if they don't go to a 51 vote majority NOW. They look like fools and are just wasting time. . . . . ." Twitter, 7/29/17, 4:32 a.m.; Donald Trump (@realDonaldTrump), "If the Senate Democrats ever got the chance, they would switch to a 51 majority vote in first minute. They are laughing at R's. MAKE CHANGE!" Twitter, 7/29/17, 4:47 a.m.

110. Donald Trump (@realDonald Trump), "Republican Senate must get rid of 60 vote NOW! It is killing the R Party, allows 8 Dems to control country. 200 Bills sit in Senate. A JOKE!" Twitter, 7/29/17, 4:20 a.m.; Donald Trump (@realDonaldTrump), "If a new HealthCare Bill is not approved quickly, BAILOUTS for Insurance Companies and BAILOUTS for Members of Congress will end very soon!" Twitter, 7/29/17, 9:27 a.m.

WEEK 38

1. Esme Cribb, "Conway Advises WH Staffers to Address Trump with 'Deference and Humility,'" *TPM*, 7/30/17.

2. Josh Feldman, "CNN's Zakaria: The U.S. Is 'Becoming Irrelevant' Under Trump," *Mediaite*, 7/30/17.

3. Andrew Roth, "Putin Orders Cut of 755 Personnel at U.S. Missions," *WaPo*, 7/30/17.

5. Kiah Collier and T. Christian Miller, "Border Agency Set to Jumpstart Trump's Wall in a Texas Wildlife Refuge," *ProPublica*, 7/28/17.

6. Juliet Eilperin and Brady Dennis, "At EPA Museum, History Might Be in for a Change," *WaPo*, 7/30/17.

7. Jennifer Wishon, "Bible Studies at the White House: Who's Inside This Spiritual Awakening," CBNNews.com, 7/1/17.

8. Palm Center, "Fifty-Six Retired Generals and Admirals Warn That President Trump's Anti-Transgender Tweets, if Implemented, Would Degrade Military Readiness," press release, assets2.hrc.org/files/assets /resources/56_Generals_and_Admi rals_Warn_Trump.pdf.

9. Kate McKenna, "Montreal's Olympic Stadium Used to House Surge in Asylum Seekers Crossing from U.S." CBC.ca, 8/2/17.

10. Ian Cummings, "NAACP Issues First-Ever Travel Advisory for a State—and It's Missouri," McClatchy, 8/2/17.

11. AP, "Kobach Appeals Order to Answer Questions Under Oath," *Kansas City Star*, 8/1/17.

12. Jacqueline Thomsen, "Top EPA Official Resigns over Direction of Agency Under Trump," *The Hill*, 8/1/17.

13. Charlie Savage, "Justice Dept. to Take On Affirmative Action in College Admissions," *The Hill*, 8/1/17.

14. Annie Waldman, "DeVos Pick to Head Civil Rights Office Once Said She Faced Discrimination for Being White," *ProPublica*, 4/14/17.

15. Rachel Chason, "He Went to ICE to Tell Agents He Had Gotten into College. Now He and His Brother Have Been Deported," *WaPo*, 8/2/17.

16. Betsy Woodruff, "Trump's DHS Ordered Agents to Block Congressmen During Travel Ban," *DB*, 8/2/17.

17. Dara Lind, "What John Kelly's Final ICE Raid Tells Us About Trump's New Chief of Staff," *Vox*, 8/2/17.

18. Josh Rogin, "State Department Considers Scrubbing Democracy Promotion from Its Mission," *WaPo*, 8/1/17.

19. Elizabeth Weise, "Hackers at DefCon Conference Exploit Vulnerabilities in Voting Machines," *USAT*, 7/30/17.

20. Tim Alberta, "Without Priebus, Trump Is a Man Without a Party," *Politico*, 7/30/17.

21–23. Ashley Parker, Carol D. Leonnig, Philip Rucker, and Tom Hamburger, "Trump Dictated Son's Misleading Statement on Meeting with Russian Lawyer," *WaPo*, 7/31/17.

24. Paul Waldman, "President Trump Is Now Directly Implicated in Trying to Cover Up the Russia Scandal," *WaPo*, 8/1/17.

25. "Investigators Want Phone Records Related to Trump Jr. Russia Meeting," CBSNews.com, 8/2/17.

26. Richard Pérez-Peña, "Former Arizona Sheriff Joe Arpaio Is Convicted of Criminal Contempt," *NYT*, 7/31/17.

27. Sean Holstege, "Ex-sheriff Is a No-show for the Joe Show, but the Case Edges Closer to Sentencing," *Phoenix New Times*, 8/3/27.

28. Ashley Hoffman, "President Trump Just Called Back to 'The Apprentice' in a White House Meeting," *Time*, 7/31/17.

29. Elaina Plott, "Ryan Zinke, Trump's Cowboy Enforcer, Is Ready for His Closeup," *GQ*, 7/31/17.

30. Kimberly Kindy, "In Trump Era, Lobbyists Boldly Take Credit for Writing a Bill to Protect Their Industry," *WaPo*, 8/1/17.

31. Nicholas Confessore and Kenneth P. Vogel, "Trump Loyalist Mixes Business and Access at 'Advisory' Firm," *NYT*, 8/1/17.

32. Carol D. Leonnig and David A. Fahrenthold, "Secret Service Vacates Trump Tower Command Post in Lease Dispute with President's Company," *WaPo*, 8/3/17.

33–34. Tony Cook, "After 6 Months, Pence Has Now Turned Over All State-Related AOL Emails, His Attorneys Say," *IndyStar*, 8/4/17.

35. Jeffrey Young, "Court Ruling Throws a Wrench in Trump's Obamacare Sabotage Plan," *HuffPost*, 8/1/17.

36. "Ivanka Trump: 'We Are Committed to Supporting the American Worker,'" video, *WaPo*, 8/1/17.

37. Erica Orden, Aruna Viswanatha, and Byron Tau, "U.S. Attorney Subpoenas Kushner Cos. over Investment-for-Visa Program," *WSJ*, 8/2/17.

38. Michael D. Shear, Glenn Thrush, and Maggie Haberman, "John Kelly, Asserting Authority, Fires Anthony Scaramucci," *NYT*, 7/31/17.

39. Josh Dawsey, "Kelly Cracks Down on West Wing Back Channels to Trump," *Politico*, 8/2/17.

40. CBS and AP, "Kelly Called Sessions to Say Job Is Safe, Sources Say," CBSNews.com, 8/2/17.

41. Shimon Prokupecz and Pamela Brown, "EXCLUSIVE: Kelly Called Comey to Express Anger over Firing, Sources Say," CNN.com, 8/1/17.

42. Nolan D. McCaskill, "Tillerson: I've Told Russia Our Relationship Can Get Worse, 'and It Just Did,'" *Politico*, 8/1/17.

43. Abigail Williams, "Tillerson Faces Many Unfilled Top Spots at State Department," NBCNews.com, 8/2/17.

44. Karen Freifeld, "Exclusive: Former Justice Department Official Joins Mueller Team," Reuters, 8/1/17.

45. Alan Shipnuck, "First Golfer: Donald Trump's Relationship with Golf Has Never Been More Complicated," Golf.com, 8/1/17; "The Latest: Report

Says Trump Called White House a 'Dump,'" AP, 8/1/17.

46. Donald Trump (@realDonald Trump), "I love the White House, one of the most beautiful buildings (homes) I have ever seen. But Fake News said I called it a dump—TOTALLY UNTRUE," Twitter, 8/2/17, 6:29 p.m.

47. "PODCAST: The Story Behind Our Trump Golf Story (and a Certain Explosive Quote)," Golf.com, 8/2/17; Robin Eberhardt, "Golf Journalist: At Least 8 People Heard Trump Call the White House a 'Dump,'" *The Hill*, 8/3/17.

48–49. Carol E. Lee and Courtney Kube, "Trump Says U.S. 'Losing' Afghan War in Tense Meeting with Generals," NBCNews.com, 8/2/17.

50. Rosie Gray, "H.R. McMaster Cleans House at the National Security Council," *Atlantic*, 8/2/17.

51. Mike Allen, "1 Big Thing: Trump's National-Security Dominoes," *Axios*, undated.

52. "A Letter from H.R. McMaster Said Susan Rice Will Keep Her Top-Secret Security Clearance," *Circa*, 8/3/17.

53. Natasha Bertrand, "The Knives Are Coming Out for H.R. McMaster," *BI*, 8/4/17; Alexander Panetta (@Alex_Panetta), "This new Russian troll-tracking tool by @SecureDemocracy shows today's top messaging priority from the Kremlin: Firing NSA HR McMaster" Twitter, 8/3/17, 3:24 p.m.

54–55. David Folkenflik, "Behind Fox News' Baseless Seth Rich Story: The Untold Tale," *Morning Edition*, NPR, 8/1/17.

56. Julia Jacobo, "White House Reviewed Fox News Story About Slain DNC Staffer: Lawsuit," ABCNews.com, 8/1/17.

57. Michael Isikoff and Hunter Walker, "Lawyer Wants Trump's Testimony in 'Fake News' Suit Against Fox," *YN*, 8/1/17.

58. Hunter Walker, "Reporter Says 'Russian Propaganda Outlet' Pushed Him to Cover Conspiracy Theory at the Center of a White House Lawsuit," *YN*, 8/3/17.

59. Jeff Stein, "How Russia Is Using LinkedIn as a Tool of War Against Its U.S. Enemies," *Newsweek*, 8/3/17.

60. David Nakamura, "Trump, GOP Senators Introduce Bill to Slash Legal Immigration Levels," *WaPo*, 8/3/17.

61. ABC News (@ABC), "Pres. Trump: The Raise Act will favor green card applicants who can speak English, financially support themselves, contribute to economy" 8/2/17, 8:47 a.m.

62. Josh Boak and Astrid Galvin, "AP FACT CHECK: Trump Immigration Pitch on Shaky Ground," AP, 8/3/17.

63. United States Conference of Catholic Bishops, "RAISE Act Will Weaken Family Bonds and Impact Nation's Ability to Respond to Those in Crisis Says U.S. Catholic Bishops Chairman," news release, 8/2/17, www.usccb.org/news/2017/17-138.cfm.

64–65. "Stephen Miller's Statue of Liberty remarks disturbed many" Twitter Moments, 8/2/17.

66. Charles P. Pierce, "The Historical Significance of 'Cosmopolitan' as an Insult," *Esquire*, 8/2/17.

67. Anne Frank Center (@AnneFrankCenter), "Nazis found Anne Frank on August 4, 1944. In 1941, U.S. denied entrance to Frank family. Reasons refugees hear now. #NeverAgain to anyone." Twitter, 8/4/17, 3:47 a.m.

68. Alana Abramson, "Boy Scouts 'Unaware' of Call Trump Said He Received from Organization Praising Jamboree Speech," *Time*, 8/1/17.

69. Robbie Whelan, "Peña Nieto Never Praised Trump's Border Policies in Phone Call, Mexico Says," *WSJ*, 8/2/17.

70. Kathryn Watson, "Sanders Forced to Revise Trump's Claim About Conversations with Heads of Boy Scouts, Mexico," CBSNews.com, 8/2/17.

71. Ali Vitali, "Donald Trump Signs Russia Sanctions Bill for 'Sake of National Unity,'" NBCNews.com, 8/3/17.

72. "Trump Statement on Russia Sanctions: My Company Worth 'Many Billions,'" NBCNews.com, 8/2/17.

73. Donald Trump (@realDonald Trump), "Our relationship with Russia is at an all-time & very dangerous low. You can thank Congress, the same people that can't even give us HCare!" Twitter, 8/3/17, 5:18 a.m.

74. Rebecca Savransky, "McCain Fires Back at Trump: 'You Can Thank Putin' for Poor Relations with Russia," *The Hill*, 8/3/17.

75. NBC *Nightly News* with Lester Holt (@NBCNightlyNews), "JUST IN: Russian PM Medvedev: Pres. Trump's admin. 'has demonstrated full impotence' in signing new Russia sanctions." Twitter, 8/2/17, 12:21 p.m.; Dmitry Medvedev (@Medvedev RussiaE), "The Trump administration has shown its total weakness by handing over executive power to Congress in the most humiliating way" Twitter, 8/2/17, 1:38 p.m.

76. Rasmussen Reports, "Daily Presidential Tracking Poll," 8/4/17, rasmussenreports.com; "Gallup Daily: Trump Job Approval," Gallup News, news.gallup.com/poll/201617/gallup-daily-trump-job-approval.aspx; Quinnipiac Poll, 8/2/17, poll.qu.edu/national/release-detail?ReleaseID=2478.

77. Quinnipiac Poll, 8/2/17, poll.qu.edu/national/release-detail?ReleaseID=2478.

78. Karoun Demirjian, "Senators Unveil Two Proposals to Protect Mueller's Russia Probe," *WaPo*, 8/3/17.

79. Henry J. Gomez, "RNC Tells Staff to Preserve All Documents Related to 2016 Campaign," *BF*, 7/31/17.

80–81. Del Quentin Wilber and Byron Tau, "Special Counsel Robert Mueller Impanels Washington Grand Jury in Russia Probe," *WSJ*, 8/3/17.

82. Karen Freifeld, "Exclusive: Grand Jury Subpoenas Issued in Relation to Russian Lawyer, Trump Jr. Meeting—Sources," Reuters, 8/3/17.

83. Noah Bierman, "As Russia Investigation Reaches New Milestone, Trump Lashes Out at 'Fake Story' as Crowd Chants 'Lock Her Up!'" *LAT*, 8/3/17.

84. "Watch President Trump's Rally in West Virginia," video, NBCNews.com, 8/3/17.

85. Sean Sullivan, "Recess Just Started for Congress, and It's Not Going to Be Much Fun for Republicans," *WaPo*, 8/3/17.

86. Jordain Carney, "Senate Blocks Trump from Making Recess Appointments over Break," *The Hill*, 8/3/17.

87. Nicole Lafond, "Interior Dept Watchdog Launches Probe into Zinke Calls to Alaska Senators," *TPM*, 8/4/17.

88-89. Anna R. Schechter, "Trump-Linked Data Firm Removes State Dept., NATO Logos After NBC Questions," NBCNews.com, 8/2/17.

90-92. "Clarification: Trump-Russia Probe-Flynn Story," AP, 8/7/17.

93-96. Evan Perez, Pamela Brown, and Shimon Prokupecz, "One Year into the FBI's Russia Investigation, Mueller Is on the Trump Money Trail," CNN.com, 8/4/17.

97. Murray Waas, "Exclusive: Top FBI Officials Could Testify Against Trump," *Vox*, 8/3/17.

98-99. Greg Miller, "Trump Urged Mexican President to End His Public Defiance on Border Wall, Transcript Reveals," *WaPo*, 8/3/17.

100. Liam Stack, "Trump Called New Hampshire a 'Drug-Infested Den,' Drawing the Ire of Its Politicians," *NYT*, 8/3/17.

101. Angela Dewan and Kara Fox, "Australian PM Turnbull Feels Heat from Spiky Trump Call," CNN.com, 8/4/17.

102. Greg Miller, "Trump Urged Mexican President to End His Public Defiance on Border Wall, Transcript Reveals," *WaPo*, 8/3/17.

103. Jay Willis, "Laziest President in American History Departs for 17-Day Golf Resort Vacation," *GQ*, 8/4/17.

104. Alexander Nazaryan, "Trump, America's Boy King: Golf and Television Won't Make America Great Again," *Newsweek*, 8/1/17.

105. Ali Watkins, "Hunt for Trump Dossier Author Inflames Russia Probe," *Politico*, 8/4/17.

106. Matt Zapotosky and Devlin Barrett, "Attorney General Says Justice Dept. Has Tripled the Number of Leak Probes," *WaPo*, 8/4/17; NPR (@NPR), "Attorney General Jeff Sessions said in a briefing this morning that Justice Department is reviewing its policies affecting media subpoenas." 8/4/17, 8:37 a.m.

107-110. Matthew Rosenberg, Matt Apuzzo, and Michael S. Schmidt, "Mueller Seeks White House Documents on Flynn," *NYT*, 8/4/17.

WEEK 39

1. Emmy Tillett, "Trump Launches 'Real' Trump TV News with Kayleigh McEnany," CBSNews.com, 8/8/17.

2. Ted Johnson, "Former CNN Commentator Kayleigh McEnany Named New RNC Spokeswoman," *Variety*, 8/7/17.

3. Lachlan Markay and Asawin Suebsaeng, "Lara Trump 'Running the Show' at 'Trump TV,'" *DB*, 8/7/17.

4. Margaret Harding McGill and John Hendel, "How Trump's FCC Aided Sinclair's Expansion," *Politico*, 8/6/17.

5. Alvin Chang, "We Analyzed 17 Months of *Fox & Friends* Transcripts. It's Far Weirder than State-Run-Media." *Vox*, 8/7/17.

6. Mallory Shelbourne, "Rosenstein: Trump Did Not Direct Feds to Investigate Clinton," *The Hill*, 8/6/17.

7. Kelsey Snell and John Wagner, "Rosenstein: Special Counsel Mueller Can Investigate Any Crimes He Uncovers in Russia Probe," *WaPo*, 8/6/17.

8. Steve Benen, "Conway Suggests Lie-Detector Tests May Be Used in White House," *MaddowBlog*, 8/7/17.

9. Editorial board, "The Trump Justice Department Joins the GOP Crusade to Shrink the Vote," *WaPo*, 8/10/17.

10. Priorities USA, "The Indiana Conference of the NAACP, Supported by Priorities USA Foundation, Files Suit Against Discriminatory and Unconstitutional Indiana Precinct Consolidation Law," press release, http://mailchi.mp/prioritiesusaaction/priorities-usa-launches-new-six-figure-digital-ad-campaign-to-hold-trump-and-senate-republicans-accountable-for-trumpcare-575357.

11. Ariel Malka and Yphtach Lelkes, "In a New Poll, Half of Republicans Say They Would Support Postponing the 2020 Election if Trump Proposed It," *WaPo*, 8/10/17.

12. Collin Binkley, "Ivy League Schools Brace for Scrutiny of Race in Admissions," AP, 8/6/17.

13. Joe Sterling, "Minnesota Governor: Mosque Blast an 'Act of Terrorism,'" CNN.com, 8/7/17.

14. "White House Defends Its Silence on Mosque Bomb," BBC News, 8/8/17.

15. FOX & Friends (@foxandfriends), "France vehicle attack leaves at least six soldiers injured" Twitter, 8/9/17, 3:17 a.m.

16. Corky Siemaszko, "NAACP Legal Defense Fund Appeals Ruling Allowing White Alabama Town to Secede from School District," NBCNews.com, 8/11/17.

17. Brian Stelter, "CNN Severs Ties with Jeffrey Lord," CNN.com, 8/10/17.

18. Ricardo Alonso-Zaldivar, "Study Says Trump Moves Trigger Health Premium Jumps for 2018," AP, 8/10/17.

19. Lisa Friedman, "Scientists Fear Trump Will Dismiss Blunt Climate Report," *NYT*, 8/7/17.

20. Oliver Milman, "US Federal Department Is Censoring Use of Term 'Climate Change', Emails Reveal," *Guardian*, 8/7/17.

21. Lara Korte, "This Woman Went to a Bon Jovi Concert for Her Birthday. An Act of Hatred Made Her Leave." *Cincinnati Enquirer*, 8/6/17.

22. Dominic Holden (@dominicholden), "JUST IN: 5 transgender troops sue Trump over his tweets/policy on trans military ban. Complaint: glad.org/wp-content/upl . . ." Twitter, 8/9/17, 7:33 a.m.

23. "Canada Military Builds Refugee Camp for Refugees from US," BBC News, 8/9/17.

24. Andrew Kaczynski, Chris Massie, and Paul LeBlanc, "Trump Pick Sam Clovis Stoked Birther Conspiracy, Called Eric Holder a 'Racist Black,'" CNN.com, 8/11/17.

25. Lydia Wheeler, "Fight over Right to Sue Nursing Homes Heats Up," *The Hill*, 8/6/17.

26. Trump Organization (@Trump), "Delighted to announce the launch of The Trump Estates Park Residences, a collection luxury villas with exclusive access to @TrumpGolfDubai!" Twitter, 8/5/17, 7:28 a.m.

27. Jonathan O'Connell, "How the Trump Hotel Changed Washington's Culture of Influence," *WaPo*, 8/7/17.

28. Jonathan O'Connell, "Trump D.C. Hotel Turns $2 Million Profit in Four Months," *WaPo*, 8/10/17.

29. Alexandra Berzon, "Trump Hotel in Washington Saw Strong Profit in First Four Months of 2017," *WSJ*, 8/11/17.

30. Peter Overby, "Hill Democrats Launch Investigation of Federal Spending at Trump Businesses," NPR.org, 8/8/17.

31. Eric Wolff and Darius Dixon, "Why Are These Billions in Pipeline Projects Stalled?" *Politico*, 8/5/17.

32. Danielle Ivory and Robert Faturechi, "Secrecy and Suspicion Surround Trump's Deregulation Teams," *NYT*, 8/7/17.

33. Josh Gerstein, "Judges Set Oct. 18 Arguments in Trump Foreign Emoluments Suit," *Politico*, 8/9/17.

34. Walter Shaub (@waltshaub), "It's not fire&fury but this should've been a headline today: OGE rejects retroactive WH waivers in letter to Senate. https://www.oge.gov/web/OGE.nsf/Congr . . ." Twitter, 8/10/17, 11:24 a.m.

35. Alex Isenstadt, "Top Trump Donor Ponies Up to Take Out Flake," *Politico*, 8/9/17.

36. Erika Kinetz and Kelvin Chan, "Trump Company Applies for Casino Trademark in Macau," AP, 8/7/17.

37. Kambiz Foroohar, "U.S. Ambassador Haley Loses Two Key Aides at United Nations," Bloomberg.com, 8/10/17.

38. Kevin Collier, "Four Top Cybersecurity Officials Are Leaving US Government," *BF*, 8/10/17.

39. Chris Morris, "California Crops Rot as Immigration Crackdown Creates Farmworker Shortage," *Fortune*, 8/8/17.

40. Daniel Dale, "Donald Trump Makes 21 False Claims in Missouri Speech about Tax Plan," *Toronto Star* [continuously updated], updated 12/7/17 as of press.

41. Jennifer Agiesta, "Trump at 200 Days: Declining Approval amid Widespread Mistrust," CNN.com, 8/8/17.

42. "Iowa Democrats Win Special Election in Trump +22 District," *Iowa Starting Line*, 8/8/17.

43. Ken Thomas and Steve Peoples, "On Behalf of Trump, Pence Carves His Own Political ID," AP, 8/8/17.

44. Louis Nelson, "Blumenthal: I Can't Explain Trump's 'Obsession' with Me," *Politico*, 8/8/17.

45. Abby Phillip, "The Curious Case of 'Nicole Mincey,' the Trump Fan Who May Actually Be a Bot," *WaPo*, 8/7/17.

46. Alex Thompson, "Trump Gets a Folder Full of Positive News About Himself Twice a Day," *Vice News*, 8/9/17.

47–48. Steven T. Dennis, "Trump Campaign Turns over Thousands of Documents in Russia Probe," Bloomberg.com, 8/8/17.

49. Richard Johnson, "Donald Trump's Tall Tales About the '21' Club," *Page Six*, 8/6/17.

50–52. Carol D. Leonnig, Tom Hamburger, and Rosalind S. Helderman, "FBI Conducted Predawn Raid of Former Trump Campaign Chairman Manafort's Home," *WaPo*, 8/9/17.

53. John Santucci and Justin Fishel, "FBI Executed Search Warrant at Paul Manafort's Home in Russia Probe," ABCNews.com, 8/9/17.

54. Aaron Rupar, "Trump Called for Acting FBI Director's Firing Hours After FBI Agents Raided Paul Manafort's Home," *ThinkProgress*, undated; Donald Trump (@realDonaldTrump), ". . . . Transgender individuals to serve in any capacity in the U.S. Military. Our military must be focused on decisive and overwhelming. . . ." Twitter, 7/26/17, 6:04 a.m.

55. Christian Berthelsen and Greg Farrell, "With Bank Subpoenas, Mueller Turns Up the Heat on Manafort," Bloomberg.com, 8/10/17.

56. "Trump Advisor Sex Scandal—Paul Manafort's Sick Affair," *National Enquirer*, 8/9/17.

57. Josh Dawsey and Darren Samuelsohn, "Feds Sought Cooperation from Manafort's Son-in-Law," *Politico*, 8/9/17.

58. Josh Dawsey, "Manafort Switching Legal Teams as Feds Crank Up Heat on Him," *Politico*, 8/10/17.

59. Benjamin Wallace-Wells, "Paul Manafort Returns to the Center of the Russia Story," *NYer*, 8/11/17.

60. Benjamin Siegel, "Congressional Investigators Want to Question Trump's Secretary in Russia Probe," ABCNews.com, 8/11/17.

61. Manu Raju, "GOP-Led Senate Panel Wants White House Responses on Kushner's Security Clearance," CNN.com, 8/11/17.

62. Joby Warrick, Ellen Nakashima, and Anna Fifield, "North Korea Now Making Missile-Ready Nuclear Weapons, U.S. Analysts Say," *WaPo*, 8/8/17.

63. Paul Sonne, Shane Harris, and Jonathan Cheng, "North Korea Threat Comes After Trump Vows 'Fire and Fury,'" *WSJ*, 8/9/17.

64. Nyshka Chandran, "Trump Just Set His Own Uncrossable 'Red Line'—and North Korea Crossed It Instantly," CNBC.com, 8/9/17.

65. Chris Dieterich and Erik Holm, "Trump's 'Fire and Fury' Comments Break Dow's Winning Streak," *WSJ*, 8/8/17.

66. Graham Lanktree, "Trump's Warning to North Korea Has Nuclear Weapons Experts Chugging Wine," *Newsweek*, 8/9/17.

67. Daniel Dale, "Did Donald Trump Accidentally Threaten Nuclear War Out of a Penchant for Hyperbole?: Analysis," *Toronto Star*, 8/9/17.

68. Glenn Thrush and Peter Baker, "Trump's Threat to North Korea Was Improvised," *NYT*, 8/9/17.

69. John Hudson, "Trump Hasn't Appointed an Ambassador to Korea and Now It's a Big Problem," *BF*, 8/9/17.

70. Andrea Mitchell (@mitchellreports), ".@SenBlumenthal: The testimony before the armed services repeatedly has been the North Koreans are proceeding from milestone to milestone" Twitter, 8/1/17, 9:15 a.m.

71. Rebecca Shapiro, "Monumental 'Trump Chicken' Roosts Near the White House," *HuffPost*, 8/10/17.

72. Jana Winter and Elias Groll, "Here's the Memo That Blew Up the NSC," *FP*, 8/10/17.

73. Philip Rucker and Karen DeYoung, "Trump Reiterates Warning to N. Korea: 'Fire and Fury' May Not Have Been 'Tough Enough,'" *WaPo*, 8/10/17.

74. Brian Stelter and Dan Merica, "Trump Answers 50-plus Questions and Promises a Press Conference," CNN, 8/11/17; Philip Rucker, "'When You Put This Guy in a Cage and Think You're Controlling Him, Things like This Happen,'" *WaPo*, 8/10/17.

75. "Trump Says He Just Wants Mitch McConnell 'to Get Repeal and Replace Done,'" CBSNews.com, 8/10/17.

76. FOX & Friends (@foxandfriends), "Trump fires new warning shot at McConnell, leaves door open on whether he should step down" Twitter, 8/11/17, 1:20 a.m.

77. Reuters Top News (@Reuters), "JUST IN: Trump thanks Putin for expelling U.S. diplomats, says 'now we have a smaller payroll' at U.S. diplomatic facilities in Russia" Twitter, 8/10/17, 1:44 p.m.

78. Warren Strobel and Jonathan Landay, "Trump Thanks Putin for Slashing U.S. Diplomatic Staff," Reuters, 8/10/17.

79-81. Chris Cillizza, "The 39 Most Eyebrow-Raising Donald Trump Quotes on Thursday Alone," CNN.com, 8/11/17.

82. Soyoung Kim and Hyungwon Kang, "North Korea Releases Jailed Canadian Pastor amid Standoff with U.S.," Reuters, 8/9/17.

83. NBC News (@NBCNews), "President Trump: 'There was no collusion between us and Russia. In fact, the opposite. Russia spent a lot of money on fighting me.'" Twitter, 8/10/17, 1:57 p.m.

84. Ed Mazza, "Former GOP Sen. Gordon Humphrey: 'Seriously Sick' Trump Must Be Replaced ASAP," *HuffPost*, 8/10/17.

85. Aaron Blake, "More Drama in Trumpland: Gorka Publicly Shuns Tillerson's Effort to Scale Back North Korea Red Line," *WaPo*, 8/10/17.

86. Donald Trump (@realDonald Trump), "Military solutions are now fully in place,locked and loaded,should North Korea act unwisely. Hopefully Kim Jong Un will find another path!" Twitter, 8/11/17, 4:29 a.m.

87. Sewell Chan, "American Allies and Adversaries Urge Caution on North Korea," *NYT*, 8/11/17.

88. Simon Denyer and Anna Fifield, "China's President Urges Trump to Use Restraint over North Korea," *WaPo*, 8/12/17.

89. Sophie Tatum, "Panetta: North Korea 'Most Serious Crisis' Involving Nukes Since Cuba," CNN.com, 8/11/17.

90. Sara Sidner and Traci Tamura, "Hawaii: First State to Prepare for Nuclear Attack," CNN.com, 8/9/17.

91-92. Adam Edelman, Ali Vitali, and Abigail Williams, "Trump Warns North Korea Leader 'Will Not Get Away with What He's Doing,'" NBCNews.com, 8/11/17.

93-94. Brian Ellsworth and Mitra Taj, "Latin America Rejects Trump's Military Threat Against Venezuela," Reuters, 8/12/17.

95. Barbara Starr (@barbarastarrcnn), "DOD spox says its not invading #Venezuala 'Any insinuations by the Maduro regime that we are planning an invasion are baseless.'" Twitter, 8/11/17, 4:32 p.m.

96. Josh Siegel, "Trump Tells Guam Governor over the Phone: 'We Are with you 1,000 Percent,'" *WE*, 8/11/17.

97. Joe Heim, Ellie Silverman, T. Rees Shapiro, and Emma Brown, "One Dead as Car Strikes Crowds amid Protests of White Nationalist Gathering in Charlottesville; Two Police Die in Helicopter Crash," *WaPo*, 8/13/17.

98. Andy Campbell (@AndyBCampbell), "Emblematic indeed #Charlottesville" Twitter, 8/12/17, 8:00 a.m.

99. Michael Edison Hayden, "White Nationalist Rally in Charlottesville, Virginia Sparks Violent Clashes, Turns Deadly," ABCNews.com, 8/13/17.

100. AP (@AP), "BREAKING: Virginia governor declares state of emergency in response to white nationalist rally." Twitter, 8/12/17; Joe Heim, Ellie Silverman, T. Rees Shapiro, and Emma Brown, "One Dead as Car Strikes Crowds amid Protests of White Nationalist Gathering in Charlottesville; Two Police Die in Helicopter Crash," *WaPo*, 8/13/17.

101. Donald Trump (@realDonald Trump), "We ALL must be united & condemn all that hate stands for. There is no place for this kind of violence in America. Lets come together as one!" Twitter, 8/12/17, 10:19 a.m.

WEEK 40

1-2. AJ Willingham, "Trump Made Two Statements on Charlottesville. Here's How White Nationalists Heard Them," CNN.com, 8/15/17.

3. ABC News (@ABC), "NEW: White House clarifies Pres. Trump's statement after Charlottesville: 'He condemns all forms of violence, bigotry and hatred'" Twitter, 8/13/17.

4. Sarah Toy and Josh Bacon, "No Bail for Charlottesville Car Attack Suspect James Fields," *USAT*, 8/14/17.

5. Tom Kludt, "Fox News, *Daily Caller* Delete Posts Encouraging People to Drive Through Protests," CNN.com, 8/15/17.

6. Matthew Haag, "Death of 2 State Troopers Adds Another Layer of Tragedy in Charlottesville," *NYT*, 8/14/17.

7. ABC News (@ABC), "Organizers say tonight's planned vigil in Charlottesville canceled due to 'credible threat from white supremacists.' http://abcn.ws/2uDY1p7" Twitter, 8/13/17, 3:11 p.m.

8. Christopher Brennan, "KKK Leader Says That He Is 'Glad' About Heather Heyer's Death," *NYDN*, 8/15/17; Katie Mettler and Avi Selk, "GoDaddy—then Google—Ban Neo-Nazi Site *Daily Stormer* for Disparaging Charlottesville Victim," *WaPo*, 8/14/17; Amy Siskind (@Amy_Siskind), ".@GoDaddy you host The Daily Stormer—they posted this on their site. Please retweet if you think this hate should be taken down & banned." Twitter, 8/13/17, 6:37 p.m.

9. Amy Siskind (@Amy_Siskind), "On their new Russian-hosted website, neo-nazis The Daily Stormer brag Trump made connection. They feel his support." Twitter, 8/16/17, 9:29 a.m.; "Daily Stormer: Cloudflare Drops Neo-Nazi Site," BBC News, 8/17/17; Rachel Sandler, "Neo-Nazi Website *The Daily Stormer* Rebuffed by Russia, China," *USAT*, 8/17/17.

10. Kerry Flynn, "After Charlottesville, Tech Companies Are Forced to Take Action Against Hate Speech" *Mashable*, 8/16/17.

11. Conor Gaffey, "Unite the Right Organizer Disavowed by Family After Charlottesville Violence," *Newsweek*, 8/16/17; April McCullum and Adam Silverman, "Man, Fired from Job, Makes No Apology for Carrying Torch in Charlottesville," *Burlington Free Press* (VT), 8/16/17; Nick Roll, "When Your Students Attend White Supremacist Rallies," *Inside Higher Ed*, 8/15/17.

12. "Gallup Daily: Trump Job Approval," Gallup News, http://news.gallup.com/poll/201617/gallup-daily-trump-job-approval.aspx.

13. Michael Edison Hayden, "Sessions Defends Trump on Charlottesville, Says

Car Ramming Fits 'Domestic Terrorism,'" ABCNews.com, 8/14/17.

14. Veronica Stracqualursi and Adam Kelsey, "Trump: CEOs Leaving Advisory Council 'Out of Embarrassment,'" ABCNews.com, 8/15/17.

15. Donald Trump (@realDonald Trump), ".@Merck Pharma is a leader in higher & higher drug prices while at the same time taking jobs out of the U.S. Bring jobs back & LOWER PRICES!" Twitter, 8/14/17, 3:09 p.m.

16. Julia Horowitz, "AFL-CIO Chief Leaves Trump's Manufacturing Council After President's Latest Remarks," CNN.com, 8/15/17.

17. Donald Trump (@realDonald Trump), "For every CEO that drops out of the Manufacturing Council, I have many to take their place. Grandstanders should not have gone on. JOBS!" Twitter, 8/15/17, 8:21 a.m.

18. David Gelles, Landon Thomas Jr., Andrew Ross Sorkin, and Kate Kelly, "Inside the C.E.O. Rebellion Against Trump's Advisory Councils," *NYT*, 8/16/17.

19. Donald Trump (@realDonald Trump), "Rather than putting pressure on the businesspeople of the Manufacturing Council & Strategy & Policy Forum, I am ending both. Thank you all!" Twitter, 8/16/17, 10:14 a.m.

20. John Wagner, "White House Disbands Another Advisory Council, This One on Infrastructure," *WaPo*, 8/17/17.

21. Gregg Jarrett, "Trump 'Seriously Considering' a Pardon for Ex-sheriff Joe Arpaio," FoxNews.com, 8/14/17.

22. Bill Chappell, "Phoenix Mayor Asks Trump to Delay Visit, Hoping for 'More Sound Judgment,'" *The Two-Way* (blog), NPR, 8/17/17.

23. Donald Trump (@realDonald Trump), "Join me at 7:00 P.M. on Tuesday, August 22nd in Phoenix, Arizona at the Phoenix Convention Center! Tickets at: https://www.donaldjtrump.com/rallies/phoenix-az . . ." Twitter, 8/16/17, 5:11 p.m.

24. John Paul Brammer, "Advocates Connect Trump to Spike in Reports of Anti-LGBTQ Violence," NBCNews.com, 8/17/17.

25. Todd Starnes, "School Letter Says AP and Honors Classes Will Be Decided by Race," FoxNews.com, 8/8/17.

26. AP, "Police: Holocaust Memorial Vandalized; 2nd Time This Summer," *Boston Herald*, 8/14/17.

27. Dan Merica, "Trump Calls KKK, Neo-Nazis, White Supremacists 'Repugnant,'" CNN.com, 8/14/17.

28. David Nakamura, Aaron C. Davis, "After Charlottesville, Trump Retweets—then Deletes—Image of Train Running over CNN Reporter," *WaPo*, 8/15/17.

29–32. Natalie Jennings and Peter W. Stevenson, "Trump's Off-the-Rails News Conference on Charlottesville, the 'Alt-Left' and Infrastructure, Annotated," *WaPo*, 8/15/17.

33. Glenn Kessler, "President Trump's False Claim That Counterprotesters Lacked a Permit," *WaPo*, 8/16/17.

34. Natalie Jennings and Peter W. Stevenson, "Trump's Off-the-Rails News Conference on Charlottesville, the 'Alt-Left' and Infrastructure, Annotated," *WaPo*, 8/15/17.

35. Hallie Jackson and Kristen Welker, "He 'Went Rogue': President Trump's Staff Stunned After Latest Charlottesville Remarks," NBCNews.com, 8/16/17.

36. Josh Dawsey, "White House Aides Wrestle with Trump's Race Comments," *Politico*, 8/16/17.

37. Rosie Gray, "'Really Proud of Him': Alt-Right Leaders Praise Trump's Comments," *Atlantic*, 8/15/17.

38. Jonathan Swan, "What Steve Bannon Thinks About Charlottesville," *Axios*, 8/16/17.

39. "An Open Letter to Steve Mnuchin; From Members of the Yale College Class of 1985," 8/18/17, lettertosteve mnuchin.com.

40. Amy Davidson Sorkin, "Roy Moore, Luther Strange, and the Lessons of the Alabama Senate Primary," *NYer*, 8/17/17.

41. Shane Savitsky, "Pence Cutting Short International Trip," *Axios*, 8/16/17.

42. Julia Manchester, "Fox's Shep Smith: We Couldn't Find a Republican Willing to Come on and Defend Trump," *The Hill*, 8/16/17.

43. Zachary Cohen, "Former CIA Director Slams Trump's 'Despicable' Comments in Letter to CNN Anchor," CNN.com, 8/17/17.

44. Andrew deGrandpre, "Trump's Generals Condemn Charlottesville Racism—While Trying Not to Offend the President," *WaPo*, 8/16/17.

45. Jeremy Herb, "Corker: Trump Hasn't Demonstrated the Stability or Competence to Be Successful," CNN.com, 8/18/17.

46. Erik Kirschbaum, "President Trump's Remarks about the Violence in Charlottesville Prompted a Fresh Round of Condemnation in Europe," *LAT*, 8/31/17.

47. Todd Franklin, "BREAKING: Articles of Impeachment Just Introduced Against Trump by Ranking Member Cohen," IR.net, 8/17/17.

48. Pete Williams, "Virginia Car Attack Possible 'Hate Crime,' Sessions Says," NBCNews.com, 8/16/17.

49. Editorial Board, "After Charlottesville, Time to Censure President Trump," *USAT*, 8/16/17.

50. Stephen Koff, "Cleveland Clinic Pulls Gala from Trump's Mar-a-Lago," Cleveland.com, 8/17/17.

51. Shannon Donnelly, "UPDATED: Keeping Track at Home? Here's a List of 25 Charities Leaving Mar-a-Lago," *Palm Beach Daily News*, 8/18/17 (updated 9/21/17).

52. Ella Nilsen, "Richard Spencer Had Speeches Scheduled at 2 Colleges, and They've Both Uninvited Him," *Vox*, 8/16/17.

53. AP, "Michigan State University Rejects White Nationalist Event," ABCNews.com, 8/17/17.

54. AP, "Lehigh University Student Petition Calls for Revoking Trump's Honorary Degree," *TPM*, 8/17/17.

55. Debbie Elliott, "Torches Replaced by Candlelight as Thousands Gather for Charlottesville Vigil," *Morning Edition*, NPR, 8/17/17.

56. John Bowden, "Mother of Charlottesville Victim Has Received Death Threats," *The Hill*, 8/17/17; Chelsea Bailey, "Mother of Charlottesville Victim Heather Heyer Says She Won't Meet President Trump," NBCNews.com, 8/18/17.

57. Chelsea Bailey, "Mother of Charlottesville Victim Heather Heyer

Says She Won't Meet President Trump," NBCNews.com, 8/18/17.

58. Donald Trump (@realDonald Trump), ". . . can't change history, but you can learn from it. Robert E Lee, Stonewall Jackson—who's next, Washington, Jefferson? So foolish! Also . . ." Twitter, 8/17/17, 6:15 a.m.

59–60. Polo Sandoval and Darran Simon, "The Descendants of Lee, Jackson and Davis Want the Confederate Statues to Come Down," CNN.com, 8/17/17.

61. "Confederate Monuments Are Coming Down Across the United States. Here's a List," *NYT*, updated 8/28/17; Andy Campbell, "Duke University Is Removing the Robert E. Lee Statues from Its Chapel," *HuffPost*, 8/19/17.

62. Donald Trump (@realDonald Trump), "Study what General Pershing of the United States did to terrorists when caught. There was no more Radical Islamic Terror for 35 years!" Twitter, 8/17/17, 11:45 a.m.; Louis Jacobson and Aaron Sharockman, "Donald Trump Retells Pants on Fire Claim About Gen. Pershing Ending Terrorism for 35 Years," *PolitiFact*, 8/17/17.

63. Donald Trump (@realDonald Trump), "Great to see that Dr. Kelli Ward is running against Flake Jeff Flake, who is WEAK on borders, crime and a non-factor in Senate. He's toxic!" Twitter, 8/17/17, 3:56 a.m.; Donald Trump (@realDonaldTrump), "Publicity seeking Lindsey Graham falsely stated that I said there is moral equivalency between the KKK, neo-Nazis & white supremacists. . . . . ." Twitter, 8/17/17, 3:19 a.m.

64. Jim Sciutto (@jimsciutto), ".@SenateMajLdr McConnell offering 'full support' for @JeffFlake after Trump criticized him & welcomed his primary opponent" Twitter, 8/17/17, 3:13 p.m.

65. Sam Ro, "James Murdoch Donates $1 Million to the Anti-Defamation League Following Events in Charlottesville," *Yahoo Finance*, 8/17/17.

66. James West, "Report: Queasy Aussies Killed Trump's Casino Bid over 'Mafia Connections,'" *MJ*, 8/16/17.

67. Jessica Schulberg, "Controversial Trump Aide Katharine Gorka Helped End Funding for Group That Fights White Supremacy," *HuffPost*, 8/15/17.

68. Julia Manchester, "Gore: Trump Should Resign," *The Hill*, 8/17/17.

69. Ed O'Keefe, "Members of White House Presidential Arts Committee Resigning to Protest Trump's Comments," *WaPo*, 8/18/17.

70. Sopan Deb (@SopanDeb), "NEW: White House responds to @kalpenn and others resigning the arts commission, says Trump was going to disband it anyway:" Twitter, 8/18/17, 1:18 p.m.

71. David Nakamura, Amy B. Wang, and Peter Marks, "Trump, First Lady to Skip Kennedy Center Honors over Concerns of 'Political Distraction,'" *WaPo*, 8/19/17.

72. Devon Ivie, "Donald and Melania Trump Are Skipping This Year's Kennedy Center Honors," *Vulture*, 8/19/17.

73. Chuck Todd, Mark Murray, and Carrie Dann, "Trump More Isolated than Ever After Worst Week Yet," NBCNews.com, 8/18/17.

74. Ashley Parker, "Hope Hicks Takes Interim White House Communications Role amid Search for Scaramucci Replacement," *WaPo*, 8/16/17.

75. Michael S. Schmidt and Matt Apuzzo, "Trump Lawyer Forwards Email Echoing Secessionist Rhetoric," *NYT*, 8/16/17.

76. Laurel Wamsley, "DOJ Demands Files on Anti-Trump Activists, and a Web Hosting Company Resists," *The Two-Way* (blog), NPR, 8/15/17.

77. Ibid.; Morgan Chalfant, "DOJ Warrant of Trump Resistance Site Triggers Alarm," *The Hill*, 8/16/17.

78–79. Michael S. Schmidt, Matt Apuzzo, and Maggie Haberman, "Mueller Is Said to Seek Interviews with West Wing in Russia Case," *NYT*, 8/12/17.

80. Emily Tillett, "Pence 'Not Aware' of Any Russian Collusion with Trump Campaign," CBSNews.com, 8/14/17.

81–82. Tom Hamburger, Carol D. Leonnig, and Rosalind S. Helderman, "Trump Campaign Emails Show Aide's Repeated Efforts to Set Up Russia Meetings," *WaPo*, 8/14/17.

83–84. Andrew E. Kramer and Andrew Higgins, "In Ukraine, a Malware Expert Who Could Blow the Whistle on Russian Hacking," *NYT*, 8/16/17.

85. Mike Levine, "Special Counsel's Russia Probe Loses Top FBI Investigator," ABCNews.com, 8/16/17.

86. Matthew Mosk, Brian Ross, and Rhonda Schwartz, "British Spy Behind Trump-Russia Dossier Could Be Forced to Talk After US Court Ruling," ABCNews.com, 8/19/17.

87–88. Tom LoBianco, "Rohrabacher Wants to Brief Trump on Assange Meeting," CNN.com, 8/17/17.

89. AP, "National Parks Service Reverses Ban on Disposable, Plastic Water Bottles," Weather.com, 8/18/17.

90. Trump Organization (@Trump), "From our Presidential Ballroom to intimate historic rooms, over 38,000 square feet of meeting and event space awaits your arrival @TrumpDC" Twitter, 8/16/17, 7:19 a.m.

91. Adam Liptak, "Neil Gorsuch Speech at Trump Hotel Raises Ethical Questions," *NYT*, 8/17/17.

92. Dan De Luce and Paul McLeary, "Pentagon Forces Out Popular Press Spokesman," *FP*, 8/16/17.

93. Matthew Goldstein and Alexandra Stevenson, "Carl Icahn Quits as Special Adviser to President Trump," *NYT*, 8/18/17.

94. Patrick Radden Keefe, "Carl Icahn's Failed Raid on Washington," *NYer*, 8/28/17.

95. Donald Trump (@realDonald Trump), "Today, I signed the Global War on Terrorism War Memorial Act (#HR873.) The bill authorizes. . . . cont" Twitter, 8/18/17, 6:30 p.m.

96–97. Robert Kuttner, "Steve Bannon, Unrepentant," *American Prospect*, 8/16/17.

98. Greg Sargent, "Steve Bannon: Post-Charlottesville Racial Strife Is a Political Winner for Trump," *WaPo*, 8/17/17.

99. Maggie Haberman, Michael D. Shear, and Glenn Thrush, "Stephen Bannon Out at the White House After Turbulent Run," *NYT*, 8/18/17; "'Populist Hero' Stephen K. Bannon Returns Home to *Breitbart*," *Breitbart*, 8/18/17.

100. Jonathan Swan, "Bannon, Backed by Billionaire, Prepares to Go to War," *Axios*, 8/18/17.

101. Joshua Green, Justin Sink, and Margaret Talev, "Bannon Says He's

'Going to War for Trump' After White House Exit," Bloomberg.com, 8/18/17.

102. Peter J. Boyer, "Bannon: 'The Trump Presidency That We Fought for, and Won, Is Over,'" *Weekly Standard*, 8/18/17.

103. Julius Krein, "I Voted for Trump. And I Sorely Regret It," *NYT*, 8/17/17.

104. "America Is Under Attack," audio/video, *Rush Limbaugh Show*, 8/18/17.

105. "'Stay Away from the Common' During Boston Free Speech Rally, Walsh Urges," CBS Boston, 8/18/17.

106. Doug Stanglin, "'Free Speech' Rally Fizzles as Thousands of Counterprotesters Swarm Boston," *USAT*, 8/19/17; Phil McAusland, "Boston Police Avoid Damage and Injuries During Rallies and Protests," NBCNews.com, 8/19/17.

WEEK 41

1. Cleve R. Wootson Jr., "Trump Mistakenly Tweeted That the Country Needs 'to Heel.' The Internet Gave Him Hell," *WaPo*, 8/20/17.

2. Max Greenwood, "Member of Trump's Evangelical Advisory Board Resigns over 'Conflict in Values,'" *The Hill*, 8/18/17.

3. Brian Stelter (@brianstelter), "No @WhiteHouse officials are on the Sunday political talk shows today. 0." Twitter, 8/20/17, 6:24 a.m.

4. Reliable Sources (@ReliableSources), "Many in Washington 'have come to believe that Donald Trump is unfit for the presidency,' says @carlbernstein" Twitter, 8/20/17, 8:20 a.m.

5. Mark Murray, "Trump's Approval Rating Stands Below 40 Percent in Three Key Midwest States," NBCNews.com, 8/20/17.

6. Sarah McCammon, "Some Liberty University Grads Are Returning Their Diplomas to Protest Trump," NPR, 8/20/17.

7. John Bowden, "Former Health Chiefs: Stabilizing ObamaCare Markets Benefits Republicans," *The Hill*, 8/20/17.

8. Anna Fifield, "Five Sailors Injured, 10 Missing After U.S. Navy Destroyer Collides with a Merchant Ship," *WaPo*, 8/20/17.

9-10. Kevin Johnson, "Exclusive: Secret Service Depletes Funds to Pay Agents Because of Trump's Frequent Travel, Large Family," *USAT*, 8/21/17.

11-12. Juliet Eilperin, "The Trump Administration Just Disbanded a Federal Advisory Committee on Climate Change," *WaPo*, 8/20/17.

13. Lisa Friedman and Brad Plumer, "Coal Mining Health Study Is Halted by Interior Department," *NYT*, 8/21/17.

14-15. Alec MacGillis, "Is Anybody Home at HUD?" *DI*, 8/22/17.

16. Eric Lipton (@EricLiptonNYT), "Interior IG confirms it's investigating Sec Ryan Zinke's apparent (failed) effort to pressure Sen Murkowski to vote yes on Obamacare repeal" Twitter, 8/22/17, 6:31 p.m.

17. Philip Bump, "3 in 10 Strong Trump Supporters Accept or Are Indifferent to White Supremacist Views," *WaPo*, 8/22/17.

18. Anne Frank Center (@AnneFrankCenter), "THIS IS SICK: ABCNews poll reports 1 in 10 adults in U.S. say neo-Nazi views acceptable - 22 million Americans. Evil epidemic of hatred." Twitter, 8/22/17, 5:48 a.m.

19. Philip Bump, "3 in 10 Strong Trump Supporters Accept or Are Indifferent to White Supremacist Views," *WaPo*, 8/22/17.

20. "Billy Joel Dons Star of David Jacket During NYC Show Encore," AP, 8/22/17.

21. AP, "Brandeis University Reopens After Emailed Bomb Threat," WHDH.com.

22. Christopher Mathias, "All the Swastikas and Broken Glass Since Charlottesville," *HuffPost*, 8/25/17; Anti-Defamation League, "Anti-Semitic Incidents in the U.S. in the Wake of Charlottesville Rally," ADL.org, 8/30/17.

23. Karma Allen, "Rabbis Cancel Annual Call with Trump over His Charlottesville Response," ABCNews.com, 8/24/17.

24. Camila Domonoske, "U.N. Panel Urges U.S. Government to Reject Racial Hatred and Violence," *The Two-Way* (blog), NPR, 8/23/17.

25. Garen Meguerian (@GarenMeguerian), "Received this remarkable letter today from the Girl Scouts. Stunned at what has happened to our country in seven months. @Amy_Siskind" Twitter, 8/18/17, 2:45 p.m.

26. John Verovek, "Charities, Nonprofits Pull Events from Mar-a-Lago amid Charlottesville Controversy," ABCNews.com, 9/6/17.

27. Daniel M Kammen (@dan_kammen), "Mr. President, I am resigning as Science Envoy. Your response to Charlottesville enables racism, sexism, & harms our country and planet." Twitter, 8/23/17, 7:15 a.m.

28. Andrew Kaczynski and Paul LeBlanc, "Trump Nominee Sam Clovis: 'As Far as We Know' Homosexuality's a Choice, 'Logical' LGBT Protections Could Lead to Legalization of Pedophilia," CNN.com, 8/21/17.

29. James Besanvalle, "Journalist Who Uncovered Russian Torture of Gay Men in Shocking Exposé, Dies," *Gay Star News*, 8/19/17.

30. Pete Williams and Julia Ainsley, "Trump Likely to End DACA Immigrant Program," NBCNews.com, 8/25/17.

31. Sarah Fitzpatrick and Julia Ainsley, "DHS to Require Interviews for More than 100,000 Visa Holders," NBCNews.com, 8/25/17.

32. Tierney Sneed, "Voting Rights Groups File Lawsuit Seeking Info About Trump Commission," *TPM*, 8/22/17.

33. Morgan Chalfant, "DOJ Drops Request for IP Addresses from Trump Resistance Site," *The Hill*, 8/22/17.

34. Morgan Chalfant, "Court Orders Company to Produce Data on Anti-Trump Site," *The Hill*, 8/26/17.

35. Melissa Byrne, "I Was Detained for Protesting Trump. Here's What the Secret Service Asked Me," *WaPo*, 8/23/17.

36. "Full Transcript and Video: Trump's Speech on Afghanistan," *NYT*, 8/21/17.

37. Michael Beschloss (@BeschlossDC), "Can't think of any other President in history who had to start a speech on war and peace by vowing that he opposed bigotry and prejudice." Twitter, 8/21/17, 6:45 p.m.

38. Aaron Blake, "Trump's Afghanistan Speech: Full of Sound and Fury, Signifying Very Little," *WaPo*, 8/22/17.

39. Mark Landler and Maggie Haberman, "Angry Trump Grilled His

Generals About Troop Increase, Then Gave In," *NYT*, 8/21/17.

40. Phil Elliott (@Philip_Elliott), "There is not a confirmed US Ambassador to Afghanistan at present." Twitter, 8/21/17, 6:26 p.m.

41. Greg Stanton, "Phoenix Mayor Greg Stanton: Now Is Not the Time for Trump to Visit My City," *NYT*, 8/21/17.

42. Jenna Johnson, "As Trump Ranted and Rambled in Phoenix, His Crowd Slowly Thinned," *WaPo*, 8/23/17.

43. Brian Stelter, "Here's How Reporters Are Responding to Trump's New Amped-Up Attacks," CNN.com, 8/23/17; Peter Hasson, "Trump Rally Leaves Media Fearing for Safety," *Daily Caller*, 8/23/17.

44. Julie Hirschfeld Davis, "Trump Widens Rift with Congress as Critical Showdowns Loom," *NYT*, 8/23/17.

45. Sean Sullivan, "Trump Hits McCain and Flake in Arizona Without Naming Them—and Appears to Relish It," *WaPo*, 8/22/17.

46. Jenna Johnson, "As Trump Ranted and Rambled in Phoenix, His Crowd Slowly Thinned," *WaPo*, 8/23/17.

47. Mark Landler and Maggie Haberman, "At Rally, Trump Blames Media for Country's Deepening Divisions," *NYT*, 8/22/17.

48. Jenna Johnson, "As Trump Ranted and Rambled in Phoenix, His Crowd Slowly Thinned," *WaPo*, 8/23/17.

49. Simon Romero, "Police Use Tear Gas on Crowds After Trump Rally," *NYT*, 8/22/17.

50. Philip Bump, "Why Ben Carson's Appearance in Phoenix Was Likely a Violation of Federal Law," *WaPo*, 8/23/17.

51. Danielle Kurtzleben, "FACT CHECK: 10 Statements from Trump's Phoenix Speech," NPR.org, 8/23/17.

52. Alex Isenstadt, "Trump Met with Potential Flake Challengers Before Phoenix Rally," *Politico*, 8/23/17.

53-55. Leinz Vales, "James Clapper Calls Trump Speech 'Downright Scary and Disturbing,'" CNN.com, 8/24/17.

56. Jake Tapper, "Intel Chief Sheds Light on 'Beautiful Letter' Trump Says He Wrote Him," CNN.com, 8/25/17.

57. Kaitlan Collins, "White House Has Paperwork Ready for Joe Arpaio Pardon," CNN.com, 8/23/17.

58. Damian Paletta, "Treasury Secretary's Wife Boasts of Travel on Government Plane, Touts Hermes and Valentino Fashion," *WaPo*, 8/21/17.

59. Citizens for Responsibility and Ethics in Washington to U.S. Dept. of the Treasury, "August 23, 2017: U.S. Department of Treasury—Mnuchin," FOIA request, 8/23/17, www.citizensforethics.org/foia/august-23-2017-u-s-department-treasury-mnuchin.

60. Drew Harwell and Beth Reinhard, "Ethics Group Wants to Know What Led Mnuchin to View Eclipse in Kentucky," *WaPo*, 8/24/17.

61. "Meeting Between Egyptian Foreign Minister and Jared Kushner Canceled: Ministry," Reuters, 8/23/17; Carol Morello, "Jared Kushner Meets with Egyptian Officials to Discuss Middle East Peace Process," *WaPo*, 8/23/17.

62. Danielle Kurtzleben, "Women Are a Huge Reason Why Trump's Poll Numbers Are So Bad," NPR.org, 8/21/17.

63-65. Alexander Burns and Jonathan Martin, "McConnell, in Private, Doubts if Trump Can Save Presidency," *NYT*, 8/22/17.

66. Jonathan Martin (@jmartNYT), "GOP senator calls just now, sez Trump consumed w RUSSIA Also: Trump must sell tax reform 'His vocabulary on healthcare was bout 10 words'" Twitter, 8/22/17, 3:20 p.m.

67-68. Josh Dawsey and Elana Schor, "Trump Clashed with Multiple GOP Senators over Russia," *Politico*, 8/23/17.

69. Aaron Blake and Callum Borchers, "Trump Has Now Tried to Call Off the Dogs on Russia at Least 8 Times," *WaPo*, updated 12/1/17.

70. Brian Ross, Matthew Mosk, and Rhonda Schwartz, "Key Figure Behind Million-Dollar Trump 'Dossier' to Face Questions," ABCNews.com, 8/22/17; Julia Manchester, "Senate Committee to Vote on Releasing Fusion GPS Testimony," *The Hill*, 8/24/17.

71. Julia Manchester, "Senate Committee to Vote on Releasing Fusion GPS Testimony," *The Hill*, 8/24/17; MSNBC "Donald Trump Dossier from Senate Judiciary Could Be Published," YouTube, 8/23/17, www.youtube.com/watch?v=AGAH7GFOIbI.

72-75. Greg Miller, "At CIA, a Watchful Eye on Mike Pompeo, the President's Ardent Alley," *WaPo*, 8/24/17.

76. Jason Leopold, "Some in Congress Don't Get the 'Gravity' of Russian Election Meddling, Former CIA Director Said," *BF*, 8/24/17.

77. Caleb Melby and David Kocieniewski, "Kushner Cos. Switches to Crisis Manager for Media Relations," Bloomberg.com, 8/23/17.

78-79. Sharon LaFraniere, David D. Kirkpatrick, and Kenneth P. Vogel, "Lobbyist at Trump Campaign Meeting Has a Web of Russian Connections," *NYT*, 8/21/17.

80. Manu Raju and Marshall Cohen, "Exclusive: Top Trump Aide's Email Draws New Scrutiny in Russia Inquiry," CNN.com, 8/24/17.

81-82. Shane Harris, "Special Counsel Examines Possible Role Flynn Played in Seeking Clinton Emails from Hackers," *WSJ*, 8/25/17.

83-84. Ken Dilanian, Carol E. Lee, and Tom Winter, "Mueller Seeks Grand Jury Testimony from PR Execs Who Worked with Manafort," NBCNews.com, 8/25/17.

85. Oren Dorell, "*Breitbart*, Other 'Alt-Right' Websites Are the Darlings of Russian Propaganda Effort," *USAT*, 8/24/17.

86. Charlie May, "Roger Stone Predicts a Civil War if Donald Trump Is Impeached," *Salon*, 8/24/17.

87. Katie Rogers, "Trump Hotel at Night: Lobbyists, Cabinet Members, $60 Steaks," *NYT*, 8/25/17.

88. Ibid., Jeremy Berke, "Richard Spencer Stayed at Trump's D.C. Hotel While He Planned the Charlottesville Rally," *BI*, 8/25/17.

89. Glenn Kessler, Michelle Ye Hee Lee, and Meg Kelly, "President Trump's List of False and Misleading Claims Tops 1,000," *WaPo*, 8/22/17.

90. Tom DiChristopher and Everett Rosenfeld, "Carl Icahn Resigned from Trump Advisor Role Ahead of Article Alleging Conflict of Interest," CNBC.com, 8/20/17.

91. Ibid.; Timothy Gardner, "U.S. Democratic Senators Seek Probe into Icahn's Biofuel Credit Dealings," Reuters, 5/9/17.

92. Donald Trump (@realDonald Trump), "Strange statement by Bob Corker considering that he is constantly asking me whether or not he should run again in '18. Tennessee not happy!" Twitter, 8/25/17, 5:25 a.m.

93. Demetri and Gillian Tett, "Gary Cohn Urges Trump Team to Do More to Condemn Neo-Nazis," *FT*, 8/25/17.

94. Damian Paletta, "Yellen Rejects Trump Approach to Wall Street Regulation, Says Post-crisis Banking Rules Make Economy Safer," *WaPo*, 8/25/17.

95. Sahil Kapur and Margaret Talev, "Trump to Rally Public on Taxes as Republicans Hash Out Details," Bloomberg.com, 8/25/17.

96. "FIRST IN PLAYBOOK: White House Rapid Response Director Is Out," *Politico*, 8/24/17.

97. AP, "Over the Groans of Some, Republican National Committee Votes to Condemn White Supremacists," *LAT*, 8/25/17.

98. Quinnipiac Poll, 8/23/17, poll.qu .edu/national/release-detail?ReleaseID =2482&utm_source=newsletter&utm _medium=email&utm_campaign=news letter_axiosam&stream=top-stories.

99. Kyle Griffin (@kylegriffin1), "Reporter: 'Mr. President, do you have a message for the people of Texas?' Trump: 'Good luck to everybody.' (via ABC News)" Twitter, 8/25/17, 1:20 p.m.

100. "Hurricane Harvey Slams Texas, at Least 1 Dead," DW.com, 8/26/17.

101. Michael R. Gordon and Emily Cochrane, "Trump Gives Mattis Wide Discretion over Transgender Ban," *NYT*, 8/25/17.

102. Jeremy Diamond, "Trump Signs Directive Banning Transgender Military Recruits," CNN.com, 8/25/17.

103. Julie Hirschfeld Davis and Maggie Haberman, "Trump Pardons Joe Arpaio, Who Became Face of Crackdown on Illegal Immigration," *NYT*, 8/25/17.

104. Editorial Board, "The Perils of a Pardon for Joe Arpaio," *NYT*, 8/24/17.

105. Bradley P. Moss, "Trump Pardoning Arpaio Should Raise Serious Alarms for the Russia Investigation," *HuffPost*, 8/26/17.

106. Alexander Mallin and M. L. Nestel, "Controversial Trump Adviser Sebastian Gorka Leaves White House Post," ABCNews.com, 8/26/17.

107. Jason Samenow and Brian McNoldy, "Harvey Makes Landfall in Texas as Category 4 Storm, Destructive Winds and 'Catastrophic' Flooding Expected," *WaPo*, 8/25/17.

108. Timothy Cama and Megan R. Wilson, "Trump Exempts Citgo from Venezuela Sanctions," *The Hill*, 8/25/17.

WEEK 42

1. Philip Rucker and Ellen Nakashima, "Trump Asked Sessions About Closing Case Against Arpaio, an Ally Since 'Birtherism,'" *WaPo*, 8/26/17.

2. Eliza Relman, "Trump Reversed Regulations to Protect Infrastructure Against Flooding Just Days Before Hurricane Harvey," *BI*, 8/28/17.

3. Donald Trump (@realDonald Trump), "A great book by a great guy, highly recommended!" Twitter, 8/27/17, 4:45 a.m.

4. Walter Shaub (@waltshaub), "Or you could start caring about govt ethics. Remember how your behaving like this led @KellyannePolls to violate the Standards of Conduct?" Twitter, 8/27/17, 7:36 a.m.

5. Andrew deGrandpre and Abby Phillip, "David Clarke, Outspoken Trump Supporter, Resigns as Milwaukee County Sheriff—Without Explanation," *WaPo*, 9/1/17.

6. Eli Watkins, "Tillerson: Trump 'Speaks for Himself,'" CNN.com, 8/28/17.

7. Fred Kaplan, "The Secretary's Rebuke," *Slate*, 8/28/17.

8. Tom Vanden Brook, "Mattis Freezes Transgender Policy; Allows Troops to Continue Serving, Pending Study," *USAT*, 8/30/17.

9. Ellen Mitchell, "Mattis Responds to Trump: US 'Never Out of Diplomatic Solutions' on North Korea," *The Hill*, 8/30/17.

10. Adolfo Flores, "ICE Left 50 Immigrant Women and Kids Stranded at a Bus Station Before Hurricane Harvey Struck," *BF*, 8/28/17.

11. Pete Williams and Julia Ainsley, "Trump Reverses Obama Policy on Surplus Military Gear for Police," NBCNews.com, 8/28/17.

12. Ms. Smith, "Trump Signs Bill into Law Allowing Warrantless Searches in parts of VA, MD and DC," CSOOnline .com, 8/27/17.

13. NowThis (@nowthisnews), "Footage shows this nurse being forcefully arrested for following her hospital's rules" Twitter, 9/1/17, 9:13 a.m.

14. Josh Delk, "Televangelist Jim Bakker: Christians Will Start a Civil War if Trump Is Impeached," *The Hill*, 8/29/17.

15. Samantha Schmidt, "Evangelicals' 'Nashville Statement' Denouncing Same-Sex Marriage Is Rebuked by City's Mayor," *WaPo*, 8/30/17.

16. Chris Kenning, "Confederate Battle Flag Sales Boom After Charlottesville Clash," Reuters, 8/29/17.

17. Manny Fernandez, "Federal Judge Blocks Texas' Ban on 'Sanctuary Cities,'" *NYT*, 8/30/17.

18. David Nather, "HHS Cuts ACA Advertising Budget by 90%," *Axios*, 8/31/17.

19. Rebecca Wallace, Sara Neel, and Arash Jahanian, "ICE Is Abusing the ACLU's Clients Because They Are Fighting Trump's Deportation Machine," ACLU.org, 8/31/17.

20. Joe Watson and Paul Ingram, "Decorated Marine Vet May Be Deported, Despite Likely U.S. Citizenship," *Tucson Sentinel*, 8/25/17.

21. Chris Tognotti, "Trump's Stance on Women's Rights in Afghanistan Is the Exact Opposite of Obama's," *Bustle*, 8/22/17.

22. Sylvan Lane, "Mnuchin: Treasury Could Scrap Plans to Replace Jackson on $20 Bill," *The Hill*, 8/31/17.

23. Allana Vagianos, "Sexual Assault Report Drops from White House Site, Remains on Obama Archive (UPDATE)," *HuffPost*, 9/1/17.

24. Ted Mann, "White House Won't Require Firms to Report Pay by Gender, Race," *WSJ*, 8/29/17.

25. Tiffany Hsu, "Administration Scraps Local-Hiring Plan for Public Works," *NYT*, 8/24/17.

26. Laura Jarrett and Daniella Diaz, "DOJ to Retry Woman Who Laughed During Sessions' Confirmation Hearing," CNN.com, 9/2/17.

27. Heidi M. Przybyla, "Report: 'Anti-protestor' Bills Gain Traction in State Legislatures," *USAT*, undated.

28. "Interior Department Watchdog Drops Probe of Threat to Alaska Senator on Healthcare," Reuters, 8/30/17.

29. Gregory Wallace and Laura Jarrett, "Government Watchdog Examining GSA's Dealings with Trump Hotel Lease," CNN.com, 8/30/17.

30. Spencer S. Hsu, "Trump Voting Panel Apologizes After Judge Calls Failure to Disclose Information 'Incredible,'" *WaPo*, 8/30/17.

31. Bryan Lowry, "Kris Kobach's New Job: Columnist for *Breitbart*," *Kansas City Star*, 8/31/17.

32. David Smith, "Donald Trump Defends Controversial Pardon of 'Patriot' Joe Arpaio," *Guardian*, 8/28/17.

33. Anna North, "Donald Trump Just Mixed Up Two Women Journalists at a Press Conference," *Vox*, 8/28/17.

34. Aaron Gregg, "Trump Says Finland Is Buying Boeing Fighter Jets. The Finnish President Called That News a 'Duck,'" *WaPo*, 8/30/17.

35. Nolan D. McCaskill, "Trump Eager to Avoid Katrina Repeat During Texas Tour," *Politico*, 8/29/17.

36. "Trump Praises FEMA Director: He Became 'Very Famous on Television,'" *DB*, undated.

37. Lyanne A. Guarecuco, "Trump Praises Crowd Size, Fails to Acknowledge Harvey Victims in Texas Visit," *San Antonio Current*, 8/29/17.

38. Trump Make America Great Again Committee, shop.donaldjtrump.com /collections/headwear.

39. Joe Concha, "Ari Fleischer: 'Empathy' for Harvey Victims Missing from Trump Remarks," *The Hill*, 8/29/17.

40. "The Latest: Interior Drops Probe into Secretary, Senators," AP, 8/30/17.

41–43. Nicole Perlroth, Michael Wines, and Matthew Rosenberg, "Russian Election Hacking Efforts, Wider than Previously Known, Draw Little Scrutiny," *NYT*, 9/1/17.

44. Isaac Arnsdorf, "Pro-Russian Bots Take Up the Right-Wing Cause After Charlottesville," BillMoyers.com, 8/24/17; Caroline O., "How Russian & Alt-Right Twitter Accounts Worked Together to Skew the Narrative About Berkeley," *Arc*, 9/1/17.

45–46. Nafeesa Syeed, "Pro-Russian Bots Sharpen Online Attacks for 2018 U.S. Vote," Bloomberg.com, 9/1/17.

47–49. Carol D. Leonnig, Tom Hamburger, and Rosalind S. Helderman, "Trump's Business Sought Deal on a Trump Tower in Moscow While He Ran for President," *WaPo*, 8/27/17.

50–51. Matt Apuzzo and Maggie Haberman, "Trump Associate Boasted That Moscow Business Deal 'Will Get Donald Elected,'" *NYT*, 8/28/17.

52. Max Seddon, "Cashflow and the Kremlin," *FT*, 8/24/16.

53. Matt Apuzzo and Maggie Haberman, "Trump Associate Boasted That Moscow Business Deal 'Will Get Donald Elected,'" *NYT*, 8/28/17.

54. Rosalind S. Helderman, Carol D. Leonnig, and Tom Hamburger, "Top Trump Organization Executive Asked Putin Aide for Help on Business Deal," *WaPo*, 8/28/17.

55. Brian Ross and Matthew Mosk, "Trump Signed Letter of Intent for Russian Tower During Campaign, Lawyer Says," ABCNews.com, 8/28/17.

56. "Trump Sought Moscow Business Deal While Campaigning for President," *Rachel Maddow Show*, MSNBC, 8/28/17.

57–58. Rosalind S. Helderman, Carol D. Leonnig, and Tom Hamburger, "Top Trump Organization Executive Asked Putin Aide for Help on Business Deal," *WaPo*, 8/28/17.

59. Andrew Roth, "Kremlin Says It Got the Trump Tower Email but Didn't Respond," *WaPo*, 8/30/17.

60. Megan Twohey and Scott Shane, "A Back-channel Plan for Ukraine and Russia, Courtesy of Trump Associates," *NYT*, 2/19/17; "New Development on the Michael Cohen 'Peace Plan' Meeting," *TPM*, 3/4/17.

61. Kim Sengupta, "The Trump-Russia Probe Contains Explosive Allegations and the President Will Struggle to Conceal the Secrets of His Past," *Independent* (UK), 9/1/17.

62–63. Michael Isikoff, "Key Democrat: Panel May Need to Hear from President on Trump Tower Moscow Project," *YN*, 8/29/17.

64. Maggie Haberman and Matt Apuzzo, "Trump Lawyer 'Vehemently' Denies Russian Collusion," *NYT*, 8/30/17.

65. Manu Raju, "Exclusive: How a Request About Russians Made Its Way from West Virginia to Trump's Team," CNN.com, 8/28/17.

66. Julia Ainsley and Tom Winter, "Mueller Team Asking if Trump Tried to Hide Purpose of Trump Tower Meeting," NBCNews.com, 8/28/17.

67. Katrina Manson, "Russian Lobbyist to Mueller Grand Jury," *FT*, 8/30/17.

68. Stephanie Kirchgaessner, "Trump Makes Policy Pledge to Senator Investigating Son's Russia Meeting," *Guardian*, 8/31/17.

69. ChuckGrassley (@ChuckGrassley), "Just had ph call from Pres Trump + he assured me he's pro ethanol +I'm free 2 the ppl of Iowa he's standing by his campaign PROMISE," 8/30/17, 7:27 a.m.; Julia Manchester, "Senate Committee to Vote on Releasing Fusion GPS Testimony," *The Hill*, 8/24/17.

70. Evan Perez, "Special Counsel Subpoenas Manafort's Former Attorney and Spokesman," CNN.com, 8/29/17.

71–73. Josh Dawsey, "Mueller Teams Up with New York Attorney General in Manafort Probe," *Politico*, 8/30/17.

74–75. Brett Forrest, "Paul Manafort's Overseas Political Work Had Notable Patron: A Russian Oligarch," *WSJ*, 8/30/17.

76. Ken Dilanian and Carol E. Lee, "Manafort Notes from Russian Meet Refer to Political Contributions," NBCNews.com, 9/1/17.

77–78. Betsy Woodruff, "Exclusive: Mueller Enlists the IRS for His Trump-Russia Investigation," *DB*, 8/31/17.

79. David Kocieniewski and Caleb Melby, "Kushner's China Deal Flop Was Part of Much Bigger Hunt for Cash," Bloomberg.com, 8/31/17.

80. Ibid.; Ben Walsh, Ryan Grim, and Clayton Swisher, "Jared Kushner Tried and Failed to Get a Half-Billion-Dollar Bailout from Qatar," *The Intercept*, 7/10/17.

81. David Kocieniewski and Caleb Melby, "Kushner's China Deal Flop Was Part of Much Bigger Hunt for Cash," Bloomberg.com, 8/31/17.

82. Peter Nicholas, Erica Orden, and Paul Sonne, "Trump Attorneys Lay Out Arguments Against Obstruction-of-Justice Probe to Mueller," *WSJ*, 8/31/17; Preet Bharara (@PreetBharara), "Note: There may never be any charges, but defense lawyers don't usu waste time on preemptive memos re: frivolous theories of criminal guilt" 8/31/17, 6:15 p.m.

83. Shannon Vavra, "Russian Diplomats Keep Dying Unexpectedly," *Axios*, 8/24/17.

84. Elise Viebeck, "Republican Congressman Floats Amendment to End Mueller Probe," *WaPo*, 8/30/17.

85–87. Philip Rucker and Ashley Parker, "During a Summer of Crisis, Trump Chafes Against Criticism and New Controls," *WaPo*, 8/31/17.

88. Annie Karni, "Trump's Shrinking West Wing," *Politico*, 8/30/17.

89. Chris Baynes, "Donald Trump's Cyber-security Advisers Resign Warning of 'Insufficient Attention to the Growing Threats,'" *Independent* (UK), 8/28/17.

90. Jennifer Jacobs and Kevin Cirilli, "Trump Punishes Longtime Aide After Angry Phoenix Speech, Sources Say," Bloomberg.com, 8/28/17.

91. Donald Trump (@realDonaldTrump), ".@foxandfriends We are not looking to fill all of those positions. Don't need many of them—reduce size of government. @IngrahamAngle" Twitter, 8/29/17, 5:26.

92–93. Derek Kravitz, Isaac Arnsdorf, and Marina Affo, "Lifting the Veil on Another Batch of Shadowy Trump Appointees," *ProPublica*, 8/31/17.

94. Alex Isenstadt, "RNC Chief of Staff Resigns amid Rash of Departures," *Politico*, 8/31/17.

95. Colum Lynch, "Top State Department Officials Step Down in 'Black Friday' Exodus," *FP*, 8/27/17.

96. Dana Bash, Noah Gray, and Jeremy Diamond, "Longtime Trump Aide Keith Schiller Tells People He Intends to Leave White House," CNN.com, 9/1/17.

97. Ashraf Khalil and AP, "19 Indicted, Including 15 Turkish Security Officials, for Attacking Protesters during Erdogan Visit to U.S.," *CT*, 8/29/17.

98–99. Stephanie Nebehay, "Trump Attacking Freedom of the Press: U.N. Rights Boss," Reuters, 8/30/17.

100. Carrie Dann, "'Abject Disappointment': Pittsburgh Voters Skewer Trump's Tone," NBCNews.com, 8/31/17.

101. "Republicans Divided in Views of Trump's Conduct; Democrats Are Broadly Critical," Pew Research Center, 8/29/17.

102. "Gallup Daily: Trump Job Approval," Gallup News, http://news.gallup.com/poll/201617/gallup-daily-trump-job-approval.aspx.

103. Dana Blanton, "Fox News Poll: Voters' Mood Sours, 56 Percent Say Trump Tearing Country Apart," FoxNews.com, 8/30/17.

104. Michael S. Schmidt and Maggie Haberman, "Mueller Has Early Draft of Trump Letter Giving Reasons for Firing Comey," *NYT*, 9/1/17.

105. Peter Nicholas and Michael C. Bender, "Trump Drafted Letter on Why He Wanted Comey Out," *WSJ*, 9/1/17.

106. Josh Gerstein and Josh Dawsey, "Trump Aides Averted More Detailed Letter Justifying Comey Firing," *Politico*, 9/1/17.

107–109. Michael S. Schmidt and Maggie Haberman, "Mueller Has Early Draft of Trump Letter Giving Reasons for Firing Comey," *NYT*, 9/1/17.

110. John McCain, "It's Time Congress Returns to Regular Order," *WaPo*, 8/31/17.

111. Aaron Rupar, "White House Walks Back Promise About Trump Donating His 'Personal Money' to Harvey Victims," *ThinkProgress*, undated.

112. Justin Baragona, "Watch as Trump Calls on a Bunch of Religious Leaders to Thank Him for His Harvey Efforts," *Mediaite*, 9/1/17.

113–115. Glenn Thrush and Maggie Haberman, "Forceful Chief of Staff Grates on Trump, and the Feeling Is Mutual," *NYT*, 9/1/17.

116. Jessica Estepa, "Eric Trump on Negative Media Coverage: 'You'd Probably End Up Killing Yourself,'" *USAT*, 8/31/17.

117. *FP* (@ForeignPolicy), "EXCLUSIVE: Here's the fire in back of about to-be-closed DC Russia trade rep building. @janawinter on the scene." Twitter, 9/1/17, 4:56 p.m.; Nataliya Vasilyeva and Josh Lederman, "Russia Claims 'Gross Violation' After Trump Orders Diplomatic Posts Closed," *CT*, 9/1/17.

WEEK 43

1. Matthew Nussbaum, "Justice Department: No Evidence Obama Wiretapped Trump Tower," *Politico*, 9/2/17.

2. Max Greenwood, "Trump Goes Hands-on in Return to Storm-Ravaged Gulf Coast," *The Hill*, 9/2/17.

3. Lynn Yaeger, "Donald Trump in Houston: 'Have a Good Time Everybody,'" *Vogue*, 9/3/17.

4. Barbara Starr and Jeremy Herb, "Pentagon Accidentally Miscalculates Number of Troops Deployed to Harvey Relief Efforts," CNN.com, 9/1/17.

5. AP (@AP), "BREAKING: AP Exclusive: Many Houston ultra-polluted Superfund sites are flooded, concerns about toxins spreading; EPA not on scene." Twitter, 9/2/17, 10:20 a.m.

6. Environmental Protection Agency Office of the Administrator, "EPA Response to the AP's Misleading Story," 9/3/17, www.epa.gov/newsreleases/epa-response-aps-misleading-story.

7. Ibid.; Jason Dearen and Michael Biesecker, "AP EXCLUSIVE: Toxic Waste Sites Flooded in Houston Area," AP, 9/3/17.

8. Juliet Eilperin, "EPA Now Requires Political Aide's Sign-off for Agency Awards, Grant Applications," *WaPo*, 9/4/17.

9. Dino Grandoni, "Government Watchdog to Launch Probe into EPA's Hiring Practices," *WaPo*, 9/8/17.

10. Ken Ward Jr., "Trump Nominates Former Coal Exec to Run MSHA," *Charleston Gazette-Mail*, 9/2/17.

11. Kenneth Chang, "Jim Bridenstine to Be Nominated by Trump to Lead NASA" *NYT*, 9/2/17.

12. Andrew Kaczynski, "Parts of Trump NASA Pick's Online Presence Scrubbed," CNN.com, 9/7/17.

13. "North Korea Nuclear Crisis: Test 'Caused Landslides,'" BBC News, 9/6/17.

14. Choe Sang-Hun, "Allies for 67 Years, U.S. and South Korea Split over North Korea," *NYT*, 9/4/17.

15. "Mattis: Trump Wanted to Hear All Military Options for North Korea," *Axios*, 9/3/17.

17. Timothy Puko, "Hundreds of EPA Workers Leave in Recent Days," *WSJ*, 9/5/17.

18-19. Jamie McIntyre, "Pentagon Scales Back Number of Reporters Traveling with Jim Mattis," *WE*, 9/6/17.

20. Ariane de Vogue, "9th Circuit Narrows Scope of Trump Travel Ban," CNN.com, 9/7/17.

21. "Trump Administration Backs Baker Who Refused to Make Gay Wedding Cake," NBCNews.com, 9/8/17.

22. Dominic Holden (@dominicholden), "US Civil Rights Commission slams Trump for pardoning Arpaio—says Trump's pardon 'damages the fabric of our nation.'" Twitter, 9/8/17, 9:29 a.m.

23-24. Julia Ainsley and Andrew Blankstein, "Homeland Security Cancels Massive Roundups of Undocumented Immigrants," NBCNews.com, 9/7/17.

25. Danny Vinik, "3 Things Trump Did This Week While You Weren't Looking," *Politico*, 9/8/17.

26-27. Benjamin Wermund, "DeVos to Scrap Obama-Era School Sexual Assault Policy," *Politico*, 9/7/17.

28. Tyler Kingkade, "Joe Biden Tells Sexual Assault Survivors Not to 'Give Up' Following DeVos Title IX Announcement," *BF*, 9/8/17.

29. Kathleen Harris, "Foreign Students Flock to Canada as Government Struggles to Get Grads to Stay," CBC News, 9/3/17.

30. Adrian Morrow, "Canada Demands U.S. End 'Right to Work' Laws as Part of NAFTA Talks," *Globe and Mail* (Canada), 9/5/17.

31. Victoria Lopez, "ICE Plans to Start Destroying Records of Immigrant Abuse, Including Sexual Assault and Deaths in Custody," ACLU.org, 8/28/17.

32. Cristina Marcos, "House Republican Causes Stir Claiming Female Lawmaker 'Doesn't Know a Damn Thing,'" *The Hill*, 9/7/17.

33. Josh Delk, "Report: FBI Probes Utah Cop Who Arrested Nurse for Refusing to Draw Blood," *The Hill*, 9/8/17.

34. Mara Klecker and Andrew J. Nelson, "Photo of 5 Males in KKK Hoods Leads to Discipline Against Students in Creston, Iowa," *Omaha World-Herald*, 9/7/17.

35. "White Nationalists Gain Path to Power Through Bannon," *Rachel Maddow Show*, MSNBC, 9/4/17.

36. Ta-Nehisi Coates, "The First White President," *Atlantic*, 9/7/17.

37-38. Brad Heath, Fredreka Schouten, Steve Reilly, Nick Penzenstadler, and Aamer Madhani, "Trump Gets Millions from Golf Members. CEOs and Lobbyists Get Access to President," *USAT*, 9/8/17.

39. Cristina Marcos, "GOP Leaders Prevent Votes to Ban Federal Spending at Trump Businesses," *The Hill*, 9/6/17.

40. Steve Benen, "GOP Again Moves to Help Keep Trump's Tax Returns Secret," *MaddowBlog*, 9/8/17.

41. Julia Manchester, "GAO to Investigate Zinke's Alleged Alaskan Threat: Report," *The Hill*, 9/8/17.

42. Esme Cribb, "Lawyers' Group: Sketchy Election Panel Using Personal Email for Official Biz," *TPM*, 9/5/17.

43. Kris W. Kobach, "Exclusive—Kobach: It Appears That Out-of-State Voters Changed the Outcome of the New Hampshire U.S. Senate Race," *Breitbart*, 9/77/17; Christopher Ingraham, "Kris Kobach Says He Has 'Proof' of Voter Fraud in New Hampshire. He Can't Be Serious." *WaPo*, 9/8/17.

44. David Weigel, "Election Integrity Commission Members Accuse New Hampshire Voters of Fraud," *WaPo*, 9/8/17.

45. Kyle Griffin (@kylegriffin1), "N.H. Senators Shaheen and Hassan want the N.H. Secretary of State to resign from Trump's Election Commission." Twitter, 9/8/17, 7:12 p.m.

46. Michael C. Bender and Kristina Peterson, "Congress Faces a Tense Agenda, with Little Margin for Error," *WSJ*, 9/4/17.

47-48. Michael D. Shear and Julie Hirschfeld Davis, "Trump Moves to End DACA and Calls on Congress to Act," *NYT*, 9/5/17.

49. Tal Kopan, "Sessions as Face of DACA Decision Reveals Internal Struggle," CNN.com, 9/5/17.

50. Javier Palomarez, "Why I'm Resigning from Trump's Diversity Coalition," *NYT*, 9/5/17.

51. Steven Shepard, "Poll: Majority Opposes Deporting Dreamers," *Politico*, 9/5/17.

52. Glenn Thrush and Maggie Haberman, "To Allies' Chagrin, Trump Swerves Left," *NYT*, 9/6/7.

53. United States Conference of Catholic Bishops, "USCCB President, Vice President and Committee Chairmen Denounce Administration's Decision to End DACA and Strongly Urge Congress to Find Legislative Solution," news release, 9/5/7, www.usccb.org/news/2017/17-157.cfm.

54. Louis Nelson, "Bannon Breaks with Trump on DACA: Conservatives 'Are Not Happy with This,'" *Politico*, 9/7/17.

55. Dara Lind, "The Government Is Already Winding Down DACA—No Matter What Trump Tweets," *Vox*, 9/6/17.

56. "Trump Says DACA Recipients Should Not Worry About Status," Reuters, 9/7/17.

57. Ryan Struyk and Tal Kopan, "983 Would Lose Protection per Day: What a DACA Phase-out Would Look Like," CNN.com, 9/9/17.

58. Jessica Taylor, "Trump Sides with Democrats in Deal on Storm Relief and Fiscal Deadlines," NPR.org, 9/6/17.

59. Amber Phillips, "With 'Good Woman,' Did Donald Trump Just Help Democratic Sen. Heidi Heitkamp Get Reelected?" *WaPo*, 9/6/17.

60. Alex Stamos, "An Update on Information Operations on Facebook," Facebook Newsroom, 9/6/17.

61–62. Carol D. Leonnig, Tom Hamburger, and Rosalind S. Helderman, "Russian Firm Tied to Pro-Kremlin Propaganda Advertised on Facebook During Election," *WaPo*, 9/6/17.

63. Ben Collins, Kevin Poulsen, and Spencer Ackerman, "Russia's Facebook Fake News Could Have Reached 70 Million Americans," *DB*, 9/8/17.

64–65. Scott Shane, "The Fake Americans Russia Created to Influence the Election," *NYT*, 9/7/17.

66. Margaret Sullivan, "Facebook's Role in Trump's Win Is Clear. No Matter What Mark Zuckerberg Says," *WaPo*, 9/7/17; Siva Vaidhyanathan, "Facebook Wins, Democracy Loses," *NYT*, 9/8/17.

67. "Facebook Gives Election Ad Data to U.S. Special Counsel—Source," Reuters, 9/6/17; Carol D. Leonnig, Tom Hamburger, and Rosalind S. Helderman, "Russian Firm Tied to Pro-Kremlin Propaganda Advertised on Facebook During Election," *WaPo*, 9/6/17.

68. Jeremy Herb, "Warner: Facebook's Russia Disclosure 'Tip of the Iceberg,'" CNN.com, 9/7/17.

69. Greg Gordon and Peter Stone, "Subpoenas Likely if Facebook Resists Russia Inquiries," McClatchy, 9/8/17.

70. Oren Dorell, "Alleged Russian Political Meddling Documented in 27 Countries Since 2004," *USAT*, 9/7/17.

71. Tom LoBianco and Manu Raju, "Nunes Vents Anger at Sessions over Subpoena, Threatens to Hold AG, FBI Chief in Contempt," CNN.com, 9/6/17.

72. Chris Smith, "Trey Gowdy's War on the Steele Dossier," *VF*, 9/8/17.

73. Darren Samuelsohn, "Trump Campaign Urges Court to Toss Out WikiLeaks Hack Lawsuit," *Politico*, 9/5/17.

74. Evan Perez, Pamela Brown, Shimon Prokupecz, and Eric Bradner, "Sources: US Prepares Charges to Seek Arrest of WikiLeaks' Julian Assange," CNN .com, 4/20/17.

75. Oleg Matsnev, "Trump Is 'Not My Bride,' Putin Says," *NYT*, 9/5/17.

76. Nicholas Fandos, "Donald Trump Jr. to Meet with Senate Russia Investigators," *NYT*, 9/6/17; "New Russia Contact Revelations in Trump Jr Senate Interview," *Rachel Maddow Show*, MSNBC, 9/7/17.

77. Nicholas Fandos, "Donald Trump Jr. to Meet with Senate Russia Investigators," *NYT*, 9/6/17; Manu Raju, Dana Bash, and Zachary Cohen, "Sources: Trump Jr. Said He Did Not Recall WH Involvement in Response to Meeting," CNN.com, 9/8/17.

78. Nicholas Fandos and Maggie Haberman, "Trump Jr. Says He Wanted Russian Dirt to Determine Clinton's 'Fitness' for Office," *NYT*, 9/7/17.

79. Ryan Lucas, "Trump Jr. Wanted Info on Clinton's 'Fitness' in Meeting with Russians," NPR.org, 9/7/17.

80–81. Tom Hamburger and Karoun Demirjian, "Trump Jr. Says He Can't Recall White House Role in Explaining Meeting with Russians," *WaPo*, 9/7/17.

82. Julia Glum, "Why Did Donald Trump Jr. Meet with Russian Lawyer? A Full List of His Changing Excuses," *Newsweek*, 9/17/17.

83. Natasha Bertrand, "Top Senator Strongly Suggests Donald Trump Jr. Lied in His Testimony About Russia Meeting," *BI*, 9/7/17.

84–85. Pamela Brown, Gloria Borger, and Jeremy Diamond, "Exclusive: Mueller Seeks Interviews with WH Staff over Trump Tower Meeting Statement," CNN.com, 9/7/17.

86. Tom Hamburger and Karoun Demirjian, "Trump Jr. Says He Can't Recall White House Role in Explaining Meeting with Russians," *WaPo*, 9/7/17.

87–89. Carol D. Leonnig, Rosalind S. Helderman, and Ashley Parker, "Mueller Gives White House Names of 6 Aides He Expects to Question in Russia Probe," *WaPo*, 9/8/17.

90–91. Betsy Woodruff, Lachlan Markay, and Asawin Suebsaeng, "Mueller Wants to Talk to Hope Hicks over Misleading Russian Statement," *DB*, 9/8/17.

92. Annie Karni and Eliana Johnson, "White House Communications Director Hope Hicks Retains Lawyer in Russia Probe," *Politico*, 9/8/17.

93–95. Gloria Borger and Marshall Cohen, "Document Details Scrapped Deal for Trump Tower Moscow," CNN .com, 9/9/17.

96–97. "New Russian Envoy Describes 'Warm' Meeting with Trump: Agencies," Reuters, 9/8/17.

98. Chuck Goudie and Barb Markoff, "Russian Thread Runs Through Chicago Extradition Case ABC7 I-Team Investigation," ABC7Chicago.com, 9/8/17.

99. "EPA Chief Scott Pruitt: Hurricane Irma Isn't the Right Time to Talk Climate Change," *DB*, undated.

100–101. Patricia Zengerle, "Senate Panel Rejects Trump's 'Doctrine of Retreat' on Foreign Policy," Reuters, 9/8/17.

102–103. Kylie Atwood, "State Department Criticized for Irma Response," CBSNews.com, 9/9/17.

104. Danny Vinik, "3 Things Trump Did This Week While You Weren't Looking," *Politico*, 9/8/17.

105. Michael C. Bender, Harriet Tory, and Nick Timiraos, "President Trump Unlikely to Nominate Gary Cohn to Become Fed Chairman," *WSJ*, 9/6/17.

106. Maggie Haberman and Glenn Thrush, "New White House Chief of Staff Has an Enforcer," *NYT*, 9/8/17.

107. "Chris Christie Accuses Steve Bannon of Lying about Him," CBSNews.com, 9/12/17.

108. Shannon Pettypiece and Jennifer Jacobs, "Key Trump Aide's Departure Rattles President's Allies," Bloomberg, 9/5/17.

WEEK 44

1. Philip Bump, "Trump Says the Coast Guard Has Great Branding Now. Google Is Not Convinced," *WaPo*, 9/11/17.

2. Mike Allen, "Why Trump Hopes the New Trump Sticks," *Axios*, 9/9/17.

3. Olivia Beavers, "White House Shares, Deletes Inaccurate 'Hurricane Irma' Video," *The Hill*, 9/10/17.

4–5. Jenna McLaughlin, "More White, More Male, More Jesus: CIA Employees Fear Pompeo Is Quietly Killing the Agency's Diversity Mandate," *FP*, 8/9/17.

6. White House, Office of the Press Secretary, "President Donald J. Trump Announces Sixth Wave of United States Attorney Nominations," press release,

9/8/17, www.whitehouse.gov/the-press-office/2017/09/08/president-donald-j-trump-announces-sixth-wave-united-states-attorney.

7. Dominic Holden (@dominicholden), "another day of dudes nominated as US attorneys" Twitter, 9/11/17, 2:15 p.m.

8. American Institute of Physics, "NASA Nominee Jim Bridenstine Has Bold Vision for Space, Unclear Intentions for Science," 9/7/17, www.aip.org/fyi/2017/nasa-nominee-jim-bridenstine-has-bold-vision-space-unclear-intentions-science.

9. Jane Stancill, "UNC Board Bans Legal Action at Civil Rights Center," *News & Observer* (NC), 9/10/17.

10. Uriel J. Garcia, "ICE Arrests Young Immigrant's Sponsor Months After Feds Assured Him He'd Be Safe," *New Mexican*, 9/9/17.

11. Antonio Noori Farzan and Joseph Flaherty, "Attorneys Suspect Motel 6 Calling ICE on Undocumented Guests," *Phoenix New Times*, 9/13/17.

12. Antonio Noori Farzan, "After *New Times* Story, Motel 6 Says It Will Stop Sharing Guest Lists with ICE," *Phoenix New Times*, 9/14/17.

13. Julie Hirschfeld Davis and Miriam Jordan, "White House Weighs Lowering Refugee Quota to Below 50,000," *NYT*, 9/12/17.

14. Briana Whitney (@BrianaWhitney), "DACA recipients now being detained for hours at Texas border checkpoints, w/ no explanation as to why. Border Patrol says it's new protocol" Twitter, 9/16/17, 7:39 a.m.

15. Jason Meisner and John Byrne, "Judge Rules in City's Favor on Sanctuary Cities, Grants Nationwide Injunction," *CT*, 9/15/17.

16-17. AP, "Congress Overwhelmingly Approves Resolution Condemning White Nationalists," NBCNews.com, 9/12/17.

18. Benjamin Siegel and Alexander Mallin, "Trump Will Sign Measure Condemning Charlottesville Violence, White Nationalists: White House," ABCNews.com, 9/13/17.

19. Mark Landler, "Trump Resurrects His Claim That Both Sides Share Blame in Charlottesville Violence," *NYT*, 9/14/17.

20. Erik Wemple, "*Politico* Editor: We Discard 'Dozens' of Potential Hires over Toxic Twitter Feeds," *WaPo*, 9/8/17.

21. Lydia Wheeler, "Trump Stirs Controversy with Civil Rights Pick," *The Hill*, 9/13/17.

22. Mike Snider, "NBC News' Katy Tur Details Unwanted Trump Kiss in New Book on Campaign," *USAT*, 9/13/17.

23. Sam Baker, "CDC Cracks Down on Communications with Reporters," *Axios*, 9/12/17.

24. Matt Zapotosky, "Justice Dept. Supports Arpaio's Post-Pardon Bid to Have Guilty Finding Thrown Out," *WaPo*, 9/11/17.

25. Madeline Conway, "Legal Groups Move to Challenge Trump's Arpaio Pardon," *Politico*, 9/11/17.

26. Michael Tanglis, "Trump Inc: Inside the President's Not-So-Blind Trust," *Salon*, 9/10/17.

27. Anita Kumar, "Trump Promised Not to Work with Foreign Entities. His Company Just Did," McClatchy, 9/11/17.

28. Jessica Garrison, Jeremy Singer-Vine, Ken Bensinger, "Trump Beach Resort Wants More Foreign Guest Workers," *BF*, 9/12/17.

29. Ariella Phillips, "Florida Attorney General Pam Bondi to Join Trump's Drug Commission Next Week," *WE*, 9/7/17.

30. U.S. Office of Govt. Ethics, Special Review of Executive Branch Agency Waivers & Authorizations, Sept. 2017, https://oge.gov/web/oge.nsf/Special%20Reports/F916A3C42996EF618525819A006D12EB/$FILE/Final%20Report%20Package%20.pdf?open.

31-32. Laura Jarrett and Cristina Alesci, "Trump Administration Withholds Almost All Mar-a-Lago Visitor Logs," CNN.com, 9/15/17.

33. Drew Harwell and Amy Brittain, "Taxpayers Billed $1,092 for an Official Two-Night Stay at Trump's Mar-a-Lago Club," *WaPo*, 9/15/17.

34. Spencer Ackerman, "Controversial White House Aide Is Now Working for Devin Nunes," *DB*, 9/11/17.

35. Carl Hulse, "As G.O.P. Moves to Fill Courts, McConnell Takes Aim at an Enduring Hurdle," *NYT*, 9/13/17.

36. Darren Samuelsohn, "Trump Ethics Watchdog Moves to Allow Anonymous Gifts to Legal Defense Funds," *Politico*, 9/13/17.

37. Cristina Alesci and Curt Devine, "Ethics Office Clarifies Rules for WH Aides' Legal Defense," CNN.com, 9/15/17.

38. Justin Fishel, Brian Ross, and Jordyn Phelps, "Treasury Secretary Mnuchin Requested Government Jet for European Honeymoon," ABCNews.com, 9/13/17.

39. Citizens for Responsibility and Ethics in Washington, "CREW Sues Treasury over Mnuchin/Linton Trip FOIA," press release, 9/11/17, www.citizensforethics.org/press-release/crew-sues-treasury-mnuchinlinton-trip-foia.

40. Ari Berman and Pema Levy, "Lawsuits, Falsehoods, and a Lot of White Men: Trump's Election Commission Meets amid Growing Controversy," *MJ*, 9/11/17.

41. Dell Cameron, "Jeff Sessions Was Lobbied to Exclude Democrats from Trump's Election Fraud Panel (Updated)," *Gizmodo*, 9/12/17.

42. Ari Berman and Pema Levy, "Lawsuits, Falsehoods, and a Lot of White Men: Trump's Election Commission Meets amid Growing Controversy," *MJ*, 9/11/17.

43. Sam Levine, "Democrat on Trump Voter Fraud Probe Slams Voting Restriction Efforts," *HuffPost*, 9/9/17.

44. Jessica Huseman, "Experts Say the Use of Private Email by Trump's Voter Fraud Commission Isn't Legal," *ProPublica*, 9/15/17.

45. Kate Linthicum, "After an Earthquake and a Hurricane—and Trump's Failure to Send Condolences—Mexico Rescinds Offer of Aid to U.S." *LAT*, 9/11/17.

46. Maggie Haberman and Glenn Thrush, "Why Did Trump Work Again with Democrats? 'He Likes Us,' Schumer Says," *NYT*, 9/14/17.

47. Judd Legum, "Scandal-Plagued Foreign Leader Gets Surprise Invite from Trump, Checks into Trump's Hotel," *ThinkProgress*, undated.

48. Mark Landler, "Trump Welcomes Najib Razak, the Malaysian Leader, as

President, and Owner of a Fine Hotel," *NYT*, 9/12/17.

49–50. Hunter Walker and Michael Isikoff, "Sputnik, the Russian News Agency, Is Under Investigation by the FBI," *YN*, 9/11/17.

51. "Fmr. Sputnik Employee: Right Wing Sites Spread Our Russian . . ." *The Beat with Ari Melber*, MSNBC, 9/12/17.

52. Megan R. Wilson, "Russian Network RT Must Register as Foreign Agent in US," *The Hill*, 9/12/17.

53. "Russian Journalist Latynina Flees Russia After Attacks," *Moscow Times*, 9/11/17.

54. Sindhu Sundar, "EXCLUSIVE: Priebus, McGahn Hire Quinn Emanuel in Mueller Probe," Law360.com, 9/10/17.

55. Darren Samuelsohn, "Russia Probes Pose Loyalty Test for Team Trump," *Politico*, 9/12/17.

56–57. Peter Nicholas, Rebecca Ballhaus, Erica Orden, and Anton Troianovski, "Some Trump Lawyers Wanted Kushner Out," *WSJ*, 9/11/17.

58. Becca Rotenberg, "Russian Politician Says on Live TV That Russia Stole U.S. Presidency," *Axios*, 9/11/17.

59–62. Ben Collins, Kevin Poulsen, and Spencer Ackerman, "Exclusive: Russia Used Facebook Events to Organize Anti-Immigrant Rallies on U.S. Soil," *DB*, 9/11/17.

63–64. Natasha Bertrand, "Shuttered Facebook Group That Organized Anti-Clinton, Anti-Immigrant Rallies Across Texas Was Linked to Russia," *BI*, 9/13/17.

65. Julia Angwin, Madeleine Varner, and Ariana Tobin, "Facebook Enabled Advertisers to Reach 'Jew Haters,'" *ProPublica*, 9/14/17.

66. Chris Strohm, "Mueller Probe Has 'Red-Hot' Focus on Social Media, Officials Say," Bloomberg.com, 9/13/17.

67–68. Deepa Seetharaman, Byron Tau, and Shane Harris, "Facebook Gave Special Counsel Robert Mueller More Details on Russian Ad Buys than Congress," *WSJ*, 9/15/17.

69–71. Chris Smith, "Did Jared Kushner's Data Operation Help Select Facebook Targets for the Russians?" *VF*, 9/15/17.

72. Byron Tau and Deepa Seetharaman, "Senate Panel Likely to Ask Facebook to Publicly Detail Russian Activity on Platform During Election," *WSJ*, 9/12/17.

73. Rachel Maddow MSNBC (@maddow), "Warner's office confirms: they really did pay in rubles. (FB's crack investigators took a year to figure out those rubles were from Russia?)" Twitter, 9/15/17, 12:44 p.m.

74. Michael Isikoff, "Pressure Mounts on Facebook to Release Campaign Ads Bought by Russia," *YN*, 9/12/17.

75–76. John Hudson, "How Putin Hoped to Make Up with the US," *BF*, 9/12/17.

77. Betsy Woodruff, "The Trump Campaign Has Begun Turning Over Documents to Mueller," *DB*, 9/12/17.

78. Kevin Liptak, "White House: Justice Department Should 'Look at' Prosecuting Comey," CNN.com, 9/12/17.

79–80. Philip Bump, "Trump's Press Secretary Offers Suggested Punishments for Two Trump Critics," *WaPo*, 9/13/17.

81–83. Michael S. Schmidt and Maggie Haberman, "Trump Humiliated Jeff Sessions After Mueller Appointment," *NYT*, 9/14/17.

84. Jim Sciutto, "Flynn Refusing New Request to Speak to Hill Committee," CNN.com, 9/13/17.

85–86. Brian Ross, Matthew Mosk, James Gordon Meek, and Allan Dodds Frank, "Flynn Concealed More than a Dozen Foreign Contacts, Overseas Trips: Democrats," ABCNews.com, 9/13/17.

87–88. Christopher S. Stewart, Rob Barry, and Shane Harris, "Flynn Promoted Nuclear-Plant Project in White House," *WSJ*, 9/13/17.

89. Carol E. Lee, Julia Ainsley, and Ken Dilanian, "Mike Flynn's Son Is Subject of Federal Russia Probe," NBCNews.com, 9/13/17.

90. Manu Raju, "Exclusive: Justice Department Declines Senate Request to Interview FBI Officials over Comey Firing," CNN.com, 9/13/17.

91. Nicholas Fandos, "Judiciary Chairman Considers Subpoenas in Trump Investigation," *NYT*, 9/15/17.

92–94. Manu Raju, "Exclusive: Rice Told House Investigators Why She Unmasked Senior Trump Officials," CNN.com, 9/18/17.

95–96. Ellen Nakashima and Jack Gillum, "U.S. Moves to Ban Kaspersky Software in Federal Agencies amid Concerns of Russian Espionage," *WaPo*, 9/13/17.

97–100. Jason Leopold, Chris McDaniel, and Anthony Cormier, "Trump Advisers Secretly Met with Jordan's King While One Was Pushing a Huge Nuclear Power Deal," *BF*, 9/15/17.

101–104. Christian Berthelsen, "Russia Laundering Probe Puts Trump Tower Meeting in New Light," Bloomberg.com, 9/15/17.

105. Natasha Bertrand, "New Details About Major Russian Money-Laundering Investigation Raise the Stakes of Trump Tower Meeting," *BI*, 9/15/17.

106. Josh Gerstein, "Another Prosecutor Joins Trump-Russia Probe," *Politico*, 9/15/17.

107. Nate Silver (@NateSilver538), "Dems flipped two very pro-Trump districts in special elections last night. There was a 28-point swing to Dems in NH. A 31-point swing in OK." Twitter 9/13/17, 7:01 a.m.

108. Jena McGregor, "U.S. Workers Have Been Giving a Lot More Money to the ACLU," *WaPo*, 9/4/17.

109–110. Mark Landler and Maggie Haberman, "Trump's Tweets About London Bombing Anger British Leaders," *NYT*, 9/15/17.

111. Tim Ross and Thomas Penny, "May Complained to Trump About His London Attack Tweets, Official Says," Bloomberg.com, 9/15/17.

112. Alan Rappeport, "More Classmates of Treasury Secretary Hound Him to Quit Trump Post," *NYT*, 9/15/17.

113–114. Byron Tau, Peter Nicholas, and Siobhan Hughes, "GOP Congressman Sought Trump Deal on WikiLeaks, Russia," *WSJ*, 9/15/17.

115–116. Jeff Horwitz and Julie Bykowicz, "Still No Charity Money from Leftover Trump Inaugural Funds," AP, 9/16/17.

117. Matthew Nussbaum, "Pence's Press Secretary to Leave White House," *Politico*, 9/15/17.

118. Eliot A. Cohen, "How Trump Is Ending the American Era," *Atlantic*, 9/12/17.

119. Richard Lardner and Lolita C. Baldor, "Transgender Troops Can Re-enlist in Military—for Now," AP, 9/16/17.

WEEK 45

1. Brent D. Griffiths, "Trump Tweets About North Korea's 'Rocket Man,'" Dings Hillary Clinton Again," *Politico*, 9/17/17.

2. Jeremy Diamond, "Trump Retweets GIF of Him Hitting Clinton with Golf Ball," CNN.com, 9/18/17.

3. Alicia Melville-Smith, "Trump Retweeted a Video from an Anti-Semitic Account Showing Him Hitting Hillary Clinton with a Golf Ball," *BF*, 9/17/17.

4. Mallory Shelbourne, "Trump Begins First UN Remarks by Mentioning His Nearby Building," *The Hill*, 9/18/17.

5. Ali Vitali, "Trump Threatens to 'Totally Destroy' North Korea in First U.N. Speech," NBCNews.com, 9/17/17.

6. Ibid.; Kelly J. Baker, "Make America White Again?" *Atlantic*, 3/12/16.

7. Anna Fifield, "North Korea Is Likely to Fire More Missiles After Trump's Speech, Experts Say," *WaPo*, 9/20/17.

8. Choe Sang-Hun, "Trump Likened to 'a Dog Barking' by North Korea's Top Envoy," *NYT*, 9/21/17.

9. Choe Sang-Hun, "North Korea Hits New Level of Brinkmanship in Reacting to Trump," *NYT*, 9/22/17.

10. Brian Bennett, "Aides Warned Trump Not to Attack North Korea's Leader Personally Before His Fiery U.N. Address," *LAT*, 9/22/17.

11. Richard Wike, Bruce Stokes, Jacob Poushter, and Janell Fetterolf, "U.S. Image Suffers as Publics Around World Question Trump's Leadership," Pew Research Center, 6/26/17.

12. Richard Wike, Bruce Stokes, Jacob Poushter, and Janell Fetterolf, "2. Worldwide, Few Confident in Trump or His Policies,' Pew Research Center, 6/26/17.

13. Kevin Liptak and Jeremy Diamond, "Trump to UN: 'Rocket Man Is on a Suicide Mission,'" CNN.com, 9/19/17.

14. Bill Chappell, "Iran Shows Off New Ballistic Missile at Military Parade," *The Two-Way* (blog), NPR, 9/22/17.

15. Josh Delk, "Trump Praises Erdogan: 'We Have a Great Friendship,'" *The Hill*, 9/21/17.

16. Christine Hauser and Katharine Q. Seelye, "New Hampshire Investigates Wounding of 8-Year-Old as Possible Hate Crime," *NYT*, 9/13/17.

17. Alex Horton, "U.S. Army Kills Contracts for Hundreds of Immigrant Recruits. Some Face Deportation." *WaPo*, 9/15/17.

18. Abigail Jones, "White Supremacists Blamed for Racist, 'Muslim-Free America' Posters Appearing at University of Houston," *Newsweek*, 9/18/17.

19–20. Franco Ordoñez, "Exclusive: Trump Team Drafting Plan to Deport More Young People—Central American Teens," McClatchy, 9/20/17.

21–22. John Burnett, "Border Patrol Arrests Parents While Infant Awaits Serious Operation," *All Things Considered*, NPR, 9/20/17.

23. Molly Redden, "Trump Is Assembling the Most Male-Dominated Government in Decades," *Guardian*, 9/21/17.

24. Stephanie Saul and Kate Taylor, "Betsy DeVos Reverses Obama-Era Policy on Campus Sexual Assault Investigations," *NYT*, 9/22/17.

25. Laura Meckler, "Trump Administration to Replace Travel Ban with More Targeted Restrictions," *WSJ*, 9/22/17.

26. Levendrick Smith, "NC Triathlon Canceled After Controversy over Trump Name," *Charlotte Observer*, 9/18/17.

27. Jacqueline Tempera, "WJAR Forced to Run Pro-Trump Programs," *Providence Journal*, 9/16/17 (updated 9/22/17).

28. Bill Barrow, "GOP Governors Launch 'News' Site Critics Call Propaganda," AP, 9/19/17.

29. Michael D. Shear, "Trump Envisions a Parade Showing Off American Military Might," *NYT*, 9/18/17.

30. Faith Karimi, "Trump Praises Health Care of Nambia, a Nonexistent African Country," CNN.com, 9/21/17.

31. The Spectator Index (@spectatorindex), "BREAKING: Nicaragua will sign Paris climate accord, leaving only the United States and Syria outside it." Twitter, 9/20/17, 4:28 p.m.

32. Aaron Rupar, "Trump Blocks Woman with Stage 4 Cancer on Twitter After She Criticized His Latest Health Care Plan," *ThinkProgress*, undated.

33. Andrew DeMillo and Ryan J. Foley, "Request Denied: States Try to Block Access to Public Records," AP, 9/17/17.

34. Jo Romm, "Trump Administration Removes Links to Taxpayer-Funded Climate Data on USGS Website," *ThinkProgress*, 9/18/17.

35. Juliet Eilperin, "Shrink at Least 4 National Monuments and Modify a Half-Dozen Others, Zinke Tells Trump," *WaPo*, 9/17/17.

36. Bruce Schreiner, "Supreme Court's Neil Gorsuch, of Boulder County, Touts Conservative Role for Judges," *Boulder County News*, 9/21/17.

37. Ed O'Keefe and Amy Brittain, "New Hotel Act Would Ban Federal Agencies from Doing Business with Trump Hotels," *WaPo*, 9/19/17.

38. Dan Diamond and Rachana Pradhan, "Price's Private-Jet Travel Breaks Precedent," *Politico*, 9/19/17.

39. Rachana Pradhan and Dan Diamond, "Price Traveled by Private Plane at Least 24 Times," *Politico*, 9/21/17.

40. Dan Diamond and Rachana Pradhan, "Price's Private-Jet Travel Breaks Precedent," *Politico*, 9/19/17.

41. Aaron C. Davis, "How Tom Price Decided Chartered, Private Jets Were a Good Use of Taxpayer Money," *WaPo*, 9/22/17.

42. Aaron C. Davis, "HHS Inspector General Is Investigating Price's Travel on Private Charter Planes," *WaPo*, 9/22/17.

43. Justin Fishel and Elizabeth McLaughlin, "Mnuchin's Travel: Investigators Now Probing Another Costly Government Flight," ABCNews .com, 9/22/17.

44. Amber Phillips, "'Regular Order' May Have Just Killed GOP's Obamacare Repeal. So What Is It?" *WaPo*, 9/22/17.

45. Phil Galewitz (@philgalewitz), "..@HHSGov plans to shut down @HHSGov for 12 hours during all but one Sunday during the upcoming 6 week open enrollment season" Twitter, 9/22/17, 12:06 p.m.

46. Chris Massie and Andrew Kaczynski, "Trump Judicial Nominee Said Transgender Children Are Part of 'Satan's Plan,' Defended 'Conversion Therapy,'" CNN.com, 9/20/17.

47. Juliet Eilperin and Brady Dennis, "At EPA, Guarding the Chief Pulls Agents from Pursuing Environmental Crimes," *WaPo*, 9/20/17.

48. Steven Mufson and Juliet Eilperin, "EPA Chief Pruitt Met with Many Corporate Execs. Then He Made Decisions in Their Favor," *WaPo*, 9/23/17.

49-50. Jenny Hopkinson, "Trump Hires Campaign Workers Instead of Farm Experts at USDA," *Politico*, 9/21/17.

51. Sarah Westwood, "Russia Probes Leave Trump Associates Struggling with Huge Legal Bills," *WE*, 9/16/17.

52. Rebecca Ballhaus, "Mike Flynn's Family Launches Legal-Defense Fund," *WSJ*, 9/18/17.

53. Patricia Zengerle, "Trump Choice for Russia Ambassador: 'No Question' Russia Meddled," Reuters, 9/19/17.

54-55. Jeremy Diamond, "RNC Covering More than $230,000 in Trump Legal Fees," CNN.com, 9/19/17.

56. Rebecca Ballhaus, "GOP Funds Donald Trump's Defense in Russia Probe with Help from a Handful of Wealthy People," *WSJ*, 9/22/17.

57. Nicholas Fandos and Maggie Haberman, "Donald Trump Jr. Gives Up Secret Service Protection, Seeking Privacy," *NYT*, 9/18/17.

58. Tierney Sneed, "Trumps Latest DOJ Nom Was at Key Meeting with Comey and Sessions," *TPM*, 9/15/17.

59. Ryan J. Reilly, "Jeff Sessions' New Chief of Staff: Mueller's Russia Probe Could Be a 'Witch Hunt,'" *HuffPost*, 9/22/17.

60. Mike Memoli, Ken Dilanian, and Carol Lee, "Senate Cancels Meeting with Trump Lawyer Michael Cohen," NBCNews.com, 9/19/17.

61-62. Jon Swaine and Shaun Walker, "Trump in Moscow: What Happened at Miss Universe in 2013," *Guardian*, 9/18/17.

63-64. Peter Baker and Kenneth P. Vogel, "Trump Lawyers Clash over How Much to Cooperate with Russia Inquiry," *NYT*, 9/17/17.

65. Jeff Pegues, "Surveillance of Paul Manafort Occurred During 2016 Campaign," CBSNews.com, 9/19/17.

66-67. Aruna Viswanatha and Del Quentin Wilber, "Special Counsel's Office Interviewed Deputy Attorney General Rod Rosenstein," *WSJ*, 9/19/17.

68-69. Evan Perez, Shimon Prokupecz, and Pamela Brown, "Exclusive: US Government Wiretapped Former Trump Campaign Chairman," CNN .com, 9/19/17.

70-72. Sharon LaFraniere, Matt Apuzzo, and Adam Goldman, "With a Picked Lock and a Threatened Indictment, Mueller's Inquiry Sets a Tone," *NYT*, 9/18/17.

73-74. Carol D. Leonnig and Rosalind S. Helderman, "Mueller Casts Broad Net in Requesting Extensive Records from Trump White House," *WaPo*, 9/20/17.

75-77. Michael S. Schmidt, "Mueller Seeks White House Documents Related to Trump's Actions as President," *NYT*, 9/20/17.

78-79. Mike Allen, "Another Potential Mueller Honey Pot: Spicer's Notebooks," *Axios*, 9/21/17.

80-84. Tom Hamburger, Rosalind S. Helderman, Carol D. Leonnig, and Adam Entous, "Manafort Offered to Give Russian Billionaire 'Private Briefings' on 2016 Campaign," *WaPo*, 9/20/17.

85-86. Kenneth P. Vogel and Jo Becker, "Manafort Working on Kurdish Referendum Opposed by U.S." *NYT*, 9/20/17.

87-89. Kenneth P. Vogel and Andrew E. Kramer, "Skadden, Big New York Law Firm, Faces Questions on Work with Manafort," *NYT*, 9/21/17.

90. Kara Zupkus, "Corey Lewandowski: If Paul Manafort, Roger Stone Colluded to Influence 2016 Election, 'I Hope They Go to Jail for the Rest of Their Lives,'" *WE*, 9/20/17.

91. Betsy Woodruff and Andrew Desiderio, "Bob Mueller Brings on 'Tough' Guy Stephen Kelly to Handle Capitol Hill," *DB*, 9/19/17.

92. AP, "Twitter to Meet with Senate Intelligence Committee Next Week," CBSNews.com, 9/21/17.

93. Barbara Ortutay and Tom LoBianco, "Facebook to Release Russia Ads, Beef Up Election 'Integrity,'" AP, 9/21/17.

94. Ben Collins, Gideon Resnick, Kevin Poulsen, and Spencer Ackerman, "Exclusive: Russians Appear to Use Facebook to Push Trump Rallies in 17 U.S. Cities," *DB*, 9/20/17.

95. Eileen Sullivan, "Trump Dismisses 'Russia Hoax' as Facebook Turns Over Ads Tied to Campaign," *NYT*, 9/22/17.

96. Elizabeth Weise, "Paper Ballots Are Back in Vogue Thanks to Russian Hacking Fears," *USAT*, 9/19/17.

97. Sari Horwitz, Ellen Nakashima, and Matea Gold, "DHS Tells States About Russian Hacking During 2016 Election," *WaPo*, 9/22/17.

98. Kevin Collier, "DHS Waited Until Now to Tell State Election Officials That Russians Tried to Hack Their Systems," *BF*, 9/22/17.

99. Ibid.; Brian Murphy, "Russian Hackers Targeted Florida, 20 Other States in 2016 Election," *Miami Herald*, 9/23/17.

100. Bryan Logan, "James Clapper: US Intelligence Assessment of Russia's Election Interference 'Cast Doubt on the Legitimacy' " of Trump's Victory," *BI*, 9/23/17.

101. Abby Phillip, "As Trump Campaigns for Strange in Alabama, He Expresses Some Doubts: 'I Might Have Made a Mistake,' " *WaPo*, 9/22/17.

102. Henry C. Jackson, "Trump Derides 'Little Rocket Man' in North Korea," *Politico*, 9/22/17.

103. Denis Slattery, "Trump Takes Veiled Shot at Kaepernick, Says NFL Owners Should Fire Kneelers: 'Get That Son of a B— off the Field," *NYDN*, 9/23/17.

104. Sam Amick, "Donald Trump Rescinds White House Invitation to Stephen Curry, Warriors," *USAT*, 9/23/17.

105. Dana Milbank, "President Trump Is Killing Me. Really." *WaPo*, 9/15/17.

106. Samantha Schmidt, Katie Zezima, Sandhya Somashekhar, and Daniel Cassady, "'Thousands of People Could Die': 70,000 in Puerto Rico Urged to Evacuate with Dam in 'Imminent' Danger," *WaPo*, 9/22/17.

107. Charlie Savage and Eric Schmitt, "Trump Poised to Drop Some Limits on Drone Strikes and Commando Raids," *NYT*, 9/21/17.

WEEK 46

1. Carol Morello, "North Korea's Top Diplomat Says Strike Against U.S. Mainland is 'Inevitable,'" *WaPo*, 9/23/17.

2-3. Gary Langer, "Trump Seen by 66 Percent in US as Doing More to Divide than Unite Country (Poll)," ABCNews .com, 9/24/17.

4. Jeremy Kohler, Christine Byers, and Erin Heffernan, "Undercover Cop, Air Force Officer, Med Student Among Those Police Swept Up During Downtown Protest," *St. Louis Post-Dispatch*, 9/25/17.

5-7. Adolfo Flores, "People Are Worried About DHS Plans to Gather Social Media Info," *BF*, 9/25/17 (updated 9/28/17).

8. Vivian Salama and Julia Ainsley, "Trump Admin. Wants to Lower Number of Refugees Allowed into Country," NBCNews.com, 9/26/17.

9. Jeremy C. Fox, "50 Immigrants Arrested in Mass. as Part of ICE Operation," *Boston Globe*, 9/28/17.

10. Reuters Top News (@Reuters), "Number of immigrants without criminal histories arrested by ICE up more than 200 percent since Jan. http://reut.rs/2yeMUIE#TheTrumpEffect" Twitter, 9/29/17, 9:53 a.m.

11-12. Jessica Schneider, "DOJ Demands Facebook Information from 'Anti-Administration Activists,'" CNN .com, 9/30/17.

13. Betsy Woodruff, "Exclusive: Read the ICE Agents' Guide to NSA Surveillance," *DB*, 9/28/17.

14. Meredith Hoffman, "Trump Sent Judges to the Border. Many Had Nothing to Do," *Politico*, 9/27/17.

15. Jonah Engel Bromwich, "Confederate Flags with Cotton Found on American University Campus," *NYT*, 9/27/17.

16. Anne Branigin, "Ohio, a Union State, Will Reinstall Confederate Monument for Some Reason," *The Root*, 9/28/17.

17. Bill Chappell, "'You Should Be Outraged,' Air Force Academy Head Tells Cadets About Racism on Campus," *The Two-Way* (blog), NPR, 9/29/17,

18. Rebecca Shapiro, "GOP Rep. Mark Walker Calls Female Colleagues 'Eye Candy' at Press Event," *HuffPost*, 9/27/17.

19. Pete Vernon, "Dancing Around the Word 'Racist' in Coverage of Trump," *Columbia Journalism Review*, 9/25/17.

20. Jim Acosta and Daniella Diaz, "Trump at Private Dinner on NFL Feud: 'It's Really Caught On,'" CNN .com, 9/26/17.

21. "South Carolina Restaurant Bans NFL Games Until Protests End," AP, 9/26/17.

22. "Trump's Fascism Spreads: Schools Now Force Kids to Stand for Anthem or Face Penalties," DeepStateNation.com, 9/27/17.

23. Chris Riotta, "Trump Administration Says Employers Can Fire People for Being Gay," *Newsweek*, 9/28/17.

24. Kate Nocera and Paul McLeod, "The Trump Administration Is Pulling out of Obamacare Enrollment Events," *BF*, 9/27/17.

25. John Bowden, "Oklahoma Blames Trump Officials for Higher Premiums," *The Hill*, 9/29/17.

26. Asawin Suebsaeng, "Trump Aides Are Confounded by His Hospital Lie: 'He's Just, You Know, Doing His Thing.'" *DB*, 9/28/17.

27. Alex Burns (@alexburnsNYT), "Not seen this before at a Senate rally: Campaign staff telling reporters they can't leave pen to interview voters before Strange/Pence event" Twitter, 9/25/17, 4:52 p.m.

28. Sari Horwitz, Debbie Truong, and Sarah Larimer, "Sessions Criticizes U.S. Universities for Their Free-Speech Policies," *WaPo*, 9/26/17.

29. Debbie Truong, Sarah Larimer, and Susan Svrluga, "Georgetown Law Students and Faculty Protest Speech by Attorney General Jeff Sessions," *WaPo*, 9/26/17.

30. Michael S. Schmidt, "Dismayed by Trump, Head of Drug Enforcement Administration to Leave," *NYT*, 9/26/17.

31. Nancy Cook, "Trump Aides Begin Looking for the Exits," *Politico*, 9/22/17.

32-33. Erika Kinetz, "Ivanka Trump's China Supply Chains Shrouded in Secrecy," *USAT*, 9/26/17.

34-35. Matthew Daly, "Zinke: One-Third of Interior Employees Not Loyal to Trump," AP, 9/26/17.

36. Adam Liptak, "Amid Protests at Trump Hotel, Neil Gorsuch Calls for Civility," *NYT*, 9/28/17.

37. Alex Howard, "Turkish Airlines Event at Trump Golf Course Tees Off Emolumental Problems," Sunlight Foundation, 9/24/17.

38. Josh Rogin, "In Private Remarks, Trump Opines on North Korea, Afghanistan and Catapults," *WaPo*, 9/28/17.

39-40. Josh Dawsey, "Kushner Used Private Email to Conduct White House Business," *Politico*, 9/24/17.

41-42. Matt Apuzzo and Maggie Haberman, "At Least 6 White House Advisers Used Private Email Accounts," *NYT*, 9/25/17.

43. Jacqueline Thomsen, "Oversight Dem Investigating Kushner's Use of Private Email Account," *The Hill*, 9/25/17.

44-45. Jake Tapper, "Exclusive: Kushner Didn't Disclose Personal Email Account to Senate Intel Committee," CNN.com, 9/28/17.

46. Josh Dawsey and Andrea Peterson, "White House Launches Probe of Private Email Accounts," *Politico*, 9/28/17.

47. Peter Nicholas, Michael C. Bender, and Rebecca Ballhaus, "Officials Expressed Concerns White House Counsel Would Quit over Donald Trump–Jared Kushner Meetings," *WSJ*, 9/29/17.

48-49. Patricia Zengerle, "Trump Slow to Implement Russia, Iran, North Korea Sanctions Law: Senators," Reuters, 9/29/17.

50-51. Adam Entous, Elizabeth Dwoskin, and Craig Timberg, "Obama Tried to Give Zuckerberg a Wake-Up

Call over Fake News on Facebook," *WaPo*, 9/24/17.

52-53. Adam Entous, Craig Timberg, Elizabeth Dwoskin, "Russian Operatives Used Facebook Ads to Exploit America's Racial and Religious Divisions," *WaPo*, 9/25/17.

54. Joseph Bernstein, "Steve Bannon Sought to Infiltrate Facebook Hiring," *BF*, 9/25/17.

55. Josh Dawsey, "Russian-Funded Facebook Ads Backed Stein, Sanders and Trump," *Politico*, 9/26/17.

56. Ben Collins, Kevin Poulsen, and Spencer Ackerman, "Exclusive: Russians Impersonated Real American Muslims to Stir Chaos on Facebook and Instagram," *DB*, 9/27/17.

57-58. Dylan Byers, "Exclusive: Russian-Bought Black Lives Matter Ad on Facebook Targeted Baltimore and Ferguson," CNN.com, 9/28/17.

59. Clarice Silber, "Famous Fake News Writer Found Dead Outside Phoenix," AP, 9/27/17.

60. Denise Clifton, "Fake News on Twitter Flooded Swing States That Helped Trump Win," *MJ*, 9/28/17.

61-62. Kurt Wagner, "Mark Zuckerberg Admits He Should Have Taken Facebook Fake News and the Election More Seriously: 'Calling That Crazy Was Dismissive and I Regret It,'" *Recode*, 9/27/17.

63-64. Daisuke Wakabayashi and Schott Shane, "Twitter, with Accounts Linked to Russia, to Face Congress over Role in Election," *NYT*, 9/27/17.

65-66. Tony Romm, "Twitter Just Told Congress It Found About 200 Accounts Linked to the Same Russian Agents Found on Facebook," *Recode*, 9/28/17.

67. David McCabe, "Top Senator Slams 'Inadequate' Twitter Briefing," *Axios*, 9/28/17.

68. Jack Nicas and Robert McMillan, "Google Conducting Broad Investigation of Russian Influence," *WSJ*, 9/29/17.

69. Timothy Gardner, "U.S. Says No Need for Puerto Rico Shipping Waiver," Reuters, 9/26/17.

70. Josh Siegel, "John McCain Asks Trump Administration to Reverse Course, Waive Jones Act to Help Puerto Rico," *WE*, 9/26/17.

71. Ruth Brown, "Trump Says Shipping Industry Opposed to Waiver for Puerto Rico," *NYP*, 9/27/17.

72. Anne Gearan, "Trump Waives Shipping Restrictions for Puerto Rico for Hurricane Relief," *WaPo*, 9/28/17.

73. Melanie Zanona, "Lawmakers Say Trump's 10-Day Shipping Waiver Not Enough for Puerto Rico," *The Hill*, 9/28/17.

74. Danica Coto and Laurie Kellman, "Puerto Ricans Say US Relief Efforts Failing Them," AP, 9/29/17.

75. Jordan Fabian, "Trump Says Puerto Rico Relief Hampered by 'Big Water, Ocean Water,'" *The Hill*, 9/29/17.

76. Cristina Marcos, "Dems Call for 'Emergency' Hearing on Trump's Hurricane Response," *The Hill*, 9/29/17.

77. Ellen Mitchell, "'Not Enough' Troops, Equipment in Puerto Rico, Says General in Charge of Relief," *The Hill*, 9/29/17.

78. Julia Manchester, "San Juan Mayor: 'I Am Begging, Begging Anyone Who Can Hear Us to Save Us from Dying,'" *The Hill*, 9/29/17.

79. David Nakamura, "On Twitter, Trump Attacks Mayor of San Juan for 'Poor Leadership' amid Deepening Crisis," *WaPo*, 9/30/17.

80. Brandon Carter, "Trump: 'Fake News' Is Trying to 'Disparage' First Responders in Puerto Rico," *The Hill*, 9/30/17.

81. Donald Trump (@realDonald Trump), ". . . want everything to be done for them when it should be a community effort. 10,000 Federal workers now on Island doing a fantastic job." Twitter, 9/30/17, 4:29 a.m.; Donald Trump (@realDonaldTrump), "Texas & Florida are doing great but Puerto Rico, which was already suffering from broken infrastructure & massive debt, is in deep trouble.." Twitter, 9/25/17, 5:45 p.m.

82. "Did Donald Trump Bankrupt a Golf Course, Leaving Puerto Rico with $33 Million in Debt?" Snopes, 9/27/17, www.snopes.com/trump-puerto-rico-golf-course.

83-84. Abby Phillip, Ed. O'Keefe, Nick Miroff, and Damian Paletta, "Lost Weekend: How Trump's Time at His Golf Club Hurt the Response to Maria," *WaPo*, 9/2/17.

85. Dan Diamond and Rachana Pradhan, "Price's Private-Jet Travels Included Visits with Colleagues, Lunch with Son," *Politico*, 9/28/17.

86. Rachana Pradhan and Dan Diamond, "Price Took Military Jets to Europe, Asia for over $500K," *Politico*, 9/28/17.

87. Dan Diamond, "Scoop: Tom Price's Travel Costs Exceed $1 Million Since May," *Politico*, 9/29/17.

88. Juliet Eilperin, Amy Goldstein, and John Wagner, "HHS Secretary Tom Price Resigns amid Criticism for Taking Charter Flights at Taxpayer Expense," *WaPo*, 9/29/17; "Pattern of Abuse of Taxpayer Money Seen in Wealthy Trump Staff," *Rachel Maddow Show*, MSNBC, 9/29/17.

89-90. Brady Dennis, "EPA Spending Almost $25,000 to Install a Secure Phone Books for Scott Pruitt," *WaPo*, 9/26/17.

91. Brady Dennis and Juliet Eilperin, "EPA's Pruitt Took Charter, Military Flights That Cost Taxpayers More than $58,000," *WaPo*, 9/27/17.

92. Ben Lefebvre, "Interior Secretary Zinke Traveled on Charter, Military Planes," *Politico*, 9/28/17.

93. Drew Harwell and Lisa Rein, "Zinke Took $12,000 Charter Flight Home in Oil Executive's Plane, Documents Show," *WaPo*, 9/28/17.

94. Jack Gillum, Alex Horton, Drew Harwell, and Lisa Rein, "VA Chief Took in Wimbledon, River Cruise on European Work Trip; Wife's Expenses Covered by Taxpayers," *WaPo*, 9/29/17.

95. Laura Strickler, Analisa Novak, and Julianna Goldman, "Trump Kids' Ski Vacation Incurs over $300,000 in Security Costs," CBSNews.com, 9/29/17.

96. Jesse Drucker and Nadja Popovich, "Trump Could Save More than $1 Billion Under His New Tax Plan," *NYT*, 9/28/17.

97. Richard Rubin, "Treasury Removes Paper at Odds with Mnuchin's Take on Corporate-Tax Cut's Winners," *WSJ*, 9/28/17.

98-99. Manu Raju, Pamela Brown, and Evan Perez, "Exclusive: IRS Shares Information with Special Counsel in Russia Probe," CNN.com, 9/26/17.

100. Brian Ross and Matthew Mosk, "Special Counsel Probing Flow of Russian-American Money to Trump Political Funds," ABCNews.com, 9/26/17.

101. Matthew Nussbaum, "Pence Sent Lawyer to Meet with Mueller over the Summer," *Politico*, 9/28/17.

102. Gloria Borger and Pamela Brown, "Special Counsel Interviews with White House Staff Could Start Later This Week," CNN.com, 9/26/17.

103. Betsy Woodruff, "Sean Spicer Lawyers Up as Russia Probe Heats Up," *DB*, 9/26/17.

104. John Hudson, "US and Russia Quietly End Diplomatic Tailspin," *BF*, 9/26/17.

105. Russell Goldman, "Trump Deletes Tweets Supporting Luther Strange," *NYT*, 9/27/17.

106. John Bresnahan, "Senate Republicans Have Never Heard of Roy Moore," *Politico*, 9/27/17.

107. James Hohmann, "The Daily 202: Roy Moore's Victory and Bob Corker's Retirement Are Fresh Indicators of a Senate That's Coming Apart," *WaPo*, 9/27/17.

108. Quinnipiac Poll, 9/27/17, poll.qu .edu/national/release-detail?ReleaseID =2487.

109. Julia Manchester, "Trump Congratulates Merkel on Electoral Win," *The Hill*, 9/28/17.

110. Ali Vitali and Corky Siemaszko, "Trump Declares Opioid Crisis National Emergency," NBCNews.com, 8/10/17; Kyle Griffin (@kylegriffin1), "Trump said he was going to declare the opioid crisis a national emergency 50 days ago. He still hasn't." Twitter, 9/29/17, 10:50 a.m.

WEEK 47

1. U.D. Dept. of Defense, "DoD Accelerates Hurricane Relief, Response Efforts in Puerto Rico," Defense.com, 9/30/17.

2. Daniel Dale (@ddale8), "'Readouts' are for Trump's calls with foreign leaders; don't think I've ever seen one for a domestic leader, let alone a former leader." Twitter, 9/3/17, 8:05 p.m.

4. Jenny Marder, "After First Tour of Puerto Rico, Top General Calls Damage 'the Worst He's Ever Seen,'" *PBS NewsHour*, 9/30/17.

5. Norma J. Torres et al. to Rob Bishop, Chairman, House Committee on Natural Resources, 9/28/17, http:// democrats-naturalresources.house.gov /imo/media/doc/09.28.2017%20 Torres%20Grijalva%20letter%20 request%20for%20PR%20USVI%20 oversight%20hearing.pdf.

6. Doug Criss, "The Las Vegas Attack Is the Deadliest Mass Shooting in Modern US History," CNN.com, 10/2/17; Dakin Andone, "The Las Vegas Shooter's Road to 47 Guns," CNN.com, 10/6/17; Jenna Johnson, "Trump on Response to Las Vegas Shooting: 'What Happened Is, in Many Ways, a Miracle,'" *WaPo*, 10/3/17.

7. Sam Levin, "Facebook and Google Promote Politicized Fake News About Las Vegas Shooter," *Guardian*, 10/2/17.

8. Ashley Parker and Jenna Johnson, "Trump on Las Vegas Shooter: 'A Very Sick Man. He Was a Very Demented Person.'" *WaPo*, 10/4/17; Ali Vitali, "Trump Signs Bill Revoking Obama-Era Gun Checks for People with Mental Illnesses," NBCNews.com, 2/28/17.

9. Bob Brigham, "Read the Leaked White House Talking Points Crafted in Response to the Las Vegas Massacre," *Raw Story*, 10/3/17.

10. Michael Hiltzik, "Time's Up: As CHIP Expires Unrenewed, Congress Blows a Chance to Save Healthcare for 9 Million Children," *LAT*, 9/29/17.

11. Brittany Taylor, "Crosby Coach Kicks 2 High School Football Players off Team After Anthem Protest," Click2Houston.com, 10/1/17.

12. Shaun King (@ShaunKing), "BREAKING: @NFL Players on 2 different teams have told me the teams are doing as Trump asked and creating policies to require them to stand." Twitter, 10/7/17, 7:35 a.m.

13. Michael K. Lavers, "U.S. Opposes UN Resolution Against Death Penalty for Same-Sex Relations," *LA Blade*, 10/2/17.

14. Betsy Woodruff, "Donald Trump's Voter Fraud Commission Just Suffered a Court Defeat," *DB*, 10/4/17.

15. Megan R. Wilson, "DOJ Investigating Affirmative Action at Harvard," *The Hill*, 10/4/17.

16. Chandelis R. Duster, "Texas Lawmaker Says He Won't Resign over Racist Remarks," 10/4/17; Chandelis R. Duster, "Texas Official Resigns After Referring to Black Prosecutors with N-Word," 10/6/17.

17-18. Dominic Holden, "Trump Just Asked a Court to Dismiss a Lawsuit Against His Transgender Military Band," *BF*, 10/5/17.

19. Dominic Holden, "Jess Sessions Just Reversed a Policy That Protects Transgender Workers from Discrimination," *BF*, 10/5/17.

20. Brianna Ehley, "Trump Rolls Back Obamacare Birth Control Mandate," *Politico*, 10/6/17.

21. Dominic Holden and Zoe Tillman, "Jeff Sessions Just Issues New Guidance on Protecting 'Religious Liberty,'" *BF*, 10/6/17.

22. Pete Madden, "Jeff Sessions Consulted Christian Right Legal Group on Religious Freedom Memo," ABCNews.com, 10/6/17.

23. Elise Foley and Mollie Reilly, "ICE Threatens More 'Collateral' Arrests in Response to California's 'Sanctuary' Law," *HuffPost*, 10/6/17.

24. Ari Berman, "Trump Election Commission Leader Sought a Radical Change to a Key Voting Law," *MJ*, 10/6/17.

25. Jordan Fabian, "Trump Leaves San Juan's Mayor Out of Praise for Puerto Rico Leaders,' *The Hill*, 10/3/17.

26. Roberta Rampton and Gabriel Stargardter, "Trump Praises Response to Puerto Rico, Says Crisis Straining Budget," Reuters, 10/3/17.

27. Jenna Johnson and Ashley Parker, "Trump Hails 'Incredible' Response in 'Lovely' Trip to Storm-Torn Puerto Rico," *WaPo*, 10/3/17; Mark Landler, "Trump Lobs Praise, and Paper Towels, to Puerto Rico Storm Victims," *NYT*, 10/3/17.

28. Janell Ross, "In Puerto Rico, Trump's Paper-Towel Toss Reveals Where His Empathy Lies," *WaPo*, 10/6/17.

29. Mary Hui, "Oxfam Slams the Trump Administration for Its 'Slow and Inadequate' Response in Puerto Rico," *WaPo*, 10/3/17.

30. Caroline Kenny, "Oxfam Criticizes US Government Response in Puerto Rico," CNN.com, 10/3/17.

31. Sanjay Gupta, "Dr. Sanjay Gupta's Dire Warning on Puerto Rico," CNN .com, 10/3/17.

32. Carrie Kahn, "Communication Issues in Puerto Rico Make It Hard to Register Deaths," *All Things Considered*, NPR, 10/6/17.

33. Philip Bump, "FEMA Buried Updates on Puerto Rico. Here They Are," *WaPo*, 10/6/17.

34. Jenna Johnson, "FEMA Removes—Then Restores—Statistics About Drinking Water Access and Electricity in Puerto Rico from Website," *WaPo*, 10/6/17.

35. Philip Bump, "FEMA Buried Updates on Puerto Rico. Here They Are," *WaPo*, 10/6/17.

36. Mary Williams Walsh and Alan Rappeport, "White House Dials Back Trump's Vow to Clear Puerto Rico's Debt," *NYT*, 10/4/17.

37-38. Josh Dawsey and Andrea Peterson, "Hundreds of White House Emails Sent to Third Kushner Family Account," *Politico*, 10/2/17.

39-40. Brad Heath, "Exclusive: Jared Kushner's Personal Email Re-routed to Trump Organization Computers amid Public Scrutiny," *USAT*, 10/4/17.

41. Mike Memoli, "Top House Democrat Asks FBI to Review Kushner and Ivanka Trump Emails," NBCNews .com, 10/5/17.

42. Alberto Luperon, "Federal Agency Found Nikki Haley Violated Law by Promoting Candidate on Twitter," *Law & Crime*, 10/3/17.

43-44. Juliet Eilperin, "As ACA Enrollment Nears, Administration Keeps Cutting Federal Support of the Law," *WaPo*, 10/5/17.

45-46. Anita Kumar and Ben Wieder, "Jared Kushner Fined Again for Late Ethics Form, Ivanka Trump Fined Too," McClatchy, 10/3/17.

47. Damian Paletta and Tom Hamburger, "Hedge Fund Billionaire Flew Top Mnuchin Aide on Private Jet to Palm Beach," *WaPo*, 10/3/17.

48. Jason Leopold and Jessica Garrison, "US Intelligence Unit Accused of Illegally Spying on Americans' Financial Records," *BF*, 10/6/17.

49. Lisa Rein, "Federal Watchdog Opens Probe into Travel by Interior Secretary Ryan Zinke," *WaPo*, 10/2/17.

50. Eric Lipton and Lisa Friedman, "E.P.A. Chief's Calendar: A Stream of Industry Meetings and Trips Home," *NYT*, 10/3/17.

51. Andrew Restuccia and Matthew Nussbaum, "Pence's Chief of Staff Floats 'Purge' of Anti-Trump Republicans to Wealthy Donors," *Politico*, 10/3/17.

52. Jacques Billeaud, "Judge Lets Trump's Pardon of Former Sherriff Arpaio Stand," AP, 10/4/17.

53. Dan Friedman, "Trump Still Hasn't Gotten Around to Appointing Someone to Protect Our Elections from Cyberattacks," *MJ*, 10/3/17.

54. Rachana Pradhan, "Cummings Questions White House About Conway's Private Jet Travels," *Politico*, 10/4/17.

55. Emily Flitter, "Energy Secretary Took Charter Flight Day Before Price Resigned," Reuters, 10/4/17.

56. Drew Harwell and Michael Laris, "Chao Used Government Planes Seven Times When Cheaper Flights Would Not Work," *WaPo*, 10/5/17.

57. Alan Rappeport, "Seven Flights for $800,000: Mnuchin's Travel on Military Jets," *NYT*, 10/5/17.

58. Keri Geiger, "Should Donald Trump Jr. Be Getting Paid for Speeches?" NBCNews.com, 10/5/17.

59. Chris Mooney and Dino Grandoni, "Interior Department Rejects 25 Endangered Species Petitions, Including Several Linked to Climate Change," *WaPo*, 10/5/17.

60. Alexander Mallin, "Secret Service Denies Having 'Visitor Logs' for Trump's Mar-a-Lago Estate in Florida," ABCNews.com, 10/5/17.

61. Darryl Fears, "Interior Department Whistleblower Resigns; Bipartisan Former Appointees Object to Zinke's Statements," *WaPo*, 10/6/17.

62. Carole Cadwalladr, "British Courts May Unlock Secrets of How Trump Campaign Profiled US Voters," *Guardian*, 9/30/17.

63. Dylan Byers "Facebook: Russian Ads Reached 10 Million People," CNN.com, 10/3/17.

64. Craig Timberg, "Russian Propaganda May Have Been Shared Hundreds of Millions of Times, New Research Says," *WaPo*, 10/5/17.

65-66. Robert McMillan and Shane Harris, "Facebook Cut Russia Out of April Report on Election Influence," *WSJ*, 10/5/17.

67. Alex Pasternack, "Russia's U.S. Propaganda Campaign Infiltrated Instagram, Too," *Fast Company*, 10/6/17.

68-69. Manu Raju, Dylan Byers, and Dana Bash, "Exclusive: Russian-Linked Facebook Ads Targeted Michigan and Wisconsin," CNN.com, 10/4/17.

70-71. Gordon Lubold and Shane Harris, "Russian Hackers Stole NSA Data on U.S. Cyber Defense," *WSJ*, 10/5/17.

72. Kyle Cheney and Elana Schor, "Trump Loyalists Lose Patience with Congressional Russia Probes," *Politico*, 10/4/17.

73. Greg Sargent, "Furious Republicans Are Working Hard to Make Trump's Russia Scandal Disappear," *WaPo*, 10/4/17.

74. Kyle Cheney and Elana Schor, "5 Things We Learned from the Senate's Russia Probe Update," *Politico*, 10/4/17.

75. Mary Clare Jalonick and Eric Tucker, "Trump-Russia Collusion? Still Investigating, Senators Say," AP, 10/4/17.

76. Kyle Cheney and Elana Schor, "5 Things We Learned from the Senate's Russia Probe Update," *Politico*, 10/4/17; "Exclusive: Trump Dossier Author Open to Senate Intel Meeting," *Rachel Maddow Show*, MSNBC, 10/5/17.

77. Mark Hosenball, "'Trump Dossier' on Russia Links Now Part of Special Counsel's Probe: Sources," Reuters, 10/4/17.

78-79. Evan Perez, Shimon Prokupecz, and Pamela Brown, "Exclusive: Mueller's Team Met with Russia Dossier Author," CNN.com, 10/5/17 (updated 10/25/17).

80. Josh Gerstein, "3 Russians Named in Trump Dossier Sue Fusion GPS for Libel," *Politico*, 10/4/17.

81. David Corn, "Did Russia Hack the 2016 Vote Tally? This Senator Says We Don't Know for Sure," *MJ*, 10/6/17.

82. Betsy Woodruff, "Exclusive: Senate 'Russia Probe' Is Not Investigating Russia," *DB*, 10/6/17.

83-85. Tom Hamburger, Rosalind S. Helderman, and Adam Entous, "Trump's Company Had More Contact with Russia During Campaign, According to Documents Turned Over to Investigators," *WaPo*, 10/2/17.

86. Elias Groll, "GOP Congressman Met in Moscow with Kremlin-Linked Lawyer at Center of Russia Investigation," *FP*, 10/3/17.

87. Darren Samuelsohn, "White House Legal Defense Fund Close to Launching," *Politico*, 10/2/17.

88. Graham Lanktree, "Billionaire Robert Mercer Is Helping Pay Donald Trump's Legal Bills," *Newsweek*, 10/3/17.

89-90. Julia Ioffe and Franklin Foer, "Did Manafort Use Trump to Curry Favor with a Putin Ally?" *Atlantic*, 10/2/17.

91. Peter Baker and David E. Sanger, "Trump Says Tillerson Is 'Wasting His Time' on North Korea," *NYT*, 10/1/17.

92. Carol E. Lee, Kristen Welker, Stephanie Ruhle, and Dafna Linzer, "Tillerson's Fury at Trump Required an Intervention from Pence," NBCNews .com, 10/4/17.

93. Peter Baker, Maggie Haberman, and Glenn Thrush, "Tillerson's News Conference Only Highlights Strains with Trump," *NYT*, 10/4/17; *CBS This Morning* (@CBSThisMorning), "'This was not like a news conference, it was more like a hostage tape.'—@Bob Schieffer on Sec. of State Tillerson's news conference on Wed" Twitter, 10/5/17, 5:19 a.m.

94. Chris Cillizza, "Bob Corker Just Told the World What He Really Thinks of Donald Trump," CNN.com, 10/5/17.

95. Dexter Filkins, "Rex Tillerson at the Breaking Point," *NYer*, 10/16/17.

96. Steve Benen, "U.S. Lost Jobs Last Month for the First Time in 7 Years," *MaddowBlog*, 10/7/17.

97. Mark Landler, "What Did President Trump Mean by 'Calm Before the Storm'?" *NYT*, 10/6/17.

98. Allan Smith, "Trump Winks When Asked Again About His Mysterious 'Calm Before the Storm' Comment," *BI*, 10/6/17.

99-100. AP-NORC Center for Public Affairs Research, "Americans' Evaluations of President Trump," undated, http://www.apnorc.org /projects/Pages/Americans-Evaluations -of-President-Trump.aspx.

101. Perry Stein, "Trump's Lewd 'Access Hollywood' Tape Is Playing on Repeat for 12 Hours on the Mall," *WaPo*, 10/6/17.

102-103. Jesse Eisinger, Justin Elliott, Andrea Bernstein, and Ilya Marritz, "Ivanka and Donald Trump Jr. Were Close to Being Charged with Felony Fraud," *ProPublica*, 10/4/17.

104. Thomas Gibbons-Neff and David E. Sanger, "Mattis Contradicts Trump on Iran Deal Ahead of Crucial Deadline," *NYT*, 10/3/17; Jonathan Landay, "Trump to Unveil New Responses to Iranian 'Bad Behavior': White House," Reuters, 10/6/17.

105. Dominique Mosbergen and Chris D'Angelo, "Trump Administration to Propose Scrapping Major Obama-Era Climate Change Policy," *HuffPost*, 10/5/17 (updated 10/9/17).

106. Liz Johnstone, "Tracking President Trump's Visits to Trump Properties," NBCNews.com [updated continuously].

WEEK 48

1. Susan Svrluga, "'We Will Keep Coming Back': Richard Spencer Leads Another Torchlight March in Charlottesville," *WaPo*, 10/9/17.

2-3. Philip Corker and Karoun Demirjian, "Corker Calls White House 'an Adult Day Care Center' in Response to Trump's Latest Twitter Tirade," *WaPo*, 10/8/17.

4. Eli Watkins, "Pence Leaves Colts Game After Protest During Anthem," CNN.com, 10/9/17.

5. Matthew VanTryon, "Mike Pence Tweets Same Picture from Colts Game That He Tweeted in 2014," *IndyStar*, 10/9/17.

6. Eli Watkins, "Pence Leaves Colts Game After Protest During Anthem," CNN.com, 10/9/17.

7. Ibid.; Justin Fishel, "Pence's Flights to and from Indianapolis Colts Game That He Left in Protest Cost Nearly $250,000," ABCNews.com, 10/9/17.

8. Rob Goldberg, "Jerry Jones Says Any Cowboys Player Who 'Disrespects' the Flag Won't Play," *Bleacher Report*, 10/8/17.

9. Daniel Roberts, "Trump Is Wrong About the NFL's 'Massive Tax Breaks,'" *Yahoo Finance*, 10/10/17.

10. Ken Belson, "Goodell and N.F.L. Owners Break from Players on Anthem Kneeling Fight," *NYT*, 10/10/17.

11. "Vice President Pence to Headline Newport Beach Fundraiser," CBS Los Angeles, 10/9/17.

12. Todd Richmond, "University of Wisconsin Approves Protest Punishment Policy," AP, 10/6/17.

13. Harriet Sinclair, "White America? Trump Praises 'Arrival of Europeans' in Columbus Day Message, Doesn't Mention Native Americans Who Were Slaughtered," *Newsweek*, 10/8/17.

14. "DHS Is Not Extending Jones Act Waiver for Puerto Rico," CBSNews .com, 10/9/17.

15. Lisa Friedman and Brad Plumer, "E.P.A. Announces Repeal of Major Obama-Era Carbon Emissions Rule," *NYT*, 10/9/17.

16. Maya Oppenheim, "Donald Trump to Become First President to Speak at Anti-LGBT Hate Group's Annual Summit," *Independent* (UK), 10/12/17.

17. Sarah N. Lynch and Julia Harte, "Exclusive: Trump Administration Reduces Support for Prisoner Halfway Houses," Reuters, 10/13/17.

18. AP, "Treasury's IG Probing Illegal Surveillance Allegations," ABCNews .com, 10/16/17.

19. House Committee on Oversight & Government Reform, "Investigation Shows Trump Transition Ignored Ethics Officials and Refused to Cooperate with GAO," press release, 10/10/17, democrats-oversight.house.gov/news /press-releases/investigation-shows -trump-transition-ignored-ethics -officials-and-refused-to.

20. Alexander C. Kaufman, "Trump's Pick for White House Environmental Post Once Said Coal Helped End

Slavery," *HuffPost*, 10/13/17 (updated 10/19/17).

21. Eriq Garner, "Donald Trump Can Destroy Records Without Judicial Review, Justice Department Tells Court," *Hollywood Reporter*, 10/9/17.

22. Lorraine Woellert, "Mnuchin Won't Fill No. 2 Treasury Post as Brooks Opts Out of the Running," *Politico*, 10/12/17.

23. Lisa Rein, "Where's Zinke? The Interior Secretary's Special Flag Offers Clues," *WaPo*, 10/12/17.

24. Courtney Kube, Kristen Welker, Carl E. Lee, and Savannah Guthrie, "Trump Wanted Tenfold Increase in Nuclear Arsenal, Surprising Military," NBCNews.com, 10/11/17.

25. Jordan Fabian, "Trump: 'Fake NBC News' Nuke Story 'Pure Fiction,'" *The Hill*, 10/11/17.

26. David Nakamura, "Trump Escalates Threats Against Press, Calls News Coverage 'Frankly Disgusting,'" *WaPo*, 10/11/17.

27. Jessica Estepa, "Sen. Ben Sasse Asks if President Trump Is 'Recanting' His Oath of Office," *USAT*, 10/12/17.

28. Tony Cook, "As Trump Slams Media, an Indiana Lawmaker Has Drafted a Bill to License Journalists," *IndyStar*, 10/12/17.

29. Fred Barnes, "Mitch McConnell Goes to the Mattresses for Trump's Judicial Nominees," *Weekly Standard*, 10/11/17.

30. Gardiner Harris and Steven Erlanger, "U.S. Will Withdraw from Unesco, Citing Its 'Anti-Israel Bias,'" *NYT*, 10/12/17.

31-33. Jonathan Martin and Mark Landler, "Bob Corker Says Trump's Recklessness Threatens 'World War III,'" *NYT*, 10/8/17.

34-35. Robert Costa, Philip Rucker, and Ashley Parker, "A 'Pressure Cooker': Trump's Frustration and Fury Rupture Alliances, Threaten Agenda," *WaPo*, 10/9/17.

36. Josh Dawsey, "White House Aides Lean on Delays and Distraction to Manage Trump," *Politico*, 10/9/17.

37-40. Gabriel Sherman, "'I Hate Everyone in the White House!': Trump Seethes as Advisers Fear the President is 'Unraveling,'" *VF*, 10/11/17.

41. Peggy Noonan, "What Bob Corker Sees in Trump," *WSJ*, 10/12/17.

42. Kyle Griffin (@kylegriffin1), "Trump this morning nearly walked out of the room without signing his health care exec. order, had to be brought back by Pence." Twitter, 10/12/17, 11:02 a.m.

43. Toluse Olorunnipa, "Trump Suggests He'd Beat Tillerson in an IQ Test," Bloomberg.com, 10/10/17.

44. Jackson Diehl, "Bob Corker on Trump's Biggest Problem: The 'Castration' of Rex Tillerson," *WaPo*, 10/13/17.

45. Josh Feldman, "CNN's Fareed Zakaria: 'We Essentially Have No Diplomacy Going on in the United States,'" *Mediaite*, 10/13/17.

46. "How Facebook Ads Helped Elect Trump," 10/6/17, *60 Minutes*, www.cbsnews.com/news/how-facebook-ads-helped-elect-trump.

47. Ben Collins, Gideon Resnick, and Spencer Ackerman, "Russia Recruited YouTubers to Bash 'Racist B*tch' Hillary Clinton over Rap Beats," *DB*, 10/8/17.

48-49. Elizabeth Dwoskin, Adam Entous, and Craig Timberg, "Google Uncovers Russian-Bought Ads on YouTube, Gmail and Other Platforms," *WaPo*, 10/9/17.

50. Ken Dilanian and Alex Moe, "Nunes Subpoenaed Firm Behind Trump Dossier Without Telling Democrats," NBCNews.com, 10/10/17.

51. Mark Hosenball and Jonathan Landay, "U.S. Congressional Panels Spar over 'Trump Dossier' on Russia Contacts," Reuters, 10/10/17.

52. Ali Watkins, "Carter Page Says He Won't Testify Before Senate Intelligence Panel in Russia Probe," *Politico*, 10/10/17.

53-54. Betsy Woodruff and Spencer Ackerman, "Russia Probe Now Investigating Cambridge Analytica, Trump's 'Psychographic' Data Gurus," *DB*, 10/11/17.

55. Nicole Perlroth and Scott Shane, "How Israel Caught Russian Hackers Scouring the World for U.S. Secrets," *NYT*, 10/10/17.

56. Shane Harris and Gordon Lubold, "Russia Has Turned Kaspersky Software into Tool for Spying," *WSJ*, 10/11/17.

57-58. Darren Samuelsohn, "President's Lawyers May Offer Mueller a Meeting with Trump," *Politico*, 10/12/17.

59. Donie O'Sullivan and Dylan Byers, "Exclusive: Even Pokémon Go Used by Extensive Russian-Linked Meddling Effort," CNN.com, 10/13/17.

60-63. Aggelos Petropoulos and Richard Engel, "Manafort Had $60 Million Relationship with a Russian Oligarch," NBNews.com, 10/15/17.

64-65. Hunter Walker and Michael Isikoff, "FBI Document Cache Sheds Light on Inner Workings of Russia's U.S. News (and Propaganda) Network," *YN*, 10/13/17.

66-67. Rosalind S. Helderman, "Reince Priebus, Formed Trump Chief of Staff, Interviewed by Mueller Team," *WaPo*, 10/13/17.

68-69. Josh Meyer, "Twitter Deleted Data Potentially Crucial to Russia Probes," *Politico*, 10/13/17.

70. Ryan Nakashima, "Twitter Turns Over 'Handles' of 201 Russia-Linked Accounts," AP, 10/14/17.

71. Manu Raju and Jeremy Herb, "Roger Stone Attorney Says He Complied with Request for Assange Contact," CNN.com, 10/15/17.

72-74. Rebecca Ballhaus and Natalie Andrews, "At the Intersection of Russia Probe and Social Media: Donald Trump's Digital Chief," *WSJ*, 10/13/17.

75. Cameron Easley, "Trump Approval Dips in Every State, Though Deep Pockets of Support Remain," *Morning Consult*, 10/10/17.

76. Chris Kahn and Tim Reid, "Trump's Popularity Is Slipping in Rural America: Poll," Reuters, 10/9/17.

77. Michelle Ye Hee Lee, Glenn Kessler, and Meg Kelly, "President Trump Has Made 1,318 False or Misleading Claims over 263 Days," *WaPo*, 10/10/17.

78. Jeff Cox, "Trump 'Likely Obstructed Justice' in Comey Firing, Could Be Impeached, Brookings Institution Says," CNBC.com, 10/10/17.

79. Rebecca Kheel, "Dems Ask for Proof Trump Consulted Pentagon on Transgender Ban," *The Hill*, 10/10/17.

80. Henry J. Kaiser Family Foundation, Bianca DiJulio, Cailey Muñana, and Mollyann Brodie, "Puerto Rico After Hurricane Maria: The Public's Knowledge and Views of Its Impact and the Response," KFF.org, 10/12/17.

81–83. Philip Rucker, Arelis R. Hernández, and Manuel Roig-Franzia, "Trump Threat to Abandon Puerto Rico Recovery Sparks a Backlash," *WaPo*, 10/12/17.

84. Philip Rucker and Ed O'Keefe, "Trump Threatens to Abandon Puerto Rico Recovery Effort," *WaPo*, 10/12/17.

85. Willa Frej, "Rick Perry Mistakenly Calls Puerto Rico a Country," *HuffPost*, 10/13/17 (updated 10/17/17).

86. Daniella Diaz, "Trump Says He Spoke to US Virgin Islands' 'President'—Which Is Him," CNN .com, 10/13/17.

87. Eliza Barclay and Alexia Fernández Campbell, "Everything That's Been Reported About Deaths in Puerto Rico Is at Odds with the Official Count," *Vox*, 10/11/17.

88. CBS/AP, "Puerto Rico Investigates Post-hurricane Disease Outbreak," CBSNews.com, 10/12/17.

89. "Doctor Quits Puerto Rico Medical Relief Team over 'Spa Day,'" *Rachel Maddow Show*, MSNBC, 10/12/17.

90. Frances Robles, "Puerto Rico's Health Care Is in Dire Condition, Three Weeks After Maria," *NYT*, 10/10/17.

91. John D. Sutter, "Desperate Puerto Ricans Are Drinking Water from a Hazardous-Waste Site," CNN.com, 10/14/17.

92. Steven Shepard, "Polls: Trump, Government Earn Low Marks for Puerto Rico Hurricane Response," *Politico*, 10/12/17.

93. Christopher Flavelle, "How the Pentagon Spun Hurricane Maria," Bloomberg.com, 10/13/17.

94. Danielle Kurtzleben and Scott Neuman, "Trump Administration to End Obamacare Subsidies for the Poor," NPR.org, 10/12/17.

95. Alison Kodjak, "Halt in Subsidies for Health Insurers Expected to Drive Up Costs for Middle Class," NPR.org, 10/13/17.

96. Thomas Kaplan and Robert Pear, "End to Health Care Subsidies Puts Congress in a Tight Spot," *NYT*, 10/13/17.

97. Michael C. Bender, Siobhan Hughes, and Kristina Peterson, "Trump Steps Up Pressure on Congress," *WSJ*, 10/15/17.

98. Zoe Tillman, "Democrats Are Launching a Legal Fight to Save Obamacare's Subsidy Payments," *BF*, 10/13/17.

99. Haeyoun Park, "We're Tracking the Ways Trump Is Scaling Back Obamacare. Here Are 12," *NYT*, 10/12/17.

100. Harriet Agerholm, "Donald Trump Boasts of 'Plunging' Health Insurance Stocks Following Executive Order on Obamacare," *Independent* (UK), 10/14/17.

101. Ashley Kirzinger, Liz Hamel, Bianca DiJulio, Cailey Muñana, and Mollyann Brodie, "Kaiser Health Tracking Poll—October 2017: Open Enrollment and the ACA Market-places," KFF.org, 10/13/17.

102. Ali Rogin and Adam Kelsey, "Trump Takes Hard Line on Iran, but Keeps Obama Deal in Place," ABCNews.com, 10/13/17.

103. Laura Smith-Spark, "US Allies in Europe Vow to Stand by Iran Nuclear Deal," CNN.com, 10/14/17.

104. Ali Rogin and Adam Kelsey, "Trump Takes Hard Line on Iran, but Keeps Obama Deal in Place," ABCNews.com, 10/13/17.

105. Asawin Suebsaeng, Spencer Ackerman, and Sam Stein, "McMaster Wants to Save the Iran Deal by Hiding It from Trump," *DB*, 10/12/17.

106. Laura Smith-Spark, "US Allies in Europe Vow to Stand by Iran Nuclear Deal," CNN.com, 10/14/17.

107. Conor Gaffey, "After Trump Travel Ban, Chad Pulls Troops from Boko Haram Fight in Niger," *Newsweek*, 10/13/17.

108. Morgan Winsor and Julia Jacobo, "Dazed Californians Brace for More 'Extreme Fire Behavior' as Death Toll Rises to 35," ABCNews .com, 10/14/17.

109. Barbara Starr and Ryan Browne, "Trump Silent as Questions Remain over Deadly Niger Ambush," CNN .com, 10/14/17.

110. Government of Puerto Rico, Status PR, status.pr/?lng=en [updated continuously].

111. Liz Johnstone, "Tracking President Trump's Visits to Trump Properties," NBCNews.com [updated continuously].

WEEK 49

1. Jessica Taylor, "Bannon: 'It's a Season of War Against the GOP Establish-ment," NPR.org, 10/14/17.

2–3. Jessica Garrison and Kendall Taggart, "Trump Given a Subpoena for All Documents Relating to Assault Allegations," *BF*, 10/15/17.

4. Jeannie Suk Gersen, "How Anti-Trump Psychiatrists Are Mobilizing Behind the Twenty-fifth Amendment," *NYer*, 10/16/17.

5. Editorial Board, "California Burns: Where's the President?" *San Francisco Chronicle*, 10/14/17.

6. Jane Mayer, "The Danger of President Pence," *NYer*, 10/23/17.

7. Callum Borchers, "Anthony Scaramucci's Media Company Asked Twitter to Vote on the Number of Jews Killed in the Holocaust," *WaPo*, 10/17/17.

8. Ashley Edwards and Emily C. Singer, "Exclusive: Army Reserve Bans Green Card Holders from Enlisting, a Move That May Break Federal Law," *Mic*, 10/17/17.

9. Ariane de Vogue, "Hawaii Judge Blocks Trump's Latest Travel Ban," CNN.com, 10/18/17.

10. Ted Hesson, "Second Judge Halts Trump's Latest Attempt at Travel Ban," *Politico*, 10/18/17.

11–12. Eric Levenson, "Protesters Heckle Richard Spencer at Univ. of Florida Talk," CNN.com, 10/19/17.

13. Susan Svrluga and Lori Rozsa, "'Kill Them': Three Men Charged in Shooting After Richard Spencer Speech," *WaPo*, 10/2/17.

14. Ryan J. Reilly, "'Crusader' Militiaman Charged in Terror Plot Targeting Muslims Will Be Jailed Until Trial," *HuffPost*, 10/20/17.

15. Andrew Freedman, "EPA's Climate Change Website Reappears, Missing the Word 'Climate,'" *Mashable*, 10/20/17.

16–17. Dan Alexander, "The Mystery of Wilbur Ross' Missing Billions," Forbes .com, 10/16/17.

18–19. Kyle Cheney, "Cummings: Trump Aides Admitted to Lawyers They Used Private Email," *Politico*, 10/20/17.

20. Anne Gearan, "Trump to Meet Philippine President Rodrigo Duterte, Accused of Extrajudicial Killings, During Asian Visit," *WaPo*, 10/16/17.

21–22. Timothy Cama, "EPA to Restrict Scientific Advisers Who Get Agency Grants," *The Hill*, 10/17/17.

23. Lenny Bernstein, Ed O'Keefe, Anne Gearan, and Schott Higham, "Trump Says Drug Czar Nominee Tom Marino Is Withdrawing After *Washington Post*/'60 Minutes' Investigation," *WaPo*, 10/17/17.

24. Yuka Hayashi, "CFPB Enforcement Chief to Step Down," *WSJ*, 10/16/17

25. Josh Gerstein, "Judge Won't Wipe Out Guilty Verdict for Arpaio," *Politico*, 10/19/17.

26. Seung Min Kim and John Bresnahan, "Trump Personally Interviewed U.S. Attorney Candidates," *Politico*, 10/19/17.

27. Laura Jarrett, "President Has Rare Meeting with US Attorney Nominee," CNN.com, 7/20/17.

28. Mike Allen, "Trump's Alternative Reality," *Axios*, 10/17/17.

29. Josh Dawsey, "Trump Gives His Own Performance a Trump-Sized Endorsement," *Politico*, 10/16/17.

30. Rebecca Savransky, "Trump: There Is No Such Thing as ObamaCare Anymore," *The Hill*, 10/16/17.

31. Abbe Gluck, "President Trump Admits He's Trying to Kill Obamacare. That's Illegal," *Vox*, 10/17/17.

32. Mike Allen, "Trump's Alternative Reality," *Axios*, 10/17/17; Kari Giger and Jonathan Allen, "Bannon's Playbook: How He'll Wreck the GOP Establishment," NBCNews.com, 10/15/17.

33. Kevin Liptak, "Trump Finally Comments on Soldier Deaths in Niger; Falsely Knocks Obama over His Responses to Dead Soldiers," CNN .com, 10/17/17.

34. Lachlan Markay and Asawin Suebsaeng, "Trump White House Uses John Kelly's Dead Son to Trash Obama," *DB*, 10/17/17.

35. Dan Merica, Jeff Zeleny, and Kevin Liptak, "Sources: Kelly Didn't Know Trump Would Publicize That Obama Didn't Call When His Son Died," CNN.com, 10/18/17.

36. Calvin Woodward and Tom Davies, "Plenty of Bereaved Military Families Did Not Hear from Trump," AP, 10/20/17.

37. Kevin Liptak, "Trump Finally Comments on Soldier Deaths in Niger; Falsely Knocks Obama over His Responses to Dead Soldiers," CNN .com, 10/17/17.

38. Anne Gearan, "'Hillary, Please Run!' Trump Jokes, Says 'Whole Russia Thing' Was an Excuse for Democrats' 2016 Loss," *WaPo*, 10/16/17.

39–40. Tom Hamburger and Anu Narayanswamy, "Trump Campaign Legal Bills Topped $1 Million Last Quarter," *WaPo*, 10/15/17.

41. Natasha Bertrand, "New Memo Suggests Russian Lawyer at Trump Tower Meeting Was Acting 'as an Agent' of the Kremlin," *BI*, 10/16/17.

42. Manu Raju and Jeremy Herb, "Senate Investigators Spoke with Russians Present at Trump Tower Meeting with Trump Jr.," CNN.com, 10/20/17.

43–44. "Russian Trolls Were Schooled on 'House of Cards,'" *YN*, 10/15/17.

45–46. Jeremy Herb and Manu Raju, "Hill Russia Investigators Probe GOP Operative Who Sought Clinton Emails" CNN.com, 10/16/17.

47. Natasha Bertrand, "Mueller Has Interviewed the Cybersecurity Expert Who Described Being 'Recruited to Collude with the Russians,'" *BI*, 10/17/17.

48. Natasha Bertrand, "An Intern at the Trump Campaign Data Firm, Cambridge Analytica, Appears to Have Left Sensitive Voter Targeting Tools Online for Nearly a Year," *BI*, 10/14/17.

49. Tim Lister, Jim Sciutto, and Mary Ilyushina, "Exclusive: Putin's 'Chef,' the Man Behind the Troll Factory," CNN .com, 10/17/17.

50. Howard Koplowitz, "Russian Twitter Bots Invade Roy Moore's Account; Senate Candidate Blames Doug Jones, Dems," AL.com, 10/16/17.

51. Natasha Bertrand, "The Founders of the Firm Behind the Trump-Russia Dossier Say They'll Refuse to Testify Before the House Intelligence Committee," *BI*, 10/16/17; Michael Isikoff (@Isikoff), "In ct. papers, Fusion lawyers argue subpoena was signed by Rep. (Nunes) 'with no authority to sign it, as part of personal mission' (1)" Twitter, 10/20/17, 3:21 p.m.

52. Chris Cillizza, "Donald Trump Just Suggested the FBI, Democrats and Russia Might All Be Co-conspirators," CNN.com, 10/19/17.

53. Marianna Sotomayor and Kasie Hunt, "Senate Subpoenas Former Trump Adviser Carter Page," NBCNews.com, 10/17/17.

54–55. Annie Karni and Josh Dawsey, "Spicer Interviewed by Mueller's Team," *Politico*, 10/17/17.

56–57. Ari Melber, Meredith Mandell, and Mirjam Lablans, "Putin Rival Ties Kushner Meeting to Kremlin Bankers," NBCNews.com, 10/17/17.

58. Gabriel Sherman, "Jared Kushner Adds Charles Harder to Legal Team as West Wing Pressure Mounts," *VF*, 10/17/17.

59. Jay Rosen (@jayrosen_nyu), "This has been reported. It needs to be interpreted. Here's Harder's areas of expertise. http://hmafirm.com /attorneys/charles-j-harder/ . . . So Kushner needs him why?" Twitter, 10/18/17, 5:53 a.m.; Charles J. Harder, profile, Horder Mirell & Abrams LLP, hmafirm.com/attorneys/charles-j-harder.

60–61. Betsy Woodruff, Ben Collins, Kevin Poulsen, and Spencer Ackerman, "Trump Campaign Staffers Pushed Russian Propaganda Days Before the Election," *DB*, 10/18/17.

62. Ali Watkins and Elana Schor, "Senate Staffers Interview Lewandowski in Russia Probe," *Politico*, 10/18/17.

63. "Senate Panel Postpones Hearing with Trump Lawyer Cohen in Russia Probe," Reuters, 10/20/17.

64. Josh Gerstein, "Judge Tosses Libel Lawsuit Against AP by Russian Oligarch Tied to Manafort," *Politico*, 10/17/17.

65. Hadas Gold, "RT Bucks DOJ Request to Register as a Foreign

Agent," CNN.com, 10/19/17, updated 12/8/17.

66. Morgan Chalfant, "McCain Says White House Blocked Cyber Czar from Testifying," *The Hill*, 10/19/17.

67. Joel Gehrke, "Nikki Haley: Russia Committed 'Warfare' Against US in 2016," *WE*, 10/19/17.

68. Greg Miller, "CIA Director Distorts Intelligence Community's Findings on Russian Interference," *WaPo*, 10/19/17.

69. Ken Dilanian and Vivian Salama, "CIA Director Wrongly Says U.S. Found Russia Didn't Affect Election Result," NBCNews.com, 10/19/17.

70. Tom O'Connor, "Putin Says Americans Should Not 'Disrespect' Trump, Because He's the President and 'Doesn't Need Any Advice,'" *Newsweek*, 10/19/17.

71. Nathaniel Weixel, "Pennsylvania ObamaCare to See Premiums Spike amid Trump Pay Cuts," *The Hill*, 10/16/17.

72-73. Lily Mihalik, "24 Hours In, Trump's Mixed Signals on Alexander-Murray," *Politico*, 10/18/17.

74. Aaron Blake, "Trump's Unmoored Week Shows Just How Aimless He Is," *WaPo*, 10/19/17.

75. Zac Auter, "U.S. Uninsured Rate Rises 12.3% in Third Quarter," Gallup News, 10/20/17.

76. John McCain, "Remarks at the 2017 Liberty Medal Ceremony," *Medium*, 10/16/17.

77. Louis Nelson and Elana Schor, "Trump and McCain Smack at Each Other over 'Spurious Nationalism' Comments," *Politico*, 10/17/17.

78-79. Julia Fair, "George W. Bush Delivers Clear Rebuke, Without Mentioning Trump by Name," *USAT*, 10/19/17.

80. John McCain (@SenJohnMcCain), "Important speech by my friend, President George W. Bush today, reminding us of the values that have made America a beacon of hope for all." Twitter, 10/19/17, 11:47 a.m.

81. Ashley Gold, "McCain Signs On to Democrats' Facebook Ad Disclosure Bill," *Politico*, 10/18/17.

82. Tom Dreisbach, "Numbers Disagree with Trump Golf Course Claim of 'Millions to Charity,'" *Morning Edition*, NPR, 10/18/17.

83. Dan Lamothe, Lindsey Bever, and Eli Rosenberg, "Trump Offered a Grieving Military Father $25,000 in a Phone Call," *WaPo*, 10/18/17.

84. "The Latest: Trump Denies Disrespecting Grieving Family," AP, 10/19/17; Alison Buckholtz, "Keep Your Money, Trump," *Slate*, 10/20/17.

85. Anne Gearan, "Trump Suggests Comey Prematurely Exonerated Clinton but Investigators Say Probe Was Largely Complete," *WaPo*, 10/18/17.

86. Matt Zapotosky, Sari Horwitz, and Devlin Barrett, "Sessions Tells Lawmakers He Will Not Discuss His Conversations with Trump on Comey Firing," *WaPo*, 10/18/17.

87. Sarah N. Lynch and Lisa Lambert, "Sessions Refuses to Discuss Conversations with Trump on Russia," Reuters, 10/18/17.

88. Dana Lind, "Jeff Sessions Just Refused to Tell Congress What Trump Said to Him About Comey," *Vox*, 10/18/17.

89. Callum Borchers, "Sessions Says He Can't 'Make a Blanket Commitment' Not to Jail Journalists," *WaPo*, 10/18/17.

90. Maegan Vazquez, "Trump, Dem Congresswoman Feud over His Remarks to Widow of Fallen Solider," CNN.com, 10/18/17.

91-94. Anne Gearan and Kristine Phillips, "Fallen Soldier's Mother: 'Trump Did Disrespect My Son,'" *WaPo*, 10/18/17.

95. Tom Vanden Brook, "Trump's Treatment of Families of the Fallen 'Sickens' Chuck Hagel," *USAT*, 10/19/17.

96. "US Soldier's Body May Have Been in Hands of ISIS Following Niger Ambush," CBS Miami, 10/10/17.

97. "Maddow: What Is Trump Hiding About U.S. Military in Niger?" *Rachel Maddow Show*, MSNBC, 10/18/17.

98. Nahal Toosi, "White House Staff Drafted Niger Sympathy Statement for Trump That Was Never Released," *Politico*, 10/18/17.

99. Ashley Killough, "McCain: Niger Attack Information 'May Require a Subpoena,'" CNN.com, 10/19/17.

100. W.J. Hennigan and Brian Bennett, "Pentagon Investigating Troubling Questions after Deadly Niger Ambush," *LAT*, 10/19/17; Barbara Starr and Zachary Cohen, "Missing Soldier Found Nearly a Mile from Niger Ambush, Officials Say," CNN.com, 10/21/17.

101. Robert Windrem and Courtney Kube, "Pentagon Sends Team to Niger to Find Out What Happened," NBCNews.com, 10/19/17.

102. Michael D. Shear, "Kelly Delivers Fervent Defense of Trump Call to Soldier's Widow," *NYT*, 10/19/17.

103. Chris Cillizza, "John Kelly's Stirring but Incomplete Attempt to Clean Up for Donald Trump," CNN .com, 10/20/17.

104. Jeremy Diamond, "Kelly Says He Was 'Stunned' by Congresswoman's Account of Trump's Call," CNN.com, 10/20/17; Jordan Fabian, "WH Stands by Kelly, Repeats 'Empty Barrel' Criticism of Wilson," *The Hill*, 10/20/17.

105. William Cummings, "Trump Repeats Claim 'Wacky' Rep. Wilson's Version of Call to Army Widow Was 'Total Lie,'" *USAT*, 10/20/17.

106. Alex Daugherty, Anita Kumar, and Douglas Hanks, "In Attack on Frederica Wilson over Trump's Call to Widow, John Kelly Gets Facts Wrong," *Miami Herald*, 10/19/17.

107. Larry Barszewski, "Frederica Wilson 2015 Video Shows John Kelly Got It Wrong," *Sun Sentinel* (FL), 10/21/17.

108. Jordan Fabian, "WH Stands by Kelly, Repeats 'Empty Barrel' Criticism of Wilson," *The Hill*, 10/20/17.

109. Ledyard King, "Video Debunks John Kelly's Claim That Frederica Wilson Took Credit for FBI Building Funds," *USAT*, 10/20/17; Herman Wong, "Here are the Four-Star Generals Donald Trump Has Publicly Bashed," *WaPo*, 10/20/17.

110. Tom Vanden Brook and Gregory Korte, "Air Force Could Recall as Many as 1,000 Retired Pilots to Address Serious Shortage," *USAT*, 10/20/17.

111. Kevin Bohn, "Leading Democrat Calls for Puerto Rico Water Investigation," CNN.com, 10/15/17.

112. Leyla Santiago and Mallory Simon, "There's a Hospital Ship Waiting for

Sick Puerto Ricans—but No One Knows How to Get on It," CNN.com, 10/17/17.

113. John D. Sutter, "About 1 Million Americans Without Running Water. 3 Million Without Power. This Is Life One Month After Hurricane Maria," CNN.com, 10/20/17.

114. Philip Bump, "Trump Rates His Puerto Rico Handling a 10 out of 10. America Rates It a 4," *WaPo*, 10/19/17.

115–116. Ali Vitali, "Trump Gives Administration a '10' for Puerto Rico Recovery," NBCNews.com, 10/19/17.

117. Oxfam, "One Month On, Millions of Puerto Ricans Still Caught in Crisis," OxfamAmerica.org, 10/19/17.

118. Matt Flegenheimer, "Is Trump Violating the Constitution? In Absentia, He Defends Himself in Court," *NYT*, 10/18/17.

119. Jarrett Bell, "Jacksonville Jaguars Owner Shad Khan: Donald Trump 'Jealous of' NFL amid Failure to Buy Team," *USAT*, 10/18/17.

120. Adam Edelman, "Brennan: Trump Aides May Need to Talk Him Out of War," NBCNews.com, 10/19/17.

121. Maria Sacchetti, "U.S. Judge Orders Trump Administration to Allow Abortion for Undocumented Teen," *WaPo*, 10/18/17.

122. Pete Williams, "Court Blocks Immediate Abortion for Undocumented Teen," NBCNews.com, 10/20/17.

123. Brianna Ehley, Josh Dawsey, and Sarah Karlin-Smith, "Blindsided Trump Officials Scrambling to Develop Opioid Plan," *Politico*, 10/20/17.

124. Chris Riotta, "Exclusive: Ivanka Trump's Security Clearance Must Be Reviewed, Senator Says," *Newsweek*, 10/20/17.

125. Lachlan Markay and Asawin Suebsaeng, "Donald Trump Has No Regrets over How the Week Went. Part XVI," *DB*, 10/20/17.

126. Christopher Wilson, "Trump Blames Rise in British Crime on Islamic Terror, Surprising Britain," *YN*, 10/20/17.

127. "Forbes 400: Introducing the Wealthiest in America," *Forbes*, www.forbes.com/forbes-400/#5b8f9a697e2f.

128. Lorraine Boissoneault, "In 2014, Americans Feared Walking Alone at Night. Now They're Worried About Government Corruption," *Smithsonian*, 10/20/17.

129. Government of Puerto Rico, Status PR, status.pr/?lng=en [updated continuously].

WEEK 50

1. Jonathan Swan, "Scoop: Trump Pledges to Personally Pay Some Legal Bills of WH Staff and Associates," *Axios*, 10/21/17.

2. Anna Mehler Paperny, "Canada Granting Asylum to U.S Border Crossers at Higher Rates: Data," Reuters, 10/20/17.

3. "Air Force: No Plan to Recall Retired Pilots to Fix Shortage," AP, 10/22/17.

4. Marcus Weisgerber, "EXCLUSIVE: US Preparing to Put Nuclear Bombers Back on 24-Hour Alert," *Defense One*, 10/22/17.

5. Scott Neuman, "State Department Reportedly Revokes Visa of Magnitsky Act Campaigner," *The Two-Way* (blog), NPR, 10/23/17.

6. Andrew E. Kramer, "U.S. Clears Bill Browder to Enter, Rebuking Russia," *NYT*, 10/23/17.

7. Natasha Bertrand, "Prominent Anti-Putin Whistleblower Bill Browder Says He Was Barred from Entering the US," *BI*, 10/23/17.

8. Andrew Restuccia and Nahal Toosi, "Trump Nominees Show Up for Work Without Waiting for Senate Approval," *Politico*, 10/20/17.

9. Lena Felton and Taylor Hosking, "Donald Trump Is Rush-Shipping Condolences to Military Families," *Atlantic*, 10/21/17.

10. Dan Merica, "McCain Appears to Mock Trump's Draft Deferments," CNN.com, 10/23/17.

11. Congressional Black Caucus, "CBC Women Demand Apology from White House Chief of Staff John Kelly," press release, cbc.house.gov/news/documentsingle.aspx?DocumentID=779.

12. Domenico Montanaro, "Gold Star Widow: Trump Call 'Made Me Cry Even Worse,'" NPR.org, 10/23/17.

13. Kristine Phillips, J. Freedom du Lac, and Rachel Siegel, "Gold Star Widow Myeshia Johnson Said Trump Stumbled Recalling Her Husband's Name," *WaPo*, 10/23/17.

14. Ben Mathis-Lilley, "Trump Says Soldier's Widow Must Be Wrong Because He Has 'One of the Great Memories of All Time,'" *The Slatest*, 10/25/17.

15. Moriah Balingit, "The Education Department Phased Out 72 Policy Documents for Disabled Students. Here's Why," *WaPo*, 10/23/17.

16. Kelsey O'Connor, "'Cornell Reviles Their Message of Hatred,' University Says After Anti-Semitic Posters Placed Around Campus, Ithaca," *Ithaca Voice*, 10/23/17.

17. Rachel Brown, "NAACP Issues Travel Advisory Against American Airlines," WCNC.com, 10/25/17.

18. Ariel Hart and James Salzer, "State Rep. Betty Price Suggests 'Quarantine' for HIV Patients," *Atlanta Journal-Constitution*, 10/20/17.

19. Stanley Kay, "Texans Owner Apologizes After Comparing NFL Protests to 'Inmates Running the Prison,'" *Sports Illustrated*, 10/27/17.

20. Heather Borden Herve, "I Have No Words . . . ," *Good Morning Wilton*, 10/27/17.

21. Kelly Heyboer, "White Supremacist Group Posts Recruiting Fliers Across Rutgers," NJ.com, 10/24/17.

22. Rich Schapiro, "New Jersey Town Proposed Rules Seeking to Stop Orthodox Jews from Moving In, Attorney General Lawsuit Charges," *NYDN*, 10/24/17.

23. Viviana Andazola Marquez, "I Accidentally Turned My Dad In to Immigration Services," *NYT*, 10/24/17.

24. AP, "10-Year-Old Mexican Girl with Cerebral Palsy Detained by Border Patrol After Surgery in Texas," NBCNews.com, 10/26/17.

25. Brigitte Amiri, "Jane Doe's Ordeal Illustrates the Trump Administration's Threat to All Women's Reproductive Rights," ACLU.org, 10/26/17.

26. Laura Meckler and Brent Kendall, "Trump Appointee Brings Antiabortion Mission to Immigration Shelters," *WSJ*, 10/27/17.

27. Kevin Freking, "Trump Official Sidesteps Questions about Pregnant Detainees," AP, 10/26/17.

28. John Wagner, "All of the Women Who Have Accused Trump of Sexual Harassment Are Lying, the White House Says," *WaPo*, 10/27/17.

29. Lisa Friedman, "E.P.A. Cancels Talk on Climate Change by Agency Scientists," *NYT*, 10/22/17.

30. Kathleen Harris, Rosemary Barton, and Peter Zimonjic, "New U.S. Ambassador to Canada Kelly Craft Says She Believes 'Both Sides' of Climate Science," CBC News, 10/23/17.

31–32. Brian Fung, "The FCC Plans to Roll Back Some of Its Biggest Rules Against Media Consolidation," *WaPo*, 10/25/17.

33. Frank Bajak, "APNewsBreak: Georgia Election Server Wiped After Suit Filed," AP, 10/27/17.

34. Mallory Shelbourne, "Oversight Dem Presses Gowdy on Kushner Personal Email Request," *The Hill*, 10/23/17.

35–36. Amy Brittain and Drew Harwell, "Private-Prison Giant, Resurgent in Trump Era, Gathers at President's Resort," *WaPo*, 10/25/17.

37. Walter Shaub (@waltshaub), "So much for the fake firewall between POTUS and the fake trustee of his fake blind trust." Twitter, 10/26/17, 9:29 a.m.

38. Dartunorro Clark, "Probe Launched into Trump Voter Fraud Panel," NBCNews.com, 10/26/17.

39. Lydia Wheeler, "Sessions Accuses Judges of Overreach in Heritage Address," *The Hill*, 10/26/17.

40. Mary Emily O'Hara (@MaryEmilyOHara), "BREAKING: Attorney General Jeff Sessions speech to Heritage Foundation says religious expression overrides civil rights laws." Twitter, 10/26/17, 10:48 a.m.

41. Clare Malone and Jeff Asher, "The First FBI Crime Report Issued Under Trump Is Missing a Ton of Info," *FiveThirtyEight*, 10/27/17.

42. Andrew Blake, "Sebastian Gorka Suggests Hillary Clinton Should Be Tried for Treason, Executed over Uranium One Deal," *Washington Times*, 10/27/17.

43. Gloria Borger, Evan Perez, and Marshall Cohen, "Trump Wants State Department to Release Remaining Clinton Emails," CNN.com, 10/27/17.

44. Eli Watkins, "Conway Confirms Trump Wanted FBI Informant's Gag Order Lifted," CNN.com, 10/28/17.

45. Andrew Desiderio, "Congress: Trump Won't Implement Russia Sanctions—and He Won't Tell Us Why," *DB*, 10/23/17.

46. Robbie Gramer and Dan De Luce, "State Department Scraps Sanctions Office," *FP*, 10/26/17.

47. Matt Zapotosky, Karoun Demirjian, and David Filipov, "Trump Administration Reveals New List of Potential Russia Sanctions," *WaPo*, 10/27/17.

48. Jane Perlez, "Xi Jinping Pushes China's Rise Despite Friction and Fear," *NYT*, 10/22/17.

49–50. Kate O'Keeffe, Aruna Viswanatha, and Cezary Podkul, "China's Pursuit of Fugitive Businessman Guo Wengui Kicks Off Manhattan Caper Worthy of Spy Thriller," *WSJ*, 10/22/17.

51. Bill Gertz, "Sessions Threatened to Quit over Chinese Dissident," *Washington Times*, 10/25/17.

52. Tim Phillips, "'Extraordinary Elevation': Trump Kowtows to Kingpin Xi," *Guardian*, 10/25/17.

53. Noah Barkin, "After Iran Shock, Nervous Europe Girds for Next Trump Salvo," Reuters, 10/27/17.

54. John Haltiwanger, "Trump Blames Generals for Niger Ambush That Got Four U.S. Soldiers Killed," *Newsweek*, 10/25/17.

55. Mark Abadi, "Trump Won't Stop Saying 'My Generals'—and the Military Community Isn't Happy," *BI*, 10/25/17.

56. Jacqueline Thomsen, "Trump: I 'Really Started This Whole Fake News Thing,'" *The Hill*, 10/25/17.

57. Philip Rucker, Sean Sullivan, and Paul Kane, "The Great Dealmaker? Lawmakers Find Trump to Be an Untrustworthy Negotiator," *WaPo*, 10/23/17.

58. Dana Blanton, "Fox News Poll: Storms Erode Trump's Ratings," FoxNews.com, 10/25/17.

59. Jasmine C. Lee and Kevin Quealy, "The 382 People, Places and Things Donald Trump Has Insulted on Twitter: A Complete List," *NYT*, 11/17/17.

60–61. Betsy Woodruff, "Trump Data Guru: I Tried to Team Up with Julian Assange," *DB*, 10/25/17.

62. Maya Kosoff, "Trump Campaign Distances Itself from Cambridge Analytica After Assange Connection Surfaces," *VF*, 10/25/17.

63–64. Rebecca Ballhaus, "Trump Donor Asked Data Firm if It Could Better Organize Hacked Emails," *WSJ*, 10/27/17.

65. Matthew Mosk and Brian Ross, "Trump-Russia Investigators Gathering Documents from Estate of Republican Operative, Sources Say," ABCNews.com, 10/25/17.

66. Ryan C. Brooks, "How Russians Attempted to Use Instagram to Influence Native Americans," *BF*, 10/23/17.

67. Manu Raju and Jeremy Herb, "Trump Attorney Cohen to Meet with Hill Investigators This Week," CNN.com, 10/23/17.

68. Nico Hines and Sam Stein, "GOP Leaders Refusing to Pay for Dana Rohrabacher's Travel Over Russia Fears, *DB*, 10/24/17.

69. AP, "The Stabbed Russian Radio Journalist Tatyana Felgenhauer Is Now in a Coma," *Time*, 10/23/17.

70. Ivana Kottasová and Samuel Burke, "U.K. Asks Facebook for Information on Russia-Linked Brexit Ads," CNN.com, 10/24/17.

71. Dan Friedman, "The Senate Judiciary Committee's Russia Probe Just Blew Up," *MJ*, 10/24/17.

72–73. Betsy Woodruff and Spencer Ackerman, "Republicans on House's Trump-Russia Probe Not That Interested in Trump or Russia," *DB*, 10/24/17.

74. Michael McFaul (@McFaul), "Recycle of inane HRC attack regarding uranium deal is classic whataboutism, perfected by Kremlin, now practiced shamelessly here. stop it." Twitter, 10/25/17, 9:36 p.m.

75. "Nunes Says He 'Would Prefer' Reporters to Stop Saying He Recused Himself from Russia Probe," video, *WaPo*, 10/24/17.

76. "Russia to Respond to Twitter Ban on Russian Media Ads—RIA," Reuters, 10/26/17.

77-79. Erica Orden and Nicole Hong, "Former Trump Campaign Chairman Paul Manafort Faces Another Money-Laundering Probe," *WSJ*, 10/24/17.

80. Josh Gerstein, "Manafort Real Estate Agent Testified Before Grand Jury in Russia Probe," *Politico*, 10/27/17.

81. Sharon LaFraniere and Andrew E. Kramer, "Talking Points Brought to Trump Tower Meeting Were Shared with Kremlin," *NYT*, 10/27/17.

82. Garrett Haake, Frank Thorp V, and Marianna Sotomayor, "Former Trump Adviser Carter Page Questioned by Senate Panel," NBCNews.com, 10/27/17.

83. Rachel Weiner, "Dana Boente Announces Resignation as U.S. Attorney for Eastern District of Virginia," *WaPo*, 10/27/17.

84. Max Greenwood, "Ex-CIA Chief Spoke to Mueller Team About Flynn," *The Hill*, 10/27/17.

85. Pamela Brown, Evan Perez, and Shimon Prokupecz, "First on CNN: First Charges Filed in Mueller Investigation," CNN.com, 10/30/17; "First Charges Filed in Russia Probe Led by U.S. Special Counsel: Source," Reuters, 10/27/17.

86-87. Steven Mufson, Jack Gillum, Aaron C. Davis, and Arelis R. Hernández, "Small Montana Firm Lands Puerto Rico's Biggest Contract to Get the Power Back On," *WaPo*, 10/23/17.

88. Steven Mufson and Aaron C. Davis, "Puerto Rico's Electric Utility Likely to Get Emergency Manager amid Criticism over Contract to Small Montana Firm," *WaPo*, 10/25/17; Anthony Adragna, "Concerns Mount over Mysterious Whitefish Energy Contract," *Politico*, 10/25/17.

89. Government of Puerto Rico, Status PR, status.pr/?lng=en [continuously updated]; Jamie Ducharme, "The Company with a Controversial Contract to Help Puerto Rico Is Feuding with the Mayor of San Juan," *Time*, 10/25/17.

90. Jamie Ducharme, "The Company with a Controversial Contract to Help Puerto Rico Is Feuding with the Mayor of San Juan," *Time*, 10/25/17.

91. Whitefish Energy (@Whitefish Energy), ".@CarmenYulinCruz and everyone in Puerto Rico . . ." Twitter, 10/25/17, 7:23 p.m.

92. John Bowden, "Whitefish Energy Contract Bars Government from Auditing Deal," *The Hill*, 10/27/17.

93-94. Christina Wilkie, "Trump Administration Rushes to Distance Itself from Whitefish Energy's Contract with Puerto Rico," CNBC.com, 10/27/17.

95. Michael Nedelman, "Suspected Leptospirosis Cases Increasing in Puerto Rico After Hurricane Maria," CNN .com, 10/24/17.

96-97. Alexia Fernández Campbell, "Nurses Returning from Puerto Rico Accuse the Federal Government of Leaving People to Die," *Vox*, 10/26/17.

98. Nidhi Prakash, "Puerto Rico Is Burning Its Dead, and We May Never Know How Many People the Hurricane Really Killed," *BF*, 10/29/17.

99. Nidhi Prakash, "Puerto Rico's Government Just Admitted 911 People Died After the Hurricane—of 'Natural Causes,'" *BF*, 10/27/17.

100. Sean Sullivan and Elise Viebeck, "Trump Meets with Republicans as Corker Slams Him for 'Untruths,' 'Debasing' the Country," *WaPo*, 10/24/17.

101-103. Eileen Sullivan, "Trump and Corker Escalate Battle over Taxes, in Personal Terms," *NYT*, 10/24/17.

104. Maegan Vazquez, "Trump-Corker Feud Explodes Ahead of Critical Hill Visit," CNN.com, 10/24/17.

105. Donald Trump (@realDonald Trump), "So nice being with Republican Senators today. Multiple standing ovations! Most are great people who want big Tax Cuts and success for U.S." Twitter, 10/24/17, 3:20 p.m.

106. Rebecca Savransky, "Protester Throws Russian Flags at Trump as He Enters GOP Lunch," *The Hill*, 10/24/17.

107. Dan Nowicki, "Arizona's Jeff Flake Announces He Will Not Seek Re-election to U.S. Senate," *The Republic* (AZ), 10/25/17; Jeff Flake, "Enough," *WaPo*, 10/24/17.

108-109. Amber Phillips, "'I Will Not Be Complicit.' Jeff Flake's Retirement Speech, Annotated," *WaPo*, 10/24/17.

110-111. Ella Nilsen, "6 Key Quotes from Sen. Jeff Flake's Speech Blasting Trump," *Vox*, 10/24/17.

112. "John McCain to Jeff Flake: 'One of the Great Privileges of My Life' to Know You," *The Republic* (AZ), 10/24/17.

113. Julia Manchester, "Trump Mocks Flake, Mentions 'Standing Ovation' for Third Time," *The Hill*, 10/25/17.

114. Jessica Silver-Greenberg, "Consumer Bureau Loses Fight to Allow More Class-Action Suits," *NYT*, 10/24/17.

115. Lydia Wheeler, "Trump Officials Quash Litigation Rule for Farms," *The Hill*, 10/24/17.

116. Julia Manchester, "Scott Brown Admits Investigation into Inappropriate Comments," *The Hill*, 10/25/17.

117-118. Margaret Newkirk and Joe Deaux, "Under Trump, Made in America Is Losing Out to Russian Steel," Bloomberg.com, 10/25/17.

119. Nolan D. McCaskill, "Trump Blasts 'Wacky & Totally Unhinged' Tom Steyer After Impeachment Ad Campaign," *Politico*, 10/27/17.

120. Donald Trump (@realDonald Trump), "The long anticipated release of the #JFKFiles will take place tomorrow. So interesting!" Twitter, 10/25/17, 12:56 p.m.; Bryan Bender, "Judge Rebukes Handling of JFK Records," *Politico*, 10/27/17.

121. Bryan Bender, "Judge Rebukes Handling of JFK Records," *Politico*, 10/27/17.

122. Katherine Faulders and Alexander Mallin, "Trump Declares Opioid Crisis a National Public Health Emergency," ABC.com, 10/26/17.

123. Ibid.; Matthew Perrone, "AP FACT CHECK: Anti-drug Ad Campaigns Fared Poorly in Past," AP, 10/26/17.

124. "Lawmakers: Lots of Unanswered Questions Remain About Niger Ambush," *VOA News*, 10/26/17.

125-126. Peter Stone and Greg Gordon "Trump Associate Cohen Sold Four NY Buildings for Cash to Mysterious Buyers," McClatchy, 10/25/17.

127. Mahita Gajanan, "'You Have No Weight Problems That's the Good News.' President Trump Gives Candy to Children," *Time*, 10/27/17.

128. Caroline Hallemann, "Anna Wintour Says Donald Trump Won't Be Invited Back to the Met Gala," *Town & Country*, 10/27/17.

129. Binyamin Appelbaum (@BCAppelbaum), "Trump releases promotional video for Fed announcement. https://www.instagram.com/p/Baw-kHQgVl2/" Twitter, 10/27/17, 2:35 p.m.

130. Doug Stanglin and Stephanie Ingersoll, "'White Lives Matter' Rallies: Opponents Outnumber White Nationalists at Tennessee Shout Fests," *USAT*, 10/28/17.

WEEK 51

1. Annie Gowen, "Trumps Set to Launch Two Real Estate Projects in India, Despite Conflict-of-Interest Concerns," *WaPo*, 10/28/17.

2. Pete Williams, "Dana Boente, Senior Federal Prosecutor and Obama Holdover, Submits Resignation," NBCNews.com, 10/28/17.

3. Mark Murray, "Trump's Approval Rating Drops to Lowest Level Yet in New NBC News/*WSJ* Poll," NBCNews.com, 10/29/17.

4. Mary Papenfuss, "Donald Trump's Approval Rating Hits New Low in Latest Gallup Poll," *HuffPost*, 10/30/17.

5. Annie Karni, "Kushner Took Unannounced Trip to Saudi Arabia," *Politico*, 10/29/17. Andrew Nusca, "Kushner Plan to Tear Down Manhattan Skyscraper 'Not Feasible,'" *Fortune*, 11/1/17.

6. Sonam Sheth, "'DO SOMETHING!': Trump Lashes Out as the Russia Investigation Heats Up," *BI*, 10/29/17.

7. Jason Schwartz, "Murdoch-Owned Outlets Bash Mueller, Seemingly in Unison," *Politico*, 10/31/17.

8. Oliver Darcy, "'I Want to Quit': Fox News Employees Say Their Network's Russia Coverage Was 'an Embarrassment,'" CNN.com, 10/31/17.

9. Paul Demko, Rachana Pradhan, and Adam Cancryn, "Confusion Clouds Open Enrollment with Republicans Still Eager to Dismantle Obamacare," *Politico*, 10/29/17.

10. Jeff Goldman and Craig McCarthy, "Racist 'Make Edison Great Again' Mailer Targets Asian School Board Candidates," NJ.com, 11/4/17.

11. Jonah Engel Bromwich, "Hartford Student Charged After Boasting About Contaminating Roommate's Belongings," *NYT*, 11/1/17.

12. Dave Philipps, "Judge Blocks Trump's Ban on Transgender Troops in Military," *NYT*, 10/30/17.

13. Ariane de Vogue, "Judge Blocks Enforcement of Trump's Transgender Military Ban," CNN.com, 10/30/17.

14. Jessica Garrison and Kendall Taggart, "Trump's Lawyers Just Argued, Again, That a Woman's Defamation Suit over Groping Allegations Should Be Dismissed," *BF*, 11/1/17.

15. Maria Danilova, "AP Sources: DeVos May Only Partly Forgive Some Student Loans," AP, 10/29/17.

16. Max Greenwood, "Sessions 'Disturbed' by Case of Immigrant Who Got Abortion," *The Hill*, 10/27/17.

17. Adam Liptak, "Justice Department Accuses A.C.L.U. of Misconduct in Abortion Case," *NYT*, 11/3/17.

18. Maria Sacchetti, "U.S. Frees 10-Year-Old Undocumented Immigrant with Cerebral Palsy," *WaPo*, 11/3/17.

19. Elizabeth Warren, "The Supreme Court Has an Ethics Problem," *Politico*, 11/1/17.

20. Darren Rovell, "Papa John's Says Anthem Protests Are Hurting Deal with NFL," ESPN.com, 11/1/17.

21. Seung Min Kim, "ABA Deems Another Trump Judicial Nominee 'Not Qualified,'" *Politico*, 10/30/17.

22-23. Timothy Cama, "EPA Blocks Scientists Who Get Grants from Its Advisory Boards," *The Hill*, 10/31/17.

24. Timothy Cama, "EPA Names Industry, State Officials to Advisory Boards," *The Hill*, 11/3/17.

25. Avery Anapol, "Perry Links Fossil Fuel Development to Preventing Sexual Assault," *The Hill*, 11/2/17.

26. Devin Henry, "Sierra Club Calls for Perry to Resign over Sexual Assault Comments," *The Hill*, 11/2/17.

27. Julia Simon, "U.S. Withdraws from Extractive Industries Anti-corruption Effort," Reuters, 11/2/17.

28-29. Fredreka Schouten, Brad Heath, and Steve Reilly, "Trump Nominates Some Club Members to Plum Government Jobs," *USAT*, 11/3/17.

30-32. Pete Williams and Adam Edelman, "Manafort, Gates Charged with Conspiracy in Mueller Investigation," NBCNews.com, 10/30/17.

33. Michael Isikoff, "Manafort Charges Grew Out of Records Seized in 'No-Knock' Raid," *YN*, 10/30/17.

34. Spencer S. Hsu, "Special Counsel: Manafort's Stated Wealth Fluctuated Wildly; He Keeps 3 Passports," *WaPo*, 10/31/17.

35. Erik Schatzker, "Rick Gates Terminated by Tom Barrack's Firm After Indictment," Bloomberg.com, 10/30/17.

36-38. Matt Zapotosky, Rosalind S. Helderman, Carol D. Leonnig, and Spencer S. Hsu, "Three Former Trump Campaign Officials Charged by Special Counsel," *WaPo*, 10/30/17.

39. Michael Isikoff, "Mueller Discloses Trump Campaign Aide Pleaded Guilty to Lying About Russian Contacts," *YN*, 10/30/17.

40. Lachlan Markay and Asawin Suebsaeng, "Steve Bannon Tells Trump to Bring in New Lawyers as He Looks for Ways to Kneecap Mueller," *DB*, 10/30/17.

41. Robert Costa, Philip Rucker, and Ashley Parker, "Upstairs at Home, with the TV on, Trump Fumes over Russia Indictments," *WaPo*, 10/30/17.

42-44. Gabriel Sherman, "'You Can't Go Any Lower': Inside the West Wing, Trump Is Apoplectic as Allies Fear Impeachment," *VF*, 11/1/17.

45. Evan Perez, Pamela Brown, and Shimon Prokupecz, "Jared Kushner's Team Turned Over Documents to Special Counsel in Russia Investigation," CNN.com, 11/3/17.

46. Brent D. Griffiths, "Kelly Reignites Feud with Rep. Wilson," *Politico*, 10/30/17.

47. Jon Greenberg, "John Kelly, the Civil War and the Compromise That Almost Was," *PolitiFact*, 11/2/17.

48. Jordain Carney, "GOP Senators Reject Talk of Defunding Mueller Probe," *The Hill*, 10/31/17.

49. Greg Farrell, David Voreacos, and Henry Meyer, "Papadopoulos Claimed Trump Campaign Approved Russia Meeting," Bloomberg.com, 11/1/17.

50. Maegan Vazquez, "Ex-Trump Campaign Adviser: Papadopoulos Was Just a 'Coffee Boy,'" CNN.com, 10/31/17; Rosalind S. Helderman, Karen DeYoung, and Tom Hamburger, "For 'Low Level Volunteer,' Papadopoulos Sought High Profile as Trump Adviser," *WaPo*, 10/31/17.

51. Rosalind S. Helderman, Karen DeYoung, and Tom Hamburger, "For 'Low Level Volunteer,' Papadopoulos Sought High Profile as Trump Adviser," *WaPo*, 10/31/17.

52–53. Michael S. Schmidt, Matt Apuzzo, and Scott Shane, "Trump and Sessions Denied Knowing About Russian Contacts. Records Suggest Otherwise," *NYT*, 11/2/17.

54. Ken Dilanian and Mike Memoli, "Top Trump Campaign Aide Clovis Spoke to Mueller Team, Grand Jury," NBCNews.com, 10/31/17.

55. Catherine Boudreau and Josh Dawsey, "Clovis Said to Be 'Cooperative Witness' in Senate Russia Probe," *Politico*, 10/31/17.

56. Evan Perez, Manu Raju, and Dan Merica, "Trump Nominee for Top Agriculture Post Withdraws amid Russia Probe," CNN.com, 11/2/17.

57. Manu Raju and Jeremy Herb, "Exclusive: Carter Page Testifies He Told Sessions About Russia Trip," CNN.com, 11/3/17.

58–59. Ken Dilanian and Carol E. Lee, "Sessions Rejected Russia Proposal by Campaign Adviser, Source Says," NBCNews.com, 11/2/17.

60–62. Leigh Ann Caldwell and Frank Thorp V, "Papadopoulos Repeatedly Represented Trump Campaign, Record Shows," NBCNews.com, 11/3/17.

63–64. Mark Mazzetti and Adam Goldman, "Trump Campaign Adviser Met with Russian Officials in 2016," *NYT*, 11/3/17.

65. Brad Heath, Steve Reilly, and Julia Fair, "Lawyers for Paul Manafort and Rick Gates Mount First Counterattack Against Mueller Charges," *USAT*, 11/3/17.

66. Emily Guskin and Matt Zapotosky, "*Post*-ABC Poll: Most Americans Approve of Trump-Russia Probe, and Nearly Half Think Trump Committed a Crime," *WaPo*, 11/2/17.

67. American Psychological Association, "APA *Stress in America* Survey: US at 'Lowest Point We Can Remember'; Future of Nation Most Commonly Reported Source of Stress," press release, www.apa.org/news/press/releases/2017/11/lowest-point.aspx.

68–69. Natasha Bertrand, "A Federal Judge Just Denied a Request for Natalia Veselnitskaya to Enter the US," *BI*, 11/3/17.

70–73. John T. Bennett, "Trump Blames Schumer for New York Truck Attack," *Roll Call*, 11/1/17; Dan Merica, "Trump Labels US Justice System 'Laughingstock,'" CNN.com, 11/1/17.

74–75. Donald Trump (@realDonaldTrump), "NYC terrorist was happy as he asked to hang ISIS flag in his hospital room. He killed 8 people, badly injured 12. SHOULD GET DEATH PENALTY!" Twitter, 11/1/17, 8:43 p.m.; Sadie Gurman, "Despite Tough Talk, Trump Follows Obama on Terror Suspects," AP, 11/3/17.

76. Paul Callan, "Trump Recklessly Endangers Prosecution of a Terrorism Case," CNN.com, 11/3/17.

77. "Trump Says Unsure if Tillerson Will Remain Secretary of State," Reuters, 11/3/17.

78. "'I'm the Only One That Matters,' Trump Says of State Dept. Job Vacancies," *The Two-Way* (blog), NPR, 11/3/17.

79. "Trump Says Unsure if Tillerson Will Remain Secretary of State," Reuters, 11/3/17.

80. Daniella Diaz, "Trump Slams Bergdahl Decision: 'Complete and Total Disgrace,'" CNN.com, 11/3/17.

81. Peter Baker, "'Very Frustrated' Trump Becomes Top Critic of Law Enforcement," *NYT*, 11/3/17.

82–83. Eli Watkins, "Donald Trump Laments He's 'Not Supposed' to Influence DOJ, FBI," CNN.com, 11/3/17.

84. Peter Baker, "'Very Frustrated' Trump Becomes Top Critic of Law Enforcement," *NYT*, 11/3/17; Jonathan Karl and Arlette Saenz, "President Trump Doesn't Know if He'd Fire Attorney General Jeff Sessions," ABCNews.com, 11/3/17.

85. Peter Baker, "'Very Frustrated' Trump Becomes Top Critic of Law Enforcement," *NYT*, 11/3/17.

86. Andrew Scurria, "FBI Is Probing Puerto Rico Power Contract," *WSJ*, 10/30/17.

87. Andrew Scurria, "Puerto Rico Governor Cancels $300 Million Power Contract," *WSJ*, 10/30/17.

88. Tim Rogers, "Navy's Largest Floating Hospital Docks in Puerto Rico," Fusion.net, 10/30/17.

89. Oren Dorell and Atabey Nuñez, "Puerto Rico's Water Woes Raise Fears of Health Crisis Six Weeks After Hurricane Maria," *USAT*, 11/2/17.

90. "Officials Slow with Info on Severity of Disease in Puerto Rico," *Rachel Maddow Show*, MSNBC, 11/3/17.

91–92. Vann R. Newkirk II, "The Puerto Rico Power Scandal Expands," *Atlantic*, 11/3/17.

93. "San Juan Mayor Estimates Actual Death Toll Closer to 500, Not 54," *The Lead with Jake Tapper*, CNN, 11/3/17.

94. David Caplan, "Trump's Twitter Account Briefly Deactivated by Twitter Employee on Last Day, Company Says," ABCNews.com, 11/2/17.

95. Sarah D. Wire, "Tom Steyer's Impeachment Petition Gets over 1 Million Signatures in First Week," *LAT*, 10/31/17.

96. Public Policy Polling, "Support for Impeachment at Record High," press release, 10/31/17, www.publicpolicypolling.com/wp-content/uploads/2017/10/PPP_Release_National_103117.pdf.

97. Mike Isaac and Daisuke Wakabayashi, "Russian Influence Reached 126 Million Through Facebook Alone," *NYT*, 10/30/17.

98. Craig Timberg, Elizabeth Dwoskin, Adam Entous, and Karoun Demirjian, "Russian Ads, Now Publicly Released, Show Sophistication of Influence Campaign," *WaPo*, 11/1/17.

99. Issie Lapowsky, "Eight Revealing Moments from the Second Day of Russia Hearings," *Wired*, 11/1/17.

100. Ibid.; Harper Neidig, "Franken Blasts Facebook for Accepting Rubles for U.S. Election Ads," *The Hill*, 10/31/17.

101. Issie Lapowsky, "Eight Revealing Moments from the Second Day of Russia Hearings," *Wired*, 11/1/17.

102–104. Nicholas Fandos, Cecilia Kang, and Mike Isaac, "House Intelligence Committee Releases Incendiary Russian Social Media Ads," *NYT*, 11/18/17.

105. Selina Wang, "Twitter Sidestepped Russian Account Warnings, Former Worker Says," Bloomberg.com, 11/3/17.

106. Gregory Zuckerman, "Key Trump Backer Robert Mercer Resigns as Renaissance Technologies CEO," *WSJ*, 11/2/17.

107. Joseph Bernstein, "Hedge Fund Billionaire Robert Mercer Will Step Down as CEO of His Company Following *BuzzFeed* News Exposé," *BF*, 11/2/17.

108. Karoun Demirjian, "Conservative Republicans Demand Mueller Recuse Himself over Uranium Deal," *WaPo*, 11/3/17.

109–111. Frank Bajak, "Georgia Attorney General Quits Defense in Server Wiping Case," AP, 11/2/17.

112–114. Raphael Satter, Jeff Donn, and Justin Myers, "Russia Hackers Pursued Putin Foes, Not Just US Democrats," AP, 11/2/17.

115–118. Raphael Satter, "Inside Story: How Russians Hacked the Democrats' Emails," AP, 11/4/17.

119. Manu Raju and Jeremy Herb, "Schiller Tops List of High-Profile Witnesses Before House Russia Investigators," CNN.com, 11/1/17.

120. Carol D. Leonnig and Greg Miller, "Longtime Trump Bodyguard to Face Questions About 2013 Moscow Trip," *WaPo*, 11/3/17.

121. Manu Raju and Jeremy Herb, "Schiller Tops List of High-Profile Witnesses Before House Russia Investigators," CNN.com, 11/1/17.

122. "House Intel Committee Speeds Up on Trump Russia Investigation," *Rachel Maddow Show*, MSNBC, 11/3/17.

123. Jeff Pegues, "Source Who Is Being Examined by Special Counsel: 'It's Every Man for Himself,'" CBSNews .com, 11/3/17.

124–125. Deborah Barfield Berry, "Trump's Voter Fraud Commission Appears to Have Gone Dark," *USAT*, 11/3/17.

126. Kevin Robillard, "Bots Stoke Racial Strife in Virginia Governor's Race," *Politico*, 11/3/17.

127. Andy Newman and John Leland, "*DNAinfo* and *Gothamist* Are Shut Down After Vote to Unionize," *NYT*, 11/2/17.

128. Jennifer Valentine-DeVries, "Administration's Nominee for CIA Watchdog Allegedly Misled Congress," *ProPublica*, 11/1/17.

129. David Corn and AJ Vicens, "Hackers Compromised the Trump Organization 4 Years Ago—and the Company Never Noticed," *MJ*, 11/1/17.

131. Javier E. David, "Trump Pitches Saudi Aramco to List IPO Stock on the NYSE, Calling It 'Important' to the US,'" CNBC.com, 11/4/17.

132. Brent D. Griffiths, "Trump Visits Trump-Branded Hawaii Resort," *Politico*, 11/4/17.

133. Huileng Tan, "China: We're the World's 'New Role Model,' and Trump Needs to Prove He Can Be 'Constructive,'" CNBC.com, 11/3/17.

WEEK 52

1. Cleve R. Wootson Jr., "Trump, Who Urged People to 'Hire American,' Secures 70 Foreign Workers for Mar-a-Lago," *WaPo*, 11/5/17.

2–3. Ruth May, "GOP Campaigns Took $7.35 Million from Oligarch Linked to Russian," *Dallas Morning News*, 8/3/17.

4. David D. Kirkpatrick, "Saudi Arabia Arrests 11 Princes, Including Billionaire Alwaleed bin Talal," *NYT*, 11/4/17.

6–7. Petula Dvorak, "She Flipped Off President Trump—and Got Fired from Her Government Contracting Job," *WaPo*, 11/6/17.

8. Ryan J. Reilly, "Jeff Sessions' DOJ Drops Prosecution of Woman Who Laughed at Jeff Sessions," *HuffPost*, 11/7/17.

9. Darryl Fears, "Powerful Lawmaker Wants to 'Invalidate' the Endangered Species Act. He's Getting Close," *WaPo*, 11/5/17.

10. Darius Dixon and Eric Wolff, "Trump Coal Backer Wins Big Under Perry's Power Plan," *Politico*, 11/6/17.

11. Lisa Friedman, "Syria Joins Paris Climate Accord, Leaving Only U.S. Opposed," *NYT*, 11/7/17.

12. Juliet Eilperin, "EPA Proposes Reversing Stricter Pollution Rules for Heavy-Duty Trucks with Older Engines," *WaPo*, 11/9/17.

13. Gregg Re, "Final Round of Layoffs Planned at Carrier Plant Trump Promised to Save," FoxNews.com, 11/8/17.

14. Lindsay Gibbs, "Wisconsin GOP Lawmaker Says Women Should Be Forced to Give Birth to Grow the Labor Force," *ThinkProgress*, 11/4/17.

15. Joseph Tanfani, "Trump Administration Ending Protections for Thousands of Nicaraguan Migrants, and Defers Decision on Hondurans," *LAT*, 11/6/17.

16. Nick Miroff, "White House Chief of Staff Tried to Pressure Acting DHS Secretary to Expel Thousands of Hondurans, Officials Say," *WaPo*, 11/9/17.

17. Juliet Eilperin and Colby Itkowitz, "ACA Sign-ups Spike at Open Enrollment's Start," *WaPo*, 11/7/17.

18. Moriah Balingit and Danielle Douglas-Gabriel, "Inside Betsy DeVos's Efforts to Shrink the Education Department," *WaPo*, 11/8/17.

19. Carol Morello, "USAID Cancels Jobs for Dozens of Applicants amid State Department Hiring Freeze," *WaPo*, 11/4/17.

20. Bethany Allen-Ebrahimian, "Top U.S. Diplomat Blasts Trump Administration for 'Decapitation' of State Department Leadership," *FP*, 11/8/17.

21. Ibid.; Barbara Stephenson to American Foreign Service Association Members, "Time to Ask Why," December 2017, www.afsa.org/time -ask-why.

22. Chris Riotta, "Lara Trump Taking on White House Duties in Troubling and Unprecedented Move, Officials Say," *Newsweek*, 11/3/17.

23–24. Richard Engel and Aggelos Petropoulos, "Paradise Papers: Leaks Show Wilbur Ross Hid Ties to Putin Cronies," NBCNews.com, 11/5/17.

25. Harry Cockburn, "Trump Expected to Nominate Notorious Anti-Feminist

Penny Nance to Be Ambassador for Women," *Independent*, 11/8/17.

26. Josh Delk, "Eric Trump's Brother-in-Law Promoted at Department of Energy," *The Hill*, 11/8/17.

27. Michael Biesecker, "Senate Confirms Trump EPA Nominee with Oil Industry Ties," 11/9/17.

28. Alex Morrell, "The Feds Are Investigating Billionaire Carl Icahn's Role Advising the Trump Administration," *BI*, 11/8/17.

29. Betsy Woodruff, "Trump Installs Tax-Dodging Expert as the Head of the IRS," *DB*, 11/10/17.

30. David G. Savage, "Trump Judge Nominee, 36, Who Has Never Tried a Case, Wins Approval of Senate Panel," *LAT*, 11/10/17.

31. Seung Min Kim (@seungminkim), "NEW: A fourth Trump judicial nominee—Brett Talley in Alabama—has been deemed not qualified by American Bar Association www.americanbar.org/content/dam/aba/uncategorized/GAO/Web%20rating%20Chart%20Trump%20115.authcheckdam.pdf . . ." Twitter, 11/7/17, 2:50 p.m.

32. Rachel Bade, "Ryan Breaks Record for Shutting Down Floor Debate," *Politico*, 11/7/17.

33. Frances Robles, "Puerto Rico Deaths Spike, but Few Are Attributed to Hurricane," *NYT*, 11/8/17.

34. Allie Yang, "7 Weeks After Hurricane Maria, San Juan Is Still Without Power, Mayor Says," ABCNews.com, 11/8/17.

35. Greg Allen and Marisa Peñaloza, "Frustration Mounts over Puerto Rico's 'New Norman' as Federal Troops Leave the Island," *All Things Considered*, NPR, 11/9/17.

36. David Begnaud (@DavidBegnaud), "'We're out of the crisis,' says 3 star Army General Jeffrey Buchanan who's announced today that he's leaving next week. Buchanan has coordinated the federal military response in Puerto Rico following Hurricane Maria" Twitter, 11/10/17, 1:40 p.m.

37. Marc Fisher, "Democrats Send Trump and Trumpism a Firm Message with Election Night Thrashing," *WaPo*, 11/7/17; Fenit Nirappil, "Democrat Concedes Virginia House Race; Three Others Will Decide if GOP Holds Majority," *WaPo*, 11/9/17.

38. Courtney Connley, "Meet the 15 People Who Made History in the 2017 Election," CNBC.com, 11/8/17.

39. Mary Jordan, Karen Tumulty, and Michael Alison Chandler, "Women Racked Up Victories Across the Country Tuesday. It May Be Only the Beginning," *WaPo*, 11/8/17.

40. Maggie Astor, "Danica Roem Wins Virginia Race, Breaking a Barrier for Transgender People," *NYT*, 11/7/17.

41. AP, "New Jersey Politicians Who Joked About Women's March Defeated," *PBS NewsHour*, 11/8/17.

42. Christina Wilkie, "House Republicans' Exodus Continues. Here's a Tally of All the Members Retiring, and Why," CNBC.com, 11/9/17 (updated 11/13/17).

43. Dan Corey, "Since Weinstein, Here's a Growing List of Men Accused of Sexual Misconduct," NBCNews.com, updated 12/15/17.

44. Veronica Rocha, Amanda Wills, and Meg Wagner, "A Conversation About #MeToo," CNN.com, 11/9/17.

45. Kathryn Watson, "Senate Passes Resolution Requiring Mandatory Harassment Training," CBSNews.com, 11/9/17.

46. Stephanie McCrummen, Beth Reinhard, and Alice Crites, "Woman Says Roy Moore Initiated Sexual Encounter When She Was 14, He Was 32," *WaPo*, 11/9/17.

47–48. Mark Maremont and Rob Barry, "Russian Twitter Support for Trump Began Right After He Started Campaign," *WSJ*, 11/6/17.

49–50. Jesse Drucker, "Kremlin Cash Behind Billionaire's Twitter and Facebook Investments," *NYT*, 11/5/17.

51–52. Julia Ainsley, Carol E. Lee, and Ken Dilanian, "Mueller Has Enough Evidence to Bring Charges in Flynn Investigation," NBCNews.com, 11/5/17.

53. Jim Sciutto and Marshall Cohen, "Flynn Worries About Son in Special Counsel Probe," CNN.com, 11/9/17.

54. Julia Manchester, "Graham: Sessions Needs to Tell Us Everything He Knows About Russia," *The Hill*, 11/5/17.

55. Warren Strobel and Sarah N. Lynch, "U.S. Attorney General Due to Face Democrats' Russia Questions Next Week," *YN*, 11/6/17.

56–57. Rosalind S. Helderman, Tom Hamburger, and Carol D. Leonnig, "At Least Nine People in Trump's Orbit Had Contact with Russians During Campaign and Transition," *WaPo*, 11/5/17.

58. Kyle Cheney and Randy Lemmerman, "Carter Page Testimony Highlights: Trump Aide Dismisses Russian Interference," *Politico*, 11/6/17.

59. Ibid.; Manu Raju, Jeremy Herb, and Katelyn Polantz, "Carter Page Reveals New Contacts with Trump Campaign, Russians," CNN.com, 11/8/17.

60. Manu Raju, Jeremy Herb, and Katelyn Polantz, "Carter Page Reveals New Contacts with Trump Campaign, Russians," CNN.com, 11/8/17.

61. Kyle Cheney and Randy Lemmerman, "Carter Page Testimony Highlights: Trump Aide Dismisses Russian Interference," *Politico*, 11/6/17.

62. Ken Dilanian, Julia Ainsley, Alex Moe, and Kasie Hunt, "Carter Page Coordinated Russia Trip with Top Trump Campaign Officials," NBCNews.com, 11/7/17.

63–64. Natasha Bertrand, "Carter Page's Testimony Is Filled with Bombshells—and Supports Key Portions of the Steele Dossier," *BI*, 11/6/17.

65. Manu Raju, Jeremy Herb, and Katelyn Polantz, "Carter Page Reveals New Contacts with Trump Campaign, Russians," CNN.com, 11/8/17.

66. Kyle Cheney and Randy Lemmerman, "Carter Page Testimony Highlights: Trump Aide Dismisses Russian Interference," *Politico*, 11/6/17.

67–68. Manu Raju, Jeremy Herb, and Katelyn Polantz, "Carter Page Reveals New Contacts with Trump Campaign, Russians," CNN.com, 11/8/17.

69. Kyle Cheney and Randy Lemmerman, "Carter Page Testimony Highlights: Trump Aide Dismisses Russian Interference," *Politico*, 11/6/17.

70. Irina Reznik and Henry Meyer, "Trump Jr. Hinted at Review of Anti-Russia Law, Moscow Lawyer Says," Bloomberg.com, 11/6/17.

71–72. Duncan Campbell and James Risen, "CIA Director Met Advocate of Disputed DNC Hack Theory—at Trump's Request," *The Intercept*, 11/7/17.

73. Ken Dilanian, "NSA Critic Bill Binney Says Trump Pushed Meeting with CIA's Pompeo," NBCNews.com, 11/7/17.

74. Spencer S. Hsu, "U.S. Judge Issues Gag Order in Manafort-Gates Russia Probe Case," *WaPo*, 11/8/17.

75. Tim Lister and Nic Robertson, "Academic at Heart of Clinton 'Dirt' Claim Vanishes, Leaving Trail of Questions," CNN.com, 11/10/17.

76–77. Josh Meyer, "Russia Investigators Probe 2016 GOP Platform Fight," *Politico*, 11/8/17.

78–79. Ryan Nakashima and Barbara Ortutay, "AP Exclusive: Russia Twitter Trolls Deflected Trump Bad News," AP, 11/10/17.

80–81. Pamela Brown, Gloria Borger, and Evan Perez, "Mueller Interviews Top White House Aide," CNN.com, 11/9/17.

82–83. Natasha Bertrand, "Trump Associates Are Getting Buried in Massive Legal Fees, and Roger Stone Says His Are More than $450,000," *BI*, 9/9/17.

84. "Washington Orders RT America to Register as Foreign Agent by Monday," RT.com, 11/9/17.

85–87. Rebecca Ballhaus and Julie Bykowicz, "Data Firm's WikiLeaks Outreach Came as It Joined Trump Campaign," *WSJ*, 11/10/17.

88. Brian Ross, Rhonda Schwartz, and Matthew Mosk, "Trump Adviser Claims He Lied to FBI Out of Loyalty to Trump: Source," ABCNews.com, 11/10/17.

89. Natasha Bertrand, "Devin Nunes Attended a Breakfast with Michael Flynn and Turkey's Foreign Minister Just Before the Inauguration," *BI*, 11/10/17.

90–91. Julia Ainsley, "Mueller Probing Pre-election Flynn Meeting with Pro-Russia Congressman," NBCNews .com, 11/10/17.

92–96. Sharon LaFraniere, David D. Kirkpatrick, Andrew Higgins, and Michael Schwirtz, "A London Meeting of an Unlikely Group: How a Trump Adviser Came to Learn of Clinton 'Dirt,'" *NYT*, 11/10/17.

97–99. Carol E. Lee and Julia Ainsley, "Mueller Probing Possible Deal Between Turks, Flynn During Presidential Transition," NBCNews .com, 11/10/17.

100. Mark Hosenball and John Walcott, "Investigators Probe Trump Knowledge of Campaign's Russia Dealings: Sources," Reuters, 11/11/17.

101–102. Dan Balz and Scott Clement, "Poll: Trump's Performance Lags Behind Even Tepid Public Expectations," *WaPo*, 11/5/17.

103. Max Greenwood, "Steyer to Spend Another $10 Million on Campaign to Impeach Trump," *The Hill*, 11/9/17.

104–105. David Folkenflik, "DOJ Set to Block AT&T Takeover of Time Warner," *The Two-Way* (blog), NPR, 11/8/17.

106. CNBC Now (@CNBCnow), "AT&T CEO: 'I have never been told that the price of getting the [Time Warner] deal done was selling CNN', never offered to sell it either http://cnb .cx/2zpJy5R" Twitter, 11/9/17, 10:29 a.m.

107. Jessica Toonkel, "Exclusive: Rupert Murdoch Twice Discussed CNN with AT&T CEO—Sources," Reuters, 11/10/17.

108–109. Josh Gerstein, "Judge Again Dismisses Clinton Email Suits," *Politico*, 11/10/17.

110. Stephen Dinan, "Corker to Hold Hearing on Trump's Ability to Use Nuclear Weapons," *Washington Times*, 11/8/17.

111. Carrie Dann, "NBC/*WSJ* Poll: In 'Trump Counties,' More Say U.S. Is Worse Off than Better Off," NBCNews .com, 11/7/17.

112. David Nakamura and Ashley Parker, "In Beijing, Trump Declines to Hit President Xi Jinping on Trade: 'I Don't Blame China,'" *WaPo*, 11/9/17.

113. Ibid.; Joanna Walters, "Trump's 'No Questions' Press Conference in China Slammed by Former Media Staff," *Guardian*, 11/9/17.

114. David Nakamura and Ashley Parker, "In Beijing, Trump Declines to Hit President Xi Jinping on Trade: 'I Don't Blame China,'" *WaPo*, 11/9/17.

115. Ali Vitali, "Trump, Putin Will Not Have Formal Meeting in Vietnam," NBCNews.com, 11/10/17.

116. Andrew Restuccia and Nancy Cook, "Trump Careens off Script on Russia After Putin Meeting," *Politico*, 11/12/17.

117–118. Julie Hirschfeld Davis, "Trump Says Putin 'Means It' About Not Meddling," *NYT*, 11/11/17.

119. Andrew Restuccia and Nancy Cook, "Trump Careens off Script on Russia After Putin Meeting," *Politico*, 11/12/17.

120. Kevin Liptak and Dan Merica, "Trump Says He Believes Putin's Election Meddling Denials," CNN.com, 11/14/17.

121. Daniel Politi, "Trump Says He Believes Putin's Denial of Meddling in U.S. Election," *The Slatest*, 11/11/17.

INDEX

Note: Page numbers in *italics* refer to illustrations.

abortion policies, 29, 196, 358, 362, 375
Access Hollywood tape, 288, 334, 396
Affordable Care Act (ACA). *See under* health care legislation
Afghanistan, 99, 178, 230, 241, 260, 269
Agalarov, Aras, 201, 202, 210, 220, 286
Agalarov, Emin, 200, 201, 202, 210
Alfa Bank, 90, 148, 166, 219, 271, 332
"alternative facts" statement, 28
American Health Care Act (AHCA). *See under* health care legislation
American Manufacturing Council, 248
approval/favorability ratings
  declines in, 23, 25, 46, 73, 82, 88, 124, 160, 164, 172, 207, 217, 232, 247, 257, 276, 312, 334, 342, 365, 373
  gender gap in, 262
  job approval rating, 106
Arpaio, Joe, 248, 261, 266, 267, 270, 280, 291, 329, 348
Assange, Julian, 18, 64, 103, 201, 254, 285, 300, 342, 366, 396
Australia, 35, 149, 234, 235, 252

Bannon, Steve
  and Cambridge Analytica, 397
  on Christie, 288
  and Comey firing, 277
  compensation for *Breitbart* work, 7
  and DACA program, 283
  on "deep state," 64
  defense of Trump, 249, 250
  disparagement of media, 31, 52
  ethics waiver of, 153, 165
  and European Union, 65
  and Facebook, 317
  financial disclosures of, 198
  firing of, 255–56
  and foreign policy, 32
  and Gorka, 117
  and Jordan's King Abdullah II, 298
  and Kushner, 92
  and McConnell, 349
  and McMaster, 230
  on media as "opposition party," 31
  and Mercer, 68
  money earned by, 81
  and Mueller investigation, 377
  and Page, 395
  private e-mail used by, 316
  and seat at National Security Council, 32, 38, 47, 91
  and Twenty-fifth Amendment, 338
  and Venezuela, 101
  and weaponizing of data sets, 120
Bharara, Preet, 65, 73, 75, 77, 109, 117, 124, 125, 163, 174, 204, 299
Black Lives Matter movement, 171, 253, 318
Boeing, 10, 15, 44, 51, 98, 173, 270
Boston, rally and counterprotests in, 256, 257
"Bowling Green massacre," 36, 41
Boy Scouts, 27, 217, 222, 232
Breitbart, 7, 14, 15, 61, 64, 89, 103
Brennan, John, 24, 77, 83, 91, 95, 215, 250, 263, 358
Brexit, 120, 161, 234, 340, 367
Britain. *See* United Kingdom
Burr, Richard, 54, 85, 108, 127, 141, 142, 166, 213, 223, 296, 316, 331, 332, 350
"Buy American" mandate, 67, 173

cabinet of Trump
  Bible lessons attended by, 226
  confirmations of, 26
  and ethics reviews of nominees, 20
  generals appointed to, 11
  Goldman Sachs execs in, 9
  lack of diversity in, 14, 24
  McConnell's wife appointed to, 11
  praising of Trump, 164
  residing in Trump Hotel, 62
  wealthy membership of, 173
California's wildfires, 345, 346
Cambridge Analytica, 120, 233–34, 296, 330, 340, 351, 366, 396–97
campaign promises, 70, 98, 101, 256
Canada, 51, 182, 226, 238, 281
Carrier Corporation, 9–10, 144, 191, 198, 389
Celebrity Apprentice, 10, 17, 19, 35, 42, 59
Central Intelligence Agency (CIA)
  and British intelligence on Russia, 95
  and Flynn, 73
  information withheld from Trump, 45
  on Russian interference with election, 11, 12, 13, 19, 91, 353
  and Russian ties with Trump team, 91
  and Steele dossier, 332
  and Syrian rebel program, 211
  Trump's intent to downsize, 19
  Trump's relationship with, 28–29
  and WikiLeaks data dump, 64, 106
Charlottesville rally and protests, 190, 245, *246*, 246–53, 255, 257, 259, 263, 265, 267, 268, 290, 291
Children's Health Insurance Program (CHIP), 324
China
  activists arrested in, 151
  and business dealings of Trump family, 45, 56, 67, 74, 80, 98, 101, 120, 151, 157, 165, 181, 291
  and G20 Summit, 193
  global influence of, 364
  "One China" policy, 41, 45, 56, 365
  and Trump's conversations with Taiwan, 10
Clapper, James, 21, 61, 122–23, 131, 152, 160, 261, 311

climate change
and Paris climate agreement, 30, 153, 154, 157, 304, 364, 388
removed from WH website, 26, 121
and Tillerson's e-mail alias, 67
and Trump's EPA, 11, 347, 348, 363
climate science/scientists, 13, 112, 257–58, 304
Clinton, Hillary
and Clinton Foundation, 9
and "Crooked Hillary" emoji, 14
and email controversy, 12, 14, 17, 124, 146, 233
and email hacked by Russians, 185, 192, 200–201, 204, 351, 366, 385, 397
and "Lock her up!" chants, 9, 233
and Putin, 15, 19
RNC's pursuit of dirt on, 78
and Russian interference with election, 76
and Uranium One sale, 364, 377
violent GIF depicting, 301
and weaponizing of data sets, 152
CNN
attacks on, 7, 34
called "fake news," 21, 42
and CNN/Trump wrestling video, 187–88
Kushner's discussions with Time Warner about, 47
Lord fired by, 238
and retraction request, 26
Cobb, Ty, 205, 233, 307, 332
Cohen, Michael
and congressional hearings, 152, 307, 352, 366
and Mueller investigation, 168, 332
and peace plan/sanctions deal, 49, 62
and real estate transactions, 372
and Russian ties with Trump team, 272
and Steele dossier, 109
and Trump Tower plans in Moscow, 271–72
Comey, James
Americans' belief of, 176
and attack ads, 159
and Clinton email investigation, 14, 17, 124, 125, 146, 277, 354
and congressional hearings, 60, 125, 154, 160–61, 162, 185
firing of, 123, 124, 125, 128, 130, 133, 137, 138–39, 146, 155, 276–77, 308, 378
and Flynn investigation, 133, 154, 159, 160
investigated by Justice Dept., 22
and investigations of Trump, 74, 127, 137, 139, 159
memos recorded by, 133, 137, 147, 160, 161, 185, 200
and mental health of Trump, 126
and Mueller investigation, 155, 234, 274, 276, 286, 308–9, 351, 378
and Page's meetings with Russians, 58
and Russia investigation, 74, 125, 126, 160
and Russian interference with election, 86–87, 161
Sanders on, 297
and Steele dossier, 21, 109, 160
and "tapes" threat of Trump, 127, 130, 160, 162, 174, 176
unwillingness to brief Congress, 22
and wiretapping claims, 61, 74, 119, 125
Confederate statues, 130, 245, 252, 314
conflicts of interest
and hunting trip with Trump, 15
and Ivanka's coffee date auction, 13
media's coverage of, 5
and Office of Government Ethics, 21, 24
postponement of press conference on, 12
Trump's comments on, 7, 11, 21
volume of, 5, 32
Conway, Kellyanne
on addressing Trump, 226
"alternative facts" statement, 28
and "Bowling Green massacre," 36, 41
brand endorsement by, 40, 45, 56, 74
on bypassing African American Museum, 24
on camera-capabilities of microwaves, 67
and ethics concerns, 45, 56, 64
husband's position with WH, 72
and leaks from inside White House, 237
misconduct complaint filed against, 53
and Mueller, 163
on nepotism rules, 13
on tax returns, 28
on transition tensions, 13
and travel costs, 329
on Trump's D.C. hotel, 182
and tweets from Russian troll farm, 352
on voter fraud, 8
Cummings, Elijah, 25, 66, 102, 108, 135, 137, 141, 316, 319, 327, 329, 348, 363

data sets, weaponizing of, 120, 152
Deep Root Analytics, 175
Deep State, 60, 64, 65, 68, 74, 129, 163, 243
Democratic National Committee (DNC)
cyberattacks on, 19, 61, 85, 109, 254
emails leaked by WikiLeaks, 24, 58, 96, 230, 285
and Kaspersky antivirus, 192
Department of Homeland Security (DHS)
H-2B visas issued by, 208
and Muslim ban, 32, 52, 227
and new immigration requirements, 313
on radicalization of extremists, 59
and Twitter lawsuit, 89
Victims of Immigration Crime Engagement (VOICE), 48
Deripaska, Oleg, 82, 131, 148, 273, 274, 309, 333, 341, 352, 387
Deutsche Bank, 75, 146, 159, 169, 179, 183, 212, 214, 220, 299
DeVos, Betsy, 43, 97, 106, 143, 189, 197, 227, 281, 303, 361, 375, 389
Director of National Intelligence (DNI), 19, 45, 141
"drain the swamp" campaign promise, 15, 88

economy and economic policies, 54, 112, 130, 333
Election Integrity Commission, 122, 183, 187, 198, 207, 217, 259, 269, 282, 293, 325, 363, 386
elections of 2016
commission reviewing popular vote, 122
and Electoral College vote, 14, 19, 111–12, 138
and fake Facebook accounts, 111
and FBI actions leading up to, 22
and illegal campaign contributions, 23
impact on schools and children, 7
leaks and exposures of voter data, 184, 193, 384–85
and Mercer family, 234
and popular vote, 29, 207, 237
recounts blocked, 8, 12
and voter data request, 183, 186–87, 325
and voter fraud, 7, 8, 29, 30, 33, 39, 41, 352
voting irregularities in, 193, 270
and voting machine malfunctions, 96
See also Russian interference with 2016 elections
elections of 2017, 391–92
empathy, Trump's lack of, 48, 276, 326
Environmental Protection Agency (EPA)
advisory board policies of, 375
and Clean Power Plan repeal, 334, 336
and climate science, 11, 112, 347, 348, 363
departures from, 121–22, 240, 280
and grants freeze, 29
and Houston's Superfund site, 279
and political reviews of scientific studies, 30
reversing Obama-era regulations, 388
Erdogan, Recep Tayyip, 86, 105, 113, 128, 133, 140, 148, 166, 276, 302
executive branch
consolidation of power at, 60, 92, 96, 113, 218
departures from, 59, 240, 315, 320
and ethics waivers, 101, 114, 140, 153, 165, 190–91, 239, 292
friends/family given positions in, 44, 52, 72, 74, 165
gender pay gap in, 189
Goldman Sachs execs in, 71
and hiring freeze, 97
internal "spies" installed in, 74, 88, 115
leaks from inside, 223, 235, 237
lobbyists appointed to, 101, 153
and one-hundred-day mark, 107, 111, 112, 113
paranoia and dysfunction in, 68
reorganization of, 68
staffers quietly installed in, 275
unfilled positions in, 26, 38, 42, 48, 52, 60, 63, 74, 92, 105, 107, 113, 143, 157, 169–70, 239, 275
Exxon, 11, 25, 42, 62–63, 75, 104, 148, 209

Facebook
and ads purchased by Russia, 142, 310, 317, 318, 330, 367, 383–84
and DoJ's demand for user data, 313
and Mueller investigation, 284, 295–96
policy-related posts on, 12
and Russian interference with election, 111, 142, 283–84, 295–96, 310, 317, 330
Russian investments in, 392–93
and Trump campaign, 342
and weaponizing of data sets from, 120
"fake news," 6, 10, 21, 42, 103, 152, 184, 318, 365
Federal Bureau of Investigation (FBI)
and Comey letter, 14, 17
and Comey's Trump memos, 141
concerns about a cabal in, 22
and Farage, 154
and Flynn investigation, 73, 78, 84, 124, 133, 154, 168, 171
investigated by Justice Dept., 22
and investigation of Clinton's emails, 14
investigations of Trump appointees, 78
and Kushner, 139, 146
and leaks to Nunes, 83
and loyalty demands of Trump, 127, 131
and Manafort investigation, 78, 134, 168, 307, 322
and Page, 168
pressured by Trump, 382
and requests for refutation of Trump-Russia ties, 53
and Russia inquiries, 123
and Russian dossier on Trump, 21, 55
on Russian interference with election, 13, 19, 103, 125, 126
on Russian money transfers, 25
and Russian visa requests, 176
and Russia-Trump investigation, 125, 126, 127, 128, 136, 147
search warrants made public, 14
and Sputnik (news outlet), 294
and Steele dossier, 332
See also Mueller investigation
financial disclosures of Trump, 140, 169
First Amendment rights, 5, 8, 337, 364
Flake, Jeff, 239, 252, 261, 370–71, 378
Flynn, Michael
and back-channel plan for Ukraine, 49
background check of, 109
blackmail vulnerability of, 122
classified information shared by, 13
and Clinton's deleted emails, 185, 264, 351
and Comey letter, 17
and congressional hearings, 73
consulting firm of, 213
and criminal investigations, 136
evidence of criminal acts, 108
FBI investigation of, 47, 73, 78, 84, 124, 133, 154, 159, 160, 168, 171
financial disclosures of, 234, 235
foreign agent work of, 65, 108, 135, 297

Flynn, Michael (*continued*)
and Gulen extradition, 66, 75
and immunity requests, 84, 124
income from Russian interests, 68, 90, 108, 141
and Jordan's King Abdullah II, 298–99
and Kislyak's meetings, 58, 118, 136, 147, 174, 181
legal defense funds of, 306
as means of Russian influence, 139, 146
and Mueller investigation, 155, 233, 235, 264, 308, 321, 351, 393, 397, 398
and neo-Nazis, 15
and Nunes, 397
and peace plan/sanctions deal, 49
and Pence, 41, 135, 138, 141
and Putin, 103
and Raqqa operation, 136
resignation of, 43
Russian support of, 24
and Russian-TV payment, 43
and sanctions on Russia, 22, 41
security clearance of, 109, 123, 141, 171, 174
as security risk, 172
and Smith, 350–51
subpoenaed, 124, 136, 141
Trump questioned about, 87
Trump's 3 am call to, 39
Trump's defense of, 43
and WH cover-up, 108
Yates's warnings about, 122–23, 127
France, 103, 106, 113, 119, 149, 190, 203, 237

Germany, 73, 80, 98, 113, 134, 144, 193
Giuliani, Rudy, 12, 17, 22, 25, 33, 69, 85–86, 127, 143, 216, 368, 398
global standing of U.S., 43, 182, 208, 226, 288, 300, 302
golden showers, 21
Goldman Sachs, 9, 11, 18, 22, 54, 71, 120
Goldstone, Roger, 200, 201, 205
golfing of Trump, 100, 102, 130, 163, 188, 190, 207, 216, 323, 334, 345
Google, 319, 339
Gorka, Sebastian, 70, 91, 99, 117, 204, 237, 244, 266, 346, 364
Gorkov, Sergey, 80, 152, 154, 157, 180, 274, 352
Gorsuch, Neil, 39, 255, 304, 315, 375
Grassley, Senator, 151, 183, 205, 217, 241, 273, 285, 298, 332, 340, 392
G20 Summit, 185, 193–95, 210, 211, 212
gun violence, 179, 324

hate crimes/acts
anti-LGBTQ violence, 248
attack at Republican baseball game, 167
funding pulled from victims of, 178
Kansas bar shooting, 53–54
mosque attacks, 55, 237
against Muslim Americans, 145, 150, 170
Portland attack, 145, 150
Senate resolution condemning, 290–91
surges in, 5, 7, 89
and threats against Jews, 35
unacknowledged by Trump, 8
health care legislation
AHCA disparaged by Trump, 169, 181
attempts to repeal Obamacare/ ACA, 50, 79, 186, 209, 210, 224, 233, 258, 269, 282, 304, 315
attempts to sabotage Obamacare/ACA, 215, 229, 238, 257, 268, 305, 328, 344, 349
and birth control mandate, 325
CBO scoring on AHCA, 144, 145
and executive order, 339, 344
failure to pass AHCA, 181
and female senators, 223
frustration of Trump with, 225
House votes on AHCA, 97, 112, 119
McConnell's efforts with AHCA, 169, 171, *177*, 177, 243, 262
and open enrollment for Obamacare, 314, 374
and popular support for Obamacare, 345
and premium increases, 238, 314, 344
and rate of uninsured Americans, 353
roll out of AHCA, 177
Senate votes on AHCA, 151, 221, 305
unpopularity of AHCA, 181
Hicks, Hope, 253, 286, 287, 351, 394
Holocaust statement by Trump, 31, 36
House Intelligence Committee
and calls for Nunes removal, 78
and Cohen, 366
on cyberattacks, 173
and Flynn, 73
and hacked voter databases, 175
and Kushner, 214, 220
and Manafort, 212
and Nunes's surveillance claims, 77
and Page, 393–94
and Russian/Trump regime collusion probe, 74, 76, 96, 103
and Sessions, 393
and Steele dossier, 273
and Twitter executives, 318
and "unmasking" subpoenas, 152, 159
See also Nunes, Devin
House Judiciary Committee, 33, 393
House Oversight Committee, 34, 43, 78, 176
Hurricane Harvey, 265–66, 267, 268, 270, 277, 278–79, 280, 293
Hurricane Irma, 280, 287, 288, 289
Hurricane Maria, 311–12, *323*, 326, 334, 343–44

Icahn, Carl, 86, 121, 143, 255, 265, 390
immigrants
arrests of noncriminals, 50, 72, 99, 104, 110, 121, 313
and DACA program, 179, 259, 283, 290
deaths of, 134
and demands for proof of citizenship, 116
and Dreamers, 104, 167, 206, 283
hotline to report, 110
negative portrayals of, 46

immigrants (*continued*)
and office for victims of immigrant crime, 48
poor treatment of, 79
and preference for Christian refugees, 31, 32, 197
round ups and deportations of, 44, 47, 50–51, 59, 72, 79, 81, 90, 99, 116, 121, 134, 151, 157, 167, 216, 280, 313
and sanctuary cities, 110, 150, 170, 268, 290
targeted in budget, 145
and Trump businesses, 104
See also Muslim ban
Immigration and Customs Enforcement (ICE), 44, 48, 50, 59, 72, 79, 81, 90, 99, 104, 110, 122, 134, 150, 151, 157, 167, 206, 216, 224, 227, 268, 269, 280, 281, 290, 313, 326
immigration policy
cases used to justify, 117
effects of, 65, 81, 82
and farmworker shortages, 240
and fast-tracked deportations, 303
information fed to media on, 57
new enforcement policies, 50
and RAISE Act, 231
targeting undocumented parents, 189
and VOICE program, 48, 110, 145
See also Muslim ban
impeachment
articles of impeachment introduced, 203, 251
considered a realistic outcome, 377
dire warnings about, 264, 268
growing support for, 36, 89, 132, 138, 154, 162, 188, 207, 259, 346, 383, 398
and obstruction of justice charges, 342
predictions of, 97
inauguration
boycotts of, 22, 25
and campaign promises, 70
corporate donations to, 102, 117, 121, 184, 189, 266
entertainment for, 15, 26
foreign business partners of Trump at, 30
funds raised for, 101, 102, 111, 300
lies regarding, 21, 28, 30
low attendance of, 26, 28, 116
and media, 25, 28
and Obama's inauguration, 28, 116
and protesters, 313
reality-TV producer's management of, 12
Russian donations to, 387
and shows of military force, 25
InfoWars, 39, 62, 74, 103, 143
intelligence agencies
and British intelligence on Russia, 95
disparaged by Trump, 18, 20, 22, 43, 194, 400
and email of intelligence officer hacked, 205
information withheld from Trump, 45
and Kushner's attempts to evade, 147
on Russian blackmail dossier, 21
on Russian interference with election, 9, 13, 18, 19
on Russian leaks of emails to WikiLeaks, 24
on Russian money transfers, 25
and Russia-Trump collusion, 141–42
Trump's intent to downsize, 19
Trump's relationship with, 28–29, 43
See also specific agencies
Iran, 105, 214, 218, 244, 302, 317, 334, 344, 345, 365
Iraq, 30, 79, 82, 89
ISIS, classified intel leaked, 131–32, 134
Israel, 132, 140, 337–38

Jewish population
and anti-Semitism, 17, 40, 45, 46, 50, 55, 64, 70, 89, 99, 110, 178, 252, 258–59, 361
and Le Pen candidacy (France), 40
and statement on Holocaust Memorial Day, 31, 36, 99
targeted by *Breitbart*, 15
threats against, 35
job creation claims of Trump, 9, 16, 18, 20, 25, 66, 79, 81, 153, 169
jobs reports, 66, 67, 88, 153
judicial nominees, 305, 337, 375, 390–91
June 9 meeting
and grand jury subpoenas, 233
and Kushner, 294
and Manafort, 200, 210, 220, 221, 241, 274
and Mueller investigation, 273, 308, 309
people present for, 205, 307
and promise of damaging information, 200, 219
and Russian adoption claim, 200, 228, 286
and Russian agent, 350, 368
and Russian intelligence, 221
and Trump, Jr., 228
Trump's role in statement about, 210, 228, 273, 286

Kasowitz, Marc, 85, 145, 161, 163, 168, 184, 189, 202, 212, 334, 368
Kaspersky Lab, 192, 298, 331, 340
Kaveladze, Irakly "Ike," 210, 220, 307, 386
Kelly, John
and Assange, 300
and chief of staff appointment, 225
and Cohn, 288
and death of son, 349
defense of Trump, 356
at Department of Homeland Security, 46, 51, 213, 227
frustrations of, 46, 277, 338
influence of, 260, 333
on Mexico, 293
and nuclear strike contingency plans, 338
and Phoenix speech, 275
and Russian interference with election, 213
and Wilson attack, 356–57, 361, 378
King, Stephen, 27, 65, 72, 104, 156, 197
Kislyak, Sergey
and back-channels communication, 147
and Flynn, 58, 118, 136, 147, 174, 181, 309
and Kushner, 58, 80, 147, 154, 181, 274
and Mueller investigation, 309
and post-meeting security concerns, 142
recalled by Kremlin, 181

Kislyak, Sergey (*continued*)
and Sessions, 58, 146, 181, 214
Trump's meetings with, 62, 124–25, *128*, 131–32, 140, 308
Kobach, Kris, 122, 183, 187, 207, 217, 227, 269, 282, 293, 326
Ku Klux Klan, 156, 190, 247, 281
Kushner, Jared
authority of, 80
and back-channels communication, 147
and Bannon, 92
business affairs of, 67, 74, 80, 120, 199
and Cambridge Analytica, 340
and Comey firing, 378
concerns about vulnerability of, 154
and congressional hearings, 161, 214, 219–20
and consolidation of power, 92
counsel hired by, 171, 180, 205, 352
and Deutsche Bank, 220
discussions with Time Warner about CNN, 47
disparaged by Trump, 378
ethics complaint against, 191
and Farage meeting, 64
FBI investigation of, 146
financial disclosures of, 115, 191, 204, 214, 328
and foreign policy, 32
and Gorkov, 80, 152, 154, 157, 274, 352
Iraq trip of, 89
and Jordan's King Abdullah II, 298
and Kislyak, 58, 80, 147, 154, 181, 274
loans of, 154, 157, 179, 199, 214, 220, 274, 374
in meetings with heads of state, 7
meetings with Russians, 91, 152
and Mueller investigation, 168, 287
as "person of interest," 139, 146
private e-mail used by, 316, 327, 363, 386
resignation of, 294
and Russian access to Clinton emails, 200, 201
and Russian ambassador, 58
and Saudi Arabia trip, 374, 388
and Saudi weapons deal, 138
security clearance of, 174, 242
as shadow Secretary of State, 46, 89, 218
and targeted social media, 296
in Trump administration, 11, 13, 20
and Veselnitskaya meeting, 200, 206, 210, 221

Las Vegas mass shooting, 324
Lavrov, Sergey, 124–25, *128*, 131–32, 134, 140, 142, 195, 244, 308, 322
Leviev, Lev, 220
Lewandowski, Corey, 9, 117, 145, 228, 310, 352, 377, 394
LGBTQ issues
and anti-LGBTQ violence, 248
and census data, 171
Clovis on, 259
and DeVos, 143
and discriminatory laws/policies, 178, 222–23, 314, 325, 326
and elections of 2017, 391
and Ivanka, 154
and Pence, 346
program funding pulled from, 258
removed from Homelessness Council website, 51
removed from State website, 29
removed from WH website, 26
and rollback of protections, 150
and Session's speech to LGBT hate group, 197
and transgender military ban, 222, 226, 238, 241, 244, 266, 325, 342, 374
and UN resolution, 325
and U.S. Census, 81
lies and false statements
about Boy Scout Jamboree speech, 222, 232
about calls to families of soldiers, 349
about Chicago's crime rate, 29
about Comey, 160
about crime in UK, 358
about diplomatic mission reductions in Russia, 243
about Electoral College vote, 14
about Finland's jet purchases, 270
about immigrants, 222
about inauguration, 21, 28, 30
about Obama's immigration policies, 35
about Philippine anti-terrorism, 252
about Podesta, 194
about Russian adoption, 200, 201, 211, 228
about terrorist attacks, 48, 62, 153
about voter fraud, 8, 29, 30
about wiretapping, 60, 61, 64
in AP interview, 109
and credibility issues, 112, 134, 147, 398
in immigration policy speech, 231
media's response to, 18, 66, 78, 87
media's tracking/cataloging of, 173, 182
in Q&A session, 349
and Russia hearings, 74
from staff members, 29, 44
in State of the Union addresses, 57, 261
Time magazine cover, 182
volume and regularity of, 52, 88, 106, 138, 173, 240, 264, 342
Lockheed, 13–14, 15, 44, 138

Macron, Emmanuel, 113, 119, 149, 190, 195
Manafort, Paul
China-related business dealings, 102
and Comey's probe, 126
and congressional hearings, 212, 215, 220, 240, 241
counsel hired by, 168, 241
and criminal investigations, 136, 395
and Deripaska, 148, 273, 309, 333, 341, 352
FBI investigation of, 78, 134, 168
FBI raid of home, 241
and foreign agent registration, 95, 180
and income from Ukrainian political party, 209
and June 9 meeting, 200, 210, 221, 241, 274
and legal expenses, 309
loans of, 209, 212, 341
as means of Russian influence, 146
and money-laundering investigations, 212, 367, 376

Manafort, Paul (*continued*)
  and Mueller investigation, 155, 264, 273, 308, 321–22, 376
  and off-the-book payments, 95
  and Russian access to Clinton emails, 200, 201
  Russian ties of, 52, 76, 82, 95, 131
  surveillance of, 307, 308
Mar-a-Lago
  events canceled, 251, 259
  New Year's celebration at, 16
  promoted by federal agencies, 107
  revenue from, 169
  taxpayers footing bill for, 54, 98, 292
  Trump's weekends at, 60
  and visas for workers, 387
  visitor logs of, 208, 292, 329
Mattis, James
  on commitments to allies, 279–80
  influence of, 260, 333
  and Iran nuclear deal, 334, 345
  and Jordan's King Abdullah II, 299
  and journalists, 184, 255, 280
  message to troops, 267
  on North Korea, 268
  and nuclear strike contingency plans, 338
  phone number published, 131
  and transgender troops, 179, 222, 266, 268, 300, 342
  on USS *Carl Vinson*, 105
McCabe, Andrew, 126, 127, 136, 159, 174, 183, 216, 234, 241
McCain, John
  and Australia, 35, 149
  and campaign donations from Russians, 387
  and health care bills, 224, 305
  on nationalism, 353
  on Niger military ambush, 356
  and Paul, 68
  and Russian interference with election, 17, 18
  on Russian sanctions, 31, 114
  on Russian threat, 151
  and Steele, 109
  and Syrian rebel program, 211
  and Trump's ties to Russia, 73
McConnell, Mitch
  and AHCA, 169, 171, *177*, 177, 243
  and Bannon, 349
  and blue slip option, 292, 337
  on cabinet confirmations, 20
  and campaign donations from Russians, 387
  and CIA report on Russia, 11
  on flag burning comments of Trump, 8
  and Flake, 252
  and Gorsuch, 304, 315
  "nuclear option" used by, 92, 304
  relationship with Trump, 262, 349
  and Russian interference with election, 18, 91–92
  Warren silenced by, 39
  and wife's political appointment, 11, 92
McGahn, Don, 122, 174, 277, 286, 294, 307, 317, 351
McMaster, H. R., 52, 54, 63, 80, 83, 105, 122, 132, 195, 212, 219, 230, 243, 244, 260, 292, 300, 345, 381
media
  access to Trump regime, 172, 184
  alt-right coverage by, 5
  arrests of, 28, 121
  Bannon's disparagement of, 31, 52
  and bullying of reporters, 21, 46
  and CNN/Trump wrestling video, 187–88
  and communication bans, 29
  described as "the enemy," 47
  disparaged by Trump, 158, 184, 276, 337, 365
  and dress codes for women, 189
  and "fake news," 6, 10, 21, 42, 103, 152, 184, 187–88, 365
  forgeries fed to, 188
  and inauguration, 25
  and Lavrov meeting, 124–25, 131–32
  and leaks from inside White House, 235
  and Mattis, 280
  and press conferences of Trump, 16, 21, 46, 72, 243–44
  and reelection campaign, 182
  restrictions imposed on, 165–66
  and Russian hacking narrative, 193
  self-examination of, 5
  and Spicer's exclusion of select outlets, 53
  suppression of, 26
  terrorism coverage questioned, 39
  and Tillerson, 44, 45, 63, 69, 94, 124, 140
  and Trump's international trip, 145, 149
  Trump's mockery of disabled reporter, 20
  Trump's relationship with, 6, 54
  Trump's schedule closed to, 61
  Trump's war on, 57
  and tweets of Trump, 5, 8
  violence against, 145, 150, 164, 188, 367
  and White House Correspondents' Association dinner, 54
  and WikiLeaks, 106
  See also specific outlets
Medicare, 101
mental health of Trump, 39, 44, 107, 126, 143, 149, 168, 257, 275, 338, 346
Mercer, Rebekah, 91, 366, 384, 397
Mercer, Robert, 68, 239, 296, 332, 384, 397
Mercer family, 91, 104, 115, 234, 239, 255, 340
Merkel, Angela, 30, 33, 71–72, 80, 130, 149, 193, 244, 250, 322
Mexican border wall, 19, 31, 194, 197, 226, 235, 260, 270
Mexico, 35, 51, 63, 173, 194, 234–35, 293
Miller, Stephen, 44, 49, 61, 396
Mnuchin, Steven, 59, 86, 107, 110, 249, 250, 262, 268, 284, 293, 300, 305, 321, 328, 329, 337
Moore, Roy, 322, 351, 392
Mueller, Robert
  appointment of, as special counsel, 135, 378
  attacks on, 163
  and Comey, 176
  firing concerns/threats, 163, 167, 176, 211, 215, 223, 233
Mueller investigation
  Americans' approval of, 380
  attempts to undermine or limit, 213, 214, 275, 307, 384
  and business dealings of Trump family, 211, 213, 234
  characterized as a "witch hunt," 137, 167, 307
  charges filed in, 368

Mueller investigation (*continued*)
and Clinton's deleted emails, 351
and Cohen, 168, 332
and collusion denial requested by Trump, 174
and Comey, 234, 274, 276, 286, 308–9, 351, 378
and Comey's Trump memos, 141, 161
and destruction of evidence, 151
and Deutsche Bank, 212
document requests of, 235
and Facebook data, 284, 295–96
and Flynn, 155, 233, 235, 264, 308, 321, 351, 393, 397, 398
grand jury impaneled, 233
indictments from, 376
and interviews of WH insiders, 253–54, 286–87
and IRS's Criminal Investigation unit, 274, 321–22
and June 9 meeting, 263, 273, 274, 286, 287, 308, 309
and Kaveladze interview, 210
and Kushner, 168, 287
legal fees related to, 287, 332, 350, 360, 396
and Manafort, 155, 264, 273, 308, 321–22, 376
and Miller, 396
and money-laundering probe, 211
and obstruction of justice probe, 147, 167
and Priebus, 286, 341, 351
scope of, 234, 296, 308
Senate Republicans' support of, 378
and Sessions, 155, 297
and Smith, 351
and Spicer, 286, 351
and Steele dossier, 331–32
surveillance in, 307, 308
and targeted social media, 342
team recruited for, 155, 158, 167, 171, 172, 193, 230, 254, 299
and Trump, Jr., investigation, 202
Trump's lawyer for, 145
and Veselnitskaya meeting (June 9), 233
Muslim Americans, 11, 145, 150, 170, 216, 317
Muslim ban
and "Bowling Green massacre," 36, 41
challenged/blocked in courts, 37, 39, 44, 49, 69, 70, 79, 81, 110, 145, 150, 164, 197
changes to scope of, 197, 280
and dangers from targeted countries, 52
and Department of Homeland Security, 227
effect on tourism sector, 50
expiration of, 164, 303
and firing of Yates, 33, 123
and Giuliani, 33, 127, 143
implementation of, 31
internal reports undercutting premise of, 69
and lawsuits naming Trump, 81
and London terrorist attack, 156
partial enactment of, 179
protests against, 32, *37*
second order issued, 61
and State Department, 33, 34
states' attempts to block, 36, 61
and Supreme Court, 151, 156, 164, 179
unforeseen effects of, 56, 72, 79, 82, 157
and Yates, 184

NAACP, 227, 237, 361
NAFTA, 105, 111, 281
National Park Service (NPS), 28, 92, 116, 254–55
National Security Agency (NSA), 331
National Security Council (NSC), 32, 38, 47, 73, 91
NATO, 23, 144, 156, 160, 162
neo-Nazis, 6, 15, 17, 70, 99, 102, 178, 231, 238, 245, *246*, 247, 249, 252, 256, 258, 265, 290–91
nepotism, 13, 20, 52
NFL anthem protests, 311, 314, 318, 324, 335–36, 362, 375
Niger military ambush, 345, 349, 355–56, *359*, 365
North Korea
Bannon on, 255
and "Rocket Man" comments, 301, 311, 312, 316, 333
and sanctions, 317
tensions with, 358
threats of war against, 92, 100, 111
and Tillerson, 69
Trump's rhetoric on, 244–45, 268, 301–2
weapons development and testing, 42, 62, 130, 242–43, 279
nuclear power plant, Russian cyberattacks on, 196
nuclear weapons
and bombers on ready alert, 360
leadership dismissed, 21
plans for nuclear buildup, 15, 337
Trump's access to, 261, 338, 399
Nunes, Devin
calls for removal of, 78
and ethics complaints, 91
and Flynn, 397
and Fusion GPS subpoena, 351
information leaked to, 78, 82, 83
on lack of evidence of ties to Russia, 55
recusal of, 138, 152, 367
reviewing intel on Russia, 138
and Rice claims, 94
and Steele dossier, 285, 340
and surveillance claims, 71, 77
and "unmasking" subpoenas, 152, 159, 213

Obama, Barack
accused of wiretapping, 60, 61, 64, 71, 72, 73, 80, 118, 125
"crooked scheme" of, 87
and failed Yemen raid, 56
inauguration of, 28, 116
and McConnell's roadblock on Russia, 91
New Year's tweet of, 17
and town hall protests, 55
and transition period, 13, 17
and Trump team's ties to Russia, 57
and Zuckerberg, 317
Obama administration
and documents related to Russia probe, 84–85
and Russian interference with election, 9, 176–77, 207
and Russian visa requests, 176
and Russia sanctions, 16, 22, 36, 118
Obamacare/ACA. *See under* health care legislation
obstruction of justice issues, 342. *See also* Mueller investigation
Office of Congressional Ethics (OCE), 18, 83

Office of Government Ethics (OGE)
on conflicts of interest, 21, 24
on Conway's misuse of position, 45, 56, 64
and ethics rules waivers, 114, 239
lack of vetting of Trump's staff, 36
on legal defense fund donations, 292
resignation of chair, 208
and rollback of ethics requirements, 217
temporary director of, 213, 217
and transition team, 20
oil and oil industry, 30, 35, 62
opioid crisis, 243, 292, 322, 358
O'Reilly, Bill, 14, 38, 55, 89, 106, 112

Page, Carter
and Bannon, 393
and congressional hearings, 117–18, 120, 340, 351, 368, 393–94
counsel hired by, 168
and FBI investigation, 94, 118, 168, 181
and FISA warrant, 94, 118, 234
and Kislyak's meetings, 58
on phone tapping concerns, 61
and Rosenstein, 131
and Rosneft stake/sanctions deal, 31, 94
and Russian contacts, 90, 393
and Sessions, 379
and trip to Russia, 379, 380, 393–94
Pai, Ajit, 115, 236, 363
Papadopoulos, George, 254, 377, 378–80, 385, 397
Paris climate agreement, 30, 153, 154, 157, 304, 364, 388
Parscale, Brad, 168, 176, 236, 296, 339, 342, 352, 396
Pence, Mike
and Black History Month, 34
and Charlottesville clashes, 250
and Comey's firing, 125
extremism on social issues, 346
and Flynn, 41, 66, 135, 138, 141
and health care bills, 224
and Mueller investigation, 168, 322
and NFL anthem protests, 335
PAC registered by, 135
personal email used for state business, 58–59, 171, 229
political career of, 240
on Russian collusion, 254
staff changes of, 300
Pentagon, 86, 108, 117, 120, 300, 342, 356
Perry, Rick, 170, 228, 329, 343, 376, 388
Philippines, 114, 141, 252, 348
Poland, 193–94, 208, 216
Pompeo, Mike, 46, 96, 172, 213, 215, 263, 289, 353
presidential pardons
aides questioned about, 273
Arpaio pardon, 261, 266, 267, 270, 280, 291, 329, 348
Gingrich on, 15
Prevezon case, 203–4, 212, 220, 299
Price, Tom, 26, 86, 121, 305, 320
Priebus, Reince, 24, 53, 54, 115, 138, 140, 146, 166, 223, 225, 227, 286, 294, 316, 341, 351
Prince, Erik, 102, 131, 147, 199–200, 298
protests and protesters
assaulted by Erdogan's bodyguards, 133, 140, 148, 166
attempts to criminalize or block, 29, 189, 269
continuation of, 42
on Inauguration Day, 313
at McConnell's office, *177*
at Nashville campaign rally, 70
NFL anthem protests, 311, 314, 318, 324, 325, 336, 362, 375
in response to Dakota Access Pipeline, 53
in response to Muslim ban, 32, *37*
in response to Spencer's appearances, 347
in response to Stockley acquittal, 312
in response to tax returns issue, 100
treatment of, 190
trips canceled over threats of, 34
Trump's efforts to silence, 10
Women's March, 10, *27*, 27
Pruitt, Scott, 86, 165, 183, 188, 226, 287, 306, 321, 328, 348, 375
Puerto Rico, 311–12, 319–20, *323*, 323–24, 326–27, 334, 336, 343–44, 345, 349, 357, 359, 368–70, 382, 391
Putin, Vladimir
and Aleppo crisis, 6
and back-channels contact with Trump, 136
on classified intel leaked by Trump, 134
and Clinton, 15, 19
and Comey, 125, 169
critics of, 77, 103, 114, 163, 173
and cyberattacks, 155, 173
and Deripaska, 309
and Flynn, 103
and French election, 106
and G20 Summit, 185
and Gorkov, 154
and Lavrov meeting, 125
and Merkel, 130
and missiles in Kaliningrad, 6
O'Reilly's characterization of, 38
and Page, 117
and Paul, 68
and Prince, 102, 131
and psychological dossier on Trump, 49
and Russian interference with election, 11, 19, 47
and Russia sanctions, 16, 31
and Sweden, 160
and Syria, 211
and Tillerson, 11
Trump's defense of, 37
Trump's meetings with, 23, 185, 194–95, 210, 211, 212, 400
Trump's phone call to, 40
Trump's relationship with, 15, 16, 24, 135, 271, 285
and U.S. diplomatic mission reductions, 226, 243

reelection campaign, 47, 173, 182, 206, 306
Republican National Committee (RNC)
and Data Trust, 175
and documents related to Russia probe, 233
and legal defense fees, 306, 350, 360
resignations from, 275
and resolution condemning hate groups, 265
and Russian hacking, 13, 19

Resistance, 64, 106, 112, 387
Rice, Susan, 87, 93, 94, 100, 136, 213, 230, 298
Rosenstein, Rod
on anonymous sources, 167
and appointment of special counsel, 124, 128, 135, 211
and Clinton's email, 124, 125, 237
and Comey firing, 124, 125, 126, 133, 137, 155, 277, 308
and Comey's Senate testimony, 126
and congressional hearings, 127, 137, 159
and Mueller investigation, 155, 307, 308
and Page, 131
and Russia investigation, 125, 126
and Russian interference with election, 165
Ross, Wilbur, 45, 55, 65, 76, 83, 85, 111, 115, 121, 347–48
Rubio, Marco, 33, 47, 85, 105, 387
Russia
bribery attempts from, 31
classified intel leaked by Trump to, 131–32, 134, 140
and Clinton campaign, 76
and congressional hearings, 74
C-Span interrupted by broadcaster from, 22
disinformation spread by, 125
dossier on Trump, 21, 29, 221, 241 (*see also* Steele dossier)
and European election interference, 285
and Flynn, 22, 24, 28, 41, 43, 78, 139, 146
and French election, 103, 106, 113, 119
funding for Trump businesses, 120, 134
and Germany election, 113
intelligence officers in, 29, 38
and Le Pen candidacy, 40
and Manafort, 146
money transfers, 25
nuclear treaty violation of, 65
provocations by, 45, 68, 104
and relationships with Trump advisors, 26
and Russian flags at CPAC, 53
sanctions against, 16, 22, 31, 36, 40, 41, 49, 94, 114, 147, 154, 166, 174, 191–92, 215, 221, 224, 229, 232, 272, 317, 394
Sessions's meeting with ambassador, 58
as source of "fake news," 6
spies and intelligence efforts of, 58, 192–93
and Sputnik (news outlet), 199, 294, 341
state oil company of, 31, 35
steel imported from, 62, 371
suspicious deaths associated with, 53, 63, 103, 114, 169, 173, 221, 274
and Syria, 92, 94, 211
and talks with Trump team, 8
Trump, Jr.'s meetings with, 6
Trump's business ties in, 40
Trump's defense of, 11, 20
Trump's inconsistency on, 24
and Trump Tower plans in Moscow, 202, 271–72, 287
and Ukraine, 24, 32, 33, 45, 49
U.S. allies' concerns about Trump's ties to, 46
U.S. diplomatic missions in, 226, 243
and Veselnitskaya meeting, 221
WH aides contact with, 43, 49
Russian collusion with Trump campaign
and collusion denial requested by Trump, 174
and cover up, 228
and distraction tactics of Trump, 181
evidence of, 185
FBI investigation of, 147
key states targeted in, 190, 203
Kushner's denials of, 219–20
and Russian access to Clinton emails, 185, 192, 200–201, 351
Sater's role in, 271–72
and Smith (GOP operative), 185, 192, 204, 264, 350–51, 366
to spread "fake news," 190
and targeted social media, 296, 317, 318, 330, 342
Trump's denials of, 244, 350
and Veselnitskaya meeting (June 9), 200–201, 210, 233, 241–42
and WikiLeaks publication of DNC information, 285
Russian cyberattacks
and ads purchased by Russia, 142, 310, 317, 318, 330, 367, 383–84
and Advanced Persistent Threat 28, 254
bots used in, 190, 271, 284, 318
and Clinton email hacked, 185, 192, 200–201, 204, 351, 366, 385, 397
on Democratic National Committee, 61, 85, 109
email of intelligence officer hacked in, 205
on European infrastructure networks, 196
Facebook used in, 142, 283–84, 295–96, 310, 317, 318, 330
and future elections, 271
and hackers' hit list, 385
House Intelligence Committee on, 173
LinkedIn used in, 231
and troll farms, 284, 339, 350, 351, 352, 366
Twitter used in, 264, 284, 285, 310, 318
and U.S. elections of 2016, 85, 94, 103, 109, 125, 155, 158–59, 164, 173, 185, 192, 193, 207
on U.S. nuclear power plant, 196
and YouTube videos, 339
Russian interference with 2016 elections
and altered voter registrations, 207
Brennan on, 142
characterized as "warfare, 353
and CIA, 11, 12, 13, 19, 91, 353
collusion of Trump campaign with (*see* Russian collusion with Trump campaign)
and Comey, 86–87, 161
and Congress, 263
and cyberattacks, 85, 94, 103, 109, 155, 158–59, 164, 173, 185, 192, 193, 204
digital forensic investigations on, 270
and documents related to Russia probe, 84–85

Russian interference with 2016 elections (*continued*)
"fake news" spread in, 152, 190, 318
and FBI investigation, 13, 19, 74, 103, 125, 126
hearings on, 85
intelligence report on, 19
lack of consequences for, 195
McCain's hearing on, 17, 18
and McConnell, 91
media coverage of, 96, 193
and methods for tampering with results, 174–75
and Obama administration, 9, 176–77, 207
and prevention of repeat of, 177
Putin-linked think tank's involvement in, 103
Ryan's acknowledgement of, 106
scope of, 173, 175
social media used in, 142, 264, 283–84, 285, 295–96, 310, 317, 318, 330, 339, 340, 341–42
in specific areas, 175
Spicer on, 172
states targeted in, 190, 203, 207, 310–11, 330
and troll farms, 284, 339, 350, 351, 352, 366
and Trump advisers, 103
Trump's stances on, 13, 17, 22, 113, 174, 177, 180, 194, 195, 196, 204, 215
voter rolls of key states shared, 84
and weaponizing of data sets, 120, 152
and WikiLeaks' release of DNC emails, 96
See also Mueller investigation
Russian ties with Trump regime
allies' information about, 57
Americans' concerns about, 54
attempts to discredit news on, 54
and back-channels communication, 90, 136, 147, 219, 229
British intelligence on, 95
G. W. Bush's call for answers, 55
and business affairs of Trump, 40, 62, 68, 95, 120, 170, 180, 192, 211
of cabinet nominations/members, 55
calls for independent investigation of, 78
CIA's evidence of, 91
Citgo's inauguration donation, 117
and Cohen, 272, 393
and congressional hearings, 23, 108, 117
cover-up of, 108
and FBI investigation, 125, 126, 127, 128, 136
first direct evidence of, 125
and Flynn, 103, 108, 117, 118, 122, 136, 393
and Gordon, 393
growing awareness of, 91
House Intelligence Committee probe on, 74, 76–77, 96, 103
Justice Department's probe on, 108
and Kislyak's meetings, 58, 62, 80, 118, 124, *128*, 136
and Kushner, 80, 90, 91, 152, 393
and Lavrov meeting, 124–25, *128*, 131
and Manafort, 76, 95, 117, 126, 393
McCain on, 73
Nunes on lack of evidence for, 55
Obama's preservation of info on, 57
and Page, 58, 90, 94, 103, 117, 118, 393
and Papadopoulos, 393
and Prince, 90, 102
and Sessions, 393
and sharing of voter rolls, 84
and Steele dossier, 24, 55, 84, 94, 109, 114
and Stein, 103
and Stone, 117
suspicious deaths related to, 114
and Trump, Jr., 393
undisclosed contacts with Russian officials, 136
and Veselnitskaya meeting, 200–201
and Yates/Clapper hearing, 122–23
Ryan, Paul, 8, 79, 106, 135, 150, 161, 391

Sater, Felix, 49, 62, 172, 193, 271–72, 334
Saudi Arabia, 157, 161–62, 374, 387, 388
Scaramucci, Anthony, 213, 215, 219, 223, 225, 229
Schiff, Adam, 76, 83, 152, 220, 380, 394
SCL Group, 233–34
Secret Service, 163, 206, 229, 257, 292
security details for Trump family, 14, 47, 48, 115, 257, 321
Sekulow, Jay, 163, 181, 206, 213, 306
Senate Intelligence Committee
and business affairs of Trump family, 123
and Cohen, 307, 352, 366
and Comey memos, 185
and Comey testimony, 125, 154, 160–61
and Facebook's Russian disclosure, 285, 296
Flynn subpoenaed by, 124, 136, 141
and Kushner, 80, 161, 214, 219–20
and Manafort, 212, 220
and Page, 117–18, 120, 340, 351, 368
request for Russia-related documents from campaign, 142
and Rosenstein, 127, 159
Russia probe of, 85, 108, 117
and Sessions, 161, 166
and Steele dossier, 56, 331
and Twitter, 310, 318
on wiretapping claims, 71
Senate Judiciary Committee
and AG nomination, 217
and Comey, 123, 298
and dossier, 241, 340
and focus of investigation, 332
and judicial nominees, 390
and Kushner, 242
and Manafort, 215, 220, 240, 241
and Rosenstein, 165
and Russian interference with election, 332
and Sessions, 354–55, 393
and Simpson, 263
and social media companies, 383
and Trump, Jr., 205, 240, 273, 285–86
Sessions, Jeff
and Arpaio pardon, 267
and Assange, 103, 254, 285
on cash/property seizures, 209

Sessions, Jeff (*continued*)
on Charlottesville violence, 248, 251
and Comey firing, 124, 133, 134, 146, 155, 355
and Comey's meetings with Trump, 159, 161
confirmation hearing of, 21, 39, 58, 64, 206, 269
and congressional hearings, 161, 166, 354–55, 393
counsel hired by, 171
and critics of Trump, 364
and DACA program, 283
and Deutsche Bank investigation, 75
disparaged by Trump, 216–17, 297
and Election Integrity Commission, 293
ethics complaint against, 64
and Fairooz case, 115, 206, 388
firing concerns/threats, 216, 223
and foreign contacts form, 204
and immigration crack downs, 42, 99, 280
and investigations of Trump, 30, 43, 124, 134, 146, 190, 211
and Kislyak's meetings, 58, 146, 181, 214
and leaks from inside White House, 235
and LGBTQ discrimination, 326
and Mueller investigation, 155, 297
and Muslim ban, 104
and new criminal charging/ sentencing policies, 122
and Page, 379
and Papadopoulos, 379
and Prevezon case, 203, 212, 220, 299
and prosecution of news organizations, 103
recusal of, 43, 58, 75, 124, 126, 128, 134, 146, 156, 160
and religious liberties, 326, 364
resignations of U.S. attorneys requested by, 65
and sanctuary cities, 170, 290
speech to LGBT hate group, 197
and transgender policy, 44, 325
sexual assaults/misconduct
and *Access Hollywood* tape, 288, 334, 396
on campuses, 150, 170, 189, 197, 269, 281, 303
and Conway's defense of Trump, 8
and defamation suits, 25
and #MeToo campaign, 392
in military contexts, 197
by Moore, 392
by Republican officials, 25
Trump accused of, 82, 189, 362
and Weinstein accusations, 392
women grabbed by genitals, 8
Shaub, Walter, 101, 165, 191, 208, 213, 217, 267
silencing tactics of Trump administration, 10, 14, 32, 38, 39
Sinclair Broadcasting, 199, 209, 236, 304, 343, 363
Smith, Peter W.
and Clinton's hacked emails, 185, 192
and congressional hearings, 350, 366
and Flynn, 192, 350, 351
and Mueller investigation, 264, 351
suicide of, 204
South Korea, 242, 279, 302
Spain, terrorist attack in, 252
Spencer, Richard, 17, 130, 250, 251, 264, 335, 347, 362
Spicer, Sean
Anne Frank Center scolded by, 50
attempts to discredit news on Russian ties, 54
on bypassing African American Museum, 24
CNN called "fake news" by, 42
and Comey firing, 309
on Comey's grandstanding, 138
on Conway's brand endorsement, 40
counsel hired by, 322
and "covfefe" tweet, 153
and "Deep State" concept, 65
exclusion of specific media outlets, 53
and Flynn's foreign agent work, 66
and Hitler/Assad comparisons, 99
on inauguration, 28
and jobs report, 66, 67
and leaks from inside White House, 59
McCarthy's portrayal of, 38
and Mueller investigation, 286, 351
on Muslim ban, 32
ProPublica defamed by, 88
resignation of, 213
and Russian interference with election, 172
Trump on "ratings" of, 109
on Trump's D.C. hotel, 25
on voter fraud, 29
on wiretapping claims, 67, 71
on Yemen raid, 35
Sputnik (Russian news outlet), 199, 294, 341
State of the Union (SOTU) addresses, 57, 260–61
Steele, Christopher, 22, 56, 84, 94, 103, 109
Steele dossier
attempts to discredit, 285, 340
BBC's verification of, 84
BuzzFeed's publication of, 109, 148, 332
Cohen's rebuttal of, 273
and congressional hearings, 42, 56, 235, 331
and FBI investigation, 55, 103
and Mueller investigation, 331–32
and Nunes, 285, 340
and Rosneft stake/sanctions deal, 94
and Sessions, 285
suspicious deaths related to, 114
Trump's focus on, 160
steel imported from Russia, 62, 371
Stone, Roger, 61, 68, 78, 96, 152, 206, 342, 377, 396
Sweden, 48, 55, 62, 160
Syria
casualties from U.S.-led air strikes, 82
and CIA training for rebels, 211
and Paris climate agreement, 304, 388
Russian meetings with Trump team on, 6, 8
threats of war against, 92
U.S. air strike on, 92–93, 94, 99, 115
use of chemical weapons in, 91, 92, 182

Taiwan, 10, 41
tax plans/reform, 33, 70, 97, 107, 151, 265, 321
tax returns of Trump
Americans' demands for, 24, 51, 282
and effects of tax reforms, 107
House Ways and Means Committee on, 45
leaked to press, 71
refusal to release, 21, 28, 100, 101, 110
terrorism
in Britain, 141, 156, 300
in Charlottesville, 290
in France, 237
mosque attacks, 33, 237
in New York City, 381
in Spain, 252
in Sweden (fictitious), 48, 62
Tillerson, Rex
and Charlottesville clashes, 267
confirmation of, 35
and daily briefings, 57, 153, 229
and departure of senior staff, 31, 63
disparaged by Trump, 339
e-mail alias used by, 67, 75
and Exxon, 25, 42, 62–63, 104, 148
at G7 meeting, 94
inaccessibility of, 157
influence of, 333
and Iran nuclear deal, 105
and journalists, 44, 45, 63, 69, 94, 124, 140
and Kushner's role in State, 46
and Lavrov meeting, 124, 322
and Mexico, 51
missing from meetings with heads of state, 45
and "moron" comment, 333, 337
and North Korea, 244, 333
and Putin, 11
and Putin's meeting with Trump, 195, 212
and Qatar, 162
on retirement plans, 76
and Russian-U.S. relations, 174
and sanctions on Russia, 94, 209, 229
shuttering of offices/bureaus, 208–9, 218, 364
SoS appointment, 11
State's budget slashed by, 69
and Ukraine, 94
and unfilled positions in State, 107, 113, 165, 381
Time magazine cover, 182
Time Warner/AT&T merger, 21, 47, 188, 218, 398
transgender population
and Department of Education, 44
and military ban, 179, 222, 226, 238, 241, 244, 266, 325, 342, 374
and Danica Roem's victory, 391
and rollback of Obama policies, 51, 170
transition team
and ethics investigations, 97, 337
ethics training canceled by, 59
and Flynn's foreign agent work, 66, 135
and Obama administration, 17, 118
and Office of Government Ethics (OGE), 20
and press corps, 23
and purging phones, 78
registered lobbyists on, 115
resignations from, 19
travel expenses, 98, 257, 293, 305, 320, 321, 328, 329
Trump, Donald, Jr.
about Russian adoption lie, 228
and conflicts of interest issues, 15, 329
and congressional hearings, 205, 215, 240, 285–86
counsel hired by, 200, 220
and foreign business deals, 373
and golf course in Dubai, 48
and June 9 meeting, 200–201, 205, 206, 210, 221, 233, 286, 299
and legal defense fees, 306, 350
meetings with Russian representatives, 6
and Mueller investigation, 202
and Russian access to Clinton emails, 200–202
and Russian funding, 120
security details for, 115, 306
and tweets from Russian troll farm, 352
and Vancouver hotel, 56
Trump, Eric
and charity golf tournament, 158
and conflicts of interest issues, 15
and foreign business deals, 373
foundation of, 158
and golf course in Dubai, 48
on negative media coverage, 278
and Russian funding, 120
security details for, 115
taxpayer-funded trips of, 34
and Vancouver hotel, 56
Trump, Ivanka
book promotion of, 114–15
business affairs of, 80–81, 214, 358
China-related business dealings, 67, 101, 165, 181, 315
coffee date auction of, 13
and consolidation of power, 92
and Conway's brand endorsement, 40, 45, 56, 74
counsel hired by, 220
and Farage meeting, 64
and financial disclosures, 328
and G20 Summit, 195
in meetings with heads of state, 7, 48, 71
and Nordstrom, 36, 40
office of, 13
official role of, 74, 80
overseas manufacturing of, 111, 151, 181, 208, 229, 315
private e-mail used by, 316, 327, 363, 386
and rules of federal employees, 114
security details for, 115
in Trump administration, 11, 13, 74
and Trump Tower plans in Moscow, 272
Trumpcare/AHCA. *See under* health care legislation
Trump International Hotel in D.C.
anti-Islamic conference hosted at, 170
as default meeting place, 62, 182, 239, 264
foreign diplomats' patronization of, 112
Ivanka's stake in, 81
and lease violation, 13, 41, 48, 75–76, 269
legal challenges faced by, 98
media banned from, 25

Trump International Hotel in D.C. (*continued*)
  and reelection campaign kickoff event, 173
  and Saudi Arabian lobbyists, 157
  Trump's profits from, 169, 239, 264
Trump Organization, 75, 90, 130, 143, 158, 192, 208, 219, 238, 239, 386
Trump SoHo Hotel, 49, 150, 172, 211, 334
Trump Tower
  and Russian money-laundering network, 78
  and Secret Service details, 229
  security details for, 47
  taxpayers footing bill for, 54
  and wiretapping claims, 60, 61, 64, 71, 72, 73, 74, 80, 100, 118–19, 125, 278
Trump Tower in Moscow, 202, 271–72, 287
Trump TV, 236
Trump University, 18, 84, 111
Turkey, 65–66, 74–75, 86, 105, 113, 133, 135, 140, 141, 235
Twenty-fifth Amendment, 244, 338, 346
Twitter
  and ads purchased by Russia, 367
  and bot accounts, 318, 341, 384
  and congressional hearings, 310, 318
  and "Crooked Hillary" emoji, 14
  data deleted by, 341
  and DHS lawsuit, 89
  Kremlin-backed support for Trump on, 392
  and Russian interference with election, 264, 284, 285, 318, 341–42
  Russian investments in, 392–93
  Russian operatives' accounts on, 384
  and Trump campaign, 342
Twitter account of Trump
  Americans' disapproval of, 215, 322
  bot followers of, 98, 190, 240, 386
  and "covfefe" tweet, 153
  and deletion of tweets, 337
  and foreign spies, 181
  media's coverage of, 5, 8, 18, 42
  number of insults recorded on, 366
  policies announced on, 17
  and proposed "COVFEFE Act," 164
  and Russian trolls, 396
  surge in followers, 149
  temporary deactivation of, 383
  threats of violence on, 318
  users blocked on, 164, 200, 304

Ukraine
  and back-channel peace deal, 49
  GOP's revised stance on, 58
  and Manafort, 52, 66
  and peace plan/sanctions deal, 49, 62, 172
  and Tillerson, 94
  violence in, 32, 33, 45
United Kingdom
  accused of wiretapping Trump Tower, 71
  and Brexit, 120, 161, 234, 340, 367
  elections in, 161
  rise in crime in, 358
  Russia-related deaths in, 169, 173
  terrorist attacks, 141, 156, 300
  Trump's plans to visit, 32, 38, 163
  and Trump team's links to Russia, 95
U.S. attorneys, 65, 289–90, 348–49
U.S. Congress
  boycotts of inauguration, 22, 25
  and communication bans, 29
  and Department of Homeland Security, 227
  and dress codes for women, 189, 198
  and Muslim ban, 33
  and Russian interference with election, 263
  and Russian sanctions, 215
  and Twenty-fifth Amendment, 244, 338, 346
U.S. Department of Defense (DoD), 137, 255, 266
U.S. Department of Education, 170, 189, 227, 361, 389
U.S. Department of Justice
  and affirmative action admissions policies, 227, 325
  and Arpaio pardon, 267
  and Assange, 103, 254, 285
  Civil Rights Division of, 191
  and Comey investigation, 22
  and DreamHost data, 253, 259–60
  Facebook user data requested by, 313
  and firing of Yates, 33
  and investigations of Trump, 30
  and Muslim ban, 33
  pressured by Trump, 382
  and Prevezon case, 212, 220, 299
  and Russia-Trump probe, 108
  and sanctuary cities, 170
  and sexual orientation discrimination, 314
  and voter suppression, 237
  and voting machine malfunctions, 96
  and wiretapping claims, 61, 100, 278
U.S. Department of Treasury, 107, 269, 321, 328
U.S. House of Representatives, 16, 18, 19
U.S. Senate, 23, 290–91
USS *John S. McCain* accident, 257, 261
U.S. State Department
  anti-Semitism monitoring by, 252
  budget slashed, 69
  cessation of daily briefings, 51, 57, 121, 153
  and coup concerns, 32
  and death of Russian ambassador, 63
  diminishing role of, 46, 56–57, 86
  and diplomatic mission reductions in Russia, 226, 243
  dysfunction in, 51
  and gender-related lists, 15
  Kushner's shadow role in, 46
  leaks from inside, 51
  and LGBT statement, 29
  and Muslim ban, 33, 34
  resignations from, 276
  and Russian sanctions, 154, 364
  and SCL Group, 233–34
  shuttering of offices/bureaus, 208–9, 218, 252, 364
  staff departures from, 31, 46, 63, 218
  and Syrian peace talks, 26
  Tillerson's arrival at, 31

U.S. State Department (*continued*)
  and Trump's conversations with foreign leaders, 10
  unfilled positions in, 105, 107, 113, 165, 242, 381, 389
U.S. Supreme Court, 34, 151, 164, 375
U.S. Virgin Islands, 324, 343

Venezuela, 101, 121, 245, 266
Veselnitskaya, Natalia, 200–201, 203, 205, 206, 210, 213, 221, 233, 241, 332, 350
Vnesheconombank (VEB), 80, 90, 134, 152, 180, 271
VOICE (Victims of Immigration Crime Engagement), 48, 110, 145
voter suppression, 237, 326

Warren, Elizabeth, 39, 72, 190, 213, 255, 357, 371, 375
Waters, Maxine, 19, 22, 57
White House
  closed to public, 39
  comment line shut down, 28
  departures from, 265, 276
  disparaged by Trump, 230
  and impulsivity of Trump, 338
  leaks from inside, 29, 43, 53, 59, 237
  and one-hundred-day mark, 96, 107
  and private e-mail accounts, 316, 348, 363
  as residence of first family, 6, 28, 35, 42, 54
  staffers' failures of background checks, 46
  visitor logs of, 97–98
  web page, 26, 32
  See also executive branch
white supremacists
  attitudes toward, 258
  Bannon on, 255
  Bush on, 354
  in Charlottesville, 156, 245, *246*, 246–53
  empowerment of, 281
  Limbaugh's support for, 256
  media coverage of, 5
  and O'Reilly, 14
  rallies of, 156, 190, 245, 335 (*see also* Charlottesville rally and protests)
  recruiting on campuses, 303, 362
  requests for tolerance of, 6
  resolutions condemning, 265, 290–91
  Trump's failure to condemn, 6, 265
WikiLeaks, 18, 20, 24, 58, 64, 96, 106, 230, 285, 366, 385
wiretapping claims of Trump, 60, 61, 64, 67, 71, 72, 73, 74, 80, 100, 118–19, 278
Women's March, 10, *27*, 27

Yates, Sally, 33, 77, 83, 118, 122–23, 127, 184, 195, 217
Yemen raid, failed, 34–35, 40, 52, 56, 63, 82, 92, 365

Zarrab, Reza, 398

A NOTE ON THE AUTHOR

AMY SISKIND is a national spokesperson, writer, and expert on helping women and girls advance and succeed. A highly successful Wall Street executive, she's co-founder and president of The New Agenda, a national organization working on issues including economic independence and advancement, gender representation and bias, sexual assault, and domestic violence. Her writing has been featured in the *Huffington Post* and *Medium*, and she is a frequent source for the national press, including in the *Washington Post*, the *Wall Street Journal*, and the *New York Times*.